HANUMAN PRASAD PODDAR
An Exalted Divinity

This work is dedicated to the sacred memory of a highly revered saint—**Bhaijee Shri Hanuman Prasad Poddar**—who was also a most dedicated campaigner of religion, divine name and ancient scriptures not only in India but abroad as well in such a cruel age of 'Kaliyug'.

HANUMAN PRASAD PODDAR
An Exalted Divinity

The philosophy of life of an ascetic – Bhaijee Shri Hanuman Prasad Poddar
and an eminent saint Sethji Shri Jaydayal Goyandka

An abridged English translation for the
comprehensive biography of*
Bhaijee Shri Hanuman Prasad Poddar
***EK ALAUKIK VIBHOOTI**
(Gita Vatika Prakashan, Gorakhpur-273006, India)
by
Prof. O.P. Gupta

Original Collector
Late Shri Gambhirchandji Dujari

Compilation and Consolidation by
Late Shri Shyam Sundar Dujari

PRABHAT
PAPERBACKS

Published by

PRABHAT PAPERBACKS

4/19 Asaf Ali Road,
New Delhi-110 002 (INDIA)
e-mail: prabhatbooks@gmail.com

ISBN 978-93-5266-781-9

HANUMAN PRASAD PODDAR: AN EXALTED DIVINITY
by Prof. O.P. Gupta

Edition
First, 2018

Price
₹ 500.00 (Rupees Five Hundred only)

Printed at
R-Tech Offset Printers, Delhi

Due to an unlimited grace of the supreme being, the english translation of the original and best seller book in hindi – 'EK ALAUKIK VIBHOOTI' by Gita Vatika Prakashan, Gorakhpur could be accomplished for the spiritual aspirants. It was possible due to divine blessings from the high ranking community of saints existing in this universe to which bhaijee is also an important member.

He alone writes and enables to write,
He alone does and gets it done,
Do not know, what is wrong,
Do not know, what is right.

Foreword

It gives me immense pleasure in contributing a foreword for English version of the original text in Hindi titled 'Shri Bhaijee – Ek Alaukik Vibhooti', which is compiled by the Late Gambhirchandji Dujari – a very close associate and fully devoted person to his mentor – Bhaijee, Shri Hanuman Prasad Poddar. It was later compiled and assembled by his able son Late Shyam Sundarji Dujari and was published by Gita Vatika Prakashan in the year 2000 at Gorakhpur. The present English version has been accomplished by Prof. O.P. Gupta, who is very well known to me and had also worked as Head, Department of Zoology, Dr. H.S. Gour University, Sagar, during my tenure as the Vice Chancellor (2004-2008).

To write anything about Bhaijee Shri Hanuman Prasad Poddar and Sethji : Shri Jaidayal Goyandka is extremely difficult. The founder editor of *'Kalyan'* and *'Kalyan Kalpatru'*, Shri Bhaijee and the man behind the Gita Press, Shri Sethji have made substantial contribution for promoting· the Indian culture. We are indebted to them for the work they have manifested to the humanity.

Perhaps, Radha Baba could understand the divine status of Bhaijee during his life. This version contains an ascendant amount of matter by Baba. The meeting of Bhaijee with divine sage Narad and the great sage Angira is also another unique event to the spiritual world. Some events included in the Preface about the impact of divinity on life and work of Dr. Gupta are also interesting.

There has also been demand by non-Hindi-speaking devotees for the English translation of its famous Hindi version 'Shri Bhaijee' – Ek Alaukik Vibhooti – The philosophy of life of an ascetic: successful in evocation of savour (Ras-siddha-sant) Shri Bhaijee: Hanuman Prasad Poddar and an eminent ascetic Shri Sethji: Shri Jaidayal Goyandka, compiled and assembled by Late S.S. Dujari, which includes fascinating contents on Hindu religion and spiritualism. An important thing of English version is also the translation of various Sanskrit words, couplets, Hindi quatrains and verses of devotional poetry into English, which are given in its Hindi version. Inclusion of various technical/ special words in English version would help the readers to intact with the real soul of its Hindi version. It was necessary to understand the text and its spirit. Inclusion of a comprehensive glossary in this English version is worth appreciating.

Another relevant part of this version is the gist written by its translator in the Preface section, which would help the reader, in advance, to have a glimpse of the most important topics of this text.

It would be interesting to know about the special mission for which Bhaijee was sent to this planet. It may give a real evaluation of an unfathomable personality of a great saint like Bhaijee. It was due to the Herculean efforts of Bhaijee Shri Hanuman Prasad Poddar that the Hindu epic like the Ramcharitmanas and the Gita are available to everyone at a very nominal price.

Inclusion of a short biography of Marwari saint with an exceptional dominion of spiritual world, Shri Sethji: Shri Jaidayal Goyandka is another attraction of the text. He established Gita Press, Govind Bhawan in Kolkata, Gita Bhawan in Swargashram in Rishikesh and Rishikul Brahmacharya Ashram in Churu. An excellent commentary on the Gita is now also available from Gita Press titled '*Gita-tatwavivechani*' due to his efforts along with Radha Baba, Swami Ramsukh Das and his younger brother Shri Hari Krishna Goyandka.

English version has become a little larger in volume but will be valuable to English readers to understand the real essence of the form, given in its original Hindi version. The language is simple, lucid and chaste. Some errors may be there, which are due to human limitations. The readers may inform them to Dr. O.P. Gupta for further improvement.

I congratulate Prof. O.P. Gupta for this appreciable work, which has been possible due to his commitment, dedication and devotion. I do hope that it will be a befitting gift for non-Hindi-speaking people. I am sure the readers in India and abroad will not only enjoy reading it, but also get divine pleasure in this process.

Teachers' Day
5th September, 2018

(Prof. D.P. Singh)
Chairman
University Grants Commission,
New Delhi

Former Director, NAAC, Bengaluru.
Former Vice Chancellor, Banaras Hindu University (BHU), Varanasi.
Former Vice Chancellor, Dr. H.S. Gour University, Sagar and
Former Vice Chancellor, Devi Ahilya University, Indore.

Preface

I feel it equally important to mention the necessary details in this section about the reason, condition and necessity to accept and accomplish this assignment for such a unique saint of this age, who could be understood in real sense after his heavenly departure only by this universal community. Earnest readers would find some of the topics of this book so impressive that they cannot be left unaffected by them. For example, this text also contains an abundant amount of correspondence between Shri Radha Baba and Bhaijee, which is a unique information for spiritual devotees.

But, before we proceed further, here are a few lines about my earlier life which has also moulded my mind towards spirituality. My childhood is passed in a native town of birth, known as Mauranipur in District Jhansi of the Indian state of Uttar Pradesh. I had been a favourite child for my late paternal aunt Kanchan Bua, who had become widow at a very young age and, hence, I got ample opportunities to accompany her during her visits to join the assembly of virtuous people (*satsang*) or to listen to the discourses by saints (*pravachan*) or to join the celebration of devotional songs (*sankirtan*), etc. It had caused a strong impact on my mental attitude and led me towards religious practices. In addition, my mother Late Durga Bai was a very simple and pious lady and was in regular habit to put lamps made of wheat flour, with butter therein below Pipal tree near Hanuman temple and I had to always join her for this ritual, being an eldest son. On the completion of my doctoral work, my teacher Prof. R.K. Shrivastava had helped and initiated me first time to begin with the devoted striving (*sadhna*) of Gayatri. There was a time when I did Gayatri Yagya daily in the morning without a single break, for six months. During 1969 to 1974, I was in close contact with a physician Late Dr. S.P. Sharma, a religious person and an ardent devotee of Goddess Durga. Due to his company, I had also an opportunity to meet saints and another highly realised ascetic late Shivram Deolia, who had also guided me for spiritual practices. A lot of saints with high caliber used to visit the clinic and residence of Dr. Sharma and I was fortunate to meet and obtained blessings coupled with spiritual guidance by them. So much strong has been my quest to search the saints and such places of spiritual importance that I have explored and visited many such places that are not very easy to locate like Kancheedham, near Nainital, Uttar Vrindavan,

Mirtola – a secluded shrine and about 25 kms. from Almora near Panuanala, where a beautiful idol of Lord Krishna was founded by Mr. Ronald Henry Nixon (during the First World War, he served as a British fighter pilot and later known as 'Shri Krishna Prem') and Yashoda Ma in 1930. I have also been successful to locate and visit the holy bungalow of Bhaijee at Ratangarh; Vishudhanand Ashram; a residential place of Lahiri Mahasaya; Dhundhiraj Ganesh and Vishalakshi temples in Varanasi and Keshwanand Ashram in Haridwar, where relics of Lahiri Mahasaya are placed. Some of these are still and strictly forbidden for general public. It has also been my habit to enquire and visit the famous holy places and well-known saints of that area whenever I had to go to attend the various types of academic assignments, in and out of the country. It has, thus, also helped me to see different interesting and sometimes rare places and to meet various people and saints with unique qualities in India as well as abroad. The few names of them are – Shri G.P. Bansod from Jabalpur, a famous Buddhist sun-gazer and an ardent devotee of the Sun God; Shri Hira Singh Markam – a saint-cum- politician who lives in Korba, Raipur. I had, per chance, made a bus journey with Shri Markam during my trip to Chhindwara. I was simply bewitched due to a sandalwood fragrance, being emitted by his presence throughout the night of the bus journey. Shri B.K. Anand lives in New Delhi, an ardent Kriya Yogi of high repute. Late P.K. Hazra was a disciple of Guru Yukteshwar, who met Shri Yogananda as early as 1932 during his very young age. One can see the picture of Shri Hazra taken in 1936 as a long-haired youth, sitting on the foreground, along with Shri Yogananda and Guru Yukteshwarji in the book '*Autobiography of a Yogi*'. I could find a unique opportunity to meet him and received his blessings at his residence in Jabalpur, with my friend Shri Sandeep Kachhwaha somewhere in July, 2011. I was so much crazy with my such habit that I even sometimes did not care even about my safety to move any place not only in India but even in foreign as well. I had to make a journey even at an early hour (3:30 hrs.) of morning in a new place of Chittorgarh in an auto-rickshaw with an unknown driver, to visit a holy shrine of Avari Mata – situated in a forest about 35-40 kms from the main city. My such habits had put me sometimes in very awkward and thrilling conditions during my visit to the great forest Lawn Memorial Park at Glendale, California on 3rd June, 2011. To visit the crypt of H.H. Yogananda, I was almost lost and felt uneasy for a while, inside such a quiet mausoleum as I was unable to locate the crypt therein, despite my continuous wandering for several minutes. But, a little later and amazingly, someone arrived (who had introduced himself as an actor in Hollywood) who had not only helped me to locate the crypt of Yogananda, but then also shown the recently made crypt of Daya Mata, Ex-President of self-realisation fellowship, Los Angeles, California. He had also put me back by his car to the main entrance of the park, which is little away from the mausoleum. Another interesting event related with this is about my earlier visit on the same day to main SRF Centre – an International HQ in California. The people over there were very courteous and had helped me to visit almost complete shrine with the help of some devotee. I had also an opportunity to visit the personal room of H.H. Yogananda where I could spend a few minutes to feel superb vibrations prevailed over the complete surroundings. On my return and after putting my remarks in the visitors' book, I moved to the main entrance and then enquired from the receptionist over there about the route and mode of transport which may be available to reach mausoleum to see the crypt of Yogananda at Great Forest Lawn Memorial Park at Glendale. She was almost shocked to learn my intention to travel to this place on foot but suggested me to wait till someone may arrive to help or perhaps the great Guru (a respectful address to H.H. Yogananda) might help me. But I have tried to move myself and was lost in between. I have then waited for someone for a lift. Within a few minutes, I have noticed a car, passing thereby and raised my hand for a lift. A nice person (who later introduced himself as Frank Margrette – a person working in press department in SRF HQ) was inside the car and enquired me about the help I may require. When I have told him about my wish to visit the mausoleum, to see the crypt of Guru Yogananda, he was also amazed and told me that it was far away from this place, then thought for a moment and asked me to jump inside his car. He was kind enough to put me right up to the entrance of the mausoleum and indicated a hint for the entry therein. These are few interesting events of my life, may be called miracles occurred, when you crave for some divine help, which is bestowed to you during your visit to a sacred place with a quest for spiritual guidance.

Due to my destiny to accelerate my spiritual quest further, I was duly initiated by my first spiritual mentor H.H. Shri B.M. Pandey, who has left a little later these worldly affairs in 1986 and is still at residence of a secret place. I have been further initiated by two other highly souled mentors somewhere in 2003 by Daddaji of Nagridham at Bhind and then in 2013 in Sagar by H.H. Shri Horamdasji of Meerut. I express here my deepest gratitude to my spiritual mentors. It was somewhere in early winter of 1988 when I had to go to conduct M.Sc. examination at Saint Andrews College, Gorakhpur, under the auspices of D.D.U. University, Gorakhpur. Dr. S.B. Singh, a senior teacher and HOD of Zoology, was my host, to whom and as per my old habit, I also enquired about important places and saints of Gorakhpur. It was only this time when I had visited Gita Vatika for the first time with him. I did circumambulation of the holy entombment of Bhaijee – Late Shri Hanuman Prasad Poddar. We both then went to a nearby place to meet Shri Radha Baba, but were disappointed to learn that he had already slept. Therefore, I requested Dr. Singh to spare some time at early hours of the next day again, so that I could pay my reverence to Baba. But due to my ill-luck, shortage of time and because of train departure,

I was unable to materialise this strong longing of mine to meet Baba. I still remember that I was extremely sad due to such instance.

Though I had been closely connected with D.D.U. University, Gorakhpur, in various academic positions since 2001, I could not visit Gita Vatika until 2011. It was an interesting story. There appeared an article in 'Kalyan' somewhere in 2009 about the appearance of the God to Bhaijee, by S.S. Dujari. I have then written a letter to 'Kalyan' to send me the address of Dujariji, which was directed to his younger brother Shri Hari Krishna Dujari, who had informed me about his death and has also sent me a catalogue with publications by Gita Vatika Prakashan. Since then, I have been in correspondence and telephonic conversations with him, looking to his simple and courteous nature. I have also asked him to send a few books from the list. Because of such literature and my good luck, I have developed a longing to attend the great festival of Radhashtami at Gorakhpur. I have contacted Shri Dujariji in 2011 and expressed my wish to attend this function, to which he gladly consented. I had an opportunity to attend it in September, 2011 for three consecutive days, which was an excellent occasion of my life and which is still an ineffable joy. I have myself seen an actual divine grace during such function. I have again tried in 2012, but due to sudden disruption of train, had to cancel my trip. Since then, I have been trying to attend it again but failed due to many compelling reasons. However, I can vouch and recommend anyone, seeking divine blessing, to attend it at least once in life this grand function in Gita Vatika at Gorakhpur. In February 2013, I was again in Gorakhpur University in connection to conduct Ph.D. viva of a student and, thereafter, went to Gita Vatika to pay my respect to Shri Dujariji. It was a surprise to me when he asked me to translate the book '*Ek Alaukik Vibhooti*' from Hindi to English, without any introduction. I have consented as if I was under some spell and asked him to give me sufficient time, for which he agreed. I had begun this work in the first week of March, 2013 and then sent a few pages (90) to Dujariji for an appraisal. This work then continued even during my sojourn to USA from May to December, 2013. It was completed in December, 2014 and then I have sent it back to Gorakhpur, except a few pages (90), which were probably lost/misplaced by the assessor. Thereafter, I had become very busy with family affairs and the pending work to rewrite the lost pages was delayed till May 2015. In May this year, I have again started to rewrite this task during my next trip to USA. But my inner instinct has persuaded me to rewrite the whole text again which I have completed by the end of February, 2016.

There was a good reason to accept this work of English translation as I had already read its Hindi version and was fascinated by its contents. I wish that people of non-Hindi-speaking region and foreigners should also have a knowledge about such an exalted divinity of the world. I have already and long back read two bestsellers of the 20th century, '*A Search of Secret India*' by Paul Brunton and 'Autobiography of a Yogi' by Yogananda and other texts of such type. I had a longing to put forward another book in the 21st century of such level in English in front of the spiritual aspirants of this world.

But a point, which I have to face while reading Hindi version of 'Ek Alaukik Vibhooti' was a pressing demand of meanings for many beautiful Sanskrit words, couplets, Hindi quatrains and verses of devotional poetry, etc., which are given by the learned compiler in Hindi version. These are often difficult to understand by a common reader who is not well versed with the Sanskrit language. It has sometimes caused a hindrance not only with the flow of reading but also creates an obstruction to grasp the related para. Thus, an effort is made with the kind help of Shri B.D. Dubey, Dr. Rajneesh Kumar Chaturvedi, Mr. Rasendu Fogla and Late S.K. Dujari to translate this part with utmost perfection. I am sure that such a step would not only help the non-Hindi-speaking readers to understand the meaning but will also maintain the flow while reading this text.

Translation from Hindi to English was not an easy job due to the reason that to find sometimes an exact and true meaning of many technical/special words of Hindi/Sanskrit to English is almost difficult and for which both Roman script and nearly accurate meaning in English have been given in English version. Furthermore, and to facilitate non- Hindi-speaking or foreign readers, an appropriate glossary is also being appended to apprise them a true definition of various technical/special words which a reader may come across in the book. Lengthy sentences are unavoidable as to cope with the soul of its Hindi version, containing also very long sentences. Few new and relevant photographs have been included in this version. An effort has been made to revise up-to-date facts of some topics like an up-to-date list of Ph.D. thesis on Bhaijee. Proper care is taken in this text to provide simple and correct English with meaning conformable to ancient Indian scriptures. Moreover, and as required, a Roman script is used in absence to locate an appropriate English word. An effort has also been made so that the language should be lucid and chaste with an emphasis that the flow and feeling of the original compiler may remain intact.

I have tried to present in the following paras a gist of this text, so that a reader may feel, in advance, a glimpse of the important portion of some topics.

The most important thing that a reader might not find elsewhere in other text is an authentic and lucid account of two actual meetings of Bhaijee – Shri Hanuman Prasad Poddar with Lord Vishnu at Jasidih in 1927 in the presence of several gentlemen and again on his arrival at Gorakhpur. The second important event is about the unique appearance of a divine saint Narad and great sage Angira in front of Bhaijee in 1936. This has never been reported with any saint in this country. Another notable thing that the readers would observe and that has not been reported or heard with other saints is a forceful involvement within the sea of act of deity (Lila Sindhu) and then continued in an ecstatic meditation for 15-20 hours even when full and futile efforts were made to indulge in bodily activities with this world. The detail about such events can be seen in text vide topics 1, 30, 60 and 139.

Another important point of this text, which my readers would find in topic 22, is the true meeting, in conversation of Bhaijee with a Parsee ghost, occurred at Mumbai in 1925. Here the Parsee ghost had very clearly and humbly pleaded to Bhaijee to perform his *Shraddha* ceremony at Gaya so that he could achieve salvation. This event is an eye-opener to those who don't believe in the existence of another world. Bhaijee had enquired many things about the ghost world, its condition and the result of the deeds of life prevailed over there. The ghost had clearly informed that every hell is true. People engaged in many types of sins will have to face very cruel treatment. Bhaijee had even established contact with divine worlds through this ghost. What is the condition of someone after the death, such track had been connected through the medium of someone living over there, with whom Bhaijee had already made a close contact.

It would also be pertinent here to include two very recent events from the Western world, which also testified the existence of another world and the importance of *Shraddha Karma*. There was news along with a photo on 13.10.2015 in '*The Times of India*', "Stallone sees dead son and sends family to Haridwar to perform *Shraddha*." Hollywood superstar Sylvester Stallone, known as Rocky Balboa, told a Vedic scholar from Rishikesh that he still sees his dead son Sage Stallone, who died suddenly in 2012. Thereafter, he has become extremely agitated and restless. An astrologer Dr. Pratik Mishrapuri, President of Prachya Vidya Society from Rishikesh, then on a visit to Los Angeles during 2014, explained to Stallone the Hindu concept of *Shraddha* and its divine effect on the departed soul. He advised Stallone to perform such ritual on specific date, after due confirmation with *Panchang* (a sacred calendar). Thereafter, a family (brother of Stallone and his wife) was seen in the crowd, along the bank of Ganga in Haridwar, performing *Shraddha* for the son of Stallone on 11.10.2015 to ensure peace to the departed soul for the son of Stallone. Stallone had quietly sent his half-brother Michael to Haridwar to perform the relevant rite for his late son Sage Stallone, who was just 36 and had also worked with his father in famous classic of *Rocky* series. His brother Michael was so much impressed by *Shraddha* ceremony that he also did the rite for his sister Toni Ann, who died at the age of 45 in 2012. Russian Cine Stars Alexi and his wife Olga were also present during this occasion. Michael also did a *Gaudaan* (gifting a cow to a Brahmin or a Hindu priest). It may be a shock to many of our Indian friends that a Hollywood star and a Christian has begun to believe in Hindu rituals. In December, 2015 issue of '*Kalyan*', an interesting instance has been given by Shri R.K. Sharma of the same nature, which anyone can look at and understand.

Under the heading in a flow of love to his motherland, the readers would find about an active involvement of Bhaijee in independence movement of India, due to which he had come in close contact with various top leaders like Gandhiji, Malviyaji, and others. Bhaijee had also helped Malviyaji in arranging financial help from various people to establish Kashi (now Varanasi) Hindu University. (Topic 12)

Bhaijee was of the firm opinion that even an impossible can be made possible by the grace of the God, which readers can find in topic 23.

Due to pinching conversation with Shri G.D. Birla, which has become the main reason for the birth of '*Kalyan*' (a very famous spiritual magazine) had also compelled the original compiler of Hindi version, the late Gambhirchand Dujari to bind up his business of Sanavad, M.P. and to move to Bombay to help Bhaijee forever. You would find its detail in topic 26.

Sincere publicity of divine name (Name of the God) made by Bhaijee and his statement that divine name benefits to all living creatures, for as much distance as it can reach, can be seen in topic 41. His efforts made for an extensive publicity of Gita Press, at the pursuit of knowledge of Gita and resulting in pious behaviour (Gita Gyan Yagya) at famous Kumbh Mela ,can be seen in topic 41.

It was not only in India but even people living abroad have received the spiritual guidance from '*Kalyan*' and '*Kalyan Kalptaru*' (topic 51). It can be seen under the headings "An Appearance to English Devotee" and "An Opinion of Foreign People about Bhaijee", respectively (topics 55, 144).

The readers would have a glimpse of the deep longing of Radha Baba in topic 67 to achieve an extremely rare type of devotion – a love like the herd girls of Braj (*Gopi-prem*) through the practice of feelings, as performed by the herd girls of Braj through their hearts, totally devoted with the love of the God.

Another interesting and important information which the reader would, obtain is that Bhaijee was not only a realised saint of spiritual world but he had also perceived the political problems, prior to seventy one years by his far-sightedness, which are still present today in India, though he had dissociated from politics in 1929. Though '*Kalyan*' is a purely spiritual magazine and never contains any criticism about other subjects, but Bhaijee had to sometimes give spiritual opinion in it during February, March and July in 1947, looking at the several atrocities on Hindus by Muslims. As the selfish leaders have not considered true warning of a saint, so the country is still facing same problems after a long duration of independence (topic 82).

For planning and construction of the temple and for an establishment of the missing decorum of Shri Krishna's birthplace, its credit goes to Bhaijee, which has brightened the face of India (topic 108).

It would be interesting to know that Bhaijee had declined many offers from various institutions and people to felicitate him, which included a great offer for rare and most coveted award of that time – "*Jewel of India*" – offered by the then President of India Dr. Rajendra Prasad and other offers like Rai Sahib, Rai Bahadur by the then British Government of India (topic 113).

Construction of the historical Bhagwat building and an establishment of four pilgrimages – The Veda building – a milestone for Hindu religion were also materialised due to genuine help and guidance by Bhaijee and can be seen under the same heading vide topics 121 and 122.

Bhaijee has not only earned the highest place in spiritual world but also produced the excellent literature in Hindi. It was at that time when Hindu religious texts were available only in small quantity, so much so that even a correct translation of the epics like *Gita* and *Mahabharat* and other ancient texts in Hindi was not available easily. Bhaijee had reinterpreted the essential part of complete Sanskrit literature in context with the present time of the country. His commentary on Narad's aphorisms on religious devotion (*bhakti*) has become a very favourite text for the path of spiritual devotion, within the tradition of Hinduism (topic 128).

The text also contains a gist of the important spiritual instructions by Bhaijee on few subjects under the heading "The Immortal Instructions" (topic 131).

Due to strong faith of Bhaijee, in repetition of the name of the God which he has propagated during his discourses, solitary discussion, trips made for spread of divine name, solitary group singing of hymns, community group singing of hymns and during group singing of hymns in the city, he had extended such work of promotional methodology through recent facilities, i.e., request made by him to publish in every issue through '*Kalyan*' magazine since 1929. Such system of repetition of divine name continues for two-and-a-half months. Readers would be happy to learn that this work is being still continued through '*Kalyan*' (topic 136).

Another important feature of the text is the compilation of a clear and an extensive description under the heading "The Divine Perceptions", which Bhaijee had created by contributing literary composition in verses towards his divine feelings and the achievement with the help of the verses given in his excellent creation, which may also be treated as an epic 'Pad-Ratnakar' (topic 138), published by Gita Press as a text.

I am deeply interested that my readers should also know about a special mission through this text, for which Bhaijee was sent by the God to this planet. One of them was to show the evidence of brightest identity of the sweet love of Radha-Krishna and to explore its feasibility for an achievement. To achieve such kind of love as that of the herd girls of Braj (Gopi prem) is said to be most difficult as given in the sub-terranean section (Patal-khand) of *Padma Purana*. But, with such simplicity, Bhaijee has assessed such worship through his discourses and texts that even the mind of an average person also feels a longing by reading or hearing these things. Second important work accomplished by Bhaijee and which readers can see in the text is the protection of Indian religion and scriptures and arranging their feasibility to an average man, as all these texts are in Sanskrit. A reader may find here how Bhaijee had to find a track of the authentic copies of these scriptures, thereafter an authentic Hindi version was produced by reputed scholars with a correct and authentic version conformable both to grammar and scriptures. Most of the religious texts are published as special issues of '*Kalyan*' and have been delivered to millions of houses. Some of the important texts have also been translated and published in English, both for non-Hindi-speaking and foreign readers. It was due to such sincere and herculean efforts of Bhaijee that has made it possible to deliver an epic like the Ramayana, the *Ramcharitmanas* in every house by making it easily available and that too at very nominal price. The third important work accomplished by Bhaijee was the publicity of divine name and religious devotion (Bhagwannam and Bhakti) to every house in such an extensive manner which is not found or heard of anywhere (topic 140).

Another important point about this book is the inclusion of a short biography of Shri Seth Jaidayal Goyandka, who was a Marwari saint with an exceptional dominion of spiritual world, to whom the people have not recognised deliberately. The whole credit to establish Gita Press, construction of Govind Bhawan in Kolkata, Gita Bhawan at Swargashram in Rishikesh and Rishikul Brahmcharya Ashram, Churu goes to him. He was such a saint who had achieved a supreme opportunity to see Lord Vishnu in an entirely vigilant condition. It was due to an initiation of Radha Baba, Swami Ramsukh Das and Hari Krishna Goyandka that Shri Sethji has produced the commentary on Gita. It was published in '*Kalyan*' in 1940 as 'Gita Tatvank'. Later, it was modified and published as 'Gita-Tatva-Vivechani', which has become an excellent commentary on Gita (topic 148).

Another important reason to take up this assignment is to apprise non-Hindi-speaking readers about the sincere efforts by a noble saint like Shri Bhaijee. Due to him only, availability of a vast spiritual Sanskrit literature is now available in Hindi, which was gradually disappearing. The *Puranas*, the *Upnishads*, the *Mahabharat*, *Valmiki Ramayan* and other important scriptures written by scholars have been published in millions of numbers and were sent not only all over India but everywhere in this world. He has himself created a huge and original literature and, thus, increased the volume of Hindi literature and provided an incomparable solid material. A literature of *Goswami Tulsidas* is made available to each and every house for a very cheap price, due to single and the herculean efforts of Bhaijee. In fact, our young readers and even future generation would not believe that a work that can only be completed by several organisations has been envisaged and successfully completed by Bhaijee alone.

Bhaijee has also presented such an ideal of service to people, for which a separate and huge treatise is needed to describe. He had been devoting in such service since childhood, which has gradually been merely increased and became just his lifeline in future (topic 127).

The readers may find spiritual and philosophical connotations as unique. It was almost difficult to translate these connotations as expounded in Hindi to English. However, sincere efforts have been made to establish a close harmony with its original, due to which few Indian words are retained in Roman script, so that to maintain their essence and significance. Pedantic style has been used to explain the concept of original compiler.

Due to usage of simple English for this version coupled with basic meaning, learned readers may find the language of this text, a little harsh than figurative. It may not appeal highly to their senses but, in my opinion, literal language is a benefiting way of expression specially for a work with spiritual contents.

Finally, it has almost been three years of laborious endeavour to translate this work. This version is well supplied with subtle and plentiful details to help, even foreign readers, to grasp the real essence of the form, given in its original form in Hindi. For the shortcomings that will undoubtedly be found in the text, I am, of course, responsible. However, a healthy, constructive criticism and suggestions, etc. may be sent which will be rectified accordingly.

Most of this work is completed during my stay in U.S.A. between June, 2013 and December and again from May to February, 2016 with my daughter Dr. (Mrs.) Eva Gupta, D.D.D. (U.S.A.) to whom I express my thanks for the comforts she extended to me. I should also express thanks for the lovely company with two of her cute children Elyna and Ryan, who always kept me in high spirits and to my son-in-law Mr. Himanshu Gupta, M.S. (Pennsylvania, U.S.A.) for an encouragement and other facilities for this work, specially for the latest PC technology. Part of this work has also been carried out during my stay at London from April to October, 2014 with my son Dr. Anurag Gupta, M.B.B.S., M.B.A. (Cantab), who has inspired me to begin with a work for charity and to whom I express my thanks for comfort and encouragement he extended to me coupled with an excellent technical assistance.

Prof. O. Prakash, former Vice Chancellor, Bareilly University and Prof. H.R. Singh, former Vice Chancellor, Allahabad University, have also helped me in various ways to improve the quality during translation. I also express my special thanks to them.

Thanks, are also due to Dr. A.N. Selwatkar, Astt. Director, CSTT, for providing me necessary dictionaries for this work. Shri D.D. Nautiyal, Ex-Secretary, CSTT, also helped me with useful suggestions. Thanks are also due to Dr. Rajneesh Kumar Chaturvedi for composing this whole text of English version with an utmost dedication and to Shri B.P. Laturkar for his help in the language improvement.

At the time of concluding this task, I was looking for an appropriate person who should not only be an eminent person but also possesses a spiritual attitude. Accordingly, I requested Prof. D.P. Singh, former Vice Chancellor, Dr. Hari Singh Gour University, former Vice Chancellor, Banaras Hindu University, former Vice Chancellor, Devi Ahilya Bai University, Indore, former Director, National Assessment and Accreditation Council, Bengaluru and now the Chairman, University Grants Commission, New Delhi to write a foreword for this version, which he kindly accepted. Prof. Singh is not only an owner with charming personality but is also an ardent devotee of his spiritual mentor H.H. Saint Shri Ravi Shankarji Maharaj from Rawatpura (M.P.). I also had an opportunity to work with him under his able leadership during my service at H.O.D. of Zoology, Coordinator, Remedial Centre and as H.O.D. in Department of Biotechnology at Dr. Hari Singh Gour University, Sagar between 2004 and 2007. I express my sincere thanks to Dr. Singh for accepting my request despite his busy schedule.

My warmest thanks are due to the light and love of my life – my learned wife Mrs. Malti Gupta, M.Sc., B.Ed., Grundstufe I & II in Deutsch (Germany) for her support and patience without which this work might have not reached to its completion.

Last, but not least, I am grateful to Shri Hari Krishna Dujariji and his virtuous wife Smt. Pushpa Devi Dujari for their confidence they have shown by assigning this task of translation to me.

Dunraven, Napeville
IL, 60540 USA

—Prof. O.P. Gupta
Former Head of the
Department of Zoology (Retd.)
Dr. H.S. Gour University, Sagar (M.P)
470003, India
opg45@yahoo.co.uk
ogdoctor805@gmail.com

*I would also like to take this opportunity to thank Late Shri Shiv Kumar Dujari (son of Shri Shyam Sunder Dujari who did consolidation and compilation of original Hindi version) for providing valuable suggestions at various instances, helping me at the crucial juncture of finalisation and further initiating publication with Prabhat Prakashan. His sudden death on 15.01.2018 has created a lacuna and I pray the almighty to grant an eternal serendipity (Sadgati) to the departed soul.

"On the name of reverend God"
A Humble Request

To write anything about respected Bhaijee Shri Hanuman Prasad Poddarji is an unauthorised effort towards his savourous heart and sight deeply absorbed with savour. The whole country will be indebted to him for a long period. I am writing something, just to sanctify my pen. Under which mental state Bhaijee has created his literature, such a hint is only available in his literary composition of the verses. Shri Bhaijee has written:

He alone writes and enables to write,
He alone does and gets it done.
Do not know, what is wrong,
Do not know, what is right.

Shri Bhaijee has agreed that Lord Shri Krishna is only writing everything, or He is only dictating all this through me. He is only doing and asked me to do all activities, through me. Lord Shri Krishna only is the performer for that. I have just no any existence in the form of a distinct person. This is the mystery by which such a great work was done by him. Philosophy of life for such a great divinity and an evidence of various aspects of his life are given in this book.

Based on the material collected by his father, Late Shyam Sundar Dujari has done such an auspicious work in the form of a homage to Shri Bhaijee. I had earlier read a book on short biography of Shri Bhaijee written by him and I was very much impressed by it. This book would play an important role as a chief support for the travellers of a virtuous pathway. Few topics are so much impressive that a serious reader cannot be left unaffected by them. Specially, topics are written by the pen of Shri Radha Baba about Bhaijee, which can illuminate a pathway of any traveller for spiritual course. A remarkably extensive quantity of such material is being published first time only. Likewise, the correspondence between Shri Bhaijee and an ascetic Shri Jaidayalji Goyandka would guide the path of spiritual aspirants. This book will be proved very useful in disclosing various dimensions of the life of Shri Bhaijee. Whosoever would read this book in this age of disbelief and would do careful study of the topics given therein, he would definitely be benefited, such is my belief. I give applause to Shri Shyam Sundar Dujari for such a sacred work and wish him good luck.

—Vishnukant Shastri
Governor, Himachal Pradesh

The reverend Ram
A Voice of Homage

During the twentieth century, founder editor of '*Kalyan*' and '*Kalyan Kalpataru*' and a boatman of Gita Press, Hanuman Prasadji Poddar was accepted as an eminent saint and realised devotee, without any dispute and his contribution for the publishing of Indian culture has been considered as an epoch-making. Such contribution is sufficient to place him in the category among the incarnated divinities like Shankaracharya, Chaitanya Mahaprabhu or Goswami Tulsidas. The biggest trust about Bhaijee is perceived because of his involvement with immortal acts by dependents of the God, due to his epic '*Pad- Ratnakar*' in which, first of all, his kind reporting has disclosed this fact. During his life-time, he had sent an article on my humble request, "for the special issue on the defense of the country" for the magazine named '*Gyan Bharti*' for which I was an editor. In addition, a letter full of humility, which he had sent to a normal young person like me, proves his greatness. During his life-time, the people had then understood only his worldly contribution while few ascetics had also knowledge of his rare background but after his heavenly departure, the universal religious community has recognised and understood him a lot.

In 1985, Shyam Sundar Dujariji had sent me a brief biography of Bhaijee and by reading of this book, I was very much pleased, and it appeared that I got the book for which I was looking for. I experienced, while reading this book, that I myself tied somewhere with his spiritual cord. Thereafter, my contact with Dujariji has gradually become increased and an intimate connection was held with him. Whatever service he did to Bhaijee through his word, I had also been provided savouring of it. Under some rare motivation and due to his suggestion only, I published a special issue on '*A Unique Hindi Philosophy*' on the birth centenary of Bhaijee. His father, Shri Gambhirchandji Dujari had continuously dedicated his complete life only in collection of reminiscences of the life of Bhaijee. Absolutely all writers who have written biography of Bhaijee have openly praised for his collection. The first book was written by Shri Radheshyam Banka titled 'Mother and *Babuji*'. He has written by dedicating it to *Shri Gambhirchandji* – "His passion was just to write the biography while the only goal of his life was to collect the topics related to his life. Even after being scolded himself by Bhaijee and non-cooperation from friends, he continued to write, just continued writing the biography in his own style." Thereafter, a huge text titled "Bhaijee – A Sacred Recollection" was published. By introducing Shri Gambhirchandji, it was written in this text – "Whatever little facts are known towards the life of Bhaijee to this world today, it is the result due to his virtuous efforts." Thereafter, in the book titled "An Auspicious Path: Founder and the Traveller", its eminent scholar Dr. Bhagwati Prasad Singh has written – "I have no hesitation in accepting this that the identity of biography of Shri Poddarji, which is in front of us today, the basic ground of its construction is due to the huge collection of events by Dujariji only. It is beyond dispute that if biography of day to day is not achieved, written by Dujariji, then most of the facts of his sacred deeds have disappeared in the shadow of forgetfulness."

On the basis of the collection of his father, Shri Shyam Sundar had published the first short biography in 1984. Two of its editions have been sold out promptly. Its third edition was published titled "An Introduction to Bhaijee" with an inclusion of some more material. In the coming *Radhashtami*, it will be a birth ceremony of his father. Therefore, again a motivation has occurred in his mind that whatever parts are left over, and which is suitable for publication from the collected material by his father, taking alongwith them into consideration and as much as possible, some extensive biography should be published. In fact, then, this book is the sixth edition of that very same book, but the title has been changed due to inclusion with a new, sufficient material in an elaborative and adaptive manner.

It is proper to mention here about two-three among many specialties from this book. A real introduction of the divine state of Bhaijee can only be realised by a divine soul like him. He was Shri Radha Baba (former name Shri Chakradharji Maharaj) whom I had myself met in Gita Vatika. Some material was published earlier by him in connection to Bhaijee, but an abundant amount which is presented in this book, of that way, is probably never published before. It is unique for spiritual devotees. Secondly, letters written to Shri Jaidayal Goyandka by Bhaijee have been published here and there – but correspondence between two eminent persons which is included in this book, of that sort, has not been published elsewhere. By disclosing the time period for some verses of devotional poetry, under the title 'Divine Perception', their usefulness has been increased. For example, prior five days to the first visualisation of the God to Bhaijee, a verse of devotional poetry which was first created shows ,which state of soul causes no delay in actual visualisation of the God. Bhaijee also met *Shri Naradji* and great *sage Angira*, who were the saints from divine time. There are several such topics which have disclosed the divineness of Bhaijee, though these are not directly related to him.

Due to normal human limitations, it is quite possible that some errors may also be found in this book by the readers. This is my request to them that they should take pain to inform about such errors alongwith their opinions related to this book to Shri Shyam Sundarji. A help is received by Shri Brijdev Dubey to look after the proofs, etc. of this book.

C-13, Press Enclave, "Saket"
New Delhi-110017

—Lallan Prasad Vyas
(International President World
Conference on Ramayan,
Editor: World Hindi Philosophy)

Contents

1

Shri Hari

Shri Bhaijee: An Exalted Divinity: A Glimpse from His Divine Life

We are fortunate that our earth has never been deserted by the presence of saints. The efforts made by the saints during the period of penance and the state of accomplishment (*Siddhawastha*) are different but they are always for the betterment of this world. Due to materialistic thinking coupled with worldly shadows, we cannot easily recognise these saints. According to Narada's Bhakti Sutra, "There is no dualism between the God and His true devotees", i.e., there exists no difference between the God and His true devotees. It is then almost foolishness to try for such comparison between saints. For a person like me, it is not at all possible to recognise even a saint. Then the question does not arise for such comparison. Prostrating with full devotion and reverence unto the holy feet of all the known/unknown saints, I am writing about the feelings of my mind.

For the last 10-15 years, I have been interested to go through the biography of saints. The reason behind this approach is to obtain a true inspiration and, in addition, to experience the special qualities elsewhere as well, which I have been observing in respected Bhaijee. Though I cannot make any claim, however, three things have been marked very special with respected Bhaijee. Generally, we can declare a saint an enlightened one only if he is merged along with the God or could really visualise the visible form (*sakar vigrah*) of the God before his eyes *(Bhedopasak)* irrespective of the fact whether he meditates on himself *(Abhedopasak)* or he meditates on other than himself (*Bhedopasak*). Both the states are particularly self-explanatory only to oneself (one who knows himself by himself in himself). As such, anyone finds it also very difficult to recognise them. Truth can only be known if the saints themselves and kindly give a signal or the almighty could create such a revealing event.

For the first time, respected Bhaijee had met Lord *Vishnu* in person on 16th September, 1927 near the hills of Marwari Arogya premises at the south-eastern part in the building of Mahendra Sarkar in the presence of 15 gentlemen, near the custard apple tree. This event has already been described in detail in many books. Even then if somebody does not believe this statement by Bhaijee or feels a little sense of pride in it, then there is no meaning to convey anything to them, nor any need to read this account. I have myself personally verified from two-three gentlemen who were present during the above event and got a fully satisfactory reply. These people lived till few years ago. The complete description of this event has been duly written in Marwari language by the reputed publisher of Gita Press, the late Ghanshyam Dasji Jalan and edited by Bhaijee himself, is still in safe custody of my respected father the Late Gambhirchandji. It is an extraordinary event of spiritual world which has put even respected Bhaijee to a great surprise. The same and second event occurred again after three days on 19th September, 1927 at the very spot. When Bhaijee himself could not understand it, he enquired with Shri Sethji about the occurrence of such event in front of many people than in seclusion, i.e., against an established fact. Shri Sethji replied with assurance that it will benefit the world. Such event has intentionally been repeated. The God blessed those by His kind presence to whom He considered a befitting person to popularise religious devotion. Meetings and talks with the God in person were held four times with Bhaijee on his arrival at Gorakhpur, which was recorded in the diary of Bhaijee and a letter written to Shri Sethji. Later, Shri Bhaijee finally joined within the acts of Shri Radhakrishna and he mentioned thus – "The self has seen and understood hundreds of divine acts, beauty and charm of *Radhakrishna* and also found an opportunity to join in some of these acts."

Not to elaborate it, it is to be pointed out here that all the realised saints worshipping the visible God have surely witnessed him in person. Different times have manifested the presence of many reputed and memorable saints and their deserving biographical literature is extensive and lucid. Biographies of most of the saints have generally been written by the esteemed scholars. It is also said that under the spell of politeness, the authors have sometimes exaggerated such events. If we accept partly such statement, even then I have not found such an authentic and lucid account in that detailed description.

The second event is about the meeting of the divine sage Narada and great sage Angira. A detailed commentary for Narada's devotional aphorism was written by Bhaijee in *Shimlapal* during his tenure of surveillance. The same commentary alongwith some changes and edition was published in 1935 by Gita Press under the name of *'Premdarshan'*. Possibly due to such commentary or other reason, the divine sage Narada along with the great sage Angira had appeared and blessed Bhaijee at Gita Vatika in 1936 and had also a long discussion with him. The detailed account of such event is also available with the material collected by my father. It is told by Bhaijee himself. Even then, I had tried to search with a hope to get some handwritten consent by Bhaijee. In reply to Shri Ramniwas Poddar of Calcutta, Shri Bhaijee has written – "when there was non-stop group-singing of hymns, divine sage Narada and great sage Angira have appeared at this place. It was an excellent occasion and also very beneficial. They had told some very inspiring things. This is a fact". The people acquainted with scriptures are all aware that Shri Narada and Shri Angira were sons of Lord Brahma and had met, inspired and gave instructions to many devotees during all the three eras like *Satyuga, Treta* and *Dwapar*. Almost five thousand years of *Kaliyuga* have already passed. During this tenure and available biographies by as many as number of saints written by the learned scholars have lucidly mentioned each and every smaller event but there was no account of the appearance of Narada. When I could not find this account in the past literature, an effort was also made from my studious friends and famous saintly scholars, but nobody could inform about such an event. I have read in the biography of Adi Shankaracharya that "Shri Vedvyas had appeared and blessed him in Uttarkashi". It is also said about few saints that they have been initiated by ancient sages. However, Bhaijee had met the God in person even nine years earlier. He had even talked with him many times as well. Bhaijee had even started working as per his actual instructions. As such, the reason behind it could not be explained, i.e., why Narada had to come to guide Bhaijee for a proper path? Even the God had also assured Bhaijee to come as and when he would think of him. There is no detailed and authentic description available about this talk held between them. However, some impression can be made with the fact that Bhaijee had been accomplished to join together the divine saint community.

The third special thing about Bhaijee was specially noted during the last 10-12 years of his life. Though Bhaijee had already entered in the divine act prior to 1940, he had kept it secret from public for about 20 years. Even thereafter, he simply tried to hide, though it was not acceptable to Lord Krishna. It had been a very crucial condition and, in fact, beyond an imagination. Bhaijee wanted that his mode of conduct remains awake and watchful on this plane so that he can edit '*Kalyan*' and continue well with other type of service activities. Even then and with continuous efforts, his natural tendency of working was merged forcefully with the divine acts of Radhkrishna. It was a wonderful compulsion. The body suddenly and completely becomes unconscious and motionless. Eyes remain open but don't see anything. The pen though was in hand, it is not even dropped. There is no activity except breathing in and out. Such state remained continued for hours. The scholars have started to call it an ecstatic meditation (*Bhava-Samadhi*). To witness and join within the acts of Radhkrishna has been invariably found in the life of many saints emotionally attached to Braja. In the biography of Yogis, there has been the description of profound meditation *(Samadhi)* not only for days, months but even for years. I have also read such story of many devotees who have ever refused to stop service or worship even when the God Himself appeared in front of them. But even with full efforts made to indulge bodily activities within this world, a forceful involvement occurred within the sea of acts *(Leela sindhu)* and then remained in an ecstatic meditation (*Bhava-Samadhi*) for 15-20 hours, was not found or heard by me anywhere. However, as per the available sources, mind of Bhaijee, while doing other routine work, remained wandering within the acts of Krishna, even then, both the works were kept smoothly running due to the lack of his deep involvement. As Bhaijee states, it suddenly happens that all the activities of mind and sense have stopped. The world is disappeared completely except to breathe in and out. Nothing can be seen with open eyes. Is it a profound meditation (*Samadhi*) or something else? Sometimes this happens suddenly if I forcefully tried my senses to involve them within this world. Earlier, such a condition occurred after many days, but it happens now and then and within short intervals.

It is not a certain meditation *(Dhyaan)* or profound meditation *(Samadhi),* which is related to a practice, and not the fruit of some activity. It is a wonderful flash of a thought by his own act or is the act *(Leela)* within his act, which is extremely rare. In fact, at this very place only, one can have a formal meeting with an ultimate being in real sense.

It is not to be elaborated here as any scholar can write a complete text towards its investigation or analysis. As my studies are not sufficient enough, I cannot claim these things as cited above are not found in the biographies of other saints. However, I would correct myself if somebody will be kind to inform me. But respected Radha Baba (Swami Chakradharji Maharaj) has written, "I have not read about such spiritual state in any religious scripture and such state has not been mentioned in the life of any devotee except Chaitanya Mahaprabhu." Respected Radha Baba was an eminent scholar and had very deep study of religious scriptures -- which is a well-known fact.

Let us now look towards his external life. Bhaijee has pointed out in his will, a little earlier to his bodily departure, that the almighty wanted some specific work to be completed by him. It is not possible for me to visualise this 'special work' nor he had given anywhere such an indication. The historical work done by Bhaijee is the availability of our vast spiritual Sanskrit literature in Hindi. Our Sanskrit spiritual scriptures were gradually disappearing and there was no possibility of their use by general public. The Puranas, the Upnishads, the Mahabharat, the Valmiki Ramayan and different texts written by the scholars have been published by Bhaijee in millions of copies and have been sent not only in every corner of India but everywhere in the world. The inaccessible scriptures are made easily accessible due to Bhaijee. Now the possibility of their destruction of such precious scriptures by the atrocities of the terrorists, to harm them, is now completely over. Apparently, if complete India is destroyed by an atom bomb, even then our scriptures will remain safe up to the devastation of earth as these have been delivered to every corner of the world not only in Hindi or Sanskrit, but in English as well. His contemporary saints, devotees, preceptors of different sects, leaders of various parties, scholars, writers, industrialists, social workers, Christians, and Mohammadens treated Bhaijee with great veneration and respect. This can be seen in the text edited "*Bhaijee Pawan Smaran*". Secondly, he himself created a huge and original literature, thereby significantly increased the volume of Hindi literature and provided solid spiritual material, which is incomparable. The literature of Goswami Tulsidasji was made easily available to each and every home of India and whole credit goes to Shri Bhaijee. Even the complete and correct Ramcharitmanas was made available only in fifty paise, which was also a special gift by Bhaijee. This work which could not be completed even by number of organisations has been done solitarily by Bhaijee himself.

The special issues of '*Kalyan*' have also their own importance as these are now well known as an encyclopedia of their own subject. It is not at all possible to count the number of persons who have made due progress on the road of accomplishment by his inspiration. To serve and help others financially was his normal nature. Though, such service was made so secretly that even his family members or very close persons were not aware about it. Nobody ever returned or seemed disappointed once he approached Bhaijee. It was beyond an imagination for any person to know that how many crore rupees have been spent for such work.

It is also difficult to imagine about his industriousness. Since 4:00 in the morning till 12:00 of the night, he remained busy in his work. During the publication of special issue of '*Kalyan*', he even worked up to 2:00 A.M. Even during his meal, he continued reading daily mail by single hand.

Let us throw some light on the eminent persons who came with his contact. Respected Radhababa firstly went to Bankura to meet honourable Sethji. He stayed there for many days with him, got his curiosity solved before Sethji who finally sent him to meet Bhaijee. Bhaijee came to meet him as soon as he received the information and greets him by touching his feet treating him as renunciant. The touch of Bhaijee had made such a magic that this saintly person and a strong follower of 'Veda' who does not believe in Radhakrishna as God, rather as an illusory character of ultimate being *(Mayopadhik Brahma)* has left studies of Veda and became a true worshipper of Shri Radhakrishna and in intervening time took zonal abandonment *(Kshetra sannyas)*, lived with Bhaijee throughout his life without a separation even for a single night and on his departure of heavenly abode, passed his entire life at the place of cremation of Bhaijee below a tree. For a suitable person, a saintly touch can make wonder, and this was an actual example. In fact, our future generations would find it difficult to believe that in this faithless time of the twentieth century, a work, which cannot be completed by several organisations – how such work beyond imagination has been done by Bhaijee alone. Like second Vedvyas, his propagation for the religion and scriptures can be highlighted better than eastern scholars. In addition, proper control of work related with conduct and views can be compared from recollectors like Manu- Yagyavalkya, etc. The creation of interesting literature belonging to religious devotion (*bhakti*) has been made by the devoted poets like Surdas, Tulsidas and others, and, in addition, an exemplary reputation is made by the saints like Chaitanya Mahaprabhu towards continuous and total involvement in the ocean of acts while an excellent unification of this altogether is clearly evident in the great personality of Bhaijee.

❐

2

An Introduction to the Family

The scriptures have clearly announced that blessed are those parents, that family, that caste, that society and that country, where divinely engrossed, supremely devoted eminent persons are manifested. In Rajasthan and in Bikaner district (at present, it is in Churu district), there is a small but famous city named Ratangarh. The grandfather of Bhaijee, Shri Tarachandji Poddar was among the famous traders of the city. He was a very religious person and had two sons – Kaniramji and Bhimramji. Bhimramji got a rare chance to become a fortunate father of Bhaijee. Shri Kaniramji took father's consent and proceeded to do business in Assam. He was the first trader among Marwari businessmen to proceed to Assam from Ratangarh. He obtained a contract to supply food-material to army. As his work flourished, he called his family to Assam. He had no children and had become aged as well. Therefore, he treated Bhimramji as his adopted son. As the mango grows on the mango tree, likewise family of Bhaijee was full of divine wealth. Shri Kaniramji had the tremendous respect for the Ramcharitmanas. He takes his meal only after daily recitation of it. His wife respected Ramkaur Devi was almost like a saint. Even without a background of normal education, she possessed a great quality to extract the gist of religious scriptures with the help of assembly of virtuous people (*Satsang*) and by consulting sacred texts. Lord Hanumanji was her deity. She had high regard in repetition of divine names and reading sacred *Manas*. If she lived in Ratangarh and could become free from her house-hold duties, she reaches and attends at holy feet of saints. There occurred Brahmin feast every month at her residence. Secret donations were also made by different means. During her Calcutta stay, she reaches Shri Sawalia temple at the early hour of three-and-a-half in the morning, after taking bath in the Ganga. After attending an early morning ceremony, which was performed by worshipping the God, she visits to the temple of Lord Hanuman and Shri Satya Narayan.

Shri Bhimramji was a very virtuous person. To save immemorial religion, he established "Sanatan Dharma Pushtikarini Society" in Calcutta. The well-known superior of Kailash ashram monastery of *Rishikesh* and a learned scholar Shri Jagdishwaranand, when took renunciation, had visited at first from Hoshiarpur (Punjab) to Shri Bhimramji. His honesty was incomparable. He can never tolerate, if at all, any outside item may arrive to his residence unknowingly. An event can be cited here. He had a cloth business in Calcutta. Due to a mistake, hundred rupees were extra added in the bill. Due to miscalculation by the trader making payment, an extra hundred rupees were delivered to him. A person named Kewal Singh with him was looking to the accounts. He could recall the mistake after two days and narrated the whole thing to Shri Bhimramji. Bhimramji, at once, told why an extra hundred rupees came into our account. Go immediately and return it. Kewal Singh replied it is already evening……. Even he could not complete his sentence. Shri Bhimramji interrupted and told what happens if it is evening. Go just now and give him back the money. I will not take meal until it is returned. This money was with us for two days and, hence, an interest for two days must also be paid. This is an example of his honesty. All such traditions of family have entered right from the childhood in the life of Bhaijee.

❐

3

Circumstances Leading to his Birth

Ramkaur Devi was more worried as there was no son of Shri Bhimramji. She had much faith in holy saints. As there were no facilities in Shillong, she took her husband's permission and went alone to Ratangarh along with a servant. Such a long travel on those days was not simple and this is an indication of her excellent courage. During those days in Ratangarh, Shri Laxminathji, Shri Mangalnathji and Shri Bakhannathji were probably the main persons among Nathyogis. They were always pleased with her due to sincere services rendered by Ramkaur Devi. Ramkaur Devi had conveyed her worry to 'Nathji'. Nathji was happy and blessed one day with a boon, that from today, grandson will be born within a year. He will be a very humble scholar and devoted saint. There will be a sign at his birth – 'Shri' sign on his forehead, hairs on shoulder and a black mole on his right thigh and he will not cry like other normal children at his birth. It is also said that he had also told that Tutiya Maharaj living with us would himself incarnate in your home. Hearing kind words of Nathji, Ramkaur Devi became very cheerful as she had no doubt in mind about the birth of her grandson.

At the same instance, one more event occurred. Ramkaur Devi was a disciple of Baba Mahardasji Maharaj from Ratangarh of Nimbark sect. Due to his inspiration, Ramkaur Devi has organised 108 recitals of *Vishnusahastranam* along with post chanting each time a sacred Mantra, in the local temple of Laxminarayan. Three other Brahmins along with Baba Mahardas himself carried out this rite. The day when 108 recitals were completed, liquid butter was poured only one time in the lamp on this occasion, but it kept burning uninterruptedly. Baba Mahardas then told her after due completion of rite – Ramkaur, your heartfelt wish has been accomplished successfully. Give this consecrated water to drink to your daughter-in-law Rikhi Bai, a saintly and religious grandson will surely be born, who would brighten the fame of your family. Please name him after the name of Hanuman. There was no limit of her joy, hearing all this message by Baba Mahardas.

She returned to Shillong as there was no need to stay at Ratangarh.

❑

4
The Birth

A little later of her arrival to Shillong, Ramkaur Devi could know about the pregnancy of Rikhibai, which made her very happy. The feelings in the heart which are waiting for the supreme and desired object cannot be understood just by hearing it from somebody. One can easily be restless by the premonition of likelihood for any complication at any moment – this can easily be realised by an experienced sufferer. At last, the ultimate and auspicious moment has arrived and Rikhibai gave birth to a worthy son on 17th September, 1892. Such an opportunity was well contrived on Saturday – the day of Hanuman. Everybody was very surprised due to the presence of all signs on the body of newly born baby about which the saint of Ratangarh had already predicted. According to her own dedication, Ramkaur Devi has named the baby 'Hanman Prasad' treating him as a kind-blessing of her deity.

❐

5

Loss of the Mother

Two months after the birth of child Hanuman Prasad, i.e., 15th November, 1892, his old grandfather Shri Tarachandji died in Shillong. On the day of his death, he enquired to his family members whether they have all taken their meal. Later, he told – Call Kaniram and took me to the cowshed of the family. Though he was 84 years old, he was able to do all his house work by his active movements. On reaching cowshed, he told – My time of departure has almost arrived. Look, the councillors of the God having four hands are standing in front of me, please do have sight of them. You should all chant *'Hare Ram' mahamantra*. He himself started chanting this *mahamantra*. Then he asked for a bath which Shri Kaniramji arranged and also put sandal spot on his forehead and got him lay down on his lap. Gradually and within a short duration, his soul left the body through eyes. He was a very great ascetic. He used to get up daily at three in the morning, after having got his hand and mouth washed and would start repeating 50 strings of beads daily of '*Hare Ram*' *mahamantra* including a complete reading of 18 chapters of the Gita prior to initiating his daily duties like calls of nature, etc. His daily routine also included 108 recitals of *Vishnusahastranam*.

The child could hardly attain two years of age when he had to witness moment of separation by his mother. Following a simple sickness, Rikhibai has to give custody of her piece of heart – her beloved son to Ramkaur Devi and then left her body made up of five elements to heavenly abode on 18th July, 1894. The whole family has become greatly distressed with grief. Grandmother must bear all the responsibilities about the upbringing of this motherless child. On becoming eligible to identify and differentiate, the child has found only his grandmother Ramkaur Devi as a mother. He started calling her 'Maa' which continued throughout life. Due to pressure from his family members, his father must marry second time. Later, he was blessed by three daughters – Kamli Bai, Annapurna Bai and Chanda Bai.

❐

6

Attacked by a Terrible Disease

Child Hanuman Prasad was hardly three years old when he became ill one day. At first, it appeared if it was a simple illness and would also be alright soon, but the condition of the child became serious due to lung disease. What would be the mental condition of the grandmother, it could only be guessed. Because of many large and elaborative worships of deities, several prayers and many rites, the child was born, which himself is lying on the cot due to attack of terrible disease. The condition got worsened even after every possible treatment. Finally, and becoming disappointed from every angle, grandmother took the child, went to Ratangarh and adopted the path of sacred recitation, divine worship, recitation, charity and sacred rites, etc. made under the guidance of saints and ascetics. The saints blessed him, and the child started recovery and after a complete recovery within a few days, had also been applausing grandmother by his sweet smile. Grandmother, then, has gone back to Shillong along with him.

❐

7

Protection from an Earthquake

Nobody can kill a person when the God is there to take care, it's another example has come soon soon. There occurred a terrible earthquake in Shillong in 1896. It was evening time. Within no time, buildings erected in the line had collapsed on the ground. An infinite property has been destroyed. During this accident, the care of child Hanuman Prasad was made possible due to the blessing of some unimaginable power. The description of this accident can be read in his language, which he himself published in *'Kalyan'*:

There occurred a terrible earthquake in Assam in 1896. At that time, I was about four years old. We had our business in Shillong (Assam). My grandfather Shri Kaniramji lived there. Father was looking after the business of Calcutta. I was brought up by my grandmother due to death of my mother at a very young age. How much pain she took for me and the affection she had for me, I cannot repay it even after serving her for one thousand births. I have not given full attention towards this aspect when she was alive. Now there is no use to repent. They have got big fortune whose parents, etc. are alive. They could earn a lot of pleasure by serving them with their heart's content, otherwise there will be no means for actual service except for repentance like myself. I was living in Shillong with grandmother. My paternal aunt had also come there. She had two children. We all three had played together. There was a completion ceremony of some fast on the day of earthquake at the place of our near one Shri Bhajanlal Shriniwas. We had to go there to take meal. Both the children of paternal aunt have refused to go. I only went alone. They remained at home. It was evening time. It would be about 5 o' clock. I took meal in the kitchen of Shri Bhajanlal Shriniwas behind his circular parapet. Returning from the kitchen, I was almost entered in the parapet that the earth trembled violently. I screamed as there was raining of stones everywhere. The complete house is destroyed within minutes. I was pressed down but, surprisingly, there were stones all around, a plank fell over them and there was a mountain of stones over it. It seems as if I am trapped in a hole like a black cave. How a space was created there for the circulation of air, it is not known but I was alive. As the earthquake came to an end, there started torrential rain and simultaneously round parapet was set to be on fire near our neighbour. There was sound of distress on all sides. There was also no information who is press down and who is saved. Grandmother started searching for all three of us. Both the children of my paternal aunt were found dead below the stones. The dead body of Shriram Goenka, grandson (and little elder to me) of my oldest paternal aunt was also found dead. Shouting and searching for us, grandfather has come down near the parapet of Bhajanlal Shriniwas. He was calling very loudly – 'Mannu-Mannu'. I heard his voice. I was a little child, was afraid and was also weeping. But don't know, by which inspiration, I could reply loudly with full strength – I am here, please take me out immediately. The pile of stones was removed. I have come out and climbed on the lap of my grandfather. He had embraced me to the heart. Both of us were weeping. There were many meanings of his weeping. Till that time, grandmother was remembering her deity – Shri Hanumanji. Hanumanji answered her prayer, the grief towards the loss of children of paternal aunt was a little lighter for a moment. The hearts of Kaniramji had been shattered due to the blow of the earthquake. Suddenly, he became sick and had left his body by chanting *"Soham-Soham"* in Calcutta on 3rd December, 1899.

❑

8

Schooling and the Initiation

(A) An Initiation: The effort of great saints provides an indication of their future life. Prior to the construction of grand palace, its foundation is automatically set according to its conformity. The same kind of spiritual phenomena was also observed from the childhood in the life of child Hanuman Prasad as well. Brought up with great affection of grandmother Ramkaur, the child was neither very naughty nor serious. He had been witnessing to his grandmother's visiting to saints. Looking to the earnest efforts of Devi Ramkaur, he had also felt concerned about many things in his heart. When the holy-hearted saints discussed about the hymns with Devi Ramkaur, at that time, the child also listens to their talks with full concentration. The child fills with full of joy by hearing the talks and the events of saints. When there was a discussion about the mentor and disciple, at that time, there occurred a manifestation of an infantly convenient elation in the heart of a child and a silent desire also created in the inner part of heart. I should also have a mentor and I should also have been initiated. Devi Ramkaur observed the serious gesture of child and just through long-looking, the emotions of both the hearts were joined by natural electric particles. In the mind of Devi Ramkaur appears pulsation with strong rhythm – he may also be initiated. My child should flourish under the shelter of feet with great saints of higher sect. Therefore, once continuous mental thoughts took the material form, Devi Ram Kaur decided one day that the initiation ceremony for the child is to be conducted. The preparations started.

During those days, a great scholar and superior of a monastery Mehardasji of Nimbark sect lived in Ratangarh. His disciple was Ramratan Dasji and disciple of him was Shri Brajdasji. Saint Brajdasji has a unique opportunity to become an initiation teacher of child Hanuman Prasad. Devi Ramkaur requested Saint Brajdasji to accomplish initiation ceremony. Saint Brajdasji also accepted it gladly. During an auspicious moment, the child took a bath. Wearing new clothes, he came unto the holy feet of mentor. An ocean of elation was rippling in the heart. The teacher observed that the child is very keen from his heart – likewise once even Lord Narad also observed Dhruva in the same manner – had initiated by the sacred verse *"Om Namo Bhagwate Vasudevay"*. It seems if the same is being repeated, Saint Brajdasji completed the ceremony. Mentor tied a necklace of small beads around the tender neck of the child and counselled a sacred verse *"Om Namo Bhagwate Vasudevay"* in his ear. *Vaishnav* initiation ceremony was conducted. This rite was held in Ratangarh in the year 1900. In the same year, Devi Ram kaur went to her father's home at Amritsar. Her affectionate grandson also accompanied. The child was already divine-initiated. Now the practical initiation by grandmother has begun. Devi Ramkaur has been favoured by Hanumanji. She had also seen an actual appearance of Shri Hanumanji. The child was already eight years old. Devi Ramkaur taught the recitation of '*Hanuman Kavach*' to the child which he learnt and started to recite daily. So strong was such sowing of seed that it had risen higher and higher. Later, this child started to recite several divine prayers like *Surya, Ganpati, Devi, Shiv,* etc. regularly. During sacred night *(Navratri)*, complete recitation of *'Durgasaptshati'* and many hymns in praise of 'Bhagwat' were also recited by him with great reverence. When grandmother goes to saint Shri Bakhnnathji for assembly of virtuous people, the child Hanuman Prasad also accompanied. Gradually and looking to the inborn faculty in child, Nathji started to teach verses of the Gita by heart. The child started to repeat the complete Gita within a year through heart. Looking at the remarkable talent and spiritual tendency, Nathji and grandmother became very happy. In between this, there appeared a necessity of a change in professional life. Shri Bhimramji has become alone after the death of Shri Kaniramji. Therefore, business at Assam had to be closed due to inability of maintaining such an extensive business, while the business at Calcutta shop (Kaniram Bhimram) was continued and since the year 1901, Bhimramji shifted to live in Calcutta along with family because Bhimramji alone had to look after, at that time for everything.

(B) Education: It is surprising that the child, who had no formal education, later on, became such a great scholar of many languages. During his subsequent study in Calcutta, he obtained sufficient knowledge of Hindi literature due to his acquaintance and contact with the then famous scholar and editors of Hindi. Even the general knowledge of English was also obtained personally by his study with the help of Shri Ayodhya Prasadji in Calcutta. The knowledge of other languages was increased by him from time to time due to his wonderful talent. The ceremony of investiture with sacred threads was conducted by Pandit Chhotelalji.

❒

9

The Marriage

Those days it was a custom to marry at a very young age. Child Hanuman Prasad was 12 years old. His shop had a good reputation in business. Grandmother had a strong desire to see him in the form of bridegroom. Therefore, engagement was made with Mahadevi Bai, daughter of Shri Gurumukhraiji Dhandhariaji of Ratangarh. An event of such occasion is really very interesting, which has brought in front the ideal form of Devi Ram kaur. Just prior to marriage, Mahadevi was attacked by smallpox. It caused spots all over her body. The whole beauty was destroyed. Her parents were distressed with a worry that the engagement would now surely be abandoned. But Devi Ram kaur has announced clearly that the words given for the engagement of a girl *(Vagdan)* is held once only, like that I am stuck to my statement about the engagement of my grandson with Mahadevi. I would never change my words until his life. The marriage ceremony was solemnised with pomp and show in 1904. But the ordinance of fate was something else. The happiness of married life could not last for a long time. Mahadevi could hardly see the face of her first child after five years of marriage and she closed her eyes herself, forever. Before the family could come out of such grief, the newborn child had suddenly died in 1911. Devi Ram kaur arranged second marriage with Suvati Bai, daughter of Shri Mangturamji Saraogi, living in *Rajgarh*. Now the death of father has come in front. Shri Bhimaramji has left his body made up of five elements in 1912 at Ratangarh. Becoming free of the last ceremony after death (Shraddha), he came to Calcutta and started to look after the full load of business attentively. In 1915, Suvati Bai was blessed with a son. But just after two days of birth, the child died, and his mother also died after six months. All such events had caused a big blow to Devi Ram kaur. She was very worried due to domestic problems. She had again started giving pressure to his grandson for marriage, who was 23 years old at that time. Bhaijee was in obsession to serve the country at that time but had to lean his head in front of the affectionate persuasion of his grandmother. She conducted third marriage of his grandson in 1916 with Ramdei, daughter of Shri Sitaram Sangneria. Smt. Ramdei succeeded as a leader of the house up to the last. She, by adjusting her temperament with the mind of Bhaijee, gave constant cooperation to his every activity by working together. Never protected even her separate existence.

❒

10

A Strength of Character by Bhaijee and a Rare Self-Sacrifice of Devi Sarojani

It is very difficult to understand in this era of attachment to sensuous pleasure about the life of an Aryan young woman. It is an account of earlier times. There occurred a battle throughout the day between Mughal army and Rajput warriors. The battlefield has been filled with corpses. Many Rajput warriors, several Kshatriya young men slept with eternal sleep on the lap of their motherland. Due to rays of evening sun, their pure and calm faces were shining. Along with these warriors, sacrificing their lives for motherland, thousands of Mughal warriors were also sleeping. There was a total silence. Yes, there was an accumulation of group of some crows and vultures and their sound collided in between with such pure silence and had disappeared in the space. The Sun God could not see such sight anymore. It had gone to hiding in the western mountain. Gradually, it became a total dark.

Mughal army had also encamped at a little distance and was alert. There may not be leftover of a small group of the warriors who are ready to play for their life and may not fight again. Therefore, the eyes continuously look forward to that mass of corpses piercing the thick darkness. Tired eyes could be opened only for a few minutes. Even the first three hours' period of the night was not concluded that the army has become unconscious with serious facial expression. Someone was awake. He was a well-built young man. Commanding presence was evident from every part of his body. He was himself the king of Delhi. He covered himself firstly with weapons right from the lower to upper side but hiding his such heroic form with the help of a sheet and began to move, putting his feet extremely slowly. He reached near the mass of the corpses. He found that a beautiful and tender girl about thirteen years of age is walking in between the corpses alongwith a lamp in her hand. She goes to every corpse, observes face within the light of lamp, then moves further. Mughal warrior was almost brought to standstill, looking at all this. Beautiful hairs of the girl were scattered on her shoulders. An unutterable peace, love and distress-like signs had covered her face. Mughal warrior presumed as if he was not dreaming. Is she not the most beautiful woman from the heaven? Alongwith lamp and watching the corpses, the girl had reached near to that Mughal warrior. Light of lamp caused to shine the white sheet of Mughal warrior. The girl now looked towards that side. The warrior looked once towards his weapons, covered body and moved two steps and remained standing right in front of the girl. Now that girl raised her eyes. She felt a little fear for a moment but right on the second moment, her complete body gleamed with an extraordinary radiance. There remained no sign of fear within the girl. The Mughal warrior asked respectfully and in silent tone – O lady! What are you doing? Keeping silent for a moment, the girl replied – I am here to search. Mixed with eagerness but with little hitch, Mughal warrior asked this time – Whom are you searching, O lady! in these masses of corpses at this numb night? The girl this time loudly replied – have come to search the body of my darling husband. He is killed today in this battle. I want his body. By pulling his body on my lap and embracing this lamp at the end of sari, I would become a virtuous wife. I am calling you as my elder brother. You should put some firewood on it.

The Mughal warrior was overwhelmed by the radiance of this girl. He had no more strength to enquire anything but gathered all his courage and asked – O lady! Please don't mind, you are in very young age! When would you have married? The girl replied with simplicity – marriage was not yet held, engagement was done. Mughal warrior asked the last question – O lady! until marriage is not solemnised, how can he be your husband? To die for him....... the girl has interrupted in between in angry voice – Shut up and attention! Don't repeat such thing again. Rajput girls select the husbands only once.

Readers would be surprised to know that Devi Sarojani had also written the same thing to Hanuman Prasadji with a change of single word in her letter prior to get rid of her life – Hindu girls marry only once. Who was this Sarojani? This event had been narrated twice to one of his friends by Bhaijee.

"It was the year 1907. Due to invitation of my maternal uncle, I was going to the house and family of maternal grandfather at Chandpur via Gualande. Sukhlal attendant had accompanied me. To reach Chandpur via Gualande, during those days, one had to go by a steamer. At that part of the steamer where I sat, a Bengali gentleman alongwith his family was also sitting nearby. With him was his wife and daughter named Sarojani, who would be about 13-14 years old. Her younger brother was about five-six years old. He also accompanied her. I had some dried fruits. Naturally, I had given some dried fruits from it to the boy. That boy also accepted the dried fruits. A little later, steamer had reached Lohganj (Narpasa). These people had got down at that very station and went further via a small open boat."

Superficially, such event looks very simple. Everyday many travellers meet exactly like this and are separated after meeting. Among them, nobody remembers anything. But no, between the interval of this meeting of Bhaijee and the family of Sarojani Devi, a sacred mysterious event is hidden and even its smell could not reach to Bhaijee himself for about four years. Memory of this meeting had already been given a farewell by Bhaijee along with sweet sound of water at Lohganj station. Since then, infinite memories have come and gone. Due to their load, such memory of meeting with Sarojani had been so much concealed that this would again start dancing alongwith sweet instrument with unsteady mind, such imagination was not possible for Bhaijee. But how does it matter? The circle of destiny was continuously moving. Day breaks, dawn laughs, afternoon becomes full of anger, evening becomes serious and the night provides consolation. An auspicious rule of God had been working in a regular order on the waves of such sequence of time. Such dance developed for a moment. A wave comes frivolously and put a garland around the neck of Hanuman Prasad. Second comes and makes a mark on his forehead, the third comes and entertains by betel leaf, fourth comes and applies lamp black then, a new arrives and provides ornaments to wear. This way each wave comes and returns after providing a prescribed destiny of sportial God as a gift and what else Hanuman Prasad can do? Immersing in the stream of pure love of his life-partner, he had bent down his head happily. Therefore:

Floating on the waves, a letter had come on 9th July, 1912. Hanuman Prasadji was sitting in his shop in the building of Parakhji at Pagyapatti in Calcutta. Calcutta city was going to rest, casting over a sheet of night but Hanuman Prasad was awake. How can he sleep? Just now an emotion has told his unknown senses, my sister is coming to deliver a letter, don't sleep and, in fact, a letter was delivered on the second moment. The letter was signed by some unknown woman. Bhaijee opened the letter. That was extremely extensive. 'Sarojani' was written at the end and was also written nearby her address for meeting at Kalighat. In the beginning of the letter, complete detail was given. How he was moving, sitting on the steamer to Chandpur via Gualande while she also sat near him alongwith her father? She had alighted at Lohganj and what can be in the remaining part of the letter, such imagination can be made by readers themselves from the following vocabulary by my helpless pen. Surely, prior to such action, immerse your heart in the stream of purest river of love, totally empty from sensual pleasure or bestial sensual conduct, otherwise you would be deprived of auspicious blessings of that respected loving Devi Sarojani.

Such thing was known by the universal thread master of the world and was known to Sarojani. Therefore, Bhaijee could know through the letter of Sarojani, who had written him and whom Bhaijee had totally forgotten even the memory of her. Sarojani was alighted at Lohganj station, but was alighted only after dedicating her body, her life, her heart, her whole of possession unto the feet of Hanuman Prasadji forever. But her such dedication was not hollow. That was filled lip to lip by the purest love of the inner heart. Therefore, it was not disclosed. Devi Sarojani was extremely clever in the external behaviour, therefore, also not disclosed anything externally, but enquired his name, caste and everything and noted in her diary from Sukhlal who accompanied Hanuman Prasad. Such thing was not allowed to be known to Hanuman Prasadji nor even attendant Sukhlal told anything to Hanuman Prasadji. Bhaijee also totally forgot her but the woman, who had dedicated her life unto his feet, can never forget it. On the roof of her heart, that sweet image was constantly dancing since that moment. How she would be passing her life, such experience can only be understood a little by some compassionate person. Although that woman had not disclosed her pure love free of deception to anyone, but her family members have decided to marry her with some other person after four years in about 1910, then a great dilemma had resulted in her mind. If she resists for her marriage, then her love comes in limelight and an appearance of love in limelight is incurable for a lover and a man strongly attached to this world cannot even imagine it. If she permits, then it is a cheating to her deity. The mind of Sarojani became restless due to such uncertainty, but an unimaginable power removed her worry. She found a way. She prepared herself and moved. She had not made any obstacle for the initiation of drama of marriage, because there was not at all any other person except her deity in her sight. The curtain of inner soul had been untied. In the purest stream of love, all impurities had been washed away. She had become a shining idol of the phrase – "There remains only one wish to a virtuous lady, there shall be no second man in this world even in her dream." In some village of Midnapore district, a drama of marriage was held. It was true from the viewpoint of this world but was totally a play in her eyes.

Sarojani reached to her father-in-law's house, lived there for four- five months, but like a bee, who lived in the garden of Champa flowers. Now the trial of love has begun. The question to protect her virtue has also arrived. What Sarojani can do? It was the story in the year 1912. One day, she had bowed last time to the drama of this world and moved out forever. The idol of Bhaijee, her deity was giving consolation in the heart While the grace of the God protecting her from outside. On the day when Sarojani was going to father-in-law's house, bidding farewell to her mother, who had given her that day thirty gold coins, when she moved to her real in-law's house after playing the game then at that time also, these thirty gold coins were tied in the corner of her *sari*.

Once Meera had gone in search of her Giridhar Gopal. Sarojani also moved today in search of her deity. In the emotion of inner heart for both, there is full similarity, but there is little difference from outside. Sarojani has changed her outlook. She has adorned herself in the form of a Sikh boy and began wandering. Reached Calcutta. In such a big city like Calcutta, she commenced to search her deity. There had been an uproar in Bardhman at that time due to flood. A news was published in newspaper to help for such an event. Sarojani observed that the name of her deity was also published in these newspapers. As soon as she has read his name, every fibre of her body began to dance with entertainment. But how she can meet? This was the question? She thought if she herself should move? But, on second instant, the rays of love burst out in the inner heart and Sarojani decides – Well! love is not the thing to be disclosed, no – will never go but instantly the heart centre started bursting with a strong longing for a sight and a craving to submit two-four words in the presence unto the feet of beloved, her soul became restless. With the access of love, she could find only one way that she should write a letter to her beloved. From the first meeting of steamer till present, whole event may be told to the master. Then if he would like to meet, he shall come. It was letter with such decision which was in the hand of Hanuman Prasadji, who was sitting as standstill.

In the pure heart of Bhaijee, a storm of emotion was moving. An electricity was passing through in red vessels due to the letter in hand. The memory of past was coming in front like cinema scenes. It seems as if the event of steamer was held just now. Bhaijee became unconscious for few moments being carried away with emotions. Till today, his life had not even touched the shadow of any sin, it had been a vow for life of complete good conduct. Therefore, this letter did not cause any sensual dirty change in his mind, an entirely pure emotion emerged but he was caught in deep thought considering his present duty. Every word in the letter of Sarojani was spilling with pure love. Such sacred love had compelled to fulfill her request of his appearance once, also awakened his pure desire. It was written in the letter – You can meet me tomorrow at 9.00 A.M. near Kalighat temple. Therefore, he moved there at the precise time. A friend named Balchand Modi accompanied him. But she was not there, and he returned from there, absent-minded. On the same night, one more letter was received on the same address, in which was written – “When you reached there, I was definitely present, but some other person was with you. Therefore, I did not meet you. Now don’t look for me, I have come to know your place. I myself only will meet you. A little later to this, a second letter was delivered on the same night – Please meet me tomorrow morning near the statue of Outramghat, second day Bhaijee has started to search that woman with eyes full of eagerness, but she was not found today as well. But a paper note was found near the statue on which was written – I am leaving as you have come late. It is not safe for me to stay here. Now I would myself come and meet you.

That long day was passed. Evening has arrived and then it was night. Bhaijee had a sort of worry in his mind. He was returning from the shop during night. His residence was at Harrison Road. There was a Shiv temple in the way but a little away from the residence. A Sikh boy met him at the very place and introduced herself – I am Sarojani. This is a forged dress. Bhaijee has also identified. In fact, she is the same girl. How the beauty of a young woman can be masked even in that Sikh dress after the introduction?

What would be the mental state of Sarojani—a love incarnates, by meeting her beloved master – it is impossible to describe by the pen. It is possible and also necessary to write this much that it was pure and sacred love. There was not even any trace of licentiousness in it. Therefore, both, though had been talking together immersed in love, had not touched even a little of the body of anyone. There was even no need of it in this meeting. Because it was a meeting of love, not the unrestrained breathing of sex.

Words were held for hours together. Truth was oozing with every word of Sarojani. Her whole efforts were through and through with internal pure love, internal simplicity, it had also no traces of forgery. The heart of Bhaijee filled with pure affection towards Sarojani, but he had given his body in the hands of his wife. According to religion and from point of relation, his wife only had the right on his body. True people don't know to give a thing by snatching it to others, which has already been disposed. Therefore, in the return of priceless love of Sarojani, question was finished to surrender his body. However, mind, soul of Bhaijee merged with the vast ocean of love with that woman. Sarojani felt that bubbles of love in her inner heart became huge waves by joining together with a fortune to the company of her beloved master. Now the practical problem of external world had to be solved.

Bhaijee told with his heart mixed with love – O lady! You should live here but in a separate house. Every arrangement will be made towards your pattern of life, everything will be arranged. But Sarojani wanted to involve in true love. She had also no self-passion in her life. The true pleasure of life was only the happiness of his master. There should not be any forceful blow in the happiness of master in future. With such intention, she said – perhaps there may come some dirtied thoughts later, between our such pure love, then it may not be a surprise. It is proper for me to live apart and is also necessary. There is definitely not at all any trace of desire to touch the body or sex in my love to you.

While leaving, Sarojani gave her gold ring to her deity. It seems that ring was worn in her finger as a symbol of her offered heart but then it is a blot to retain the symbol once you have given the heart. With this contention, the symbol was also placed at that very place where the heart was.

After a few days, a last letter was delivered by the loving hands of Sarojani. It was written therein – "Body is incapable to bear the pain of separation, now

I would not retain it." On the receipt of letter, Bhaijee made a lot of efforts to find her, but no trace was found. It was told, later, that she buried herself in the water at the Triveni Sangam in Prayag. The symbolic ring from the heart of love idol Devi Sarojani was changed into the form of a medal. There was no change in the shape of symbol. Earlier, it was round, now also it remained round. But it was hollow, which it should be. Heart has also become hollow due to continuous melting as pain of separation by the beloved and it seems today if the melted soul of her beloved reached near to that hollow place which is now filled. It was not a medal, was a symbol of two melted and united loving hearts. Medal was given by Bhaijee as a prize to one of the students in Girls' Degree College of Jalandhar. On one side was inscribed – **"In the memory of Sarojani"** while, on other side was inscribed – **"A young Hindu girl only marries once."**

Describing about this event after many years, Bhaijee said that though showing due respect for the sacred love of Sarojani, there had never been created any sense of worldly pleasure in my mind and Sarojani remained also firm with the Aryan tradition.

❐

11

A Meeting with Seth Shri Jaydayal Goyandka

Supreme saint Sethji, Shri Jayadal Goyandka was such a Marwari saint, whom people have never recognised though already familiar of him. His age-old way of life, dress, Marwari-mixed Hindi language, everything was so simple that people had not recognised, though observed him very closely that he is a special dominion of the spiritual world. Generally, persons connected with assembly of virtuous people (*Satsang*) called him by the name of 'Sethji'. With an intention to conduct assembly of virtuous people, he had been visiting various places. Bhaijee had also heard his praise during his professional tenure. During 1910-1911, Shri Sethji had come to Calcutta. Fortunately, arrangement towards his assembly of virtuous people was made in the shop of Shri Haribuxji Sawalka at Pagyapatti. His shop was in front of Bhaijee's shop. Therefore, Bhaijee also went in his assembly of virtuous people. His loving behaviour, original thinking, inner faculty without pride, spiritually realised experience with strong waves of affection started attracting Bhaijee. Although, at that time, it was leading status of political and social thoughts in the life of Bhaijee, even then, such was the attraction and so much joy was obtained by Bhaijee during the assembly of virtuous people (Satsang) with Shri Sethji that he started to take advantage from the assembly of virtuous people regularly on the visits of Shri Sethji at Calcutta. In addition, under the influence of his personality, Bhaijee started to introduce his friends to him. Shri Jwala Prasad Kanodia, Shri Banarsi Dasji Jhunjhunwala and others were introduced to Shri Sethji.

❑

12

In Passion and Love to the Motherland

Bhaijee had even an earlier interest in social and political activities but due to non-interference of father, started to take part with full freedom in such activities. He had main and active cooperation with Vaishya general assembly, Hindu club, Hindi literature council, Savitri Kanya Pathshala, Marwari relief society, Calcutta Hindu general assembly. It was at that hour when independence movement was going on in the country and the place of Bengal was especially notable. It was impossible to keep aloof from it for a sensitive person like Bhaijee. His heart was filling more and more with the love of his motherland. On the other side, maintenance of shop had been continued to relax. Bhaijee considered extremist principles only suited to time. Secret societies have been made at various places. Bhaijee was also an active member of such secret society. Every activity of it was kept as secret. Few members of the society were in contact with Bengal revolutionary society in which Shri Vipin Chandra Ganguli. Shri Vaidyanath Vishwas and others were chief members. Shri Jwala Prasadji Kanodia was the chief of the society and the meetings of the society were held with Shri Phoolchandji Chaudhary at Belur and in Birla Palace at Lilua. The aim of this movement at that time was to offer body, mind, wealth and everything to the country. From this, Bhaijee received the practical training of compliance as per rule, self-control, sacrifice and simplicity. During such incidence, he got an opportunity to come in close contact with many and to meet again and again with reputed people of various fields like Shri Arvind, Shri Surendra Nath Banerjee, Shri Vipin Chandra Pal, Shri Chitranjan Das, Shri Virendra Nath Thakur, Shri Shyamsundar Chakravarti, Shri Brahmbandhav Upadhyay, Shri Satyacharan Shastri, Shri Sakharam Ganesh Deuskar, Shri Shardacharan Mitra, Shri Krishnakumar Mishra and others. In addition, he had also come in very close contact of successful editors and scholars, prominent literary persons of that time in Calcutta like Pandit Govind Narayanji Mishra, Pandit Durga Prasadji Mishra, Shri Bal Mukundji Gupta, Pandit Jagannath Prasadji Chaturvedi, Pandit Ambika Prasadji Vajpayee, Shri Panchkadi Banerjee, Pandit Jhabarmalji Sharma, Pandit Laxman Narayanji

Garde, Shri Ram Kumarji Goenka, Shri Babu Vishnu Paradkar and others. Just after a little later to it, he has also developed close contact with Pandit Madan Mohan Malaviya, Dr. Rajendra Prasad, Mahatma Gandhi, Shri Purushottam Das Tandon, Lokmanya Tilak, and others.

When Malviyaji reached in Calcutta in 1914, Bhaijee also arranged financial help by meeting several people for Kashi Hindu University. Since then, Bhaijee established a contact of permanent love with him. When Mahatma Gandhi arrived in Calcutta in 1915 while returning from South Africa via Rangoon, Bhaijee felicitated him with congratulatory address as a minister of Hindu General Assembly. A relation was also developed with Gandhiji later.

❐

13
Inside the Alipore Prison of Calcutta

The name of Bhaijee also appeared in police diary due to his help to prosecute in law suit of revolutionaries and taking an active part in secret society. His activity was now under supervision. Without any fear, he continued to participate in his activities. Prior to one month of his being a prisoner, he got an information that the government is in process to make him prisoner, once it got some or the other suitable occasion. Though he was familiar with it, he did not run or hide at any place nor deviated by his activities. One day, an armed police force reached at his Clive Street shop and took him as prisoner in an offence of treason on 20th July, 1916. His friends Shri Jwala Prasad Kanodia and Phoolchand Chaudhary were also arrested. In the beginning, these people were placed in Duranda House and, thereafter, have been transferred in Alipore Jail.

It was not even three months of his marriage and there were only three women in his home. It was also not known that for how many days he will stay in prison. Thinking about all these circumstances, he became even once perturbed. What was his mental condition at that time can be read in his words only:

"Along with Jwala Prasadji, etc., we were many friends. But since the day of arrest and then our transfer to jail on the same day caused me a great pain. My heart became restless. Distress has swarmed upon my heart and a dark was visible all around. When no support was found, at last I could recollect the name of the almighty. To recall 'The shelter for Unsheltered' (The God) only was found as a support by me. I started repeating the divine name. As soon as the singing of hymn begins that the peace has been manifested. Gradually restlessness had gone, and the Kingdom of peace has covered the heart. At this very time, I could realise the importance of divine name. I then felt a need of string of beads. The first beginning of my progress had been started from this very place."

He requested a string of beads from the guard who showed him inability to comply but gave one solution that after completion of a string of beads by counting, draw a line on the wall with this nail. He has given him a nail. His repetition of divine name in low tone began. Government tried fully to put a case of treason, but it could not be possible due to lack of solid grounds. It was not possible to retain him in the prison for a longer time on the ground of doubt. Therefore, and according to Indian Defence Act, an order was issued to put him and companions under surveillance for an indefinite time. All the companions were sent at different places. He received an order to move to a village named Shimlapal, 24 km from Bankura. Prior to his departure, he could meet his family members for one hour. During the meeting of one hour, the mental condition of his family members can be well imagined. ❐

14
Surveillance at Shimlapal and His Spiritual Practice (*Sadhna*)

If the God snatches something, he also sanctions infinite times than that. He appears to snatch only to sanction. The God has snatched from Bhaijee his complete ambition for love to the motherland, separated friend-circle, dissociated family members. No family member could live with him, but in lieu of this, sanctioned such an object, in which comparison, all these tempting objects are extremely negligible and totally insignificant. That object was the auspicious remembrance of the God. Daily routine of Calcutta was different while at Shimlapal, it was something else.

During the time of surveillance, there has become an extraordinary change in Bhaijee. The life of Shimlapal became an occasion for a harsh devoted striving. According to the order by the government, he cannot go out of village. He can also not meet even any one of the villagers after evening. Not permitted to meet anyone related to education, cannot go outside the hut from 6:00 of evening to 6:00 of morning, letter could be received only through the police. Government had sanctioned ₹ 80/- monthly towards his expenses, out of which he keeps ₹ 30/- for himself while ₹ 50/- were sent to grandmother for the maintenance of family. During those days, Bhaijee generally awakes between 3:00 A.M. and 4:00 A.M. in the morning and after counting of thirty strings of beads of 'Hare Ram' – a sacred verse then proceeds to toilet and bath. On the completion of bath, prayer at sunshine, noon and sunset, study of the Gita and Vishnusahastranam, he meditates based on picture made by Ravi Verma of Dhruva-Narayan. Within a few days, his mode of life has adapted with the aim and so much beautiful has become his practice that three hours each had been spending during morning, noon and night in meditation. The remaining time was spent in the repetition of divine name and study of religious texts. Becoming free by the necessary routine work for the body in a very short time, the rest of the complete time was spent like this very style, for devoted striving and practices. Later, such had become the practice of meditation in six months that whatever was held in the mind towards the God in place of any object by opened eyes, at the very place, the idol of Lord Vishnu seems to appear in front of sight. Later, Bhaijee had told it several times that this is not any supernatural skill or miracle. Whosever would do such practice, he can also experience it.

So much interest was developed in chanting of divine name that it was intolerant to forget it. It appears in mind that nobody should talk to me and if there is some urgent need, then I should not speak as far as possible. Tongue was constantly engaged in chanting of divine name. When a casual visitor had to sit for a very longer duration, Bhaijee told in humble words – Look! I am a useless person. It is already late. You might have some work. Therefore, please go away. It was his effort to meet the least people. It is just possible when chanting of divine name is transformed as mercenary activities.

If he behaved roughly that time to anyone then he feels sad. Once he was busy in reading religious texts. A person has come to lend a knife. He does not like to be disturbed that time. Therefore, he told him with this intention – Not now, collect it later. The person though had departed, but Bhaijee was so sad that he went to him running, given the knife, entreated for forgiveness in humble words and satisfied him. At this very time, he also made commentary of aphorisms in **'Narad Bhakti'**. Later, it was published by Gitapress titled *"Prem Darshan"* with some changes and additions. He had made such serious commentary of the love having the form of religious devotion in such a young age that it has become a noble text of careful study for a longer period.

During such exile of time, he was also spending time in another type of service – that was to distribute the medicines. A civil surgeon, who had come to check his health, arranged some homoeopathic drugs and books, with his cooperation and on that basis, he started serving the sick people. Later, his wife was also permitted to live with him and she had also been extending a helping hand in such activity of service.

The God granted him inconceivable success due to his true emotion for service. Once cholera was spread there, he treated sixty-one people – out of which fifty-eight recovered. A Muslim was dumb since many years. His family members came for his treatment. Firstly, he could not decide about which medicine should be given to him, then had prescribed a medicine looking at symptoms from the book. He was very surprised to note when that dumb entered inside and was talking along with a large crowd and the people had started congratulating him. He had developed family-like relation with too much love with everyone, police personnel and other people over there.

He had one more extraordinary experience. Once he received a message that his grandmother is sick and wants to meet him. He cannot go out according to rule. Due to special affection of grandmother, he had developed a strong desire to meet her. He sent a telegram to the government but was refused. His mind had become extremely restless and for this reason, he began chanting divine name. On the same day, a Muslim Deputy Collector had come for inspection. Bhaijee told him the full story. He was very generous and so said to him – you would receive an order tomorrow only. Bhaijee could not believe because the order can only be issued by the Governor. He started with his chanting of the divine name. On the second day precisely, he was permitted by an order to proceed on parole for seven days and feeling surprised and experiencing the grace of the God, he has immersed in it.

During such life of surveillance, Bhaijee had been progressing on the stairs of devoted striving. Mode of his life had been turned inwards. He was given an order of release by the Governor after a duration of twenty-one months – to leave Bengal within twenty-four hours.

In fact, Bhaijee had settled in new family, living in one and three quarters of year in Shimlapal. By extending hand during joy and sorrow of villagers and by serving them, he had control on their hearts. When the people over there were told about the information of the order for expiry of surveillance by the government, they were stunned and pained. Alas, who looked daily after our welfare, gives medicines by his hand, to whom our sorrow was told and had been lightening our hearts, who had given love and respect to everyone, he shall go among them forever. Villagers could not check the tears from eyes and all surrounded Bhaijee. On the other hand, bullock cart was ready to proceed to Bankura. He had been consoling by embracing each of them with internal affection and by spreading his hands, was also wiping their tears. He asked for an excuse for his faults from anyone and requested blessing that his life may progress with fast speed towards the God. Everyone blessed with full heart. Both sat on bullock cart. The cart moved, it appeared as if the heart of Shimlapal people was also moving out, the cart was moving ahead while it was being followed by the crowd of Shimlapal, children, old men, men and women. Bhaijee was pointing them all to return by his hand, but it was difficult to check its speed once the dam of emotional flow is broken. Shimlapal village had already been left far behind. Bhaijee was worried for the return of villagers. Therefore, he gathered his courage and made request with folded hands in unclear voice due to choked throat, my dear brothers, you have come very far, now please return, now do not come forward. How long you people would accompany? Love and affection of you all will be remembered by me throughout the life. That will be an ultimate treasure of my life… The words came from his inner heart, affected the villagers and they had stopped there itself. Bhaijee had been gazing them with his face turned towards them. He reached Bankura after a journey of several hours. He came to Asansol by rail after meeting relatives and family over there. Grandmother and other family members have already reached Asansol earlier. From there, he proceeded by rail directly to Ratangarh accompanying everyone.

❐

15
A Life in Mumbai

Though Bhaijee reached Ratangarh with his family members, but there was nothing except a house. The earning of grandfather had already been offered in the earthquake in Shillong. Something was earned of the business in Calcutta, but it was dedicated to politics, social service, saints and ascetics. Bhaijee had looked after the shop at Calcutta after the death of father, but there was only debt remaining, due to his absence. Under such disorganised condition, there was a problem of earning for livehood to the family. Bhaijee had no anxiety in his mind because he had earlier thought all these things and opted politics. Time was passing happily due to favourable wife and tolerant grandmother. But some arrangement had to be done for the business. He was worried for this very reason that suddenly a letter was delivered from Seth Jamnalalji Bajaj with an advice to come to Mumbai. Some work will be started. On an auspicious day, he went alone to Mumbai in August, 1918. Stayed there with his paternal aunt. Second day, he went to meet Shri Jamnalalji Bajaj. He was overwhelmed looking to his affection. Such affectionate relation has remained increasing continuously.

At first, he started work of brokerage for cotton in partnership with Gulabraiji Nemani. Three-four months later, inclined towards the brokerage of shares and began brokerage in partnership of Shrimadanlalji Chaudhary. This work continued for twelve months, but there was no special income. New planning is to fall into thought. Started brokerage of shares by the name of 'Ganga Vishnu Hanuman Prasad' with Shri Ganga Vishnu, a family brother of Shri Jamnalalji. Though there was also a profit in it, the expenses were also increased due to the presence of family in *Mumbai*. Due to combination of such pair like Bhaijee as grandchild and Ramkaur as grandmother, the merit arising from liberality had also increased. In 1920, a new arrangement for brokerage of shares was made with the name of 'S.D. Poddar' in partnership with the owner of firm 'Tarachand Ghanshyam Das'– Shri Balkrishnalalji and Shri Shriniwasji Poddar. Business started for millions of rupees. Suddenly, three lakh rupees had to be recovered from the business. Two lakhs were somehow recovered while one lakh could not be raised. Accountant made complaint against Bhaijee. But Shriniwas had scolded the accountant – Everything is done with my consent. Let it be if there occurred a loss. It was a great shock on the heart of Bhaijee and due to this loss, he became sick. He had to proceed to Nasik for the recovery of his health. It was recovered due to his stay there for one month. When it was known to Jamnalalji, he had arranged to start work with his brother-in-law Shri Chiranjilalji Jajodiya. The work had begun of brokerage business and personal trade, brokerage of commercial transaction for linseed, etc. by the name of 'Chiranjilal Hanuman Prasad'. Such work had made good progress till his tenure in Mumbai.

❐

16

Renaissance of Tendencies for Social Service and Patriotism

When Bhaijee attained his senses, since then a strong desire to serve country and society has been continuously increasing. If limitation of surveillance had not come in between, then it was difficult to predict its idol-shape by now. But the God had sent him for other work. Therefore, he had no faith for violent politics after his devoted striving at *Shimlapal*. Every instinct again awakened due to the presence of favourable atmosphere in Mumbai. The company of Jamnalalji had been an extraordinary help in it. He was a protector in one way of national leaders of that time. Every leader generally stays in his guest house only and full load of their arrangements was also on Bhaijee. Bhaijee had already an introduction with national leaders from Calcutta itself, now more closeness has flourished. An extreme intimacy had developed also with Gandhiji. To this extent that whenever Gandhiji comes to Mumbai, a visit was surely made his home to meet to his Grandmother Ramkaur. A close relation was also developed with Shri Balgangadhar Tilak and Lala Lajpat Rai. In 1919, an all-India Congress session was held in Amritsar under presidentship of Pandit Motilal Nehru. At that time, Bhaijee was a follower of the extremist group of Lokmanya Tilak. In 1920, the session of Congress was held in Calcutta under the presidentship of Lala Lajpat Rai, he went there as well. In the same year, Congress has accepted non-cooperation movement with a little change at Nagpur under the presidentship of Vijay Raghvacharya. Bhaijee was also present at this session as well. In 1921, he had also participated in Ahmedabad in the session of Congress, held under the presidentship of Hakim Azmal Khan. But the conclusion for active cooperation with Congress has been made from here itself. Spiritual tendency of Bhaijee was the main reason behind it. Due to an increase of spiritual tendency in life, he had a difference of opinion with Congress leaders regarding religious leanings. Gradually, he became aloof from the politics. Due to his close contact with top leaders for so many years, Bhaijee had an opportunity to meet and exchange ideas with top leaders of the country. Out of these were Shri Vitthal Bhai Patel, Shri Vallabh Bhai Patel, Shri Vinayak Domodar Sawarkar, Shri Kaka Kalelkar, Shri Khan

Abdul Ghaffar Khan, Shri Vinobaji, Shri Mohammad Alijinnah, Shri Shaukat Ali, and others.

Bhaijee had been totally attached with full sincerity in the service of the country as well as to serve the society. He was an active member of the chief organisation of that time – All India Marwari Agrawal Committee – right from 1919. The first session of general assembly was held in the same year at Hyderabad. He went to Hyderabad neglecting his newly started business. In 1920, he was elected secretary of Mumbai branch of general assembly. As a state secretary of general assembly, Bhaijee had served a lot to Agrawal general assembly. This year the session of general assembly was held in Mumbai and the credit of its success goes to Bhaijee. The third session was held in Calcutta while fourth in Indore and Bhaijee also took an active part in both the sessions.

Just as the spiritual tendency had become chief, negligence started appearing in social activities, but he extended service activity at personal level. Once he had saved a girl from the clutches of dissolute persons, but these people have reported against Bhaijee to the police. C.I.D. inspector Shri Patvardhan called Bhaijee and advised him – though you are involved in this work totally with an intention to serve, but it is a dangerous work, you should not involve in such work. We are also industrious as much as possible. Bhaijee considered this advice reasonable. Therefore, he withdrew himself of such activities.

In addition to such activities, he had been serving to sick people by his body, mind and wealth, financial help to widows, help to poor students and service to orphans secretly. Even without sound financial condition, he had arranged money for such activities by cutting his own family expenses. Due to such activities, he had become affectionate to all.

❐

17

Bonfire of the Foreign Garments

Bhaijee took an oath of patriotism on the announcement of partition of Bengal by Lord Curzon in 1905. He was 13 years old at that time. Such decision made during his childhood was not only fulfilled throughout his life, but it had become more brilliant. Bhaijee had begun to wear *Khadi*, one-and-a-half years prior to Gandhiji and which continued till his death. During his tenure in Mumbai, he had also given an active cooperation in propagation of Khadi, when an intimacy had developed with Gandhiji. To this extent that Bhaijee and his companions had been visiting various houses along with bundle of *Khadi* on their shoulders to sell, extracting time from their own profession.

Thereafter, when the national movement of Gandhiji acquired strength, not only foreign items had been banned, but were even put in fire. Gandhiji was of the opinion – when it is sinning to wear foreign garments, then it is also justified to burn them than to give them to others to wear. Gandhiji had come to residence of Bhaijee and demanded foreign garments also from his grandmother Ramkaur and set them to fire.

Bhaijee was in full support of this movement. He had an information that even after the imparting of foreign garments by grandmother, his wife had foreign garments. He asked his wife – Let all the foreign garments in home be set in fire if you give your consent. His wife believed these may be distributed to poor in place of burning. But Bhaijee explained to her putting arguments of Gandhiji in front. When she found it is also heartfelt desire of Bhaijee, she had collected all foreign garments of the residence and placed in front of him like a faithful lady. No consideration was made that such Sari is very costly.When a heap of garments was collected, Bhaiji again asked – do you have any other foreign garment left over in the house. Came the reply – No. Bhaijee warned her – please check it again, probably something may be left over somewhere. That very was the reply again – there is nothing anywhere at all. Bhaijee was looking for a Sari, therefore, he looked at the Sari worn by his wife. Now she could understand the meaning of repeated persuasion by her husband. I will come back just now – saying this, she went inside the room, changed her Sari and placed that last remainder of Sari on the heap of garments. Within minutes, that heap was changed into a heap of ashes.

Like this, the second event occurred when Bhaijee lived in a garden near Gorakhnath temple at Gorakhpur. A relative had given some foreign garments to his only daughter Savitri. It was known to Bhaijee when he returned from Gita press in evening. At that very instant, he demanded garment and celebrated bonfire by burning them also in his courtyard.

❐

18

Revival of Spiritual Perception

To a spiritual work for which Bhaijee was sent by the God, an attraction to that side has begun even living in the luxurious professional life of Mumbai. This can be said as an exception of simple rule. Doing business mainly and fully participating in political and social activities, if someone climbs to the stairs of devoted striving in life and that too living in a metro city like Mumbai, then it shall only and be called divine wish. This very thing also occurred in the life of Bhaijee. Just after ten months of his arrival in Mumbai, Bhaijee had to proceed to Bankura for the marriage of his younger sister Annapurna. Due to this reason, an assembly of virtuous people (Satsang) with Shri Sethji was also acquired. No such opportunity prior to this occurred for both to live together continuously for many days. This union of sacred hearts was occurring this time by an extreme closeness. The heart of Bhaijee was full of gratefulness because Shri Sethji had visited to family of Bhaijee when he went to Calcutta during the time of his surveillance. Bhaijee has now more attachment towards Shri Sethji after this meeting. Even after his return in Mumbai, a longing had always been occurring for such meeting. The God has arranged accordingly when there is such longing. A little later, Shri Jamnalalji Bajaj was going to Chakradharpur to meet Shri Sethji. Bhaijee also accompanied him. Though benefit of meeting, i.e., an assembly of virtuous people (*Satsang*) with Sethji was obtained. In addition to this, he entrusted Bhaijee to improve the language of his two books – "*An Attainment of the God Through Sacrifice*" and "*Prem Bhakti Prakash*". Bhaijee not only corrected its language but, in one way, made its rejuvenation. Shri Sethji has become ecstatic looking at his expression in effective literary style and with an extreme clarity of his original feelings. He found an introduction of the feelings of heart and an ability of Bhaijee. He returned to Mumbai in July-August, 1920.

In 1921, a devotee from Bhiwani, Shri Luxminarayanji had come to Mumbai for the spread of divine name. He was the follower of saint Shri Ram Karnji – a follower of Gauriya saint – resident of Navdeep. Wandering from place to place, engrossed with group singing of hymns, they spread divine names. When Bhaijee found them dancing during group singing of hymns, he was very much impressed by his devotion to group singing of hymns. Mind, soul, speech and body of Bhaijee had begun to immerse with the God due to their company. Again, that very flow due to an assembly of virtuous people, singing hymns and group singing of hymns have washed away the life bending away from this world towards the eternity. Near about January 1922, devoted striving of Bhaijee had begun again with more intensity. During those days, few such events occurred of miracles by the grace of God that Bhaijee developed indestructible faith for the grace of God. Even the creation of verses in devotional poetry also began during these days.

❐

19

A Strange Marriage of the Sister

Chanda Bai was the younger sister of Bhaijee. The burden for all his younger sisters was on the shoulder of Bhaijee. Went to Ramgarh (Rajasthan) from Mumbai. Marriage of Chanda Bai was conducted with Chiranjilal Goenka of Ramgarh in1922. The marriage was different from other marriages. Bhaijee was fully immersed in the flavour of religious devotion. The main aim in the life of Bhaijee was only singing hymns (*Bhajan*) and group singing of hymns (*Keertan*). Therefore, this very flavour remained to be the main thing in this marriage as well. Different types of songs have always been sung at the occasion of marriage in Hindu culture. During this marriage, instead of such simple songs, songs with flavour of religious devotion (*Bhakti*) were sung in sentimental language. Bhaijee himself had created these songs in sentimental language. These songs have also been published in the form of a small booklet titled "*Marwari religious songs*". A new awareness was shown to the society by these songs. Improvement was also noticed in many customs.

Bhaijee had insistently invited famous saint of that time and broker of divine name – *Ram naam*, living in Laxmangarh, to attend this marriage. He had initiated a stream of flavour in religious devotion for the society by singing hymns (*Bhajan*) and group singing of hymns (*Sankeertan*) at the occasion of marriage.

Sweets were definitely distributed after marriage, but it was not only distribution of sweets, but the religious books were also given to everyone. A religious consciousness has appeared in the society through reading such texts.

❐

20

The Arrival of Shri Jaydayalji Goyandka to Mumbai due to an Invitation of Bhaijee

Shri Jwala Prasad Kanodia was a close friend of Bhaijee right from his living in Calcutta. In this present age, friendship of Jwala Prasadji Kanodia is found completely genuine at the criteria of friendship. He and Bhaijee had met many years ago. During these years thinking, living and workplace of Kanodiaji were all kept changing according to time, but one thing did not change – that thing was his friendship with Bhaijee. From the first moment of friendship, hearts of both were filled towards each other. Both had considered pleasure of each other as their own and grief for each other as also their own. Even after occurrence of several turnings in the life of Shri Kanodiaji, these two things remained unbroken.

As Bhaijee introduced Shri Jwala Prasad Kanodia to respected Shri Sethji, since then an attraction had gradually been increased by Shri Jwala Prasadji towards respected Shri Sethji. The intensity of attraction of Shri Jwala Prasadji was far in excess than the attraction of Bhaijee towards Shri Sethji. In view of Shri Jwala Prasadji, respected Shri Sethji had been thriving as something different. So much deep was the effect on them of the purity of respected Shri Sethji by joining his assembly of virtuous people, talking with him, raising various spiritual questions that he is robbed on him. Offered himself mentally towards respected Shri Sethji. There was no other person so much spiritually powerful at that time in the opinion of Kanodiaji than respected Shri Sethji. By surrendering himself unto his holy feet, he felt forgetful of self in bliss but to enjoy such pleasure alone hurts him. Though he remained immersed in supreme bliss, he could not forget his friend Bhaijee. During these days, Bhaijee was living in Mumbai. Enjoying the assembly of virtuous people (*Satsang*) with Shri Sethji, he has remembered his friend. But Bhaijee was not near. He was in Calcutta and Bhaijee was in Mumbai. He does not find it proper to call Bhaijee from Mumbai. He decided to write a letter to Bhaijee that he may make efforts insistently to invite Shri Sethji in Mumbai. Shri Sethji cannot avoid insistent efforts. Respected Shri Sethji will definitely come to Mumbai and this way his friend Bhaijee will definitely also acquire benefit with his assembly of virtuous people (*Satsang*). Shri Kanodia was aware of this as well that his friend Bhaijee is getting busy in other activities in Mumbai. Therefore, he considered it very necessary to bring him together to respected Shri Sethji again. To a small extent, it will be an accomplishment of duty towards his friend. As soon as such thought appeared, Jwala Prasadji had written a letter to Bhaijee in Mumbai to make efforts for the arrival of Shri Sethji in Mumbai for the assembly of virtuous people (*Satsang*).

On this end, it seems as if Bhaijee was only waiting for letter from his friend. Though Bhaijee sent a letter and telegram to respected Shri Sethji, he had even asked his friends to send repeated telegrams and letters insistently with a request to Shri Sethji that he should definitely come to Mumbai for assembly of virtuous people (*Satsang*). During winter of 1922, Mumbai city became sanctified by acquiring the sight of the highest of high saint of the world. There was no limit of enthusiasm of Bhaijee. He was standing with full of elation along with hundreds of reputed people at the station. The train arrived, and respected Shri Sethji had come down alongwith his 20-25 companions. At the time of meeting, every pore of the (one's) body of public was enraptured with joy. Everyone moved just on foot engrossed in joy. If Shri Jaydayalji moved sitting in car, then only four-five persons to the maximum could sit near him and acquire an opportunity of his auspicious company. But a true saint just knows no unevenness. In his every action flows love with equal feelings to everyone. It is not so that they try for it, divine harmony is continuously and naturally maintained in them. Respected Shri Sethji belong to all and everyone belong to him, a bottomless infinite and absolute ocean of love was rippling in his heart for everyone and very high waves were soaring in the ocean of love at that occasion. Everyone was bathing in it. Why should he differentiate to donate the waves of love to anyone? Does the ocean ever also make difference to give away the waves? Never. Therefore, respected Shri Sethji preferred just to proceed on foot as well. A procession was formed automatically. To a saint who already came up from honour and dishonour, there was not even a little importance of procession. He was then naturally placed in a true form, his body only dancing on the lively waves of ocean (Chinmaya Swaroopanand) and was moving forward with a determined speed of destiny. The procession reached in the alms-house of Sukhanand.

Shri Sethji stayed for ten days at Mumbai. The first lecture in the alms-house was given on disinterested performance of one's proper duty *(Nishkam karmyog)*. In the temple of Shri Narayan, group singing of hymns (*Sankeertan*) began. During such sacred stream in the assembly of virtuous people (*Satsang*) for ten days, an innumerable number of people have taken a dive. On the day of return, Shri Sethji has requested for a befitting farewell in the assembly of virtuous people. Humbly announced – You should all come together daily in the assembly of virtuous people after my return. Shri Shivnarayanji Nemani said in his reply – an assembly of virtuous people (*Satsang*) must be held. I have allotted a place in my garden for a period of five years, but you should arrange for a speaker. Shri Sethji has instructed Bhaijee to discuss something for some time in the assembly of virtuous people. Initially, Bhaijee felt a little embarrassment, but had leaned his head due to his mandate. Though Shri Sethji has returned from Mumbai, but left the stream of an assembly of virtuous people in his absence. Such stream started to flow with speed due to Bhaijee. Bhaijee also started an exposition on the Gita in detail. For many years, such routine continued. Two repetitions of the Gita were completed in detail. On 66th verse of the 18th chapter, an exposition was held for one month. In the beginning, the assembly of virtuous people was held in day, but it also began at night after few days. To attend an assembly of virtuous people, absolutely all people, speaking different languages like Marwari, Marathi and Gujrati, etc. arrived. Whenever Shri Jamnalalji Bajaj came in *Mumbai,* then arrived daily. A follower of Gandhiji, Shri Krishna Das Jaju comes daily. Later, Bhaijee had started an exposition on the Ramcharitmanas. Such exposition had been extremely full of feelings and audience listened to it enchantedly. In between, holy men also arrived. Then Bhaijee also managed an assembly of virtuous people with them. Due to this, Bhaijee had become familiar with very good saints. Out of them, chief saints were Swami Achyutmuniji, Shri Bhole Babaji, Shri Udiya Babaji, Shri Hari Babaji, Swami Shivanandji, Shri Prabhudattji Brahmchari. Bhaijee also developed affectionate relation with spiritual preceptor of Ramanuj sect, Shri Anantacharyaji Maharaj and spiritual preceptor of Ballabh sect, Shri Gokulnathji Maharaj. During these days, Pandit Haribux Joshi started to come to assembly of virtuous people. He had been narrating beautiful verses of Sanskrit to Bhaijee. He developed friendship with Bhaijee. Bhaijee also become familiar with famous musician Pandit Vishnu Digambarji Maharaj, who had also developed a great affection for Bhaijee. During intercalary month of 1923, his sacred legend was held in the building of assembly of virtuous people in morning from seven to nine o'clock. During recitation of sacred legend, a stream of flavour flowed. He also arrived sometime at night. From time to time, celebration of devotional songs (*Sankeertan*) for city was also held. On *Ramnavmi* – ninth day of the light half of month Chaitra, Janmashtami, Charandi – a huge procession of city celebration of devotional songs was produced. Thousands of people had participated. Bhaijee used to get unconscious sometime during the celebration of devotional songs. Impressed by his exposition, local Marwari school invited Bhaijee to educate children on the Gita. He started exposition on the ultimate mystery with great interest to these students daily for one hour. Famous leader Dr. Ram Manohar Lohia was a student during those days in this school. The teaching of the Gita by Bhaijee was even remembered by him throughout his life, which he disclosed even in his lecture at several occasions. It was all the result of Mumbai visit of Shri Sethji. The devoted striving (*Sadhna*) of Bhaijee also lit up.

Grandmother Ramkaur was ultimately happy from the daily routine of his grandson. Since the blessings of saints up till the sight of present movement were in front of her. Now her play had come to an end. Grandmother Ramkaur reached unto the feet of thread-holder on the day of *Narsimh Jayanti,* i.e., 29th April, 1923. Prior to her heavenly departure, everyone noted that grandmother Ramkaur was repeating in low tone an incantation of *"Soham-Soham"* in happy mood. She was only boatman for family of Bhaijee and the family had once become empty. Bhaijee successfully conducted the last ceremony in honour and for the benefit of deceased relatives by spreading money with great generosity presuming if it was some special occasion of joy.

❒

21
Instructing through Dream to an Unknown Person for Necessary Arrangement

During his stay in Mumbai, one more unusual event occurred. Once Bhaijee went in a city named Mhow near Indore due to some work. By the time he reached there, it had become dark. He went to an alms-house and requested a place to stay with the manager of the alms-house. The manager told him – there is no empty room. Bhaijee again requested – I must stay here for night only, even any small place would solve my purpose. The manager replied with rough tone – I have told you once that no room is vacant here. You can stay in any hotel. There was just no question for Bhaijee to stay in a hotel. Therefore, he went outside silently. He was thinking it is already quite late, but rest has to be made somewhere to pass the remaining part of the night. His eyes found a place near the alms-house. On visiting there, he found it, as stable. On one corner, there was a place to tie the horses, while the other corner was empty. Bhaijee decided to take night rest at that very place. He cleaned that site by his hands. He was tired of full day, prepared his bed and fell asleep without food or drink. Due to tiredness, he has just managed to sleep once he fell asleep.

The owner of the alms-house was a very religious and devoted person. He had dreamt during sleep that the God is telling him – one of my devotees is sleeping hungry at the stable near your alms-house, you should go and make proper arrangement for his food, drink and his stay, etc.

The owner of the alms-house got awakened. He jumped to his feet in haste. Went immediately to alms-house at night and found that a person is sleeping in the nearby stable. Looking at true happening of the dream, his heart became an ecstatic. He was full of emotions observing an extraordinary sympathy by the God. Reached near and got Bhaijee awakened with great respect, bowed him respectfully. Bhaijee asked him with great affection – Who are you? Why you have come at this time? Please tell me if there is anything I can do.

Due to an ocean of emotions, even the words were not coming out from his mouth. The eyes were moist with that very condition, has put his forehead on the feet of Bhaijee. Bhaijee asked caressing his shoulder by his hand – Tell me, what is the problem?

He replied after a little pause – the God has adopted me today due to your kindness and entrusted to serve his devotee (You). He narrated the whole event of the dream. He rolled up the bed by his hands and requested Bhaijee to come along with him. Bhaijee had to accept his hospitality. He brought Bhaijee and arranged for his sleep there itself. Hearts of both were full of gratefulness due to sympathy of the God.

❐

22
A Conversation with the Parsee Ghost

Such event occurred near about 1925 during his stay in Mumbai. Bhaijee had told this description during a context: As the devoted striving (*Sadhna*) begins, it has got intensified. I had begun to move daily near the sea at Chaupati after evening meal. Several benches remained lying, sitting over there, had been engaged for recitation of divine name and meditation to the God. It was a secluded place; a little darkness was also prevalent. One day I was reciting the divine name, sitting on the bench. Suddenly and right in front of my bench, a Parsee gentleman appeared standing near my feet. As the priest of Parsee wears special type of costume, of just that sort of costume, was worn by him. I continued repeating divine name for a long duration while he remained standing there. For a sake of courtesy, I said – "Gentleman, please sit down, it has become long delay since you are standing. He replied – Please don't be afraid, I am a ghost." Hearing this, I was in fear and perspired. He said further – you should not be afraid, I will not harm you. I want a help from you and you would also receive blessing. I have become a little reassured hearing this. He continued – if you had not talked with me first, then I cannot make a sound. Therefore, I was waiting that you start talking. I have no power to speak first, with persons of this world. There are several stages in ghost world, various powers are possessed by the ghosts. I can go at all places, can also be seen by all, but cannot talk until somebody talks to me at first. I am not in a good position in the ghost world. Please send somebody to Gaya and arrange to offer cake of rice to the spirit of ancestors for me. Then it would also cause a good fortune for me. I said – "You are Parsee, you people don't believe in ceremony in honour and benefit of deceased relatives. Then why do you insist to perform such rite? He replied, "Truth, if it is a truth, then it is not comparable with caste. There is no difference of caste with the soul. He then narrated the name, address of his residence in Mumbai. Thereafter, he vanished. As told by him, on second day, I reached his address. He lived in the region named Bandra. He died six months ago. His name and full address, etc. were found. Though he was Parsee, but had been reciting the *Gita* text.

Once everything was found correctly, I sent Hariram Brahmin, living near me to Gaya and managed successfully an offering of rice cake to the spirit of the ancestors and a ceremony in honour and for the benefit of deceased relatives. On that day when an offering of rice cake to the spirit of ancestors was made for him in Gaya, on that very day, he reappeared in front of me, once again at Chaupati. He said -I have come to express gratefulness to you, you have done my work. I am now proceeding from ghost world to higher world. I was very much satisfied hearing his talk.

I have enquired many things of the ghost world, about the condition of the ghost world, result for deeds of life over there, etc. He informed a person who dies alongwith an enmity for someone must meet many cruel treatments. He finds much pain in hell. Every hell is true. People engaged with many types of sins have also to face very cruel treatment. There are many ghosts with goodwill and many with ill-will. They have nature and action according to mode of life. They remember relatives of this life and tried to behave in the same manner with the people over here. Good ghosts are retained there for a few days and then send to the paternal world. According to their earlier practice, tendency to sing hymns is maintained there as well. **Family members should always donate grains, water, garments, etc. in the name of those persons, living in the ghost world**. To provide good fortune to the ghosts, an offering of rice cake in Gaya ceremony in honour and for the benefit of deceased relatives, recitation of Gayatri verses, recitation of *Bhagwat*, recitation of *Vishnusahastrnam* and prayers to the God, according to their respective religions, will provide good fortune (*Sadgati*) to them. Thereafter, Bhaijee contacted some souls of there, through the medium of that ghost. Even contact was established with some divine worlds. What was the condition of someone after death, such track had also been connected through the medium of some living beings over there, with whom Bhaijee had made close contact. People, who were in close contact with Bhaijee, had been attempting to find about the recourse of the family members. Bhaijee had delivered the name of the deceased persons, extra gamous subdivision of his caste, group, place of death and address of the place of his act of cremation, to living creatures of other worlds. Due to their efforts, exactly a correct information was found for few persons, incomplete for few and just nothing in some cases, was received. Ten to twenty such cases had always been ready to be worked out.

Some years ago, in a hotel of Varanasi, a person was murdered by his friend. His wife belonged to Gorakhpur. She was very sad. Due to her pursuance, Bhaijee found out with the help of living creatures of other world and asked her to comply a method, directed by them. That person met with good fortune. Like this, a person from Calcutta requested Bhaijee to find out the condition of his father. Then Bhaijee told by obtaining a clue after a few days that he was proceeding towards the higher world.

❒

23

Four Extraordinary Events Motivated by the God

How much concerned the God is towards his real devotees, such events point out a small sample of it. The devotee may pray or may not, the God materialised the things in such a natural way, which seems to be impossible. Bhaijee believed even impossible can be made possible due to the grace of God. He had not said such things because of scriptures. Such event of this sort had taken place in his life which had made his faith unshakeable. Here four of such events are being described:

1. Bhaijee had one companion in Mumbai – Hariram Sharma, who was engaged in the brokerage of cotton. A very intimate friend Shri Ramkrishna Dalmiya incurred huge losses in commercial transactions during that period. With a consideration of his welfare, Bhaijee advised Shri Hariram Sharma that he should not take this time commercial transaction with his friend. He had a big loss just now. If any further loss occurred, then he cannot repay it. But greed and ordinance of fact are very bad things. Hariram made a big deal with him due to greed. More loss occurred again in it while Dalmiyaji was not in a position to repay it. Hariram may lose his prestige in case no payment is made. Having been extremely sad, Hariram went to Bhaijee, sat near him and explained the whole story. Bhaijee replied – I had already warned you. I have no any solution for this. He started weeping and said – What should I do now? Bhaijee replied – What else will you do? Shed tears in front of the God. He surely listens to a distressed prayer. He went inside a nearby room and began praying, by closing it from inside.

A little later, a phone call was received from a friend of Bhaijee Shri Bal Krishna Poddar – Will you accompany me to turn around at *Chaupati*. If you agree, then I may come along with the car. When Bhaijee gave his consent, he came along with his car. Both went for wandering. Many things were discussed. On return, he asked suddenly Bhaijee – Where is Hariram nowadays? Bhaijee narrated the whole story. He was a very unliberal person towards money-lending, but said, due to some unknown inspiration, to collect a blank cheque tomorrow from his residence. After his departure, Bhaijee made due consultation with his two-three friends, if it was not a misuse of friendship, to ask for such a big amount this way. A friend asked Bhaijee, you did not extend clothing for *Draupadi*? You have not said anything to him. Bhaijee called Hariram personally and told him the full story. He became an ecstatic. All things have been told to Dalmiyaji, who had sent a signed receipt and attached alongwith the lease documents of his paternal property. On second-day receipt and the lease documents had been sent to Shri Balkrishnaji. He replied – I had never given the money against the security of house documents. I even never lend money, but I don't know how it has come in my mind? He threw away the lease documents and sent a signed blank cheque. Everyone was struck with wonderment. Payment of money was done timely. Shri Dalmiyaji returned the money after two months along with interest.

2. The second event is of more surprise than earlier. Just as in the words of Bhaijee, the story also belongs to Mumbai. We had a partnership firm. Once and during an emergency for a person, I must make a payment of rupees ten thousand in cash to him without consulting my partner. Though such money was arranged by him from somewhere, a big disaster appeared to that person through whom he had brought this money. This person had come to me and wept so much that anyhow if the money may be arranged for two-three months, then it would be returned from somewhere. He was a person of a very reputed family. He belongs to a family of very high, great and respected leader of the country. What should I do now? I have only divine name with me. During those days, I did sometimes desirous (*Sakaam*) repetition of the divine name but very seldom. Such event occurs prior to 1924. I never did the desirous repetition thereafter. I don't want to describe the experience thereafter. I started repetition of divine name. The poor person was very nervous. I got down from my shop with him. We both together had begun to move towards his office. When we reached in front of India Bank, we met with one of our friends. He enquired – Why both of you are dejected? I told him the full story. He replied expressing his sympathy – India Bank is just in front. I have an account in it. I am expecting money from Africa. If it is already received, then I can lend money just now. He was thinking that money will arrive after two weeks. In this way, money will also not be paid, and friendly behaviour would also be fulfilled. But the act of the God happens to be very unusual. Though money is needed today, but the arrangement has already been made in advance by the God. We went to the footpath in front of India Bank. He enquired about his present balance in the account. Came the reply – There was nothing till yesterday, but just now a D.D. is received of rupees twenty thousand from Africa. As we stood nearby, we had all heard his reply. Now what he can do, he must lend the money and had given Rupees ten thousand. His work has been fulfilled. Thereafter, the money was returned to him. Divine name has made this work possible. Like this, I have many experiences of lifetime from beginning towards divine name.

3. It is not only a matter of money. How the protection of life occurs due to the grace of God, one of such miracles was already seen at the time of earthquake in Assam. Now one of such events took place in Mumbai by which an excessive faith was gained in the mind of Bhaijee on the God. This event was published in *'Kalyan'* through his pen only:

This event belongs to the year 1919. I lived in Mumbai. I had been sleeping and eating in the evening at the residence of my uncle, Shri Laxmichandji Lohia, who lived in the bungalow of Pandit Shivduttraiji, a lawyer near B.B. & C.I. Railway (Western Railway in present time) Santacruz station, a little faraway from Mumbai. One day, it was 8.00 P.M. and was dark phase of the dark half of lunar month. Coming by local train, I came down at the platform of the Santacruz. Now platforms are built on both sides. It was just on one side at that time and that, too, without light. There was no searchlight in the engine as well. To reach to the bungalow of Shri Shivduttji, one had to cross the railway track by running in front of the engine. I did foolishness of running in front of the engine to cross railway line. Local trains stop for one minute only. I was a new person. I thought I would cross the track prior to the departure of the train but as soon as I placed my foot on the track, the train departed. But at the same instant, due to Godly inspiration and arrangement, some unknown person forcefully pulled me, catching my hand. I had fell on the other track. The train moved on swiftly. Three activities were performed simultaneously – crossing of the track, departure of the train and the pulling by an unknown person. A delay of even one or two seconds would have broken my body into pieces. But the God already arranged for my escape at that place and in that dark night. I was trembling with fear. My heart was very ecstatic due to the kindness of God. Tears were flowing from eyes. I observed in dim light of station a young boy of *Bohra* community was laughing, remained standing and was telling with great affection – now don't repeat such mistake, the God has only saved your life today. I praised silently and expressed gratefulness. I had fallen on stones at the track but except a little penetration due to stones on my right foot, there was no wound to me. I went home almost running and started meditating to the God.

(Ishwarank p.614)

Under what conditions and how many times the eternal compassionate God would have saved us, even saves at present as well but we, the unfortunate people, have forgotten of such sudden and unexpected kindness. Such events do not awaken his sweet memory in our mind but Bhaijee was aware to respect the experiences by heart, therefore, did not assess through mind, but tested by heart and enjoyed. One more similar event occurred that Bhaijee published in '*Kalyan*' in the following manner:

It was the story of 1926. I was going from Mumbai to participate at a festival in Rishikul which was established by the money and labour of Bhai

Shri Lachchhiram Chudiwale of Laxmangarh. From Ahmedabad, I proceeded by Delhi Express. I was in second class. A Brahmin boy was with me to take admission in Rishikul. I was sleeping on a berth of this side, while on the other front seat, he was asleep. It was about 5 o'clock in the morning of the second day. A T.T. gentleman entered in our compartment at Beawar station. On the seat, where I was asleep, he sat near my feet. I was awake and did not like sitting someone near my feet. Therefore, I got up due to courtesy. While I was asleep, my head was near the last window of the seat. Then that window got empty. I sat near the middle window and the T.T. was sitting near the third (first) window. These windows were closed. I was talking to the T.T. gentleman. With this, there heard a very strong sound from behind and the Brahmin child screamed, who was sleeping on the other seat. We were all aghast. We all looked back. It was found that a very big stone attacked the window glass. Very thick glass of window had been smashed due to breakage and its pieces had scattered all around. A very small piece of it was hit on the head of the boy, due to which he screamed. Had I slept there, my head would have definitely been near the window and that must have burst open by the blow of stone and glass. But the rescuer inspired me by sending a T.T. I could wake up and was saved. This incident occurred in between the Sarghana station and Makrera station near *Ajmer*.

(Ishwarank p. 614)

❒

24

Spiritual Quest for Formless and the Prevalent State – A Vision by Lord Shri Ram

After ten days in the assembly of virtuous people with Shri Sethji, much intensity had appeared with the devoted striving of Bhaijee. During those days, Bhaijee was engaged with the worship of an unqualified, formless, impersonal ultimate being (Brahma), but his devotion had been as usual in the God and his name. The company of a true saint is always unfailing.

A lot of things had also been discussed with Shri Sethji about the meditation, and an aptitude for informal impersonal ultimate being *(Nirgun Nirakaar Brahma)* for ten days. Accordingly, he started meditating regularly. Within a very short time, how much higher state had been achieved by Bhaijee – this description is available through the letters written to Shri Sethji from time to time by Bhaijee.

During letter-writing, the natural state is almost evident with blissful perceptible supreme spirit *(Anandmaya Bodhswaroop Parmatma)*. Words are being written by the pen. Whatever sudden blaze is appearing towards writing, it is said to be fabricated under an ultimate being. Sometimes it also does not occur. No perception remains for the existence of anything except an ultimate being – it seems as if a shape of snowball had to feel convicted in the bottomless ocean in infinitude water, which is also erased, only water and water remained........even then pen is running and continued writing, yes there appears no evidence of any difference with the state of perceptible bliss (*Bodhswaroop Anand*) and the earthly bliss *(Bhumanand)*. What is such state that cannot be expressed......? After a long duration, there appears an idea with a sudden blaze to pen again, but the feelings are with that very type........

The present state like this does not always continue. This seems a little changed in between, but even during transformation, at the most, such changes occurred from inconceivable state and to a state of type of an experienced bliss and even a little below of the state of bliss, a state like as an onlooker occurs, at the time of work, when the sudden urge for worldly enjoyment is felt. At that time, all worldly pleasures along with the body seem to appear just doubtful collectively in all-pervading consciousness but definitely acknowledged. Yes, sometimes such type of occurrence also destroyed altogether even the existence of sensual enjoyment. There remains no residue of any mode of life. A state is achieved of the past through sense, mind and intelligence for an excellent, ineligible, abundant bliss, such state cannot even be remembered well, later on.

Religious discussion had not been the thing of only to hear and to tell for Bhaijee. On the contrary, it had really entered in his inner heart. These things had found a home in his mind. The world had been no more a true object for him, but it should not be understood by it, that in addition to consider this world to be false, he also considered an idolatry incarnation of the God to be fake and illusory like learned and proud person of the present age. On one side, such high was the state of his meditation that he had remained absorbed in meditation for continuously nine hours at length during night. During an assembly of virtuous people, he had told himself that I had not at all any sense of my body at that time. If someone pricks a needle on the body, then I don't feel it at all, so much dense state has prevailed, and this was also evident during his daily routine that this world is deceptive in a pure infinite bliss, perceptible ultimate being *(Shuddh Anantanand Bodh Swaroopanand Brahma)* like a sensation of dazzlement in the sky. But even after such an occurrence, his faith remained unaltered on the God and his divine name. There was no feeling in his mind towards the real idol that this is also a false conviction like a sensation of dazzlement. He had been continuously experiencing the God, grace of the God and grace through divine name at every step.

During those days, he had such an experience for which even great ascetics and saints also crave for, eagerly. During an assembly of virtuous people at Gorakhpur and describing its detail, he himself said – It occurred in Mumbai. I had nearly to go to see a drama on Surdas along with Sagarmal Ganediwale. Residence of Sagarmal was also on the way. Sagarmal said – Let us go to residence to drink water. I agreed and both of us reached his home. Discussion had begun regarding divine name (name of the God). Sagarmal believed there is special benefit of recitation of divine name if someone also remembers the God simultaneously. I told him it is not so, but if you have pronounced two words 'Ra' and 'Ma' from your mouth at the time of death with any intention or unknowingly the person must achieve good fortune (Sadgati). There is also not any doubt in it. Such is the power only in the words akin of sacred verse. Hearing this Sagarmal said – Meaning of 'Ram' in English is billy-goat. If some English man invoked Ram with the intention of billy-goat at the time of his death, then will he also obtain good fortune? In his knowledge, there is just no any meaning of Ram except a billy- goat. He asked me: Tell me what is your opinion? I replied – With my faith, he should achieve good fortune.

Such thing was being discussed that suddenly my external consciousness has disappeared. Though my eyes were opened, but there was no consciousness externally. I sat with open eyes, unaltered on that very place. I only remembered that I obtained a sight of Lord Shri Ram, Laxman & Sita at that time. How long such visit lasted, I don't remember it. Even talks were also held, but everything is not in memory. Two things only remained in my mind. Firstly, the God had said – repetition of divine name with any intention shall cause good fortune to the person. Secondly, that the God had referred in this context, the name of his devotee Vishnudigambarji – a scholar in singing. Except this, I don't remember anything else. On becoming conscious on the second day, Sagarmal told me – you were repeating that "this is the God, catch hold of his feet," etc. But I had no external consciousness nor had uttered anything in my knowledge. Therefore, whole night passed like this. I did not regain external senses. Now Sagarmal became perturbed what had happened to me. At last, he asked me to stand by catching my hand and took me down from the stairs in the same condition. Then like in that very condition, he brought me to my residence. On reaching home, he asked me to go to the toilet, but I had no any senses as to what was going on outside. Therefore, I did not reply to him. When he observed me as totally lost of outward wisdom, he asked me to sit under the water tap. A water stream was flowing on my head while Sagarmal himself started chanting a devotional song. Gradually, I could regain outward senses. On the same day, Shri Vishnu Digambarji met me at noon. I narrated him the full story and hearing it, he started weeping.

Now one can imagine how both mind and heart of Bhaijee were gradually merging with the God. The flame of generalised and all- pervading spirit of universe was illuminating the brain. Here the charming emotion was gradually accumulating in his heart. Though all this was materialising in his life due to the grace of God, for the motives it can be said that his devoted striving (*Sadhna*) had also been extraordinary. His ever-readiness for the achievement was such that he did not sleep more than two to two-and-a-half hours in the night. The body and mind had to do a lot of hard work for daily routine and other spiritual propagation. Even then he continued his spiritual striving during the night with due integrity. But the body, at last, remains in the captivity of natural laws only. Due to problems with sleep, he developed intense pain in his head. He was treated by reputed ayurvedic and allopathic physicians. Thousands of rupees were spent but without any benefit. When he left the practice of Vedanta after two-three years, the pain also subsided by itself. To get rid of the practice of Vedanta, it was actually manifested by the God Himself.

❐

25

To Help His Spiritual Aspirants

As the devoted striving (*Sadhna*) of Bhaijee was getting very dense, in the same manner, there also started an accumulation of crowd of the devotees. He made twenty rules for the devotees to follow for spiritual development. There were about fifty members in this committee (Sadhna committee) who followed these rules with due enthusiasm. During these days, Bhaijee has written a book based on his experiences titled "*Means to Control the Self*" (*Mann ko vash mein karne ke upay*).

Famous musician Shri Vishnudigamberji was a close friend of Bhaijee. He was managing an institute 'Gandharva College'. Due to his generosity, he was spending money openly. So, there became a debt of about seventy-five thousand rupees and a stage has reached for an auction of Degree College. Bhaijee was informed about such situation. He was himself not in such a condition that he could give him that much of amount. He was compelled to take a loan due to his strong desire to get rid of his friend from dire difficulty. A loan was arranged on his name from Shri Balkrishnaji Poddar, Shriniwasji Poddar, Birla Brothers, Shriniwasji Bajaj, Shri Laxmandasji Daga and the debt of college was paid. Pandit Vishnudigamberji felt extremely obliged to him. Due to such debt, Bhaijee had to face great difficulty and which could be corrected after twelve years in 1935.

Once a treasurer Shri Rajaram of 'Marwari Agrawal Community Fund' had withdrawn rupees two thousand towards his own expenses from the ready cash. The police had been asked to arrest him as soon as it was known by the officers. He started weeping in front of Bhaijee as he could find nobody as his saviour. During those days, there was not at all any freedom for money within the hands of Bhaijee. But Bhaijee did not care about it and borrowed money from two-three of his friends and got him released. He was fully leaned due to such kindness of Bhaijee. Bhaijee, without caring about his own problem, freed others many times from their sufferings.

There was also a second event – his firm 'Chiranjilal Hanuman Prasad' had to recover about ten thousand rupees from the firm named 'Sangidas Jaisiram'. Bhaijee knew that the financial condition of Sangiramji had got down due to a loss in commercial transaction. So, instead of demanding money, he tried to hide away from him, even Sangiramji met him on the way, just to let him not feel embarrassed. On one side was his such saintly behaviour while his partner Chiranjilalji was totally adamant to recover the money. He knows that it is not possible to recover the money if Bhaijee is aware of it. Therefore, without telling him anything, he made a complaint due to which a warrant was issued. As soon as the warrant was sent and Bhaijee could know about it, his first and prompt effort was to inform Sangidasji telephonically that it was all done without his knowledge. The people are arranging to arrest you. Please manage your safety. In fact, attitude of his partner Chiranjilalji had badly pained his mind, but he could not apparently say anything to him due to courtesy. Whatever may be, people had strong faith in him due to such type of many and extreme efforts full of benevolence. Therefore, when Bhaijee went to Rishikesh, he had to return immediately due to insistence from his friends to Mumbai. In addition, the maintenance of building for association of virtuous people was also disturbed due to his departure to outside. The work for association of virtuous people was most liked by his mentor (Respected Shri Sethji) and by himself as well. As such, it was also a reason for his return in no time.

❐

26

An Auspicious Beginning of '*Kalyan*'

Bhaijee had relation with 'Marwari-Agrawal community' – only looking to the service for society. It was not at all a special aspect of his spiritual practice. By the way, all good efforts are helpful in spiritual practice, but as his field of accomplishment only as a disinterested performer of his proper duty (*Karmyogi*) is to be an auspicious work, likewise it was not related with such efforts. Even then he was attending to every meeting.

The eighth meeting of Marwari-Agrawal session was held in Delhi in 1926. This time Shri Jamnalal Bajaj was the chairman while Shri Atmaramji Khemka was the welcoming president. In the beginning, Atmaramji, due to some reason, had denied accepting the designation of welcoming president, but had consented due to insistence from Jaydayalji Goyandka and Bhaijee. The question arises upon the receipt of acceptance that it is very difficult to prepare an overall presentable lecture of the welcoming president in such a hurry because it was difficult to speak on second day after getting it written and published within twenty-four hours. Khemkaji put this responsibility on Bhaijee. In fact, there was nobody except him in such a hurry to prepare this lecture seriously. He could also not overlook the affectionate wishes of Khemkaji. He prepared a lecture by writing it during night and got it published. It was read on second day in the session. People liked it very much. Shri Ghanshyam Dasji Birla was also attending this session. Though there was difference of opinion between Birlaji and Bhaijee, they were friends since childhood. This lecture was also liked by him inspite of the differences of opinion. After the session, he told Bhaijee regarding the session – Bhaijee, what are the views of you people, how do you like it? How far are they justified? I don't want to criticise it, but its propagation in the world is being done by you people. Even the public is also agreed up to a certain extent. If you people possess a magazine related to your thoughts, then you people would get more success. You should start publishing a paper reflecting your ideas.

Birlaji actually conveyed a pinching thing in the form of suggestion, but such discussion in real sense became the main reason for the birth of a monthly magazine '*Kalyan*'. Everyone returned to his native place upon the completion of this session. Bhaijee also went to Mumbai. Shri Jaydayalji was visiting Bhiwani during these days from Churu. He had to go to Bankura. He stayed in Bhiwani for association of virtuous people. Bhaijee thought why he should miss opportunity to meet him. I can go to Bhiwani and will proceed to Rewari with him. From Rewari, I will go to Mumbai and this happened as well. Shri Jaydayalji started for Bankura after conducting the assembly of virtuous people at Bhiwani. There began a discussion about the Delhi convention in the train. Bhaijee had also narrated the advice in this context by Ghanshyam Dasji to start a magazine. Lachchhiram Murodia was sitting nearby. Hearing all this, Murodiaji told instantly – Yes, yes, it is excellent, it must come out. Not only this, he took Bhaijee to a corner of the train and also took his words, convincing him with extremely affectionate persuasion that he shall do editorial work as well daily for two hours. He then went to Shri Jaydayalji after receiving words from Bhaijee and requested to start this magazine. When Goyandkaji heard that Bhaijee had accepted the responsibility of editing, he also consented to it happily. It was also decided in the train itself in 1926 that the name of the magazine shall be '*Kalyan*' and arrangements were made to start its publication from Mumbai. There was no limit of joy prevailing amongst the assembly of virtuous people sitting nearby. Soon the train reached Rewari. Goyandkaji moved for Bankura while Bhaijee went to Mumbai. Reached Mumbai alongwith a new ambition, new affection and a new temperament of service in his heart.

The preparation for '*Kalyan*' started. At first, there was a problem for its registration. He had no idea for the various formalities of such work. Therefore, he became somewhat puzzled. But the puppet master of the world, the supreme lord, who really intended for the inception of '*Kalyan*', had automatically arranged every coincidence. Shri Shriniwas Bajaj, owner of Venkateshwar Press, was also one of the friends of Bhaijee. He had taken all responsibilities regarding the work of publication once it was explained to him. He took Bhaijee along with him and arranged all the formalities for registration, etc. and preparation for the first issue of '*Kalyan*' had ensued.

Meanwhile, Bhaijee had to begin again for Rajasthan. There is a refuge for asceticism of Lachchhiramji Chudiwala in Laxmangarh and it was the annual function of that refuge. Lachchhiramji had extremely persuaded Bhaijee to attend the function and, as such, he had to go.

On his returning to Mumbai, he had become seriously busy with the publication work of '*Kalyan*'. Due to an intense effort of Bhaijee, the first issue of '*Kalyan*' was published by Venkateshwar Press in Satsang building in 1926, which was entirely correct and fully devoted to spirituality. The first issue contained two articles and a letter from Shri Sethji. There was an article by Mahatma Gandhi. In addition, there was a collection from the speeches of ancient and very old saints, collection from scriptures and the remaining part consisted the articles of Bhaijee. During those days in Mumbai, Bhaijee had to look all the works alone, right from collection of articles up to its distribution to the customers. There was a hindrance in the editing work for '*Kalyan*' due to his pre-engagement in Mumbai. In a letter written on 13^{th}August, 1926 by Bhaijee to Dujariji – 'To maintain for proper work of editing of '*Kalyan*', it is necessary to get me rid of the trouble of publication and distribution, etc. to the customers as soon as possible, then only the proper work of editing is possible'. As soon as Dujariji received such signal, he closed his shop at *Sanavad* (in Madhya Pradesh) and came to Mumbai to extend his full support to Bhaijee, as it was not possible to appoint anyone during those days with salary, looking at the weak financial condition of '*Kalyan*'. Due to an inspiration of Shri Gambhir Chandji Dujari and from the second year, the first special issue of '*Kalyan*' was published titled '*Bhagawannamank*'. Therefore, many new customers have been enrolled for '*Kalyan*' by Shri Dujariji with the help of his companion Shri Ramkrishnaji Mehta.

❐

27

A Preparation to Leave Mumbai and the farewell

Just as Bhaijee could become little bit carefree after the publication of the first issue of '*Kalyan*', he had to face another trouble. The health of Shri Sethji got unusually worsened. There was no cure by the medicines. Bhaijee arranged special rites for him by Pandit Ganeshdutt Vyas of Bikaner, his teacher at the place of sacrifice. Due to the grace of God, Shri Sethji was cured soon after the completion of this ritual. Due to adoration and behaviour of Bhaijee, he earned a high reputation in Marwari society of Mumbai. However, he wanted to get rid of all such honourable receptions.

In the mind of Bhaijee, there was a rapid increasing of alienation from such worldly affairs and entanglements. His mind was always entangled with the Lord even during performing different types of work. The God was pulling him with great intensity. He was planning to spend his life solitarily on the bank of the Ganga. Since May 1927, he started visualising Lord Vishnu with his open eyes like Shimlapal in lieu of meditating on the formless. During these days, Bhaijee was living along with Shri Ramkrishnaji Dalmia, Shri Banarasidasji Jhunjhunwala and Shri Gambhirchandji Dujari in the house of Tarachand Ghanshyamdas.

He had to go to Calcutta with a work of Agrawal general assembly due to an inspiration of Shri Sethji. From that place, he went to his birthplace in Assam. His mother-in-law and father-in-law were living in Gauhati and were sick during those days. As such, he also went to Gauhati. Bhaijee with his mind full of an intense asceticism had decided there itself to dissociate himself from the shop of Mumbai. He sent a telegram from Assam to the shop-owners in Mumbai to regularise the household transaction. From there, he went to meet Shri Sethji at Bankura.

He was feeling uncomfortable now on each day to live in Mumbai. He had to collect his share from his firm 'Chiranjilal Hanuman Prasad'. Though he had not accumulated any property at that time, the firm was in a good financial condition. So, he proposed firmly to collect his share with the partner, who had not agreed in the beginning being well- informed of his asceticism mode of life, separated him arbitrarily from the incomes and expenditures. Bhaijee never cared for wealth and, as such, gave due consent in writing as desired by his partner and became fully engrossed in the act of accomplishment as well as in singing of hymns, becoming totally aloof of his business.

On this side started planning of publication of '*Kalyan*' from Gitapress, Gorakhpur. He received a telegram from Shri Sethji from Jasidih to proceed soon to Gorakhpur alongwith full staff of '*Kalyan*' and publish second special issue of second year from there itself. Bhaijee was already and keenly willing to leave Mumbai. He had apprised Shri Sethji about his intense desire to spend his life at the bank of river Ganga. He got the reply – Stay in Gorakhpur for two-three months and explain related work with the people of '*Kalyan*' living over there, you would be then free to move to the place of your choice and then keep sending material for publication every month from there itself. Bhaijee found his advice favourable to his own thinking. The news had spread all around like a fire that Bhaijee is bidding farewell for singing and worship to some secluded place. Everybody felt restless by hearing such news. Though Bhaijee was persuaded insistently to stay in Gorakhpur, he remained unshakable to his decision. Pandit Haribaxji Joshi came to meet Bhaijee as soon as he could know about his decision. He said – "Bhaijee, you are leaving. My mind is very burdened. I wish that your future life should remain such a sacred one and you make more and more progress in your devoted striving. But please never make any contract of money with any virtuous person." Bhaijee had noted such advice firmly and maintained it throughout his life. Prior to ten days of his departure to heavenly abode, Joshiji came to meet Bhaijee at Gorakhpur. Then Bhaijee reminded him – "Panditji, you have asked me to be careful from a big sin. I have always kept it remembering and was saved of many sins due to it. By the grace of God, I could manage my vow uninterruptedly."

Preparations have been started for the departure to Gorakhpur and on 11th August 1927, at the young age of thirty-five, leaving altogether his business, he moved out from Mumbai for his spiritual journey. He had to go at night by Delhi Express. Hundreds of his fans were present at the station and were all talking about only one thing – Whether Bhaijee is leaving Mumbai forever? Many reputed people of the society had come to see him off. Bhaijee had asked for an excuse towards his faults and also begged his pardon to remain blessed throughout the life. The train started. There was a big applause on the name of Bhaijee and everyone was full of tears. Bhaijee, by keeping his hands folded, remained looking at everybody affectionately. His name 'Bhaijee' was given in Mumbai itself. This name was adopted by everyone like children, old people, men and women at later life.

❐

28

Away from the Entanglement of Temptation

After his arrival at Gorakhpur, Bhaijee once stayed in Gitapress and became busy with the work of '*Kalyan*'. During that time as well, the work of Gitapress was looked after by Shri Ghanshyamdasji, Shri Shukdeoji, Shri Ganga Prasadji and Pandit Ladhuramji. All his companion friends were eager to meet Bhaijee. Their intention was true. As such, that sort of arrangement was made by the God. Accordingly, it is not even 15 days had passed of his arrival in Gorakhpur that he had to go to Mumbai with some special work of Shri Ramkrishnaji Dalmia. There must be an examination prior to the appearance of the God. The time for test had arrived. He had been an affectionate and esteemed person for all and every respected Marwari friends of Mumbai. There was a firm named 'Harinandrai-Ramnarayan Ruia' with a vast wealth. They possessed three-four large mills during that period. The owner of the mill Shri Ram Narayan Ruia had come from Pune to Mumbai as soon as he could hear about the arrival of Bhaijee in Mumbai. He took him to a corner and narrated him a message of his heart that he had become an old man, but his children are still young. Therefore, please stay in Mumbai now and look after my firm and children. You will be paid rupees fifty thousand annually along with a bungalow to stay as well as a motor car. In addition, you can also be a partner in any work you deem fit. Extending all rights in your favour, I will arrange to put in writing according to your liking. It was, in fact, an attractive offer to Bhaijee. But to one who is more eager for meeting with the God, all sorts of attraction are futile. Bhaijee replied in a very polite language – "I have already decided to leave Mumbai. Therefore, I am totally unable to manage your work at Mumbai." Though he was continuing with entreaty, Bhaijee was firm with his decision.

It was the almighty who wanted to examine him, to which Bhaijee stood totally successful.

❑

29

A Longing to Meet the God

On 30th August, 1927, Bhaijee again returned to Gorakhpur and became busy in editing *Kalyan*'s third issue for second year. Though he was planning every work externally, his heart was longing strongly every second to meet the God. Except it, he did not like anything. Bhaijee was restless, i.e., why the God does not appear to him?

We cannot imagine anything until we pass ourselves through such condition. Bhaijee was ready to sacrifice anything for it:

The one whose soul feels extreme lamentation,
To meet his sweetheart,
He does not care the distance of the path,
In any way,
Even also never looks a little towards
The countless obstacles,
But runs madly where the flute is being swiftly played
By Nand Kishor.

(Pad-Ratnakar)

The same condition was the feelings from the heart of Bhaijee.

Every time he was dreaming only about one wish:

Only one wish implanted in my heart (soul),
To always gaze for Natnagar under Banyan tree at the bank of Kalindi.

(Pad-Ratnakr p.1052)

Following his spiritual path, Bhaijee had almost approached very near to God. His intense desire to meet the God was increasing everyday. Shri Sethji was also deeply encouraging his efforts. Shri Sethji went to Jasidih on health grounds during this period. Even in Jasidih, he was quite aware with the mental condition of Bhaijee and was also observing it minutely. He was in search of the right moment.

❑

30

An Actual Vision of Lord Vishnu, Twice in Jasidih

Bhaijee was already examined and his devoted striving (*Sadhna*) had also been fully matured. Virtually body, mind and soul had all been agitating to have a glimpse of the heavenly beauty of the God. There was no comfort during day nor any sleep at night. A strong restlessness by the heart of his devotee is reflected in the heart of the God and then He built a basis towards his appearance. Bhaijee considers Shri Sethji as his mentor. Therefore, the God had fulfilled this work through his medium. Sooner Shri Sethji found an occasion. He called Bhaijee at Jasidih near him by sending a telegram. As soon as the telegram was delivered, Bhaijee was set out from Gorakhpur along with Shri Ghanshyamdasji Jalan on the same evening.

Now the event to be occurred was a very scarce event in the spiritual world. Whenever the God appears in person, it is generally in a secluded place and on the completion of achievement (*Sadhna*) of devotee, but it is a strange phenomenon of His appearance to Bhaijee in front of 15-20 eminent people, about which Shri Sethji had disclosed this mystery later on. Now the main event has been written in Marwari language by Shri Ghanshyamji Jalan and is being given here in its Hindi translation from the main piece of paper edited by Bhaijee.

First Event
Om Shri Parmatmnenamah

Date: 16.09.1927
Place: Jasidih, Marwari Arogya Bhawan
Time: Afternoon 11.00 A.M.

Shri Sethji was lying on the cot in his room of Arogya Building. Bhaijee and Shri Ghanshyamdasji Jalan were sitting on the floor. Shri Sethji discussed on meditation with Bhaijee.

Bhaijee narrated the event in the way Lord Ram appeared and his attitude in **Shimlapal**, where he was meditating on Lord Vishnu even by open eyes, which was discontinued for a while but again started, it was all narrated.

Shri Sethji replied – Spiritual wisdom must prevail soon after the appearance of God. If there remains any hindrance, then it does not occur at that hour. Even then its responsibility comes on the God who blessed him with spiritual wisdom, through his once or twice appearance. There should be no doubt for liberation. Then Shri Sethji asked – You meditate on 'Lord Vishnu'. What is your opinion on this aspect? Is it a meditation or a meeting? Then Bhaijee replied – It appears as a meeting except speech or touch. Shri Sethji continued – You consider it a meeting. Then why don't you try to touch the feet? It may be only your strong will. Bhaijee said – I also considered it as strong will. If I meditate…… I visualise the idol even through moving, sitting alongwith the vision of the nearby objects. Then Shri Sethji said – It can be considered a deep state of meditation. Thereafter, Bhaijee and Ghanshyamdasji both returned as it was resting time of Shri Sethji. Bhaijee had again developed a strong desire for a virtuous appearance of the God and wanted to pray Shri Sethji for this purpose. A little later, Bhaijee and Ghanshyamdasji went to Shri Sethji at 2.00 P.M. Shri Sethji said immediately – There is a plan to go to the hill for meditation. Meanwhile, other people have also arrived.

Everybody has reached on the hill. Shri Sethji was first in the row and was searching many places. Even the people recommended some but was not approved by Shri Sethji. Then he selected and informed about a place, the place was near the custard apple in the east-southern part of the building of Mahendra Sarkar. According to the handwritten page by Shri Ghanshyamdasji at that place in Jasidih, following persons were present – 1. Shri Jaydayalji Goyandka; 2. Hamuman Prasadji Poddar; 3. Ghanshyamdasji Nuwewala (Jalan); 4. Rameshwarlalji Nuewala (Jalan); 5. Dwarkadasji Nuwewala (Jalan); 6. Sukhdevji (Gitapress); 7. Prahladraiji Jaluka; 8. Shubhkaranji Chudiwala; 9. Ramlalji Chudiwala; 10. Dungarmalji Bagla; 11. Jwala Prasadji Kanodia; 12. Kedarnathji Kanodia; 13. Shivdayalji Goyandka; 14. Daulatramji; 15. Vaidyanathji Shekhpurwala.

All sat towards one side while Bhaijee was sitting in front of Shri Sethji. On his one side was Jwala Prasadji, while on the other side was Ghanshyamji. Shri Sethji said – Hanuman meditates on the God keeping his eyes opened, he must do and should speak like this. Bhaijee agreed to it totally. Then Vaidyanathji Shekhpurwala requested Sethji for his guidance. Shri Sethji then said – I have come here with an idea that Hanuman will only deliver things to the people. Therefore, you should follow the method of Hanuman for meditation and also ask others to follow. I have also a plan to speak later. Hearing it, Bhaijee promptly replied – I am ready to speak with your permission. Then Shri Sethji directed to sing a verse in praise of the God and also '*Yada-yada*' from 4/7 chapter of Gita and meditate on the God. Then Bhaijee had recited four verses of Gita, i.e., '*Shantakaram*', '*Sashankhchakram*', '*Yada- yada*' and '*Paritranaya*' and explained the method by which he did meditation on the God in Shimlapal and became silent for some time. Then he spoke suddenly – I now explain the procedure by which I have seen an appearance of the God. You people also meditate in the same way. Bhaijee started explaining the essential nature of the God. Then Vaidyanathji Shekhpurwala enquired whether the God is sitting or standing. Bhaijee replied – He is sitting on the lotus and then became silent after narrating the essential nature of the God for some time. A little later, Bhaijee said – I extend the hand to touch His feet, but the hands stopped and could not move further. A little later again said – Hands moved further but the seat of the God has moved backward. A little later again said – Look here, the feet of the God have come near to me. I will touch now, you can also touch. Meanwhile, he spoke loudly the God has disappeared. All these things were told by Bhaijee with open eyes. Then Shri Sethji interrupted – I don't know the reason of His disappearance, but a sudden blaze appeared for me to ask Hanuman this thing – Whether he would explain about meditation or I shall do it? Then Bhaijee replied – I will only narrate about the meditation, but I must touch the feet. Shri Sethji then said – The way in which meditation was held, it is just normal for such type and regarding touching of feet depends upon the consent by the God.

Meanwhile, Bhaijee came as usual and again started worshiping the God. Keeping his eyes opened, he asked – If someone wants to see Him, please do it by coming near to me. Here are the lotus feet of the God. I am touching, then you all can also touch. By telling this, he extended his hands forcefully, caught hold of right foot of Shri Sethji and fell, loosening all his external senses. Then Shri Sethji asked – Ghanshyam, lift him up. But Ghanshyam could not lift him up. Shri Sethji then continued – Jwala Prasadji, please raise Hanuman. Then Jwala Prasadji carefully picked Bhaijee up and allowed to sleep on his lap. Like this, Bhaijee remained motionless and in fixed state for about one-and-a-half hours.

Meanwhile, Shri Sethji started describing the meditation for Shri Lord Vishnu. During his description of meditation, following people also joined – 1. Badri Prasadji Goyandka; 2. Kunjlalji Sultania; Sitaramji Poddar. In the beginning, he pronounced verse like *'Twamev mata', 'Sashankhchakram'* with great affection and then described the beautiful shape of the God. Therefore, he said like this afterwards – I have taken minute body form and now worshipping, let the God recligning him on *Shesha* in my heart. Informed like this and then worshipped according to the method given in the book '*Prem Bhakti Prakash*'.

Thereafter, he prayed the God in very compassionate words. Bhaijee opened his eyes and then closed instantly. Later, he opened his eyes and said – The God has gone. Then Shri Sethji said – Let us all depart. Therefore, everybody started to move. Shri Sethji was moving ahead of all full of passion. The body was shaking while his feet were falling here and there. Rameshwarji and Shubhkaranji were accompanying Shri Sethji. Bhaijee was following them and Ghanshyamdasji and Jwala Prasadji were escorting Bhaijee. He had no sense at all as his body and feet were trembling. On the arrival in the building,

Shri Sethji had gone to his room. Bhaijee had laid down on a cot outside the room of Jwala Prasadji. Ghanshyamdasji was near to him. He started speaking remaining laid down on the cot unconsciously (The main part of his speech is given below):

The God is reclining on Shesha.
Remnant of the food offered to The God is there. Do you still remember?
How many Pedas and Laddoos were there?
'Om' was written outside of the room. Looking at it, Bhaijee said – Look the God is sitting inside 'Om'. Where will He go from this place? He is extremely beautiful and is sitting inside the 'Om'.
Please look at his excellent beauty surrounded by flashes of light all around.
That very is also your place and my place is that very region as well. Where will He go?
Came here and put me up to this place by catching my hands and then gone away. Gone, but where can He go? He is omnipresent.

Then Ghanshyamdasji asked Jwala Prasadji to accompany Bhaijee and went to arrange his meal. Shri Sethji asked Ghanshyamdasji – How is Hanuman? Will he take meal? Ghanshyamdasji replied – He was telling that he has eaten a lot of *laddoos* and *pedas*. Shri Sethji asked Ghanshyamdasji – Please provide him a glass of milk also. Tell him to drink milk after eating *laddoos* and *pedas*. Ghanshyamdasji brought a glass of milk and told Bhaijee – Shri Sethji has sent this milk. Bhaijee said – Distribute it among everyone. Then Ghanshyamdasji had given it to Dwarka, Shubhkaran, Rameshwar, Kedarnath and also took a little for himself. Remaining milk was consumed by Bhaijee. He then asked after drinking milk – Should we go to Shri Sethji? Then went towards Shri Sethji and sat on the wooden cot. Meanwhile, Shri Sethji was also arriving. Looking at his arrival, Bhaijee said – The God is arriving! Get up! And fell on the feet of Shri Sethji in the state of unconsciousness. Thereafter, returned to sleep after staying for some time with Shri Sethji. There has been extreme pleasure throughout the night without any sleep at all.

The details of the above event have been dictated in the following words, later, as spoken by Bhaijee:

It has been my eager desire to witness some mysterious event personally. However, there had never been any desire to visualise the God in my life. My talk with Shri Sethji about visualisation of Lord Ram and the discussion with Jwala Prasadji about the feeling of love for Shri Sethji had much increased my longing to witness such an event.

Due to such reason, requested.......... Ghanshyamdasji was with me. On our arrival, Shri Sethji asked even without our request – Come on, we will go on the hill for meditation. Regarding the visit on the hill is written separately.

When I tried for meditation, all scenes have vanished suddenly. A very strong sunshine suddenly appeared all around.

The place where Shri Sethji was sitting, I could visualise the four- armed idol of the God with open eyes, like two persons sitting facing each other. There was no limit of my joy. I described the beautiful shape of the God for some time. Modes of life have altogether detached externally. I have tried many times to extend my hands to touch the feet of the God but could not extend my hands. But the seat of the God moved backward. On my further request, the seat of God came near to my hands. I wanted to touch the feet, but in the meanwhile, the God had disappeared, and Shri Sethji appeared in His place. I asked – What happened? Then Shri Sethji said – I feel like a sudden blaze to describe. Bhaijee then replied – I can describe but I must touch the feet of the God. Then Shri Sethji said – As noticed earlier, such meditation can be made easily, but touching of the feet depends on the consent of the God.

By telling this, there occurred suddenly an infinite sunshine. I again began to see the vision of the God as I did earlier. Being full of bliss, I caught the right feet of the God and fell on His feet forcefully. The God placed his hand on my head. Interrupting in between – the people said – you were laid on the feet of Shri Jaydayalji. But, in my conscience, there was nobody at all at that place except Lord Narayan. Even Shri Jaydayalji was also not there. Shri Narayan Devji was only there. I remained under such state for a long duration, while the God was continuously smiling putting his hand on my head. I realised after a short while that some extraordinary person is worshipping the Lord with an orderly manner. I became very happy by looking at such reverence. A little later, I have observed a visit of several sages. Lord *Narad, Vyas, Sanatkumar, Hanuman*, etc. were present amongst other sages. On arrival, they introduced themselves and started praying their reverence like me unto the feet of supreme Lord and also became very happy by finding me prostrating unto the feet of the Lord. Thereafter, the food offered by that extraordinary person during his worship, the Lord asked a child of sage to distribute the *Prasad* to everyone which he has distributed to all as per the instruction of the God. The Lord has further instructed – Give it to Hanuman as well. The child then also gave *Prasad* to me, which I ate with great pleasure. I have never felt such an extraordinary taste of it in my entire life. A little later, the Lord has vanished causing restlessness in my soul and I have opened my eyes and said – The Lord had now gone. Then Shri Sethji said – Let us also move. I found that my head was on the lap of Shri Jwala Prasadji. The people asked me to stand but I was under such bliss of flood that I have again lost my external senses. I personally visualised that the Lord was moving along with me. I was running with great pleasure. I was asked then to sit in the building. Even then I was visualising the same Lord. Then I was brought in front of Shri Sethji. I again visualised the Lord there as well and I had prostrated myself. Thereafter, I regained my body consciousness.

Second Event

Date: 19th September, 1927

Place: Jasidih, South-eastern part of the building of Mahendra Sarkar

The people were gathered at 2.00 P.M. in the library of Arogya Building. On the persuasion of Hardattji Goyandka, Shri Sethji asked Bhaijee – As desired by Hardatt, therefore, effort should be made to visualise the Lord in person by opened eyes like the previous day. Thereafter, Bhaijee remained silent for some time. A little later, Shri Sethji suggested to start with verses of prayer and verses like '*Ajoapi*', etc. (Gita: 4/6). Thereafter, he himself became silent after pronouncing *'Twameo mata cha pita twameo*. Thereafter, a few minutes later, Bhaijee pronounced three verses *'Shantakaram'* (A prayer to Lord Vishnu) (*Gita*: 4/6), *'Ajoapi'* (Gita : 4/6), *'Yada-yada'* (Gita : 4/7), *'Pavitranaya'* (Gita : 4/8), and asked the people present to pray jointly and in a single voice to request Lord with restless soul to come over and also instructed not to make any type of sound. If there occurs a sound, nobody should pay any attention to it. The mind should fully concentrate on the Lord as far as possible. Even if there occurs thunderbolt, no one should feel it. Thereafter, Bhaijee started praying to the Lord.

He prayed – O Lord! O kind-hearted, I don't have enough devotion, I don't have any strength, I don't have any ability, no power under whose spell you had appeared that day in person. Please be mindful again to appear today as well in front of us, under the same spell of love and power. O Lord! I have no capability to pray. With the same inspiration, this prayer is being made to you. During prayer, Bhaijee was instructing in between. Keeping silent for some time, he asked – O Lord! Why don't you appear, what is the reason today? A little later, Bhaijee told Shri Sethji – There is no result of today's efforts. I performed meditation simply by open eyes, but even then, it is not giving results. What is the problem today? Now please permit me once so that I could visualise as usual. Then Bhaijee said – Now a little meditation is successful. Hearing it, Shri Sethji told – I am intensely feeling that the hillside is an appropriate place for this work. This place is royal while that place is sacred and natural. Listening to it, Bhaijee said – Well, let us go there. Everyone was ready. Shri Sethji also stood up and moved in front of them. By observing a place on the hill way, he said, this place is also good, but we have to go today on that very place. At last, everyone reached to that region of hill, where the God had visualised last time. Reaching that place, Shri Sethji asked Bhaijee – Have you washed your hands and feet? Bhaijee replied – I have washed my hands and feet. Mohanlalji had taken along water with him and he had washed his hands and feet. Shri Sethji and Bhaijee occupied the same place they had been on Friday. Alittle later, after his sitting, Bhaijee felt interruption while pronouncing three verses – *'Twamev mata'*, *'Yada-yada'*,

'Pavitranay', keeping silent for a while, he said – Everyone should be attentive. Concentrate your mind and try to visualise the Lord. By open eyes, if someone feels distracted, he should then close his eyes. Agreeing to his statement, Shri Sethji said – Both the statements are true. Either close your eyes or concentrate your sight on the tip of the nose.

Bhaijee continued – I had been narrating previously to Hanuman Goyandka about meditation. The Lord should be remembered by that very way. Hanuman had also been trying to meditate, likewise everyone should meditate on the image of the Lord. Keeping silent again for some time, Bhaijee told – Like that day, the Lord has again appeared on that place. Today has an extreme peculiarity of bliss. It is the same grand seat of lotus. The lower colour of the lotus is white, pink in between and blue above. On it likewise the Lord is sitting, keeping his right feet towards the lower side. My senses had almost stopped. As far as I can dare to narrate the form of the God, I did. You should all accordingly meditate on the form of the God. Thereafter, Bhaijee said

There is an extreme radiance of the light coming from the nails by the feet of the God. I don't know the names of his ornaments. Thereafter, Bhaijee stopped talking. Then Shri Sethji asked – Why have you stopped talking? Describe clearly the form of the God. Shri Sethji repeated it but Bhaijee did not reply. A little later, Bhaijee fell and became unconscious. The head of Bhaijee fell down in the lap of Ramjidasji Bajoria (*Bhagalpur*). Shri Sethji asked Ramjidasji – Let him sit. He tried but informed that he is not capable to lift him up. Shri Sethji said Hanuman, meditate attentively. Then Shri Sethji started singing:

'Shri Krishna Govind Hare Murari, He Nath Narayan Vasudeva'

A little later, Ramjidasji helped Bhaijee to sit. Then Shri Sethji asked – Why don't you speak? Bhaijee replied – I had tried to speak, but in vain. Then Shri Sethji asked – How the people will be benefitted until you describe his form. Why have you asked so many people to come along? If you don't wish to speak, then why have you not come alone? Listening to this, Bhaijee started talking – I had earlier tried a lot, but I was unable to speak.

Thereafter, Bhaijee started describing the form of God. As soon as he concluded his description about an appearance of God, Shri Sethji asked – When you were lying, what was the arrangement? Bhaijee then replied – How can I say, don't you know? Were you not listening? Now listen to what he is telling now. By saying this, he again fell unconscious. Then Shri Sethji started singing hymns –

'Jai Raghunandan Jai Siyaram, Janki Ballabh Sitaram'

A little later, Bhaijee opened his eyes and said – I am not that much allowed to be heard. Everyone can visualise if you ask for it. Then Shri Sethji said – Why should I ask? The God may do as He feels proper. Then Bhaijee said – Everybody does not wish for His appearance. Shri Sethji said – Those who wish for, should be blessed by it. Then Bhaijee replied – If you demand, then these people can visualise. Shri Sethji said – If he asks, then I can tell the names. Bhaijee insisted – If you say it, he is ready to do so. Then Shri Sethji replied – Why does he not speak in front of them so that everyone can also hear it? If he does not wish to appear in front of them as occurred earlier, a voice from heaven can also be announced now, so that all can hear. Then Bhaijee replied – It is against the law of nature, you are not aware of it? Thereafter, Bhaijee again closed his eyes and became unconscious. A little later, Bhaijee opened his eyes and said – If you insist, then the appearance is possible. But Shri Sethji said why should he insist? Bhaijee had again closed his eyes. A little later, Bhaijee again opened his eyes and said – The Lord wants if Shri Sethji desires, then His appearance is possible. Then Shri Sethji said – You do visualise Him. Then Bhaijee replied – It does not matter to me. But if you recommend, then everybody can visualise Him. On such statement, Shri Sethji clarified – If He desires, then he can visualise. I have no interest. I am not a flatterer. If He wants, He can appear, otherwise it is His goodwill to do so. I am happy as He desires. Then he again closed his eyes. Bhaijee again opened his eyes and said – The Lord has due interest, i.e., why He agrees to your desire. Then Shri Sethji said – I have come here with a due loss made to my work. Even then if He wants fawning, then I can sing hymns for His name and can also dance for Him. Thereafter, Bhaijee said – you can just speak for it. On hearing this –Shri Sethji told him – I do not speak in such manner. Thereafter, Bhaijee said seriously to everyone – According to the ways shown by Shri Sethji, the Lord can be visualised. A little later to this, Bhaijee said loudly – Listen, what does the Lord want to convey:

1. To obey him (Shri Sethji) will be to obey me.
2. To please him (Shri Sethji's) will be to please me.
3. To fulfill his (Shri Sethji) wish will be to fulfill my wish.
4. To visualise him (Shri Sethji) will be the same as to visualise me.

Thereafter, Bhaijee said – The God has vanished.

Bhaijee wanted to proceed to Gorakhpur on 19th September 1927, but due to an extraordinary event of an actual appearance occurred on that day and it became already night due to it. So, Shri Sethji and Bhaijee along with other fellow friends proceeded to Varanasi on the same day. Bhaijee, in the way, asked Shri Sethji – in Jasidih, there occurred an extraordinary event. This time in front of all. Why such event took place in front of everyone when it is generally occurred in lonely place. What is the reason behind it? Shri Sethji replied – It shall benefit the world. Such an event should not come to limelight during lifetime, then it would be better.

Bhaijee asked – It is not the complete answer of my question. I wanted to know the reason of occurrence of such an actual impression in front of so many people.

Shri Sethji replied – The Lord blessed a person this way, with whom he finds maximum possibility of publicity of divinely devoted service. Even to others, He can also visualise but not in front of all.

Later, it was proved that the kind of publicity of religious devotion (*Bhakti*) which was made by Bhaijee had been almost rare to be found elsewhere. The visualisation of the God in Jasidih was conveyed by the people present there to their relatives and friends so that it was soon circulated to many places. Letters from people started pouring in to Shri Sethji and Bhaijee.

❐

31

Repetition of Extraordinary Events for an Appearance of the God at Gorakhpur

There started an assembly of virtuous people (*Satsang*) daily in the garden of Kantibabu at Gorakhpur at the place where Bhaijee was also residing. These people asked many questions to know about the events occurred at Jasidih, but Bhaijee was too shy to reply. Respected Bhaijee had written letters in detail to Shri Sethji about the description of such talks held during these days. To acquaint himself in a better way, one should read the letters which would be published in near future. The events that were noted by Bhaijee in his diary are also being mentioned in ditto as follows:

First Event

Day and date: Sunday, 2nd October, 1927
Place: Garden of Kantibabu (Outside of Gorakhpur), central large room near the hall from the southern side.
Time: Morning at about 7.30 hrs. in the presence of several people came for assembly of virtuous people (*Satsang*).
Presence: Shri Chetramji, Badri Prasadji, Rameshwarji, Ghanshyamdasji and Shankarlalji.

The discussion was in progress about the meditation, which was also being accomplished. Suddenly, there occurred an extreme flash and Lord Vishnu appeared. He was standing in the sky. Visualising Him for about five-six minutes, I was almost speechless. A lot of blessings were emitting by his face and eyes. As the father to his son and a friend to his friend looks with affection and love, such feeling was, in fact, prevalent there. It was also being realised that Lord Vishnu wants to convey something and, even then, ready to come and appear whenever there occurs such desire from my side or Himself. A little later, he disappeared suddenly. A sort of an alienation prevailed throughout the day.

Second Event

Day and date: Saturday, the 8th October, 1927
Place: Garden of Kantibabu, a room facing south just in front of the gate, previously used as an office.

I felt highly alienated at about 12 o'clock in the afternoon. I was sitting outside. Trying to inspect the labourers busy in white-washing, I went inside suddenly like being attracted by someone to a small room and closed the door. I sat on the chair near the north-side window and placed instantly a chair to sit for someone. Suddenly, there appeared a flash. A total peace prevailed. I cannot describe my internal state at that time. Immediately, the Lord appeared. His feet touched for a while the chair placed in front of me. Thereafter, He again continued to appear in the sky. I was almost enchanted. There was no limit of my joy. The Lord prevailed in front of me was showing great bliss with His kindness and love. I could not at all speak nor pray but touched his feet instantly. Looking to extreme kindness of the Lord, I was myself feeling extremely happy. Such state prevailed for a longer time. Then the Lord pronounced as if the sea of bliss had overflowed. Do you still have any wish? With great effort, I could utter only one or two words – Not all, expect you only………… .

During this occasion, the sweet smile of the Lord was very extraordinary. The Lord has supported me smilingly. Thereafter, He conveyed few things slowly with casual gaps:

1. It would be beneficial not to describe about my appearance.
2. The people fighting for the sake of religion do not know my power.
3. There is still delay checking a complete cow-protection.
4. There is still time towards my incarnation.
5. If you wish to do good to the world, then make the propagation of my name, overlooking caste and religion, declaring that his name would do everything in this era. Even for my incarnation, the name would be the reason.
6. Those who extend shelter to sin, taking help of my name, warn them that they shall never be liberated even by *Yamraj*.
7. To destroy sin and obtain lustful life with the help of my name will be the greatest foolish work. The sin can be destroyed even by enjoying or suffering the consequences of one's action or repenting them. One should not care about momentary pleasure. There is no harm in coming or going of enjoyments.
8. Name is more important than anything else. As such, it should be used cautiously.
9. Pride has enhanced immensely. The proud is a great hindrance as far as my acquisition is concerned. Beware of the proud persons and warn

them that they would meet a fateful end at last. Pride is worse than anger or sex.

10. Do not assure firmly anyone about my appearance.
11. Do not publicise about these things with my name except Jasidih.
12. I will now not come as such. I had come twice even without invitation. Since I wanted to convey these things, therefore, you can call me by remembering whenever you wish to, but do not commit mistakes thereafter.

Thereafter, the Lord maintained silence. I remained gazing towards Him with great pleasure and I did not prefer anything during this time except Him in the world. Even there was no sudden blaze for anyone in my mind. Suddenly, the God disappeared. My fixed gaze had also been disturbed. I observed that Shri Rameshwarji was peeping from the window of eastern side. I opened the gate by removing the front chair separately. It was about 2.15 hrs. in the clock. Thereafter, an alienation remained prevailing for about 40 hours.

Third Event

Bhaijee again went to Jasidih on 17th October, 1927 to talk with Shri Sethji. Bhaijee was blessed by the actual appearance of God right on the second day of his arrival to Gorakhpur. The detailed description for the third and fourth events of the God's appearance was written by Bhaijee to Shri Sethji in the letter of 24th October, 1927. Such letter is also being given in the text towards the correspondence made between Shri Bhaijee and Shri Sethji, which would be published soon.

Thereafter, Bhaijee discontinued to note down about the appearance of the God. The events may be noted if they are countable. When it has become a normal event in life, it is difficult to take note of the same. On arrival of Shri Gambhirchandji Dujari, Bhaijee took him into a lonely room and narrated the event of Jasidih in words mixed with great love. Shri Dujariji was listening enchantingly and thinking that there can never be any price of such kindness from Bhaijee. Let me sacrifice myself unto holy feet of him and then decided his aim of life to note down every event of life of Bhaijee. It was duly followed by him till the end of his life. Bhaijee though unwillingly had to tell him something, sometime due to his extreme and insistent requests.

It was just impossible during these days to realise the restrained joy prevailed in Bhaijee. He was getting the rare opportunities of frequent meetings, touch and discussion with the God. Even the people living close to him, during these days, could feel such divinity. Bhaijee was inspired during these days by the God to maintain his external life very simple so that nobody could identify. Bhaijee followed it till his last day so that the people living very close to him could not identify his real personality. Many people knew him only as an editor of 'Kalyan'.

❐

32

A Vision to His Better – Half by the God

When the wife of Bhaijee reached Gorakhpur from Ratangarh, she also heard everything about the actual appearance of Lord Vishnu to her husband. She thought – A person forgets this world after meeting an actual appearance of the God. He has no interest in anyone except the God. So, what would happen to myself? Sometimes she feels lonely and tears trickle down from her eyes. Once when Bhaijee found her weeping, he asked why do you weep? What happened? She replied – If I don't weep, then should I laugh? You are blessed by the actual appearance of the God, but my world is finished. Bhaijee replied smilingly – Well! I am still the same to you as I was earlier. Saying this, Bhaijee placed his hand on her head. An extraordinary miracle happened instantly, and she started to see the actual appearance of Lord Vishnu with four hands. Not only this, such miracle continued for many months, when she kept on visualising such form during her daily routine and homely movements. Later, it was discontinued.

Likewise, she went once to Varanasi with Bhaijee. Soon after his morning routine, Bhaijee started to observe the proof material of *'Kalyan'*. She asked Bhaijee for a visit to Baba *Vishwanath* temple and *Maa Annapurna*. Bhaijee replied – As I have come to inspect some important proofs, so I will not go anywhere. Even on insisting several times, when Bhaijee could not agree, she went to the room, feeling dejected, telling herself that she could not visit that place even on her arrival at Varanasi. Instantly, Baba Vishwanath and Maa Annapurna actually appeared before her and said – Why are you feeling dejected? You wanted to visit our place to see us, now let you satisfy. In this way, after showing their appearance, they disappeared a little later.

❑

33

A Letter to Shri Ghanshyam Dasji Birla

There were a lot of talks in the society about the actual appearance of God in Jasidih, at various places. People had been criticising according to their own feelings. The famous industrialist of India, Shri Ghanshyam Dasji Birla had been a friend of Bhaijee since his childhood. On hearing about this event, he wrote to Shri Sethji that such divine things should not be published as such. According to him, such things should be treated as secret. Shri Sethji replied to him, which is being given as below:

|| Shri Hari ||

Dear Shri Ghanshyamdasji Birla, Let us remember his (divine) name with great affection. Received the news about appearance of God to Bhai Hanuman Prasad. He has visualised the actual form of four-armed Lord Vishnu. Such news can be trustworthy because Bhaijee Hanuman Prasad does not appear as a liar. You have written about the condition of Bhai Hanuman Prasad. As such, the conditions of everyone do not remain same always nor any other person can realise well the condition of others. Regarding this condition, it is your faith to accept or reject such event. You have mentioned that to encourage in spreading and discussing such things will not be justified. It may be true, but Bhai Hanuman Prasad is not the guilty for it. I myself have enquired everything against his wishes and disclosed amongst the people. So, in fact, it is my fault.

Gitapress, Gorakhpur, Sincerely,

Jay Dayal Goyandka

December, 1927

❐

34

Life at Gorakhpur

Gorakhpur city at that time was far below many aspects like climate, houses and roads, etc. Gorakhpur was not at all suitable to live for Bhaijee who was living in a good house in Mumbai. The main reason to stay in Gorakhpur was '*Kalyan*' and '*Gitapress*'. Bhaijee always considered Shri Sethji at par to a mentor. Respected Sethji issued an order that '*Kalyan*' should be published from Gorakhpur and Bhaijee should manage it. Bhaijee had selected a place of living in Gorakhpur about 2-2½ miles away from Gita press in the garden of Kantibabu near railway line and ***Asuran*** bridge. The garden was taken on rent. The road to Gita press from the garden of Kantibabu was almost rough. Such rough road becomes very dangerous especially during rains. No passenger can travel in such weather nor was there any arrangement of light. During rainy season, the black cotton soil becomes very slippery. On such road, Bhaijee travels daily to back and forth Gita press. During the rains, dark night and without any light, Bhaijee travelled on foot daily to and fro Gitapress. He had also no umbrella with him at several occasions as he had to start suddenly. In the beginning, Bhaijee was living alone with Shri Badridasji Acharya (joined Bhaijee due to inspiration of Gambhirchandji Dujari) in that garden. Later, family of Bhaijee also joined him at that place. Presently, the world-famous '*Kalyan*' and '*Gita press*' are the result of continuous efforts made by Bhaijee. Bhaijee had no interest to live in Mumbai nor any disinterest to live in that garden. He wanted to complete his work of his beloved God. Bhaijee lived in that garden of Kantibabu at Gorakhpur for about 28 months from 1927 to 1929.

There is an inspirational event to move away from that garden. There had been a spread of plague epidemic in Gorakhpur during those days. Many people were infected by plague and were taken away by the jaws of death. The plague was spread in the ninth month of the Hindu lunar year in 1929. People have started to move here and there from Gorakhpur. The city people also took shelter in the nearby gardens. A poor Brahmin Shri Banarsiji from Sahebganj area was infected and died due to plague. His family had become orphaned. They had no shelter. This family requested shelter from Bhaijee in his residence at the garden. It was necessary to extend shelter to this orphaned refuge. As such, Bhaijee permitted to give one room.

Bhaijee had actually seen the God several times at this garden and also received his divine instructions. As such, this garden had become gradually famous due to the presence of Bhaijee. The Jalan Brothers of Gorakhpur pay due respect to Bhaijee. So, they had also understood the importance of this garden. They had then purchased it.

One of the members of Jalan family did not like his action as to provide shelter to that orphaned family. It was then known to Bhaijee. Bhaijee found himself helpless. But Bhaijee felt very much hurt in his heart. 'I could not provide shelter to an orphaned family'.

Bhaijee instantly decided. Another house was searched for his living. A small and extensively damaged house made by tiled roof of Shri Balmukundji was situated on the southern part of Gorakhnath temple. This house was taken on rent. Though the place was far away from the garden of Kantibabu, but when one had to live under control and a refuge cannot be provided shelter, it was not tolerable by Bhaijee. He did not care at all of his own sufferings. He wanted to spend minimum on his own self. So, an extensively damaged house was taken on very low rent. Bhaijee has never taken a single coin for his expenses from Gita press – '*Kalyan*' throughout his life. He was spending very little on himself throughout his life. During this time, Bhaijee and his fellow companions were living in a very simple way. He had come to live for some time and then wanted to proceed on the bank of the Ganga but had to live in Gorakhpur as desired by the almighty.

The spiritual state of the most respected Bhaijee had been the main reason for the development of '*Kalyan*'. His life had been an ideal incarnate form of the work without desire, divine faith, divine love, divine devotion and knowledge. The characters of divine wealth described in the 16th chapter of the Gita were present in him in simple and natural forms. Whatever he writes in '*Kalyan*' was all present in Bhaijee. A constant, continuous and worldly sacred divine essence with non-stop stream of nectar had remained flowing through his sacred life, sacred speech, sacred writing, sacred sight and sacred idol and was providing nectar of the God to the living creatures of this world in a natural way. It is the reason that small plant of '*Kalyan*' developing in a normal manner has now been serving in such a way to the common people. Respected Bhaijee had sacrificed every moment of his life and every particle of his body to the service of '*Kalyan*'. Actually, Bhaijee and '*Kalyan*' have become the synonyms for each other.

Bhaijee was always ready for every activity of '*Kalyan*'. Since the inception of '*Kalyan*' as a monthly magazine, it had started publishing characters of a saintly composed immemorial religion at a very fast speed in India about divinely religious devotion, divine name, good conduct, knowledge, asceticism, disinterested performance of one's proper duty, etc. Bhaijee produced special issue for third year in August month of 1928 titled '*Bhaktank*' containing double pages than earlier and more pictures, etc. in a quantity of 12,000 as first edition, which had amazed everyone. Though at the end of second year, there were only four thousand permanent customers of '*Kalyan*', even then Bhaijee had produced it with great elation, without paying serious attention about any great loss. The account of '*Kalyan*' was maintained separately from Gita press during that period. The loss occurred towards '*Kalyan*' was the personal responsibility of Bhaijee. Bhaijee had been helping others by taking millions of rupees as debt. As such, he also did not care for the loss of '*Kalyan*'.

Due to some reason, Shri Atmaramji Khemka of Delhi had resigned as a trustee of Govind Bhawan. The immediate director Shri Mahavir Prasad Poddar had also separated himself from the work of Gita press. At that crucial time, Shri Bhaijee and his close friend Shri Jwala Prasadji Kanodia had been fighting in that complicated situation and worked together with Shri Sethji.

The maintenance department of '*Kalyan*' was also looked after by respected Bhaijee for some time. On the inception of '*Kalyan*' on Gorakhpur, Shri Dujariji inspired and called Shri Badri Prasadji Acharya from Bikaner to Gorakhpur. Shri Acharyaji had not only managed the maintenance work for customers of '*Kalyan*' but also taken the responsibility to cook meal for Bhaijee during his living alone at Gorakhpur. Shri Badri Prasadji Acharya was such an industrious person that he had never allowed any deficiency for the maintenance of '*Kalyan*' without caring about his own health. In such a crucial condition, Bhaijee suddenly uttered that present number of customers of '*Kalyan*' though is four thousand, it will soon be forty thousand. His words no longer need any delay in materialising this fact. Even at the time of Bhaijee, the number of customers has increased more than one lakh sixty thousand. It is also a strange thing that there was a ban to enroll new customers of '*Kalyan*' for some time due to insufficient supply of '*Kalyan*' magazine.

❒

35

Spreading of the Divine Name and Message

As desired by the God, Bhaijee attached himself with full concentration in spreading divine name. There also began celebration of devotional songs (*Sankeertan*) at his residence which was generally conducted daily at night between 11 and 12 o' clock, but on Deepawali on 25.10.1927, Bhaijee enchantingly continued it till 1:45 hrs. of midnight. At last, he said – There is eternal benefit by recitation of the names of the God. The sound of divine recitation benefits all living creatures for as much distance as it can reach. Really, the importance of divine recitation is unutterable.

Many times, Bhaijee also arranged group singing of hymns standing with great affection and dancing. With the permission of Shri Sethji on 19th November 1927, Bhaijee proceeded to Assam via Calcutta alongwith other fifteen fellow companions to make propaganda for the divine name. Hundreds of affectionate people were eagerly waiting at Howrah station to have a glimpse of Bhaijee. Several people in the form of a procession reached Shri Govind Bhawan at Banstalla Lane along with Bhaijee, walking and chanting divine names with great elation right from the station. Bhaijee had given a fascinating lecture. On the conclusion of his lecture, many affectionate people requested Bhaijee for an appearance of the God. Due to several requests, Bhaijee declared in ardent words that whosoever wants to visualise the God with pure heart may kindly stand up. Nobody could understand divine inspiration by which such unalterable sentence was uttered, everyone was sitting at that hour except Doongarmal, who was standing. Even he sat immediately. No one could stand up. Like this, such events occurred at many places in the life of Bhaijee. It is not possible to describe here in detail about this journey. But, Bhaijee completed the journey of places like Calcutta, *Nalbar, Gauhati, Shillong, Tinsukia, Dibrugarh, Naugaon, Bhagalpur,* etc. with great elation and looking to his keen attention given to spread divine name, people have acknowledged it, as repetition of spreading the divine names like *Chaitanya* occurred four hundred years ago. A large procession has come forward in Calcutta on the eve of Gita birthday celebration. It was the first and last chance to dance on the streets of

Calcutta by Bhaijee. Bhaijee also met Pandit Ambika Prasad Vajpayee, editor of '*Swatantra*' and Shri Laxmi Narayan Garde, editor of '*Bharat-Mitra*' in Calcutta. The editorial work of '*Kalyan*' was also continued during journey. The rules have been framed for the people who wanted to accompany him, which were duly followed by everyone.

The rules were:

1. To study one chapter of Gita daily.
2. To do meditation regularly.
3. The sacred verses of 16 words of '*Hare Ram*' should be recited daily with 14 strings of beads.
4. To recite '*Gayatri verse*' daily in morning and evening each with one string of beads.
5. To wear hand-woven clothes.
6. To avoid sweets.
7. Do not smoke.
8. To follow chastity.
9. Do not lie.
10. No fashionable garments.
11. Do not keep a servant.
12. Do your work without the help of others as far as possible.
13. To bear your own expenses.
14. Do not be angry as much as possible.
15. Do sleep and get up at the right time.
16. Do not expect respect/appreciation nor accept it.
17. Do not accept physical or financial help.
18. Protest peacefully.
19. Do not feel proud of your opinion.
20. Keep away from the women.

Even after his return after fifteen days to Gorakhpur, the second journey was started to spread divine name on 31st December, 1927 to Mumbai. Bhaijee stayed there at Nemaniji Wadi and an assembly of virtuous people (*Satsang*) was arranged in 'Satsang Bhawan'. The Mumbai people were waiting of this occasion with great interest. A request was made by visiting various homes to repeat divine names in low tone. People living in the lane of Dadi Seth Agyari promised to repeat divine names in low tone – the sacred verse of '*Hare Ram*' with 400 strings of beads daily. Bhaijee also met his affectionate Shri Yadavji Maharaj and Shri Anantacharyaji of Ramanuj sect. There had not been any obstacle for the work of 'Kalyan' as the editorial department also accompanied him.

Bhaijee reached Ahmedabad from Mumbai on 9th January, 1928. He met there with the wife of Shri Jamnalalji Bajaj, Kaka Kalelkar, Mahadeo Bhai

Desai and Sister Mira (Miss Sled, the daughter of Navy chief of England). Attended the prayer meeting in the Sabarmati refuge of Gandhiji at evening and had a discussion with Gandhiji in seclusion up to 9.00 P.M. To know about the rules of accompanying people busy in spreading the divine name, Gandhiji became very happy and also praised highly of such type of work. Bhaijee also requested Gandhiji to contribute an article in '*Kalyan*' which he had agreed upon happily. Bhaijee went Borabar (Jodhpur) from Ahmedabad. Mahant Mukunddasji from *Chaitanya* sect had given a heartily welcome and persuaded to make promise by the people of village to repeat in lower tone three and-a-half crore sacred verses of 'Hare Ram' during religious observances of Holi. He reached Bikaner on 13th January, 1928 in morning via Mundva where he stayed for a day. Bhaijee was given a grand welcome at the station. Around the city, celebration with devotional songs was arranged on second day. During his four-day stay in city, an uproar was created by celebration of devotional songs in the city. During this journey, Shri Chimmanlal Goswami first time met Bhaijee and was also impressed.

Creating an uproar for the spreading of divine names in *Bikaner*, *Ratangarh*, *Sardar city*, *Chhapar*, *Sandva*, *Bidasar*, *Sujangarh*, *Losal*, *Maulasar*, *Didwana*, *Churu*, *Bhiwani*, *Rohtak*, Bhaijee reached Delhi. From there, he went to *Khurja*, where Shri Haribaba came on foot from very far away distance to meet him at station. From there, causing the river of divine names to flow, at various places like Firozabad, Kanpur, Lucknow, etc., he returned to Gorakhpur on 17th February, 1928.Meanwhile, Bhaijee told once to Dujariji in seclusion that there had occurred an extraordinary condition on 1st November, 1927 for two days after the questionnaire made by Shri Sethji and again on 10th November, 1927, during the time of devotional singing at the field, there occurred even more extraordinary condition. Thereafter, two days in morning, when I was explaining mental worship, to get it done in front of all, I could not control myself. The things that are to be kept as secret, should not be revealed.

❐

36

Impact of Group Singing of Hymns (*Keertan*)

Where there is an emotion, devotional singing by the saints creates an instant effect but where there is no emotion, its effect can also be realised as well. Such an event occurred at that hour when Bhaijee was moving at different places to spread the divine names like Chaitanya Mahaprabhu.

Shri Ravindraji (Editor of '*Purodha*' and '*Agnishikha*', Pondicherry) had been an Arya Samaji since his childhood. He considered group singing of hymns a show only during those days. He heard once that Bhaijee performs devotional singing alongwith his group. Under the spell of childhood, Shri Ravindraji also went to witness Bhaijee during his group singing of hymns. He had come only to see his group, considering it only a show. But on hearing the group singing of devotional songs (*Keertan*) and looking an access of emotion of Bhaijee, his body feels a thrill. An extraordinary effect was imposed on his mental roof of emotion by Bhaijee that he writes himself at one place, even today after a gap of thirty-five-forty years, it is difficult to forget the access of emotion of Bhaijee. It was not only a devotional singing, but it was like showering of nectar by the God.

❐

37

The Benefit of Declaration about the Appearance of the God after Death

Within a very short time, an information of actual appearance of the God at Jasidih had reached to far distant places – specially where the people known to Shri Sethji and Shri Bhaijee were residing. This news could not be delayed spreading even to several professional friends of Bhaijee in Mumbai. Materialisation of the event was such that everyone could not believe it. Few friends had been very close to Bhaijee. Such persons started writing letters to Bhaijee, some of them wanted full details, others wanted affirmation from Bhaijee. Everyone was sure that Bhaijee shall never write false at all. There was a reputed industrialist friend. Shri Bal Krishna Lalji Poddar (Messrs Tarachand Ghanshyamdas), who had written from Mumbai and made several questions regarding the actual appearance of the God. The reply of Bhaijee is being given as follows in which Bhaijee had specifically written that these things should not be published during his lifetime, there will be no objection after his death, rather it would benefit the people.

This much can be said without confusion that the saints declared the name and form false and also opposed the propaganda of false. The real saint shall never publicise his name or form. But it is also an ultimate fact that living beings are always supremely benefitted by the biographies of saints and the spiritual aspirants got special help and inspiration. As such, our scriptures are full of biographies of saints and Shri Sethji and Bhaijee published extensively about the details of life sketches of ancient saints through Gita press. In general, Bhaijee himself opposed strongly to write his biography and whenever his scholar friends made an attempt during his lifetime, Bhaijee instantly and strongly asked to discontinue it. So much so that he mentioned for such protest in his will, written during his last days. But it definitely benefits people by such true incidences, known after one's life, this is very clear by his letter. Shri Sethji himself also started dictating his life events to Bhaijee during 1927. Such notes written by Bhaijee are still safe. Such work had been continued for several days. Then there occurred such an accident in between so that the work was discontinued forever. Not even this much, a letter written by the hands of Shri Sethji himself to Jwala Prasadji Kanodia was found, in which he asked to prepare his photo, to be sent to Bankura and it was also mentioned there that if he prefers, then it can also be retained by him. It is clear that Shri Sethji, who was against photo and biography, started doing it only after that accident. The letter of Bhaijee is being given below.

Dibrugarh, Ninth month of the Hindu lunar year (Nov-Dec.) 1927: Dear brother Balkrishnalalji Poddar,

Let us remember the divine name with love. Your letter was delivered here last night through Gorakhpur. As I have come here, this reply is delayed, please excuse me. You have written me after a long gap but kindly keep remembering me. I am obliged to you for the same. I often remember you. I am attracted due to remembering your simple nature.

There is one more request, please try to reduce the increasing interest in Western culture and fashion as far as possible.

At present, I am unable to reply to your question regarding the God, with specific details. This subject is actually needed to be kept as supreme secret than secret. Such things caused the possibility to degrade the tradition than its publicity. The publicity and propaganda of any such thing should not be made in his lifetime. There is no harm after his death but actually will benefit the society. Such extraordinary things of many saints have not been published even after their death. Because they kept it so much secret in their lifetime that except omnipresent almighty and them, the third person does not know about it. The secret action of the affectionate and abode of love should not be published. He who gets an opportunity does not need any publicity. Publication can be made for two reasons: (1) To benefit this world; (2) To obtain respect and get worshipped.

He who published it to secure second aim may not actually visualise the God at all, make false statement or do not understand its meaning. He who gets such grand opportunity will never accept respect or appreciation by this world. When he has secured the highest honour, is there any other higher honour than this? The respect or appreciation from this world is a nominal or very nominal thing and he shall never look towards this side at all. The worldly respect or insult does not worry him. He is only engrossed by the unrestrained love of meeting his beloved. Actually, in his opinion, there remained only one beloved and nobody else. Then why will he expect respect or appreciation and what for?

A chaste woman selects her man only once. There shall never be another person of this world, even in her dream.

When it comes to the benefit of the world, even this shall also not be met by the publication of that secret mystery. It is not possible that he managed an actual appearance of the God to everyone, like sinner, virtuous, logician, fake logician, bad or good person because the almighty is not a puppet which dances as per his nod. Secondly, it is not the law that everyone could really see him. If it happens then who is going to believe it? Lord Krishna has shown his universal form to all in the assembly house of *Duryodhan*. Witnessing it, the people with an acquaintance have become enchanted. Non-believer Duryodhan said that it is an illusion by illusionist, is magic he had not believed.

When people do not believe in the actual God, then if somebody says by his mouth that such incident occurred to him, then who would believe in his statement? You may meet many people who can create doubt or suspicion, make false logic, make taunt and put protest. Though he does not fear or care for anything from suspicion to false logic, nevertheless this caused an insult of his dearest beloved as important as his own life and with this thinking, he does not publicise such secret things. If he does, there occurred actually no harm to him or his beloved at any time, but it harmed the people due to various reasons. As such, it is not advisable to convey, nor such things benefit even the world at every place. Most of the listeners and interrogators wanted to enquire only due to curiosity. On listening to the things and after putting some logic or false logic, the curiosity is subsided. Like the last scene of drama, the play is concluded, which generally caused an actual insult to such great events. Under such circumstances, nothing is said in this context under any simple reason as well. Such words have been written with an intention to your satisfaction and to inform the law of subject. For the time being, this much can be written to you that if you feel it proper, then you should believe on such things that with deep ambition and an act of adoration coupled with blessing by the God, it can be possible to anyone.

I also wish strongly for one more request. Please increase the number as far as you can to chant the divine name. It can do anything. It must be remembered just with virtuous feelings of love. There should not be left any stigma of lust.

It is a private letter, which may be returned after reading or should be retained safely and separately or it should be torn and thrown. It would be better if others may not investigate.

Yours, Hanuman

❐

38

An Excellent Example to Cope Up with the Friendship

You have already read about an incidence of Shri Hariram Sharma. He was resident of Ratangarh and had become a friend of Bhaijee in Mumbai. Bhaijee had obliged him many times in such a manner, had averted of difficulties in such a way that he cannot adjust to return it even by sacrificing his life. The kind-hearted generosity of Bhaijee was only a great support to his livelihood. But what can be done towards his company. On his arrival at Ratangarh, he was trapped in a bad company. He became sick and reached near to death. He was misguided by the people, wrote a letter to Bhaijee and asked him to repay two thousand rupees, pending in his name, which he had borrowed in front of many people. Thereafter, he died. If Bhaijee had declared the fact to everyone, then they could believe him, but a stigma might be placed to Hariram. Bhaijee did not like that anyone could know his friend as liar. During these days, there was no freedom of money to Bhaijee. Therefore, he sold his paternal property and decided to pay two thousand rupees to his family. Such event was conveyed to his close friend Shri Ramkrishna Dalmia. He instantly wrote a letter that it is type of injustice to pay Hariram for a false account and you should, therefore, not at all sell your paternal property. It is an altogether misutility of your generosity but Bhaijee humbly replied that Hariram is no more today in the world. I treated him as my friend. If I tell the truth, then everyone will blame him that who always looked after his livelihood, he was himself blamed falsely by Hariram at the time of his death. If I could do a minute service to a poor Brahmin, there would be no harm to me. People would defame me which is always dear to me. I feel pleasure to bear this stigma for my friend on my head. I have, however, decided to pay this amount.

Such an elegance to contribute money may not probably be found even after a thorough investigation.

❒

39

Setting an Accomplishment Society (Sadhan-Samiti)

During these days, Bhaijee had been arranging an association of virtuous people (*Satsang*) to worship and sing hymns daily in the morning. On 5th May 1927, he asked in front of seven-eight affectionate people that few rules are to be framed and it is vitally important to follow them by spiritual aspirants (*Sadhak*), who are busy in act of accomplishment. No peace is sanctioned without an accomplishment. So, if you are ready, then some rules may be framed to its members by setting up an accomplishment society. Rules should be followed strictly with due respect so that the aim of the human life may soon be achieved. Everyone agreed upon happily. Fifteen laws and bye-laws were framed with due consultation. The rules were as follows:

1. Meal: Renouncement of all spices except salt, meal should consist maximum of five items, i.e., (i) Flour or rice; (ii) Butter; (iii) Pulse; (iv) Salt; (v) Vegetables or dairy product.
2. Garments: Should be made by hand-woven local cotton and not more than four garments (except underwear or towel).
3. Repetition of divine name in low tone: Be in a habit to complete three-string beads with 16 sacred words of verse necessarily, prior to eating anything and to do 14 strings of beads in total, prior to sleep.
4. Good conduct: Do not get angry at all and no action towards anger should be exhibited.
5. Chastity: Do not intercourse with your wife more than once in a month. Do not look at another woman with bad intention.
6. Prayer: Be in a habit to attend prayer daily with a passion for one hour at definite hour and specific place compulsorily
7. Instructions: Instructions of the society must be followed without raising any question.
   (i) Repent according to instruction of society.
   (ii) Do not describe anything about society without its permission.
8. To study one chapter of Shrimad Bhagwat Gita daily, by grasping its meaning.

9. Be in a habit to do evening religious rites, Gayatri and study of religious texts daily. Be in a habit to do religious rites along with an oblation in five utensils with devotion and respect, sitting on one seat at least for half-an-hour. Religious rites should be performed at the suitable time in morning and evening.
10. Prayer must be made daily alone for half-an-hour.
11. Speak Truth: Do not utter false speech knowingly for the past or present.
12. Exercise regularly at least for five minutes.
13. Try to visualise the God everywhere and specially with those people you are dealing with.
14. Try to remember the God for every 15 minutes and try not to forget once you are accomplished.
15. Fill up the diary of rules daily prior to sleep.

Bye-laws: The following are the bye-laws, excluding basic rules:

(i) Do not feel proud.
(ii) Do not harm anyone by mind, speech or work.
(iii) Avoid jokes.
(iv) Avoid excess of talking.
(v) Renouncement of every type of narcotics.
(vi) Love everyone.
(vii) Do not hate anyone due to illness, caste, creed, religion or views of country.
(viii) Do not look towards the mistake of others.
(ix) Try to do work by yourself as far as possible.
(x) Do not take service from anyone.
(xi) Be in the habit to remember the God always at the following occasions:

Leaving the bed in the morning, going to bed at night, during bath, during gargling, during meal and during drinking water.

The overall in-charge of this society were respected Shri Sethji and Shri Bhaijee. The main members were: (1) Shri Gangababu; (2) Shri Shukdeoji; (3) Shri Ghanshyam Babu; (4) Shri Biharilalji Jhunjhunwala; (5) Pandit Ladhuramji Sharma; (6) Pandit Chimmanlalji Goswami; (7) Shri Gambhirchandji Dujari; (8) Shri Nandlalji Joshi; (9) Shri Shiv Krishnaji Daga; (10) Shri Rameshwarji Bajoria; (11) Shri Ramkrishnaji Kabra; (12) Shri Madanlalji Chudiwala; (13) Shri Ishwardasji Daga; (14) Shri Ramjidas Bajoria; (15) Shri Badridasji Acharya; (16) Shri Muralidharji; (17) Shri Venimadhavji; Pandit Govardhanji Sharma.

A scheduled activity of the accomplishment society was held daily. Everyone prayed daily for 10 minutes of the 36th-46th verses of the 11th chapter of Gita. Thereafter, there occurred an exposition of religious text by Bhaijee. The following prayer written by Bhaijee was recited thereafter:

O Lord! incomparably supporting us, O my life supporter

(*Pad-Ratnakar, no. 147*)

Such prayer was held. Thereafter, Bhaijee prayed alone loudly to the God with due meekness. Rest of the people also tried to make up their mind according to his words.

Likewise, such was the effect of the prayer by Bhaijee that within a few days and suddenly the aim of the life had changed altogether by the members of the accomplishment society. Every member of the society tried to follow respectfully such rules in ditto. They also even accepted the hardest punishment happily. Once everyone reached about a half minute late to the society, to repent it, everyone did one-day fast. Shri Bhaijee himself followed the above rules with very much strictness. Therefore, all other members also felt highly elated to follow such rules.

The work performed by Gita press is highly acknowledged with high respect in every field of the society. It all occurred wonderfully due to sacrifice, ascetic fervour and faithful longing by all the people. They had all been the cornerstones for the palace named Gita press.

❒

40

The Birth of Daughter

During July, 1920 and in fifth lunar month of Hindu calendar, Ramdei Bai gave birth to first son but he expired after about eighteen-nineteen months. The God wanted now to get his work done by Bhaijee, retaining him in domestic life as well. Therefore, on 22nd November 1922, a girl was born early morning, who was named Savitri. It was just natural that his child inherited the specialties Bhaijee was already engrossed in.

❐

41

A Pursuit in Resulting of Knowledge for Gita at Prayag Festival

During the festival held every twelfth year of January-February in Allahabad, millions of people assembled from far away at Prayag– a king of pilgrimage. Such a huge shape of Gita press is prevalent today that wherever the Hindus are residing in any corner of the world, the books from Gita press can be seen in most of the houses. An indefatigable effort of Bhaijee is the reason for such an extensive propaganda and publicity.

The famous saint of Gujarat, Shri Akhandanandji Maharaj (founder of cheap literature association) had come to meet Bhaijee. He had requested to arrange a pursuit of knowledge of the Gita by Gitapress *(Gita-Gyan-Yagya)* at twelve-yearly Kumbh festival to be held in 1929 at Prayag. He had also requested Bhaijee to accept a good amount to meet the expenses for such activity. To do an extensive propaganda of Gita press, Bhaijee accepted such an obligation. Looking at a very good opportunity to spread the divine names, sacrificial act of knowledge for the Gita was arranged there with due consultation from Shri Sethji. He himself arrived while Bhaijee along with Shri Gambhirchandji Dujari also reached there on 13th January, 1930. It was inaugurated by Pandit Madan Mohan Malviya. Famous musician Pandit Vishnu Digambarji also came and very sweet group singing of hymns was held daily during night. A very famous scholar from Varanasi, Shri Madan Mohan Shastri did an exposition on Shrimad Bhagwat in morning while Shri Sethji gave discourse on religious text during the day. Bhaijee had already been making brilliant expositions. An exhibition was also arranged for the Gita. Smt. Swarup Rani, mother of Pandit Jawaharlal Nehru attended it regularly. Such an arrangement was continued successfully for one month.

❐

42

A Hindi Literature Meet at Gorakhpur

The annual meeting of all-India conference of Hindi literature started on 1st March, 1930 at Gorakhpur. The friends and affectionate people of Bhaijee agreed to stay with him in a damaged house covered with tiles near Gorakhnath temple. The names of the main scholars were Shri Banarsidasji Chaturvedi, Shri Narottamji and Thakur Shivmurti Singh. Shri Ramdasji Bajoria was asked to look after these visitors, who had impressed them up to the brim by his services, hospitality and reception. Shri Banarsidas Chaturvedi was so much pleased by his hospitality that he had even written later to Bhaijee that if at all a college of hospitality starts, then Shri Ramdas Bajoria may be appointed as a principal in it.

❑

43

A Dominance for an Instinct of Detachment

Bhaijee had come to Gorakhpur from Mumbai thinking that once the management of 'Kalyan' will be in order, he will go to the bank of Ganga and would live in seclusion. But the Lord perhaps wanted to set a new example to the world that how a person can remain settled entirely in the act of deity (*Lila*) despite fully occupied in service activities. The work of '*Kalyan*' and 'Gita press' was increasing by leaps and bounds and it was also causing a state of being busy to Bhaijee. Looking at the present circumstances all around, Bhaijee could not spare even a break for a minute. Even with all this, Bhaijee was still longing internally to live in calm and quiet ambience. As soon as the special issue of 'Bhaktank' became ready, Bhaijee had decided in mind to go to the bank of the Ganga and went to Bankura to take permission from Shri Sethji. By explaining all his mental condition, requested permission insistently to hand over the charge of '*Kalyan*' and 'Gita press' to someone else but Shri Sethji explained him that it is also the work of the God Himself and the world would be greatly benefitted. No person is yet available like you. Therefore, you should not feel detached by it. Bhaijee had given due honour to his advice, suppressing his own feelings, but his craving had become stronger and he has again written a letter to Shri Sethji and the reply of which was given from Bankura by Shri Sethji on 4th January, 1930 – you have written that to perform further duty in coming days seems difficult by yourself. But nothing is difficult as per the desire and permission of the God. You have also mentioned that your mind feels alienated since many days, it is alright. What is the benefit to discontinue the special issue of '*Ramayanank*' of '*Kalyan*'? .... What else can I say about your departure? I am foreseeing great benefit to this world by '*Kalyan*' and 'Gita press'. According to my mind, you should live in Gorakhpur itself in seclusion and look after the work...... If I and you could proceed to Prayag, then everything can be discussed therein alone.

When both met in Prayag and arrangements were set right, Bhaijee had placed his heartily desire to him in seclusion when Shri Sethji was ready to leave for Bankura on 29th January, 1930. Shri Sethji had told him with great affection that he does not approve his visit to anywhere leaving such a noble work of Gorakhpur. Looking to your intense desire, you may be permitted to leave for a few days, but it would be your responsibility to edit '*Ramayananк*', which you can do from anywhere.

Nobody knows that such an affectionate relation between Bhaijee and Shri Sethji had been continued since how many births. A complete knowledge of this thing is possible to a person who knows about his previous births. Bhaijee has never disclosed such mysteries but once respected (Radha) Baba told that Shri Sethji was the father of Bhaijee in an earlier birth. Bhaijee fully respected his instructions which had caused postponement of his desire to go to a quiet place.

He had again written a letter to Shri Sethji that he is curious to go to Chitrakoot soon. Bhaijee received a letter dated 14th January, 1930 from Shri Sethji. It was mentioned:

You have mentioned your visit to go to Chitrakoot in March, 1930 and asked my consent; as such, there is no idea to retain you in Gorakhpur to do the press work. We could not discuss everything alone in detail at Prayag...... if it does not matter, then you can go to Chitrakoot after Holi festival. During my departure to Rishikesh in February, I want to discuss with you and decide this matter again.

Similarly, Bhaijee had continued making requests while Shri Sethji kept on averting it. Such correspondence and persuasion for meeting remained continuing for years together. On extreme persuasion, he went somewhere to live in calm and quiet for a few days but the Lord who wanted to get his act done through his medium brought him again to this worldly affair.

❑

44

Refusal by Shri Sethji to Permit Civil Disobedience for Salt

Shri Ganesh Shankar Vidyarthi of Kanpur and editor of 'Pratap' reached Gorakhpur in April, 1930. He was going to join Civil Disobedience of salt at Padrauna on the invitation of Baba Raghavdasji. It was high time for those days for civil disobedience of salt. Gandhiji has written Bhaijee to join him. Several friends also persuaded to join this civil disobedience. Bhaijee was also sympathetic for such work with his body and mind. He took Shri Gambhirchandji Dujari with him and went to Padrauna with Shri Vidyarthi to take an actual part in civil disobedience for salt. Ardent lectures were made and when salt was auctioned, Bhaijee purchased very little salt for twenty-five rupees. He had insistently made request to Shri Sethji to permit him specially in this movement. Bhaijee had written to him that many of my friends have been arrested in this movement and I also wish to join it, please accord your permission. Shri Sethji replied instantly through telegram – Do not join this movement and wait for the letter. Shri Sethji replied in a detailed letter which can be seen in the book alongwith the collection of letters, to be published soon. The heart of Bhaijee was melted due to sorrow of his affectionate companions. Therefore, his mind remained completely unchanged. As per the advice of Shri Sethji, Bhaijee went after 10 days to Churu to attend a function in Rishikul. Shri Sethji had clearly restricted Bhaijee not to attend this movement. Bhaijee had been telling some time as a joke that Shri Sethji possesses a fabulous weapon, which was also known to him and me as well. He had used this weapon seldom but on my continuous insistence, if he does not like it, then he said, "Look, I said, it should not be done." I must keep silence and have to agree. Due to such check made by Shri Sethji, Bhaijee could not make progress in politics.

Staying in Churu for two-three days, both saints went to Bikaner with Shri Gambhirchandji Dujari. Took meal there at his residence, visited the local saint Shri Lalimai. She was a lady saint of high order from Bikaner. The lives of many widow sisters of women association of Bikaner was made joyous due to her. Whenever Shri Sethji and Bhaijee visited Bikaner, they had always met her. Shri Lalimaiji had also a great respect for both people. Stayed in Bikaner for one-two days, Bhaijee proceeded to Ratangarh and Jaipur to collect pictures for '*Ramayanank*', then returned to Gorakhpur after 10-12 days and got busy in preparation for '*Ramayanank*'.

❐

45

An Inscrutable Help by Divine Power (Leela Shakti) of the God

It was always said by Bhaijee in his discourse that power of divine act of the God is such an extraordinary thing that everything is prearranged about what and when the God will bequeath, due to which pledge of the God and the fulfillment of the pledge occurred simultaneously. Many of such examples can be seen in the life of Bhaijee. Mahamana Madan Mohanji Malaviya was in very close contact with Bhaijee. Being living in Mumbai, he became also intimate with his son. His nephew Krishna Kant Malaviya was at that period in Naini prison. An order was issued to shift him from Naini to Basti prison. The road from Naini to Basti passes via Gorakhpur. He sent a telegram to Bhaijee – 'Reaching Gorakhpur station in evening along with ten people while shifting to Basti, please arrange for our meal'. The telegram delivered in Gita press at about 10.00 A.M. During that period, Bhaijee was living in a small and old garden of Shri Balmukund near Gorakhnath temple. The people of the press have sent this telegram to Bhaijee in the evening when there was only half-an-hour left for the arrival of train. On the receipt of the telegram, Bhaijee was thinking that it is unfortunate when press people have opened it, it should have been sent by then itself or they could have sent the meal to station, by getting it prepared somehow in community eating centre. Now the meal cannot be prepared in half-an- hour nor a vehicle is available here. The phone was also not available during that period. One must go on foot for a distance to get one horse vehicle. Once he also decided to go on foot to station. Bhaijee has narrated that he had not prayed to God for the same. It was prior to 1924 that I had to make contended prayer or repetition of sacred verse in low tone for himself but did never afterwards. He was under confusion that with this, he found two, Ekkas (-an earlier form of Tonga) were approaching and halted at his residence. A person got down with sweets, fruits, vegetables and *puri* and said there was a function at Balmukundji's, place who sent it. Looking at all these arrangements, Bhaijee was very much surprised and pleased. He sent everything by these vehicles to station with those persons along with one of his own family members. The train arrived 15-20 minutes late. Shri Krishnakantji and his companions had eaten *puris*, sweets & fruits up to their satisfaction. Bhaijee then said – Look! How the things are arranged by the God. Such meal might be prepared in the morning or in the afternoon. If it comes one hour earlier, it is eaten by all of us or if it comes after half-an-hour, it has no use to them. As soon as the telegram is received, instantly everything like *puri*, vegetables, sweets and fruits as well have been arranged timely by the God including the one-horse vehicles. Such was the quantity of meal that ten to twelve people could eat it satisfactorily.

❐

46

A Shelter to an Orphan Boy

Such event belongs to 1931. Once a person reached Gita press in sad condition. His wife expired. He had two children – a son, 14 years old, named Anand Mandolia and a daughter, who was 8 years old. There was nobody in the family who could look after the children. He cannot go anywhere in search of an employment leaving his children alone. The reputation of Gita press had reached to distant places. He came to Gorakhpur as he could not get shelter anywhere and requested help for his children, explaining everything in Gita press. The workers in the press had clearly refused telling that it is not an orphan house or an alms-house. We cannot keep here your children, you can get them admitted in any orphan house. Being in distress, the poor man returned to station. When Bhaijee could know about it, instantly he sent his worker to station and called them back at his residence. The man had requested him to retain his children for few days so that he could arrange for his livelihood. Bhaijee had kept both children with him cheerfully and with great love. That person had left the children and gone happily. The children were very naughty. So, they keep doing arrogance. Bhaijee told in Gita press in front of all if the Gita press is only the name of machines publishing biographies of famous saints, is it not our duty to help others during their bad times? Likewise, Bhaijee has given many times a shelter to such sad and orphaned persons.

❐

47

A Trip to Braj

With an aim to make preparation for 'Shri Krishnank', Bhaijee had started his journey to Braj and reached Vrindavan on 20th March, 1931 by attending a celebration of devotional songs in *Aligarh* with his family and twelve companions. He stayed there for three days and visited the important temples and arranged for photography. Also met prominent saint and made discussion. Then came to *Mathura* and made arrangement for collection of items for 'Shri Krishnank'. In addition, he had also made visits to like famous places, Shri *Nandgaon, Barsana, Radhakund, Kusum-sarovar and Govardhan, etc.*

Attended the knowledge of sacrificial act of Gita at *Kazimabad* on his return and also met saints like Shri Haribaba, Shri Bholebaba, Shri Achyutmuniji, etc. At the assembly of virtuous people, Bhaijee had given a special exposition regarding the importance of divine name and also shared his experience.

There occurred a type of flood in the stream of celestial Ganges due to arrival of Bhaijee at *Rishikesh* on 23rd April, 1931. From there, he went to Kazimabad to meet Shri Udiya Baba. Wandering like this, he reached Gorakhpur on 7th May 1931 and became busy in editing of 'Shri Krishnank'.

❐

48

Meeting with Swami Vishuddhanand

Swami *Vishuddhanandji* was a teacher of Mahamahopadhyay *Pandit Gopinathji Kaviraj*. He had a great fame, during that period, in spiritual world. Bhaijee also went to meet him at Varanasi on 23rd March, 1932. He was very famous to show miracles. Bhaijee was introduced after an assembly of virtuous people. He asked Bhaijee – tell me what you would like? Bhaijee did not ask to show any other miracle but asked him to experience the smell of divine body of Lord Shri Krishna and also requested for His appearance. Accepting his request, 'Gandhi Baba' (he was famous by such name) smiled. A little later, the room was full of divine smell. The revered persons present there had never experienced such a divine smell. Then he said to Bhaijee – look into my eyes. Bhaijee has begun to visualise Shri Krishna in his eyes. A little later he asked – let me finish this show now. The visualisation of Shri Krishna had stopped after some time and the divine smell in the room also ended.

❐

49

During the Dam-Function of Shri Haribaba

Swami Haribaba arrived suddenly at the residence of Bhaijee on 6th February, 1934 without any prior information. On his arrival, he said – There had been a large function held for the celebration of devotional songs (*Sankeertan*) on Holi since many years at dam. Such celebration was discontinued since three-four years as there was no benefit as expected by it. Since the celebration of devotional songs had been discontinued, there occurred various types of riots in the nearby villages. Disturbed by such incidences, many people had come to me and requested to start the function of celebration of devotional songs as earlier, on yearly basis. The permission was sought from Udia Baba who consented and suggested that celebration of devotional songs must be held. I went at the dam on the same day and got started twelve-hour non-stop celebration of devotional songs and it was decided to arrange twenty-four-hour non-stop celebration of devotional songs till coming 14th February, 1934. To arrange and make request for maximum attendance of saints and sages in this festival, I came here through Prayag to request you and Shri Sethji. As you are extremely busy, as such, instead of making request through letter, I myself have come to take your positive consent. Bhaijee had given him a heartily welcome with great affection and went to Shri Sethji with him and explained everything. Shri Sethji said – it is doubtful for me to attend due to health grounds but Bhaijee will do the needful.

On 26th February, 1934, Bhaijee alongwith his affectionate companions went to attend this festival at Dam. Next day at 4.30 A.M., Bhaijee joined the celebration of devotional songs. Haribaba danced during the celebration of devotional songs in standing and intoxicated manner, which was enjoyed by everyone remarkably. Bhaijee met there with various saints – Shri Udiababa, Shri Nagababa, Shri Shivanandji, Shri Krishnanandji, Shri Bholebaba, Shri Prabhudattji Brahmchari, etc. Bhaijee had attended this function for three-four days and also gave a highly impressive discussion on the importance of repetition of divine name and group singing of hymns. He returned to Gorakhpur on 4th March, 1934.

❑

50

Shri Chimmanlalji Goswami

Shri Chimmanlalji Goswami was born on 27th June, 1900. His family was full of religious instincts and he got impressions of Ballabh sect right from his birth.

The female ascetic Shri Chandra Kala Devi and Shri Brajlal Goswami had the honour to be his parents. Passed high school in 1916 and went to Varanasi to study English, Philosophy and Sanskrit at Queen's College. During his studies, he received special attention and guidance from Mahamahopadhyaya Pandit Shri Gopinathji Kaviraj. On completion of his studies from Queen's College, he passed his M.A. in Sanskrit in first division in 1922 from Kashi Hindu Vishwavidyalaya. Thereafter, for some time, he worked as personal assistant to Mahamana Pandit Madan Mohan Malaviya. On return to Bikaner from Varanasi, he also worked as principal for four years. Thereafter, he worked in politics department of government at Bikaner for six years and then remained a personal secretary of the chief council of state, respected Shri Manu Bhai Shah.

As desired by the God, Bhaijee went to Bikaner in 1927 to spread divine names. At the same period, Goswami had seen Bhaijee and was extremely attracted towards him during his first meeting. Such was a deep effect on his mind of his first meeting that a strong desire was born naturally to accompany him a little more. This desire was gradually increasing while Shri Gambhirchandji Dujari was also persuading him continuously to live near Bhaijee. Due to his inspiration, he took leave and came to Gorakhpur on 15th May 1929. He got a rare opportunity to live near Bhaijee for about one-and-a-half months. An accomplishment society was already formed during that period and its rules had been followed with great zeal. By joining it, he had also started to follow these rules sincerely. During such a short time, he got an occasion to know the experiences and God-related matured thoughts of Bhaijee, as well as to see very closely his life, deeply immersed with the God. Such was an effect on his mind by the public-censured personality of Bhaijee that he took a decision just after ten-fifteen days to live at the holy feet of Bhaijee, leaving everything while rest of the life may also be passed under his kind shelter. He had insistently placed his desire in front of Bhaijee. Bhaijee told if you are firm and have taken permission from your father, then you can join editorial department of '*Kalyan*'.

Though such decision was difficult to comply but being firm is surely blessed by the grace of the God. That very thing occurred, he resigned of a high position from Bikaner state and came to Bhaijee in January, 1933 alongwith his wife to live permanently.

Bhaijee was very much pleased to get an assistance from Goswamiji. To spread divine name and Godly devotion in the society and spirituality in public life as well as the reputation of morality, Bhaijee was continuously energetic and to give it more momentum for such an aim, the monthly magazine '*Kalyan*' had been strongly helpful alongwith many other reasons. This monthly magazine was published only in Hindi. On the arrival of Shri Goswamiji, a monthly magazine in English had also started its appearance. It was titled '*Kalyan Kalptaru*' which had the same aim as '*Kalyan*' except the difference of the language. Shri Goswamiji was an eminent scholar of Hindi, Sanskrit and English. He had an extraordinary command on the grammar of all three languages.

The publication of '*Kalyan Kalptaru*' started since the year 1934. Though Goswamiji was, its chief editor he also started helping Bhaijee for Hindi monthly '*Kalyan*' and his name began appearing as assistant editor of '*Kalyan*' since 1936. On the demise of Bhaijee, the complete load of editorial work had come to Goswamiji. Now Goswamiji had to control the work for both the magazines i.e., '*Kalyan*' and '*Kalyan Kalptaru*'. During his editorial tenure, three special issues had been published – '*Shri Ramank*', '*Shri Vishnuank*' and '*Shri Ganeshank*'. With an opinion of the material and decoration, all these three special issues of '*Kalyan*' had also been exactly the same as other issues published under editorial team of Bhaijee. During editorial tenure of Goswamiji, the glorious tradition and spiritual reputation of '*Kalyan*' had been unbroken. After heavenly departure of Bhaijee and taking the responsibility as an editor of '*Kalyan*', such a request was made by him in which one can see an excellent clarity of his heart. He had written in his reporting

– "Leaving his mortal body to become eternally engrossed within an act of the deity by our supreme Vaishnava devotee Shri Poddarji, I have to carry the responsibility for editing '*Kalyan*' and myself feel totally unable to bear it. Till now, the complete load of 'Kalyan' was carried away alone by Shri Poddarji. As a courtesy to give me inspiration and to fulfil the passion of my honour, he had included my name along with his glorious name. I don't have the strength of devoted striving nor spiritual experience, nor sacrifice, nor penance, nor any divine wealth, nor personal matured thinking, nor such study or thinking over of scriptures, nor my pen has such a strength. Under such a condition, I found in myself totally absence of the ability like and as far as to become the editor of magazine like '*Kalyan*'. I consider myself totally inappropriate to serve '*Kalyan*' but I am looking in anyway the work of '*Kalyan*' as a desire to fulfill my duty towards my supreme relative like supremely respected Bhaijee. In the real sense, I feel as if the work of '*Kalyan*' is being done by Bhaijee himself. At every step, he took care of it in his thoughtful form, otherwise continuation of such a grand duty is totally impossible by such an incompetent, less intelligent, non- resourceful and an insignificant person like me. I feel myself surprised that how and in what ways the work is completed. Looking at his courtesy at every step, I cannot believe that Shri Bhaijee is separated from '*Kalyan*'. I do consider that '*Kalyan*' belongs to him and he belongs to '*Kalyan*' or, better to say, he himself has become in '*Kalyan*' form. It is not our belief but an experience that Shri Bhaijee even today in invisible form is still managing the '*Kalyan*' and due to this reason, this work is being carried away well.

Such words are generally heard and said about *Shri Ramcharit Manas* that credit for its creation goes to Goswami Tulsidasji. Then circulation of this epic to each and every village or cities through Gita press is due to Bhaijee. Prior to publication of Ramcharit Manas, Bhaijee had asked Goswamiji to correct it. A Hindi scholar Pandit Shri Nand Dulare Vajpayeeji also gave an important cooperation for its correction to Shri Goswamiji. Thereafter, Bhaijee had himself written the Hindi meaning of Manas. Due comparison was made of Manas copy of Malihabad, copy of *Ayodhyakand* from *Rajpur*, *Sundarkand* copy from *Dulhi* village, *Balkand* copy from Shravan Kunj (Ayodhya), Manas copy from Golaghat (Ayodhya) and some other texts, and it was then only that Shri Goswami had made a comparative study with a due correction in the sacred text of Manas. The Manas text which is being published nowadays by Gita press was duly presented by the studious personality of Goswamiji.

Goswamiji had been keeping busy in translation and editorial work so that he could not meet Bhaijee for many days. A daily attendant of Bhaijee Shri Krishna Chandji told Goswamiji – you should meet Bhaijee at least once in a day. The people from far off places have been coming to meet him and you, being here, do not meet Babuji (Bhaijee).

Goswamiji replied in a sweet tone – if I go to meet him, it would take at least half-an-hour. If I use this time to complete the work as directed by him, would it not be nice? The time is not sufficient to complete the work assigned by him. If I start going to him daily, it would also harm his activities. How can I explain my mental status? Who would not prefer his proximity and to visit him. To talk or to visit him would definitely please me but it is more joyous to obey him. My internal desire is to fulfill his work. Listening to his reply, Shri Krishnachandji became silent.

During 1959, a message was sent by Baba to Goswamiji. Such message should be called an information. The information was that the king of Bikaner Emperor Shri Gangasinghji had entered in the divine act. When Goswamiji was working in the administrative section at Bikaner, he had a close contact with the Emperor Shri Gangasinghji. Goswamiji was pleased to receive this information but was more surprised than pleased. He was surprised to know that he had already expired since many years ago, but entered now in the kingdom of divine act of Shri Radhakrishna and if it happened now, which was the auspicious act or practice or grace for such an achievement? Goswamiji knows that Emperor Shri Gangasinghji was the only best Hindu king who lived his life with all kingly comforts. Goswamiji expressed his surprise. Then Baba explained that emperor Shri Gangasinghji had not achieved such state by any practice, but it was actually a beautiful result due to his contact and relation with Shri Poddarji Maharaj (Shri Bhaijee). Hearing such fact, how much internal faith and feeling of Goswamiji would have become more strong and joyful towards Bhaijee, it is beyond an imagination.

Goswamiji worked in editorial section of '*Kalyan*' and '*Kalyan Kalptaru*' published by the Gitapress, only due to his inspiration to serve. Though there was not at all any intention to earn the money, even then and yet he had received a little but to meet his livelihood.

Goswamiji had a very sweet voice. Even at old age, his singing charm was maintained. The discourse of Babuji (Bhaijee) was held daily for one hour in the morning at Gita Vatika. At later years, Goswamiji could not get even little time but during early period in Gita Vatika, Goswamiji had been singing one verse of religious poetry prior to such discourses. When the pilgrimage train was proceeded, Goswamiji had also accompanied Bhaijee in this train. Wherever the train reached, Bhaijee was given warm welcome and he also had to give an exposition amongst the devotees present there. Even there, Goswamiji had also been singing poetical verses prior to an exposition. Goswamiji also received umpteen temptations. The main temptation was the chair of Shankaracharya. Impressed by his simplicity and scholarliness, the chief of the seat Shri Gowardhan chair and situated in Jagannathpuri, an eternally prosperous Shankaracharya, respected Swami Shri Bhartikrishnatirth Maharaj expressed his desire to nominate him as his successor.

As soon as the offer from Shankaracharya was sent to him, there instantly occurred a crucial condition of religious crisis to Goswamiji internally. Respected Shankaracharyaji is our religious teacher. He is perpetually and supremely respected, it is only his kind blessing to be selected for such a grand position of Shankaracharya, his sheer hint only is at par to an order and it should have been accepted at once looking to his inclination but Goswamiji had expressed his inability to accept such an offer.

Goswamiji was of the firm opinion that the primary dominion present in the role of Shankaracharya and the great work of religious foundation which is performed during that period by then first Shankaracharya, the same great work is being carried out at present by Bhaijee. To remove the depression from the religion and to make an arrangement for a reply to social questions like sacred work is being carried away by Bhaijee, not only this much, in the way in which a huge and best literature is created by him and just as looking to his previously Vaishnavi state full of great feelings, it appears that in the tradition of great divinities of spiritual preceptors like Shankaracharya-Ramanujacharya, like religious founders, Manu-Yagyawalkya like recollector saints, Tulsidas-Surdas like great saintly poets Chaitanya- Mahaprabhu, Vallabhacharya like great connoisseurs, Bhaijee is also to be counted around.

Baba has always been appreciating the beliefs of Goswamiji. In this context, there is a very interesting incident regarding sixteen songs. In compilation of sixth line of tenth stanza of sixteenth rhyme, there is an utterance by Shri Radha – The supreme Goddess of the groves of Vrindavan:

O Lord! You continue to live throughout twenty-four hours in my temple of mind.

Baba feels a sudden blaze in his mind that in this line, there should be another word in place of the 'Lord' – any loving word without any sign of supremacy, then the complete feeling of the poem would be more charming. Baba and Bhaijee both agreed for a distinct faith that Shri Radha – a perpetual owner of meeting place for her and Krishna at Vrindavan and Shri Krishna a perpetual owner of the meeting place of him and Radha at Vrindavan are both actually, the God and Goddess, but such a sense of supreme being is not evident in the sweet kingdom of supreme love. The supreme sweet ocean of love for this couple of eternally supreme abode of love and their supreme being are hidden in the unfathomable bottom of that ocean. The manifestation of such God occurs seldom only and occurred only when the God is required in fulfilment of some act. Sometimes only in fulfilment of that act, the dominion power of supreme being got an opportunity to serve a little, otherwise this supreme being remained totally asleep and hidden. The sixteen songs (*shodash geet*) is a creation of supreme elegant thing consisting of virtuous thoughts in the kingdom of love, as such Baba explaining his feelings told to Bhaijee – if another sweet word is used in this line in lieu of the Lord, then the freshness of the poem will be more enriched.

Bhaijee replied – as you say and as you wish, I will do the same. The line which has suddenly throbbed at that instant, that very same has been conveyed to Bhaijee – 'O charming Lord! You have remained engaging my attention entirely throughout twenty-four hours of the day in the pool of my mind'.

Bhaijee highly appreciated the suggestion of Baba and this line was accepted in toto. In poetry, new line was replaced in lieu of old line. Bhaijee was happy of such change.

Then this thing was told to Goswamiji by Baba. Goswamiji humbly asked Baba if such change was really necessary?

Baba explained his feelings as conveyed to Bhaijee. This was not the thing that Goswamiji was not accepting such feeling or its importance. With such an understanding and with intense meekness, Goswamiji had started telling feelings of his mind – Baba, I accept your suggestion in totality but there is a small thought in my mind. According to my faith, I don't consider the sixteen songs or its terminology as an object of simple level. These poems are not only a literary composition. During the state of emotional meditation (*Bhava Samadhi*) of Bhaijee, the act (*leela*) or the expression of strong feeling had materialised in his range of sight and or range of hearing, the same have been drawn together in the limit of the terminology of these poems by blessing of some inconceivable power. As the sixteen songs are related with that state of emotional meditation, I don't approve any type of modification or change in it. In my opinion, the original line should be retained as such.

Baba very much appreciated opinion of Goswamiji and he had given due honour to such thoughts from his heart. Thereafter any change in that tenth poem had been deleted. Of course, Babuji had made one thing necessary that the line suggested by Baba had been accepted in the form of 'one another lesson'. Such 'another lesson' stands published at the end of tenth poem of sixteen songs.

Looking at his simple dress of white cotton sari, long shirt (*kurta*) and his simple behaviour, nobody can imagine that he is an eminent scholar in Sanskrit, Hindi and English. He had a simple and honest behaviour for everyone. It seems that shadow of very sweet behaviour of Bhaijee had also been casted on him. He did not speak beyond requirement but do enquire about well-being of everyone during his meetings. He never praised himself but if somebody praised in front of him, then he felt an awkward position and made due resistance of it, with due humility. The people coming in close contact with him were left deeply impressed by his behaviour.

During the last span of his life, Goswamiji had been very sick for five-six months. He was living in a house very near to Gita Vatika. Looking at his pain and sickness, Baba brought him in Gita Vatika. He was placed in a room in the same building of Gita Vatika where Bhaijee had lived. The medical treatment and care of Goswamiji had been started with full sincerity. Lying on the sick bed, the body of Goswamiji was suffering with extreme pain. The way in which time and attention had been given by Baba towards treatment and care of Goswamiji was a thing of an astonishment. Even during such condition of pain, Goswamiji was uttering only one sentence – O Lord, let your wish be fulfilled.

Looking at the chronic illness of Goswamiji, Baba had started saying that it is a time of final departure and Goswamiji might now live no more. People busy in discussion found if Goswamiji probably wanted to change the position of lying or wanted to say something by speaking. Some of them asked – What do you want?

Goswamiji told them – Not to wish anymore, I just want only this. Suffering with extreme pain, Goswamiji did not say that he needs medicine or treatment. Looking at his immense pain, if somebody showed sympathy, then Goswamiji always told him – Every action of the Lord is auspicious – even in such sickness, an auspicious touch by the God is still active and the same is being experienced constantly.

Goswamiji had written at one place – My relationship with Bhaijee for more than forty years has been a priceless treasure in my life, which has been suddenly bestowed to me by his blessing without motive, due to my own good conduct of many births. Such was the wonderful affection extended by him during this period and did caressing to me, which cannot be described in words. I cannot be indebted by his debt even in many births, nor I wish it to do. Flowing in strong stream in the river of life, he had lifted by his normal kindness to an extremely wicked person like me and made eligible to the blessings of the God. Never paid attention to my errors but also appreciated extremely even for a minute and favourable conduct, inspired by him only. He is not only my elder brother, friend and mentor, but also my guide and everything to me and still he is. His simple memory has moved my heart with compassion. Well! The rest of my life may pass in the memory of Bhaijee and my Shri Radhamadhav, this is my only wish.

Lying on the sick-bed, Goswamiji had been often observing to the sacred place for cremation of Bhaijee through the window of his room. Such place of cremation had remained painted by the *attar*-mixed yellow soil. Few days prior to his departure of heavenly abode, Goswamiji expressed his last wish in front of near relatives and said – the yellow soil painted on the sacred place of cremation is my wealth of life. Shri Bhaijee is a symbol of yellow shawl of my beloved Shri Krishna and it is always kept alive as the sacred memory – a treasure to my life. The last bath of my dead body should be made through the water collected from washing of that sacred soil.

Goswamiji died on 5th May 1974. He lived on this earth for about 74 years. He had no child. A little later, his wife also expired in *Bikaner*.

❐

51
Initiation of '*Kalyan-Kalptaru*'

Since a long time ago, Bhaijee was realising the need that a monthly magazine in English like '*Kalyan*' should also be published so that the English-speaking people and the persons living abroad may find easily the message from '*Kalyan*'. To manage such an important work, an emotional scholar was required. By arrival of Shri Chimmanlalji Goswami, such lacuna was fulfilled, and a decision was taken to publish '*Kalyan-Kalptaru*' in English. Its publication took place since 1934. Bhaijee acted as a controlling editor while Goswamiji was editor. For some duration, Shri Krishnadas Bengali worked as a joint editor who was the disciple of Shri Satish Chandra Bengali. This magazine was in great demand from abroad and the people were also highly benefitted by it. Scriptures like the *Shrimad Bhagwat, the Shrimad Bhagwat Gita, the Balmiki Ramayan, the Ramcharit Manas, etc.* have been authentically translated and presented in English language due to this medium. There occurred two-three occasions to suspend the publication of '*Kalyan-Kalptaru*' for few months due to many problems. But the difficulties have been removed by the grace of God and publication continued. But it was discontinued after the death of Goswamiji. According to website of this magazine, "Since 1934, (with a brief gap) it is being published regularly with a special number on spiritual theme or ancient scripture followed by eleven monthly issues."

Protection of Shri Shukdeoji in an unusual way

To note the approaching of terrible weapon, realising it that my duty is to destroy the trouble of a refuge.

(Ramcharit Manas/Lankakand/93/1)

One of the milestones of Gita press was Shri Shukdeoji Agrawal, who served Gita press throughout his life. He had an excellent devotion and respect for Shri Sethji and Bhaijee. The event occurred in 1934. He was returning from *Swargashram* to Gorakhpur. The mother and wife, etc. of Bhaijee had accompanied him. Bhaijee was at Gorakhpur during that period. Shri Shukdeoji was extremely eager from inside to see and meet Bhaijee soon by any means. Prior to arrival of *Khalilabad* station, he had made himself free by completing his morning routine, i.e., mental. and morning religious rites and meditation. Yet the Khalilabad station was still far away. The train was still moving but due to his eagerness, he felt as if Gorakhpur station had arrived. He opened the door of the compartment and tried to get down. The iron handle fixed near the door was in his hand and he was hanging outside the compartment in a moving train which was fast moving. He was unconscious for some time but became conscious later and thought I am now near to death. With this, he had visually seen that Bhaijee was assisting him bodily and getting him down by holding his hand on arrival of Khalilabad station and also helping to stand at the station. Thereafter, Bhaijee was no more visible. Khalilabad station is about 20 miles from Gorakhpur. Bhaijee was at Gorakhpur station. But he took care of Shri Shukdeoji. Shukdeoji narrated this incidence to Bhaijee on his arrival to Gorakhpur. But Bhaijee expressed an ignorance about it.

❐

52

An Arrival of Shri Shantanu Bihariji Dwivedi (Swami Akhandanandji) at Gorakhpur

Impressed by the articles published in '*Kalyan*', Shri Shantanu Bihariji Dwivedi came first time in June, 1934 to Gorakhpur. By reading special issue '*Bhaktank*' for third year of '*Kalyan*', he decided to meet Bhaijee. It was such an intense desire of meeting that irrespective of thinking about finances, he started as such empty-handed. Came up to *Dohrighat* station by rail and from there came on foot to Gorakhpur which is about 40 miles. On meeting Bhaijee, he made first question – how to love the God? To his reply, tears have been trickling down from the eyes of Bhaijee. He embraced him and replied:

'O Uma! Those who are aware by the nature of Ram shall never remember anything except to repeat His sacred name.'

He was attracted by the affection extended by Bhaijee. He stayed there for three-four days, second time he arrived during the time of celebration of devotional songs (*sankeertan*) in Gorakhpur on 30th June, 1936. He started working in editorial section in Gorakhpur as he had a strong desire to live near Bhaijee, as well as took special interest in different activities and singing devotional songs. He had made a great contribution to his work of Hindi translation of the *Shrimad Bhagwat* and also for editorial work. He had high regards for Bhaijee. Consequently, he took renunciation of the world and became famous as Swami Akhandanand.

❐

53

To Bestow Spiritual Instruction Unconsciously at an Autumn of Full Night Moon

Shri Bhaijee has always been making efforts for spiritual progress for the people working near to him. From time to time, he was arranging special activities – rites, etc. for this purpose. Looking at the extreme eagerness of his close associates during 1934 and by framing very strict rules, Bhaijee arranged for the celebration of devotional songs (*sankeertan*) at night by forming a committee for devotional songs. Due to an extreme eagerness of practitioners throughout, it was completed in a very good manner and during which few people had special experiences.

During the next year in 1935, Bhaijee had again arranged a celebration of devotional songs again at night. Bhaijee utters few such words, anew again during celebration of devotional songs by which everyone felt highly elated. Celebration of devotional songs of poem continued throughout the full month of June. The minds of everyone were highly elated during the full moon of autumn night. On the completion of celebration of devotional songs of poems, Bhaijee had begun describing sweetly about the fifth chapter of Krishna festival including an enactment of the round dance. Hearing the flute played by Shri Krishna, the herd girls of *Braj* had proceeded from their homes – describing all this in melodious voice, Bhaijee had become ecstatic and started singing devotional songs. A little later and becoming normal, he began to speak that Lord has described the duties of women and ordered them to return, the herd girls of Braj had felt disappointed, later after examination and by describing the enactment of round dance, he again became ecstatic. Again, the celebration of devotional songs started. A little later, Bhaijee started speaking with harshness – the Lord had vanished. Then the herd girls of Braj had begun praying submissively. Again, the Lord appeared – telling this, Bhaijee kept quiet. Bhaijee alongwith the rest of the people started dancing and singing celebration of devotional songs while in standing. Bhaijee was performing very emotional dance but, while dancing, he fell and became unconscious. The celebration of devotional songs had been concluded after a long duration. Everyone sat down. Shri Ramjidasji Bajoria was sitting in front of Bhaijee.

He asked – We should also be blessed by His appearance. Bhaijee did not reply as he had not yet returned in this world. He repeated many times. Then Bhaijee said – everyone has gone, we are left. He was asked – what do you mean by we people? Replied – there were only two – Shri *Vishakha*ji and me. Ramdasji did not understand anything and asked again – Who were those two people? Bhaijee started laughing very loudly A little later, Ramdasji again requested for an appearance. Then Bhaijee said – who wants appearance? Are you looking for some show here or performing any trickery or dissimulation? Trust on Shri Radhakrishna. If you want his appearance, then repeat a sacred verse – *'Om kleem Shri Radha Krishnabhyam namah'* three thousand times daily for one year with an asceticism. Mohanlalji asked – Whether *Lalitaji* was there? Hearing it, Bhaijee asked loudly – Who is there? Thereafter Bhaijee regained his consciousness. He then asked the people – What happened? Someone enquired about the sacred verse. Then Bhaijee said – Which verse? I don't remember anything. What have I said? Then everyone was given *kheer* as a food offered to the God. A little later, Bhaijee asked with an affection and persuasion from Bajranglalji Bajaj that I am asking in a very simple manner that since I stopped talking during celebration of devotional songs, what happened since then till now, I don't remember anything. Did I make any mistake? Who made question in between and what was my reply, I also don't know anything.

Thereafter, Bhaijee became very much attentive. He did not arrange celebration of devotional songs by his initiation, nor uttered such things which may cause emotional provocation.

After some time, Bhaijee went to attend a function in *Rishikul* at Churu during dark half for ninth month of Hindu year. From there, he went to *Bikaner* alongwith some people. He took meal at the residence of Shri *Gambhirchandji Dujari* and started talking there itself in seclusion with his affectionate companions. In addition to Bhaijee, there were also other people like Shri Chimmanlalji Goswami, Shri Shukdeoji, Pandit Govardhanji, Shri Gambhirchandji Dujari, etc. Shri Dujariji said – it is such a great occasion after many days. Therefore, please tell us some sweet and affectionate things like that during autumn night of full moon.

Shri Bhaijee said – I don't remember any word of that incident. Shri Goswamiji told – You had become unconscious on that day. So, how could you remember those conversations. But let us also have that experience. Shri Bhaijee replied – Look, you people are all are very close to me. Therefore, I will clear my position. There is no doubt that I have more with that thing than you people. But whatever thing is in my possession cannot be shared by others because that is not within my power. It has been my desire that my companions should also achieve the divine affection. But to let achieve anyone such an affection, I don't have such an ability. I have tried for one person but could not get the result because such a strong sin was committed by him in this birth and due to such restriction, there was no benefit.

❑

54

Receipt of the Book Written by Bhaijee During Dream

Shri Deshpandeji, a gentleman in a village near *Nagpur*, had seen a saint in his dream during night, whose look was like Shri Bhaijee's. He gave a book '*Sadhan-Path*' during his dream written by Bhaijee. On his awakening, the book was found lying on his bed. As such, he was very much surprised. Citing such event, he had written a letter to Bhaijee, which was destroyed by Bhaijee. A reply, which was sent by Bhaijee, is being given below:

|| Shri Hari ||

April-May, 1935

Dear Shri Deshpandeji,

Let us affectionately remember His divine name.

Received your letter. If the words written in letter are true, then it is a matter of great surprise. Please do not be under false notion that I have doubt in the quality of being true of your letter. I can definitely say this much that I do not know anything about it. Prior to receipt of this letter, I was not aware about it. I can let you believe that I do not possess any attainment at all. '*Sadhan-Path*' book was given by some saint in your dream and was found on your bed on your awakening, will definitely be the result of your devotion. Who was that saint, I have no information? What is the mystery behind it, I do not know anything. Please do inform if that saint had conveyed anything. If so, what did he say? The personality as mentioned by you is like that of Lord Shiva. You are fortunate that a saint has appeared in your dream.

Whatever has been given in '*Sadhan-Path*', it is all written based on scriptures. What is my contribution? When I observe, then all these things are not present in me. Therefore, how can I give you spiritual instructions. I have even no right to bestow spiritual instructions. By consulting '*Sadhan-Path*' if you acquire peace, treat it as gift by that saint. Do not consider anything from my end. You wish to achieve the God, it is really a thing of great pleasure.

Yours,

Hanuman Prasad Poddar

❐

55

Appearance to British Devotee

It is not possible to count number of people living abroad who had received spiritual guidance through '*Kalyan*' and '*Kalyan-Kalptaru*'. To find such an example, following letter and its reply written to an English devotee of Krishna named Shri Radha Krishna-Prem-Bhikhari (*Ronald Nixon*) can be seen:

Dated-17.01.1935

Respected Mr. Editor,

About 11 years old, dark, savorous and supremely beautiful boy named 'Hrishikesh' came at 12.00 o'clock in the afternoon. During that period, this Radha Krishna-Prem-Bhikhari was reading 6th number of volume nine of '*Kalyan*' with deep concentration. With great humility, that boy had requested a small locket-sized Gita from this Bhikhari and asked, 'Please teach me 22nd verse of chapter 9 of the Gita and elaborate it as well. As soon as this Bhikhari started reading 'One who ponders on me entirely devoted..... (Gita: 9/22), he instantly intervened and said, " **Gita is the form of the God, there is not at** all **any doubt in it.**" This Bhikhari then asked, 'Hrishikesh' – friend! Where do you live and what do you do? He replied most humbly with love and ecstasy – I live in '*Kalyan*' and took care of all the living beings through '*Kalyan*'. The devotees are infinitely precious to me. The God and devotees and devoted Vaishnava all three are one. Then this Bhikhari asked him – friend, where is your home? He replied in slow and sweet voice – my place of residence is in *Sewakunj, Vrindavan*. Shri Radhakrishna from Vrindavan is my favoured deity. Hearing all this account, I wanted to provide some refreshment to him. This Bhikhari immediately went to internal department to arrange refreshment. On his return, he found Hrishikesh had gone somewhere. Conjecturally, it took about five minutes. This Bhikhari has tried a lot and had ran himself for about four miles but could not locate him anywhere.

When this Bhikhari met 'Hrishikesh', then perchance, there was nobody at that place. Please inform me this much only whether the boy named 'Hrishikesh' worked in your office and whether he lives in Sewakunj, Vrindavan. This Bhikhari shall be extremely grateful for such information.

Yours sincere refuge,
Radha Krishna Prem-Bhikhari

Letter written by Bhaijee to Shri Radhakrishna-Prem-Bhikhari

Gorakhpur,

Dated-20.01.1935

Respected Shri Radha Krishna Prem-Bhikhariji,
let us remember divine name with great affection,

Received your letter dated 17th January, 1935. No such and supremely beautiful boy named 'Hrishikesh' lived in '*Kalyan*'. Sewakunj-Bihari Shri *Shyam Sunderji* does live everywhere. Therefore, also lives in the '*Kalyan*' office. Also, if he lives in '*Kalyan*' can be confirmed by him only. He has never visualised to us in the form of a Brahmin boy. Really if Hrishikesh came to you to give begging of love at your place, then you are very lucky. You have committed definitely a mistake that you have not caught him and not took him alongwith you for refreshment. How and when he told you about his name 'Hrishikesh', please do inform.

Yours,
Hanuman Prasad Poddar

❐

56

A Directive to Obtain an Initiation During Sleep from Bhaijee

06.05.1935

Respected Mr. Editor may receive '*Om Namo Krishnay*' from Krishna Kumari. I had a dream on 02.05.1935. I had seen that Lord *Vrindavan Bihari* is giving an order in dream to achieve him and develop love of him by taking instruction from Hanuman Prasad.

'Nobody cares for lineage!
If you remember the Lord, you belong to him!

Hearing this, I was awakened. It was about 2.00 o'clock at night. I thought – whose name is 'Hanuman Prasad'? I have not heard anybody's name as '*Hanuman Prasad*'. Thinking such, I fell again asleep and heard again 'you are confused that who is Hanuman Prasad'? Well, he is known as Hanuman Prasad Poddar, the editor of '*Kalyan*', Gorakhpur. It's over then. I felt a bliss supreme. Now it is my repeated request that treating me as you daughter, please keep me guiding with necessary instructions from time to time. Please also excuse me for any type of mistake.

The reply sent to the above letter by Poddarji is being also given as follows:

Jyeshtha Sudi 1, Vikramaditya year 1922, Gorakhpur

Dear sister,

Let us remember His name with great pleasure. It is long since I received your letter. I could not reply timely, therefore, pardon me. Could know about the event in dream. Those who could hear the voice of Shri *Vrindavan Bihari* in dream, they are always blessed. It is my request that you ask Vrindavan Bihari himself that way to meet him in person. Request him why does He cheat by mentioning other's name. It is my faith that if your request possesses tenderness and strong will, then he can himself tell you the way to meet Him. Lord Shyam Sundar is such kind-hearted that he provides the rope by himself and then came to tie himself. Please make such request and have strong faith, then He will definitely visualise. Do not make such a doubt that the supreme Lord, who has given you instructions during dream to meet me, may not meet even with your true eagerness. This is my sincere suggestion.

Your brother,
Hanuman Prasad Poddar

57

An Extraordinary Event and Life Transformation

The life of Shri Deochandji, a resident of *Indore*, has changed extraordinarily. Later, he had been visiting Bhaijee many times My father (Shri Gambhir Chand Dujariji) has asked him to write his extraordinary experience. Such description is being presented in his language. He has used the word 'devotee' in place of 'I'. Such an event had occurred in 1935.

He was totally an atheist. To behave and show a temperament of insult only was his religion towards the people, society and saints who followed and believed in God. It may be due to mainly being logician or volatility, but he does necessarily utilise it and did opposition to followers of the God with piercing words on many occasions. So much so that poor and simple devotees started weeping by remembering the God or else they made humble requests in a bemoaning manner, to let the God correct his attitude.

It occurred once. The prayer of devotees cannot go as blank and at last the Lord heard it. When he was returning on that day with his friends from evening walk, there occurred a discussion about the God. One of his friends was very emotional and narrated many events of the divine acts by the God and the effect of things, due to his eternal love which had been very charming. But it was a habit of this atheist to do opposition of anyone whosoever met him and also abused loudly in words with disrespect to the God. So much conversations were held that this emotional friend started weeping, left him and moved to other place. His crying was heart-touching and the sound came through his pure heart and delivered such prayer near to the God. The crying of the emotional friend has seriously touched the heart of such atheist due to unknown reasons. Such things had also occurred previously several times, but there was no effect on his harsh heart but today his mind knows no limit of sorrow caused by his emotional friend. He reached home immediately and went to bed, that too without eating or drinking anything and fell asleep due to excessive repentance.

From here begins a change of his life. In sleep, he felt a great sunshine coupled with bliss. In that incomparable beautiful sunshine, a person appeared with very serious mood, placed a book and vanished. The book was in front of him, titled '*Tulsidal*'. By reading this much only, the pages of the book itself started turning back to front. On turning two pages, there was a picture of the God, a verse was written on the upper side while at the lower side was inscribed 'Revered crown prince of *Braj*' and there was one more verse on the lower side. A little later and like real, the God has appeared and was looking with great affection, sitting there, at him through his lotus eyes. After about 10 minutes, He spoke in a very sweet voice by raising his hand:

Resigning all your duties to me, the all-powerful and all-supporting lord, take refuge in me alone. I shall absolve you of all sins, worry not. (Gita, 18:66) and vanished.

The devotee could remember 'Tulsidal', Gita press and that verse. How can one just forget the charming look of the God? On awakening, the devotee was busy in thinking the complication of these things. He recollected that elder brother of one of his friends is religious in nature and fond of reading spiritual books. He went immediately to him and enquired about '*Tulsidal*' published by Gita press. He was told that such book is published by Gita press and has been written by respected Shri Hanuman Prasadji Poddar and is a very good text. I also have this book and brought it and showed to him. Sooner he found it, he observed same verses of the God and everything else therein. He immediately went to the shopkeeper to procure this book independently and brought it with him.

On the completion of the study of this book, he also read another book '*Sadhan-Path*' written by Poddarji and from here itself, the devotee begins an extraordinary practice which was just opposite to the external life and such practice started secretly.

Hare Ram Hare Ram, Ram Ram Hare Hare,
Hare Krishna Hare Krishna, Krishna Krishna Hare Hare

Repetition of the above sacred verse in low tone has started in number of 64 strings of beads daily alongwith the meditation of Lord of Revered crown prince of Braj. It has continued for three months. Meanwhile other books of Gita press have also been studied. Glory of saints was also listened to. Such has become the condition within three months of practice that meditation and chanting of divine names have begun constantly. It was an experience by his family members that even during his sleep, repetition of divine name in low tone had remained continued.

Even on this much of practice, if the Lord did not appear or some special thing may not materialise whichever is considered befitting, by the God, to the devotee? It is just not possible.

Meanwhile one day, there occurred tremendous happiness in his heart and the world also looked so beautiful and divine which could even never be described. There was an extraordinary happiness in heart alongwith a voice that the Lord shall definitely appear today. There has been unrestrained joy throughout the day, don't remember any hunger and was almost in an unconscious state. The close friends have also noticed and had told them on their query that it is very much bliss and happiness today and also feeling that the Lord would appear. More friends came in the evening, but the family members did not allow them for a frequent meeting due to his unconscious state and an arrangement was made to sleep early. One friend was emotional, and he slept near him with lot of insistence and with a hope to witness such an event.

It should be eleven o'clock of night, everybody of the family had fallen asleep. During ecstasy, the devotee remained under the state of half-drowsy-like condition coupled with an unrestrained joy.

Devotee was lying on the cot with his friend and found that a very beautiful and divine four-legged platform, which was extremely radiant and was studded with divine jewels was descending towards him. The divine platform had a width of about 9' × 12' and from downside can be clearly seen well decorated things by jewels, garments, and sacred verses, etc. are written on the upper side. This platform was dismounted and placed on the cot. Devotee was lying, therefore, he got up. His friend was still asleep alongwith his nearby other sleepers.

It was not only a platform but a large room. The jewels-studded platform had an upper roof of about 12'. In the middle of the roof, the following very sacred verse was written from which were also emitting lights of various colours:

Hare Ram Hare Ram, Ram Ram Hare Hare,
Hare Krishna Hare Krishna, Krishna Krishna Hare Hare

Possibly the light was emitted from the studded jewels. All around the sacred verse, the verses from early Indian scriptures have been inscribed, from which had also been flowing a source of light. Though there were walls all around, but the air had been continuously flowing through them and internal things can be seen through its every particle. Two doors were situated near the walls of eastern side. In the middle region, thrones studded with divine gems had been placed close to each other. Various verses had been inscribed along with pictures on each side of the wall and the light was emitting from each of them. On the middle of the wall, there were some broad lines like tricolor flags, which were emitting lights of various colours. Devotee was sincerely observing such view that instantly a gentleman began appearing and walking on it. He was wearing a long white shirt of Khadi and a rough white sari. He was a medium-built person and was moving there. He asked the devotee – get up, wash your hands and feet and come up on the platform. Devotee got up, there was clean water near in a small round pot. He washed his hands and feet and moved above near that saint. The saint said – as decided by the God, there will be a meeting of His group at your place. Several saints – high, souled of noble nature, will attend it. On the completion of devotional singing, the Lord will talk something Himself to new devotees; thereafter which arrangements must be made for comfort, peace and conservation of this world, it would be discussed. This committee meets as per rules which consists of ninety members, out of which forty-five are ancient sages and ascetics while remaining forty-five are the saints and high-souled persons working bodily in this world. According to the wish of each of them, the meeting of committee was held four times in a year at four places. Like this, the whole year is completed, the meeting has been arranged at your place according to my wish. I, Hanuman Prasad Poddar, work as an editor for '*Kalyan*', a religious magazine published at Gorakhpur in India. Exactly at 11.30 hours, the sages and high-souled persons with noble nature had gradually started approaching. They all came one by one and sat on their allotted seats. The way in which saints arrived, in the same manner, Bhaijee introduced everyone by their names. Like this, everyone arrived.

The group singing of hymns (*kirtan*) had begun after arrival of everyone. The sages and ascetics started the singing which was followed with its repetition by saints and high-souled persons.

The group singing caught its momentum, and everyone stood up after half-an-hour of group singing. During group singing, many of them started dancing and jumping, while few of them had been feeling very emotional.

This devotee and Bhaijee had also been busy in group singing. In between, Bhaijee told devotee God is now arriving and after three months from today, there will again be a meeting of this committee at your place.

Prior to the arrival of God, there flowed a very sweet and enchanting fragrance of a specific nature. A special effect was appearing in the group singing due to such fragrance. A little later, a flash appeared and the Lord Himself arrived. Gradually entered through various doors and sat on the throne. Devotee was engrossed in group singing with his body and mind. By the grace of God, he was observing the whole act. As soon as the God assumed the throne, the devotee had got an access of emotion. Dancing due to unrestrained joy, thrill and shedding tears with eternal bliss, he fell unto the feet of the God. What happened thereafter, no description is available. It was beyond the capacity of the devotee. At last, devotee was found unconscious on his bed. His friend and other nearby sleepers had awakened. The devotee could return to consciousness after six hours.

❐

58

An Arrival of Pandit Jawaharlal Nehru at Gorakhpur

It was in the year 1936 when Bhaijee had arranged a nonstop celebration of devotional songs (*sankeertan*) for one year at *Gita Vatika* in Gorakhpur. Important saints and many dignitaries of the country had attended this function. During that period, Pandit Nehru was very famous. He was being appreciated for his sacrifice, renouncement and his stamina to face the hardship for the freedom of the nation. In relation of protest to Simon Commission, such was the intensity of torture and manhandling with him and *Pandit Govind Ballabh Pant* by the British government, which had caused an intense pain in the hearts of people of India. People had also very much interest in him.

During that period, there had occurred a strong flood in and the nearby region of Gorakhpur in which Bhaijee helped the flood-affected people by body, mind and wealth. To inspect the condition of flood during that period, Pandit Jawaharlal Nehru also came to Gorakhpur. During those days, an English man was the collector and it was an apprehension that whosever will lend his car to Nehruji, his vehicle will be forfeited. In such a condition, who can dare to lend his vehicle? Baba Raghav Das came to Bhaijee and requested – Bhaijee, I am not getting the car and our prestige is at stake. Bhaijee had a car during that time and so said – Please take the car. Nehruji went to the nearby region in the same car, returned to Gorakhpur after due inspection and by making speeches. On the same night, C.I.D. inspector Ram Prasadji visited Bhaijee and told jokingly – You have lent your car to Panditji today. Bhaijee replied – I have not given it secretly. Most of the leaders during that period always stayed with Bhaijee, which was known to everyone. Collector said – I know that Bhaijee has given his car, but no action will be taken. It was his faith that Bhaijee is not a political person. He provides an accommodation to everyone with love. Nehruji was invited in that great rite of celebration of devotional songs. He came to the sacrificial act and bowed to the Lord of Hall of Sacrifice. He also enquired – whether such celebration of devotional songs remained continuing throughout day and night? Were these small drums and cymbals also being played throughout? He was not aware by that time of all these things. Bhaijee gave an exposition in front of him on the quality of Indian religious devotion (*Bhakti-bhava*) and importance of celebration of devotional songs. Nehruji was wonder-struck and heard his exposition, feeling impressed by it, went back with due appreciation.

❒

59

Second Plan to Spread the Divine Name

In *Kaliyuga*, the divine name is only above all solutions and the Lord Himself by appearing in person had instructed Bhaijee to spread it. Bhaijee also considered it to be entirely simple and best of all methods in the present era. In a farewell to one of his affectionate friends, **Bhaijee had said regarding the importance of divine name that my first, last and latest discovery is that a person longing for his good fortune (Sadgati) should catch up to the shelter of divine name.** If he can do any other practice, then he must do. There is no contradiction but if nothing can be done, then continuous repetition of the divine name should be made only through tongue.

To his first plan, Bhaijee went himself with his attendant at various places to set people to repeat the divine name by explaining its importance. When Bhaijee was not satisfied with this much, it was planned like the devotees of *Chaitanya Mahaprabhu*, who went to different places to spread divine name. Accordingly, few true devotees should be trained who could visit different villages, arrange for celebration of devotional songs and persuade the people to do repetition of divine name and celebration of devotional songs. With such intention, the very first correspondence was made with Shri Prabhudattji Brahmachari, explained him the details and framed few rules just for such spiritual aspirants (*Sadhakas*). A rite was arranged for six months' non-stop *Hari naam* – celebration of devotional songs at the end of 1935 in *Jhunsi*. About 35-40 spiritual aspirants (Sadhakas) had attended it but due to absence of devotees with true devotion, Brahmachariji felt discouraged. To give him a new inspiration, Bhaijee with affectionate attendants had gone to Jhunsi on 27th August, 1935 to attend the celebration of devotional songs. Due to his arrival, celebration of devotional songs had become livelier and with a new encouragement, Shri Brahmachariji had extended it for another six months. To encourage Brahmachariji further, Bhaijee had promised to send five selected spiritual aspirants from Gorakhpur. On reaching Gorakhpur on 2nd September, 1935, Bhaijee had sent five selected spiritual aspirants at Jhunsi. Due to arrival of these spiritual aspirants, other devotees had also felt highly inspired. The main rules practitioners were to remain silent for six months, to repeat one lakh divine names daily, to join in for four hours in non-stop celebration of devotional songs, to eat little fruits. It had caused a solid progress in the life of spiritual aspirants. Due to its successful completion, Bhaijee was highly pleased.

Bhaijee did not sit idle even after the revival of rite for non-stop celebration of devotional songs at Jhunsi. By inspiring religious student Satyabratji, a disciple of Baba Raghavdasji of a refuge from supreme soul of Barhaj, Bhaijee himself went to Barhaj on 1st November, 1935 to organise the arrangement for non-stop celebration of devotional songs in Barhaj as well, like Jhunsi. Due to his visit, decision was taken to start non-stop celebration of devotional songs. He again went on 7th November, 1935 to Barhaj and helped to start this rite by inspiring the spiritual aspirants by his brilliant discourses.

On his return from Barhaj, Bhaijee had firmly decided in his mind that to inspire everyone and to provide solid benefit to spiritual aspirants, a grand non-stop celebration of devotional songs should also be arranged at his residential premise for one year in Gorakhpur. At first, decision was taken by due consultation with Shri Sethji. Then Munilalji (Swami Sanatan Devji) was sent to Shri Prabhudattji Brahmachari in *Ayodhya* and requested him to share the responsibility as the main director of the function for which he consented. Thereafter, arrangements had been made for large pavilion and cottages in *Vatika* premises for residence of spiritual aspirants and guests. Bhaijee went to *Kanpur* in March- April, 1936 and arranged for the consent to join the non-stop celebration of devotional songs at Gorakhpur from Swami Nardanandji – chief disciple of saint Ekrasanandji, Swami Shukdevanandji and Swami Bhajnanandji and then returned.

Great rite of non-stop celebration of devotional songs has begun on 30th June, 1936. Shri Prabhudattji Brahmchari alongwith his group reached Gorakhpur in the morning. Bhaijee was present to welcome them at the station with his attendants. Different parties for non-stop celebration of devotional songs had also arrived from outside. Right from there, in a form of procession of devotional songs, people have moved towards Gita Vatika enthusiastically. Shri Prabhudattji Brahmachari was keeping silence since many years. In the afternoon of 2nd July, 1936 in Gita press, this great rite was convened as city celebration of devotional songs with a great pomp and show to which an unlimited group of people had participated. Dancing with boundless joy with his attendants, Bhaijee had become without external sense several times during the celebration of devotional songs. The fortunate people who had seen Bhaijee at that instance completely immersed in unrestrained joy of celebration of devotional songs, could never forget his bodily postures. Such an unlimited group of people immersed with celebration of devotional songs had reached at the residence of Bhaijee at 9 o'clock at night. The convention of that day was concluded in Vatika after the distribution of prasad.

To describe completely about this one-year non-stop celebration of devotional songs is not possible due to fear of an expansion. Emotional people can well imagine. Many saints from outside have been attending to this rite from time to time. Due to arrival of holy- souled people like Swami Ekrasanandji, Swami Nardanandji, Swami Shukdevanandji, Swami Bhajnanandji, Nagababa, Swami Akhandanandji (from Ahmedabad), Shri Jairamdas 'Deen' Ramayani, Swami Ramdasji Maharaj, etc. in the presence of Bhaijee, Shri Sethji and Prabhudattji Brahmachari, such rite has been very successful. Pandit Jawaharlal Nehru also came to vatika to see the celebration of devotional songs. Divine sage *Narad* and great sage *Angira* had also visited in between to Bhaijee in person and had a discussion with him. Many saints and highly souled of noble nature had also come, attended and left the venue without any introduction. Likewise, a silent saint arrived on 10th January 1937, settled in the building for sacred legend. Took meal if someone had given, otherwise even never asked for anything else. It also happened that spiritual aspirants had come to attend the celebration of non-stop group singing of hymns but stayed there throughout their life. Shri Daulatramji Tambi, a resident of *Ujjain* had come to attend as a spiritual aspirant for four months in non-stop group singing of hymns, but deeply inspired by the divine atmosphere and he stayed there for the rest of his life. This non-stop celebration of devotional songs was concluded on 24th June, 1937. Speaking with a very extraordinary exposition at that time for importance of divine name, Bhaijee declared that it was that divine name only which had managed this rite for one year. Due to His grace, every type of hindrances had been averted. Though it caught fire, yet no one got affected. Plague was also prevalent, but nobody became sick even without vaccination. You must undertake for repetition of divine name. If it continues, then remember my words, you shall achieve God. Such a benefit has been bestowed on me by repetition of divine name that I have no words to narrate. **The divine name can not only make impossible things possible, it virtually does it**. Make a declaration to repeat divine name and it would be looked after by Him (The God).

Shri Prabhudattji Brahmachari had written in his memories regarding such celebration of devotional songs:

Every arrangement of such rite had been done by Bhaijee. But he had never mentioned his name at any place, everything was being carried away on my name. I had ten-twelve spiritual aspirants with me, so much good arrangement to stay, for meal, for transport had been done to everyone. When I remember these things, I feel like an ache in my heart. What a beautiful assembly of virtuous people (Satsang) was held during those days, innumerable and eminent scholars had been discussing about the divine things by sitting together. Alas, those days have gone in such a manner as not to be returned thereafter.

❐

60

An Actual Meeting with Divine Saint Narad and Great Sage Angira

Describing such an extraordinary event, Bhaijee had narrated – non- stop celebration of devotional songs (*sankeertan*) was held in 1936 at Gita Vatika, Gorakhpur. I had written an extensive commentary on *Narad's* short rules on religious devotion (*bhakti-sutra*) in *Shimlapal*. Such commentary was being published during those days. Even in an exposition of sacred legend of the God, I had heard the topic regarding Shri Naradji. Due to such reason, I was very much attracted during that period towards Naradji. A desire had been aroused repeatedly for his appearance.

Two glorious Brahmins had appeared one night in my dream. I could not recognise them. On requesting for their introduction, they informed that they were Narad and Angira. Then they informed, "We shall come to meet you tomorrow at 3.00 P.M." Such dream while I was almost awake and was so realistic that I had no doubt about it. I had managed to clean a hut near tamarind tree on the backside of garden, placed a bench in front of it and then arranged for two seats on it. I did not disclose it to anyone. I myself sat in lounge outside my residence and was waiting for their arrival. Two Brahmins came exactly at 3 o'clock and expressed a desire to meet me. I recognised them. Exactly in same form, same shape, in which I had seen earlier during dream. I began to move towards backside of the garden while they were following me. We had reached to that hut at a secluded place. I requested them to take seats which I had already arranged on the bench, while I sat down. Both the Brahmins had put on white dresses, but both had disclosed their actual appearance as soon as they sat on the seat. It was very grand and worth-seeing appearance. They sat there for some time and said few things to me. At last, they said, "Whenever you remember us, we will appear." They were talking in our language. When they appear to someone, they speak in the same language which can be understood by the other person.

Naradji had disclosed many hidden elements in front of Bhaijee, which are not given in religious scriptures extensively. Thereafter, whatever Bhaijee had spoken in his discourses or had written in '*Kalyan*', it was an affirmation of these principles. He was not in a habit of opposing anyone.

Thereafter, Naradji, etc. like divine saints had been visiting regularly to Bhaijee for discussion because Bhaijee had been associated in the divine sphere of saints.

❐

61

Swami Chakradharji Maharaj (Shri Radhababa)

When one year non-stop celebration of devotional songs was in progress at Gita Vatika in Gorakhpur, at that period, Swami Chakradharji Maharaj arrived in Gita Vatika. In due course of time, he had developed a very strong relation with Bhaijee. His introduction is being disclosed as follows in brief:

Fakharpur is a small village in the district of *Gaya* in *Bihar*. In the same village, Baba was born on 16th January, 1913 in a traditionally rich, in a scholarly and title holder of 'Mishra', Brahmin family. His father's name was Shri Mahipalji, while mother was known as Smt. Adhikarini Devi. Shri Mahipalji was very honest with good character and passed his time in worship and reading religious texts. Mother had also been extremely kind-hearted, emotional and religiously devoted. All these had also influenced Baba right from his birth.

Baba had spent his life in political work from 1928 to 1931. In 1928, Baba was a student of ninth class in district school of the city and was only 15 years old. Due to his active involvement in political and revolutionary activities, he had to go to prison twice and each time he was sentenced a punishment to spend six months in prison. In the prison, he had to bear terrible, painful conditions. In such extremely cruel and painful conditions, Baba had many wonderful divine experiences of true prayers and the grace of God at every step. Such long and memorable experiences had diverted the life-stream of Baba towards spiritualism. Since his living in prison, he had been thinking that he would spend spiritualistic life as soon as he was out of prison. When he had come out of prison second time in 1931, his elder brother took him to Calcutta and got him admitted in ninth class in Sohrawardi Begum Memorial School. In 1934, Baba passed metric examination in first division. Thereafter, his family members had got him admitted in intermediate class of Rippon College (Surendra Nath College in present time). In 1935, Baba passed first year. After passing first year, such a change to the root had occurred during the life of Baba which had particularly changed the shape of his future.

Baba had opted renunciation of the world on the day of the autumn night of full moon for round dance in the seventh Hindu month of lunar calendar (Saturday, 12th October, 1935). Then Baba was studying in second year of intermediate class in Calcutta. Having taken recourse to saffron garments, he told his elder brother – You have invested a lot for one-and-a-half years towards my intermediate education. I don't feel it proper to waste such expenditure. Therefore, on completion of study for intermediate, I would appear in the exams so that you people can feel satisfied. Such studies of six-seven months would also conclude my studies towards the worldly subjects.

He had stayed for a few years with respected Shri *Jaidayalji Goyandka* at *Bankura* after living for some time in Calcutta. Respected Shri Sethji had kept him with great affection. During that period, he was a worshipper of a normal impersonal and unqualified ultimate being (*Nirgun Nirvishesh Brahma*). Being well-versed with supreme spirit, Shri Sethji had also been describing qualified incarnate form (*Sagun Sakaar Roop*), which he was not interested in. Therefore, he began exchange of ideas with Shri Sethji. Shri Sethji had explained him immensely with proof available in scriptures, but he could not accept his logic. Then Shri Sethji once asked him to meet Bhaijee, but he had not shown any interest. But something had been planned by the ruler of this world. Shri Sethji was planning to go to Gorakhpur and he also asked Baba to reach there by a particular date. He arrived in *Gorakhpur,* but Shri Sethji could not reach due to certain reason. On his arrival at Gitapress on 26th October 1936, he was told that Shri Sethji had not yet arrived. He enquired about residence of Bhaijee and reached at Gita Vatika.

As soon as Bhaijee received an information, he came and bowed him by touching the footnails of Swamiji. Swamiji had felt such an extraordinary experience due to touching of his feet by Bhaijee as if complete essence of Braj from this world had been poured in his mind. Being a staunch follower of Vedas (any of four early Indian scriptures) in his early life, Swamiji could not check such changes. Thereafter, Swamiji had stayed for a few days below the tamarind tree behind the vatika. Feeling a hindrance to his devoted striving due to crowd present for celebration of devotional songs, he had left this place and moved to the other corner of the city near *Hanuman Garhi*. He had stayed there for four-five months.

Swamiji was an eminent scholar of *Sanskrit*, *Bangla* and English and his knowledge for scriptures had been unfathomable. He had also a good experience of music. There was an excellent flow and attraction in his speech.

On the pursuance of Shri Sethji to dictate commentary for Gita, he went with him to *Churu* and completed commentary dictation in April, 1939 by staying there at Bankura in his company.

On completion of commentary writing, Baba had decided to go to Vrindavan, met Bhaijee and informed about his plan. Bhaijee told – You can only go when I would permit. Baba did not understand what the actual plan of Bhaijee was? He replied – You can only refuse my ticket. I would go along the railway line on foot. Such discussion was held in Calcutta. Bhaijee smiled. Baba went to his room. As soon as he was absorbed in meditation, he received a clear instruction from Lord Shri Krishna that you wanted to come to Vrindavan only for me. I am present in the body made up of five elements of Hanuman Prasad. Then why are you leaving him for my sake? Baba now could understand that the body of Poddar Maharaj was in fact in Vrindavan form and to stay with him daily means to stay daily in Vrindavan area. On the same day, i.e., 11th May 1936, taking an oath of 'exclusive renouncement to an area' – (*Kshetra sannyas*) to stay always alongwith him, he informed about it to Bhaijee. Thereafter, Baba did not separate himself from Bhaijee even for a single day.

In about 1941, Baba was ready to go for an exposition. Then Bhaijee pointed out – You had come here for some other work but had become busy in the work for the public well-being. Baba promptly understood this hint and since that day, he became silent. He began talking through writing on slate. Thereafter, in 1956, on full moon night of autumn, Baba took an oath for silence as strict as the wood. Prior to opting for silence, Baba had explained through his last exposition on religious text – "If Poddarji Maharaj is a small plant of rose, then I am a small flower in one of its branches. This plant has the capacity to bloom not only one but several rose flowers more beautiful and better than me." During such dumb silence as wood, Baba had kept an exception to resume sometime to talk with Bhaijee only. During such strict silence as wood, only Baba developed a strong feeling for a literary composition and a poem for beloved was written during this period.

Once Baba called me on 2nd July, 1980. On that day, he was in a very good mood and was telling me with great affection about something. In that context, he told me that he remembers things of his four earlier births. When I had showed eagerness, he continued – prior to this birth, I was born as a woman in some Bengali family of Mymensingh in *Bengal*. I did not eat meat or fish even there as well. Prior to this birth, I was born in a family of *Chanakya.* Prior to about 1700 years to this, I and Bhaijee had been born as real brothers and Shri Jaydayalji Goyandka was our father. Prior to 3500 years to this, I was in the Eastern Greece in the city named *Athens*. When I reminded for Socrates, he replied – though Socrates was not there but he was near to a person to whom he had asked to do something while leaving. You are now not supposed to know more than this.

I was sitting second time near Baba on 14th May, 1984 alongwith other people who had also been sitting nearby. Baba told – When I was living in the front hut, I used to get up generally daily those days at 2-3 o'clock at night. Once I got up and sat keeping my face towards the north direction. I found that

Mahaprabhu Vallabhacharya had appeared suddenly and had placed one hand on the cow standing nearby. I got up and bowed before him. Then he said – I am still in domesticity and you should have not vowed as such. I replied – You are still supremely respected by ascetics. Then he did not reply but began smiling. A little later, he disappeared. Like this, once *Mahaprabhu Chaitanya* also appeared, but the place and incident have not yet come to my mind.

Once I was in *Ratangarh* and likewise got up at 2 o'clock. I found that *Lord Krishna* had appeared in front of me. During that period, Bhaijee had been greatly suffering from piles for three years. At last, it was cured when treated at Ajmer. Shri Krishna told me laughingly that such a great trouble tolerated by Bhaijee had to be experienced by you. I told – I did not understand. Then came the reply – It was a deed performed by you. Then He disappeared. At the dawn, I went to Bhaijee and enquired. For some time, he was avoiding. But I told him with some force, I could know from a source which is above and all. Then he began laughing and told – You and me also are no more two entities. Let me work for '*Kalyan*' and will talk on some other day.

Bhaijee had chosen to end his act (*Ih-leela*) on 22nd March, 1971. Baba had carried through uninterruptedly this great oath (from 11-05-1939 to 22-03-1971) to live with him daily. Bhaijee's pyre was put to flames at Gita Vatika itself. Since that day, Baba had left his old hut situated in Gita Vatika and started living under a small tin shade below a tree at the other side of the cremation ground. He spent his last days of his life by staring daily at the supremely sacred cremation ground with tearful eyes. On the day of 13th October 1992, respected Baba had renounced his body of five elements. His sacred body had been given a land-cremation on 14th October, 1992 at the same place. A beautiful cremation temple had been built at this place which remind about his supremely auspicious memory.

❐

62

Letters of Radhababa to his Elder Brothers

When the elder brothers came to know about the fixed rules of Radhababa to live with Bhaijee like a shadow, they were greatly surprised. They were very much aware of the eminent scholarliness of Baba, unbroken devotion for Vedas and his nature to follow strict rules as an ascetic. Their hearts had not been permitting them well to accept the reason about his younger brother to live constantly with a grocer. From time to time, they had been enquiring to solve their doubts by sending letters to the respected Baba. Following are the few excerpts from these letters, which respected Baba sent them as reply.

Sawan Krishna 11, Vikramaditya year 1996

Respected brother Devdutt,

I vow to you with due respect and affection.......... writing one more thing of great mystery. It should be disclosed in front of very few people as far as possible. This is a very special request to you. You have met Shri Jaydayalji and Hanuman Prasadji. Though you may not have little respect, but its last result particularly is to achieve the God. In appearance, Shri Jaydayalji and Hanuman Prasadji are merchants. It is not that I am telling this thing only without restraint, and exactly the same will occur as is being said by me. The time only can prove the quality of being true to my such statement. If you will read about the event for salvation of *Yamlarjun* in *Shrimad Bhagwat*, there is a verse:

It is just not possible to become tied by such people

Who have an impartial vision and have fully dedicated their hearts towards me.

It will be like as to appear dark in front of the eyes of people at the time of sunshine.

(*Shrimad Bhagwat 10.10.41*)

The thing which has been beneficial by the appearance of Narad to Yamalarjun, the very same thing shall be applicable to the people who had been meeting these two. There may be or may not be true regards by the people coming to visit them. It is possible that due to less devotion or due to some other restriction or to give up the practice due to your involvement in bad company, you must take one more birth. Likewise, Yamalarjun had got the stupidity. But one who will be born this time, such shall be his destiny, which shall compel him to achieve the God. But why should you retain a loan? Do the act of an accomplishment (*Sadhna*) with full intensity and make your life successful by achieving the God in any small portion of this life.

Yours, Chakradhar
Ashwin Krishna 4, Vikramaditya year 1997

Respected brother Devdutt and Taradutt,

I vow to you with due respect and affection. .... With sacred and supreme intention only, to retain versatile moments of my life towards the God, I have taken an oath to live throughout the life with Bhaijee, Shri Hanuman Prasadji Poddar, which I am still continuing. As desired by the God, lifelong association with Shri Hanuman Prasadji may not be possible. Such an information is only available to the controller of this universe. But if wish of the God is like this, I have no definite intention nor my interest to move even a single step to this or that way, leaving Bhaijee aside.

Believe me that any association with Bhaijee has been not at all due to some dealings. It is not so that there are same worldly problems due to which I am not meeting you people. Bhaijee can arrange very easily for me to and fro ticket. But the fact is that neither I can tell the reason, nor I will be able to come or go anywhere leaving Bhaijee behind. What will happen tomorrow, I don't know.

I had already written this thing as well in some of my previous letters that I had experienced the virtuous visible form (*Sagun Sakaar Swarup*) of the God of supreme core of supreme element due to kindness of Bhaijee only. Who is in possession of – what is worthy to perform or not to perform and which can also be performed beyond these two – such capable is God and is competent to be blessed by the God love to anyone by his stimulation, can catch hold of any person near to death and can provide him an appearance of the God, capable of arranging his journey to heavenly abode. You can imagine the possible reason about my strong wish to live with such person throughout the life like a shadow.

Yours
Chakradhar

In this context, respected Baba had also given in writing about Shri Bhaijee to Shiv Kumar Kedia on 20th February, 1941 at Ratangarh, its small portion is being given below:

The state of Bhaijee should not be taken like an ordinary person because even highly achieved virtuous people cannot understand these things....... in my knowledge, no such a highly accomplished and divinely blessed person had ever been appeared with such highly spiritual caliber since many ages but, if existed, then it is not in my knowledge. I have not found any reference of it. The highly realised and affectionate devotee, Naradji definitely, mentioned about such state in his principles of religious devotion (*Bhakti-Sutras*).

All the living creatures from this world of illusion, they may be flies, mosquito, birds, animals, ancestors or divine entities, whosoever be, will get salvation one day on coming to His contact. The existence of his natural body is supremely sacred and auspicious to this universe.

❐

63

A Handwritten Letter by Swami Shri Ramsukhdasji Maharaj

Shri Gambhirchandji Dujari had a feeling of friendship with respected Ramsukhdasji Maharaj at Bikaner. Both had been discussing together about the God. Dujariji had narrated the event of an actual appearance of God to Shri Bhaijee at Jasidih to him in detail. He had already developed an attraction for Shri Sethji on reading articles of '*Tatva-Chintamani*'. Hearing about this event, he made up his mind to meet Shri Sethji. On the dark half of the lunar month of tenth Hindu calendar in 1934, Dujariji took him to Churu and introduced to Shri Sethji. Later, he also introduced Swami Ramsukhdasji to Bhaijee. A new book was published by which it was known that he had become busy to spread divine emotions right from the age of nineteen years. One of his friends was a virtuous person Shri Chyawanramji. Both had developed a great attraction towards Bhaijee. This handwritten letter by Swami Ramsukhdasji to Shri Chyawnramji is being mentioned as below:

Legible part of the letter has been translated as follows:

Bhaijee has been, at present, giving discourses on '*Prem-Darshan*' for about two hours in Gorakhpur and if new devotees enquire about some irrelevant things, even then he replied intelligently while assembly of virtuous people, discourses and group singing of hymns are also being continued. He likes the devotees. Rest of his time, he allotted for discussion in seclusion. His behaviour has always been pleasing to the mind. Please convey my deep regards by his obedient pupil to the holy feet of Parmal Dasji and greetings to other companions.

Ashwin, *Krishna* 5, *Vikramaditya* year 1993

Yours,
Ramsukhdas
Govind Bhawan, Calcutta

❐

64

Residing at Ratangarh

Even when managing editing of '*Kalyan*' and other types of services, the mind of Bhaijee had been agitated from time to time to live totally aloof. Whenever he founds such an opportunity of any means, Bhaijee proceeded to an isolated place. On similar occasion, he proceeded to *Laxmangarh* on 18th September 1932, alongwith his friend Lachchhiram Chudiwala on his persuasion. He discussed there the arrangement in relation to management of *Rishikul* and then moved to Ratangarh. He wanted to live there. Therefore, he called the editorial department of '*Kalyan*' at Ratangarh. Due to a need of seclusion, he selected *Dhari* of Motiram Bhartiya to reside, which was about one- and-a-half miles from the city. In addition to editorial work for '*Kalyan*', his solitary practice started from there. During that period, workers of *Gita press* had gone on strike and the whole set-up of '*Kalyan*' had come to a standstill. Then there began a persuasion to call back Bhaijee to Gorakhpur to solve this issue, but as Bhaijee wanted to pass some time in solitary practice, he had sent a letter in the form of a direction from there itself, containing seven points. On these grounds, there once occurred a compromise. Then he went to Calcutta for treatment and returned to Gorakhpur on 24th March, 1933 via *Gauhati*.

On completion of one-year non-stop celebration of devotional songs (*sankeertan*) during publication of special issue of '*Kalyan*' – '*Santank*' and by obtaining permission from Shri Sethji to live in Ratangarh, he moved from Gorakhpur on 15th August, 1937. He wanted to live there for a longer time. So, he took alongwith him the whole editorial department of '*Kalyan*'. He had described the symbolic picture of his mental condition in a letter, part of which is being given below:

Gorakhpur, 9th August, 1937

Dear Brother........,

Let us remember His holy name with great affection. This is only a point, at present, to visit Ratangarh. Though my purpose will not be solved by leaving Gorakhpur and to live in Ratangarh. I wanted to live totally alone for four to six months in complete seclusion, but respected mother and others did not permit me to live alone and it had become almost necessary to retain my work companions alongwith.

If I worked, I did it with full sincerity like a responsible person and felt pleasure to do so, perceiving the hints from that active God (*Leelamaya*). Despite this, whenever I felt to run away from the work, the main reason of it seemed to be my nature characterised by an asceticism. It is not a new thing. Since I became conscious, till then and moving in various fields like customary, social, political and religious, such stream characterised by an asceticism is found flowing continuously with the same extent in the soul. But it is a matter of surprise that my whole life had been full of applications except twenty- one months of *Shimlapal*. Though there has not been any scarcity of an application during these twenty-one months, even then, the soul has always been looking particularly for completeness. It is possible that I may be some renouncing ascetic in the previous birth. I am observing since many years that ochre-coloured garment, wooden water pot, loin cloth, etc. have appeared like my clothes and objects. The rivers, pilgrims and huts of ascetics look like a home. Found pleasure in renouncement than accumulation. If somebody took away anything from residence or it is given to someone, then I feel good. Living alone and not talking to anyone I feel comfortable. Feel to run away from the crowd. Let nobody come to me, should not meet anyone, not to speak with anyone, not to know any new thing, such has been my desire… with such an inclination, I had planned to proceed separately. Health, etc. are secondary. But such plan seems not to be successful. There is definitely not at all any other desire to accept renunciation, but a desire definitely prevails to live like an ascetic… such is the state of my soul.

Yours,

Hanuman With Bhaijee, companions like Prof. Nand Dulare Vajpayee, Pandit Chimmanlalji Goswami, Shantanu Biharji Dwevedi (Swami Akhandanandji), Bhuvaneshwar Nath Mishra 'Madhav' Krishnadasji Bengali, Pandit Deodhar Sharma, Daulatram Tambi, Pandit Govardhan Sharma, etc. had gone to Ratangarh.

On arrival at Ratangarh, Bhaijee had been sitting alone daily in morning for three-four hours. In fact, he had come here only to utilise such a solitude. Later, he had given a hint to his affectionate companions that generally in such solitude, the God himself had come to explain in the form of clues about the things of mystery.

Shri Goswamiji had been narrating the story from *Ganesh Purana* and on its completion, Bhaijee alongwith his associates went to Bikaner on 7th September, 1937. He met there Shri Lalimaiji and Shri Swayam Jyotiji Maharaj. The son-in-law of Shri Champalalji Kothari died untimely during that very period. So, he went to his house and consoled in such an excellent manner that his full family had begun to attach with the God (the death of Shri Champalalji occurred at Calcutta in a very extraordinary manner in front of Bhaijee during visualisation of the God). On second day precisely, he returned to Ratangarh. During Bhaijee's stay at Ratangarh, the zeal towards group singing of hymns (*kirtan*) and assembly of virtuous people (*Satsang*) had begun to increase amongst his affectionate companions. Twenty-four hours' non-stop group singings of hymns had been arranged for several times while non-stop group singing of hymns had also been held often for three-four days of duration.

Bhaijee had decided there to arrange a special rite during his stay between full moon night of *Ashwin Shukla* and full moon night of *Phalgun Shukla*. An alms-house in which the people of the editorial staff of '*Kalyan*' were living, prayers and group singing of hymns were held daily at 5 o'clock in the morning regularly. An assembly of virtuous people with Bhaijee was arranged daily. Affectionate companions had also come from faraway places to meet Bhaijee. On the completion of rite, the alienation of Bhaijee had become even more aggravated.

On 10th March, 1938, Shri Prabhuduttji Brahmachari had arrived in Ratangarh and then a city group singing of hymns had been arranged. Shri Sethji also came to Ratangarh and due to his and Bhaijee's efforts, a communal riot had been subsided. Bhaijee went once to Gorakhpur due to non-pacification of turmoil by the workers in *Gita press*. On arrival of Bhaijee, their leaders had agreed instantly to the promises by Bhaijee and, thus, a commotion was subsided. Due to persuasion of Shri Sethji, he had to live in Gorakhpur for several months.

❐

65

Conquering the Opposites Being Unaffected by the Heat and Cold

There was a terrible famine in Ratangarh during 1938. In such type of activities, Bhaijee had always been the first in the line. During that time, an arrangement was made to secure famine-affected people. Bhaijee went to Bikaner to consult Shri Sethji for such type of relief work. He was returning from there to Ratangarh. It was the month of *Pusya* and a severe cold was prevalent. Baba was also with Bhaijee. Bhaijee observed that Baba was feeling cold and so he also wrapped around his blankets on Baba. Baba asked – Will you not feel cold? Bhaijee said – What do you know about me? I have decided about it. Since this very moment, if I become an observer for cold, then I can never feel at all any cold. Likewise, in Gorakhpur, during working in summer days, a stream of perspiration remained continuously produced from my body, but it did not make any hindrance in my work, neither a fan was needed nor cool air. Hearing this, Baba said – You may not feel cold but due to effect arisen therefrom, the body may be sick. Bhaijee replied – even this can also not happen. Thereafter, what Baba can say and began smiling.

❐

66

A Living in Seclusion at Dadri

Since 1938, an eagerness to live in solitude of Bhaijee had again increased. He was busy in work but was not sincere. At this, time Shri Sethji was arranging to dictate '*Tatva-Vivechani*' commentary on the Gita which is to be published as a special issue of '*Kalyan*' (year 1939). Due to such work, Bhaijee had to live sometime at *Bankura*. But he had decided in his mind that he had to go definitely thereafter in solitude from Gorakhpur. '*Gita-Tatvank*' was printed and became ready in 1939. Meanwhile, due to beginning of Second World War (18th September, 1939), Shri Sethji asked him to postpone his visit for 15-20 days. Bhaijee was not interested in any activity during that period. Editing of '*Kalyan*', article-writing, etc. everything was discontinued. Visit to the office had also become futile due to disturbances in his mind. Finally proceeded to *Dadri* (Haryana) on 25th September, 1939. Prior to his departure, Bhaijee called his affectionate companions and said with great love – if you love me, I may live at any place, but I am near you. There cannot be anything at par with love. Wherever I live, I will be indebted to your love. Maybe I can come earlier or may stay a little longer there, according to the wish of God. It is not my decision that I won't come back. On living distantly, a letter of mine can affect a lot. I am going due to divine inspiration only. The sight at the time of departure was particularly very heart-piercing. Standing at the station, hundreds of people had been looking at Bhaijee with great compassion. The reason to select Dadri for solitary living was due to cement factory of Dalmia Brothers and it was their persuasion that all arrangements would be made for the solitude as desired by Bhaijee. Bhaijee had a friendly attitude with Dalmia Brothers since many years.

Therefore, this offer has been accepted. A separate bungalow was given there to Bhaijee on his arrival and every arrangement was made in the way towards solitude as desired by Bhaijee.

Now the question arises that when Bhaijee had been in support and opportunity to see and talk with the God, why was Bhaijee required to do practice in solitude even after twelve years of this? The exact answer is known only to the supreme being, but a hint is apparent. Once few affectionate companions of Bhaijee in Gorakhpur were persuading him for an actual appearance of the God. When you talk with God, then also tell Him about us. Bhaijee then replied – I knew about the thing, which has been bestowed on me, is not available to you people. But I cannot arrange it for you even if I wish. My affectionate friends should also be benefitted only by my sheer wish. I wanted to try such an effort. But the mode to achieve such state is even very difficult. Just to make such base, one has to live in total solitude for six months in an unknown place and with an indolent life. How much time it would require for complete success is not known.

As desired by the almighty, Bhaijee could stay in Dadri for three months only. The following was his daily routine at Dadri:

Morning 4 to 5 o'clock: To relish sweet act of the God.

5 to 6 o'clock: Toilet, bath and morning religious rites, etc. 6 to 7 o'clock: To reply of incoming letters by hand.

Day 7.30 to 8.30 hr: To do religious practice in solitude by fastening the door.

10.30 to 11.30 hr: Toilet, bath and afternoon rites, etc.

11.30 to 12.30 hr: Repetition of divine name silently in low tone.

12.30 to 13.30 hr: Lunch.

13.00 to 13.30 hr: Break the silence to talk a little bit.

13.30 to 14.30 hr: If needed, then to talk in writing.

14.30 to 17.30 hr: To fasten the door and practise in solitude.

17.30 to 18.00 hr: To read incoming mails.

18.00 to 19.00 hr: Toilet, bath and evening rites, etc.

19.00 to 20.30 hr: To sit on the grass outside and read a little bit of the daily newspaper, meal, to break silence and discuss important matters.

20.30 P.M: To sleep after name-chanting (one lakh) of the God.

A letter written by Bhaijee from Dadri to Shri Goswamiji

Dalmia, Dadri
7th October, 1939

Dear Shri Goswamiji,

Let us remember His divine name respectfully with love. Received your letter.

I live in solitude. Nobody generally comes to me, but this environment belongs to the mill. There are other things as well. Therefore, to stay at this place permanently had never been planned by me nor it is today. But it is not yet decided where to proceed from this place. Ratangarh is not as per my requirement and to live in other places permanently will be unsuitable to respected Maaji and mother of Savitri. Although wherever I live, they agreed to that place and will always be, but it is not suitable to them, such is my opinion. Let us see where I can stay in such a condition… like motionless and silent is my life and this very much seems to be favourable, at present.

Yours,
Hanuman

Baba (Swami Chakradharji) and Gambhirchandji Dujari only lived with Bhaijee at *Dadri*. Part of the things which had been performed in writing by Bhaijee are being summarised as follows:

It has been a great bliss on today morning between 7.30 and 10 o'clock. Decided to be alone for six hours… to recite daily at least one lakh repetitions of divine name. More than this is not possible… body is dying every moment. Therefore, did not stop name repetition even for a moment if one is conscious. If such happens, then the God would look after in unconsciousness… If the God is worried about us, then it proves that there is at least some reason of our worry…. When the God belongs to us, then where is the reason for worry?... Do not worry about the future, just try to attempt at present, as per the inspiration received in mind through the God, simply try in that manner. Whatever is planned for future, it shall particularly be fulfilled. I have no aim, don't know, what is demanded by the mind tomorrow. Whatever is destined by the God is my vow… don't give importance to the union of body but give due importance to the union of soul. Therefore, if lovers must live mutually separate and the union of soul is true, then daily meeting is possible even though living separately… the best is that there should not be any aim; if it is, then let the God's desire be fulfilled. … Even if it is not possible, then it should be a spiritual and auspicious vow. Want to remain seated in solitude, if I must get up in between, then work achieved of many days turns into somewhat contaminated … many times I have remained in a very serious stage.

… Worry should only be carried out to do a constant mediation upon the God. However, if you are not mentally well, then it does not matter. By the grace of God, whatever will be, will be even without the adjustment of mind. If the mind is required to be set right, then even it would be corrected suddenly by His grace… You should believe this; we people are highly blessed by the God. It is not totally a solitary accommodation. Therefore, a little could be felt (about the arrival of any new person). If it is completely solitude and no one arrives, then it is felt very soon. That much only is required for such practice. Otherwise, due to adultery of place, the environment does not help in practice…. garments and purity of seat are also not proper at this place. An exchange of serious correspondence on practice of love (*prem- sadhna*) has begun from this place only with Shri Krishna's devotee and a learned woman, Raihana Tayyabji. During this period, there occurred severe famines in Ratangarh. Bhaijee started service activities under his own direction from there itself around Ratangarh. As a reward for this work, later, Bhaijee was awarded '*Shiropava*' and 'Special note' by king of Bikaner, Shri Gangasinghji. Later, Bhaijee went to Ratangarh from Dadri.

❐

67

Self-Experiences by the Pen of Respected Baba

(1)

Baba (Swami Shri Chakradharji Maharaj) had handed over his self-experiences to Bhaijee in his handwriting which are being given in the succeeding paras:

I am writing things after the publication of '*Gita-Tatvank*'. I had strong faith on you but was afraid that if I will tell loudly, then you may say that I am blinded by lust, therefore, not eligible but was also thinking that how can I explain you such form of lust. Woman is an object to be enjoyed by me – such an attitude had never prevailed nor exists at present, but my mental condition is unusual even today. Whenever I see a beautiful woman, I seldom think – Look! She is beautiful, and God has given her even such a body illusion that she considers herself as a body according to her actual form. I am in body of a man, even though being a part of *Radharani*, also possess body illusion of a man, I am unlucky. Then I thought it is a mortal body, is dirty. There is no difference of body or soul for Radharani. It is not just a mortal beauty; the body lives here. If it is the part of Radharani, it means the part is beautiful and not the body – such types of thoughts of hate and attraction in innumerable shapes and types seldom appeared when I had extroverted mood. In addition, one more thought comes as sudden blaze that if I were a woman. Therefore, I was also moving forward alone with such standard of mind during that period as well. The meaning to the form of asceticism and attachment were something else to me. Since the beginning and even today, such faint desire has been working in my mind that to remain happy in the happiness of Shri Krishna means love should be imprinted in my life. Inspired by such desire, which may also include cheating of mind, the efforts till today have been continued willingly or unwillingly. I had already told that *Chaitanya* literature had a strong impact on me because the thoughts of my mind, which had appeared on its own, I was the follower. By gradual reading, the temperament to serve has become stronger. In the beginning in a form of woman, there had remained hidden a lust for some of my pleasure, which had become weaker. Then I thought to find a mentor. Who should be mentor, such question is raised, then thought a little and accepted *Shri Rupmanzari Devi* as a mentor in the mental world without any formal function. I have forgotten to tell that whatever has happened entirely from beginning till today is being done, has been done, performing at present. During such happening and during all these, what is the condition of my mind, this I cannot understand precisely. Sometimes an ardent restlessness, sometimes disappointment, sometimes an attachment sometimes fear to downfall, without any aim, without thinking, such things have been appearing in my mind, but mostly or even all, may be even artificially motivated. How can I belong to *Shri Kishna*, this has been due to passion? Therefore, during repetition of divine name, a thought has approached to serve by framing a course for the act or by the grace of God performed during the eight stages of the day (*asht kaleen leela*). In addition, the article of *'Purushottam Tatva'* (element of supreme Godliness) had been added in daily routine. I was reading daily, even studying at present as well and was thinking this and still think that I am a part of Radharani, the smallest part, but let it be my place or anywhere but I am built of the same metal. Such thought has been making me restless, where to find course for the divine act, whom to ask and who will guide me, who would understand my mental condition. Few would consider it as my degradation, others may laugh. I had shyness of you. I had no money to arrange and consult the complete Chaitanya literature – with a hope that course of the divine act will be found. Once in the afternoon, I was sitting near you, then got up and returned (it happened in Gorakhpur), then you called me and narrated the *Padmapurana*. You had called and said – Look! I would tell you something. After narrating a little, you directed me to read it all. I was in a hut near you, started reading, could find three such chapters which have become like breath to my life. In the same text, I found a very beautiful course for the act through eight times *(asht kaleen leela)*. Lord Shankar has told in it – As he wanders with displayed act in Vrindavan, of just that sort of act also performs daily. His acts, daily acts still continued. I have very much liked this verse. I was thinking – What! Even today and at this moment as well, this time also, He is performing the act, I am not observing Him (I have used feminine gender at some places because my prayer, etc. have all been made through such form in mental world). Every time such verse appeared through my mind and still appears:

As He walks for pleasure with a revealing act in *Vrindavan*, as described in ancient Indian scriptures, in that same manner He also performs divine act daily in Vrindavan on this earth.

I thought such are the words of omniscient and entirely truthful sages.

Such is the application for performance of divine act by the deity (*Nityalilayam*) and peace *(shanti)*. The words are by Lord *Shankar* while *Narad* is an audience. Then they are also today in this form, they remain in such type, remain eternal, will be eternal. This was asked by Narad visiting Vrindavan and *Vrinda* explained the course for the act. Lord Shankar had also told this to Narad that one should presume himself as a woman and should serve with such an act. This was also a support to my thinking. So, the devoted striving *(Sadhna)* began slowly, sometimes with great momentum, like this, like that, mental service started on this basis, became pleased with a hope of success in life. Repetition of sacred verse *Hare Ram, Hare Ram* and doing everything also mutually, the mental service had begun. It remains continued. The attraction for Vrindavan has gradually been increased but particularly for you as well. I was at that time thinking about you that I am away from the nature. I am a part of Radharani, then Bhaijee himself is also the same. The difference is that my body illusion is not yet completed, I have no right to serve, Bhaijee is always higher than this body and is blessed to find an opportunity to serve. Therefore, went to Dadri from Gorakhpur. The devoted striving was kept as it was but suddenly a change occurred. A question had always been coming to mind since arrival from Bankura – "**One should follow only one aim and one religion, to live with the holy feet of his beloved (Husband) through body, speech and mind**" often thinking – the body is not fit to serve but mind and body can be for the same. I tried my level best from mind but how can I serve through speech, what type of speech would please Shri Krishna. Suddenly, a thought appears that Radharani is most dear to Shri Krishna and, hence, her name shall definitely be liked by Him. Like this, not very clear but few supporting characters of this sort have been found in many verses of '*Brahmvaivart*'. Therefore, suddenly such thought became so strong that the rule to repeat three lakh names has been discontinued, forcefully discontinued. Without following your advice, I started to repeat 'Radhe-Radhe-Krishna'. Later, it was conveyed to you. I found an excellent verse in text named '*Radhasudhanidhi*', which made my faith stronger that name of Radha is very dear to Shri Krishna – then chanting of '*Radhe Krishna-Radhe Krishna*' silently and worshiping the God mentally through eight times (*asht kaleen*) has begun.

The life of Ratangarh has begun. Suddenly found a book containing a verse and according to which – who pronounced 'Ra' – I bless him with supreme adoration and who, no sooner 'Dha' is pronounced, I began to follow him with a greed to hear. Such are the words by Shri Krishna Himself for Radherani. This verse is from *'Brahmavaivarta'*. In the beginning, I could not find it, with an abundant search, then found it one day in an extraordinary manner. Though I found this verse recently in '*Brahmavaivarta*' but have got sufficient faith even earlier that the one, who has created this quotation, shall never quote it falsely. During the treatment of wife of Mahananda in Delhi at the residence of Mathura Prasadji, I could receive too much faith by looking at this verse quoted in '*Shreya magazine*' – these words are definitely from Shri

Krishna. Thereafter, such name of 'Radha' became achievable and became also an act of achievement (*sadhan*). By repeating 'Ra', I would be blessed by supreme adoration and 'Dha' means Radha satisfied the sense of hearing to Shri Krishna. So much satisfaction is achieved that he follows the person repeating Radha, he does not get such satisfaction by anything because such narration – to follow is only available in the Bhagwat, but that has a limitation. Here the thing is higher, such thoughts have caused a rise in thought waves to repeat the name of Radha and such habit has continued to increase. I was also thinking that my *Radhakrishna* would be pleased by name of 'Krishna'. Therefore, the name of Radhakrishna has become the dearest thing in my life. Such temperament increased sometime up to such an extent that a thought appeared this time in Gorakhpur that there are many female attendants to serve through the body of herd girls of *Braj*. I only wish a pleasure of senses for soul, having the passion to be in woman body in the form of a herd girl of Braj. So, it is better if I become a parrot in Vrindavandham and by flying and continuously chanting 'Radhakrishna' might give pleasure to Shri Radha and to her beloved. Then thought, the parrot is man and, hence, I should be mynah. For, a few days, such temperament was so strong that I was thinking in mind about the look of mynah and wish to see my future body. I have not seen mynah. Though its figure can be found in English dictionary, I was not aware of the meaning of mynah in English, then enquired with Shri Goswamiji and Madhavji but even they could not explain it. Then I thought to request you to arrange for a mynah. I would observe it. Then thought it would be shown as and when decided by Shri Krishna. I will not say anything. Gradually, such temperament has subsided and become in this form – let me leave it to him, let him provide that very body by which he would like to be served, the kind of service desired by Him is for His comforts I have to serve. So be it.

Likewise, the name of 'Radhakrishna' and the service remain continued. Prior to opting for silence, I was afraid due to several reasons that I may not tend to fall but what can be done, whom to ask for shelter, who is mine? Such things and these thoughts appear only when natural tendencies becoming extroverted moved downwards for a longer duration below the world of mental service… Then such verse *'Namchintamanikrishnah'* (Lord Krishna is also called Chintamani – a supposed jewel granting all desires to its possessor) appeared in my mind, which has caused flow of temperaments, thought that 'Krishna name' is 'Chaitanya'. So, if Krishna is near to me in such form, then what is the fear and my devotee is never perished (Gita : 9/31). Such statement is not false. By pronouncing 'Radhe', I am even and at least His devotee. It appears also and had also appeared at Dadri and appears now in any form of that if I fell, then what will happen, if it is His desire, let it be so. Infinite births have passed, many more may pass. But feeling a fear to fall – such an attitude during that time has become somewhat weaker, had no desire to fall. Now there is no feeling of fear to fall but felt a blow in my heart that if I would fall, then I would not find that service but recently such thought is becoming very strong that whatever happens, it is all due to Shri Krishna. Let His wish be fulfilled. Neither I am a body, nor I am a name, I am His dearest object. What is the problem if He finds pleasure by sanctioning a hellish body? Sometimes there is a prayer – O Lord, take me! Wherever you wish to, if you wish me to be in hell, then take me to the hell. If you wish to devour by splitting my body as a messenger of death, eat it. Well, you would also become this body by tearing it to pieces. Regarding the present condition, I would mention later. Now I return to silence. Don't remember precisely and after giving several thoughts, it is decided to pronounce 'Radhakrishna' and nothing else. ... since one-and-a-half- year repetition of 'Radhakrishna', group singing of hymns and mental service as before, are being continued.

Now I am writing regarding fundamental thoughts considering it even necessary to write something. The speeches of Shri Krishna may be by some chance or in any scripture appear very sweet and, in this world, I trust mostly on your words, your words attract me more than others. Now the question arises who am I? The thoughts have been arising and then thought – Chakradhar and the body called by this name are also not me. The relation by this name, my relation to this body have been only since twenty-nine-thirty years, then who am I? Reply comes from within – Bhaijee has said who is more trustworthy than him, I am a part of Radherani. Then why I am within this body, why is this illusion, why is such an affection? Sometimes it appears in mind to ignore this body. As I have forgotten the earlier bodies, likewise should also ignore this body even in living and unto the holy feet of Radherani, as I am in mental world, should immerse with them. The body would be left, and I will not be informed. I would be in the country, which will never cease to exist that opportunity will never be concluded. That divine kingdom shall prevail. I shall also be serving till eternity living near the holy feet of Radharani. Then why did I not forget this world? Why does not a strong desire to be forgotten arises? ... Sometimes it appears that which view I am looking in front, what is this world? You have told me in Gorakhpur – Shri Krishna has not only told just by speaking but by showing the whole universe inside Him – He is everything and everything is under his control as well. ...all these words have impressed very strongly... Thereafter, in the castle of mental world of Radharani, I had been thinking by sitting near the holy feet of Radharani – That Shri Krishna who is milking the milk at present has scrapped together such a large universe in Himself. During evening, Radharani is observing the glory of Shri Krishna from the balcony of her castle, who is returning from the byre, Shri Krishna being among the herds of cows, has always been looking towards Radharani while I am also sitting near Radharani, such type of thoughts appeared in the evening. Such thought also appears several times at that period – O my wealth of heart! You have planned this much act, sometimes begun praying due to restlessness that – O Lord! Please remove this from before me and retain in this very *Shyam Sunder* identity and I may forget everything. Sometimes also starts praying to Radherani! I am a part of your body only, may be smallest, I am yours only. Therefore, call me for once... likewise several prayers have been made at different intervals.

... The Bhagwat is my dear text, specially wherever I read speeches of *Shri Krishna*, mind is attracted to that very place. Sometime back, a thought again appeared that the world prevailed in front of these eyes, what is that in real sense? Based on tradition by the words from several scriptures, the mind declares that it is precisely all Shri Krishna... likewise and moving in dilemma, once a verse was found in eleventh section – through mind, through speech, through sight and whatever is perceived by other senses, that particularly everything is nothing but me and me alone, there is nothing at all except me, treat it like this. This is an instruction to sages like *Sankadik* by Shri Krishna in the form of a Swan. This verse has attracted me very much – then continued thinking it every time that the same Shri Krishna, who is in mental state, is being seen in so many forms but where is Radherani. Where is Shri Krishna, there is only the Radherani because she is the soul of Shri Krishna. From a work celebrating the Bhagwat of the *Padmapurana* and the *Skandpurana* and from many places such an attitude has been implanted in the mind that Radherani is the soul of Shri Krishna, Shri Krishna is Radha and Radha is Shri Krishna. So, for a few days, whenever I see a creature or an animal, a man, it appears that Shri Krishna is inside him and Radherani is in his heart. Then this verse [Whatever is acknowledged through mind, speech, sight or other senses, it all represents to me. No one exists except me. You should instantly and logically accept this principle. (*Shrimad Bhagwat* – 11/13/14)] has started throbbing in such a way that whatever I say, hear or touch, everything and absolutely all are Shri Krishna. I think, when hungry – that hunger is felt through mind means Shri Krishna has precisely come in the form of hunger. Shri Krishna comes in the form of satisfaction, then which type of object the mind is? A verse 'I am the mind among sense' (The Gita: 10/32) appears that mind is Shri Krishna as well, then why it appears sometime dirty, why it contains dirty agitations, lustful passion? On advancement of mood, prayer says – O Lord! you are also inside in the form of mind, my master! Why you appear in dirty form, please change your form in the same Shyam Sunder identity in front of me, I did not like your such horrible form... then comes a second thought – a noble lady does not love anyone...Loves her husband only... O Lord! be in the form in which you would like to be... I know I am a poor woman, please be mindful to me, O store of grace. Then again thought – he has only come in the form of this prayer, that is all I am looking at, observing in eternal forms, but had never realised but identified only today. Such final temperament has been gradually increasing, whenever I ponder in a mental state during time of service, during that service, such thoughts appear sometime that the body of herd girls of Braj by which I am serving, the mind is also experiencing the sight of that body. I am feeling then that the realised thing through mind is Shri Krishna only... what would then happen? It seems this would happen that once my body is dead, I would enter in that body and will immerse with Shri Krishna. I would join in the acts of Shri Krishna till eternity, this very is supreme spirit. That is, to a point where mind can reach, it is the ultimate element. Then comes the thought that why I have come into present world by returning from that mental world... that time.

❐

68
Radhe-Krishna

The above paras were written yesterday up to 12.00 A.M. There were a lot of things to be noted yesterday, but no order is appearing to my mind today. Such enormous talks – such is a wave of enormous thoughts, which could not be concluded even writing continuously for many days. How is the condition of mine at present, I cannot explain it even with my willingness? If I wish to explain, then I would write quite the wrong way. There has been a flow of stream for dirty, insensitive, lively, distressful thoughts, don't know what my state in future will be? The sample of present status is being written as a conclusion.

… I am thinking… I am observing the divine act, looking to the act by my Lord. Uptill when this act would change… don't know… all good and bad thoughts, sudden blazes have been appearing before me as thoughts through mind, through speech by which the practice is being done, that very is also the same in the form of practice with anger due to jealousy *(Manvati-Sadhna)*, that will also be coming because of spiritual practice. I am only observing who am I. I am the smallest part of Radherani who is in mental world… but that is not the complete act, it is also beyond to this aspect, what is that, don't know…. He is eternally actful. If I could feel even a particle of any such act, then would feel gratified. Why did I not feel it? Don't like. Why did I not like? I am charmed. Who is causing infatuation? I am the most loving thing of Shri Krishna? Who can captivate my mind except Shri Krishna? Let you charm me. O Lord! You should be happy….

Sometimes I used to forget these fundamental thoughts. Become extremely restless, I would sob. Being in extreme helplessness, have started weeping due to a feel of a shelterless poor woman. Prayed… there is no one to me except you, who would listen to me... Please remove such sight in front of me, send me near to Radherani, that is all… sometimes pray... you have set the fire of separation in my mind, that's it. Should I remain weeping continuously for you till eternity… sometimes tells that Radherani is immersed in every respect with your love, is an ultimate limit of simplicity. Omniscience, etc., properties exist in them or not, don't know. Please remind her once about me, you know my condition well.

... Sometimes think He is omniscient, omnipotent, our good wisher, our mentor, I am extremely dearest to them that is it, felt lot of pleasure, then comes a flood of pleasure. Let your wish be fulfilled, thinking such, I used to remain silent.

Mahaprabhu has made a commentary on the verse 'May embrace or may crush who is clinging to feet' in his life from the learning octet. It is the highest description of the form of desire for love towards Krishna. By reading 'Such an affirmation by Shri Radhaji is a sign of purified love which is enjoyed by *Gour Rai*' (Chaitanya Mahaprabhu), I ponder, what a height of such loving form of Radherani is, I am only a part. If even a particle comes into me, I would be gratified. You have mentioned in the article 'Devoted striving (*sadhna*) with a temperament of herd girls of *Braj*' that the heart of herd girls of Braj has always been in such a call-out. The highest illustration is to surrender everything. I also thought to possess such type of temperament, though superficially. If it could enter internally, then I would be gratified. Such thoughts appeared in the mind much earlier. I have read your article and biography of Mahaprabhu several times. It is possible that such instincts have been initiated due to these reasons, but when I had read the commentary of the verse by Mahaprabhu and your's article, then could know it was quite correct illustration for temperaments of my inner heart. Such commentary of Mahaprabhu on 'I am a female servant for the feet of Krishna' and in a part of that, from your article, have the highest depiction of those characters, sometimes by reading them, I have become so much immersed in temperament of such a highly and generous surrender that there remain not even any grievances…

...When the external states prevail, then sometimes remember with great respect to everyone like the dog, an outcaste, cow and the ass renouncing my outlook and regard for public opinion. Thought, my Shri Krishna, my master is only in such forms… He asked me to bow… whenever a dog, donkey, ox or a bullock are in sight, I begin to move to my hut having such thoughts in mind. Sometimes become restless and ask – O Lord! Come at least for once and explain. It is you only, in every respect you are or there is some difference? How can I serve you? Then there comes a thought, service will be through body, through mind, through speech. I am not out of three. He is just there in the form of these three. I would then see, He may serve Himself according to His own wish. I will be witnessing.… Thought sometimes O Lord! How can I make you happy? Why are you angry with me, which fault I have committed? I am adulterous. Therefore, you are angry? Tell me O Lord! How many days such dull life, loveless life, dirty life shall prolong? Please fill it up, my Lord, my heart with your love. I may remain swimming or floating in it.

...Why I am separated from you, O Lord! ...Then I remember such words – O herd girls of *Braj*, I am separate from you. Being a star of your eyes, I am still separate, but I am separate so that you could constantly remember me, every mode of your life may be immersed in me. I am far, being far away, mind is more attached with the beloved than when He is near. Such is the message sent by *Udhav*. Thought sometimes, because He is set apart, therefore, should do non-stop thinking. That's it, thinking of him only. But why did I not do? Which is such an attraction? Who can remove it? Intensity of meditation, upon realising such thought, has increased.

The Bhagwat is my favourite literary work, still remember a little *Sanskrit*. Specially of the verses which are favourite to me. I have studied many commentaries on such verses. But after publication of 'Bhagwatank', now do not consult any commentary. Thought sometimes, though written by Shantanuji, but all verses have been seriously inspected, once from the sight of Bhaijee and the meaning is only published when it is approved by him. That's it. Hence, this is now a proof for me. Gradually, reading such text, also studied the '*Bhramargita*' – this was written in it – as in dream a man can see many objects, which are false. Just like this. If man should consider such vigilant visuals of the world to be false, like dream and may become alienated and then should try for my actual appearance. Thought it is said by Shri Krishna and that too to His beloved herd girls of *Braj* and *Bhaijee* has published its meanings with due screening, then, am I dreaming? Probably have slept by sitting near the feet of Radherani and the dreams have begun to appear, is it such a thing? But who would disturb my dream? O Lord! Please disturb my dream such a prayerfulness was there. Then it comes again in mind – it may be visuals of vigilant, may be visuals of dream, both are felt by the mind and 'I am the object perceived through mind'. Such is the statement of Shri Krishna. Then where is the dream? It is an act of Shri Krishna, is His illusion, precisely He is. O Lord! It is Your wish. I will love you, I should love you, not your beauty, if it is a horrible form, should I not like you?

...As much as, such type of various thoughts has appeared which are difficult to describe. Sometimes dirty instincts have got awakened. Then I thought, you have come in this dirty form to take me along to hell, then as you wish, let your wish be fulfilled … in this context, strange things appeared, which are difficult to describe.

That varied emotions I had for you, it is also a long history. You would laugh a lot by hearing it, but it is not the right time. If I live, remain conscious and if He (The God) would prefer which is the foremost condition, I would then tell you my feelings towards you but not today.

...It was a strange condition today at Govindramji's place, but cannot explain properly, there is no need as well.

I live with you, am thinking what is the interest of Bhaijee in retaining me? Comes the reply there is entirely nothing. I am here entirely due to my own interest. Yes, then should I leave? Because love is self-denying but so much interest from affection exists (surely this affection is just of a strange type) and such type of thought appears that I felt to tremble by the premonition to abandon you.... prayed surely, O Lord! if you don't like, then release, you should be happy, O Lord! please do that only. Sometimes prayed, don't release me. Then again requested – your wish be fulfilled.

The body style moves differently. Don't know how long it would continue. Sometimes I think… to continue writing but it has now become a habit not to write anything in this very context.

I don't know if I could explain to you my exact condition by writing this much as well. A strange state prevailed nowadays, what will happen, have no idea.

By hearing these words, don't know if you would hate or love me or extend sympathy. I am flowing in solitary stream. Sometimes think, have given thought many times that I am an instrument for His pleasure. I may be placed anywhere in that form, should retain in that very form, this in my foremost happiness. What is the devoted form of striving, I had already explained as above. Due to writing something or the other, there have been lots of cuttings. As was thinking in mind, I have used feminine gender and sometimes masculine gender with verb. Please sanction an excuse if there is anything causing a hate, looking at my heart. Because kingdom of love belonging to Shri Krishna in every respect is a thing beyond mind and speech. I have not yet been free by the touch of dirty world. Then to talk of love is yet an irony. But *Bhaijee,* this is the condition of my mind. Becoming stubborn and arrogant in every respect, I was thinking that even at present the same stubbornness is being continued irrespective of the fate, whatever is the real state of affairs, I should catch it. What may come I don't know. Have definite desire to obey you till my consciousness, but it does not work. Considering me also as extremely small and dirtiest, please do favour with your love and be kind to me. By writing this much, I conclude.

It happened once. It appeared in mind that my name is Manjulali. Had got an inkling since that very day. Exactly this very emotion was reflected upon many times.

Well, I am a milkmaid of village, without beauty, without youth, then why you love me? O sister, you know it why this Shyam Sundar loves me? No beauty nor youth, then why He should love me? O God! What happened if I have become mad? Yes sister, I have become of no use. I have been observing Shyam Sundar through day and night. O confidante, I proceed to give up my life. But during submerging in water, I don't lose my breath, remain observing that Shyam Sundar is laughing by standing therein. He says – You have come to give up your life, then how I will live if you give away your life? O sister, then I can neither live nor die, what should I do?

But O sister! What happened to me after all? Well, is there any magic as well in this Vrindavan. True, therefore, this occurred. Sorry, how was to ascertain. O sister! I know only churning the curd, knew to make butter milk and knew nothing. I was comfortably busy in domestic work. Rani loved me very much. She told – Manju to bring some flower for worship. O sister! I went to pluck flowers, somebody said in sweet voice – Manju! Attention! Whosoever plucks flower in this forest, he has become in my command. That becomes my property. O sister! I felt astonished, but I went to pluck flowers for Rani. I replied in loud voice – Who are you? Someone laughed, comes the reply. What would you get from seeing, if you pluck flowers, then the same thing again, do you understand? O sister. Rani may not be delayed, Rani will be waiting for me, considering such, I plucked flowers and tied in my border of sari and moved. Then again heard that sweet laughter – Manju, you are trapped.

O sister! I never imagined but could know later, He was Shyam Sundar only.

O sister! How can I tell you? Wherever I look, I find Him only. O sister! I am sick but don't know the type of sickness. Shyam Sunder in eyes, Shyam Sunder in ears and Shyam Sunder in every pore of the body. In fact, He has deserted me. O sister! I don't know how He could know the things of mind. My Rani laughs looking at us.

O sister! I was once combing my hairs. Putting flowers in them by plaiting, I found Shyam Sundar is standing behind and telling – Manju, you don't know how to comb, I am very well aware, may I adjust. O sister! I ran and went to Rani, started sobbing by hiding my face. Rani asked – My dear Manju, what happened to you? I have narrated everything. She said – He is very naughty, but it does not matter, and embraced me affectionately. I am sorry sister, actually I came to serve Rani, was not aware what is the condition of Rani, who will be looking after her? I have become mad for Shyam Sundar, cannot eat and sleep. Many days have passed. I am still awake throughout days and nights. Found Shyam Sundar in dream, he is laughing and asking – Manju, will you swing the cradle? I used to get startled and got up.

O sister! Please tell me the truth, eventually who is Shyam Sunder to me? Why should I love Him? I am sorry, what rubbish I am speaking? O Shyam Sunder! wealth of my life! Everything to me! Really, I have become totally spoiled due to you. Life has gone, family has gone, religion has gone, everything has gone. That is good, what will I do by retaining this. O sister! Where Shyam Sundar is not present, what will I do by visiting such places? But sorry, I have become actually mad. Shyam Sunder is standing there. Don't know what happened to me? Mother began to weep and called an ayurvedic physician. She asked – please check what happened to my Manju. She has been chattering day and night. Alas! She had been doing all my household work, served me day and night. Took care of my daughter-in-law Radha but now is getting totally sick. O sister! This very Shyam Sunder had also become the physician as well. My mother did not recognise him. By examining my nerve, He said – this is a very serious sickness, it is also difficult to cure it, this can never be cured. Yes, it can be subsided for a while. Well, old lady, tell me whom she had loved the most?

Mother replied – My daughter-in-law Radha.

The physician said – Look here, you must do two things. Your daughter-in-law should go wherever she wants to move and don't interrupt in any of her assignments, otherwise she would be sick again. O sister! Rani was laughing from the corner of her sari. The physician went back. I was near to cry and began to weep by putting my head on the lap of Rani. Said – Rani, I have become mad. What will happen now, who will look after you? Rani said by embracing me near to her heart – My dear Manju, your madness is not like a disgrace, it is to be rewarded only due to an eternal good fortune to some unusual person. The people of this world are longing for it. By telling this, Rani had begun to kiss by putting me near her heart.

O confidante! Rani also smiles, Shyam Sundar also smiles but I am gradually becoming frail. Don't know sister what happened to me? Thinking beyond such nonsense imaginations, the forehead becomes almost like hot. That thing does not appear frequently during writing. At one time, something, sometime anything, from time to time throughout the day. Sometimes repetition of divine name in low tone is being continued for a day or two. Sometimes something else.

Thought many times to enquire from you. Then appears in mind not to leave knowingly, may be left, memory may not be there, then.... Please do not misunderstand that my mind is, in fact, competent for such things. Inside me is your touchstone-emptiness for passion of love that does not at all exist. It seems someone is exporting me by pulling forcefully.

I had to ask for an advice. The thing is my daily routine is somewhat fixed. What occurred in it, some study, careful study of few special verses and the number has also been fixed prior and after the meal. There has now been no rule or number left for repetition of divine name.

It happened that evening. I told you – Bhaijee, time is short while there is long way to go. You have replied – Maharajji, the vehicle is so fast that there is no comparison with the way. But don't remember that the path is yet to be travelled. There appears a slight disappointment in mind by such comment, but instantly became automatically reflected upon with that temperament. Went outside to nearby wall of sand, began to chatter in myself as follows:

O Sister! What should I do? I did not come on my own, but someone forcefully brought me. Yes, I have been brought to die due to such restlessness. But O sister! I cannot die. What to do? Did not allow to die, went many times to drown in the Yamuna.

Like this was continued on that day for hours. Such thing was to be asked that when the mind is at peace, then think what to do, may I leave this knot of such rule. Because memory reminds to keep the promise prior to begging. But as the eye opened, a change in mood occurred.

Though it does not matter, but such uncertainty has occurred daily. Then that has not yet completed and once it is released, then released forever. Sometimes few words of text are retained in the memory and the mind is half engaged with an imagination of just that sort and change of mood has come to an end somewhere. But I am afraid to break the bond of rule since many years with this apprehension that by chance, mind may not deceive.

❐

69

An Unexpected Help to Shri Ramnathji 'Suman'

Bhaijee had an excellent way to help others. There are many examples when the person himself, who was given help, was obviously never informed what to say about others. Such an example can be seen in the words of Shri Ramnathji 'Suman' as follows:

How he could know about my grievances, I have never understood even when no visit, no message and no correspondence were made for months together. This event occurred in 1939. I have brought my wife suffering from extremely killing diseases from Delhi to Prayag just for a change of climate. Without means, destitute, without any wealth as I was very much impressed by Bapuji, during those days, who called and considered it as an atheism to think and accumulate for tomorrow. It was the last day of the month. I was totally immersed with worry by sitting outside on the platform. There were only three-four rupees left with me and I had to pay the milkman, maid, cook and landlord, etc. on the first date of the month. I was new to this place and was not known to others. Why should others believe me? Therefore, was calling the God by sitting and closing eyes how it will happen, what will happen, the ornaments of wife had already been sold one by one. The eyes are closed with a sincere request being made to the Lord of destitute; tears are trickling due to my helplessness and in a condition without assistance. Suddenly, a postman arrives. I was so much engrossed in myself that I did not mark anything. Postman said – *Babuji*, you have received an insurance (money order). Now I think that it should belong to a person who was previously living in this room. Therefore, laughing falsely told – Brother, it may not be for me. But please look at it – saying this, he handed it over to me. Really it was only for me. It is an insurance for three hundred rupees and has come from '*Kalyan*'. Due to this sickness, I had not written any letter to Bhaijee since last one-and-a-half year. He was not aware about anything. I had written few articles on his request. Generally, '*Kalyan*' does not pay any remuneration, nor I made any such request, nor demanded anything. I could not understand till today that how Bhaijee could know all these things. How he could find my immediate address and how he has sent money like a friend of poor hidden behind the curtain without any introduction or letter? On query, he was simply smiling but never disclosed.

Now listen about my condition. I forgot to receive insurance, the eyes had closed again, and tears began trickling. Postman became restless and remained looking for something, astonishingly. Then moved my shoulder and said – Babuji, what happened? Please do sign on receipt. I signed it but am being continued weeping uninterruptedly. This is a divine appearance in life and Bhaijee is an appellant to the God.

❐

70

A Repetition of Solitary Living in Ratangarh

Subsequent to his arrival to Ratangarh, daily routine of Bhaijee continued, with little change just like *Dadri.* He remained five to six hours in a lonely room or went on sand bank outside the city in the evening. Once he had given a hint to one of his loving companions that perpetual sweet acts of Shri Krishna have been seen always in new forms better in Dadri than in Gorakhpur and best in Ratangarh than Dadri. At this very period, one more special event occurred. One procession was taken out on Gita's birthday celebration on 22nd December, 1939 in Gorakhpur, due to which few Muslims had created a turmoil near the *masjid* of Sahabganj and also fabricated a law suit against several people in the court of law. Due to absence of Bhaijee, absolutely all had become perplexed. Several letters with a request of persuasion had been sent to Bhaijee to call him back, but he was not in a mood to go back leaving his solitary living. He was consoling them through letters. He writes in a letter:

It is my request that efforts from outside should definitely be made with full enthusiasm and integrity. There should also not be any fault for this work which can be manipulated by money. Every effort should also be made seriously. But some people should also be like this, who could make humble efforts to materialise the spiritual instructions of the Gita and speeches of saints into reality.

Suppose *Gita press* will be deserted, views of Gita press will not be accepted. They will be treated guilty fraudulently and will be punished. The prestige of press and its reputation will be removed in front of the people. Sometimes I think what will be lost if this also occurred? It is a fact, if we accept it leaving pride that the present status of Gita press has not been developed under any scheme or power and if we would like to save its reputation by scheme or power (and if the power, by which it is made, would like to destroy it), then it won't be spared. That's it. Live comfortably by fixing your faith on that entirely auspicious system. If you wish to worry, then ask why there is shortage in meditating on him? What else can I write?

I request you with folded hands that whatever I am doing, I may be allowed to do so. Please console the people so that no more persuasion be made to call me back.

The affectionate people at Gorakhpur had faith that Bhaijee will set right everything by transmitting power from there itself and that happened as well. People felt extremely surprised when the law suit was placed in front of the court and the judge had dismissed it without any evidence or argument.

A letter sent during this very period to Shri Goswamiji, Bhaijee has written:

...Let this inertly mad person be left far aside. If this madness has come outside, then everyone will have to be perplexed. I must place a check in front of all, though madness is then often increasing internally. The decision to publish special issue of '*Kalyan*' – '*Sadhanank*' was taken for the next year. But it was difficult to prepare '*Sadhanank*' due to alienation of Bhaijee. Therefore, Shri Sethji arrived at Ratangarh on 12th March, 1940 and talked to Bhaijee in solitude and asked to proceed to Gorakhpur for the preparation of '*Sadhanank*'. Bhaijee humbly replied that he is not in a mood to go to Gorakhpur nor his mind is in proper shape to do any sort of activity. Shri Sethji had understood his mental status and directed him to call the editorial department at this place and get it prepared from this very place. Bhaijee said – I can get it ready by calling them here, but I am not in a mood to go with them to Gorakhpur.

During these days, the 'Hindu-code-bill' was presented for consideration in the Indian Parliament. Bhaijee believed there will be an increase of dishonest conduct in social life of Hindus by the approval of such law, which will be a basis of moral decline to the whole country, keeping it in mind; Bhaijee had planned a detailed signature campaign against it. Several articles had been published in '*Kalyan*' with such intention. Bhaijee had sent telegrams to the President, ministers and political leaders in this context and also inspired several people to send telegrams and letters.

❐

71

A Unique Death of Shri Govind Ramji Poddar

During his trip to Ratangarh, one more extraordinary event had occurred. Shri Govind Ramji Poddar was a reputed wholesale grain merchant at Ratangarh. He was honest in trade and very simple in nature. Most of his work regarding his trade had been looked after by his son and an accountant while he had been spending most of his time generally in repetition of divine name in low tone. He had an unbroken regard on Bhaijee, but it was known to very few people. He had been visiting daily in the assembly of virtuous people (*satsang*) with Bhaijee and had high respect for the liking of Bhaijee. One example will be sufficient for this purpose.

Once there was Brahmin feast on the eve of twelfth day departure to next world for a rich man of Ratangarh, possessing crores of rupees in which all Brahmins of Ratangarh had been invited. But few Brahmins from nearby villages had also come without invitation. They had not been provided meal and were ready to return hungry and disappointed. When this information was known to Bhaijee, he became restless and moved with a firm decision to return only after meal was served to Brahmins. When such thing was told to Shri Govind Ramji, he arranged to prepare *Puris*, vegetables and sweets and served meal to all Brahmins with great respect and affection and also did farewell along with proper donation. Then he informed Bhaijee that proper arrangements had been made as per his definite intention. Hearing this, Bhaijee became very happy.

Once he told in an ecstatic voice to Bhaijee, though my action does not look like but looking to your kindness, I want to make one request, please do a definite favour for visualisation of the God at the time of departure from this world. Bhaijee replied if you have certain faith, then it is not a big problem.

He became ill prior to his death. A poisonous blister appeared on his back and its poison had begun to spread in his body. Physicians had also become disappointed. Whenever Bhaijee went to meet him in between, he reminded him about the visualisation of the God. Looking at his grave condition, Bhaijee had arranged to begin non-stop celebration of devotional songs (*sankeertan*). He also fervently kept on chanting the divine name.

A man came running from his home to Bhaijee on *Kartik Shukla* 15 in the year 1941 and requested to come to his residence as his condition was very grave. Bhaijee took Baba and went to his house. Bhaijee had perceived that he should live only for a short time. Bhaijee told Baba – "Please do not leave this place till I come back, I will come soon." Baba had been consoling him in-between to continue repetition of divine name without any gap. Shri Govindramji replied in a very tender voice – "Swamiji, I have an extreme pain and am almost unable to repeat the divine name."

Bhaijee came with his carefree movement, two hours prior to his death. During such occasion, facial expression of Bhaijee had an extraordinary look – a serious facial expression full of contentment as if he had come to bid farewell to someone. Bhaijee had sat near to him and said – "Please repeat the divine name and visualise the God in front." He started suddenly repeating divine name in speed. Bhaijee said – Look how fast he is repeating divine name. Everyone noted if some magic has occurred. At present and a few minutes earlier, he was unable to repeat divine name due to pain. Now his tongue was repeating the divine name like a machine. Bhaijee was calling and showing to everyone like a play. He said – Look at this person with good deeds. How fast he is repeating the divine name, people have been observing him with an aghast look. Bhaijee asked him – Look! Do you still visualise the God? He has expressed his consent by moving his neck. Bhaijee was mentioning to the people present there like a child – look and note, he says that he is visualising the God. Now a line was begun by the people without interruption to enquire about it. The family members were present and about 20-25 virtuous people had asked him – Are you visualising the God? And he had given his consent each time by moving his neck. Though his eyes were closed, but he was full of senses. There was no sign of paralysis. Bhaijee had been repeatedly telling – what an extraordinary event it is? He has also been smiling extraordinarily. Thereafter, Bhaijee had made a prayer – O Lord, well it is, the universe exults and is filled with love by chanting your names, virtues and glory; terrified demons are fleeing in all directions and all ascetics with great powers and saintliness are bowing to you (Gita-11/ 36), and also narrated seventh chapter of Gita as if he was also offering knowledge. Thereafter, his soul had left his body.

❑

72

Marriage of the Daughter – Ms. Savitri

An auspicious marriage of the only child of Bhaijee was solemnised on *Margashirsha Shukla* 10 in the year 1941 with a great pomp and show with Shri Parmeshwar Prasadji, son of Shri Shiv Bhagwan Fogla at Ratangarh. The marriage pavillion was created at his residence and famous Pandit Shri Madan Mohanji Shastri from Varanasi had arrived to accomplish all activities fully conformable to scriptures. Due to a very vast field of acquaintance to Bhaijee, reputed people came from distant places at that occasion. Many saints and sages also arrived. During this period, one event needs to be mentioned:

At the time of main feast *(Sajjangoth)*, there was a row of people coming for meals. Different types of sweets had been prepared. Everyone was aware about the nature of Bhaijee. His door was opened for everyone, whether he received an invitation or not. Many people were taking meal. Custodian of the store felt that the sweets may be shortened; even the people from marriage party did not take the meal, while it was extremely difficult to find out an exact number of people coming to take meal. He was worried looking at the quantity of food items. He had expressed his worry in front of few important persons of the family. Such information also reached to Bhaijee. Bhaijee came in the store for sweets and asked – Show me the quantity of sweets, everyone says that sweets have been in shortage. By saying this, Bhaijee had run his eyes in the direction of every sweets and said – People mentioned it senselessly that sweets were in shortage. Where is the shortage of sweets? By repeating this, he went outside and got busy in other activities. There was no limit of surprise to the custodian of store, when he found that sweets were still left over even after taking of the meal by marriage party. He had a faith that it was only due to inspection of sweets by Bhaijee.

In due course, four children were born to Savitri, two boys – Suryakant and Chandrakant – and two girls – Radha and Pushpa.

❑

73

Regarding Respected Shri Bhaijee from the Pen of Respected Baba

An introduction about Shri Chakradharji Maharaj has already been given in the preliminary pages. During his time of silence (1941- 42), he had given in writing a few things about Bhaijee in front of some unique devotees. He prevented them from describing these things in the lifetime of Bhaijee and himself as well. This text is being presented with an intention that devotees may be benefitted by consulting them.

(1)

During the night of Paush Shukla 13 in the year 1941, respected Baba gave in his handwriting in front of Shri Chimmanlalji Goswami, Shri Gambhirchandji Dujari and Pandit Govardhanji. Part of the text is being given as follows:

The dust from the feet of Bhaijee is not at all lesser than the dust of Braj. To live near Bhaijee is likely to live in Braj. Rather is higher than it which I don't want to mention due to certain reasons. The internal structure of Bhaijee has expressed even stronger reasons than the reason by which Braj is important. Dujariji and Goswamiji could somehow guess it. This is such an extraordinary thing that by its repeated declaration, it is difficult to understand even a little bit of it. But, it is even then such an excellent object that nothing can be declared. Till today and at this particular time, the people have not imagined up to that extent that it is such an excellent thing. And it is my strong faith that an appropriate knowledge of its actual form, i.e., what is this in real sense and to know it very precisely will not be possible even by saying this thing. It is only possible by a look of favour from Bhaijee. People may hear or can say anything about Bhaijee, conformable to the scriptures but spiritual condition of Bhaijee is such an extraordinary that even various commentaries cannot touch the shadow of the real state of affairs (Parmarthiksthiti). It is only to advise that whatever may be the reach of the height of your highest imagination, just imagine up to that extent and dedicate unto the holy feet of Bhaijee.

Radhe Radhe Radhe Radhe Radhe

Bhaijee is a tree that grants all desires of present life in real sense. Therefore, I say to request the best thing from him is to love unto his feet.

(2)

On Margashirsha Shukla 2 in the year 1941 at Ratangarh,
Shri Chakradharji Maharaj wrote the following things in reply
to a question raised by Shri Dujariji at the residence of Bhaijee
at 10 o'clock in the night:

Presence (i) Shri Chakradharji; (ii) Shukdeoji; (iii) Madanlalji Chudiwale; (iv) Shiv Krishnaji Daga; (v) Govardhanji; (vi) Kedarnathji Kanodia; (vii) Shiv Bhagwanji Fogla; (viii) Gambhirchandji Dujari.

Swamiji: What is your question?

Dujariji: How to develop love and respect to great people?

Swamiji: (i) You may tell sometimes your sufferings solitarily in front of him whom you considered as a great person. (ii) You can also convey in such a way that I don't want to be needy in front of you all the time, what else can be such lowness greater than this. (iii) It means to cast your image occasionally in his divine inner heart. (iv) It is totally one thing only, whether it is the God or great person, he would do salvation by any means. To accompany him with ill-will would be blessed by religious devotion (*bhakti*) only while to receive love, one must do only favourable service. Just like this, the essential property (*Vastu gun*) of great people caused salvation but to receive the divine love, you must do efforts to be in his accord.

I was thinking today that you (Dujariji) would definitely ask something, then what should I reply. I should think this in advance. After thinking for a longer duration, I could only think to request you to bless me with a true heart so that I should get at least little attachment unto the holy feet of Bhaijee. If I could not love, then at least this much may be maintained that wherever I may be (probably Bhaijee may or may not like, don't know), I may also be longing with true craving to remain laid with the feet dust of Bhaijee. It is true whether Bhaijee would retain or reject me, I don't know about it. It seems that he would not leave me if I wish. He would never like to leave, but I am a person with a very weak heart. Don't know if such an illusion may enter in my mind, compelling me to move somewhere. Due to such fear, I am with true self-seeking the blessing from you all. It is a fake thing, it is not a joke that if Bhaijee and I live, till then my love remains increasing daily without gap unto his holy feet. At present, Bhaijee has taken care of me with utmost respect but I can say this thing by making the God as witness that please give your blessing so that even after humiliation or insult, if I am permitted to live there, even then I should live in that insulting life, I should not think to leave him because I shall never get such company in life, shall never obtain, it seems totally correct. I don't know even the entity responsible for my support, i.e., Radha, Krishna or Bhaijee because he does not tell me anything clearly. But whatever actual peace, real pleasure is in my possession or is in process of increasing, it has begun only after my meeting with Bhaijee. And it also appears quite correct to my mind, had I not met Bhaijee, then how uninteresting would my life be? Believe me, the temperament I retain towards Bhaijee is yet to develop but sometimes feels so agitated by emotion that I cannot explain to you.

We are not aware of his actual identity, not at all aware but whatever comes to mind and whenever his kindness showered sometimes, I cannot explain, how I felt at that time, cannot explain even willingly but can say this much that so much attraction prevailed at that time towards Bhaijee which cannot be explained through speech. There have been some important things that are informed through one of his reliable sources about him. When I remember those things, then again, I think whether that day will come or not. When I will sacrifice unto his feet? Today at 8 o'clock, I was thinking to request Bhaijee to let me know who would die first, himself or me, but if he dies earlier, will he be kind enough to show his appearance to me? Because I don't know such an ability to sacrifice for you and I also think that due to some fortune, I have been given such an opportunity and otherwise I will have to repent.

That's it. This is sufficient and let me go now.

A saint wrote to me specially some words about him, but also instructed clearly that such words should not be disclosed to anyone. This letter was delivered firstly into the hands of Bhaijee who had given it to me after 10 days – it consists of some account written in such a normal way which I can say after due consideration that even an imagination for such a high spiritual condition cannot appear in our mind. Firstly, I could not even believe it once I have read such letter. But now as per the gradual passing of days, the mystery of that thing is slowly going to open and names of saints I have heard through various scriptures, I have never read such a state in life for any one of them. It was mentioned by the saint about his meeting with a sage, who was 300 years or older with high calibre, who had already joined within the act of Shri Krishna and he enquired about spiritual status of Shri Jay Dayalji and Bhaijee. I am giving gist of this conversation as follows:

Last year, I gave a hint to Goswamiji like I have given to you, but the style of Goswamiji had changed from the next day, but did not even mention it to him as well. It was because of two reasons. Though Goswamiji may be in very high status, but believe me, I did not know who you are, who he is. I don't know about anybody, but it appeared in mind that the saint will never be angry to me, what would be the harm if I tell this thing to few people, then again thought that these people would not utilise the real benefit. It may be dirtiness of my mind. But, firstly, there is a prohibition; secondly, there is doubt in my mind that until the inner heart becomes not pure by the devotional songs (*bhajans*), till then nobody could understand such thing. Thirdly, still I am afraid that if Bhaijee would know about these things, then he can utilise some strong method to threaten me because his thoughts seem to me only such that an inspiration specially from Shri Krishna has been bestowed on him, due to which, he wants to expose himself as very simple. Now if I do anything against him, then it is natural that he will say now go and enjoy. Till now, you could know this much secretly about me due to my sympathy, but if you have now started misuse of it, then go. Not this much only, I also feel afraid of such fear that if he will utilise a little rough method, then my present progress shall altogether be checked. Such things may not be in his mind. It may be altogether my imagination as well, but such temperament still prevails in my mind. And it is true that Bhaijee would feel extremely shy to expose such things. I demand this much fee only from you that please do not discuss such things in front of Bhaijee. And I am also feeling this fear that Bhaijee has seen me. What he may think, I have no idea. In my opinion and in my comparison, you people have high regards. I feel like there is definitely a difference in the type of temperaments with everyone?

(3)

On the road and in the morning of Margashirsha Shukla 3, in the year 1941, written following things remaining standing in front of Shri Dujariji

...Because whenever I shall be eligible, Bhaijee would not spare even a little deficiency. At present, my life has been prolonging in such a way by his kindness or kindness of Radhe Krishna that there is no need to ask anyone, no need to know, unknowingly and by other means. When front path appears closed regarding any question, then such an effort is made by Bhaijee automatically that I got the light. Then why should I go and inquire?

I have forgotten to tell one thing at night that none should misunderstand me anyway that I am criticising Shri Jay Dayalji and Bhaijee being in a higher or a lower state. I can never be indebted to Shri Jay Dayalji even by becoming a shoe for his feet because he has made me in such a position by retaining me with him for three years that I could achieve ability to live with Bhaijee. But what can I do, I have been more attracted towards Bhaijee. Therefore, even with a desire to sacrifice by all means unto his (Shri Sethji) holy feet, I cannot follow his advice due to some very special spiritual reasons. I love him very much and can vouch without any doubt that I respect from the core of my heart to the dust of feet of Ghanshyamji, Ramsukh Dasji, etc. who possess religious devotion (*bhakti*) unto his holy feet. But there are such things that a man may understand by the explanation from the God in my opinion. Otherwise, I have no stamina for such an explanation, why I don't agree to any of his advices though I possess a very high temperament towards him. People have misunderstanding can make imagination as an elder and younger for Shri Jay Dayalji and Bhaijee and discuss many types of things but there are few such things which can be only understood with due practice (*sadhna*). Nothing will occur here by random knowledge of scriptures. Also, the kindness of the God only can let you understand this. Therefore, whatever I have told you during night, such thing should also be included therein. It is good for me that there is no one greater than Bhaijee because I have knowingly insulted Shri Jay Dayalji first for the sake of him and have also considered his kindness as insignificant. I have no faith in pride, believe me. I have totally no power that I can say something to anyone, but faith of my mind is such that though willingly many things have come to an end by coming in front. If you can see in my heart, then look properly that whosoever has even a little respect to Bhaijee, is extremely dear to me. I don't want to hide anything from him but when there comes a break between talks, then it comes to my mind, not to disclose for the time being. But, in mind, so much love enhances towards all of you that I bow my head considering respect from my heart to you all because you all have so much respect to a person like Bhaijee in your mind. I don't raise anything for anyone in front of Bhaijee but am compelled sometimes to raise about you people. It is my nature that if someone asks about Bhaijee, then I do not feel satisfied even narrating it throughout the night. It appeared sometimes that people felt like bored.

I was telling this thing that though I did not know at all about Bhaijee, but I only loved discussion about him to the maximum. There is only some such sort of things particularly and there are some reasons as well, which I cannot describe to anyone. Nobody can understand, if described. Only Bhaijee knows and if Shri Jay Dayalji knew it, I have no information. Though I wanted to tell but did not know that after saying, the mind is filled with an alienation for a longer duration. I have been thinking this for a longer time in the night that why I went in that room. What was the benefit? My mind was totally alienated. Such condition is also occurred by pledging love very much, to you people. If Bhaijee would like to enquire, would like to see these pages, then can be shown without hesitation. But nothing is to be done without his information. Good or bad, whatever will be, he would surely extend his kindness. Fear still exists but the fear is of an extraordinary type. If he feels angry, he would even then refer only to Radha Madhav. But there is a desire in my mind that I should be according to his expectation. It should not act against him. The main fear is that by reading such text, he will say why you are exaggerating than singing hymns. When fear will go, don't know, then what would happen. If you trust me, I consider you people in a very respectful way, but even then, many reasons forcefully entered the mind causing an alienation.

(4)

Given to Shri Chimmanlalji Goswami and Shri Gambhirchandji Dujari on Pausha Krishna 30 in the year 1941 during mid-night between 10:15 P.M. and 12:30 A.M.

Believe me, the things that I am going to narrate, if I would have complete faith in them, then my life would be extraordinary – such would be the behaviour and my attraction towards Bhaijee that it would have been an ideal to this world with an implicit confidence, but it is not so. And by God's will, I don't even wish that it should be. If there exists any wish, believe me, Shri Krishna and Bhaijee are such trees longing by the devotee which grant every wish, they would definitely fulfill. There occurs no desire in my mind which I should pray for. I only wish to raise the curtain in its usual way in which it is being gradually raised. Otherwise, Bhaijee would fulfill my wish without fail at the same moment. But since the day I have heard this thing, I have been extremely benefitted spiritually, specially from that day which I cannot also fully disclose.

The thing is that a saint wrote me a secret letter one-and-a-half or two years ago, about which I have already written earlier. He personally met a sage of high calibre who had already joined in the divine acts of Shri Krishna and he enquired many things from this sage. I would have shown this letter to you, but it is clearly written there – You will not show this letter to anyone. This is also a reason for not showing this letter, which also contains information about many other people and I am also not showing it due to few other reasons. It is with me, I have kept it like my breath alongwith my texts of daily routine. If this is not lost and chance comes like this till my death and if you are alive and still crave, then you can see it or if I change my mind soon, then I would show it to you. So, be it, I presume like this and, according to my knowledge of history, these saints must be manifested when King Akbar was on the throne of Delhi. When this saint enquired with this sage (after repeated inquiries) to tell him about Shri Jay Dayalji and Shri Hanuman Prasadji, what he had told in his reply is this (he began smiling and said): You are examining me, you are already aware "that subtle body of Hanuman Prasad has become truly in the form of Shri Priyaji".

Now to explain this thing from my point of view, I am writing a little, very concisely. Think – what is a subtle body? The body of Bhaijee is made up of five elements (along with eyeballs), means five elements structure along with eyeballs, only that much is left. Remaining altogether, the whole has been transformed into the form of Radhaji. I never read about such spiritual state in any scripture till this day and no account is available of such state in this life of any devotee except Chaitanya Mahaprabhu. I did not mean that Bhaijee is the first example in the history of this world. There might be some exceptional saints, but it is not in record and it seems that sages have knowingly not mentioned such state in the scriptures. And if it has been mentioned, then I have not seen it. In fact, the act of such temperament by the herd girls of Braj to Shri Krishna and all events are altogether an unutterable object. Manifestation of that element is found in fortunate eminent people after an achievement of the all-pervading spirit of universe. It is altogether a thing beyond mind and speech, but I am telling you people few things in a very precise form as per the lawful advice. Fortunately, if due to awakening of excellent opportunity, someone is involved with the practice of worshipping as herd girls of Braj and if his devotion of striving becomes successful due to infinite blessing of Radha-Krishna, then he transforms into dispositional body (*Bhava-deha*). The examples are transformation of '*Arjun*' to '*Arjuni*' and *Narad* to herd girls of Braj. The element of such characteristic body has altogether been blissful. And after the achievement of such characteristic body by some or the other unique person, obtains the right to enter in the act. Thereafter, following the death, such characteristic body is appointed in the service. But even by the characteristic body, when someone is proud of the beauty, it is due to the body devoted to love of God (*Manjarideha*) or due to confidante of Shri Radhaji. Being follower as a confidante of Shri Radha and to play suitable part in the act in the service is the nature of flower buds. The confidantes are eternal and are with a possibility to enter in the bodies, devoted to love of the God (Krishna). Whatever is the number of highly skilled herd girls of Braj, they are either as flower buds or somewhat below the level of confidante, means in the form of highly skilled herd girls of Braj earned the right to serve but to transform into suitable body of Radha Rani, is a different thing. To become in such condition, there will be no feeling of outer world even for a moment. It is only reported during last days of Mahaprabhu when he had a befitting rapport with Radha Rani. But it is such a belief regarding him among devotees that he was himself Shri Krishna. Therefore, such state does not possess any special importance to him. But looking at the life of Bhaijee, it appears that he had definitely achieved once natural state (*jivbhava*) of life. Therefore, such state is extremely rare and is the result of ineligible blessed state, this can be estimated easily. In other words, Bhaijee does not come to outer world even for a moment. Then the question arises how the normal activity goes well, its reply for the logician is different but the devotee should understand like this when Radha Rani herself is acting inside the curtain of this structure made by five elements, then her universally competent power will also be developed. Therefore, the concept of "An intention with which the people accept my shelter, I grant reward according to that very motive" is also being applicable altogether to Bhaijee.

Radha Rani is present in this structure of five elements of Bhaijee and even for a moment by such knowledge of existent identity (*Swaroopbhoot*) – i.e., I am Radha, he never deviates by this knowledge, but as will be the belief of the people towards him, accordingly and due to his universally competent power, his behavior will be like a machine. These are so many things in this context that even if full night may pass, even then it cannot be explained completely. It is related with an achievement. It means Bhaijee (Radha Rani) only may explain its mystery by his kindness and that very person only can imagine very little that the conduct will remain continued in such a way. There is no space for logic. Therefore, please be sure that Bhaijee used to be continuously possessed with the thoughts of Radha, likewise as a worshipable incarnation (*archavatar*) may appear for the worship able idol (*arch-vigraha*), causing a possibility of impossible occurrence in an excellent manner, in the same way and, in other words, one can understand like this that in the structure of five elements called by the name Bhaijee, has been blessed by the incarnation of Radha Rani. If such structure lives, there is no need to respect, once you tend upwards, due benefit would be given according to your capability. So much so is the personality trait (*vastuguna*) of Bhaijee that whosever comes or will come into his contact, everybody will move towards the God either in this birth or will take one more birth (only one more) and will obtain divine ending (*Bhagwati gati*) according to their longing. It would occur due to existent influence *(vastuguna)*, emotion is not required. It is because the natural power *(swarupashakti)* of Lord Shri Krishna has been incarnated. The thing what we have heard about *Mahaprabhu*, the same thing towards solution of the world will also be applied in his case. Even being this much and according to **'O Arjuna, however men seek me, even so do I respond to them' (Gita: 4/11)** in the lifetime, he would appear according to the feeling of people. As a husband to Savitri's mother, as a Hanuman to his mother and whosoever would like to get his work done, with that feeling, he would do it, if it does not harm him. Relief to a sad from sadness, wealth to a poor person, i.e., whatever is the request, will be granted. Like devotees, he would not make efforts for salvation from this world. Editing of '*Kalyan*' which is being done should be taken as it is reflecting the reflection of real affection of customers as well as the longing of Shri Jay Dayalji. Bhaijee cannot be judged now by that standard. He should be judged by divine standard. As two types of opposite particles are visualised in Lord Shri Krishna one-time infatuation and one-time omniscience in the same way Bhaijee being possessed with the character of Radha simultaneously can also charm this world becoming a proud person as Hanuman Prasad. His speech, efforts made for the act of an accomplishment, to look sad in the absence of devoted striving, to be observed for making efforts for progress, it is altogether merely a sport for a teaching to this world. In fact, he is instantly and also abundantly endowed with such knowledge that he is Radha and at the same time, someone observes him giving daughter in marriage, observes him talking with somebody for some trade, exactly at that time and at the same moment, such a lively act still continued to take place in the divine country of that structure about which our dirty minds cannot even imagine.

In a very concise form, I have written so many things to you that what is the change of subtle body in the form of Shri Priyaji, based on my human brain. I have no idea if you can think better than this, but discussion will be auspicious. Therefore, I have written. If you could not think, then you may definitely get a little help. Just imagine about one thing that the body available after death as a corpse alongwith senses and eyeballs is known as gross body, body of the remaining seventeen elements is called subtle body and that sage said it, as a complete form of Priyaji and a subtle body. I have learned an unaltered version of his letter by heart by reading it yesterday.

It is beyond doubt that opening and closing of eyes to see someone, all such efforts are the efforts by Radha Rani. Believe me that to find such a rare opportunity is very difficult. If someone looks intently, then he would not require searching the proof of its quality of being true. And the one who can surrender to him looking intently for him, it is beyond description. At the time to bless someone, it must be understood it happened exactly like that someone worshipped Radhaji and she is pleased with him and Radhaji comes to reward him. Then the knowledge of Radhaji at that instant that She is Radha is unbroken. Just as this, Bhaijee also rewarded Dujariji as per his feeling, to me as per my feeling, to you according to your feeling, remained continuously possessed with the characteristic of Radha. His inner heart would be specially informed by that devotee who would surrender himself. He would be brought forward on the road of achievement, otherwise whatever is the law for normal properties of substance (*vastuguna*), that same would be applicable to everyone. Otherwise, in him, defect of unevenness would also appear like the God. Therefore, though relation may be with him in any form, the result would be eternally auspicious, it is for sure. Like everybody has accomplished a purpose by the sight of Shri Krishna during his incarnation period, but *Duryodhan* had always considered Him as magician till the end, while *Bhishma* visualised Him as supreme being. Just like that, all the persons in contact with Bhaijee shall accomplish their purpose, it will be definitely done but to become aware of his actual identity and to really enjoy his company is only possible to a person who can surrender himself.

When I have heard it first time, I did not believe it immediately and thought how could it be? Several genuine doubts appeared. But these words were bewildering me forcefully. One day Bhaijee himself spoke several such touching sentences while giving discourses on the love of Braj, love by herd girls of Braj. Then I could find its key. I realised that day that such state was possible and definitely possible but would certainly occur, would have occurred and was occurring in the life of some rare saint.

(5)

Radha Baba gave in writing on *Paush Krishna* 9 in the year 1941 to Goswamiji, Rameshwarji Jalan, Govardhanji and Dujariji

The best thing in my opinion is that any close associate of Bhaijee should join his company just for the sake of company and should not place any aim. He has an identity and only to wish his company and should try with his best – I am improving or falling, progressing or degrading – I have not yet recovered from my mode of habits – he should never think about such things. Then take it surely for granted that Bhaijee would bless with such an excellent gift, which nobody can imagine. This is the best thing which I can say about Bhaijee. Believe me, if somebody can be like it, then Bhaijee shall make it a point to facilitate his entry in the act of Shri Krishna along with him. It is a bad-to-worst life, not to worry, terrible and sudden blaze due to sin arises in mind, sins are being done, not to worry at all but you must accompany Bhaijee. Such accompanied person would definitely go alongwith Bhaijee. Being so easy, there is no one in my opinion, who accompanies him for the sake of company, at least I am not. No means are necessary. The best thing I have told you from the core of my heart. Do meet the great people, do talk, do make company of virtuous people, but there should not be adultery in mind that Bhaijee will abuse, will irritate or would warn. There is one condition which I have forgotten to tell you, there should not be a feeling of association with any other great person in it. There are great people in the world and I salute to the feet dust of them, but I have to follow Bhaijee. Believe me, due to insufficient repetition of divine name, an extremely low form is present in front of us. Do try to repeat divine name. Then his kindness would surround you from all corners in such a way and would show such an enlightened divine identity, about which an imagination is altogether impossible at present. But even the repetition of divine name would be possible only due to his kindness. Towards such a trustworthy person, he would extend at least this much courtesy in advance that his warning will not disturb his soul. If a follower having faith in Bhaijee observes, then there is no problem. Then wait for such an occasion, that moment, while terminating his act, may also bestow something to you from the offering without motive. The condition is to give up any hope in your mind from him till the end. As you wish, with the strength due to your kindness only, Bhaijee, I would not leave, this is my firm decision. By retaining such temperament, I might have to live anywhere due to destiny but by maintaining mental contact, would also cause physical contact in between, due to his kindness. Sometimes he also behaves like a child. There is no need of recommendation towards the God or Bhaijee, absolutely not. But due to childhood, I have tried to recommend whomsoever praising him with very good words, then I noted that Bhaijee was ready to bestow his blessings, but he was not ready to accept, then what could be done?

If you could somehow grasp one croreth part of moment of his kindness, then you would never forget the name. I am the one who is near to him, his kindness has been retaining us altogether. As many number of people are here in my sight, I am mostly attracted towards Goswamiji amongst them and I think if he prefers, he can try to be like him. There is no unevenness in the favour but due to lack of longing, people have been restrictive due to several circumstances. But if you wish due to your longing or unutterable good fortune, you are in such a condition that you can do its practice. There is no scarcity or excess in the affection by Bhaijee, but I found it displayed in some way with you....

There is scarcity like for that group and secondly to pay very little attention on his instructions. Thirdly, there is an excess of toils of the world. If there is an absence of point two and three and may form a group with true integrity, who have real faith in him and also possessed an attachment to hear then an inspiration may compulsorily occur from the side of the God in the mind of Bhaijee, by which he may entirely change the situation laughingly. Such thing may appear in my knowledge that Bhaijee has been moved very high from this world. And he is being continuously raising. Therefore, now to make efforts to increase faith and affection among people from his end seems almost impossible. But if the group could act in such a manner having no aim to harass Bhaijee but with a longing to listen to his words through heart, then such an effort can be made by him automatically that everybody may be attracted. When he says to do, then if a person does with an effort to proceed further and with true intention to obey, then it is all right, but it is not a condition that you would be completely successful. The condition is to try for movement, even this much cannot be done by us. Therefore, the flow of his grace, though continuously touching us, our mind could hardly believe it. The solution for this is very beautiful – to weep in front of him with true mind. But believe me such desire is also not present from inside. These efforts should be made for the benefit at personal level. And its initial technique is to make sincere efforts for singing hymns with your true intention (after completion of the important work) and see the effect of singing hymns and you would realise the flow of stream of his grace. And an identity which is seen of him presently, you would see an extreme and extraordinary identity than that. An uninterrupted remarkability would be just increased. So much is an attachment of the family that such temperament prevails only because you are at present here. You will forget it once you leave this place.

Shri Radha Rani worshipped *Tulsi* to materialise her meeting with Shri Krishna. I was reading the importance of *Tulsi* – a holy basil in *Kalpbheda*. If you would hear it, then most of the people won't believe it that it is not this much of importance for holy basil. Even Lord Shankar has said up to this much of extent that if the smallest piece of wood from *Tulsi* is placed on the burning pyre due to good luck of the person, then instantly the messengers of

Lord Vishnu will take him to heaven. Doing mistrust on ancient sages is due to dirtiness of our minds. If you can sing hymns (*bhajan*) in real sense, then everything starts appearing in consciousness like real. Without singing hymns, there cannot be grace of God or great people. Then why it does not occur? I have experienced such reality in my life that everything occurred due to his grace. Egoism will not do anything at all. Such should be our desire that I should do singing of hymns, then singing of hymns is possible but it would occur only due to his grace. We did not do it just as you have said. We don't know its answer but sometimes think why did we not do it, what is its reply? It seems to me if we retain such pride that we will do it till the time it would not happen.

Look at it, if you have no enthusiasm, then some other time. It happens that several types of emotions have arisen in mind forcefully yesterday and there appeared a feeling to say something to you again. I may forget after many days. Therefore, I have decided. So, there is no hurry from my side; everything depends entirely on your contentment only.

(6)

Instructions to Shri Vasudev Singhania on *Paush Shukla* 1, in the year 1941 by Swamiji

I know very little, least and nothing about Bhaijee. Dujariji knows too much. But if it is a persuasion that I must tell something, then follow my request to do one lakh repetitions of divine name daily for one month. Repeating of divine name should be performed for the pleasure of the God. It is not that you have to listen to something from Swamiji. Then I would be really pleased and will also obtain enthusiasm and if the God desires, then I have a definite plan to tell you according to my intelligence.

I am a very small being but advise you affectionately and by my heart that if you do for one month at least one lakh repetitions of divine name daily and then if you ask me to tell something about Bhaijee after one month, then I may feel highly inspired and may wish to tell something. Please don't get angry. At present, I am not at all willing to say. In the language of love, I can say to give me my fee as one lakh repetitions of divine name daily for one month, then I can talk.

...if your mind is entangled with him, then possibly the confidence may decline. Please maintain spiritual relation only. Your wife has recovered. Suppose she did not, then would Bhaijee not still be a saint? But it is not proper if your mind is affected by such worthless instincts. If you respect Bhaijee, then it should be taken for granted that he can do possible from impossible. Why are there such talks? It is likely to request five-rupee note from the treasury of king of kings of the whole world and then becomes happy on its receipt, likewise to become happy by the imaginations of such worthless miracles in the case of Bhaijee. In this first place, thought of any type for Bhaijee is auspicious but if such things are even slightly seized by the mind, then in my opinion, it would take a lot of time to get real benefit by Bhaijee. Is it not a harm to become so late? Then the progress would be checked.

In my view, the saints have been of very high status. Please stop examining about the omniscience of Bhaijee through the worldly things in future, which is my repeated request. If someone misguides you, even then you don't listen, you can hear such things superficially.

But, in your mind, at least an influence has been laid due to such things.

Those things are of such lower status, so worthless, so simple that it may cause reduction in faith due to them in future.

As you treat him, he would be the same to you. If you think about him that he would know only when conveyed, then you would see his act only to the point and if you are really and firmly determined from your inner heart that Bhaijee knows everything, then indeed he knows everything. You can experience it only when you believe him completely with certainty.

Even then I request you that please get rid of these worthless concepts from your mind. In the real sense, such a thing may cause a decrease in the glory of a true saint. You have a clear heart as you have told me clearly. Therefore, I am very happy. As such, I can dare to say with an affection that, in fact, nobody can describe the glory of a saint. Whatever is the glory of the God Himself will be the glory of a true saint. If with true inner heart you can believe that Bhaijee is a saint, then indeed at that moment, you would yourself be changed to such an extraordinary person that people may be surprised looking at you. At present, based on hearing something, a temperament has developed superficially that Bhaijee is a saint, but its basis at present has not been established. Such superficial temperament has been even developed due to eternal fortune and due to highly virtuous act, it is a very beautiful temperament, but its basis should be made firm. There will be no home without a firm base. If you begin treating Bhaijee as a saint, then you would need not do anything. Because to get a true saint means to meet the God. But it is not a true recognition. If our inner heart is dirty, such recognition cannot prevail. Likewise, if there is a blind person and who cannot see any light, and if you say about any extraordinary object in front of him, he cannot understand exactly about that thing, though would listen everything carefully. When he will regain eyesight, then he would be surprised to see that this is such an extraordinary object. Likewise, we are blind, mean that our inner heart is dirty. We don't understand at all even by hearing the words of saints that, in real sense, what object a saint is, how much glory he possesses. When our inner heart will be pure we would understand that such is a saint, and such is his glory. Therefore, if you intend to increase your faith for Bhaijee, and would like to receive benefit from Bhaijee in real sense, then I am requesting you with a least advice from heart that try to save yourself as much as from sins and should repeat at least one lakh divine names daily. If you are already doing it, have been doing more than it, then it is a matter of great pleasure. Until you do such practice, till then the knowledge about real glory of Bhaijee is almost difficult. Bhaijee or the God Himself may let you provide the knowledge about His glory without repeating the divine name, then it is something else. Those people are independent. It is a universal law that repetition of divine name must be performed. If you really did the repetition of divine name, then you need not consult anyone. You will know everything automatically.

Whatever are the things without repetition of divine name have been all superficial. The people can never understand that indeed it is a play like childhood.

Tell me first, what do you think about Bhaijee? If you really need it, then such things would automatically be informed to you by the inspiration of the God Himself. But it is beyond your right that you could hear about his glory. Then do it, try it. And my condition is to repeat one lakh names daily for a few days. If I remain alive and you still wish, then come to me. I would be gladly encouraged to tell you things about Bhaijee.

(7)

Swamiji gave in writing to Sri Krishnaji Daga at night between 10 and 11 o'clock at Ratangarh on *Magh, Krishna* 7 in the year 1941

Radha Radha Radha

To associate him with your body, mind and speech.

If and as far as you find an opportunity by grace of God, till then try to live as much as you can near to him.

To ponder over things whatever are known to you about him by your mind.

To discuss among people having real faith in him through speech. These three things should be followed as far as possible and with utmost readiness and sincerity, which would enable you to receive with that promptness the blessing of great people and also allow to see their actual identity. Once you realise it, then you would wander happily in it, would become speechless and the body will be surrendered unto his holy feet.

You should have a desire to serve living near him, means you should dance like an instrument according to his wish. But it is a thing of mind. Please do not tell him anything openly but if he makes a wish or asks you to live in any place, live in that very place, means never say it openly that you wish to live near him. True saints know everything, nothing is hidden from them about your mind. Even with such longing, if he wants to keep you separately, then it would be auspicious for you, by retaining you separately would cause an increase in your faith, therefore, would be retained separately. There have been many reasons, but everything is very clear to him. He would do that very thing only which would increase your faith.

It is better if you live with a person whom you are most attracted to. Both are indeed great persons, means you should have a desire to live with the one whom you are most attracted to, but don't reveal openly to him. Whatever is ordered by them, do it with full sincerity of your heart. Then whatever is suitable to you will happen automatically. Repetition of divine name is such a thing that without approaching anyone, without consulting anyone, everything would be known by itself. It would be illuminated in the heart itself. Informers would tell you forcefully without asking them. They should tell you everything even non-willingly. Such thing has been embarked into my life up to a great extent with a true experience. Do not go to anyone, do not ask anything from anyone, only repetition of divine name from your tongue and remembering it through your soul, that's all, only two activities are the best which should be continued. Then you don't require anything. But do not feel proud for repetition of divine name in your mind means I am doing sincerely while other people are of lower status and have been wasting time unnecessarily.

Do whatever you deem fit,
Though the world is full of good and ill,
You should sit and clean yourself (thoughts).
I respectfully greet this whole world with folded hands,
Recognizing it as consisting of *Shri Sita Ram.*

(*Ramcharit Manas/Balkand* /7:17)

You are venerable, they are also venerable, but we must do repetition of divine name.

(8)

Swamiji gave in writing to Vasudev Singhania at Ratangarh on *Magh Shukla* 4, in the year 1941 while Shri Dujariji was attending, nearby during sleep

Radha Radha Radha

When did you prefer it, today or tomorrow? How would be my mood tomorrow? The things have been discussed today towards the implicit confidence since 5 o'clock. It would not be for your personal benefit. With great affection, I will tell you a thing of your interest, please trust me. Whatever would be the best thing to you in my opinion, I would try to explain with my little intelligence. Everyone is not benefitted by the opinion of every person. Specially, you should be careful that by listening to everything may harm you instead of benefitting. In front of a person, very high words of faith may even react in such a way that his faith may be reduced. And it is not a check that I should not teach you, if it appeals me, then I can teach you everything. But, at present, it does not suit.

Do not teach more than four persons – Dujariji, Goswamiji, Govardhanji and Bajrang Bajaj. Do not teach anybody except them. It is a condition even not to your brother Purushottam as well. Do not lie to anyone. With great affection, you can declare it that Swamiji has taken a promise. We will talk today for one hour, then sometime later. It is not a rule that everything must be completed today. But if you break the rule repeating one lakh divine names daily, then it won't.

You have asked me that day if Bhaijee is omniscient or not (to know inside the mind, to acquaint with everything like the God).

Think about one thing. In front of you, there is the structure of Bhaijee made up of five elements. What is inside it? As we were born, in the manner a soul is born, like the same Bhaijee was born. In other words, an individual soul was born 40-50 years ago from today who was named Hanuman Prasad. But due to God's grace and devoted striving (*sadhna*), he achieved such a higher status, which we can never imagine. To explain you in a better way, suppose the God comes five- seven years ago from today and blesses Himself with the highest status, best spiritual state to the soul present inside this structure of five elements of Bhaijee, then hid him in his heart and then the God Himself started working in his place, exactly that way things happened here. The soul present in this structure of Bhaijee has achieved the highest spiritual condition and has joined in his blissful act in his heart. Now the God Himself is working at his place and will continue to work if such structure of five elements lives. Now you can treat it like the God is maternal uncle, is omniscient, all-powerful, he would behave in front of you exactly like a maternal uncle behaves towards his nephew. Would say, yes brother, Vasudev, do you agree? Poor Vasudev did not know that his maternal uncle has already gone long back. In his place, the God Himself replies to my query, listens to my words, and gives due advice to me. The poor chap would understand this only if his maternal uncle is responding. He may think this much only that 'maternal uncle' is a saint but he could not even imagine that the God Himself is playing with him. Likewise, he would be son to mother, father to Savitri and husband to mother of Savitri and nobody could find about it at all. Exactly such a condition also prevailed here. Now you can imagine in a general way that it is a laughing matter for him to know about everything. But the knowledge about the omniscience would only be known to the one who will have a complete doubtless faith on him. Whatever you have heard about the God in the scriptures, all such things also existed inside this structure but what is God, it would be known exactly when due to continuation of your practice, he would let you experience it by raising his curtain. And then if they like and you still remember this thing, then show me that state which you have provided to maternal uncle. Please show me in which form the soul of maternal uncle is at present. Then, in fact, you could understand the spiritual status of maternal uncle. In other words, firstly you would achieve God. Thereafter, by His grace, you would know about the real state of Bhaijee. Except this, there is no other way. Firstly, I even did not know I am entirely a worthless creature, but whatever I would say by the grace of God, you would not at all understand. Rather it will be even beyond your mental ability to guess it. With great affection, I am writing you such words. Please do not get angry. Nobody can understand without devoted striving. Whatever is the superficial state at present, that is, the God Himself is replying from the inside of that structure. But we don't know such a thing. Giving his daughter in marriage, editing the '*Kalyan*'. But we don't believe this thing. Therefore, someone gives advice to him, someone mistrusts him, few vilified him, but he smiled hearing such things. Under such circumstances, what should be the duty, you can decide yourself. To become carefree by surrendering yourself unto his feet by making your full efforts with your heart. It is a good occasion. Once the destiny is completed, the play is over. The body stamina is dependent only on the destiny. The God would indeed be there if the destiny continues. One must do ascetic fervour till eternity to find the one who is God. He is himself so simple to achieve. It is unfortunate that you don't believe it. Curtain of illusion has been covering him. By his grace, some rare people would be blessed to believe in such statement. In fact, when the God has come, then its eternal benefit would be given to everyone. Whosoever comes under His sight, he would be purified unknowingly and successfully but it would occur at last, a pleasure of his company would be obtained only by surrendering the self (due to many reasons, I cannot write every word openly. I also wrote few things under cover).

Yours…is. This condition is exactly like you grind the sauce by a touchstone. Maternal uncle, will this thing be costlier? Will such thing be cheaper? By asking this much only and from its answer only he is satisfied. Alas, he does not understand that for which saints and sages have felt tired towards their involvement in ascetic fervour for hundred crores of years, he himself is playing with us by hiding himself at this moment. Such thing cannot even appear to his mind. He cannot understand even with due explanation because his mind has a passion for wealth, he needs wealth. There is no such thing in this world. What to say about wealth, which cannot be granted by Bhaijee but he has no faith on Bhaijee, no dependence on him. He will be, at last, benefitted surely because he has developed contact with the God by any temperament. It is not only him, as far as all living beings of the world, who will meet him, everyone will achieve salvation. It may be possible that by not obeying him, they will have to take one more birth. Such birth may be in any origin. May get any womb like dog, ass, man but the destiny of origin will be such that the visualisation of God shall be occurred. Such living beings are fortunate who have visualised him once. They don't realise that it is the only deficiency. Your welfare is decided but if you don't make efforts by your heart to follow him according to his advice, coupled with proper surrender, then probably you must take one more birth. Shall it be, I do not claim but who would persistently request him for worldly pleasure, then in my opinion, he shall have to take one more birth. For example, yours…is. He desires wealth from him. Now one out of two shall occur. Either he would develop asceticism by his grace in this life, but if it does not occur, then to make him possessor of a crores of rupees, to make him a possessor of hundred million of rupees, he will take one more birth because he is like a tree that grants all desires by showering parental kindness to devotees. Otherwise, there will be no value of desirous devotees. The wealth is the root of sorrow, the God will not grant to him who has the probability to descend on achieving the wealth. If he must give, he would give to him alone who has got no fear to fall. If through devoted striving, he could achieve such state in this life as becoming unattached to wealth, he can utilise it, could ascend from the path of decline, then he could make him a possessor of hundred million of rupees in this very birth. But neither he has faith in him nor dependence. A devotee seeking motive shall certainly have to act accordingly. The qualities that should prevail in him are absent. He wanted a contract from Bhaijee, wanted to examine Bhaijee, but Bhaijee does not require any certificate that he should appear in an examination. If he really believes in him and becomes dependent on him even for wealth, then his mind would acquire asceticism in this very life or will make him a possessor of crores of rupees by creating such a way to escape. Whatever is requested from him, you will get it because he is like a tree that grants all desires, showing a parental kindness to devotees. Take whatever is required. Someone enquires about rates, while other enquires about fluctuation. He knows which person is asking him about what thing and with which intention. Sometimes he will indeed tell the truth. Sometimes, he would tell lie knowingly so that the faith should decline. He would tell such few things which shall never occur correctly. Don't know if he did it to reduce the faith or with other intention and to whom, but he does everything with proper ordainment without any fault because maternal uncle no more exists in the structure. Now the God Himself is there, whose single nod makes or deteriorates this world. But brother, if the inner heart will not be clear, till then, even by hearing this much of description, things cannot exactly and practically enter inside. To come down is impossible. There are two ways, one to give custody of your life in his hands according to his wish, with a longing through your heart to sacrifice unto his holy feet and secondly, to repeat divine name continuously from your tongue. Please take it as a truth if you have not repeated one lakh divine names daily, then you may hear or read from others, but I could not dare to tell you such an important information. There are still higher things to describe but I don't wish to do so. Please don't be angry. Just do two tasks. When there is the God, His kingdom is also of just that sort, then what is the problem? If He likes, then His grace would get the work done without a diligence. Due to several reasons, I have written things under a heavy cover. I have great love to you. On the one hand, I naturally love a person who talks about Bhaijee with interest, secondly you have taken an oath to repeat one lakh divine names daily. But you may not be probably benefitted at present to hear more than this. I have such a feeling. Dujariji, Goswamiji, Govardhanji (and, today, Foglaji is also present), except these four – I have not described things so openly to anyone. I am describing due to lack of love, it is not at all a reason. If Bhaijee will hear such things, he will definitely be angry to me superficially. You have not to hide from him. If you like and he prefers, then he can read each single thing. I did not say to hide from him. But it should not be disclosed to others. It is my repeated request. I have myself told you this much of things under heavy embarrassment. It had appeared to mind repeatedly to take permission from Bhaijee, but he may refuse on query though it is not hidden from him. I am, in that case, a very wretched person. There are themselves many errors in me. I consider you to be of lower grade, this is not at all a reason, but I don't even wish to speak. Keep on repeating his divine name then whatever is necessary for you, someone will tell, by the inspiration of the God. If someone desires to tell then listen to him, but don't ask from anyone openly. Longing should be there in mind. You may wish through your mind but never ask from the God. The God is then all-powerful. I don't have any fear. If you stop repeating divine names, then faith may not increase. Both things should be maintained with great readiness and with an altogether sacrifice of worldly interests… like if you are also entangled in such dilemma, then it is likely to delay. Do both. A rule for repeating one lakh divine names and then study along with the repetition of name. You can study 25th – 30th chapter through heart. It is possible by practice. Mental worship, pronunciation of divine name by tongue and to ponder. How will it be possible to pronounce the divine name and worship simultaneously? I have told you the best thing previously, of course, covering it a little bit. Be in a habit of repeating the divine name and also develop a true longing to hand over a halter of life in the hands of Bhaijee from your heart, then the teller would explain you forcefully. You can act as in childhood. Maybe in habit to hear or to tell, then it is also alright. There are many benefits as well in it, but the true benefit would be delayed. There is nobody except Dujariji in my opinion, who can really achieve from heart a complete benefit properly towards the path of devoted striving by hearing the instructions from Bhaijee.

(9)

Baba gave in writing to Shri Gambhirchandji Dujari on 24th January, 1942 in the presence of Shri Chimmanlalji Goswami

On the day Bhaijee was blessed by the appearance of the God in Jasidih, there are a lot of differences between that achievement and the present achievement. It was then an appearance of the God, who is highest amongst the triple deities. Whatever had been the appearance, thereafter, it was like the state prevailed in him, like an appearance of God to Dhruva. And, thereafter, then again, a more higher state is achieved by the arrival of Lord Shri Krishna. And, even so, a higher state is achieved and the couple God arrived. Then, even a higher state has also achieved in such a manner when his pride has entirely been immersed within Shri Radha Rani. It means he has become immersed with the eternal idol of Radha Rani. Though such condition is inexpressible and beyond speech, intelligence and mind, but as far as can be commented, that very thing is being described as per the lawful advice. That is such an extraordinary condition that the day on which someone amongst us will really be transformed to a herd girl of Braj, by practicing alongwith the emotion of herd girl of Braj, he would understand it that day exactly and he will also not be able to explain to any other person. It is about an achievement but explanation about a higher state of devoted striving can also never be explained. There is only one way to experience it through devoted striving (*sadhna*). In fact, whatever is the commentary, it is all superficially.

Just think about it, as soon as Bhaijee immersed with Radha Rani, Shri Krishna Himself has become attribute of such five materials. To explain you better, I can say that suppose as is the appearance of five material structures and the behaviour is maintained by it, that is entirely being conducted in the same way as Lord Shri Krishna is expressed in it in the form of Shri Radha-Krishna and then due to his power of total competence, acting as entirely divine being alongwith Bhaijee (with Shri Radha Rani) simultaneously, also took care of the activities of this lifeless world. Precisely, at the same time, when Bhaijee is listening to radio, it appeared to people as if he is being listening to a radio with great interest, but, simultaneously, an entirely blissful act is continuing there evidently. There is only this much of hindrance between that act and you, that there existed a curtain of five materials. Whereupon if a picture is drawn of the act of entire *Vrindavan* and covered it with an earthen pot, then the one who doesn't know the mystery inside the earthen pot, he would find it, as an earthen pot only, what is inside, he can never know, that the sound is coming from the structure of five materials – brother Dulichand, please bring the medicines. This sound has been spoken by him due to inconceivable divine power by the total competence of Shri Radha-Krishna for a destined conduct and has been told at exactly that time when an extraordinary act is being continued there. The words have no power that I could explain to you; my intelligence is perceiving correctly for one thing which cannot be expressed precisely through speech. It is only possible due to his kindness only. You are in lower or upper state, it is not the question. Question is that I cannot express exactly through language even with due thinking about it with proper care. Then what can I do? Therefore, consider like this that Shri Krishna, who is a base form of entire act for present, future or past, He himself has been manifested since five to seven years earlier in this structure and shall remain there if this structure of five elements lives. What would happen here that, as will be the feeling of a person, so shall be his experience accordingly. If *Beni Madhav* likes, then He will visualise in the form of *Sita Ram* because *Lord Shri Krishna* is precisely the *Ram* and *Radha Rani* is precisely the *Sita*. On the very completion of devoted striving, that divine act will only appear in place of this structure. Such is the difference between incarnation of Lord Shri Krishna Himself and the condition prevailed here that descending during the incarnation period does not occur based on structure of five elements. It is entirely self-illusory, where there is no relation of five elements. The curtain belonging to creative power of the supreme spirit (*Yogmaya*) is also not the curtain of five elements. Therefore, an incarnation which prevails here, you can treat differently if Lord Shri Krishna himself has been incarnated alongwith His delightful power, Shri Radha in the form of a frenzy incarnation. He has been incarnated five-seven years earlier from today and such incarnation would prevail till the remaining part with destiny of five materials structure.

It is my opinion and worthless understanding that Shri Radha Rani accompanies only with some great persons of an impenetrable and rare quality for which only one example is Mahaprabhu till today and there is no one in my knowledge or given in the scriptures or among modern saints. The gist is that in the order by which the devoted striving is increased, raising gradually in the same order, Bhaijee has gained such a height that visualisation of Radha Rani Herself, about which *Sage Narad* has been told in the '*Padma-Puran*' by the cowherd people of the Braj themselves, that such a visualisation of Her beauty is even rare to *Lord Shankar and Brahma*, such visualisation of that form, O *Narad* ! has been occurred to you, the same visualisation has also been accomplished by Bhaijee and then he immersed in it. It means the pride without good qualities of a devotee like a concubine, or of a close female friend have all been released and become blessed by getting benefit of beatified state of commission of the soul totally with Radha Rani. The soul which was born 40-50 years ago taking shelter of the structure of Hanuman Prasad, I am that and dissolving this pride altogether in the form that I am Radha, I am dependent on Shri Radha Rani which is enlightened entirely by that blissful kingdom. Whatever speech comes through the sense of the speech that belongs to kingdom of consciousness. Each effort of every sense is active for us based on such conscious, it means the effort made by the subtle body due to presence of soul only, instead of this, the eyeballs, which have been left only in five materials, the light comes in them from that kingdom, which is entirely complete and blissful, it is not like molecular as of the soul. Therefore, future of such people coming into his contact will be the highest and radiant.

Due to inconceivable power of the God, nobody will know it. You can even believe up to that extent by hearing, in which extent the inner heart could be able to accept such thing due to repetition of divine name, being illuminated by his kindness. I also experienced myself this thing that such as an experience has been continued gradually as highly unusual. There is no value of my worthless talk or worthless experience because had it been a true experience, I would already have told you, then my life, my spiritual condition, my attitude towards Bhaijee would have been an ideal to this world, but it does not occur even minutely then these all are pretentious remarks, just so it to be accepted. Therefore, whatever may be. An effort could be made to explain by writing such description, that's it, to let you trust which is not in our control. It is under the control of Shri Radha-Krishna, which is according to my faith, may be incomplete faith, is expressed there in that structure. Therefore, omniscience, omnipresence or whichsoever things have been described in the scriptures till today about Lord Shri Radha Krishna Himself, will be described, absolutely all are present there. But it would be realised to him only who will have an entirely doubtless faith. A little bit of an introduction can be sought if you intend to be a true devotee. But it is to be concealed to those who are non- believers, not to be concealed to believers. His faith shall compel to describe. In this context, Bhaijee himself uttered two-three times such important things in a few words, which caused such an impact on me, not only an impact, but has become totally clear that the state, as explained by Bhaijee, has himself achieved it. In other words, Radha Rani Herself kindly disclosed that I have myself come in to this structure about whose feet you are searching. The soul of Hanuman Prasad has been immersed in me and on its place, I am now with my beloved Shri Krishna. If you want to meet Radha Rani, then you are already with Her since last three years, there is only a curtain of five materials that would be raised timely. Like as in incarnation period, an idol of Shri Krishna established at one place is all-pervading, it can be better understood during the appearance of universal form and during an act of fastening by a rope. Overall, even with restricted-like appearance in one country, he is all-pervading. At that moment, you or someone else will actually visualise Him, it will no more be just a question of country at that time. That country will be totally blessed, which is entirely inexpressible. Bhaijee told me once, during an appearance, there is no existence of this country, which becomes totally blissful. I have understood your question, please accept this answer that you are being fastened in the limit of five materials until you are not visualising such an act. Because that one act only is omnipresent element and is also present in your heart, also present in every atom but that is expressed there. As Lord Shri Krishna who had also diffused in all the acts, in all forms for one hundred and twenty-five years, in the same manner and from the day of achievement till the remaining part of destiny, it is expressed in front of everyone, taking the cover of that structure by blissful act of the supreme twin (Shri Radha Krishna). Being expressible,

He is also all-pervading. Do not know if it has been contemplated or not. It also consists of a heaven but is not expressible.

I can tell you very sweet things. This very thing I wanted to get done. He is attainable and this I have repeatedly told. There had been a sudden blaze to explain today morning. I thought it many times. Though I have no proof, according to letter of Mahatmaji, proof is available only to change the subtle body into blissful form. But there appeared one thing in mind, taking consideration of the real nature of Shri Vrindavan. With the proof available in scriptures and from various means, it is verified that if an incarnation itself exists, not only for that much duration, but that place becomes alive forever. Therefore, such proof is available for the presence of the ultimate being (*Sachchidanandmayee bhoo-rekha*) even after the disappearance of incarnation not only are the thousands of speeches, in thousands of poems of saints residing in Braj, but also in scriptures composed by saints. Therefore, when land of soil has become alive, soil structure of five materials should have also become alive. Because there is no difference particularly in the earthen elements, I have seen at least that much of evidence in scriptures that five materials body of divinely achieved Vaishnava is not made by ordinary five materials. But except like Haridasji, Prakashanandji, and others, others have also found is as lifeless, just like that five-materials body structure of Bhaijee has become divine, but ineligible will found it as lifeless, such feeling has come in mind many times. I have not even a capacity to prove it, but may be assumed for the time being. Though according to my belief, just as much as that is the importance of the dirt of the body of these five-materials structures as much as the dirt of Braj of that time during incarnation period of the God, not of the present age, but Braj dust of that time. An incarnation is now also here, but if there is no faith, then what is the meaning? When idol of Lord Shankar is covered by the brass on the thirteenth day of lunar fortnight and then water is poured on it, will it get the same result by pouring the water with respectful temperament? What is the problem if the idol is covered when it is an idol of Lord Shankar, likewise if there has been thinking of five materials, then according to my doubtless faith, he should also get that result, which is the result by thinking about an actual act, because that is only a cover of actual act and it is that very curtain. O Lord! We are mean, our eyes cannot see inside, we cannot see you behind the curtain, if the worship has been performed with such an intention, then it is my belief that the act would merely be manifested definitely in his inner heart.

(10)

Chakradharji Maharaj replied to the question of Dujariji at Ratangarh on *Bhadra Krishna* 6, Year 1942

Two things are precisely coming to my mind: (i) to pray to God silently with an ardent longing; (ii) if you could do an association of true saint, then tell him with open heart that how I can be attracted towards the God. Such are just these two things that are in actuality and immediately at that moment, at least his craving would definitely be increased.

You would be so much intoxicated at one-time meeting and having affectionate discussion with him that you will yourself feel surprised. It means that such an attachment does not occur in our mind. If there is an attachment, nobody would know it, but the mind will always remain restless and there will always be a hate towards disappointment, sorrow and passion. Where to go, what to do like that nothing would appeal you. On then achieving such a state, the God would Himself start helping in the form of supreme being or will inspire some saint for his help because if it does not happen, then there may occur error just between the affectionate relation of devotee and the God. I grant rewards according to that only, in the way people took shelter in me (The Gita; *4/11*) … as the more restlessness would prevail here. With that same proportion, there would precisely be same restlessness also in the inner heart of the God. Even, at present, and to a small extent, among us, whatever longing of such type appears in our mind, that also influenced the God. And he replied of such mild longing. But until the longing becomes not so strong, till then the reply from the God does not appear exactly in our experience and, therefore, restlessness is felt.

You had told me to discuss something. Probably, this particularly would better suit you. What is the real problem, the God knows it, I don't know it at all. But such is the saying of scriptures that whatever is visible- the God exists there in full form. To experience it – there is a need to establish your divine temperament with someone. For this very reason, there is teacher succession in scriptures, the pupil considers his teacher as the God and tries to sacrifice unto his holy feet, surely such teachers and pupils both are almost scarce today. But there is no scarcity of the God and saints are also not in scarcity, it is only the pupils who are in shortage. Look, a devotee is needed to wait patiently alongwith longing only and his inner longing only has been reflected in the God, in the saint – which are entirely different elements – and then an activity has begun accordingly.

Saint is an active substance and the God is completely and entirely expressed there in every form. The structure only tries according to worldly act, while the complete God who is in his interior, He only acts. Because, in fact, the pride of the saint is entirely disappeared and if it is left, then that pride is such an extraordinary quality that normal person possessing it, cannot just understand it. Therefore, the complete power of the God is expressed there. In the inner heart of every person, though the God is present definitely with His full strength, but there remains a curtain of pride between him and the God, therefore, the God, though already present, is not visible there in all these people, but when that curtain of pride in saint is removed, then he has become entirely divine. Therefore, until remaining part of the destiny, this should be taken for granted that the God is Himself present in the form of a saint. If you don't agree to it, even then the things would be very same, but like *Duryodhan* who, even after visualising the actual Lord Shri Krishna, after teaching many times by him, had not considered Shri Krishna as the God. Therefore, he could not enjoy the benefit of pleasure of his co-residence in the life time, likewise on the day a person achieved the God, since that day, the God Himself in His place, but the non- believer (non-devotees) could obtain little pleasure of His co-residence in their life time. Everyone coming to his contact shall definitely achieved salvation. In eleventh section, the God has Himself counted the names of thirty-forty devotees in relation with the glory of an assembly of virtuous people (Satsang). Commentators have also described about the biography of each of them, i.e., who is benefitted by whom (company). Looking at such an account, it appears that most of them achieved the God in that very life while few of them must take one more birth. Like this, the glory of saint is still the same today. According to time, the faiths of people have reached to a lower level but how can it reduce the glory of the true object, i.e., the God and the saint. It would be all the same even in three eras. Therefore, the saints, who exist today, their glory is still the same, quite unaltered, but it does not come to light due to lack of faith. In earlier times, the glory of saints was displayed soon to the people due to their honest tendency, which is delayed a little at present. The reason is not due to the scarcity of power of saint, the reason is the error in the faith of devotees. It is often misunderstood that there have been saints like *Mahaprabhu Chaitanya*, etc. who have granted salvation to all even without emotion, then I really did not know its reply, but it appears that even an affection bestowed by him to the people has also got difference and an enlightenment in the life of everyone does not occur instantly. Few of them must do devoted striving (*Sadhna*) for a long duration up to this extent that Ramchandrapuri did not also receive affection by him, because he has insulted his teacher. One more thing also prevails here. There is also a general assumption about Mahaprabhu that he was himself the God. If we don't agree to the above statement, then it is also given in scriptures that the God had been specially bestowing His grace from time to time and the saintly people like this have also granted an affection due to divine grace without any obstruction. Now why such grace is bestowed, when it occurs, what is its rule, nobody knows except the God. Therefore, the saints are that very, their capacity is also exactly that but – (i) there is no inspiration by the God to exhibit such miracles (ii) there are also no such devotees due to which miracles may at least appear for them.

I might have seen in your diary or some other place. I don't remember but I have definitely seen it somewhere. Bhaijee had raised a question on problem of cows at the time of actual appearance of the God and the reply given to him was that the plight of the cows will be increased more, it is not the time for their salvation. Now just think yourself, if cows are not dear to the God. Being Gopal, He is still supporting towards this plight that the time is yet to come. Like this, among the devotees without any obstruction, without any temperamental faith, probably there may be any such precise mystery to bestow affection, then I have no information due to which even with the presence of very high, uncommon, extraordinary saints (and with an excessive power, when the God Himself is a saint, then his power must be very much), no such events have come to limelight.

The gist is this that power of the saint is same and that would work as well, in future also that will work. But from themselves, the people should try in a way so that we could feel his grace, but only necessary prerequisite is the desire to develop divine temperament towards saints.

Second thing while I was writing is this, that when the God appears in the statue of lifeless stone due to emotions then where such feeling already existed, if He also appears there, this means on developing divine affection in saints and then visualisation of the God in them, one may begin visualising the God everywhere, then it will not be a surprise.

(11)

Chakradharji Maharaj has given in writing to Dujariji at Ratangarh on Kartik Shukla, 8, in the year 1942

Radha

Look, one thing is faith while the other is an aspiration.

The meaning of faith is that the God exists, the success of life is in His achievement only. Saints are there, to love them is just only success of life and to secure unshakable faith, doubtless faith on such thing, is important. Tomorrow will have sun rise, as you don't have any doubt on such thing, needs no proof, one who says tomorrow will have no sun rise, you will call him mad, like this to develop faith in the God and saints and to achieve their love is precisely known as faith.

The second thing is an aspiration and it is a thing of great importance. Look when there is an incarnation of the God, at that time in his idol and also when there is some saint on this earth, there is just no and entirely no need to show faith towards them, the need is for aspiration because then the power of object (*Vaastu shakti*) remains entirely uncovered (displayed). Now the clear reply of your question is that if you consider Bhaijee as saint then you will have to do faith in him, it is not the question that the substantial power (*Vaastu shakti*) uncovered here. The God did exist at this moment but is not uncovered here (is covered here), at this moment if you have no faith here till then the God will not appear at this moment, but whenever you see a saint, the power of the God (*Bhagwati shakti*) remained entirely evident there, therefore, can appear there even without faith, but the need of aspiration will also be required there. Aspiration means a direction towards him, it means by your mind, by your intelligence, by your soul, by your speech, by your body, join him with all your every particle. In it, it is not entirely necessary to know the elements, to know his form, only this much is needed that without knowledge, without understanding, connect your mind and senses to him, then believe me that object will itself immerse in him in unaltered form. You may not believe it. Take an example of a servant. If he lives with Bhaijee and does not at all know about the spiritual calibre of Bhaijee, but if he could devote himself completely alongwith his mind, etc. and with all his senses, etc., then complete power of Bhaijee himself would immerse in him unknowingly. Such is the glory of physical properties (*Vaastu shakti*). Put faeces in fire. It will form same fire from such dirty smelling faeces, just as the fire forms by sandalwood. Like this, where divine energy (*Vaastu shakti*) is quite evident as an incarnation idol or in the form of a saint, it is a matter of connection only, just connect yourself and you will achieve the goal. The same thing you should also consider in the case of Bhaijee. You have not aspired, not connected otherwise you would have become like him.

When you are now living separately from body, your mind also does not aspire about him, then there is a possibility for the aspiration of money, naturally you will surely join him. Under such circumstances, what can I tell you? No faith, alright, but at least, aspiration should prevail. If you join him only through mind, through speech and through body, he will change you exactly like himself even without faith. It is entirely not desired that you should know the spiritual status of Bhaijee and then put your faith on him. Whatever may be, what can I tell you, you have asked me with due affection and I am also replying with an affection. There was a solution, which you have ignored knowingly and the last solution is now left, for which I had already told that whatever you are: (i) Spare one hour time regularly to connect with Bhaijee, whatever you have heard about Bhaijee, read it in the form of an essay which you might have already possessed; (ii) Pray regularly to the God or to Bhaijee in your mind, O Lord! O Bhaijee! I am trapped in greed of passions. Please be kindful, please fill my inner heart with your love, entirely by yourself; (iii) Whenever you find time or possessed by the feeling, then instantly remind him about yourself through letters. Try to awake your memory in his sacred inner heart irrespective of his proper and timely reply.

Radha Radha.

It is such a befitting solution that if you can exactly believe it that I am caught and everything of mine has been fulfilled, then indeed believe it that without performing anything, you have been definitely caught and everything for you has been achieved. Make sure that no scarcity of faith should occur. Let other confuse you but no disappointment should appear even for a moment, then the entire responsibility goes on his shoulders. He would precisely do everything. The fact is that all the living beings have been dancing as per His will. Your visit to that place, to query with me, my reply, all these activities are being controlled by his cord.

The fact is if there remains a pride, till then, there are joy and sorrow, when the player once comes in front of the puppet, knows truly to himself that I was dancing with the help of cord, that's all, then there remains only joy and bliss to him.

(12)

Swami Chakradharji Maharaj has given in writing during chronic sickness to Shivdayalji Goyndaka at Churu on Paush Shukla..... in the year 1942.

Look, teacher tradition has been disappeared now because there has been a scarcity of deserving pupil and deserving teachers. But look to every scripture, a guide has generally been found in the life of every saints. To me, I only remember each time both Sethji and Bhaijee who can help you completely with great accessibility. It is quite true that the God is completely independent, and a true saint mixes his desire to His desire but as I have requested, it does not go in vain to make repeated requests from your heart to a saint because the God Himself begins to answer your prayer.

Look! I have knowingly not shown my faith to Bhaijee or Sethji. We entirely do not have real faith towards these persons, but such trust has been thrust in my mind by some extreme reliable sources that these two grandeurs are very extraordinary, and it is entirely my doubtless faith that your request coupled with love can materialise one out of two things, entirely at this moment and today itself.

(i) Either your mind becomes entirely quite free from all types of worries, may become dependent on the God, such may be the condition of mind having no worry to this world with a feeling that I would definitely be blessed by an appearance, such firm faith, such strong faith should prevail so that it should appear that in the way Bhaijee has gone to city and has informed to come back soon, just that sort, the God will also come soon.

(ii) Or may actually visualise because believe me, it is my high of highest belief which is with us, i.e., whatever has been spoken by Sethji/ Bhaijee, that sentence is clearly related with the kingdom of the God without any hindrance. Look, whatever good or bad words have been spoken by each individual, it is also related with kingdom of the God, but it contains of a curtain of pride. In my opinion both persons are such where there has been entirely no such hindrance. I cannot let anyone trust me. I myself did not know anything. It can be just my temperament but whenever you will ask me then I would say the very thing only which will be the best thing to you in my opinion.

(13)

Chakradharji Maharaj at Churu has written to Shivdayalji on Paush Shukla in 1942

In fact, we do not at all know the glory of the God, otherwise a person who could get an opportunity to visualise the God, one who achieved the God, how much rank can be of such person, how much power is possessed – by assuming such things all pain disappears and the God appears in each and every atom. Whatever I can emphasise if I could have achieved such a higher state then you have probably believed it.

But two rarest of the rare divinities are in front of you, if you wish then can take benefit just now from this moment. Believe on the words given in scriptures:

The seventh type of religious devotion (Bhakti) is to recognize with an equality, the whole world as consisting of me (Shri Ram) and treat the saints higher than me.

(*RamcharitManas/Arayanakand/35:3*)

It is an entirely a true thing. In fact, the glory of the saint is precisely the glory of the God but the God Himself has thrusted the honour for appearance of Himself just on the forehead of saints, such has been a law forever. In views of saints there is no one is greatest than the God and in the view of devotee himself there is nobody higher than the God. But where an actful identity (*Lilamay Swarup*) of the God exists, the devotee is responsible, everything is a prerogative of the devotee. Such prerogative is due to the knot of love. But it is so strong that you can actually see its example even today if you desire so.

Ram may be the Lord of universe, but He is brother of *Laxman* and not the Lord of universe. Such pleasure occurs by the sight of saints and should occur.

(14)

To Dujariji, Goswamiji at the evening of Paush Shukla 2, in the year 1941

Shri Sethji is himself a highly eminent person and I cannot be indebted to him, he only made me so deserving that I could be able to experience a little kindness of Bhaijee. In fact, to live three years with him, how I have felt being separated from Bhaijee, it is a long history and it has all done due to an inspiration of the God but those who are with him, everyone is not Sethji. I have great love to Ramsukhdasji, he has committed a mistake which he does not know. Once, don't remember the place, he had uttered in front of someone, to mediate just on Sethji. I have been informed by reliable sources that such statement has caused a very bad impact on many persons. Such statement made by Ramsukhdasji is quite correct and is a thing of entire benefit, he said a true thing, but those who had no such faith on Sethji, it has caused just a bad impact on them. It has become entirely a misutilisation of a true statement. A great person like Shri Sethji is born rarely but the status of Bhaijee in front of the devotees of Sethji is very inferior. Take it as truth, I love very much to Sethji and I have regards with his every single association of virtuous people but also never did any criticism of Bhaijee in front of anyone even on any account. Just to imagine that I had any enmity with Sethji would be a great injustice to me. But when the question arises of faith and love, such is my feeling, there in relation to Bhaijee which cannot be described. Despite this, if these people slightly criticise Bhaijee then I wish to leave that place or bear it. Sometimes with my high and real feelings towards Sethji, I begun discussing it to make him happy. The gist is that I did not like it at all the effort by anyone for an eminence to be set up of Bhaijee even at that assembly. I feel such an afraid of Govardhanji that he may misuses somewhere of my such statement due to his simplicity. One of the defects in him is this that he does not repent for it even by performing such fault. I have also noticed that once informed, he can also say it – what is the harm, if the people know, it would benefit them, he probably cannot think of such idea that Swamiji would be highly irritated. I am writing it, just to let him read, he will also discuss with me affectionately but if he wishes to listen to my words and wants benefit from it, then I did not like that he should follow me, but then he should agree to my terms. If such words are described by both of you, then it will be by mistake or if it will be made knowingly, then it is my faith that this much shame will be in your mind that Swamiji has forbidden it. But I will treat such condition as if it was desired by Shri Krishna, thus is alright. Though whatever he will do, will do with the wish of Shri Krishna, but it should also be surely accepted by him, that if he assumes it would benefit the people as desired by Shri Krishna, i.e., why I have spoken such, then it should also be considered that is it not an inspiration by Shri Krishna of denial from my end? I like him from my heart but unless he is not ready to resume such of his faith till then I am a hesitant. Take it as an ascertainment that who will be benefitted by such word, i.e., you or someone also would automatically reach to him by some destined coincidences. Because everything is being managed only under the control of all powerful God. Therefore, even being enthusiastic one should think patiently. Tell them frankly that I don't consider him less than Dujariji and Goswamiji but due to two of his weaknesses means lack of faith directed towards one object, (it may be my suspicion) secondly his habit to disclose the things atonce to others, due to these two reasons, I am naturally hesitant in my mind. If he decides truly himself by a clear mind to remove these two faults, then I have no objection. I would have then even shown it that very day. And if he would have forced me a little bit, then I would have told him that very day to experience it, but it will reduce his benefit.

Look, as far as Radha Rani is concerned, nobody has such a power in world that it may be misused. If it occurs, it would be only towards his prosperity. We should definitely be careful from our end, and then we are not attempting, by any means, any wrong thing for which we are required to weep and wail.

I wish to repeat such thing again and again that Shri Sethji is also a rare divinity of the world, but for me, I follow the *phrase like, that Lord **Shiva** is a residence of defects.* Whosoever are his followers, I put the dust of their feet on my forehead.

(15)

Place – Ratangarh Time – Night
Date – Paush, Shukla 13
Presence – Shri Goswamiji, Dujariji, Govardhanji

Look, there is no need to be disappointed or dejected even for a tiny amount. The company in which you are moving nowadays, if it does not break, then no second question arises. Probably, if we are caught in some terrible bad company, then only this association may break, otherwise we have all been tied once by the rope of grace by Bhaijee. Now there is no any power which may allow you to separate even willingly. Even if you move, then you must return after wandering for few days. Cannot live without such company, because you are living due to his grace, it is also not due to your manliness even for a tiny amount. If he likes, in other words, he would like to play with someone, then may go for few days, otherwise it's impossible, no one can leave. Therefore, just utilise the company as much as possible and take it for granted and accept it without any doubt that at least five-seven persons, who are under my watch, if these people become deserving person to the true company of Bhaijee whose grace will eliminate complete dirt in a moment and will bless them and in case Bhaijee prefers to end his life earlier then he would take care of them till the remaining part of their destiny. If even aspired a little bit, then will control by making an actual appearance, otherwise would control in an invisible form. The gist is that few people who are going to maintain such an intention (like the way just now shown by Dujariji) towards Bhaijee, they may be wicked up to any extent. Bhaijee within a moment would make them entitled to move alongwith him by his grace without any motive. There is nothing impossible for him. No circumstances can make any hindrance for the completion of his desire, like no rule is applicable for Shri Radha Krishna, He is also all independent, of just that sort, no rule is also applicable for him. There is no binding of any type even for a tiny amount. He can just do whatever is his desire. Therefore, to appoint anyone to a very high office within a moment is a play of laughing matter to him. I have already narrated to you about the matter given in 'Padma Purana'. Shri Krishna asked to a herd girl of Braj for a devotee – Please transform him like you. Instantly that herd girl of Braj has transformed him into a herd girl by performing an identical thinking and put him unto the holy feet of Shri Krishna and asked him by supplying him a lute – you should sing hymns to my Lord. Like this or by an extraordinary way than this, Bhaijee will put alongwith him those 5-7 people by transforming them like him within a moment in the service of Shri Krishna, such is my firm belief. Due to such strong faith, I can say that I did not enquire such things from Bhaijee, but I have no doubt, there is absolutely no doubt even for a little amount. Yes, I am definitely afraid sometimes, due to such reasons about which it cannot be said that what is the motive in those feet, if Bhaijee desires to play, wishes to lead a round someone for a few days, then this poor man would reach him after some delay. Why would such act will occur, nothing can be said – there is no unevenness that to accept one and refuse to other? But you might have heard about the story in scriptures about *Jay-Vijay* attendants, likewise there will be no surprise if such an act may also occur by him. If it does not occur, then these five-seven people, all without an exception would achieve best destiny. In other words, as far as is the limit of speech, is the approach of mind, accordingly to that, would achieve best spiritual state, being remain follower of Bhaijee for eternity to never-ending duration and would also obtain right in serviceful act of Shri Krishna.

I have asked you again several times to be his follower with a reason that grace of Bhaijee should not be misutilised to misutilise the grace and also for delay in accompanying him, probably he should definitely be ready for punishment. Every fault can be excused for followers, their every fault will be considered as his own by Bhaijee. Therefore, for it, an entirely doubtless, without fear, fearless future, extraordinary auspicious future is decided, but out of these 5-7 who would not show an effort to be his follower, though to become his follower will be only due to his grace, but an effort, longing, a light of heartily longing in the inner heart should definitely prevail there. Otherwise, think about it, think with intelligence that only who has become his follower, if he does not receive some special prize, then it is useless thing to be his sincere follower. Then there will be no difference between good and the best. Then what is the meaning if Bhaijee has done that very thing to a person who had sacrificed totally everything than he has done to a normal devotee. It is not the rule of the God, though he is all-independent, has no restriction but to fulfill correctly and completely for his own act, it generally creates a difference of haste and delay between those who are followers and those who are not. It is in order if he becomes follower up to last moment, then it does not matter because he has joined the line of follower then there is no such thought that he is a follower since so many days or he has joined just now, there is no question of the period, there exists everything in present tense. Therefore, a longing should definitely be awakened to be a follower. It requires no efforts even for a little amount. Dujariji and Goswamiji would understand my such words in some better way due to many reasons. Such an extraordinary object is present in these five material structures that whatever amount of faith is present, no more faith is needed than this, only need is to aspire. Once you have become aspired, that extraordinary existent property (*Vaastuguna*) which is expressed there in that structure in extremely clear shape, would itself attract towards him like a magnet. If it is not attracting, then I can say this according to my worthless intelligence that though the faith is sufficient, but without aspiration. Attachment for sensual pleasure, attachment for family, worldly interest has been in between, which inhibits the stream of grace. Though so much is the strength in the existent property that it will win, these all would have flown in the stream of that kindness but when such faults still exist with us, then it should be assumed that they have yet to come with the contact of stream along power of grace otherwise must have floated by now, so be it. Now no need to worry. Like previous day, I repeat the same thing – to remain in the maximum company of him with your mind, speech and body. A very good mental association exists between Bhaijee and Dujariji. It is the best method to meditate day and night towards his teaching. It would give an extraordinary result. **The herd girls of Braj had treated Lord Shri Krishna as supreme beloved**. But they had not immersed ultimately with him (*Brahmbhava*). According to such an ethic, even not being aware about the real form of Bhaijee, his actual form will definitely come in front without doubt, it would not be required to acquaint, everything will start to be visible clearly, present inside that structure.

The method of Dujariji is one of the best methods, though there is definitely a more higher method than this, which may bring in front of the form of Bhaijee, very quickly but you will have to do that practice from the beginning. But that is somehow not required to us. Whatever we have heard about Bhaijee, that very is sufficient, it is to be thought over again and again with your mind and to be discussed entirely amongst devotees by accumulating your total intelligence, total patience, until it is possible, till then try to accompany Bhaijee as much as possible. This will be a mental union through speech, through action and through mind. By performing such behaviour, an attraction will increase in such a speed towards Bhaijee that it will feel as if it is being done due to magic. Suddenly Bhaijee will look in between towards you extraordinarily with such an affection that you would be carried away by love.

At present, you observe his laughing, also touch his hands, you also receive much pleasure, but that bliss is so boundless and of such an extraordinary type which you have just not yet seen. The inner self would be entitled to experience that pleasure with three such efforts, i.e., through work, through speech and mentally and then such bliss will be increasing more and more. Such scene and feeling which are brought in front of you today due to his laughing shall really bring you back many times more than that, about which an imagination cannot even occur at present. The importance of the structure of five materials is not yet taken up at present in front of us. I can tell you one thing of high importance. The feet dust of Bhaijee is not at all less than the dust of Braj. To live alongwith Bhaijee is precisely like the living in Braj. Rather it is higher than this, which I don't want to write due to several reasons. The various reasons due to which the Braj has received importance, stronger reason than that is expressed inside this structure. Dujariji and Goswamiji can imagine a little bit about it. It is quite such an extraordinary thing that even on its repetition again and again, it is also difficult to guess a little. But it is such an extraordinary thing that nothing can be said. The imagination of people has not reached up to that extent till today that is such an extraordinary thing. It is my firm faith that true knowledge for real identity of him, it means what he is in real sense, its exact knowledge will not be known even by several repetitions of such thing by me. It is only possible due to blessing of Bhaijee.

Whatever you may, hear or speak about Bhaijee on the basis conformable to scriptures but such is an extraordinary spiritual stage with Bhaijee that various commentaries cannot touch even the shadow of the real stage of affairs (*Vastusthiti*).

It is only to convey that as much as higher an imagination of you can reach, imagine up to that extent and dedicate unto the feet of Bhaijee. In fact, Bhaijee is truly a tree that grants all desires of the devotees.

Therefore, I suggest that request him for the best demand, i.e., to love unto his feet.

❐

74

Financial Arrangement

It has been a curiosity in the mind of several people that how Bhaijee managed his expenses. He had already given up his trade at the age of 35, had no big amount with him. Then what was the arrangement towards the expenses? Many people had the wrong notion that Bhaijee was managing his expenses through '*Kalyan*'. Once a familiar person came to Bhaijee and had enquired during general talks that how much he had saved from '*Kalyan*'. Bhaijee explained to him that there was generally always a loss in '*Kalyan*' or it was almost at par, i.e., no profit, no loss. The person further asked – it is alright, but I am asking this being your own family member. Actually, it was not coming into his understanding that why a person will take such pains without profit. Bhaijee then further said to him that I did not take even a single paise from '*Kalyan*' and '*Kalyan*' has not been published with an intention to earn money. It had come to his understanding or not, but Bhaijee had not at all any financial relation from Gita press or '*Kalyan*'. This thing is indisputable. So much so that the place, where he had lived at Gorakhpur, was purchased by Shri Sethji and one of his relatives had given it to a trust, later which was managing Gita press. Bhaijee had then started to pay rent towards his part of living to Gita press once it was transferred to the trust. When Bhaijee left Mumbai and had come to Gorakhpur, at that time, some good wisher deposited rupees twenty thousand in the name of his mother and his wife and the household expenses were met by the interest received from this deposit. The frugality had existed right from childhood in the life of Bhaijee. He never permitted unnecessary expenditure on himself even up to an end. One can feel such an impression of changed time upon the new members of family. Bhaijee had written in this context in his will – "… but due to grace of God, I never approached to any friend for financial help. The financial contact had remained only with that one family and normal person who does not normally believe in the difference of 'self-other' between himself and me. Rather, who feels sorry by such an imagination."

❐

75

Third Plan to Spread the Divine Name

According to the instruction of God, Bhaijee has started for an arrangement to spread divine name, wherever he lived for several days. On arrival from Dadri, he had a mind to live few days this time at Ratangarh. Therefore, he became active here as well, with his favourite work. In the beginning on 26th November 1939, he began non-stop celebration of devotional songs (*sankeertan*) and also an arrangement for an exposition of religious texts with great zeal. Several people have come from outside, many saints have also arrived. An arrangement was made for exposition of religious text in the afternoon while Bhaijee had managed assembly of virtuous people (*satsang*) during night. Like this, non-stop celebration of devotional songs and other types of arrangements had also begun since 28th August, 1940, 9th November, 1940 and 16th January, 1941. Due to lack of space, it is not possible to describe them all in detail. Since the night of Lord Shiva (25.02.1941), a non-stop celebration of devotional songs has started for seventeen days at the residence of Bhaijee. Such function was planned to continue till Chaitanya birthday celebration, but this non-stop celebration of devotional songs was continued day and night for more than two years due to distinctive grace of God. Then it began again and continued from April, 1943 to July, 1944 from 6 o'clock in the morning till 11 o'clock at night, i.e., seventeen hours daily. Meanwhile, Shri Prabhu Dutt Brahmachari and Shri Haribaba have arrived at Ratangarh. It has inspired Bhaijee more and it was decided to arrange a grand celebration of devotional songs and a saint-ceremony for seventeen days. Due to Second World War in that period, several Marwaris have returned to their homes at Ratangarh from Bengal and Assam. Such occasion was especially suitable to spread the divine name. A short description can be seen as follows in the words of Shri Prabhu Dutt Brahmchari:

"I went to meet Bhaijee to his paternal place at *Ratangarh*. He asked me to stay for, few days at Ratangarh. I told – what for? No function has been arranged though, there are so many rich people in this place. He replied seriously and very slowly in great enthusiasm – whenever you like, as you like, function can be arranged. I replied – I must arrange for new year celebration this year at *Muzaffarnagar*. We will do it some other time. Bhaijee said – 'Sooner is the better'. Please arrange new year celebration at this place only. It may be arranged here for fifteen days while the remaining fifteen days may be held at Muzaffarnagar. Discussion was held properly and due to his promise, such was a grand success of the function at Ratangarh that every person from *Marwar* had declared that such type of function had never been held nor would be held in future. The children of highly rich people had been available entirely to do all types of small services like to arrange shoes for the audiences, to broom the road, to fan with hands, etc. How much influence he had on the wealthy society, I have only witnessed such sight for a fortnight, being present at Ratangarh. Due to Second World War, most of the money-lenders have returned to their states leaving Calcutta. They love Bhaijee more than their breath and Bhaijee by putting hands on the shoulders of those tender teenagers like an extremely affectionate father talks to his dear sons, just in that manner, he gives them order for insignificant and inferior type of services and those teenagers from the families endowed with crores of rupees and millions of rupees, obeyed his orders with great zeal. They take it as their great opportunity, who obtains an order from Bhaijee.

He was so cheerful that he remained laughing at all occasions. Whatever had been observed at my end, he would burst out in laughter. A procession was held at Ratangarh. There are many camels in this desert. I sat, my back in front, on the camel and moved out with city- group singing of hymns. My face was towards the tail of camel. Seeing me sitting thus, during procession, he just kept on laughing indiscriminately……"

Shri Brahmachari sat facing backside on the camel so that he could see the magnificence and grandness of the procession. His camel has arrived from station to railway bridge, even then he could not see the other end of the procession. There were several group-singing of hymns, an exhibition of Lord Ram, an exhibition for the act of Shri Krishna and musical instruments, etc. Great saints, devotees and best narrators on the *Manas* and *the Bhagwat* have also arrived from several places. An arrangement was made for the assembly of saints in the background of the building of Bhaijee. The following was the daily routine:

Morning:

5-6 : Group celebration of devotional songs (*sankeertan*) by Hari Baba.

6-9: A group engrossment for *Shri Ramcharitmanas*.

9-11: An exposition for the act of Shri Krishna by the group of round dance from Vrindavan.

11-12: Group celebration of devotional songs by respected Hari Baba.

2-6: Discourses, etc. Evening:

7-8: Group celebration of devotional songs by respected Shri Hari Baba.

Night:

8-11: An exposition of the enactment of Shri Chaitanya by the group of round dance (*ras-mandali*) from Vrindavan.

To witness such an assembly of saints, people have come from hundreds of miles. Many have stayed throughout the duration. Shri Raghunathdasji from Shri Ramanuj sect, who was chief of Shri Rangji temple of Vrindavan, sang '*Shri Dashawatarstotram*' by Shri Jaidev during his access of emotion. He has not only remained engrossed himself in the ocean of existence (*Bhava-sagar*), but also immersed the devotees.

On the conclusion of function, Bhaijee had given a farewell, full of feelings to all saints and sages. Everybody had returned with an immutable impression of the function in their hearts.

A vast *'Vishnu Yagya'* was arranged on 9th April, 1943. Many people from outside had also arrived to attend it.

❐

76

Recuperating at Ajmer

Bhaijee went to *Delhi* to attend marriage of Vishnu Hari – elder son of his friend Shri Jay Dayalji Dalmia on *Vaishakh Krishna* 11 in the year 1943. From there, he went to *Swargashram* for the assembly of virtuous people. From Swargashram, he went to Mumbai due to sickness of Shri Parmeshwarji Fogla. He had arranged an assembly of virtuous people (*satsang*) several times in the *satsang* building. On his arrival back to Ratangarh, Bhaijee had become sick. He was caught by a new disease of piles alongwith other diseases. On the next day of *Janmashtami*, he moved to Delhi for treatment, but instead of improvement, his condition had become very bad due to terrible headache and malaria fever. It appeared as if he would retain his life or not. Therefore, each of the family members was called through telegram at Delhi. Due to unsatisfactory improvement, he moved to *Ajmer* on 10th October, 1943. From there, he went to *Pushkar* for sight-seeing. There was one-time relief in Ajmer by the treatment of Dr. Ambalal. By visiting *Kankroli*, *Nathdwara* and *Udaipur*, he returned back to Ratangarh on 9th November, 1943. Again, due to increase in pain, he moved to Ajmer via Bikaner. He was operated for a blister in his anus. Shri Pyarelalji Daga, Baba, Ram Sanehiji and Dr. Ambalal had served him with a highly affectionate readiness. Later, it was also known that such disease was taken on his body in lieu of some other person. From there, Bhaijee had written the description about that period in a letter:

!!Shri Hari!!

10.12.1943, Ajmer

Dear Brother…… ,

Let us remember the almighty with love.

You have enquired about my health, it is as usual, the condition of wound is improving according to physician. Bandage was applied with castor oil after operation which has caused pain. There remains somewhat more pain and restlessness. Today, the condition is better than yesterday. I felt ecstatic by reading your letter. Brother, it is a fact, you all belong to me. There is no anxiety in my soul. I have been experiencing the grace of God at every step. Though this time the sickness has been very painful… but an exposition of the auspicious grace by the God has been evident, from time to time, here as well. This world is a platform of theater of the God, which requires the acting with all flavours. But within the interval of each acting, he is evident. In fact, play and players both are his auspicious identities....

Yours, Hanuman

Bhaijee returned to Ratangarh on 3rd July, 1944 from Ajmer. There occurred pain again due to piles, then it had become cured automatically. At Ratangarh, Bhaijee has arranged an offering of eye donation camp and organised a grand camp by inviting a famous eye surgeon from *Bhiwani* in which thousands of villagers had been benefitted by the operation and people returned back by acquiring eye-sight.

On 25th March 1944, a rite had begun for 108 repetitions of the *Shrimad Bhagwat* by sixteen Brahmins at the residence of Bhaijee and thereafter non-stop celebration of devotional songs (*sankeertan*) was arranged for seven days. ❑

77

Swami Shri Sharnanandji at Ratangarh

During July 1944, a non-stop recitation of the verses on the glory of Lord Shiva was arranged for several days at the residence of Bhaijee. Swami Sharnanandji Maharaj arrived at Ratangarh on 22nd July, 1944 and stayed just with Bhaijee for many days. Then Bhaijee had gone to Bikaner with him to meet the king of Bikaner for the inauguration of tap for water to the public through his hands at Ratangarh. He had consented for the inauguration due to request made by Bhaijee. On 5th November 1944, Shri Karpatriji Maharaj arranged a grand rite in Varanasi and Bhaijee went to join this celebration. Bhaijee had given there an impressive lecture to oppose 'Hindu-code-bill'. From there, he attended the meeting of Govind Bhawan Trust at Gorakhpur and then returned to Ratangarh. A rite for group commeasuring of 108 Ramcharit Manas and non-stop repetitions of the Bhagwat for 18 days had been made in Ratangarh from 17th December, 1944 to 3rd January, 1945 for the welfare of the World. Then again from 22nd March, 1945 to 13th April, 1945 during whole inter-calary month, an arrangement has been made for non-stop repetition of the Bhagwat with great zeal. During these days, Bhaijee was also elected as a member of legislative assembly of Bikaner, which was treated that time also as a reputed position as well but Bhaijee has immediately sent a letter of resignation.

❒

78

Feeling an Intimacy with Malviyaji

In the words of Bhaijee:

My acquaintance to the worth remembering at early morning and noble-minded Shri Malviyaji and whose feet are to be revered, had been since 1906. At that period, I was living in Calcutta. Whenever he arrived, I went to see him. He was very kind to me from the beginning to the end and which enhanced more and more. I had family-type relation with him. He treated me like his son and I also treated him more than a respectful father and, as such, I did not call him '*Panditji*' but always 'Babuji'. He conveyed all his family matters to me. I have been in his very close contact for some time. Therefore, I found an opportunity to see and understand him very closely. He had multifarious talent and his field of activity was also very vast. In addition to be ultimately religious, he was also an unravelled politician. Defending an ancient immemorial religion and education, expansion with an extension of true education in public was the main aim of his life. By mentioning few reminiscences of his sacred life here in brief, I am feeling myself as sacred:

Once he came to Gorakhpur and just stayed with me for two-three days. On second day morning of his arrival, I was sitting near his feet. He was alone. With great affection, he told – Brother! I want to give you a rare and precious thing. I have received it from my mother as a boon. It is very a wonderful thing. I did not give it to anyone till today, but giving it to you, it may look very small but is in a great benefaction form. Like this, he continued speaking on its importance for half-an- hour. My curiosity has been gradually increasing. I told him impatiently

Babuji, please hurry up, someone may come in. He said – It is an incidence of about forty years ago. Once I went to my mother and requested her for a boon with great humility – "Please grant me such a boon by which I may get success wherever I go."

Mother placed her hand on my head affectionately and said – "Son! I am giving you a very rare thing. When you intend to go to any place then, at that time of departure, pronounce '*Narayan, Narayan*'. You would always be successful. With due respect, I vowed my head and accepted the sacred verse from mother. Hanuman Prasad! I still remember since then till today, whenever I forgot to pronounce '*Narayan*, *Narayan*', then I became unsuccessful. Otherwise, in my life, due to effect of pronouncing '*Narayan, Narayan*' at the time of departure, I have never been unsuccessful. Today the supreme thing given by my mother, such a great sacred verse, I am giving it to you, you may get benefit by it, by saying this Malviyaji became ecstatic.

I have accepted his boon by putting it on my head and received high benefit from this. Now such a thing happened that everyone at home learned it. Now during movement outside by anyone from the residence, instantly children have begun to pronounce '*Narayan, Narayan*'. Like this daily and several times on the same day, '*Narayan*' along with sacred memory of respectful Malviyaji had been refreshed. When I was residing in Mumbai, a Congress convention was held at Amritsar. Lokmanya Tilak was its President. I reached Amritsar from Mumbai alongwith one of my young friends. It was the month of December. There occurred a terrible rain that year in Amritsar, a few days ago. The winter is famous in Punjab and due to such rains, there had been a high increase of cold. We did not see such winter in Mumbai.

Therefore, I went there with normal clothes. Both had one bedsheet and light a blanket as bedding.

We stayed at a halting place of Malviyaji in Amritsar. An accommodation was provided for us in a large rest house for pilgrims. Probably, Mahatma Gandhi was also staying in it. We both slept on the cots during night. The body was shivering. We had been lying holding our knees close to our chest. We covered our faces by blanket, but our bodies were trembling. It should be 9 o'clock at night. By observing everyone, Malviyaji came near to our cot. By observing us drawing together and covering our faces, he asked – Who are you, where have you come from? Have you eaten something? I have removed cloth from my face. I immediately jumped on my feet and touched his feet. My friend also got up and touched his feet. We both were shivering. By identifying us, he asked – Where are your beddings? I said this is just my bedding which I have laid and covered. He was surprised – Is this all your bedding? Don't you know how much cold prevails here? How could you treat Amritsar as Mumbai? Expressing such fake anger, he asked one of his accompanied Punjabi persons – Bring eight blankets immediately. Then he again asked us – Have you eaten something? I said – Yes, we did it. Then he said – Look, you have made a great mistake by not informing me. I have come by the way, otherwise you people would be in great trouble at night and don't know what would have been its effect? Why have you been so formal? What can I reply? Meanwhile, few people have brought eight blankets. Two blankets each have been spread on our cots while the remaining two have been left for use as cover by us. He arranged for the tea and had given us to drink. Until we had not slept after drinking tea, till then he remained sitting there on a chair. We wanted to sleep only after his departure, but he insisted – Until you sleep by covering yourselves, till then I will not go. Therefore, we had to sleep. Our souls had moved by looking at his such an affection.

Malviyaji had four sons – Ramakant, Radhakant, Mukund and Govind. Out of them Malviyaji had sent Mukund to me in Mumbai. He had stayed there for a longer duration. Later, Radhakant also left his practice of law and moved to Mumbai from Allahabad – to start commercial transaction. Due to faith and advice of his friend, Radhakant has begun the business for commercial transactions. But Radhakant was ruined. During the same period, I had to go to Varanasi. I went to see Malviyaji. He was very sad due to destruction of Radhakant.

On my return to Mumbai, I received a telegram from Malviyaji in which it was written – Tell Radhakant to recite '*Gajendramokshastrotra*' with confidence and distressfully his debts will be refunded. I informed about this instruction of Malviyaji to Radhakant, but he did not take any note of it. Later on, I have received a letter from Malviyaji. He had written about the experience for importance of recitation of '*Gajendramokshastrotra*'. I have been ruined up to brim, due to debt. I have faithfully and distressfully recited '*Gajendramokshastrata*' and my debt has been repaid.

We had gone to Malviyaji after meeting with Gandhiji along with Baluramji, a broker for divine name of Ram. Malviyaji had stayed in the house of king Govindlalji Pitti. On reaching there, we bowed before him. Malviyaji asked for an introduction of Panditji. I gave him full introduction and also told the reason to bring him along with. Malviyaji heard it in full detail with great affection, enquired several times and highly appreciated Panditji. Later, had signed. he was very eager. Exactly just are his words – Since when I have become conscious, from then I recite daily the divine name and if I am alive, I shall do it regularly.

There are several more recollections towards affection of Malviyaji.

❐

79

Solution of Water Problem in Ratangarh

To get rid of hindrances for construction of proposed waterworks and to solve water problem of Ratangarh, Bhaijee had arranged its inauguration by the hands of king of Bikaner. The following is its foremost background.

Due to lack of water tap in Ratangarh, the residents had to face lot of problems. There was also a well of Shri Durgaduttji Tharad. Vacant land was also there, and he wanted to solve the water problem by constructing a water tank with his own expenses but the vacant land near the well, where he wanted to build water tank, had been used by Muslims to exhibit their *tazias* and utilised for other activities. If a work of water arrangement is done on that vacant land, then it may receive a blow in the interest of Muslims and other neighbours. Therefore, such planning had not been successful due to their protest. He could not succeed even by meeting with government officers. They informed Bhaijee everything that due to some selfish people, such work for general interest was not getting success. Bhaijee did not agree to interfere in between because there was an apprehension of riot unnecessarily, when even government officers had also not been cooperating in it. Success was difficult. As such, Durgaduttji had become more disappointed. But as *Tulsidas* requested through Jankiji to pray to Lord Ram – at an appropriate time, mother may find out a suitable occasion. Likewise, in the life of Bhaijee as well, people at many occasions had also took shelter of Maiya (wife of Bhaijee) to get any work done by Bhaijee. In this very manner, Durgaduttji told Maiya on a suitable occasion that the well, land and money are all ours but even then, such arrangement is not being managed by which everybody may be benefitted with water. Bhaijee was also requested but he did not accept it. If you can speak to him on a suitable occasion, then this work probably may be completed. Maiya replied – It would cause a benefit of water to whole city, come on, I ask him just now. Both have come to Bhaijee and Maiya asked – Why don't you get this work done for them? Bhaijee replied – Is it the work of my home? There is an apprehension of riot in this, with Muslims. Maiya had boosted his moral – When will your ability and acquaintances be utilised? The whole city will be benefitted with water. Bhaijee then replied – I will think over. After thinking a little bit, Bhaijee then suggested – There is a solution, your work will be done, but publicity of name will not be given for Tharads. Durgaduttji had accepted such a solution.

The queen of that time of Bikaner had treated Bhaijee as his adopted brother and had high regards. She had also sent '*rakhi*' on *Rakshabandhan*. Bhaijee had written a letter to her that one of his close persons desires to construct water-work at Ratangarh, so that water facility may be available to whole of the city. The name of this water- work will be in the name of king of Bikaner "Shri Shardul free-supply water-works". Some local people are creating hindrances. A letter of request is also being written to emperor, the king of Bikaner. Please make a personal request so that the royal command may be issued about it by him.

A letter of request was sent to the king of Bikaner. When Bhaijee went to Bikaner on 30th July, 1944 alongwith Swami Sharnanandji, he also met the king and queen of Bikaner and discussed about it. An approach made by Bhaijee was found quite correct. A royal command was issued for construction of waterworks and the emperor also agreed to come for inauguration. The Muslims could know about it and tried to run to and fro but were unable to do anything against royal command and "Shri Shardul-free-supply waterworks" was constructed which had solved the problem of water scarcity for the whole population of Ratangarh.

❒

80
An Affectionate Relation with Mahatma Gandhi

In the words of Bhaijee:

I have been in very close contact with *Bapu* and I have found an opportunity to watch him very closely. My acquaintance with him was very old (since 1915) but when I lived in Mumbai, Mahatmaji was living at Sabarmati refuge at Ahmedabad. At that time, I had been visiting refuge in between at several times. When he comes to Mumbai, due to working in business matter with late Bhai Jamnalalji Bajaj, I was responsible for the complete hospitality to Mahatmaji from his end. Mahatmaji visited my residence several times in Mumbai. Such was his relation pertaining to a family with me, as it was with his son Bhai Devdas.

There are many sweet remembrances in relation to Bapu. Some of them are being given below:

1. Gandhiji had arrived in Mumbai and was staying at Juhu. He was a little bit sick. I alongwith Sister Shanti Devi went to meet Gandhiji. During these days, a newspaper '*Navjivan*' was published by Gandhiji in Gujarati. When we were going to Juhu, got a copy of '*Navjivan*' on the way. It was published in it – 'Gandhiji is sick, no one should go to meet him'. By that time, we have almost reached near Juhu. We thought we are already very near, can go up to bungalow, but will not meet. On reaching at the residence, we found Bhai Devdas at the ground floor. We have enquired about the health of Bapu and tried to return. Bhai Devdas said – you have come here, let me inform at least to Bapu. Wait for a while, why you wish to return. Bhai Devdas went upstairs and said on his return – Bapu has called you all upstairs. We were then helpless. We went upstairs and bowed to Bapu. He abused us laughingly and said – why you were returning? I replied – Bapu, it was published in '*Navjivan*', therefore, was returning. He said – is it published for family members? Whether Devdas will not stay here? Then he explained, it is for those who come here, and I have to speak

due to courtesy – maybe even if I feel pain in speaking. If I don't speak to them, then they may feel pain, feel sorry. Therefore, I have checked them to come over. But if you come, I may not speak a single word to you. You remain sitting here, If I did not speak to you, you would never mind it. Therefore, what sort of hesitation I may have on your arrival. As you have come, please sit for some time and then return.

2. Bapu had come to Mumbai and stayed at Labournam Road. At that time, a person named Baluramji from Rajasthan stayed with me, he was known as broker for divine name of Ram. Shri Jamnalalji Bajaj was also in Mumbai. I, Jamnalalji Bajaj and the broker for divine name of Ram, all three have gone to meet Gandhiji. Gandhiji asked full introduction of Panditji. Baluramji opened his register and placed in front of Bapu and requested – 'Sign here and start repetition of divine name'. He was in habit to speak like this only. We have explained everything to Gandhiji. He became very happy. He said – Look, if you insist, then I can sign but one thing is there, when I was in Africa, then I did repetition of divine name by number, but now I did repetition of divine name throughout the day. When I myself did not count it, why you wish to put a binding of number? On this, Jamnalalji said – Bapu, you do not require to sign here. Bapu then did not sign it.

3. '*Bhagvannamank*' of '*Kalyan*' was ready for release. I went to Bapu along with Seth Jamnalalji to request him to write something about '*Ramnaam*'. Bapu said laughingly – Why you have brought Jamnalalji? Will I write due to his recommendation? Why did you not come alone? Sethji smiled. I told Bapu, it is true that I have brought him so that you will definitely write. Bapu said laughingly – O.K., I excuse this time, but never show such mistrust. Then he immediately took out his pen and wrote a message as follows: 'Tulsidas left nothing to speak towards the glory of divine name. Twelve sacred verses, sacred verse with eight words have all been peaceful to the people trapped in such network of delusion. There is also no doubt in it. One should rely on that sacred verse by which he can get peace. But who had no experience of peace and who is in search of peace, to him 'Name of Ram' can definitely be a touchstone. The God is known by thousands of names. It means His names are infinite, properties are infinite. Therefore, the God is beyond the name and beyond the properties. But to an embodied, it is very important to take the shelter of name and in such an age, even a stupid and illiterate can also take shelter of a single word, single verse in the form of *Ramnaam*. In fact, its pronunciation '*Ram*' is just a single word and there is no difference

between '*Omkar*' and '*Ram*'. But the glory of the name cannot be proved by belief in reason but can be established by an experience with faith'.

On completion of message Bapu asked smiling – 'You have come to collect message only and counsel the world or do you also perform something? If you take an oath for repetition of divine name daily, then you will receive the message, otherwise, I won't give'. I replied – Bapu, I just did divine repetition daily, but now I will further increase it. By saying this – 'Look such precious thing is not given without price' – Bapu gave me the message. Sethji had to discuss something, and he stayed. I have touched his feet, took permission and returned.

4. On my arrival to Gorakhpur (in August, 1927), I went to Mumbai with some work and then was proceeding to Ratangarh from there. At that time, the train runs via Ahmedabad. Moving from Mumbai when I got down at Ahmedabad to change the train, I went to his refuge to meet Gandhiji. I reached at the refuge. A copy of '*Kalyan*' was in my hands. Just, per chance, a prayer for the repetition of divine name of the God was published in it. Gandhiji took that issue of '*Kalyan*' in his hands and began to turn over its leaves. On observing an article "A humble prayer for the repetition of divine name", he asked – 'What is this?' I explained how the request is made each year in '*Kalyan*' for the repetition of sixteen words – a sacred verse, i.e., *'Hare Ram, Hare Ram, Ram Ram Hare Hare, Hare Krishna, Hare Krishna, Krishna Krishna Hare Hare',* and how the male and female readers did the name repetition with great enthusiasm. Instantly, he enquired – How much repetition is completed? I replied – many crores have been done. He was happy and has encouraged – you did very well. If even 10-15 people in them will do repetition with true feeling, then they will achieve salvation. Then said – Look, I also did repetition of divine name and took out the string of beads of *Tulsi* below round pillow and said by showing it – I do the repetition of divine name at night by it. Per chance, his string of beads was broken, and I had one string of beads of Tulsi in my pocket. I thought – I may give him new string of beads in place of broken one. I have requested Bapu – 'Bapu, your string of beads is broken, give it to me and please take new string of beads.' I took out new string of beads from my pocket and advanced it to him. Bapu was very cheerful and has cut a very affectionate joke. He told – you come to deliver string of beads? Means you have come to make me your disciple? I and all other people sitting there burst out in laughing. I said – Bapu, string of beads is separated, therefore, wanted to replace, how can I dare to give you string of beads? He became happy to my reply and said – if you give me new string of

beads, then you will have to give some fee alongwith. With donation comes the fee as well. I said – Your grace is there, please tell me what I have to donate? Then he said seriously – please increase the repetition of divine name by one more string of beads with what you have been doing at present. Then I will accept your string of breads. I replied – I am ready for the same. Bapu then has accepted new string of beads with pleasure. Since that day, I have been doing one more string of beads, in addition to my own repetition of divine name and have maintained this practice without break till today.

5. It was the event in 1932. Bhai Devdas Gandhi was in prison of Gorakhpur. He had become sick in prison due to typhoid. The incharge of prison could not look well after Bhai Devdas. Bapu was informed. He wrote to me – Devdas is sick in prison at Gorakhpur. You are now fully responsible to look after welfare and treatment for him. In that period, Bapu was in *Yarvada* prison. On the receipt of instruction from Bapu, I started serving Bhai Devdas. To go and meet inside the prison was not possible legally but the officers have been always very sympathetic to me. They have given permission to meet Bhai Devdas daily. Within a few days, Bhai Devdas has recovered and been released from the prison. I have accompanied him up to Varanasi.

I had been informing continuously about the wellbeing of Bhai Devdas to Bapu through telegrams and letters. Bapu became so much influenced due to such little service that he has written a letter:

Yarvada Mandir, 21-7-32

Dear brother Hanuman Prasad,

Received today your letter and telegram. I will never worry about Devdas because you are there and Devdas has also written to me that you loved him very much. Nowadays, I would be always waiting for your letter.

Blessings from Bapu

6. The memory of Bapu is always linked with '*Kalyan*'. The principle of refusal to publish outside advertisements and critical review of articles was accepted only due to his advice which is still being maintained by the grace of God till today.

❐

81

A Strike in Gita press

Bhaijee left Ratangarh and reached Gorakhpur on 11th June, 1945. There was sufficient displeasure among the employees of Gita press. Bhaijee discussed the matter with trustees and provided financial facilities to the employees. For the time being, the problem was solved. But the leaders incited employees and again gave a notice of strike just after some time. Bhaijee has tried again to solve the problem, stayed several times in press throughout the day but the problem could not be solved. Employees were firm on their stake of claim. The organisers have put a notice on the gate to close the press indefinitely on 6th July, 1946 as they could not solve the problem. The strike continues for one- and-a-half months. This was the longest occasion of such lockout in press during the life-time of Bhaijee. At last, Baba Raghavdas, due to persuasion of Bhaijee, agreed for mediation and the strike was called off due to his efforts.

❐

82

Heartfelt Wailing and Warning through Tormented Heart Prior to Partition of Our Country

A saint like Bhaijee had already perceived the problems prior to 50 years only by his far-sightedness, which are prevalent today in our country. Though Bhaijee had been entirely dissociated from politics after 1921 because he had realised at that very time that spiritualism had no importance in the view of current leaders. Bhaijee knows that social problem and politics of Hindus is related with the religion and which is an important organ for spiritualism. Even during his active participation in the battle of independence for country and also after experiencing dire sufferings under house arrest, he dissociated himself from politics due to such reason. Despite it, leaders of all parties had maintained friendship with him.

'*Kalyan*' was a pure spiritual magazine. Bhaijee very seldom wrote review on other subjects but whenever he did, it was only under spiritual opinion. The serious atrocities which had been smeared on Hindus prior to partition of country had tormented the heart of Bhaijee. Even then, he has written at that time in '*Kalyan*' – 'The God is the same for Hindus and is the same for Muslims. If a Hindu is a form of God, then a Muslim is also a form of God. If a Hindu causes pain to a Muslim or beats him or if a Muslim causes pain to a Hindu or beats him, then he dissatisfied his God irrespective of whether the name of the God is 'Allah' or '*Parmatma*'. In fact, you may be a Hindu or Muslim but firstly you are a human being, thereafter you are a Hindu or a Muslim. '*Kalyan*' has never harmed anyone nor it can ever demand. '*Kalyan*' not only desires an overall welfare of everyone of the entire world by its heart, but also for the whole human race.

With such an intention, Bhaijee has written with a warning to political leaders in the issue of '*Kalyan*' in February, 1947 – An intrigue and the work of conspiracy by political Muslims is continuing successfully. Due to attachment of nationality, most of the influenced people amongst Hindus are involved for the practice of an independent state by losing 'self' and are flowing in the stream of new destructive ideas. For the sake of peace, by snatching all types of rights of Hindus, to destroy them, one such cruel arrangement of wickedness, insincerity and deceitful behaviour is in progress very secretly with extreme expertness and to check it or any active action to avoid it, has not been initiated till today from the direction of Hindus. Such type of laziness will be very dangerous for the future of Hindu community. It may be called tolerant nationality or thoughtless negligent suicide, nothing is clear about it. A motive to write such a thing is so much so that Hindus should be alert and begin to follow their prescribed duties. Please remember that Hindu caste is at present under terror.

Bhaijee wrote in the March 1947 issue of '*Kalyan*' –

"During last September, an article was published in '*Kalyan*' – 'What a Hindu should do?' in which a description was given about the terrible atrocities done in Bengal with a suggestion that what step should be taken by Hindus for self-defense and a welfare to all'. At last, it was given in the article 'Remember that Hindus, Muslims, Parsis, Christians all possess the same characters of just one God. To do bad for one would be bad for others and to do good for one will decide the good for others. Let the God may do good to all and provide good advice and good fortune to all'.

'*Kalyan*' is a reputed spiritual magazine accepted by all in India." Surprisingly, instead to be alert, the current Congress government,

Bihar and United Province government have issued order to confiscate these issues of '*Kalyan*'.

In issue of May 1947 of '*Kalyan*', Bhaijee wrote:

"For last several months in India, everyone knows there has been a vast expansion of atrocities and dishonest conduct. Living men and women are being thrown in burning fire. Innocent women and children are being killed with cruelty, wealth and property are being looted, women are kidnapped, and they are raped. It is unfortunate still is, that even witnessing this much of injustice and atrocities, our leaders have not changed their attitude. They are still following the same policies to please Muslims by suppressing Hindus. Our leaders have still been repeating the same old tune for peace. The result has been continuously evident clearly, in front. Hindus are facing terrible misfortune at every place and Muslim caste is trying to obtain improper benefit constantly due to such an attitude of Mahatmaji, etc. It has caused a harm to Hindus but in result there will be no benefit to Muslims or to this world as well.

"By considering all these things and the clear-cut statements by honourable Congress leaders like Nehruji, etc. to confine an introduction for the acceptance of Pakistan – it appears that if Hindus – they may be inside or outside of Congress or followers of any opinion or theory, have not made a strong and active opposition with one intention and in one tone unitedly, then the country will be divided into pieces. It will be beginning of an outrageous ruling of Muslims and will be extremely bad and evil plight for Hindu culture and Hindu caste. Under such circumstances, the Hindus should consider these conditions very seriously and should express the facts, putting aside their differences fearlessly, remained with honour towards Mahatmaji, Congress and leaders of Congress. In fact, if Congress government will suppress Hindus under injustice and due to pressed down by Muslims, till then, Muslims will never come forward for cordial relations. Very little time is left. An effective action must be taken towards this aspect very soon. In real sense, we don't want a little harm to anyone or even Muslims. We want to destroy an injustice, atrocities and tyranny which may exist in Muslims or Hindus or in any caste. We had no enmity with Englishmen. The conflict was due to their injustice thrusted on India but an injustice by Muslims has been changed today entirely as tyrannical. If such tyrannical attitude is not destroyed immediately, then it will also cause intense pain once to them, who are affected by tyranny but finally it would also cause an extreme harm to the tyrants. Such is an opinion of Hindu scriptures."

Bhaijee again wrote in the July, 1947 issue of '*Kalyan*' – "Mahatma Gandhi had said with such an intention, prior to a day or two of the declaration of planning for partition that India may burn to ashes, but Pakistan will not be allowed to form due to fear of violence. But then the same division of India, the same non-innocent Pakistan has been accepted happily. It is a matter of great surprise that Mahatmaji himself begun to issue instructions for its acceptance, who was earlier called an acceptance for planning of partition is an insanity. To understand the mutually opposed statements by Mahatmaji has become a fearsome puzzle today. It is clear by the speech of Pandit Nehru and Sardar Patel that such planning has been accepted due to dispiritedness by dire events of atrocities and cruel murders of the citizens. In addition, it is also a burning fact which they have accepted, i.e., unable themselves entirely to control the violence by the people of Muslim league. Therefore, the citizens may ask such questions that when such inability and weakness already existed, then why Pakistan was not accepted just or one or two years ago? Such strong terms and conditions would have not been stipulated at that time nor such racking of brains would be needed and even the people of Muslim League would have also not gesticulated in such a way.

"Looking at the circumstances, it is very clear if such had been the play of our leaders, being in attachment of nationality, if Congress does not change its policy completely of flattering and not opted the path of justice with intelligence and full strength, then don't know, how many straight problems will have to face in future. Whatever is evident till today due to submissive policy of Congress, such of their policy is not yet discontinued.

"I have regards to Mahatma Gandhi for a long time but whatever he is doing at present and endorsing with a reference to Gita, it is definitely harming Hindus and also creating a misuse of Gita.

"We have been changed so different, just in our own home, due to an attachment of nationality, that we considered it to be a harm of generosity by saying and declaring ourselves today as Hindus. Our national leaders will definitely respect Muslims but would never like Hindu name. Hindus are considered as non-Muslims. It causes an indication of shame in naming 'Hindustan' of a Hindu place. It is entirely true that policy of Mahatmaji is to please Muslims, which causes cowardice on the name of non-violence to the devotees of Mahatmaji, thereby increasing an arrogance and savagery amongst tyrants due to their victory. Hence, this has happened and is being continued."

What else a far-seeing and realised saint will write? Bhaijee had considered Gandhiji like his father, while Gandhiji had also an affection like a son on him but when he adopted a harmful policy for the whole country, Bhaijee must write looking it's all effects. It was just our ultimate misfortune that our selfish leaders have not considered timely on a true warning of a saint and this is the reason that the country is still facing of same problems even after seventy years and no real solution of it has been sorted out. Our life would have been happier if the then current leaders have adopted an appropriate policy, paying an attention on the warning of Bhaijee.

❐

83

Reaching and Helping to the Hindu Victims of Noakhali Riots

In 1946 and at the time of obtaining India's independence, there occurred a heart-rending sight in the country. Thousands of people entered death's maw, countless people also lost their families, house and everything, heart-rending atrocities were thrusted upon the younger women of an extended family. To remember today such of that time still caused a feeling of thrill in body hairs. It was not just easy to keep quiet, looking at such inhuman atrocities to the innocent public for a sensitive person like Bhaijee. A stream of tears had begun to flow from the eyes of Bhaijee by hearing the sad stories of people came running from East and West Pakistan. Bhaijee has begun every possible effort. *Noakhali* was the main area for such atrocities. Mahamana Malviya was sick during those days and it caused a big shock to his heart by hearing the stories of such atrocities and he died. Bhaijee published a homage issue of '*Kalyan*' in his memory which contained many plans to protect Hindu religion. Later, this issue was also confiscated by the government. But Bhaijee remained always fearless on such occasions. Bhaijee has sent a volunteer group from Gita press to Noakhali for help. The main people were – Shri Giridhari Baba, Shri Krishnadasji Bengali and Shri Krishna Chandraji Agrawal. During these days, a railway employee from Bengali family of Gorakhpur was living in Noakhali. Looking at the plight of his family, he came running to Bhaijee and began to sob. Bhaijee moved with emotion and called Shri Giridhari Baba immediately to apprise him the circumstances. Due to blessings of Bhaijee, Shri Giridhari Baba could successfully bring away that family from terrible disaster and has sent the family safely to Gorakhpur. During his trip to Noakhali, Giridhari Baba met Mahamana Madan Mohan Malviya at Hindu University, Varanasi. He was on bed due to sickness. The person sitting outside the room asked – Where do you come from? Shri Giridhari Baba replied – From the residence of Bhaijee Hanuman Prasad of Gorakhpur. The person immediately went inside and informed Malviyaji – A person has come from Bhaijee and wants to meet you. He was instantly asked to call him.

Shri Giridhari Baba bowed before him. Then Mahamana asked – How is Bhaijee? How did you come here? He replied – I was going to Noakhali. Bhaijee has started a camp there to help the people. Malviyaji said – Bhaijee is now life of Hindu religion. He is such a pious person who provides a lot of strength to me. Giridhari Baba realised about a very high status of Bhaijee in the heart of Malviyaji. He gave his blessings and moved to his journey ahead. Bhaijee had been continuing activity for such type of help as and when, an occasion occurs.

❐

84

A Miracle During a Trip to Assam

In October 1946, Bhaijee went from Gorakhpur on a trip to Assam. Once he was going to *Tinsukia* from *Golaghat* by bus. It was night time. The bus was moving at one place through a narrow lane. That very moment, a passenger cried loudly – Water, Water. Due to sudden and loud out-cry, hands of driver have trembled, causing a dislodge of steering. The bus was on the slope, the wheel of the bus had slipped away, and the bus begun to move towards the trench. There was no other helper at that instant except God. Bhaijee has made roar in a high tone of '*Narayan, Narayan, Narayan, Narayan*' by raising both his hands. It was just a delay to raise the voice of divine name – '*Narayan*' that bus stopped at one place. By colliding with stem of a tree, it stood firm by sticking with stem. The bus was damaged a little and the driver and few other persons have got a slight injury but Bhaijee and rest of the people have saved clearly. Bhaijee returned to Gorakhpur safely from this trip.

❐

85

A Session of Hindu General Assembly at Gorakhpur

During the time of partition of the country and to consider the solution of the problem, which caused inhuman atrocities to Hindu community – a session of Hindu, General Assembly was held at Gorakhpur on 24/25 December, 1946. About six-seven thousand representatives took part in it. Arrangements for meal, etc. to everyone had been done under the leadership of Bhaijee. Bhaijee had completely been busy in it for two days and he also gave very brilliant lectures from the dais on those days. He had suggested to work jointly towards dire event of Noakhali. Session was conducted with full success. On 13th January, 1947, Bhaijee went in the love conference for celebration of devotional songs for Hindu-national-service Organisation in Shri Vishnu temple and affectionately met all by clasping from heart to heart. The close friends, thus, have fulfilled an elation of themselves on this day.

❐

86

Non-stop Celebration of Devotional Songs on the Half Kumbh at Prayag

Non-stop celebration of devotional songs (*sankeertan*) and an assembly of virtuous people (*satsang*) coupled with sermons were arranged between 3rd and 16th February, 1948 by the Gita press on the eve of half-Kumbh at *Prayag*. Bhaijee went from Gorakhpur to attend it. People assembled from distant places at Prayag during such occasion and due to this reason, such arrangement was made to spread the divine name. Several people were benefitted by non-stop celebration of devotional songs and the discussion by saints.

❐

87

An Appearance of Sages like Sankadi and Others

A person of dignity, whose life was chiefly based on singing hymns and worship (*bhajans*) and was closely associated with Bhaijee, once narrated – he went once to meet to Bhaijee. The room was closed, therefore, he sat outside. He felt that there had two or four persons sitting inside the room of Bhaijee. Some discussion was progressing with Bhaijee. Suddenly, it was covered with complete silence and door opened a little later. Bhaijee was still appeared in an access of emotion. That gentleman then just enquired – Bhaijee, with whom were you talking? Comes the reply – These were just Sages, *Sankadi* & others. Both became silent. Bhaijee did not yet become completely normal. On his becoming completely normal, he asked – Which things you have been discussing about Bhaijee has instructed him to keep such things as completely confidential.

As divine saint community is set to keep in action since the time immemorial in the inner world, to spread the religious devotion (*bhakti*) and religious arrangement. Bhaijee had also been associated for this community. Therefore, the members of this divine community had been arriving for discussion with Bhaijee.

❐

88

A Trip to Ayodhya for Deliverance of Shri Ram's Birthplace

It is said that the grand temple built by emperor *Vikramaditya* on the birthplace of Shri Ram had been destroyed by *Babar*. Since then, there have been many Hindu-Muslim riots at that sacred place, but the Aryan community somehow has maintained its control. During December, 1949 in Ayodhya, such a miraculous ray was splashed by the idol in the temple of Shri Ram's birthplace that all the devotees have become fully immersed with an access of emotion due to its radiance. Such an auspicious message has spread all around like an electric current. This news reached to court of law. Shri Vir Singhji, a civil judge of Faizabad, issued an order to the government – until the case is finally decided, till then this idol shall be placed safely, where it is presently situated and its worship, service, etc. alongwith the reading of religious texts should be continued in a proper manner.

An information about such miraculous event was also known to Bhaijee. He was requested to help in this matter. Bhaijee became very happy from this message. He himself went to Ayodhya in December, 1949 and encouraged the volunteers and public, who had been disappointed by the activities of government, through his sermons and spiritual instructions. On this occasion, there was a need for a monthly expenditure of about fifteen hundred rupees. The responsibility of total expenses was happily borne by Bhaijee. Bhaijee asked for an attention of millionaires of the country on this aspect for this great work by which it became very easy to arrange financial help for this work. Sometimes special fund was also required for an accusation of related expenses apart from the usual expenditure and to this purpose, the gate of Gita Vatika was always accessible for the managers.

Not only this much, Bhaijee has also found track of such an educated and eminent Muslims of Islam religion for such dispute, who had proved logically Shri Ram's birthplace against Islam religion and not considered it as a Muslim's place of worship. To build an environment in favour of birthplace, one or two out of these Muslim gentlemen were also sent to Ayodhya. In addition, Bhaijee has also again and again written letters to chief government officers, leaders and academicians and inspired them to cooperate for such social work. Likewise, Bhaijee did noble services for this work.

❒

89

Events of Rescue from Suicide

How many people have been saved from suicide by Bhaijee cannot be counted because he had treated such events as secret. It had been with all his mighty efforts that no one could know about personal things of other person. Few of such events are being presented here – One who has received service from Bhaijee but who is now happy and is in prosperous condition, such a reputed person had narrated this event a few days ago in choked voice, after demise of Bhaijee. His eyes were full of tears, shivering of body due to hiccups and memories of past were jolting his seat of heart. It is an incidence of about 12-13 years ago – Sickness and scarcity surrounded me all around. The success worshipper world considered me almost disclaimed, humiliated and neglected. The sickness was increasing the scarcity and scarcity was nurturing the sickness. It was not a simple disease but asthma – even a small movement causes breathlessness. If I must go even for a short distance, then have to stay at many places. Entire sources of income had been exhausted. I was unable to do any labour, there was no one to help. Family members also neglectected me. I almost got disappointed from life. It was difficult to live while an imagination of death was pleasant. The death should be peaceful and somewhere at the bank of the Ganga – such intention has inspired me to proceed to Swargashram. I expressed my desire in front of my family members. Permission was given instantly and with pleasure as I was already a burden to them. I reached Swargashram entirely friendless, unsupported in sick condition. There was no place in '*Gita Bhawan*', could find somehow a place in '*Parmarth Niketan*' with repeated requests. Incapable from body, disappointed by self and without money I have almost decided to opt for loss of life by drowning in the Ganga – purifying the sinful. Then suddenly I came to know that Bhaijee is here. I was an old lover of '*Kalyan*' – had high regards to Bhaijee. I thought why I did not weep and lightened myself in front of him. He is capable, possibly he may also do something for me. To this decision, I have just given an action form as well.

Where do you come from? Bhaijee asked me, sitting amongst several people.

I was badly panting due to my movement from such a distance. I replied with hesitation – Yesterday…only...came…from…Cal... cutta. Bhaijee might have probably understood, looking to my way of speech, my condition. He asked me again – Is your health alright? Why are you so much panting?

Hearing such an affectionate tone which had touched my heart while the eyes replied – throat was choked.

'Comein, let us sit inside'– by saying this, he got up and I followed him. What is the problem, tell me without hesitation? Have faith for the auspicious ruling of the God – the voice of Bhaijee echoed in the room coupled with dignity of faith.

I explained wearingly my complete condition in front of him. With much confidence and patience, he heard complete details, in between once or twice, someone tried to enter in the room but Bhaijee had refused with a hand gesture to him.

'Suicide is not a sin but is the greatest sin; you don't get freedom from the troubles, but it is to invite new and terrible sufferings. Suicide brings a ghost reincarnation and individual must bear terrible pains in this reincarnation. Please have a faith on the grace God, who is kind hearted, He will definitely hear your prayer and your problem will be solved. I will come tomorrow after the assembly of virtuous people (*satsang*) in Gita Bhawan, please remain there at that time.'

I became overwhelmed due to affection, kindness and greatness of Bhaijee. I came out of his room slowly and have begun to wait for tomorrow – he will come himself to meet me in my room.

'Had an ayurvedic physician come to you?' Shri Bhaijee asked me while entering my room with a sweet smile on second day.

Yes! He was here, he also gave in writing about medicines, but… I have not arranged.

Please give me this paper, I will arrange. You can take your meal in dining hall of Gita Bhawan. And yes! The milk will also be delivered to you in the morning and evening I told him hesitantly… I have to tell you something. Tell me, what is the problem?

No there is no such thing; in fact, I had a desire to talk to you in alone – I told him looking at few people standing behind.

Alright, alright, I will come tomorrow again, then you can talk to me. Please give me that paper. Today I am in little hurry – Bhaijee said while getting up.

I tried to convey with extreme hesitation, by putting the prescription in his hand – the fact is that I have….

'I have an urgent work today, will talk tomorrow'….by saying this, Bhaijee left the room.

I was under a very strange condition. The love of yesterday… an alienation of today – an inner conflict has begun in the heart. How will I say that I have no money for medicines, milk or even for my meal? What he will think, what he will reply? An alienation of today had also caused to appear many more thoughts in my heart. I was cursing myself, being immersed in such thoughts – but I was helpless, without remedy, I was under a very pathetic condition.

On second day, Bhaijee came at the same time, but no one was with him today. I have also become free from the anxiety – 'O.K. I will feel now a little hesitation in explaining my condition'.

'Had you received the medicines, you might have begun to consume' – Bhaijee said in normal and in an affectionate voice.

'Yes! I got it' – by giving such a short reply, I have again immersed in an uncertainty – How to convey? What to say? I was just thinking all this that Bhaijee told in slow voice – what you want to say, you can say, later, but, at first, listen to me.

By saying this, he took out an envelope, gave it to me and said – Keep it, there are some rupees in it, you can use it towards your expenses. Look, I request you with an extreme humility – I beg of you in the name of the God that don't disclose it to anyone and don't feel any embarrassment in your mind for it. I am your brother, you are mine and I belong to you. I will tell the physician to recover the money used for check-up and medicines. Well, I go now and will come again. By saying this and running his hand over my head affectionately, he moved out of the room.

I was thinking, being speechless about the service full of love by Bhaijee, which had been so much unknown, so much secret and far from the desire for respect, very far, what to say for the compensation. Tears were trickling through eyes, I continued thinking that this is the true form of service and love.

Second incident occurred about 40 years ago. Once at 8-9 o'clock, two people suddenly entered the room of most respected Bhaijee – one was in police uniform while the second had covered himself from head to toe with clothes. Shri Bhaijee, at that time, was busy in inspecting the proof of '*Kalyan*'. Both people bowed to Bhaijee. Bhaijee reciprocated their gesture and requested them to sit down. Giving his introduction, the person in police uniform said – I work in spy department and accompanying person is my elder brother. Then he told with great hesitation – My brother is suffering from leprosy. He is a good advocate but since the day he had this disease, he has discontinued to visit court of law. The leprosy is considered as most hated disease in the society and society exiled him who suffers by such disease. My brother knows the intensity of this disease. Therefore, he does not now like to live. He used to sob day and night and abstained from meeting anybody. Bhaijee, I heard about your greatness by several of my friends. Therefore, I have brought him intentionally to you. He does not want to show his face to anyone. Therefore, he has come here by covering whole of his body with clothes. Shri Bhaijee was listening everything carefully and with much eagerness. It appeared if he as was listening something in relation to one of his close relatives. On the completion of our discussion, he moved towards his brother and by putting his hand on his shoulder, told him – Dear brother! you should also tell something. Remove clothes from your face and let me examine the condition of disease.

With such feeling of intimacy, love and above and all bodily contact of Bhaijee had stirred up the soul and mind of my brother and he burst into tears and has placed his head on the lap of Bhaijee. The eyes of Bhaijee also filled with tears and he had begun to tickle his forehead by his tender hand. A little later and on reduction of the intensity of pain, brother told – Bhaijee, I don't want to live. I have come to you on the persuasion of my younger brother. It is my first and last respectful greetings … by saying this, brother had again begun to cry profusely. Bhaijee had continued to tickle his head by hand. The surrounding had become very serious. A little later, said Bhaijee Dear brother! Why have you become so much disappointed? There is not at all any place of disappointment, when an all-powerful and totally affectionate Lord is here. The Lord is capable for: What is worthy to perform or not to perform and which can also be performed beyond these two. Therefore, get rid of such disappointment.

The heart of my brother was little consoled by such an arousal and assurance by Bhaijee. He sat down and raised the cloth, laid on his face. Bhaijee observed his face with very close attention and then said

"You have been unnecessarily so much fearful. The disease is in its primary stage. Then the body is just a temple of diseases. You should not worry if a disease has come in front of you in a clear shape. I call an ayurvedic doctor, who will arrange medicines for you. If the God desires, you will be completely healthy within a few days. You have shown your inability to retain your body which is not justified. The people who have knowingly ruined their life and body, by consuming poison, burning in fire, drowning in water or attacking themselves by some weapons are just very unfortunate and are worthy for sympathy. The human body is a means to achieve the God and is obtained by the grace of God and due to just very auspicious action. To destroy such a rare body is a great sin. Suicide will not permit to get rid of the pains. The destiny will have to be experienced in future as well. A man commits suicide to get rid of momentary dejection or remorse which multiplied and will be painful to him in next world till eternity. Therefore, no one should think about suicide. The God is supremely merciful. With complete faith on his grace coupled with due reverence, you should make sincere request to the God and take proper treatment.

"The God shall definitely hear if you call Him earnestly. There is no such work which cannot be fulfilled by the grace of God. Therefore, believe on my suggestion, you should pray to all-powerful and entirely affectionate God through your heart in your own tender language. The prayer made with due confidence can destroy all type of diseases – mental and physical. A gentleman named Gilbert Henry Gaze has written in a monthly magazine of England – 'Science of thought review' – A person in Germany had been suffering due to infinite paralysis during the first year of birth. Both of his feet have become useless due to paralysis. A prayer has been arranged for him. A message was received after few months that both of his feet have got new strength. The muscles which had died since last 48 years have become active. His life has become joyful, free from every type of worry and faithful to the God. "It was an old event. A famous merchant from Calcutta was affected

by plague. There was fever between 104-105° and large swelling of glands have appeared on both the legs. In Calcutta, a reputed doctor has declared after his check-up, there is entirely no hope of life, but he had faith on God. He closed the room and placed an idol of Lord Shri Krishna in front and began to repeat the sacred verse – "*Hari sharnam*" by totally surrendering himself to Shri Krishna. By the time of early morning, he has become completely healthy by the grace of the God and lived long.

"I have seen many such events accomplished in my life as well as in the life of others. The diseases like cancer, T.B., etc. have also been cured miraculously due to prayer. It is my firm belief that even an impossible can be made possible by the sincere prayer to the God. Therefore, please make prayer through your heart and also repeat the sacred verse 'Hari sharnam' by your heart."

My brother heard the conversation of Bhaijee with due curiosity and respect. An impulse of hope appeared in his heart. When Bhaijee stopped talking, he said – Bhaijee, your affection, love and intimacy have overwhelmed me. The words which you have spoken about an affection and capability of the God, I have now faith on them. I am no more disappointed in life. Whatever medicines you will arrange for me, I will take that sincerely and will make sincere request to the God, as directed by you, through my heart.

By hearing such words of hope uttered by Bhaijee, the police officer was also pleased. Both brothers bowed to Bhaijee and bid him farewell.

On second day, Bhaijee called a famous, local ayurvedic doctor and arranged for medicines from him. By that time, English medicine named 'Sulphane' was not popular by which it is possible to eradicate leprosy. My brother began to use the medicines. The real medicine was to do sincere prayer faithfully and repetition of divine name, both continued equally. Within a few months, my brother was fully cured and begun to work in the court of law.

Such an event inspired the tender heart of Bhaijee to do something also towards the people effected by leprosy. A little later, fortunately, a famous social worker Baba Raghavdas decided to establish 'a refuge for service of leprosy' in Gorakhpur and Bhaijee joined him as his closest assistant. Few months later to the establishment of this refuge, respected Baba has joined grant of land movement of saint Vinoba Bhave and full responsibility for leprosy service refuge has come just on Bhaijee. Shri Bhaijee extended this work in such a beautiful manner, by also sparing time from his extreme busy life that the leprosy service refuge of Gorakhpur is **one of the important leprosy centers of the country** and it is providing hope and life to many thousands of disappointed people.

❐

90

Shri Riyaz Ahmed Ansari was Saved from Suicide

Third event is extremely surprising. Under compelling circumstances, a Muslim brother decided to commit suicide. He did not allow anyone to know about it. It became still a mystery how Bhaijee could know about it. It is not known how many such secret events would prevail, which cannot be imagined. This event was known only when Shri Ansari himself described its mystery.

By reading the feelings of Shri Ansariji in the newspaper regarding 'Shri Ram birthplace temple', Bhaijee called him to meet. Since then, his introduction had begun to increase with Bhaijee and he met Bhaijee several times. Due to some reasons, he was facing extreme financial difficulty. But he had never shown his problem in front of Bhaijee. The condition had reached up to this much of extent that there was nothing left to eat at home. No meal was prepared at his place continuously for three days. His body had become weak and appeared as sick. The younger, amongst other two daughters, Shahida who was four years old, began to cry badly due to hunger. Looking at the condition of home, specially observing plight of his daughter due to hunger, his power of tolerance was exhausted. With long and due consideration, he decided to commit suicide in the forthcoming night. Unable to find other alternative, he laid down on the bed according to his decision. It was 10 o'clock of the day. Suddenly, somebody knocked at the door. He came out and found Bhaijee standing on the road near his car. He requested him to come inside and Bhaijee entered inside and sat on a chair. Bhaijee said smiling – Brother, you look very sick. What could he reply now that sickness was something else, nothing available to eat since last three days except water and condition was prevailed due to such consequences. Therefore, only said this much – 'Yes'. Bhaijee instantly asked – what problem do you have? Which disease is it? Shri Ansariji did not reply anything, remained silent. Looking at his silence, Bhaijee said by consoling him – Brother! This world is just a place of sorrow. Everybody must face here pains and the true people have to face even more troubles because the God examines them. There has been no effect on him by the suggestion

Shri Jaydayal Goyandka & Shri Hanuman Prasad Poddar

Shri Radha Baba and Shri Hanuman Prasad Poddar
during a religious celebration

Shri Radha Baba and Shri Hanuman Prasad Poddar
during a religious congregation

Shri Radha Baba

Shri Hanuman Prasad Poddar

Smt. Hanuman Prasad Poddar

Shri Radha Baba Samadhi in Gita Vatika

Shri Hanuman Prasad's place of activity and presently
a sacred and worth-seeing place in Gita Vatika

Smt. & Shri Hanuman Prasad Poddar

Shri Jaydayal Goyandka

Sethji (with turban) & Bhaiji (with glasses)

Shri Jaydayal Goyandka a little before his departure to heaven with Shri Radha Baba and Bhaiji

Gita Press Gate, Gorakhpur

Sankeertan Palace in Gita Vatika, Gorakhpur

Place where sage Narad and sage Angira met Shri Poddarji

Shri Hanuman Prasad Poddar

Shri Radha Baba, Shri and Smt. Hanuman Prasad Poddar

Shri Hanuman Prasad Poddar's samadhi in Gita Vatika

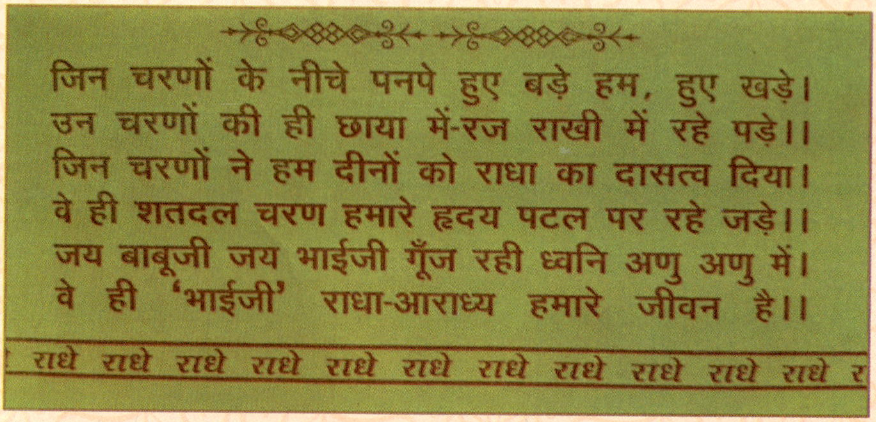

जिन चरणों के नीचे पनपे हुए बड़े हम, हुए खड़े।
उन चरणों की ही छाया में-रज राखी में रहे पड़े।।
जिन चरणों ने हम दीनों को राधा का दासत्व दिया।
वे ही शतदल चरण हमारे हृदय पटल पर रहे जड़े।।
जय बाबूजी जय भाईजी गूँज रही ध्वनि अणु अणु में।
वे ही 'भाईजी' राधा-आराध्य हमारे जीवन है।।

राधे राधे राधे राधे राधे राधे राधे राधे राधे राधे राधे

Prayer

Shri Gambhir Chand Dujari—The original collector of Hindi script

Shri Shyam Sundar Dujari—Compilation and combining of Hindi version

Parikrama at Gita Vatika

Shri Hanuman Prasad Poddar's samadhi in Gita Vatika

Shri Hanuman Prasad Poddar

Shri Radha Krishna

given by Bhaijee because he had decided of suicide in forthcoming night and he was immersed to get rid of all troubles thereafter. He simply shook his head instead of any reply, it seems as if he was endorsing the suggestions by Bhaijee. During conversation, Bhaijee moved an envelope to him and said – "You need it, please take it. Refusal will cause pain to me. Surely, I will try to arrange money for your business. He said – Bhaijee, how could I repay your such obligation? Bhaijee replied – what obligation, what repayment? I only wish that you should be comfortable. There is one more request about the decision you have taken to do with your life in coming fortnight, which is not good. The life has been given by the God and he has only the right to finish it. Please bypass your decision. He felt as if there is lighting to fall. He had not disclosed anyone about his decision, then how Bhaijee could know about it. Definitely he had some divine power in him. He jumped to his feet and said – Bhaijee! you are not a human, but an angel. How you could know about my feeling? Bhaijee replied – Whatever has come to your mind, it has caused sudden blaze to my mind. Permit me, we will meet again. Bhaijee began to laugh.

After departure of Bhaijee, he opened the envelope and found twenty notes of hundred rupees. One who had not even two rupees, how much happiness would prevail to him on receiving two thousand rupees, one can well imagine about it. These two thousand rupees of that time were equal to more than two crores to him. Bhaijee also gave him an additional eight thousand rupees after almost twenty days and said there is no need to return this amount. To prepare clothes from the handloom was his paternal occupation and by engaging happily therein, he led his life by supporting his family.

❐

91
Reorganisation of an Accomplishment Committee (*Sadhan-Samiti*)

Looking at special enthusiasm of many devotees like Shukdeoji, etc. Bhaijee has reorganised an accomplishment committee on his return to Gorakhpur from Ayodhya on 7th January, 1950. The rules were framed to follow, which had been accepted by the members enthusiastically. It was a favourable work for Bhaijee because he had always wanted to see the life of a person close to him, as remained always ready for spiritual practice. To encourage the devotees, an assembly of virtuous people (*satsang*) has also been accepted by visiting Gita press at night. During the time of coming and going – a loud recitation of group singing of hymns for the sacred verse '*Hare Ram*' remained continuing. Such activity was continued for several days enthusiastically. Bhaijee often enquired about the observance of rules by the devotees and continued to encourage them.

❐

92

Conformity of Pictures in '*Kalyan*' on the Basis of Scriptures

Whichever pictures had been published in '*Kalyan*', their basis was explored in Hindu scriptures. There had been many such occasions when it took sufficient time to search out suitable basis, but as long as scriptural evidence was not found, it was not published. The description of such an event is being given as follows, through the words of Pandit Mangalji Uddhavji Shastri:

Such an event belongs to 1949-50, when I first met Bhaijee. I found *Gita vatika* like a garden in which ascetic practices are carried out. Bhaijee affectionately embraced and asked me to sit on the cot by holding my hand. The initial preparation had been in progress for the special issue of '*Kalyan*' – "Hindu-culture issue". In the picture above the title was just to publish the sight of an assembly of Shri Ram. Members of editorial department had been discussing regarding that picture. A member asked Shri Poddarji (Bhaijee) – "The topic seeking justice by the dog is not traceable in the Valmiki Ramayan. Now it could be searched out in some other Ramayans".

"I have seen that topic" – I have intercepted in between. "Give me Ramayan, I will just find out."

That person has brought a copy of the Ramayan and given to me. Even through careful examination, the topic could not be traced in that edition. The person emphasised – "We have checked it two-three times that topic is well known but it is not described in Valmiki Ramayan." "Then as long as such an evidence is not found, how can we publish the picture related to this topic, over head of title" – said Poddarji.

I could then understand, by hearing such words of Bhaijee, how scriptural evidence is considered as basis for publication of things in '*Kalyan*'. This is the main reason for reputation of '*Kalyan*'.

"I have then just seen in the Valmiki Ramayan, but I have a copy of Nirnay-Sagar-Press," – I conveyed.

The copy from Nirnay-Sagar-Press was consulted and that topic was found there. Everyone was happy. Being full of contentment, Bhaijee embraced me. ❒

93

Bhagwat Week at Gorakhpur by Swami Akhandanand

During earlier days, Swamiji worked by the name of Pandit Shantanu Bihari Dwivedi for many years with Bhaijee in editorial section of '*Kalyan*'. He had become a family member of Bhaijee. In the words of Swamiji – I did not accept renouncement from my hereditary domestic life but took it from the family of Bhaijee only. Swamiji was an eminent person on the Bhagwat. Bhaijee has arranged his narration as Bhagwat-week in 'Shri Krishna – Niketan' at Gorakhpur. A function was arranged at a grand scale and Bhaijee, his family and his close friends attended this narration. An organisation of this programme was held between 26th February and 5th March, 1951.

❐

94

A Trip to Bankura to Attend Marriage of the Grandson of Shri Sethji

Bhaijee reached Calcutta by flight on 19th April, 1951 and moved to Bankura by train at night after meeting his friends during day time. There was a marriage ceremony for Madhav, son of Shri Mohanlal (whom Shri Sethji considered to be his son) – younger brother of Shri Sethji on 21st April, 1951. The presence of saints always creates spiritual atmosphere only at every occasion. Bhaijee has given a very mind captivating exposition towards the child act of the God at Bankura. At the time of departure of marriage procession, Shri Dongarmalji Lohia had been managing celebration of devotional songs as dancing ahead of Bhaijee and Shri Sethji. Just by performing celebration of devotional songs (*sankeertan*), the marriage procession reached at the place of marriage. An auspicious moment for marriage was after midnight. Therefore, Bhaijee stayed there whole night. Leaving Bankura on 25th April, 1951, he reached Gorakhpur via Asansol and Varanasi.

Bhaijee became extremely sick during the dark half of lunar month between November and December. The pain caused by disease lasted for several days, but benefit beyond expectation was achieved in health due to an observance of a rite.

❒

95

Service to Famine-Affected People at Gorakhpur

There occurred an aweful famine in Gorakhpur during 1952. Bhaijee had always arranged for charity work on such occasions. This time as well Bhaijee along with Shri Sethji served grain and clothes for famine-affected through their hands by visiting various villages in a jeep. The volunteers felt a great enthusiasm due to presence of Shri Sethji and Bhaijee. Just thereafter, Shri Sethji developed chronic pain in stomach and body condition became serious. Bhaijee arranged a rite by the people of confidence for the benefit of his health by which there occurred a prompt relief in the health of Shri Sethji.

❐

96

Protection of Sinking Motorboat

Bhaijee had controlled many times the horrible accidents in such a normal way that spectators were left shocked by a surprise. Such an incident occurred in Swargashram on 13th July, 1954. About 20-25 people have embarked on motorboat to go to Rishikesh from Swargashram, Gita Bhawan, in morning at about 10 o'clock. Maybe due to destiny! When the boat reached in between the current of the Gangaji, the engine of boat had stopped suddenly. The driver of the boat had tried a lot to start it, but his efforts went in vain. Boat was caught in current and had begun to move fast into whirpool. One can simply just imagine the mental condition of travellers. It seems as if the boat was just about to drown. All the passengers had begun to call loudly 'help-help' out of profound grief to the God and Bhaijee. No other help was visible.

It can be said as miracle by God. Exactly at that very time, Bhaijee moved out from Gita Bhawan number two. He could see and hear the loud noises and drowning boat with passengers. Staring towards the boat, Bhaijee had raised his hands and repeated three lines loudly – "*Narayan, Narayan, Narayan*". The boat stopped then and there in midcurrent unexpectedly. The driver again tried to start the engine, but in vain. Corner of a very thick rope had been tied with the stem of a strong tree, while the other end was tied to boat and it was sent towards motorboat. Then it was pulled back at the bank of the river. With an unwearyingly effort of four-five hours, all passengers were rescued safely at the embankment of Gita Bhawan by boat. Each passenger was realising that they had recovered new life due to kindness of Bhaijee. All passengers with grateful hearts had gone to Dalmia building, residence of Bhaijee and bowed to his feet. Bhaijee met everyone with great intimacy and simply said – You all had to endure lots of pain, but the God helped. The hearts of everyone had become ecstatic.

❐

97

In the Kumbh Fair of Prayag

In fact, Bhaijee generally had been arranging function to spread divine name at the time of Kumbha at Prayag and also attended it himself but, in 1954, Bhaijee stayed along with his family in Prayag for one- plus-quarter months during Kumbh. A very large pavillion was created by Gita press, where two times weekly commissioning of 108 for the Shrimad Bhagwat and nine times commissioning of the *Ramcharit Manas* had been conducted. An assembly of virtuous people (*satsang*), an exposition, narration, celebration of devotional (*sankeertan*) songs, etc. have also been arranged from morning till night. In addition to Bhaijee, saints and eminent scholars like Swami Sharnanandji, Swami Akhandanandji. Shri Pathikji, Shri Ram Kinkarji, etc. had been delivering their discourses daily. Bhaijee was asked by many other saints to accompany in their respective pavillions for an assembly of virtuous people. A short biography of Bhaijee was published in 'Bharat' – a journal of Prayag during such occasion. Bhaijee alongwith the delegation of several saints and scholars met there with the Prime Minister of India Shri Jawaharlal Nehru and insistently requested to check the killing of cows. At the occasion of the *Kumbh*, Shri *Purushottam Dasji Tandon* also arrived at Prayag and as soon as he could find the news about the presence of Bhaijee, he came to meet Bhaijee alongwith his attendants. If he stayed there, he generally came to meet Bhaijee and talk with him by sitting on the sand at the bank of the Ganga. Bhaijee stayed in Prayag between 11th January, 1954 and 18th February, 1954 and then returned to Gorakhpur along with his family.

❐

98

A Man of Simplicity

It occurred in 1954. Under the presence of Swami Karpatriji Maharaj, a cow slaughter prevention movement was in progress in Calcutta. News was received that Respected Bhaijee Hanuman Prasad Poddar was arriving at Calcutta due to some work. The local volunteers wanted to take benefit of his arrival and arranged a private meeting on that occasion.

The meeting had to begin at 3 o'clock of the day. In addition to Bhaijee, special volunteers had also been invited. Generally, everyone had arrived. But there was no sign of Bhaijee. It was already 3 o'clock. Everyone was waiting for Bhaijee. At last, at about 3.30 P.M. a person uttered – Bhaijee may come or may not come, let us start the meeting.

Meanwhile, an old man sitting just near the door of room in a very simple dress said – "Well, I have already come."

Everyone was taken aback. No person among them knew respected Bhaijee by face. Therefore, nobody had made any objection nor felt any need to ask for more introduction to that ingeniously simple person, sitting near the shoes.

But when it was known he was indeed Bhaijee, everyone had suffered greatly with shame and respectfully requested him to sit on a particular place.

❒

99

An Assembly of Virtuous People (*Satsang*) at Swargashram (in Gita Bhawan)

Uttarakhand has been a place of devoted striving (*sadhna*) for centuries in our country. Shri Sethji had begun a session for assembly of virtuous people in this sacred land of Uttarakhand – in Rishikesh. Such trend, which had started during 1921-22 is being continued uninterruptedly till today. Each year Shri Sethji stayed most of the time in that very place from Chaitra to Ashad along with the group in assembly of virtuous people collected together with great faith, relished the essence devoted to the God on the sandy river bank of the Ganga which echoed due to sacred stream coupled with a continuous indistinct noise. A little later, such programme had also begun on the bank of the Ganga, known as Swargashram. There was a dense forest that time and there were only few huts to live in. Stream of divine joy continued to flow below the shadow of a huge Banyan tree at the bank of the Ganga.

Bhaijee went first time during *Chaitra Shukla* in the year 1924 from Mumbai to receive the benefit of this programme. Prior to this, people involved in an association of virtuous people (*satsangi*) of that place, had perceived a lot about his achievement through Shri Sethji. Bhaijee had taken there, benefit of the impressive discourses by Shri Sethji, in addition to that and on the insistence by the people involved in the association of virtuous people had also given some hints about the reason of his progress during devoted striving. Though Bhaijee could stay there only for three days at that time, but everybody was impressed to hear the realised things of his inner heart. Due to his busy schedule of '*Kalyan*', Bhaijee had not, thereafter, visited there regularly but had been visited often. In the first month of Hindu year (March- April) in 1929, when Bhaijee went there, he met Swami Shivanandji and in the same year had written the experiences of an achievable life of Shri Narayan Swami on his meeting with him. Shri Narayan Swami was born in a rich family and was a highly learned person. At that time, he had been repeating name of 'Narayan' by maintaining a continuous silence and did not accumulate anything with him. Later, his experiences had been published in the form of a book named '*An Experience of a Saint*' by Gita press. That year Bhaijee had been arranging celebration of devotional songs (*Sankeertan*) in an excellent manner by performing beautiful dances under lustful condition at night at the bank of the Ganga.

Shri Sethji actually wanted to call Bhaijee every year, but Bhaijee was unable to come. To investigate the future and for residential purpose for assembly of virtuous people, a large building named 'Gita Bhawan' was constructed there at the bank of the Ganga. A hall for the assembly of virtuous people was also constructed and vast river banks were also built as a facility for bathing. The expositions of Bhaijee had been very heart-touching and passengers of spiritual path would wait for such session of assembly of virtuous people, eagerly. The complete responsibility of this programme had also come just to Bhaijee after the death of Shri Sethji. Thereafter, Bhaijee visited Swargashram every year and had stayed there for two to three months. The editorial work for '*Kalyan*' was also performed from there itself. During the presence of Shri Sethji, assembly of virtuous people had continued for about 12-13 hours daily and Bhaijee was also giving an exposition daily for 4-5 hours during those days on the persuasion of Shri Sethji. After the death of Shri Sethji, Bhaijee generally was arranging an assembly of virtuous people (*satsang*) for two times, each for an hour of duration. The ardent devotees who had tasted such essence once, they generally made efforts to come every year. An arrangement was also made to invite other saints and sages for discourses. In addition to discourses, devotees had been requesting Bhaijee for some extra – time to solve their personal problems in solitude. During the time of discourses, people present in assembly (*satsang*) of virtuous people delivered their written questions to Bhaijee which were solved timely by Bhaijee. During night and at the residence (Dalmia building) of Bhaijee, poetry singing and celebration of devotional songs (*sankeertan*) were held while celebration of devotional songs was arranged in Gita Bhawan on the day of full moon, a day without moon and eleventh day of lunar fortnight. Bhaijee had been visiting continuously till 1969 except for one year when he was not well.

❐

100

An Arrival of Shri Sitaram Omkarnath Maharaj at Gorakhpur

Shri Sitaram Omkarnath Maharaj was a famous Bengali saint. People considered and respected him as a realised person. He was attracted to Bhaijee through '*Kalyan*'. Therefore, he had begun to study the special issues of '*Kalyan*' with an awakening interest. He met Bhaijee first time in about 1953. His articles had been appearing in 'Kalyan'. Thereafter, he became silent and during that period, translated the books in Bengali, published by Gita press. At that very time, he had a desire to bow and prostrate at the door of Gita press. He had given up silence in 1955 and arrived at Gorakhpur by spreading the divine name. He prostrated at the gate of Gita press even though immersed in mud and Bhaijee accompanied with him and had shown the entire press. The affectionate behaviour of Bhaijee had completely taken over the control of his heart for a long time. He had translated Shri Ramcharit Manas in Bengali with the help of commentary on language by Bhaijee during the repetitive period of silence and had dedicated such translation on the name of Bhaijee and Shri Chimmanlalji Goswami. He had written in letter of dedication:

"Whatever is being done to spread about the religion to spread the divine name, to spread scriptures in such cruel *Kaliyug*, with the help of two superhuman instruments through the eternal and entirely compassionate supreme Lord, I have never seen such type of thing or publicity in any voluminous work in *Sanskrit* dealing with an aspect of ancient Indian history or not heard if any religious promulgator, who had ever made such a worldwide publicity of religion. Bengali translation of their excessively dearest 'Shri Ramcharit Manas' is dedicated in the sacred name of two beautifully risen and charming moons by supreme abode of love and an entirely revered person, the editor of '*Kalyan*', Shri Hanuman Prasad Poddar Sir and the illustrious Chimmanlalji Goswami."

He came again in 1964. That time Bhaijee had arranged for his stay near to himself in Gita vatika. He was extremely influenced by the affectionate behaviour of Bhaijee. Thereafter, he continued a letter correspondence with Bhaijee. During April 1969, he arrived at Swargashram at the residence of

Bhaijee. It was last year of his stay at Swargashram for Bhaijee. Bhaijee had severe pain in his stomach but neglecting it, he engaged himself towards his hospitality. Pleasant discussion, group singing of hymns and an assembly of virtuous people (*satsang*) were held and Bhaijee accompanied him up to the bank of the Ganga. He was given a farewell along with sufficient quantity of fruits. As soon as he went back through boat, the sharp pain in his stomach had again appeared and Bhaijee could reach his residence with great difficulty.

He wrote for Bhaijee:

"Our Lord has acted by such a novel propaganda for scriptures and religion through the body of Shri Poddar Baba (Bhaijee) which is not yet found nor will be found. The head is automatically bent down unto the holy feet of such saint. …Shri Poddar Baba was an excellent instrument for the propaganda of religion of the God… by taking permission of his heart, the holy God Himself only was performing the activities. Shri Poddar Baba was free. An arrogant person cannot perform such type of propaganda for scriptures and religion.… to protect existing form of an ancient religion in this age of proliferation and just to fulfill the supreme welfare of the world, monthly magazine '*Kalyan*' has been emerged, taking the shelter of the body of Shri Poddar Baba due to will of the holy God. An infinite number of men and women continuously suffered and fell by the road due to grief, sorrow-diseases- blaze and sufferings, have been contented by resting under the peaceful, comfortable and very cool shadow of '*Kalyan*' and are being still contented. Surprisingly, during this Kali-impure-defiled era and at a time of abandonment of scriptural religion, number of customers for '*Kalyan*' – a proclaimer of the religion and immemorial scriptures, is more than one lakh fifty thousand… as example for the sea is the sea only and an example for sky is the sky. Likewise, an example to our Poddar Baba is only our Poddar Baba himself."

❒

101

An Inauguration of New Gate of Gitapress by the President

Jaydayalji Goyandka and Poddarji had been thinking for long that the construction of main entrance of Gitapress and '*Kalyan*' should be according to its ideal and repute. He could succeed of such planning in 1957. For construction of Gita press, inspiration was sought from the chief symbol of ancient temples through the glorious architectural style of the country. The main gate consisted of seven types of symbols:

(i) Word symbol in the form of sentences from the Gita and the *Upnishads*.
(ii) An animal symbol in the form of ox and lion & serpent.
(iii) Flower symbol in the form of a lotus.
(iv) Sign symbol in the form of a Swastika or tetraskelion.
(v) An object symbol in the form of pitcher and conch.
(vi) An armament symbol in the form of conch, wheel, club, lotus, trident, a small drum, bow and arrow, etc.
(vii) Instrumental symbol in the form of a string of beads, book, lamp, fragrant gum, a dish holding lamp, etc. have been shown suitably.

For construction of entrance gate, support has been sought by the art employed in the construction of *Ellora, Ajanta, Kali temple of Dakshineshwar, Vishwanath temple of Varanasi, Dwarkadhish temple of Mathura, Jagannath temple of Puri, Lingraj temple of Bhubaneswar, Sun temple of Konark, Meenakshi temple of Madurai, Golden temple of Amritsar, Mahadeo temple of Khajuraho, Stoopa of Sanchi, Jain temple of Abu, Mahakal temple of Ujjain, Shiv temple of Kedarnath, Buddha temple of Bodhgaya, Buddhist tower designated in Burma.* In the second part of main entrance, there is a chariot with four horses built of marble on which statue of Lord Shri Krishna is in facial expression to indicate Kaurav army to Arjun. The length of chariot is six-feet-one-inch and the weight is about 1500 kg. It was shaped and arranged from Jaipur.

To inaugurate such a grand entrance gate of Gita press, the President, Dr. Rajendra Prasadji had arrived at Gorakhpur during *Vaishakh Shukla* in the year 1955 due to special insistence of Bhaijee. Poddarji had given him a hearty welcome from Gita press. The President expressed his views during the inaugural speech as follows:

"You have obliged me by inviting on the occasion for the inauguration of Gita entrance. With the help from various portions of many temples, hemispherical structures and Buddhist towers, you have built a magnificent entrance. You have built an entrance by selecting from the architectural samples built in thousands of square miles in thousands of years and by looking at them, anyone can imagine the style of all those structures.

"Whenever I found any such organisation, which is practically industrious in spreading such type of thoughts, I have naturally become emotional. Therefore, whatever work has been done in Gita press till today and being done, I pay respect to it and I wish that it should expand more from day to day.

"You are fulfilling an extremely important need of life. The one who had inspired you will also succeed your efforts. This is my hope and good wishes."

❐

102

Protection of Life of Sudarshan Singh 'Chakra'

A famous author of '*Kalyan*', Shri Sudarshan Singhji 'Chakra' had high regards for Bhaijee. How Bhaijee once took care of his life can be seen as follows in his own words:

This incidence occurred in 1955. I had returned from a trip of *Kailash Mansarovar*. I had proper enthusiasm instead of tiredness. While I am at it, but also wanted to make trip to *Muktinath, Damodar- tank,* which will nearly complete my visit to all pilgrimages of Uttarakhand. I requested Bhaijee of his permission to proceed and it was granted.

The journey was needed to be commenced by the second week of September to October. That was the best suitable climate. All preparations had been completed. I thought to board such a bus from Gorakhpur so that the flight may also be available on that day. Staying at night at *Bhairahwa*, the journey on foot may be begun on the next day.

The luggage was ready. rickshaw was called for bus stop. Then I went to bow Bhaijee in his room.

Bhaijee was inspecting the papers, sitting on the mat in his room near editing office of Gita vatika. I bowed before him.

'Oh! You are leaving? Bhaijee suddenly had suspended his face. His voice became heavy and sad. He said – O.K. go, the pictures of special issue of '*Kalyan*' – 'Satkathank' have not been decided; artists have not yet been instructed. I will work hard and will just do it, anyhow. It was an entirely unexpected condition. I had already asked him well in advance about this trip. He had consented happily. He had also helped to secure important certificates. The selection of pictures, instructions to artists regarding it had always been issued by Shri Bhaijee. I had seldom given just a very little help in it.

The most peculiar condition was that it was my first occasion to hear Bhaijee in such tone. In future also, I never heard to speak in such tone. His such tone was intolerable to me. Therefore, responded – why do you speak like this? If you wish to deny, say it frankly.

Listening to just this, Bhaijee called in complete trial of strength and voice, full of joy, current manager of editing department Shri Dulichandji Dujari and said – "Brother, please send back the rickshaw. Sudarshanji is not leaving."

Now there was nothing left for me to say. I left silently. Rickshaw was sent back. The luggage was unfastened. I was a little sad.

Next day, I had become just free from my daily routine that Bhaijee had come and stood up at the door of my room. He told in a very serious tone – Sudarshanji, a serious accident has occurred.

"What happened" – I asked.

He replied – there was a phone call, just now, by collector. He had enquired that the person from your place who wanted to go to Muktinath had gone or not. I told him that he had not gone. He informed that the plane that took off yesterday had met with an accident. All its passengers had died.

Later, there was a news in newspapers that not only the plane was destroyed by dust storm, thunderstorm and the terrible rain of hailstorm, but even the road for motor route had also been damaged up to several miles. There was no possibility to open that route at least for 15-20 days.

❒

103

A Trip to Distant Pilgrimages

A special train for pilgrimage from Gita press was arranged in 1939 under the patronage of Shri Sethji. Bhaijee was also persuaded that time to accompany but he was immersed with the fever-like solitude and he went to Dadri for a seclusion. Therefore, his close friends had been persuading him to accompany and Bhaijee kept it postponing. Several people have been requesting insistently to Shri Sethji about it because it was their belief that Bhaijee would not deny about the words from Shri Sethji. Due to continuous persuasion, Bhaijee must agree under compulsion but had separated himself entirely from the managing department. Finally, the programme was finalised to start in January, 1956. Although this news was not circulated, otherwise a problem may arise about whom you would say 'Yes' and to whom 'No', but even than a number of accompanying persons had exceeded so much that it was not possible to take everyone along and an excuse with folded hands had to be made from them. Despite this, there were about six hundred ladies and gents to accompany. To arrange eating and drinking and other arrangements of full trip for about three months was an extremely arduous task.

On 19th January 1956, Bhaijee reached Varanasi along with one hundred people from Gorakhpur. It was decided to begin journey just from Varanasi. In the beginning, the journey was to proceed firstly to *Puri*, but that programme must be postponed due to riots held during that time in Odisha. Due to change of programme, they must stay in Varanasi for seven days. It was decided after a serious consideration that journey may begin firstly from *Chitrakoot, Prayag* side and north India could be seen at first instance. The whole programme of special train was changed accordingly. On 26th January, 1956, Shri Sethji arrived to Varanasi from Calcutta along with 225-250 people. By collecting every accompanying passenger, Shri Sethji, Bhaijee and Swami Ramsukh Dasji had informed them about important things which should be remembered during journey. Worship by sacred verses of 'Vedas' for Shri Ganesh and other deities has been performed by the chief scholars of Varanasi. Thereafter, worship of the engine and planning for an auspicious moment have been conducted by Shri Sethji. With a roar of victory for divine names, the journey began on 27th January, 1956. The train reached at *Karvi* on second day morning and morning prayer and celebration of devotional songs (*sankeertan*) were conducted under the guidance of Shri Goswamiji. Bhaijee had informed about the important rules to be followed by the passengers. Such a trend framed throughout the journey, i.e., once the train reached a station in the morning, all passengers were collected together there itself and prayer and celebration of devotional songs (*sankeertan*) had been performed under the guidance of Shri Goswamiji and then they were told about the nearby sight-seeing places. Everyone reached *Chitrakoot* from Karvi by bus and stayed there for two days. It is not possible to describe about complete journey. Therefore, a brief description of few places can be given. A huge community of people had welcomed Bhaijee under the direction of Shri Purushottam Das Tandon and Prabhudutt Brahmachari at Prayag and Brahmachariji had presented an honorary address to Bhaijee. At *Ayodhya* station, after completion of prayer, celebration of devotional songs and discourses, everyone had moved to take bath on foot by performing group-singing of hymns (*keertan*) from station to the new embankment of *Saryu.* In the evening, after sight-seeing of main temples, a vast meeting was arranged by the citizens of Shri Ram birthplace to welcome Bhaijee in which all chief saints of the city were present.

Bhaijee was informed on his arrival at Indore that Shri Sitaram Dasji Onkarnathji Maharaj engrossed in deep yoga and ascetic practice at that time in the refuge of *Onkareshwar* pilgrimage. Being in silent state, he did not meet anyone, but he instantly came out as soon as Bhaijee reached and by giving few Tulsi leaves and a garland of flowers has become immersed in profound meditation at that very place. In Mumbai, Bhaijee was given a grand welcome because several people from there had very long acquaintance with Bhaijee. Each one was extremely happy to accompany Bhaijee during pilgrimage. During the assembly of virtuous people (*satsang*) also, an incomparable public was collected together.

When Bhaijee reached South India, an assistant editor of chief paper – "*Hindi-Prachar-Samachar*" of South India Hindi promoter committee, Shri S.R. Sharangpani accompanied him as a translator. Most of the important pilgrimages of South India have been seen. Amongst those, few names are – *Tirupati, Kalhasti, Kanchipuram, Tirunnamale, Shrirangam, Madurai, Rameshwaram, Kanyakumari Shrivilluputtur, Tenkashi, Kumbhkonam, Tirunevalli, Alvar, Tirunagri, Thiruanantpuram, Guruvayur*, etc.

Bhaijee had his own special way to analyse the events. For example – Bhaijee was going to *Tirumallai* from *Tirupati.* Looking at shortage of time, the journey was undertaken bus or car by instead of foot. Bhaijee sat in vehicle only when he was satisfied that everyone has got a comfortable seat in buses. Whence on the mountain, there was a road of stairs, for climbing for foot travellers, each vehicle had stopped at that crossing and all travellers had got down. Bhaijee had explained in devotional fervour – the special thing of the place is that like worshipping incarnation (*archavatar*) of the God, his emotional incarnation (*vibhvavatar*) is also considered as respectful and important. This 'Sheshshell', which is actually a group of seven hillocks, is considered a form of an ancient serpent. The God is known here as 'Sheshshell Shiromani'. Shri Ramanujacharya Swami has considered it improper to climb this sacred mountain by foot and, therefore, reached temple with the help of his knees and hands wrapping the clothes around them. But alas! we are powerless and are compelled. By saying this, Bhaijee closed his eyes and become absorbed in meditation for some time. Thereafter, he had prostrated towards *Sheshadri* and applied its dust on his forehead. The discourses given by Bhaijee during pilgrimage had been extremely important from the literary, cultural and religious viewpoint. The programme of welcome address, arranged in *Meenakshi temple, Madurai* was also very interesting. Local devotees had recited religious songs in *Tamil, Sanskrit* and *Gujarati* language and hence eulogised Bhaijee with a very big garland to wear, praising his religious services and also presented, to repeat in loud, an honorary letter of appreciation. In his reply, Bhaijee told seriously that to worship the name and personality of anyone, to eulogise by garlanding him is not good. Local people were surprised looking at the exceptional meekness of Bhaijee. He paid great respect lying flat to scholars of Vedas, well- versed in scriptures and used to get extremely pleased by hearing their proper accent for recitation of Vedas. They were given due honour and gratuity as well. According to local people, it had not only provided sufficient strength for spreading of religious devotion (*Bhakti*) in South India due to such trip of Bhaijee but had only provided more strength to spread Hindi. Emotional devotees at many places over there had also walked around in reverence of the pilgrimage train.

When Bhaijee reached Calcutta via Puri and Bhubaneswar, a very large number of public had assembled at Howrah station to welcome Bhaijee and had got benefitted by joining there at the functions in assembly of virtuous people (*satsang*).

An authentic description had been prepared for all pilgrimages, which was published next year as a special issue – '*Tirthank*' in '*Kalyan*'.

❐

104

Nobody Should Know Anything About My Inner State

The shivering winter was over while the scorching summer is yet to come. It is morning time and gentle breeze is flowing. During such a pleasant weather, a lady is sitting in an implicit belief in front of the picture of her idol. She is not aware of winter or summer. The tears have been trickling due to severity of emotion. Due to an abundance of emotion of today, when did the stream of tears in lieu of trickling have soaked her border at the end of *Sari* cannot be known to her. How much time has lapsed as sitting since morning while the Sun God has almost arrived in the middle of sky, even this was also not known to her. Her condition can be described in words, indeed:

No clue for day or night,
And also, no track of the evening or morning.

(Pad Ratnakar – p.505

It is not a new thing. She had been sitting adamantly with a longing, retained in the secret corner of the heart, nobody knows since how many years, that let me see once my idol. If the worship is in the form of an omniscient divine idol, then such state can be occurred to several lucky devotees. But the one whose appearance is not yet made, though convenient, the condition of her heart cannot be described. But nothing is hidden by supreme being and its arrangements have been made, as being improper to ask further to wait.

In 1956, Bhaijee reached near Baijwara in South India during his trip to the complete pilgrimage of India. He went to a residence of a known reputed pleader. During conversation, he said that an adult lady just in his neighbourhood sings hymns day and night in solitude. Endowed with divine wealth, she remained engaged generally in worship with reading of religious texts. As you have come, you should meet her once. Due to his persuasion, Bhaijee went to meet her. He asked the accompanied persons to sit outside and he went inside alone in her room earmarked for spiritual accomplishment (*Sadhna kaksha*). He found that a lady was sitting with an access of emotion in a genuine atmosphere, in front was an idol of the God and a picture of Bhaijee himself was also placed nearby. The lady did not open her eyes, presuming someone would have come, as usual, to receive remnants of food offered to the God. Looking at all this, Bhaijee is carried away with an emotion. A little later asked – O lady! Whose picture is this? Just bending her head, she replied – I had read something about him since many years ago. Since then, I have a feeling of surrender to him. I could get this photo by much efforts from Mumbai. Since then, I am worshiping him in the form of a favoured deity. Bhaijee asked – Do you know him, ever met him, where does he live?

The lady replied – I know his name but have never met him. When I have surrendered him myself, then no need to know about the address or whereabouts.

Bhaijee said with great embarrassment – Will you please look up for once?

Through the eyes full of great modesty, the lady had cast off her gaze and by seeing her deity in front, had become ecstatic and had placed her head unto the feet of Bhaijee. A little later, she got up and adorned with a mark of sandal paste on forehead of Bhaijee, offered flowers by putting sandal paste unto his feet and said slowly – You can go now.

Bhaijee asked – O lady! May I know your introduction?

She replied – You are not required to know my introduction. An introduction which I have, it should also not be conveyed to your people, otherwise there will be a crowd at my place.

Bhaijee said – You can at least note my address.

The lady replied – I don't need it. There has been only one longing in my mind that I should meet you once. The Supreme Lord has fulfilled this longing in a very strange manner. I don't wish anything else. I do live just near to you through my mind. Let my dedication succeed to the end.

Looking at all this, Bhaijee has become perturbed with emotion and went outside by blessing her through heart. Bhaijee had narrated this incident after many years to one of his close friends. On consistent persuasion though, he had disclosed her name – Chinmayee Devi but never disclosed name of place and address up to the end. If asked, he said – she does not like that anyone of this world should know her unselfish and silent dedication.

Once a while Bhaijee was sitting, her emotions have revived some memory and the pen begins to move –

Dedicated to divine feet, whatever belongs to me or mine,

Permanently dissociated from deeply accumulated and every temporary shelter of the world and worldly affairs.

I have now relation to the God only with all my affection,

Love, faith, and engagement have all vanished, causing to open all the knots.

To love him in his temperament while the whole world just existed in him only,

Except him, there is no one left whom I can deal with. Don't like if someone knows anything about my condition,

My brother, it should also be kept always confidential even from the God.

With beautiful flowers and fresh fragrant soil, I did worship daily, it is very secret, he should never know it, I am afraid of this.

Such of my pious worship may continue safely till eternity,

May live anywhere, in whatever condition but it should never be concluded.

With such of my worship, I may continue to receive just contentment till eternity,

I may always progress with my interest in worshiping, may increase in an ultimate bliss till eternity.

Let an increasing worship yield only a sacred outcome of worship, I may observe his very pleasing form constantly.

But he may never observe me or my worship,

If he will see, then only it will be a completion of an emotional interchange.

Then I may not retain such secluded sacred existence,

Then there would arise new desires to be satisfied by the beloved.

(Pad Ratnakar/p. 472)

An actual ideal of such feelings was presented by Chinmayi Devi.

An infinite salute to that lady and to such secret lovers.

❐

105
A Circumambulation of Giriraj

Bhaijee became sick on his return from pilgrimage. He went to Ratangarh from Gorakhpur on 22nd November, 1956 for the recovery of his health. Most of the time, he remained there in solitude, by closing his room. From there, he went for circumambulation (*parikrama*) of the sacred mountain of Mathura between 10th and 11th February, 1957. He was accompanied there with close friends, in addition to his family members. The circumambulation of Shri Giriraj was conducted enthusiastically with pleasure. From there, he also went to obtain a sight of Shri Radhaji at Barsana. On 13th April, 1957, he returned to Ratangarh.

❐

106

Death of Shri Ghanshyam Dasji Jalan

Though Bhaijee had not recovered completely, but due to serious sickness of Shri Ghanshyam Dasji Jalan and an extreme insistence of Shri Sethji went to Swargashram on 20th May 1958 from Gorakhpur. Shri Jalanji has made an unwearied effort throughout life for the progress of Gita press and remained a publisher and printer of Gita press until death. He has left his body during celebration of devotional songs (*sankeertan*) in the presence of Shri Sethji and Bhaijee at an embankment of the Ganga at Gita Bhawan in Swargashram on 24th May, 1958. Thereafter, the responsibility of printer and publisher was also given to Bhaijee.

❐

107

An Indication of Spiritual State

Just to write anything about the spiritual state of any saint will be an effort without an authority. Firstly, then the spiritual condition itself is a self-existential (*Swasamvaidya*), secondly, no one can guess about it. Such thing can only make a home in one's heart when someone could achieve that state of devoted striving (*sadhna*) by the grace of God. Then to restrain few words about Bhaijee, is even more difficult because such an act is presented by the God through him, was an excellent coordination between a scholar of high caliber, saint and highest saint of *Braj* temperament which is normally not seen. Bhaijee has sometimes given few indications in the presence of few close friends and this is merely an effort to connect only those words without an authority.

An initial accomplishment (*Sadhna*) of Bhaijee was highly influenced due to Shri Sethji. Shri Sethji had been mostly narrating meditation for Lord Vishnu or to a form without good qualities and without shape (*Nirgun* and *Nirakaar*). Accordingly, Bhaijee started devoted striving in Shimlapal and had been meditating on the picture of Lord Vishnu painted by Ravi Varma and within six months, an idol of Shri Lord Vishnu has fixed into his eyes even during his various day-to-day movements. It was not considered as any attainment by Bhaijee, rather, was treated as seriousness of practice. When devoted striving (*Sadhna*) had begun again in Mumbai, he had achieved a high state without good qualities and without shape (*Nirgun* and *Nirakaar*) and in between also visualised *Shri Ram*. Then, prior to one or two months of the publication of *'Bhagvannamank'*, meditation had begun of Lord Vishnu automatically in place of an unmanifested one (*Avyakt*). It was his opinion that which is unknown, that very is known, who is without qualities and shapeless, that very is with good qualities and shape. Therefore, due to strong longing for visualisation for the God, an actual appearance of Lord Vishnu was occurred in front of several people in 1927 at *Jasidih*, this was a very rare event of spiritual world which cannot be retained as confidential by any means. Such appearance was the visualisation of the highest deity among three deities (Brahma, Vishnu and Mahesh) and was not of an incarnated great

Vishnu. A little later, the incarnated great Vishnu also appeared. Such mystery was disclosed by Shri Krishna, then it was known. During the preparation of publication for '*Shri Krishnank*' in 1931, serious thinking and continued study have been made towards the acts of Shri Krishna. Some of religious texts from region of Gaur sect have also been studied. Due to such activity, a longing was emerged to witness the act of the God. An instinct had already been present since the time of study of the Shrimad Bhagwat in Mumbai. He feels, as if the God is saying – there occur only two types of acts in my *Vishnu* identity – An incarnation act and eternal act of the heaven. An act is completed in the highest form and entirely as an identity of Shri Krishna. You will now be empowered to know the identity of Shri Krishna. On that night, Bhaijee was very pleased in himself and has visualised Shri Krishna in dream. Firstly, visualised as narrator of Gita and later as a resident of Vrindavan – Shri Krishna. It appeared instantly that He is saying – the narrator of Gita is also a resident of Vrindavan (famous as *Vrindavan Bihari*). He is very kind to you. He has accepted you. You will now see his acts. On second day, during the time of meditation of Lord Vishnu, *Vrindavan Bihari* Shri Krishna has begun to appear in meditation automatically. During change in meditation, an appearance of acts of Vrindavan have also begun to exhibit. Bhaijee had said once – 'an inspiration to remain as simple in life externally had already been arisen after an event of Jasidih but a clear instruction has only been given by Shri Krishna. Therefore, if you try to remember during 1927-1937, then seriousness was more prevalent in life'. During the observance of divine acts, I had also become one with them. He explained in this context – an entry in the act is not due to initiation of my desire. When he desires, it suddenly attracts me and permits to join in the act. Neither can I go willingly, nor can I ask others to accompany. You cannot go there with this body. Found an opportunity to attend these acts for four to five hours each. This event occurred during 1937. He had remained immersed in the Kingdom of divine act even being as externally busy in editing '*Kalyan*' and other service activities. Then he had gone to Dadri to live in solitude, that time he had remained occupied with the sweet acts of Radha Krishna. A high soul of noble nature had virtually seen *Mirabai* in about 1940. He had raised some questions and also enquired about the state of Bhaijee. Then Mirabai replied that the subtle body of Hanuman Prasad has transformed totally into an own form of Shri Priyaji. To believe on it completely or not depends on the condition of one's own inner faculty. But Bhaijee has never disclosed such state for several years in external life. When Bhaijee has remained devoid of an external consciousness unwillingly for hours after 1961 which is known as temperamental profound meditation (*bhava-samadhi*), then the people could feel a little bit. It is not possible to comment of such state in words. *Naradji* has described it as an identity of love – 'An identity of love is inexpressible in words and it's like describing about the taste by a dumb'. To give a hint for such state – any word can be used like an emotional meditation (*bhava samadhi*), divinely state (*Bhagwati sthiti*), great emotional state (*Mahbhavmayi sthiti*), natural state (*Swaroop sthiti*), a state in the kingdom of divine love (*Divya prem rajya sthiti*), etc. Bhaijee had achieved such state possibly in 1941, but its external characters have come to light after 1961. This was just the condition of inner state of Bhaijee while externally the God wanted him to do extraordinary service of spiritual world. Therefore, realisation was made of every main character like *Shri Ram*, *Shri Shiva*, Goddess, etc. When Bhaijee was preparing for '*Shivank*' in Ratangarh in 1943, *Lord Shankar* appeared and gradually transformed to *Lord Vishnu* and from Lord Vishnu again transformed to Lord Shiva and remained laughing in both forms. Likewise, when he was preparing for *'Shaki ank'*, Bhaijee was blessed, during those days, by an energy element (*Shakti-tatva*). The same thing happened in relation to other characters. Like this, the body of Bhaijee was just allowing time to pass while he himself remained immersed within the charmed savour (*Madhurya ras*) of his deity.

❐

108

An Inauguration of Temple for Shri Krishna Birthplace at Mathura

Like Shri Ram birthplace in Ayodhya, the glory of Shri Krishna's birthplace in Mathura had also been almost vanished. An ancient temple of that place had been destroyed by Mughal Kings. Due to inspiration of Mahamana Malviya, Shri Jugul Kishor Birla has taken this work in his hands for its restoration. But for planning and its implementation for construction of Bhagwat building and the temple and fix the reestablishment of missing dignity of Shri Krishna birthplace, the credit goes to Bhaijee. Its introduction was framed during the pilgrimage of Bhaijee. When Bhaijee arrived at Mathura, a person asked during his welcome function – millions of travellers have been coming to Mathura each year. There is no one whose heart is not torn apart himself looking at the present wretched condition of Shri Krishna birthplace. When Bhaijee stood up to express gratefulness at the end of function, he declared with eyes full of tears – whatever has been said towards birthplace, I am totally agreed with it. I am also ready to offer my little effort for this purpose. Soon ten thousand rupees will be sent to you for this work. In fact, this work expects to do your duty by yourself. Hearing this, the people present over there have become happy beyond limits.

Bhaijee immediately sent rupees ten thousand on his return to Gorakhpur. In addition, he has also inspired Dalmia brothers for the construction of Keshav temple at Shri Krishna birthplace. Shri Ram Krishna Dalmia has arranged to construct Keshav temple in the sacred memory of his mother. Bhaijee went to Mathura to inaugurate this temple and on 6th September 1958, on Shri Krishna's birthday, and has inaugurated this temple through his hands. Bhaijee has spoken in his lecture at the time of the inauguration ceremony – "Due to raising of such issue of Shri Krishna birthplace – the face of our country has brightened."

❐

109

To Exert Transfer of Power (*Shaktipat*) by Radha Baba

Shri Bhaijee had also adopted one more way to hide himself. To a new person, he saved himself to reveal by putting Baba in front. On one hand, faith of religious public is just like this, which is attracted more towards ochre garments than to domestic attire and then Bhaijee had also maintained his efforts as well, just like that. During previous years, when he visits city like Calcutta, etc., a time was fixed for a meeting to Baba. Whosoever had come to meet at that time, they had to sit near Baba, who did not utter to anyone nor see to anyone. Bhaijee continued to tell about the name of person, whosoever bowed him. The attention of new person does not move to maker of saint than just to the saint and a thing desired from the heart of Bhaijee also fulfilled. Bhaijee received phone calls many times to fix time for a visit to Radha Baba. It was a general feeling that Bhaijee is working as secretary to Baba.

Like this, if there is certain thing to be given to a particular person, then it is arranged through Baba. This event occurred in 1959. Few days ago, to eighth day of celebration of Radha's birthday, respected Baba told to Bhaijee to call five distinct persons on the eighth day celebration after Radha's birthday. I will give something after examining them. Baba had been following, during those days silence strictly. Nobody can go near him. Bhaijee only could arrange meeting of anyone by leading away with him. Bhaijee has written a letter to one of the persons among five, mentioning all names that Baba had told to reward something after examining those people. Therefore, you all five should reach prior to eighth day of celebration of Radha's birthday. All those five people were familiar with the rule of silence of Baba and evidently do not have also a direct contact with Baba. Looking at his kindness, they have been feeling pleasure of such opportunity. As per written direction, they reached a little earlier and Bhaijee went inside the hut of Baba alongwith those five persons at the precise time and day. What is examined by Baba and what they have received are only known to Baba or his beloved. But after half-an-hour, all five persons have come out of the hut in a very happy mood. There is not only one but several events, when Bhaijee had to hide himself due to apprehension for disclosure of some distinguishing property, by putting Baba in front.

❐

110

A Narration of the Childhood Exploits of Shri Krishna

On the whole, Bhaijee had been several times narrating childhood exploits of Shri Krishna in his discourses, but few sentimental people wanted that such acts should be narrated comprehensively. Such persuasion continued for several years but waiting just sustained for some good opportunity. Finally, Bhaijee agreed to narrate an elaborative description of childhood exploits of Shri Krishna in morning daily for two hours for about one month from December, 1959. People from faraway places, who were waiting for it, assembled in Gorakhpur. Based on various commentaries, the sacred legend has begun from the first chapter of tenth part of the *Shrimad Bhagwat*. Although, during those days, Bhaijee had engrossed in an ecstatic state (*Bhav samadhi*) for a longer duration, Therefore, he becomes indifferent looking to the crowd of audiences. But, when begins the narration* then took up describing it lively, being immersed in it and then Bhaijee becomes again detached on the completion of narration. The people, who had enjoyed that charming-narration, they only realised the intensity about shower of emotions which occurred during that one month.

**The cassettes of such discourses, which have also been recently condensed in a pen drive are available for sale with the Gita vatika Publication, Post Gitavatika, Gorakhpur, 237006, India.*

❐

111

Laying of Foundation Stone for the New Building of Govind Bhawan

An endowment named 'Govind Bhawan Office' was established since many years ago. Gita press of Gorakhpur and Gita Bhawan of Swargashram are managed by this trust. Due to an increase in sphere of its activity, the old place of Govind Bhawan in Calcutta was not sufficient. Discussion was in progress for new building since many years. According to the decision of organisers, a land was purchased for the construction of new building on Mahatma Gandhi Road. Laying of foundation stone was decided to carry through by the hands of Bhaijee.

On 26th January, 1960, Bhaijee went to Calcutta from Gorakhpur. Several people have given Bhaijee a hearty welcome at Howrah station. An arrangement for the residence of Bhaijee was made in Panihati about 12 miles away from Calcutta city. Bhaijee stayed there for about fifteen days. The residents of Calcutta had found after several years an opportunity for the benefit by assembly of virtuous people (*Satsang*) with Bhaijee for as long as this much of duration. During the time of this visit, laying of foundation stone of the new building of 'Govind Bhawan' was suitably completed in sumptuary way by the hands of Bhaijee.

❑

112

Revisit of Shimlapal

Most of his affectionate companions had been requesting Bhaijee to accompany to Shimlapal where Bhaijee had first started his spiritual quest. Being a nearer place from Calcutta, such persuasion has increased. One more coincidence has appeared for this very time. Shri Sethji had to be operated of eyes at Bankura. Therefore, Bhaijee went to Bankura from Calcutta alongwith some attendants. From there, Shimlapal was about 24 miles away. Therefore, on request of attendants, he travelled to Shimlapal by Motor Car alongwith everybody. Everyone, firstly, has seen that hut where Bhaijee had lived for about forty-four years ago. Inside its small room was written 'Nrityagopal' by Bhaijee in *Bangla* with red clay soil from those days. Bhaijee has narrated about the memories of past. Then everyone visited to a small river nearby where Bhaijee had taken bath during those days. Thereafter, went to the police station of Shimlapal and observed the documents written by Bhaijee. Prior to return to Bankura, garments, money, etc. have been distributed to the villagers.

❑

113

Away from the Titles

Everybody is interested to earn a degree. At present, people are trying various means to earn degree. Flattering is done, and money is also spent for it. Bhaijee had run away from such degrees though have been bestowing even without any effort. There occurred several occasions in life when many institutions, people had desired to felicitate him but Bhaijee did not accept any such proposal.

At first, Bhaijee was offered a designate of 'Rai Sahib' (a title during British rule in India). The current collector of Gorakhpur Shri Pedley and the president of city municipality, Babu Adya Prasadji had been the proposer for this. Both were overwhelmed by the services rendered by Bhaijee. Bhaijee has requested an excuse with folded hands – "I am not suitable for it." Both had an affectionate relation with Bhaijee. Therefore, they understood his feeling and agreed.

Thereafter, in 1935, during raining season, there occurred a terrible flood in nearby areas of Gorakhpur. Several villages submerged in water and repeated calls have been made from all around. Bhaijee himself along with the workers of Gita press joined to help through body and mind. He himself was delivering grains and garments in the villages by the boats. Meal was given daily to about 6,500 people. One can well imagine the expenses incurred for such an activity of service. Looking at the devotion to his work and readiness, the current Commissioner

R.C. Hobart has sent a telegram and letter of thanks and wanted to award the degree of 'Rai Bahadur' (a high-ranking title during British rule in India). Bhaijee has humbly refused.

A little later, the Governor of United Province (U.P.), Sir Harry Hague has thrown a net as 'Sir' (knighthood). On the insistence of Bhaijee, he also agreed. The Governor felt happy for it. Bhaijee had friendship with Sir Harry Hague. When they met, Bhaijee asked without any hesitation due to friendly relation – What do you mean by the award of such an honour? He replied laughingly – "To put a strap around the neck of a dog......" before he could complete his statement, Bhaijee interrupted, "Then you were putting a strap around my neck." The Governor said laughingly – you are telling it because you have rejected it. If you had accepted, then we felicitate you and would have expressed thanks that you have accepted it.

Thereafter, he has acquired the biggest of all a temptation, to accept the degree as 'Jewel of India' (Bharat Ratna). This event occurred in 1955. The President of India Dr. Rajendra Prasadji wanted to award 'Jewel of India' to Bhaijee for his uncommon contribution of campaign for religious awakening and freedom struggle of the country as well as a true campaigner of religious texts and literature, which was awarded to very few people at that time. Rajendra Babu has given this responsibility to the then Home Minister of India Pandit Govind Ballabh Pant, to take consent by Bhaijee. He came to Gorakhpur and met Bhaijee. Talking with great intimacy, he took away the pen from the hands of Bhaijee and then took out a letter from his pocket and requested him to sign in it with his consent. There was a proposal in that letter for 'Jewel of India'. Then he told – "Can I retain this pen as a gift?" Bhaijee replied – there is no need to ask for such thing. But he has expressed his refusal towards its acceptance. Bhaijee continued – I have feeling of high respect in my mind towards Rajendra Babu, but I will not accept his such an appeal. Looking at the pain prevailing in the inner heart of Bhaijee, Panditji has taken back that paper. On his returning back to Delhi, Panditji has narrated everything to the President. Rajendra Babu told this much only that with great difficulty, I had obtained this consent from Jawahar Lal.

❒

114
A Divine Experience to the Home Minister of India

A Shri Govind Ballabh Pant few days after the above incidence, Home Minister, Shri Pant had a supernatural experience regarding Bhaijee. He wrote about his dream and the things related to the actual miracles in detail to Bhaijee. He wrote – You are such a great and eminent person that not only India but whole world should be proud of you. In addition, he has requested to burn his letter. Bhaijee has burnt his letter as directed by him. The reply sent to his letter by Bhaijee is being given as follows:

Respected Shri Pantji, Respectful greetings.

Received your letter. It is pleasing to note that you have reached Delhi safely. I am surprised to read your letter in a new style. Don't know what is going to happen due to an auspicious rule of the God.

You have written to witness dreams and actual miracles which have not come into my understanding. Well, these can be the impressions by some instincts of your unconscious mind. What you have seen and written about me, I can say this much that, nor I am ascetic nor a realised great person, or an achieved saint neither have a power to bless by divine appearance to anyone or to bless with a boon. I am a normal person with full of weaknesses. I have infinite blessings from the God without motive, I have faith in it. I had no knowledge prior to receipt of this letter about your dream and to witness miracles in vigilant state. Therefore, what can I say? The impressions received about your future death have definitely caused a worry to me. If you think it proper, then do the repetition of sacred verse *'Mahamrityunjay'* and ask some faithful devotee of 'Shiva' to do one lakh twenty-five thousand repetitions of above sacred verse. I know it that you are a religious person. You have faith in the God and religious scriptures. You have written – Jawahal Lal is also religious though may utter anything externally, which is alright. I also consider the same about him.

You have just written about me – You are such a great, such a great person that not only in India, but whole world should feel proud of you. Wanted to honour by awarding a degree of 'Jewel of India' to you, without considering your identity or its importance. You did very well that you have not accepted it. You are of a very high state than this degree. I greet you just from my heart. I am feeling an excessive embarrassment by reading such of your words. I don't know under whose inspiration you have written all this. You have always been venerable to me. In the way, I was like earlier, I am also at present, not changed even a slightest. You have always been affectionate to me and considered one's own. I want you to do same affection always on me and consider me one's own. I don't expect your regards but ask for your love and favour and also ask for your kindness. If there is anything I can do for you, please do write to me. According to your instructions, the letter has been burnt. You should please also treat this letter as confidential.

Yours
Hanuman Prasad Poddar

❐

115
A Great Festival – Shri Radhashtami

On the whole, proclaimed ceremony for all the incarnations like *Narsingh* – fourteenth day, *Vaman* – twelth day of lunar fortnight, *Ram* – ninth day of lunar fortnight, *Janki* – ninth day of lunar fortnight etc. had been generally celebrated here at place of Bhaijee. But *Shri Krishna* – eighth day of dark half of the month and *Shri Radha* – eighth day of lunar fortnight *(Radhashtami)* functions had been celebrated in special manner. Among them, place for *Radhashtami* remained on the top. To spread for celebration as great festival of *Radhashtami* had begun specially just by Bhaijee only. Though this ceremony had been celebrated in *Barsana* but it has not much publicity in other places. Prior to thirty years of his heavenly departure, its great festival form has begun. Gradually, it got expansion and the affectionate people have begun to arrive to join from outside. Its shape has become very vast since 1955 after pilgrimage and this great festival has become an immortal tree of wisdom for devoted striving (*sadhna*). Thousands of men and women have experienced peace by the shelter under its dense shadow. A person who has joined it once need not ask anyone for revisit. The preparation of the great festival begins about a month earlier.

Painters, masons, carpenters have all joined together for this work devotedly. The groups of the people from outside have begun to arrive two-three days earlier. Bhaijee himself managed for an accommodation to everyone. Hundreds of people from outside experienced themselves on their arrival as a member of 'Radha-family'. Direction for singing of devotional poetry, celebration of devotional songs (*Sankeertan*) and discourses (*Pravachan*) in morning and evening have been made by Bhaijee himself. People remain immersed in bliss.

During the eighth day of the lunar half by sixth month of Indian lunar calendar, the beginning of this great festival began, early at 4.30 in the morning with the playing of great flute. Thereafter, morning procession begins at 5.30. People inspired by the emotion went dancing upstairs to Bhaijee and he also came out on the roof. At about 8.30, Bhaijee, a dignity personified came and sat in a huge pavillion. In the beginning, Bhaijee talked an exposition in the pavillion. Thereafter, Bhaijee brought out Baba from the hut. Both then ensconced on the dais. Baba remains engrossed in the kingdom of emotions. Recitation of poetry, celebration of devotional songs, discourses, etc. continued throughout the day. By closing the eyes for five minutes, everyone waits for the birth at about 12 o'clock and due to sound produced by conch, bell and gong, the wide sky made to resound at that time of birth. The function concludes at about 4 o'clock, the distribution of *prasad* was followed by special exposition by Bhaijee after the discussion by distinctive scholars, saints and ascetics at night. Night wakefulness was conducted by emotional devotees in which celebration of devotional songs (*sankeertan*) and recitation of poetry (*Pad gayan*) have been performed. *Dadhikardmotsava* (a ritual of Radha's birthday involving throwing of curd mixed with saffron, etc. over devotees) was held on second day in which curd mire is made with large quantity of curd mixed with turmeric, saffron, camphor, attar, rosewater, etc., which offered firstly to Shri Radha Kumari and then tossed up over to devotees during unrestrained group singing of hymns (*Keertan*), everyone would be immersed by such an essence. Later, after recitation of poetry for festivities, Bhaijee gives concluding exposition which was eagerly awaited by the existing people. He says – this function is now concluding – not finished, it will indeed never finish, it is now continued daily. Today we can wish – we should also get a mist by the grace of *Shri Radhaji*. Everybody coming to this place has to bear pains, it is your affection, your grace to whom I can thank. Everyone is just one's own.

To describe the picture of pleasure prevailed during these two days through words is not possible. They only can experience it who have attended it. It is not the subject of description that whom and what you had achieved in the kingdom of emotion. Its beginning had started with a particular intention and how far such intention has been achieved – the almighty can only decide its result. The great festival is still celebrated in the same manner in Gita vatika after the heavenly departure of Bhaijee and the presence of Bhaijee is also felt on such occasion by some of the lucky devotees. Now, such great festival is also being celebrated at many other places.

❐

116

An Extraordinary Miracle due to Joining in the Unrestrained Name Celebration of Devotional Songs during the Great Festival of Radhashtami

This event occurred in 1961. About 30-35 people among us were going to attend the great *Radhashtami* festival from Calcutta. A boy also accompanied us, who had always to tie a leather and iron strap around his backbone due to bone tuberculosis in the vertebral column. If it is removed, then he was just unable to sit or stand without any support. When we took bath in the *Ganga* at Varanasi, two people have arranged his bath in Ganga by grasping him carefully due to his extreme desire. On the day, these people have reached Gorakhpur, Bhaijee has disclosed in his discourse that some trustworthy person told him that Shri Krishna is moving around to watch this great festival of Radhashtami for 7-8 days and He will remain here for 3-4 more days. If someone has strong longing, then he can also appear before him. This boy had a longing just from Calcutta and has come to Gorakhpur for the first time by hearing the importance of this great festival.

On the second day of great festival of *Radhashtami*, as usual, an unstrained name celebration of devotional songs was in process. This boy was also performing celebration of devotional songs (*Sankeertan*) of 'Radhe' – 'Radhe' – dancing with full passion, just tying a strap around. In between, he became unconscious and fell. When people have informed his companions, they lifted him out at one place. Some of them went to call a doctor while others have informed Bhaijee. Bhaijee said – It does not matter. He had totally no external sense but was continuously uttering '*Radhe – Radhe*' by his tongue. A little later, Bhaijee came and said in his ear – Look! I have come. We have helped him to sit. He grasped feet of Bhaijee. Bhaijee said – Get up, you have been blessed by a special thing. Then told us. He should not be gone out of this pavillion. There is no need of any doctor. Grasping his hand, Bhaijee brought him back again in pavillion. Tears were flowing continuously from his eyes and he sat down by grasping feet of Bhaijee. Then he placed his head on the lap of Bhaijee. Bhaijee uttered something one or two times into his ears and becoming ecstatic, he put his string of beads of Tulsi in his neck. Then he announced during his exposition

– This boy was still unconscious. I have not asked him yet, but I believe that he received special experience. If someone desires, then can enquire with him. Who is a deserving person, no one knows it? By saying this, Bhaijee has become ecstatic and silent. Thereafter, this boy remained in semiconscious state for about 40 hours.

Regarding special experience is known to him only, but we have also seen from our eyes that one who cannot even sit without strap was walking well without strap after this incidence. The people who came alongwith him were struck with wonderment. At last, he returned from Gorakhpur just leaving strap behind. It was difficult to guess about his bone T.B. which had just vanished suddenly.

❐

117

Miracle of the Power to Resolve

Shri Bhaijee made things which appeared as impossible to simply possible many times, by his power of the commitment (*sankalp shakti*). But he has always tried to keep such events as secret. Sometimes some events had been disclosed by some reasons. Out of such, an event is just presented here –

Shri Ghanshyamdasji Sharma from Vrindavan had gone, that time, to Calcutta. Earliest he was acting as Thakur in Krishna's dalliance and dance with herd girls of Braj and had become extremely affectionate since that time to respected Baba. Therefore, everyone calls him 'Thakurji'. Baba had taken an oath from him with a promise to always come to Gorakhpur during Radhashtami. His mother fell sick in Calcutta and, therefore, his stay there was important to look after her. It occurred in 1959 and Radhashtami was fast approaching. He wanted to reach to Gorakhpur on Radhashtami while it was also necessary to stay in Calcutta to look after his mother. Under such circumstances, he had written a letter to Bhaijee that I could not reach to Gorakhpur on Radhashtami due to such compulsion. The letter was delivered two days earlier of Radhashtami. Bhaijee explained everything to Radhababa. During those days, Baba had maintained silence and talked only to Bhaijee. Baba told him – Thakur should come on Radhashtami. My show will be spoiled due to his absence. Now there is no time that a message can be sent to him. Therefore, please call him through your will power.

Bhaijee listened to Baba and returned to his room without any comment. How Bhaijee used his power to resolve is known to him only but on the same day, Shri Sharma boarded the train for Gorakhpur without any arrangement of reservation. On arrival to Gorakhpur, he went straight to Bhaijee. When he bowed, Bhaijee told him smiling – you have written to me that you will not come on Radhashtami, how you have come now? He could speak this much only that circumstances had not been suitable to arrive, but you have pulled me here. Then Bhaijee told him everything affectionately and has directed to do daily routine later, firstly to come alongwith me and meet Baba. Bhaijee said by entering the hut – Baba! Your Thakur has come. Baba was very happy. During those days, on the great festival of Radhashtami, Bhaijee was producing new verses for devotional poetry to be sung every year. Baba had called him to sing these verses along with Chimmanlal Goswami. How many such things have been done by his power to resolve are known to Bhaijee only.

❑

118

A visit to Puri and Navdeep

Some of his close friends had a heartily wish to visit Puri and Navdeep with Bhaijee. This programme was planned many times but was always postponed due to some or the other reason. Few sentimental devotees from Calcutta had also persuaded for it. At last, it was decided that when a programme is finalised for Calcutta in the marriage ceremony for daughter of Shri Mohanlalji Goyandka in March, 1962. Then a trip of Navdeep and Puri may be made from there itself. On 5th March, 1962, Bhaijee has moved alongwith his attendants at night from Gorakhpur to Varanasi. He took flight next day and reached Calcutta. An arrangement was made of Bhaijee to stay in Panihata away from city. Wherever Bhaijee went, the programme of celebration of devotional songs was definitely organised at that very place. Bhaijee has departed from Calcutta during night to Puri on 13th March, 1962 after successful conclusion of marriage ceremony. About 200 people have accompanied him. Bhaijee stayed there with the family at the place of Bangurs while the remaining people in the rest houses for pilgrims. Everyone along with Bhaijee had the sight of temple of Shri Jagannathji and the melodious celebration of devotional songs was held inside the courtyard of temple. During celebration of devotional songs (*sankeertan*), external senses of Bhaijee were lost. With lot of efforts, Bhaijee could regain external wisdom after celebration of devotional songs and recitation of verses from devotional poetry. Everyone took bath in the sea at evening. Everyone has also travelled to Sakshi Gopal and Bhuvneshwar on second day. From there, returned to Calcutta and after few days concluded trip of Navdeep.

❐

119

Saving of Shri Dulichand Dujari

On completion of his education, Shri Dulichandji had come to work with Bhaijee in 1933. He was a nephew to Shri Gambhir Chandji Dujari and on his persuasion only, he came to serve Bhaijee. Since then, he remained in service of Bhaijee continuously. Due to his sincerity and ability, within a few years, he became an obligatory attendant to Bhaijee. He was alone managing the work of two-three people. He had become just like a family member of Bhaijee.

Thieves have entered in his home in the night of 4th April, 1962 and beaten him badly. Due to an injury, his head was split and whole body was drenched with blood. Dulichandji became entirely unconscious and almost like dead. He was immediately sent to a hospital and an arrangement was made for the best treatment. Bhaijee himself goes to hospital and remain seated near to him for hours together. Full arrangements have been made towards his proper treatment. Even with sufficient treatment, he could not achieve complete consciousness and his condition has deteriorated on 16thApril, 1962. Treating doctors also got almost disappointed. It appeared if the last fight is in progress with death and there is very little hope of his life. Bhaijee was informed about it. Now there was no visible effort to save him, everyone was looking towards Bhaijee. Family members were also requesting Bhaijee insistently. At last, Bhaijee asked everyone to leave the room and then closed it. What Bhaijee did inside the room is known to him only, but the people have observed thereafter that condition of Dulichandji has improved beyond expectation. Gradually his condition has been improving. Within a few days, he returned home with good health. Although his body could not be healed as earlier due to injuries, even then he would do his utmost to serve Bhaijee.

Likewise, Bhaijee also saved life of Shri Dileep Kumar Bhartiya, when surgeons had become totally disappointed during his second operation.

❐

120

Laying Foundation Stone of Bhagwat-Building

An opinion was being considered for many days for construction of Bhagwat-building on the basis of Manas temple of Varanasi for which it was planned to put eighteen thousand verses of complete *Shrimad Bhagwat* – a great epic, to be engrossed on marble and then should be attached on its different walls. Proposals have been received from various places but at last, it was decided to build this building just in Mathura at Shri Krishna birthplace. Laying of foundation stone was decided for 11th February, 1965. With this intention, Bhaijee left Gorakhpur and reached Mathura on 8th February, 1965. About 150-200 in number, a group of attendants joined him from places like Gorakhpur, Lucknow, Kanpur, etc. Saint community and reputed citizens have given Bhaijee a grand welcome at Mathura station. Bhaijee was almost covered with garlands.

Massive preparations have been made for the festival. Reputed people have arrived from various states. The whole pavillion was emitting a dazzling light by the electricity. About 250 scholars had been reciting the Shrimad Bhagwat for the entire week in a huge pavillion in front of Shri Krishna platform, what an extraordinary sight it would have been, when 250 people will be reciting the scriptures in chorus. The elderly people have declared that such ceremony has not yet occurred, nor will occur in future. In addition to this, a week-long narration of the Shrimad Bhagwat was arranged by the *Braj*-fame respected Shri Nityanandji Bhatt.

Bhaijee arrived at Shri Krishna birthplace on 11th February, 1965. The worshipping of the Gods and Goddesses has been performed by the most eminent Brahmins. About 12-13 feet-deep pit was dug to lay the foundation stone. An arrangement was made to get down through stairs. Bhaijee alongwith his wife had come down and sat on a seat. The work for the worshipping of Shri Ganesh, Vastu God, etc. had been performed for about an hour in proper manner. Bhaijee has put bricks for the foundation of Bhagwat-Bhawan and then applied mortar on them by a silver trowel. Shouting in triumph has prevailed for divine name with a humming. On second day, its descriptions along with photos were published in prominent newspapers of North India. Bhaijee delivered a brilliant lecture on this occasion. Its excerpts are being given below:

"It is first occasion after the destruction of temple by the tyrannical Aurangzeb about three hundred and fifty years ago, when an auspicious recitation of the Shrimad Bhagwat is being done by scholars of Braj at this sacred land. Casteism and Statism have been thriving on the name of nationality. Leadership, hungry for power, is fighting badly and the riots are being emerging here and there, making our country feel ashamed, by inciting meek students and public. We, who believe just in one God, living in just one India, are attacking disdainfully to each other. It is just an indecent and unfortunate thing to us. Our country is free today, is republic. There is no difference between Hindus and Muslims. In such a condition, the temples and the religious places, which have been taken away by polluting them with savageful attack, it is also a duty of our present Muslim brothers that they should return this sacred place with great affection. It is beneficial to Hindus and also beneficial to the country. They may agree or not, God knows, if don't agree willingly this time, then the almighty and the time shall make them agree who may not be agreed today. The rich men should donate open-hearted. Life will not be permanent to anyone, wealth is not retained permanently by anyone and who knows if such an auspicious occasion may come or not? Therefore, maximum cooperation should be given to such sacred work."

Hundreds of Brahmins from Mathura-Vrindavan were given fee for religious session while a help was extended with garments and money for friendless and sad people, donation was also given to many organisations, services had been extended to saints. A trip was made alongwith the family and attendants to Barsana-Govardhan, etc.

Felicitation was made from Vrindavan municipality to Bhaijee as a supreme and passionate religious devotee, symbol of Indian culture, great protector of religion, centre of spiritual inspiration. Like this, Bhaijee went to Rajasthan after a long stay in Braj up to 27th February, 1965.

❐

121

An Establishment of Four Pilgrimages – Veda Building

Vedas have the highest place in the form of first expression of the world literature. The then Governor of U.P., Shri Vishwanath Das was a devotee of Vedic literature. Once during a trip to Badrinath- Dham, he gave due consideration of an arrangement for daily recitation of the sacred Vedik verses. It was decided during that trip to establish a Vedic building in Jagannath Puri. On his return, he went to Gorakhpur and discussed in this context with Bhaijee. Bhaijee liked this idea. Bhaijee suggested – Why only in Puri-Vedic building should be established in all the four corners of India – all the four abodes – Badrinath, Jagannath, Rameshwaram and Dwarka. Shri Vishwanathji also appreciated such advice. Bhaijee had requested the head of cow protection seat, respected chief of the monastery Shri Digvijaynathji to accompany him for this assignment. He accepted it happily. As a result, a foundation was laid to form a trust in the joint meeting held at the sacred place of Gorakhnath temple on the day of 27th January, 1965. As a general secretary, Shri Vishwanathji became an active secretary and Bhaijee as a joint secretary to this organisation. To note only this thing that Bhaijee is involved for this work, several people have donated the wealth. Jagatguru Shri Shankaracharya from all over India have accepted as patron due to persuasion of Bhaijee. Nowadays, branches of Veda-Bhawan at many places in India are busy in fulfillment of their objects. The present main centers are Badrinath, Jagannath Puri, Rameshwaram, Dwarka, Rudraprayag, Kaldi (Kerala), Shri Rangam and Prayag.

❐

122
Bhaijee – A Social Reformer

Our society had accepted defects in many of its traditions just with the flow of time. The attention of Bhaijee was already to this point right from his young age. During his stay in Mumbai, he tried his level best to get rid of current evils, being an active member of 'Agrawal general assembly'. '*Kalyan*' though was a complete and spiritual magazine but even then Bhaijee tried his level best to check such bad traditions through his discourses, through '*Kalyan*' and assembly of virtuous people from time to time. The dowry system which has perturbed our society even today was already perceived by the farsightedness of Bhaijee fifty years ago. He had written in June, 1955 issue of '*Kalyan*':

"...To demand dowry is a great sin. An appeal has been made several times in *'Kalyan'*. I don't know to what extent our temperament is degraded. I am very much surprised when well-educated progressive young people from colleges are determined for dowry from the father of poor girl. ...I appeal to the people of this country, to the grooms and their guardians on the name of the God and humanity that they should take an oath for not to demand dowry and save themselves and society due to such an increasing sin and pain."

He also warned even with very harsh words in his discourses. When he could not get desired result with repetitive writing made one appeal again in '*Kalyan*' –

"I again make a special appeal to the rich, middle class and educated young people and their guardians that they should progress by sacrifice, put an ideal example in front of all, by accepting marriage proposal without dowry. The kind-hearted people should frame such community at various places and explain humbly and respectfully about the evils and sins of dowry to young persons and their guardians and detach them by such sin. The wealth from dowry will never be sufficient for life but it is only an attraction. ...

"I have also a request to the people from daughter's side not to search a groom richer than themselves instead find a suitable poor boy and marry your daughter to him. To marry your daughter at par to your status can make her happier."

He had only been giving advice, it is not so. He made an excellent ideal as well during his life time. Though he had no son except two grandsons. An engagement of elder grandson Suryakant was held in October, 1967. He declared clearly even at that time – we will not accept any dowry; every rite should be performed according to the method conformable by scriptures and marriage should be simple and within limitation. To make such thing clearer, he repeated – nothing will be accepted in the name of dowry. Whatever the father wants to give to his daughter should also be under a limit. There should not be anything else. According to the tradition of Agrawal community, nothing will be accepted under the tradition like – 'Dant', 'Angi mewa', 'Hara-bhara', 'Badi milni'. Such expenses for wastage of money and an ostentation should be placed far away from the community. Country is not in such a condition that the community could tolerate such manners and customs.

Not only this much, even unnecessary expenses and false exhibition were also prohibited at his residence. It became a tradition to distribute sweets and feed sweets to the newcomers at the time of engagement. Bhaijee decided even in beginning that sweets will not be distributed at the time of engagement, nor given to eat at that occasion as well. Shri Ramdasji Jalan, son of Shri Ghanshyam dasji Jalan was also sitting at that time. He was like a family member of Shri Sethji – Bhaijee and was little unsteady in talking. He said – "*Tauji*! You have found a good way to save the money. To celebrate the engagement even the sweets are not served for those who have come on this occasion." Bhaijee made a clarification – "Such tradition was not existed earlier in our community. Since then, on this occasion over here, such tradition has begun that sweets should be offered to the family members who arrived at the time of engagement. The scriptural mode and limitation should be followed in toto, but the community should be saved by an unnecessary attention and wastage of money. As far as feeding of sweets is concerned, you are most welcome at any time at residence but not at the time of an engagement. Regarding the question for saving the money, it should not be understood like this. Money saved by this way, will be utilised elsewhere and ₹ 1001/- will be spent for poor in distress." Those people in the community, who have been gradually increasing the wastage of money for an ostentation at the time of marriage, etc. should definitely consider this suggestion by Bhaijee.

Likewise, Bhaijee was also against the marriage of widows. He had been narrating in his discourses – I have given a serious thought, I have found no benefit for the widow nor to the community by the marriage of a widow. Therefore, I cannot support the marriage of a widow due to persuasion of someone. Likewise, he was also against of multi-marriages. His third marriage was solemnised at the age of 23-24 years on the persuasion of grandmother. He said – though I had married thrice. Therefore, I have no right to say but don't consider it proper specially at the elder age or in possession of a child. It is my request that a person, who has a son and become elder, should not marry again. He had also written a book titled – "*A Community Reform*", which was published in 1928. Unfortunately, this book is not being managed to publish nowadays.

❑

123

A Movement for the Protection of Cow

Bhaijee was sad due to non-elimination of stigma for killing of cows even after setting India free. Therefore, whenever anyone starts a movement for this purpose, Bhaijee gives complete cooperation in it. But it does not give special pressure on the government due to failure of joint efforts by everybody. When Bhaijee was in Swargashram in 1966, a chief volunteer had come from Delhi and requested Bhaijee to make efforts so that everyone should join for cow protection. It was an extraordinary work to satisfy all virtuous persons, sects and political parties to work from one stage. During those days, Shri Prabhudutt Brahmachari had come to meet Bhaijee on his return from Badrinath trip. Bhaijee talked first of all to him and satisfied for this work by narrating him everything. Fortunately, at that time, Shri Karpatriji Maharaj was also in Rishikesh. Bhaijee went to him alongwith Shri Prabhudutt Brahmachari and other chief volunteers and requested by explaining him everything. He was also influenced by the factual facts of Bhaijee and agreed for a joint effort. On the same day, Shri Karpatriji, Shri Brahmachariji and Bhaijee signed on an affidavit. From this very place, sowing of a seed was made in the form of the all parties movement. Later, chief religious persons, political and social organisations and reputed persons have also signed on same affidavit. On 12th September, 1966, a meeting was convened in Varanasi under the leadership of Karpatriji in which Bhaijee and other prominent people have also participated and a decision was taken to form "A great all- party cow protection campaign committee" and other main topics. Various hindrances for this movement have appeared but have been solved by the humility, intelligence and devotion, etc. of Bhaijee. Shri Karpatri has declared – Brother Hanuman, you are wholly, responsible for financial arrangement. Bhaijee has agreed to bear total burden for lakhs of rupees. For it, a letter was written to Bhaijee by the soul of Sanatan Dharma Pratinidhi Sabha, Punjab; Swami Ganeshanandji – I am happy to know that you have accepted to be a host for this great rite. Though the financial burden has been looked after by several people but the work which was done to collect money by Bhaijee secretly was more important. In addition, Bhaijee has also started to include materials for cow protection in every issue of '*Kalyan*'. There were about one lakh fifty thousand customers just for '*Kalyan*' while it was difficult to imagine the number of readers of '*Kalyan*' and for this reason as well, this movement has got much strength.

A historical convention for the splendid procession was planned in Delhi on 17th November 1966, in which Bhaijee himself has joined. There was an apprehension that Bhaijee probably may be arrested in Delhi. Bhaijee had no fear even about a little bit in his mind. He has joined that procession of Delhi along with his attendants and when tear gas and shooting took place near the stage at Parliament Street, Bhaijee was present on that very stage. The God has taken care of everything. Since 20th November 1966, Shankaracharya of Puri and Shri Brahmachariji went on hunger strike till death. In proportion, as duration of hunger strike prolonged, Bhaijee had been sending daily telegrams or letters to the President, Prime Minister, Home Minister and several government officers. Likewise, he had also been inspiring to prominent people like Jagatguru Shankaracharya, Shri Vinobaji, etc. by sending telegrams or letters. Also informed to Anandmayee Mata to inspire Indiraji for cow protection. Bhaijee did that time vigilant and inexpressible efforts. He had been receiving news of prayers, rites, repetitions of divine name from the various corners of the country due to his efforts. People have been turning up into prison willingly. Bhaijee has sent his own volunteers to look after this movement. Although this movement could not succeed to stop the killing of cow family throughout the country because an ordinance of fate was just so, even then, efforts made by Bhaijee for protection of cows shall remain long memorable.

❑

124

Fourth Plan to Spread Divine Name

The work that Bhaijee did for the spread of divine name can be marked as unique. In such age of atheists, thousands of men and women will get inspiration by that. In due course of time, people had not such faith as was seen 40-45 years ago by Bhaijee. Therefore, he thought now for a new method to spread divine name. People in the number of thousands had already been coming every year to Gita vatika, their ears may receive involuntarily just the sound of celebration of devotional songs and name with celebration of devotional songs (*sankeertan*) may be uttered to a small extent from their mouth as well, with such intention he has a thought about a non-stop name celebration of devotional songs (*Naam-sankeertan*) from Radhashtami of 1968 in Gita vatika. The singers for devotional singing have been called from the birthplace of Chaitanya Mahapabhu, Navdeep, Bengal who with their enchanting tone kept on pouring the divine nectar of sacred chant – *'Hare Ram'* in the ears of spiritual aspirants residing in and visiting to Gita Vatika. Till today, such activity is continued uninterruptedly for twenty-four hours and nobody knows how long such rain of favour by Bhaijee will be pouring in this way on thousands of men and women.

❐

125

A Service During an Extreme Famine of Rajasthan

During 1968-69, a fearsome famine occurred in Rajasthan. In such terrible famine, the condition of men and specially of cow family has become very pathetic. Although Bhaijee was unwell during those days, when he was informed about this condition, he could not remain quiet. Just during his sick condition, a vast arrangement has been made for the service activities at many places. Services to cows have been given specially in Bikaner. By arranging a small amount of five thousand from his wife, Bhaijee has begun this service activity and fifteen lakhs were spent for this work by the grace of God. Whenever such occasions have appeared in the life time of Bhaijee, he had made arrangement with full sincerity. Service task has also been extended in storm-affected areas in Assam in 1969 and a help was also given to eastern Pakistan (now Bangladesh) to the storm-affected people during 1970.

❐

126

An Ocean of Service – Shri Bhaijee

Just as Bhaijee immensely enriched to Hindi literature, of just that type, Bhaijee also presented an ideal of service for which one separate and huge treatise is needed to describe this thing. Since his childhood, Bhaijee had been devoting his body-mind and wealth in service activities. He never missed any occasion for such type of work. Once approached to him, he had never disappointed anyone. Such temperament of childhood has gradually been merely increased and become his just life-line in future. Although his working about the help was such – "If something is given by right hand, then left hand should not know it." Even then, many events which have come to light, it is not possible to describe them all in detail. He himself was also serving through body but on above circumstances whatever vast amount of money has been spent for service activities, it is difficult to believe it. Although after his arrival to Gorakhpur, neither had he earned any money nor taken any money from *Gita press* or any other institution nor taken money as a present of gift, up to an extent that he has not given his name in the appeal published for collection of money. Whatever service is extended, it is done through the self-inspired donation by his own people or relatives. Even their names had also never been disclosed to anyone.

Few events are being given here, only as hints, by which readers themselves could guess about his services –

1. 'Respected Bhaijee! It appears that the body will now not prevail to more period. I had wished that the death of the body should be near to you but there is one problem, by which I am feeling a little shy in mind. You already knew it that I am suffering from T.B. and gradually it has laid down over my body. T.B. is a fearsome epidemic and the physicians have been advising to keep and reside a patient separately. Why should I reside near to you with this disease? But the mind could not come in terms with it. I wish repeatedly that I should take last breath just near to your vicinity.'

The famous saint of Ramsanehi sect Shri Chyawanramji expressed this desire of his inner self to respected Bhaijee (Hanuman Prasad Poddar). During those days, Bhaijee was living at his paternal place in Ratangarh. Saint Shri Chyawanramji had a unique faith on the repetition of *Ram- naam*. His life had been very simple and full of good and saintly qualities. He has high regards, much affection and close relationship in his mind for Bhaijee. He had considered Bhaijee as an ascetic of great power and saintliness and it was the reason that he had wanted to end his life in his vicinity. There is an unerring power near great person – saint Chyawanram had a firm faith on it.

Shri Bhaijee was then already an embodiment of affection, in addition he had a high regard since his childhood towards saints-ascetics in his heart. He believed to serve merely saints, is a religion for a householder and he himself was in domestic life – was an ideal householder. Therefore, when he heard such desire from the mouth of true saint that his body of five elements should end just near to his vicinity, then Bhaijee requested with a temperament of normal contentment, "*Maharajji*! This house just belongs to you. This house is beseemed just due to feet dust of saints. I am fortunate that you are offering me an opportunity to serve you. I would be happy to do my best, to serve you with my best ability. Please do not feel any embarrassment. How does it matter if it is tuberculosis? Everyone must die. Disease occurs to him only upon whom it must attack. Nobody is affected from a disease by saving others without an ordinance of the God.

By hearing such affectionate and intimate words from Bhaijee, the heart of Shri Chyawanramji was moved with compassion. To perform a service properly is supremely obscure. It is difficult to fulfill it. Not only his personal pleasure and selfishness but also after dissolving his 'ego', a man deserves to be eligible to serve. In Bhaijee, these things merely existed in normal sense by the grace of the God. Therefore, service to saint Chyawanramji has begun in decent and organised manner. Shri Bhaijee arranged for the stay of Shri Chyawanramji just in his own residence. He was given a large room to live in front of his perpetual drawing room so that Bhaijee can keep an eye constantly towards his maintenance. Whenever Bhaijee goes inside for meal, etc., by coming out of his room, at that time he always enquired to saint – tell me Maharaj! How do you do? And Maharajji replied – I am alright, Bhaijee! And Bhaijee then goes inside smiling. Not only this, but he himself had attended to the service of Maharajji for some time, daily. That time, discussion was held for his body pain, an exchange of ideas had also been made in relation to the arrangement for medicines and wholesome, etc. In addition, discussion was also held about the God. The saint was present in the form of a patient and saint was there in the form of a servant, whosoever got an opportunity to join with the discussion in that period, have considered themselves as blessed.

To increase the reputation of their devotees, the God examines them. It seems if the God precisely had a wish to examine Bhaijee in the form of a patient. A strong change was produced with the nature of supremely endurable and indifferent saint Shri Chyawanramji by the God. In any utensil which he took meal one day if he finds the same utensils next day then he said – I have taken meal in these utensils yesterday, bring other utensil for today. Shri Bhaijee arranges for other utensils immediately. Like this, six sets of utensils had been allotted to him so that one set of utensils was repeated only after six days. The same thing also occurred about the blankets to wrap around. Bhaijee also arranged many sets of blankets. Many types of complex situations had been creating from time to time, but Bhaijee felt highly delighted in the service of the saint. His supremely virtuous wife, devoted to service, also cooperated happily and with much delight towards the arrangements of such service. Like this the service continued. But everyone from society had an affinity towards Bhaijee. Several people had an attachment towards his body. Such eminent people have begun to arrive to Bhaijee and requesting him – 'Bhaijee! the decision you have taken to permit Maharajji to live with you is not appropriate. You are already watching that a lot of phlegm is thrown daily by Maharajji. Tuberculosis is a terrible disease. It attacks very soon. You are sitting daily near to him. Sometimes he puts his head on your lap. You are requested that an arrangement may be made for Maharajji at some independent place and away from your residence'.

Shri Bhaijee listened to the heartfelt advice by his well-wishers and smiles. There was no effect of awesomeness of the disease to him. Swami Chyawanramji also remained engrossed his mind with the God. He had continued reading a book – "Twenty-five hundred priceless verses" – published by Gita press and edited by Bhaijee, alongwith the repetition of *Ram naam* daily.

The disease had been gradually increasing. Respected Swami Ramsukh Dasji Maharaj had also been visiting from Ratangarh and looked after Maharajji by his hands. Respected Swamiji and Chyawanramji were pupils of same spiritual guide. Both had a great affection.

The time has come for an abandonment of his life. Respected Bhaijee, Swamiji, Shri Goswamiji, etc. were all present. Group singing of divine name (*sankeertan*) was going on. During such supremely sublime moment, saint Chyawanramji took his last breath.

Shri Bhaijee has properly arranged the funeral rite of his dead body according to religious sect of Maharajji. A large procession along with the celebration of devotional songs (*Sankeertan*) had accompanied the funeral procession. Bhaijee himself was walking on foot by performing group singing (*Keertan*).

In the room when Maharajji died, Shri Bhaijee has arranged to begin a non-stop group singing (*Keertan*) for divine name after thoroughly cleaning of that room. Due to cooperation of devotees, affectionate friends and relatives, non-stop celebration of devotional songs (*Sankeertan*) has begun with great ostentation. Bhaijee had also attended daily in group singing of hymns (*Keertan*) by sparing some time from his busy life. As his own room was right in front of it and as such, he was constantly also managing for group singing of hymns (*Keertan*). Non-stop group singing for divine name continued for two-and-a-half years.

This is an identity of service by a saint to a saint.

2. It is an old event. Discourse by supremely respected Bhaijee was being held in the Radhashtami pavillion of Gita vatika. During those days, eastern districts of Uttar Pradesh were suffering with terrible famine. Under the supervision of 'Gita press-service group', Bhaijee had begun service activity. Drought-affected people had been served by grains, garments, etc. Even being unwell, Bhaijee had been visiting to inspect the famine-affected areas. The heart of Bhaijee was highly suffered from the pitiful condition of starved public and animals. Fortunately, some rich and reputed people from Calcutta and Mumbai had come that day to meet Bhaijee for consultation regarding their family and business. Shri Bhaijee began an exposition:

There is a poetry by Narsi Mehta which was very much liked by *Bapu* (Mahatma Gandhi):

Who can feel pain of others,
Can be considered as a devotee of Vishnu.

He would try his best to get rid of the pain of others, without feeling any pride in his mind.

In fact, '*Vashnava*' – that one only liked by the God who feels the pain of others and tries his level best to get rid of it. In this, whatever is possessed by anyone, everything belongs to the God and is just for the service of the God. Likewise, everyone has the God in him – in the form of every living being, the God is just manifested. Therefore, to whichever forms of the God, whenever anything is required and if we have it, then the thing of the God is offered to the God – with such intention and without any pride, it should be offered humbly.

Shri Bhaijee has explained this disposition in detail during his discourse. The audiences were listening to his discourse quite seriously. On conclusion of discourse, the people of the city have departed. People from Calcutta and Mumbai surrounded Bhaijee. Meanwhile, a young person in torn and dirty clothes had come and stood in front of Bhaijee. Looking at weak and poor person, concentration of Bhaijee diverted from those people and he asked to that young person. Brother! Where do you live? What for have you come? Such were the affectionate words of Bhaijee that the young man did not utter a single word, his eyes have begun to trickle. That's all, the heart of Bhaijee has moved with agitation due to other's distress. He at once stood up and reaching to that youth placed his left hand on his right shoulder and began caressing his head by right hand. By receiving such an unexpected affection, the heart of youth also moved by compassion; he now began to weep quietly. Shri Bhaijee continued caressing his head as usual. A little later, when an intensity of pain decreased, Bhaijee asked from the youth – "Brother, why do you weep this much?" "Babuji! I have got nothing to eat for two days. Old parents and younger brother and sisters at home are all hungry, it's winter time. There are no clothes for the protection of cold. Sister is grown up and to take care of her dignity, she had also even no old clothes or wrapper. No grain is sprouted in the field due to failure of rains. Due to reputation of our ancestors, we cannot disclose our sorrow to anyone. Due to your fame, I have come under your shelter, controlling himself, the youth has placed his trouble in front of Bhaijee."

Shri Bhaijee consoled him and sat at that very place on the mat by holding his hand. The rich people, came from outside, were astonished by watching all this that how Bhaijee concentrated his attention towards that weak and poor person, becoming entirely detached from them.

Shri Bhaijee instructed his attendant to take away this brother with him. Give him a long shirt and *dhoti* and ask him to take bath at the well.

An attendant accompanied the youth. Shri Bhaijee remained sitting in that pavillion. A little later, the youth has returned to Bhaijee after bath and wearing the new clothes. Shri Bhaijee arranged breakfast and milk from his residence and asked him to eat in front of him, youth was carried on drinking milk and was also wiping his eyes continuously. He was observing – how Bhaijee though surrounded by five-seven illustrious people, becoming alienated from everyone, was looking just after him. Meanwhile, Bhaijee sent one of his companions to his wife and arranged for several *sarees*, long shirts and *dhotis* and clothes for voluminous skirt and three-four blankets to the family of that young man. He gave all this to the youth, called a rickshaw and asked him to sit on it and bid him farewell. When the rickshaw was near to start, Shri Bhaijee said – "Brother! You may now go today, come again later. I will be in room upstairs, but you can meet him (pointing towards an attendant). He will inform me of your arrival. Don't weep nor feel disappointed, the God will arrange everything."

Shri Bhaijee then addressed to people came from outside, after bidding farewell to the youth – Excuse me, I have spoiled one hour of you people. But what to do, looking at any sad person, I cannot control myself. The condition of nearby villages is very lamentable. I have myself visited there and observed it. Looking at the condition over there, a man had to burst into tears compulsorily. There are many such people in the country nowadays who are living with great pleasure and if they like then can eliminate the hunger of stomach for several people. Edibles and grains and fodder, etc. may be available in large quantity on payment. At such juncture, thousands-lakhs of men- women and animals are suffering today without grains and fodder, few have already died – it is a matter of great concern. I am merely a weak person; how can I disclose my condition. When I sit to eat and find bread and butter and many types of vegetables in front of my plates, my eyes have become moist and did not like the meal, but I concealed this state from my family members. Likewise, at the time of sleep, when I wanted to sleep covering with quilt, putting pillow below the head on the cotton mattress, then picture of those hungry-poorest of the poor men-women often appeared in front of my eyes and the sleep is vanished and I had been praying to the God to eliminate their pain as resting on the bed. I concealed such helplessness but had to disclose today due to its relevance.

While disclosing this, the heart of Bhaijee moved by compassion and an inner pain has appeared on his face. The rich people were enchanted and surprised by obtaining a real introduction to the heart of Bhaijee. Everybody assured Shri Poddarji to extend cooperation for such work according to their capacity.

3. It is an old event. The pavillion of Gita-Bhawan in Swargashram for assembly of virtuous people (*Satsang*) was full of audiences. Most respected Bhaijee was the brilliant speaker. Dense peace was prevailed all around in his exposition even there was sufficient public. On the conclusion of the exposition, an important information was announced by a speaker, among the persons belonging to the assembly of virtuous people for which a service was expected.

   A reputed but poverty-stricken Brahmin reached from Rajasthan. Due to sudden attack of dangerous cholera, his condition had become grave. Due to such weak condition, he needed a help. Energetic people may please enroll names, four persons are needed to serve throughout the night. On its first announcement, only two energetic people enrolled themselves. The speaker repeated the announcement, due to embarrassment, one more person gave his name this time. The person spreading the information slowly said – “Bhaijee – only one more name is required, please repeat the announcement once again.” “It is not needed” – by saying this much Bhaijee stood up from his place. The person who announced the information was caught up in the problem – how three persons would suffice throughout the night – how the clothes socked with vomiting and excreta will be changed without the help of two people and one person also cannot carry out service continuously for eight hours, but he was unable to repeat this request in front of such a splendid personality.

On leaving Gita-Bhawan, Bhaijee asked to the person spreading the information, by casting a glance on the public – “One person will reach on the time and place as per your instructions”. “He may reach in the hut situated behind the temple of Swargashram exactly at 10 o’clock at night. He shall have to stay up to 2 o’clock thereafter, second group will replace him.” “Alright” – giving such a short reply, Bhaijee moved forward. It was an almost 10 o’clock at night. In the lap of mother Ganga, the moon like an infant was playing fractiously. That very moment, Bhaijee has slowly entered inside the hut, by opening its door.

“You…. you…” feeling a strange astonishment, the person who had announced the message said – “You may please leave; we will manage everything”.

“Why? Can I not serve?”

“No, it is not so – his clothes are being soaked again and again with vomiting and excrement, these have to be cleaned and then clothes have to be changed.”

“Then, what happens?” Bhaijee replied in a simple and normal voice.

“No… it gives terrible smell, I am telling you for this reason,” he tried to convey these words in the ear of Bhaijee.

“The body is full of filth, how the good smell would appear instead of bad.” Bhaijee said with a dull smile.

The service continued by Bhaijee without any reluctance – to change clothes soaked with excrement, to clean vomiting, to give medicines, to let him gargle, to provide water. It was all being performed as a worship to the God, with full sincerity, love and affection, what to speak about a dislike. In recognition of limitless ‘Self’ of Bhaijee, the sick person was not a different person but was his own, was own from one’s own, was his own identity.

The person who spread the message was observing with a surprise. He was enchanted that Bhaijee is not only an expert to counsel, but he is more expert to serve, is also more eminent. By the touch of a saint like Bhaijee, his affectionate service, his glorious presence has caused a great peace to the patient. By the time, the term of Bhaijee became over, his condition improved sufficiently and when Bhaijee was ready to return, he felicitated Bhaijee temperamentally with moist eyes.

4. On his arrival to Gorakhpur, Bhaijee had not a single paise of his own nor had any deposit anywhere. He did not just earn anything. He had no financial relation with Gita press – *'Kalyan'* or any other organisation. He had also never expected a single paisa from anyone as a gift, worship, present, etc. Under such condition, the service activities had been arranged adequately by the donation received from relatives, friends and devotees duly inspired by the self or by the God. But, sometimes, such occasions had also appeared when donation received for service activities is fully utilised and it was again necessary to arrange a definite amount to get rid of the pain of the person present in front. Under such compelling conditions, the heart of Bhaijee had caused to melt and he took debt from someone and not this much only, had wiped the tears of that poor person by even selling ornaments of his wife. Only some part of a letter is being presented of Bhaijee, by which you can realise about the great sensitivity by the heart of Bhaijee – !!Shri Hari!!

Gorakhpur…
Jyestha Badi, Vikramaditya Year 2010

Dear…,

Let us affectionately remember divine name with due respect. Received your letter dated 27th May 1953. A post-card is also received from Jaipur. Wife of…please keep collecting receipts by giving… monthly.

You have written about… it is alright. I am myself much worried about him that I cannot do anything even by knowing about his sickness. Whatever arrangement can be made, I have given that much to him and in future (decided for six months) also I have told him to send hundred rupees monthly, but you know it, I am entirely a pauper, I don't have money. The financial condition of the world has become so weak, that earlier the people had been telling to invest money in good work by themselves, which has now entirely been checked, does not work now even on request. I have assured to Mr. … but I don't have a single paisa. I have taken loan from the ready cash of Gita press and have given to him but could not yet repay it. During few days back, I had to give … rupees as help. When I could not arrange from anywhere then have sold an ornament of mother of Savitri (my wife). This is the real condition how I am maintaining giving and taking, you can imagine the factuals from this very account. To whom should I disclose? What is the benefit as well? For this reason,… I have not replied to Mr. … his two letters are received…one was received earlier, second has come today. Please give him one hundred rupees from my side.

He has written … rupees approximately towards the debt, monthly expenditure has also been shown approximately at 150/- per month and has also written to visit some colder place. All these things are correct but what I can write to him. I have no arrangement. I would somehow be sending one hundred rupees monthly for six months but I am not in a position to do more than that….

Yours Brother,
Hanuman Prasad

5. One who is familiar with the life of Bhaijee knew that how much conformity was in his speech and the action, he told that much only, which he had followed himself in his life. He had nothing individually, but it is difficult to find a generous person like him. He had been donating day and night with open hand, nobody ever returned empty-handed from his residence. The store-room of Bhaijee was always full by grace of God.

   He had been adopting new methods to serve. From the beginning of winter, distribution of woolen sweaters, bedsheets and blankets, etc. had begun from his place. Not only this much when the wind attacks like a tip of spear during cold-shivering nights of *paushya month*, Shri Bhaijee, a servant of poor, jumps to his feet from his bed during that bone-shivering cold. When the whole city and every single resident of city remain immersed with sleep, covering themselves by silky quilts or tattered garments in a hut or concrete building to their capacity, that grief-agitated person could hear the groaning of those destitute lying below the trees, frightened brothers and sisters attacked by an awesome cold. Shri Bhaijee forgot his old decrepit body and complete body pain and moved outside in jeep to arrange for prevention of cold of destitute. Few devoted companions also accompanied him.

   The trailer attached with the back-side of jeep remains full of blankets and by riding over the city, his jeep forward to that ruined building of that road where brothers and sisters without clothes had remained swept together shivering with cold. Jeep was put to stand aside, and Shri Bhaijee covers grief of those unfortunates from his hands by coming down from jeep – covers them by woolen blankets and at once moves away from that place. Accompanying children also covered those shivering brothers and sisters by blankets. When all people, lying there, had been covered by blankets, then with an apprehensiveness that someone may not deprive them by these new coverings, a person of the group warns them a little, calling in low voice. During such an action, someone may get up and by observing a woolen blanket over him, looks surprisingly here and there with a longing to see the donor, but just prior to this, jeep alongwith Bhaijee moves further from there to the other corner of the city, where just as this, other brothers and sisters would be found suffering with cold. Like this, sequence of such secret activity for the protection of cold just continues every year. Wherever, Bhaijee was unable to go there, he arranged such service by his relatives or faithful attendants. Alas! We could also somewhat follow such an ideal service like Bhaijee.

❐

127

A Contribution to the Hindi Literature by Bhaijee

Bhaijee has already the highest place now in spiritual world, but the material, he has provided in Hindi literature is also an excellent one.

When Bhaijee has begun to publish Hindi literature through Gita press, prior to this, availability of Hindi religious texts was very meager up to the extent that even correct translation of the *Gita* also was available only with difficulty. An authentic translation of the '*Mahabharat*' and ancient texts in Hindi was rare. The existence of texts, which was just not known to the people, the same texts are now available in Hindi today in the number of millions, its credit only goes to Bhaijee. Not only the translation, but an increase of Hindi literature, which is performed by Bhaijee through *'Kalyan'*, is incomparable. He has produced authors and has given an encouragement to promising authors. Authors had themselves a feeling of pride by the publication of an article in '*Kalyan*'. Special issues of '*Kalyan*' published on various topics, contained in them such solid materials, that they have become world encyclopedias of their discipline. In addition to this, Bhaijee himself has not left any subject of spiritual world, untouched by his writing but rather produced a vast material.

As the great sage *Vedvyas* had made the commentary on the secret language of Veda with the help of ancient texts, with that same style, Bhaijee has reinterpreted an essential part of complete Sanskrit literature in the back ground of present time of country through *Hindi* medium. Every text written by Bhaijee has its own standing, but if only two of his great texts like ***"Radha-Madhav-Chintan"*** **and** ***"Pad-Ratnakar"*** are presented to the history of Hindi literature, then their usefulness and greatness shall be unfailing in comparison to any great author.

In the opinion of Bhaijee – "Virtuous literature can be said as footprint of real literature. Only language cannot be called literature. Language in that case is only the medium of literature. The literature, which inspires everyone to proceed on the virtuous path with equal gesture in various fields, cares for welfare of everyone, that very literature provides self-guidance in various forms, to lead a life of the person towards good fortune and has always enabled a man to march ahead just on the path of righteousness". Every article of Bhaijee whether as prose or poetry are full of such great classic. His first article was published in monthly paper '*Maryada*' in January, 1911 titled 'Worship to the Motherland'. Since then, to his last writing, whatever he has written irrespective of the subject, has remain been inspiring the mankind to opt for a path of good fortune. Creation of spiritual literature has begun from the time, of surveillance at Shimlapal when he had written first time a commentary on *"Narad Bhakti Sutra"* during his prime state on devoted striving *(sadhna)* at the age of 25 years. In due course of time, this very commentary was published by Gita press by the name of "*Prem-Darshan*", with some modification-changes. Maintaining such a high object only, the field of literature created by Bhaijee has become extremely vast. His pen has created literature in Hindi as poetry, essay, prose, poem, reminiscence, editorial comments, review, letter, discourse, etc. It is not even possible here for the acquaintance with an introduction to his articles. If an evaluation is made of his complete literature, then a very vast text can be created. His literature of about twelve thousand pages has been published. All these texts are priceless possession of Hindi literature. It is also a thing of pride for Hindi literature that many of his texts have been translated in Sanskrit and English, Bengali, Tamil, etc. and other languages. Tamil translation has been published by the press of 'South India Hindi Promotion Committee". In South India, where a Hindi publicity is little, publication of translation of his Hindi texts in Tamil, is a thing of great importance. Translation of 'Shri Radha-Madhav-Ras-Sudha' was done into various languages like Sanskrit, Tamil, Telgu, Malyalam, Kannada, English, French, German, Sindhi, Oriya, Marathi, Urdu and Russian. Not only this much but the people of South India have studied Hindi to read *'Kalyan'* and other texts written by Bhaijee. What else than such a solid medium can be adopted for the publicity of Hindi. Shri R. Shouri Rajan writes:

"I have an indirect introduction with Bhaijee since 1949. I was studying in higher class of '*Tarkshiromani*' in Maharaj Sanskrit College situated in the current *Tanjore* district of *Tiruvaiyaru*. I had learned a little Hindi through self-study. The small booklets for furthering knowledge by Gita press have stimulated an interest in hundreds of students like me to learn Hindi. A useful publication like '*Shape of Hindu culture*', '*Fourteen Gems of Upnishad*', Annual Special Numbers of '*Kalyan*', etc. have remained extending us to a new guidance. I have heard from the mouth of many scholars and normal people – the timely spreading and an expansion can be made of our prestigious Hindu culture just by such books. The people of Gita press are just extending a very praiseworthy service. If even one scholar and generous person like Shri Poddarji exists in every Indian language, then the rejuvenation of India would have been easily attainable.

It was the result of perseverance just by Bhaijee that the number of customers of religious magazine like *'Kalyan'* had surpassed more than one lakh fifty thousand even in his life time, superseding the number of customers from all monthly magazines of India, during such an atheistic time without any advertisement. The general scholars have appreciated it openly. Only two opinions are being given here –

A famous scholar from Varanasi Shri Baldev Upadhyay, M.A., Ph.D. writes –

"The special numbers of *'Kalyan'* are better than another but *'Tirthank'* is precisely an encyclopedia of Indian pilgrims. Such an authentic useful information is not available in the text of any language what to say about in Hindi. Please do not treat it as financialism, it is realism. For the publication of such special number, the religious world will ever be indebted to you people."

A reputed, senior scholar Dr. Bhagwan Dasji, D. Litt. writes – "Whatever appreciation is made of your true endeavours, shall always be as an insufficient. '*Tirthank*' is seen, it is a complete directory of such pilgrims of India and consists of very beautiful pictures. Every Hindi-speaking Indian is indebted to you."

When the serious text *'Shri Radha-Madhav-Chintan'* was published by Bhaijee, every reputed scholar of Hindi literature has abundantly praised it.

Dr. Prof. Shri Hazari Prasad Dwivedi, D.Litt. has written –

"I have read '*Shri Radha-Madhav-Chintan*'. Glory of religious devotion (*Bhakti*) is evident in all articles by Bhaijee Shri Hanuman Prasadji Poddar, but this text has an excellent coordination of scriptural thinking coupled with religious devotion. This can only be written by the pen of a devotee like Bhaijee."

National poet Shri *Maithili Sharan Gupta*ji has written –

"Creation like '*Shri Radha-Madhav-Chintan*' is only possible by a devotee and thinker like Shri Hanuman Prasad Poddarji. He did an immeasurable obligation to the religious devotees."

The President awardee, Dr. Krishna Duttji Bhardwaj, M.A., Ph.D. has written –

"... by the creation of such a virtuous literature, Shri Poddarji has not only made a successful enhancement of saintly literature among Hindi literature but has also provided a recent support to the feelings for emotional devotees of religion."

Dr. Baldev Prasadji Mishra, M.A., L.L.B., D.Litt., has written – "The literary gems which have originated by the competent pen of Shri Poddarji (Bhaijee) have not only made literary field of Hindi, fairly rich, but the worshippers of sweet flavour have also achieved choice of thing in a very appropriate quantity, as desired by their hearts."

Prof. Shri Gulab Raiji has written –

"I have read the topics of *'Shri Radha-Madhav-Chintan'*. We all are proud of service for literature by Bhaijee. This book has not only just its religious value, but its literary value is also notable."

A prestigious person for discussion, Pandit Madhvacharyaji has written –

"A literature like *'Shri Radha-Madhav-Chintan'*, etc. definitely cannot be a special creation of any person as his own, I am now realising if Shri Radhe Rani herself has granted the boon in the form as complimentary present along with some of her touching expressions accompaning strong feelings to religious devotees."

Like this, an extensive literary composition of verses *'Pad- Ratnakar'* is a priceless possession of Hindi literature. The authors were already aware from the prosaic literature of Bhaijee, even so, Bhaijee did literary composition of verses abundantly as well and such knowledge was available even in a very little extent prior to publication of *'Pad-Ratnakar'*. It was given absolutely a due attention by all scholars in Hindi world. Deeply versed with *Braj* literature Dr. Prabhu Dayal Mittal, D.Litt. has written –

"A life-pervasive immortal practice by most respected Bhaijee Shri Hanuman Prasad has done so much benefit for the individuals of this world which is well known. But he was also much laudable for the devoted striving (*Sadhna*) of literary field which is not known to most of the people. I had earlier enjoyed reading some of the literary texts of respected Bhaijee, but he had such an abundant amount of literary creation, it is known to me only from the text of *'Pad-Ratnakar'*."

Dr. Vasudev Krishna Chaturvedi, D.Litt. has written –

"The literary blessing from the Goddess of speech and learning of respected Bhaijee will not only equally be appreciated among the treasure of Hindi literature but it will also have a personal identity in the field of music."

Dr. Ram Kumar Verma, M.A., Ph.D., Ex-Professor of Hindi, Moscow (Russia) has written –

"By repeated reading of this text coupled with excellently flavoured perception, one can feel pleasure like diving in the literary river of saint *Surdas*. I could realise today only by reading this – *'Pad-Ratnakar'* that how much renowned religious devotee and a poet Bhaijee was."

Dr. Awadh Bihari Kapoor, M.A. D.Phil. has written –

"I have not even imagined it that his verses of devotional poetry may contain such a vast collection. Even being occupied uninterruptedly in writing several books, booklets and editing 'Kalyan', he could produce so much of precious poetry stimulated with devotional feelings, full of philosophical facts, mandate, and an indicator for as many as this much of relationship and the highest truth, thus it appears that how much devoted, how much lively and musical was his life.... it would be better to call him a great voice and not a versifier."

Dr. Ramchandraji Mahendra, M.A. Ph.D. has written –

"There was an urgent need for such publication of poetries in one text only by an eminent scholar of Hindu culture like Shri Poddarji. It was not known that Bhaijee has made such an original contribution in the field of literature. Such a clear evaluation may hardly be available just in other places through the medium in literature of Indian culture.

...Many books have been written towards an ethical awakening of India and will be written in future but a literary composition in verses by a single author of permanent importance and originality like '*Pad-Ratnakar*'– is published very little in any country and time. The author of this book is not an ordinary poet but is such a literary creator, who has created a new era of literature in religious devotion by his creation." Babu Purushottam Dasji Tandon wanted to publish *'Brhamvaivart Purana'* in Hindi. He got translated in Hindi with much efforts and expenses and submitted it for publication to 'Hindi literary conference'. It could not be published for several days due to many types of inconveniences. Suddenly, Tandonji found one day '*Brahmvaivart Purana*' was published as a special number of *'Kalyan'* in Hindi and that too for a very small price. He was very much surprised and has at once sent a letter of congratulations to Bhaijee in which he has written – "The work which cannot be accomplished even by an organisation like 'Hindi-literary-conference', has been conducted by you in a normal way. We are now carefree at this end."

The reason for the completion of such an extensive work of Hindi literature in such a normal manner was this, that some divine power was working through the medium of Bhaijee. Once a representative of Indian-news-conference made an enquiry in this context, then he replied – "I did not edit '*Kalyan*', only my finger moves but even I don't know who is this hidden power which forces my fingers on the pen. Sometimes I become so much engrossed in this work that if someone may come and stand in front of me, even then I did not take notice of him".

Dr. Shri Jagdish Gupta has written –

"I have seen comparative data of Indian publications and found if publications of Gita press are deducted, then position of Hindi language will come down than many other languages of India."

Like this, one can well imagine that Bhaijee by serving excellently and quietly to Hindi literature has made it very much well off. Name of Bhaijee will always be shining intensely amongst the history of Hindi literature.

❑

128

Shri Bhaijee – An Epoch-Maker of Hindi Literature

Shri Bhaijee had a multi-faced literary talent. To read good books was his passion just from the beginning. He himself told once that during my primary state at the street of Calcutta College, I had read good books by purchasing them where the old books were sold at cheap price. In addition, his thinking was very broad. The service and the good standing he had made to Hindi literature is itself a topic of an independent text. The limit of that splendour is just not as much as can be seen through the eyes till this moment. Whatever cannot be perceived, that is far more than it. A famous poet and writer Dr. Kishor Kabra has written at one place that Hindi authors have isolated the creation of Bhaijee up to this moment, by marking it as religious.

If an attention of Hindi writers, critics and history writers will not be diverted to this aspect, till then the valuation of literary contribution of Bhaijee is not possible. Although whatever has been written by Shri *Tulsidasji* and *Surdasji* was all just religious, these saints have not paid any attention on any other subject, but they have been accepted in the form of the 'Sun for Sur and Tulsi as the moon' but even with the lavish praise shown by his contemporary and every author, Bhaijee has not been yet given an appropriate place in the history of Hindi literature. An epoch-maker of Hindi literature like Professor Mahaveer Prasad Dwivedi, Prof. Hazari Prasad Dwivedi, Prof. Gulab Rai, Prof. Kishori Dasji Vajpayee, Dr. Ram Kumar Verma, Dr. Baldev Prasad Mishra, Dr. Prabhu Dayal Mittal, Dr. Vijyendra Snatak, and others were all impressed by the services of Bhaijee to Hindi literature. One of the famous critic scholars of Hindi has told me that just set apart to discuss about other subjects – it is also a subject of important research that how many new words have been created in Hindi literature by Poddarji. The religious literature which has been published prior to '*Kalyan*' and religious literature, which is being published thereafter, by observing both carefully, my statement would be justified.

About ninety books of Bhaijee have been published. The boundary for his edited literature is so huge that even its imagination cannot be completely fulfilled without thorough observation. His pen has not taken any pause from 1911 to February, 1971. Prior to and until few days of his heavenly departure, his pen carried on writing while lying in the bed. How many of his literary genres will be timeless like the *Ramcharit Manas*, nobody can take this decision, nor we will live to witness it. But according to statement by a realised saint that just as the Ramcharit Manas is known to every home, of just that type, the literature of Shri Poddarji will also be known someday. In fact, by casting a glance distantly on the pages of the history, one cannot find even a single multi-dimensional talented author like Bhaijee.

Sufficient propaganda has been done for the Christianity and still being done because they are exploiting our weaknesses but even then, it will not be an exaggeration to express that sufficient inhibition is applied on it due to spreading of literature by Bhaijee. Like this very type, his knowledge of various languages like English, Bengali, Gujarati, Marathi, etc. helped him translate the best part of literature of these languages in Hindi.

The way Bhaijee kept his spiritual achievements as secret till last, in the same manner, he tried his level best to keep his services to Hindi literature as secret. How many articles he had written by various nicknames, it is a difficult task to count. All his literary collection published during his life time, never contains his name for any one of them. The literary composition in verse which was appreciated openly by several eminent scholars, about it he has written extending a clarification by the name of 'Deen' – "This 'Deen' neither had any experience nor had just any temperament. He is not a poet in any means nor had a little knowledge of literary composition for verse. He is even incapable to do a successful and correct versifying. Therefore, he feels shyness with a sense of modesty to introduce himself.'

Among those scholars, who have examined him closely, one of them was a famous scholar of Hindi, Dr. Bhagwati Prasad Singh. He has written at one place – "It is not an exaggeration to say that this era can be better and rightly known as **'Poddar Era'** in the history of Indian literature because Shri Poddarji had made so much growth of Indian literature during these almost 50 years which nobody has ever done it solitarily. Probably our coming generation may not believe that editor of special numbers of '*Kalyan*' and producer of such a vast literature was only a single person."

❐

129

To Train the New Authors

The notable services that have been rendered by Bhaijee for Hindi literature, among one of them was to train new authors in Hindi. By the publication of solid spiritual and totally useful matter in '*Kalyan*', its reputation has begun to progress by leaps and bounds. During its inception time, there were not many authors from outside for '*Kalyan*'. Sometimes Bhaijee writes himself, while some matter was given by Sethji in Marwari Mixed Hindi. This text was published into simple Hindi by Bhaijee himself, it also consists of collected matter of some ancient saints. But soon Bhaijee tried to contact reputed saints and inspired them to write. Bhaijee has also requested Gandhiji to write articles for '*Kalyan*'. The saints who had remained immersed in their religious practices isolated were also requested by Bhaijee to write articles, by inspiring them for public well-being. He had himself been visiting at few places and requests for the same, sent his relatives to some places, to other places he sends letters for this work.

For example, Shri Narayan Swami was a realised saint. He had remained silent for twenty-four hours. In other aspects, he was a high educated person of a rich family but by becoming with an intense asceticism, had to put a loincloth of sacking, tied with the help of a rope around his waist. He had not kept anything with him as stockpile. He would sleep only for two-and-a-half quarter hours during night. Rest of the time, he was continuously busy with divine repetition in low tone. He was in Rishikesh in 1930. Bhaijee himself went to him and requested him to write his experiences. In the beginning, he did not accept due to his simple and alienated nature. On the repeated requests by Bhaijee, agreed to write by sparing sometime during night. He said that whatever has been written by him is that, which he has himself experienced. It was published by Bhaijee in the 4th year issue of '*Kalyan*' under the heading 'An Experience of a Saint'.

Some Bengali scholars and saints, who are known to Bhaijee, were asked to contribute in Bengali and translated himself it to Hindi. He has also asked the saints of *Ayodhya* and *Vrindavan* to contribute and then refined their language himself. In the beginning, he also went to Pandit Gopinath Kaviraj.

He has dictated an article by shutting his room. Also approached Pandit Madan Mohan Malviya and requested him to contribute. He was weak in writing but was a very good orator. He asked to shut the room. It took him six hours to dictate while he spoke, Bhaijee kept on writing. Then he read the article and has given it with his signature. A large crowd was collected outside in six hours. On his exit outside, he said – Look, you have wasted my lot of time. Therefore, he sends his man to them (Malviyaji and Gopinathji) and they have dictated him. In future, he has appointed a special person even in Varanasi just for Gopinathji Kaviraj, who kept on persuading him for writing because he was a very busy person. Later on, Gandhiji began to send his articles just by the receipt of his letter. Whatever articles are received from new authors, these were duly rejuvenated by Bhaijee himself and then published in '*Kalyan*' by their names. When the authors found modified version of their articles, they feel enchanted and also inspired to write again. Not only this, the new authors also feel themselves honoured that their articles have been published in a reputed magazine like '*Kalyan*'. Like this, many new authors have been trained in Hindi. In addition, Bhaijee had requested for writing to reputed Hindi scholars and poets as well. Due to his decent conduct, humility and respect, everyone accepts his request with love. Poets like Maithili Sharan Gupta, Sumitra Nandan Pant, Nirala etc. sent their articles regularly with pleasure. Prof. Mahaveer Prasad Dwivedi, Prof. Gulab Raiji, Shri Ram Nath 'Suman', Shri Vasudev Sharan Agrawal, Pandit Kishori Das Vajpayee, Shri Viyogi Hari and others always sent their articles regularly.

The people, who do not write on spiritual subjects, Bhaijee also inspires them to write on spiritualism. Generally, everyone knows the name of the novel-king of his time Shri Prem Chand. He was considered the best of that time in writing social novel and stories. Bhaijee also managed a spiritual article to be written by him as well. His letter is being given here:

OFFICE OF THE 'HANS'

Dated:16.02.1931 Lucknow

Dear Hanuman Prasadji,

Received your kind letter. I agree to your statement that I had not written anything in 'Kalyan' for three years, but it has a reason. It is a religion concerning magazine and I an ignorant of the religious subject. To write anything on religious elements will be an effort without any authority. Being a competent person, you wanted something to be written by an incompetent. Therefore, I will now follow your order. The subject 'Shri Krishna and Future World' would suit me and I will write something on it.

Yours sincerely,
Premchand

Chirgaon (Jhansi)

Dear Poddarji,

I bow to *Jankiji*. It is difficult to access the special numbers of '*Kalyan*', which are complete literature in their representative subjects. It seems to me also for '*Yogank*' as well. How I can congratulate you for it. I respectfully bow to a most devoted *Vaishnav* like you.

Yours,

Maithili Sharan Gupt

A letter written each by Shri Suryakant Tripathi 'Nirala' and Sumitra Nandan Pant is being given here, which tells that Bhaijee had been contacting the poets, who stressed an importance for expression of the poet's individual sensibility, to write for 'Kalyan'.

Garhkola, Magrayar (Unnao)
17.10.1931

Dear Shri Poddarji,

I bow to you.

Received your kind letter. I have become ill in Calcutta during my visit for a conference. On my return I was busy in several domestic problems. I could not write anything for your reputed magazine. Even though thinking several times about it, I could not write anything. I am very much ashamed for your kind and gentle behaviour. I will be sending something for your forthcoming issues. An article will be sent to you within a few days.

Yours,

Suryakant Tripathi 'Nirala'

16th June

Dear Shri Poddarji,

Yours, Suryakant Tripathi 'Nirala'

I bow to you. Thanks for the letter. I am sending you one of my poems to your perusal for the issue 'Hindu culture'. I will reach Prayag by the first week of July. Hope you are fine. Be kindful to me.

Yours,

Sumitra Nandan Pant

An attention and humility of Bhaijee can be seen in the letter written to editors of '*Didi*' magazine – Thakur Shrinath Singh and Dr. Shri Lokesh Chand –

'Kalyan', Gorakhpur

Assad, Krishna 10, in the year 1946

Respected Thakur Sahib,

I bow to you. It is decided to publish next special number of '*Kalyan*' as '*Balakank*'. Several types of disorders like disobedience, lack of restraint, disbelief towards culture and religion, work indifference, attachment towards luxury, etc. are increasing among children and youth, you know it better than me. Our children should be virtuous, healthy, devotee of the God, patriotic, devoted to work, actionable, generous and great hearted – with this intention it is decided to publish '*Balakank*'. You are stem of Hindi, scholar in child psychology, reputed producer of child literature, lover of culture and religion and considered '*Kalyan*' as your own form of heart. Therefore, it is specially requested to you send something in writing to '*Balak-ank*' by yourself and also persuade other suitable eminent persons to contribute useful articles and essays and kindly forward them to me. This issue will consist of the ideal short biographies of Indian and foreign children, men and will also include few articles helpful in awakening of the life of children. I hope you would kindly cooperate in this work.

Your grace is indeed already here.

Yours,
Hanuman Prasad Poddar
25.03.1966

Dear Lokeshji,

Let us remember the almighty affectionately.

You will be happy to learn that special number issue of '*Kalyan*' '*Shri Ramvachanamrit Ank'* is going to publish next year. Three years ago, '*Shri Krishnavachnamrit Ank'* was published, which was well received by the public. You must have already seen it. In the same manner, it is planned to publish '*Shri Ramvachnamrit Ank*' this year, which would have a vast collection of speeches of Shri Ram, delivered on various subjects including Shri Ram Charit at various events. The countries related with great India like Thailand, Combodia, Sumatra, Java, Bali, etc. wherever the literature related with *Shri Ram Charit* is available, if you can collect the selected and useful lectures from there, available on various subjects on Shri Ram and could forward this collection, then it will give proper help for the usefulness and ornamentation of this issue. The lectures should consist of name of texts, pointing names of places, etc., while the original lesson should be given in *Devnagari* script. Those events should also be described for which such lectures are included. Please reply by the return post that until when you will be sending your priceless collection.

Everything is fine due to the grace of God.

Yours,
The Editor

How the non-interested scholars had written due to influence by the personality of Bhaijee, a letter in this context can be seen by *Guru Golvalkarji* –

A National Volunteer Organization Centre, Nagpur
(Rashtriya Swayamsevak Sangh, Nagpur)

Director: Head of Organisation Dr. Hedgewar Building
M.S. Golvalkar, Nagpur-2, Janpur

Dated – 25.12.1949

Respected Bhaijee,

I am not an author. Nor I have studied much. But you have made persuasion that I should just write something for the special number of Hindu culture in '*Kalyan*'. A respectful reverence which I have in my heart for you and an affection, you bestowed to me due to such compulsion, I have tried to write something. An appraisal is becoming faulty due to very short, prescribed limit of the author itself and the very extensive subject. I am not sure if you will like it or not. If you don't approve, just discard it.

Yours faithfully,
M.S. Golvalkar

Swami Shivanandji was sending his articles by himself. Dr. Radha Kumud Mukharji, Shri Akshay Kumar Bandopadhyay, Bhupendra Nath Sanyal, Swami Bhole Baba, Shri Raj Gopalachari also sent their articles. Most of the people had written considering '*Kalyan*' as their own. Even on payment for remuneration, it was duly refused but rather some of them felt insulted. Those who write just for remuneration or the one, about whom Bhaijee was familiar with weak financial condition, to them remuneration was sent by Bhaijee. It appeared that whole intellectual energy, total ascetic practice – sacrifice, total adoration for the country had begun its longing to extend their contribution in helping the 'special activity' of Bhaijee. It was informed while demanding articles for special number that the essays can be sent in any language among Sanskrit, English, Hindi, Bengali, Marathi, Gujarati or Urdu. Goswamiji was translating the English part. Familiar with several languages Shri Gauri Shankar Dwivedi was living near Bhaijee. He was also acquainted with foreign languages. The work related with Gujarati and Bengali was looked after by Bhaijee himself. Other officers were also consulted. Shri Kanhaiya Lal Manika Lal Munshi sent in Gujarati which was later translated by Bhaijee.

Moreover, even Christians and Parsis had also written for '*Kalyan*'. Several Christian priests were good friends of Bhaijee. Many Muslims had great affection for Bhaijee. Professor of Philosophy at Allahabad University Dr. Mohammad Hafiz had visited Bhaijee, Bhaijee took him to his residence for a sight of his Lord Shri Krishna. Bhaijee was a true follower of immemorial (*Sanatan*) religion. In his opinion, worshippers of every religion are worshipping only one element by different names and shapes. He would always write neither Temple should be destroyed nor Mosque or Church. Each of them is a place of worship. He has written even in his poetic verses –

According to him, *Arhat, Buddha, Jesus*, *Ahurmazd*, Allah are all the same characters of one truth. In fact, an immemorial religion is such which gives honour to every religion. Can any Muslim or Christian tell that his religious preceptors have placed their object of reverence at par to *Ram, Krishna*,

Brahma. It is just a propaganda by selfish political leaders that to create a vote bank, they have oppressed an immemorial religion (Sanatan Dharma) by naming it a secular and misguided the public. The shape of a true immemorial religion, which has been disclosed by his pen, through his working and speech by Bhaijee, nobody can deny it as being a true human well-wisher. Bhaijee would hang along a picture of Jesus Christ in his office room. Once a narrow-minded person asked – Why have you put this picture? Bhaijee replied – I like Jesus. I agree that his religion is only a part of our immemorial religion but why we should object to follow the good things it consists of. Alas, if the religious preceptors of other religions could also speak just such non-insistent thoughts in front of the public, then our world would have been extremely happy. This is a true reason for the fame of '*Kalyan*' by which it was gladly immersed by all in this country and abroad.

❐

130
The Development of the Gita press

Gita press was established by Shri Sethji in 1923 at Gorakhpur. At that time, Bhaijee was at Mumbai. In August 1927, Sethji has sent a telegram from *Jasidih* for Bhaijee, to proceed for Gorakhpur immediately along with staff of '*Kalyan*' and publish second issue of second year from there itself. Up to this time of about four years, few editions of the *Gita* and two small booklets – '*Ram Bhakti Prakash*' and '*Conversation with God in Meditation*' written by Sethji were only published. Due to installation of pen-flat-bed cylinder machine, sufficient material for publication was not available and the machine was remained empty for a long time. Shri Sethji believes that this problem will be solved on the arrival of Bhaijee at Gorakhpur. A few days later to the receipt of telegram, Bhaijee arrived at Gorakhpur. On his taking the responsibility for publication of literature, the work has brought forward with fast speed. Due to his efforts, the authors and translators had joined the work of Gita press, which increased by leaps and bounds. The main reason of development of the press like an electricity was the divine personality of Bhaijee, by which worthy people are attracted and have begun to cooperate in this work. He was especially careful that there should not be any mistake in printing. Every proof was read thrice out of which it was inspected twice by Bhaijee.

The proof which was received at 6 o'clock in the evening, was returned with due correction up to 7 o'clock in morning by Bhaijee irrespective of its quantity. In addition to this, verses of each contextural reference were checked with an original text. Thus, authenticity of each publication was increased. Due to such of his perseverance, the reputation of Gita press has made progress in every sphere. In addition to this, beautiful pictures have also heightened the beauty of this work. About 575 books, printed in various shapes, were spreading divine wealth in this country and abroad in the life time of Bhaijee. Editions of several books have surpassed in millions. One more specialty of Bhaijee was this that he was taking complete care of each worker and every worker was giving due respect to Bhaijee, considering him as his guardian and had looked after the work of Gita press.

If it is assessed through the point of price, then no other publisher was capable to provide books in such a low price. Take the case of *'Kalyan'*, for the total pages of twelve issues of first year were 384, while an annual subscription was two rupees only. Prior to heavenly departure of Bhaijee, an annual price of 44th issue of '*Kalyan*' in the year 1970 was nine rupees and the number of pages were 1356, i.e., three times more. From different means, Bhaijee had maintained an annual fee of '*Kalyan*' to that level of the price of paper, which was prior to forty-four years while price of everything had increased more than one thousand percent during these forty-four years. It is a wonderful record in the work of journalism without any advertisement which can be a milestone to anyone. Such record was not only desirable by the editors of our country but even the foreign journalists have also accepted its dignity.

A number of good books mainly on Bhaijee (about 60) have been published by the Gita Vatika Prakashan, Gorakhpur and are available for a reasonable price. This process is still being continued with the sincere and persistent effort of Shri H.K. Dujariji. One can request a recent list of publications from the address given on front page.

❐

131

The Immortal Instructions

Respected Bhaijee produced an extensive material on every aspect of spiritualism. A list of published work has already been mentioned above. Important instructions, which have appeared through his pen on few subjects only, are being given here –

1. **Means for a religious devotion *(Bhakti-Yoga)*** – An uninterrupted attachment towards his deity – the God by state of mind or an ultimate affection or an impartial unique love with the God is only known as religious devotion. There are many ways for religious devotion, many levels and many departments. The sages have defined the religious devotion very nicely. In fact, the God can be mostly in power of control by religious devotees than anything else... convenient practice is befitting for Lord Krishna, that very is known as religious devotion. Convenient means, to do that work which is interesting to Shri Krishna, which gives happiness to Shri Krishna, to do that very work continuously through body, speech and mind... *Shri Ram,* Narsingh, *Vaman*, etc. each divine form can be considered here as Shri Krishna.... There are three types of religious devotion – An accomplishing devotion *(Sadhan-Bhakti*), temperamental devotion *(Bhav-Bhakti)* and loving devotion *(Prem-Bhakti)*. The one that can be accomplished through senses, such an act of hearing – like group singing of hymns, etc. is known as an accomplishing devotion. An accomplishing devotion (*Sadhan-Bhakti*) is of two types: (i) Conforming to rule and; (ii) Conforming to love... an honest quality – with special identity of interest like the rays of loving sun means presence of a mentality which is dearer to soul through a longing to achieve the God – that is known as an emotion/sentiment... a matured state of emotion is known as the love.

   (Divine discourse*, Part-5)

2. **Means for true knowledge (*Gyan-Yoga*)** – That is such a supreme element which can never be seen nor can be taken nor it has any subdivision of a caste group, nor it has any class, nor it has eyes, ears or hands or feet, etc. nor outer wisdom nor both types of wisdom. He

has no inner wisdom nor outer wisdom nor both type of wisdoms, nor main property, not learned, not unlearned, he cannot be seen, nor anyone can make contact with him, nor can he be caught, nor he had any sign through which nothing can be thought of by mind nor can be said anything by speech. An essence of the implicit belief of the soul and away from the toils of the world is peaceful, beautiful and supreme.... When a seeker has seen that divine form of light of an ultimate Brahma, creator of complete universe and also a primary cause of Brahma, the God of all, then that clear-hearted saint has achieved an ultimate harmony leaving behind all sins and virtuous acts.

(Divine discourse*, Part-5)

3. **Disinterested performance of one's proper duty (*Karma- Yoga*) –** In fact a man has right to work but has no right in fruit of action. No one can claim that I will achieve that goal just by doing duty only. On this, such question can be raised that when the result is not in your hands, then why we should perform our duty? By sitting an ideal as well, whatever is to be happened, will be done. Therefore, the God has already warned that your mind should not be attracted as a shirker from duty. Because you have right to work without any hope for the result. It is true that there will be no work without any aim. Therefore, some object or aim will also be there in the duty of a man.

(Divine discourse*, Part-6)

Get rid of an attachment and hope for the result, just continue virtuous duty to achieve the God, maintaining an equal conduct to victory or defeat and for convenience and inconvenience, attachment in acquisition, benefit-loss, etc. will be a real disinterested performance of one's proper duty (*Karm-yoga*).

(A reform of world-paradise*, Part-5)

4. **Bodily disciplines where eight parts of the body touch the ground in an elaborative obeisance *(Ashtang-Yoga)*** – To make useful the philosophical knowledge of his mind, a Yogi should remain involved with the thinking of the supreme God, discharge studentship disinterestedly, study through balanced mind coupled with purification, satisfaction and to carry out ascetic practices. These are ten types of laws of religious observance and self-restraint. To follow them under similar norms, one can achieve an excellent result while a follower without desires achieves salvation. By depending one of the postures among postures like *Bhadra,* etc., a virtuous person should practise yoga through mind overpowered by the law of self-control. An action controlling the air known as vital breath through practice is called breath exercise. Breath exercise is of two types depending on the difference of living and non- living.... A Yogi should gradually,

by withdrawing and controlling of strongly attached senses, sensual enjoyment like speech, touching etc., transform them to follower of mind... When as devotee is entirely engrossed just only within the form of the God by becoming totally indifferent to other subjects, that very state is called meditation. Thereafter comes the profound meditation (*samadhi*). Being entirely away by all imaginations and to remain stuck just only within own identity is called profound meditation. Every profound meditation is achieved through meditation.

(From Divine discussion*, Part-4)

5. **Means towards meditation *(Dhyan-Yoga)*** – The first thing is to concentrate your mind. An object, which you want to achieve, considering it as most important, your mind normally and repeatedly just meditates on that object. In his mind, an aptitude towards his determined matter becomes firm and later on that very aptitude is transformed in the form of meditation due to total intentness and due to trend of thoughts. ... There is great importance of meditation. The Lord has declared in the *Shrimad Bhagwat* – A person who continuously thinks for the sensual enjoyments, his mind is trapped with sensual enjoyments and who meditates on me, he is merged in me. Absolutely all types of Yoga have importance and need for meditation in some or the other forms. There are many types of meditations, a devotee should also practise any type among them, looking to easiness of practice, his interest and capability... It is necessary to acquaint him, prior to know some methods of meditation that, which is the best place, time and posture for a devotee of meditation.

(Divine discussion*, Part-3)

6. **A theory of love *(Prem-Yoga)*** – There is no difference between love and the God, like the way description of supreme being is not possible through speech, Vedas have become silent by uttering 'Neti-neti', like that way, love also cannot be described through speech. The love which can be described through speech that is entirely external form of love. The love is indeed a thing to realise.

   The love is experienced through mind and mind is always lives near his abode of love. Then, in the absence of mind, how the speech could get the real information even for a little to describe. Therefore, whatever description is available about love, that is only symbolic, is external. Without an achievement of love, no one then knows about love and on its achievement, he has simply given up his mind.

   The love is beyond the qualities. There is also no desire in love and it continues to increase. There is by no means of conclusion in love.

   An identity of Radha – An identity of nature of Shri Radha is a constant alert condition intruded in consciousness for the love of Lord Shri Krishna. The gist of lightning (*Haladini*) is love while the essence of love is the great emotion coupled with renowned rapture and Shri Radha herself possesses renowned rapture with great emotional identity. She is a practical lightning power (*Haladini shakti*) in an incarnate form, is only a single self-identity (*Atma-swarupa*) for the most sacred love. The one, who has only one work just conducive to the bliss of Shri Krishna by her purest perpetual service regarding with the pleasure of Shri Krishna, as such, Shri Radha is the best in the group of beautiful women of Krishna and is supreme Goddess to everyone. Shri Radha is complete power. Shri Krishna is all-powerful. Similarities and differences both are considered towards power and powerful. In the form of similarity is Shri Radha while Shri Krishna being immemorial, eternal and perpetual, are one and they are only ensconced in two forms perpetually since time immemorial for the savouring of the acts (*Leela- rasaswadan*). Even Shri Radha and Shri Krishna, both even on being ultimate love form for an entire experience of love, are just expressed as Shri Radha only for the special support to an essence of act (*leelaras*).

* * * *

Shri Radha, who is established as a half part of body of Shri Krishna is merely an identity of Shri Krishna. Two types of appearances are there for the savouring of acts (*Leela rasaswadan*). Both ultimate beings are just one supreme sprit. There is no woman or man in them. Only revelation of act is there, both are divine idols with virtuous characters, free from smell of sex. They do not possess the body made from five elements, formed by the action, conceived by the exploitation of semen. Therefore, there is also no question of possession of even a little bit of sex or anger, etc. in them. Everything is an ultimate being.

Love of the herd girls from Braj – Among the countless powers of Shri Krishna, powers which are fostering the lightning power (*Haladini shakti*), these are only the associate female friends – the herd girls of Braj of Shri Radha. All the communities of cow herds of Braj are just the eternally different embodiments of that lightning power. Their lives are naturally just offered to the God. Their actions are naturally also devoted to the service of the God. They do not attempt any such action in which there is any other intention except an adoration for pleasure of meeting with Shri Radha-Krishna, except accomplishing of love to the God. Their intelligence, mind, senses, body including the soul are always dedicated just to Shri Krishna. Continuous service of Shri Krishna only is performed by them.

The temperament of herd girls of Braj is the temperament with total dedication. There is an entire sacrifice of personal pleasure in it. For such temperament, there is no need to wear Sari, voluminous skirt, blouse; nor any need of hollow anklets containing pieces of metal in feet and the nose ring in nose. To achieve temperament like herd girls of Braj, one should follow the path of herd girls. A heart of devotee, when really considered the God as His husband and beloved, at that time, he deserves for the achievement of temperament as of herd girls of Braj and exactly like a wife, when the God is chosen in the form of a husband, instantly they are called beloved and husband.

(*Tulsidal)*

7. **An importance of divine name** – Like the way, the fire had a natural power of burning, in the same way, the divine name has naturally a power to burn the sin prevailed due to attachment of worldly sensual pleasures. It does not require feelings in it. Divine name should be recited through tongue by any means, then one, which is the natural reward for recitation of divine name that would be also achieved without faith. Even when, there is no feeling, even then repetition of divine name in low tone should just be done. Divine name is at par to divine form (divine form of the God). Everything will be done due to the live property of divine name, due to its power in divine name. Specially in the era of *Kaliyug*, there is just no other way except divine name. Laziness and logic, these two things are hindrances in the repetition of divine name in low tone. Be in the habit of repetition of divine name. With the help of repetition of divine name, you will achieve salvation from ocean of life without efforts and also obtain divine love.

(Satsang ke Bikhre Moti**)

8. **Dedication** – A complete genuine dedication is not to be executed, it occurs automatically. If, there is any righteous man to do dedication, till then, the pride is leftover and there is deficiency in total dedication. There occurs such a condition, when the body, senses, vital breath, mind, intelligence, pride – or an entire group of all these – is governed by the God Himself. Under such condition, no one can be an entirely different from Him. To achieve such state, firstly one has to accomplish the method of a refuge. Such method of refuge consists several emotions:

1. To sing hymns, entirely devoted to the God, continuously and constantly.
2. To have a complete trust on the God.
3. To do entirely and always a work, which is favourable to the God.
4. To consider everything belongs to the God and never expect anything from the God.
5. To join the company of people, who understand the meaning of refuge or who obtained real refuge by the God.

(Total dedication – Divine discussion*, Part-6)

9. **An adoration on the divine grace (*Kripa Sadhna*)** – Everyone has got the grace of the God always and infinitely. As much as we can just trust on such grace, we can achieve that much of benefit. Whatever has been entrusted to the grace of the God, that very has become well protected. Nothing is impossible or non-attainable by the grace of the God. …an experience is achieved for an ultimate pleasure by every action to be made, due to his grace by dedicating towards that highest grace and everyone feels that a thing which he considered to be impossible, it has become suddenly possible due to grace of the God. And the gate of the God's grace is opened to everyone.

(A reform of world-paradise*, Part-1)

10. **A prayer** – The God understands all languages and to do a normal prayer, there is no need of special type of words. And such firm belief should be there that the God will at all costs fulfill of my innocent prayer. Wonderful result is certainly achieved by performing confident prayer for fulfillment of worldly shortage, achievement of flawless wealth and honour, get rid of sickness, recovery of health, get rid of trouble, etc. But all these prayers are just like as to demand small amount of money from an infinitely powerful and generous king.

(Prarthana-Piyush**)

But O Lord! May I ask you one thing, I bring disgrace of crime repeatedly and you wash it repeatedly. It is not fair that I just did not commit crime. You may say – Don't do, who asked to do? But O Lord! Being aware that my kindful Lord is compelled to become so much alert and energetic to retain a neglected person like me as thoroughly washed and cleansed, I did crime just habitually. O merciful! Now it will go away just by you only. Please grant me this prayer necessarily, O my treasurer of mercy.

(A Prayer*)

11. **The Celibacy** – The loss of celibacy is just the reason for decline of age. When there was proper promotion for celibacy, then there were not this much of diseases here nor anyone had generally died during youth. But the condition, at present, is contrary to earlier. We have forgotten celibacy, the very basis of life, for this very reason, we have been facing such wretched condition. It should be remembered that as long as the celibacy is not reestablished in our country, till then, it is just very difficult to achieve our awakening. No building can be built on false basis. If it is built, then it is so weak that it may collapse just by a little jerk. Like this, life cannot be sustaining without celibacy, if exists somehow then also just for a short time. This is the reason that we are always in such misery.

(The Celibacy*)

12. **An Asceticism** – To possess an aversion in every respect by the whole seen and heard or unseen and unheard substances of this world and paradise is known as an asceticism. As long as, there is an attachment in sensual enjoyment, till then a man cannot act firmly for an ultimate object, i.e., to achieve the God. The condition of sensual enjoyment begins by an aversion from worldly enjoyment. An attachment of mind in worldly enjoyment is mainly due to four reasons – (i) An existence of worldly enjoyment. (ii) Feeling of charm in worldly enjoyment. (iii) Feeling of happiness in worldly enjoyment. (iv) Feeling of love in worldly enjoyment. To realise all these four by discernment will help to achieve the asceticism. Therefore, there is a basic need of the regular and everlasting objective discernment (*vastu-vivek*). An asceticism is awakened by discernment and the discernment can be refined and become permanent through asceticism. Both are differently based methods.

    (A Path of Accomplishment)*

13. **The truth** – The aim of our life should be truth. Truth is the name of the God. Therefore, just the God should only be our aim. If there is anything else without the God, then that is entirely unreal, just do not exist. Nowadays use of word 'truth' is mostly just applicable only in meaning of a genuine lecture. Therefore, special attention is to be given on it. In the way we have heard or understand a subject, exactly with that pure intention to explain it in the same manner, we should speak in words with facial expression, sign etc. The truth should also be conveyed in such words which may not hurt to listener as far as possible. One should speak with humility in very sweet and humble words. It is just false to speak something secretly with cleverness. To speak anything secretly and cunningly will also be a sin. Therefore, one should not speak with a deceitful intention.

    (An immediately effective medicine for snares of the world*)

14. **Non-violence *(Ahinsa)*** – Non-violence is a supreme religion and is an ultimate penance, it is an ultimate truth, the religion is originated only from non-violence. According to the above words just from the *Mahabharat*, one can come across about the glory of non-violence and an inhibition of violent meat- eating generally in all scriptures and body of sacred and profane *Brahmanical* tradition but a man is so selfish and tongue-desirous that he kills the innocent animals to fulfill his hobby of hunting and tasting the hated meat and to fill up his poor belly. Meat-eating is a very big sin and an extremely harmful fornication. The man who brings the animal for slaughter, the man who allows to kill the animal, the man who kills the animal and who purchases, sells and cooks to eat, these are all considered just meat-eaters and murderers of animal. Non-violence religion is a head ornament of all religions.

    (*Bhagvacharcha* part-4**)

15. Free from Anger (*Akrodh*) – Desires are precisely averted and transformed in the form of anger. A man becomes extremely foolish during the anger. Natural purity, constancy, feelings of happiness, peace and thoughtfulness of his mind are destroyed. In fact, an angry man cannot be a devotee of the God. His inner heart has just no place than for the knowledge. It can be suppressed by following four methods – To consider every unfavourable event, accepting it as an auspicious ruling of the God and accept it with favourable mind, considering it beneficial in final stage.

Treat the sensual pleasure as a feeling of an asceticism. Enhance your tolerance.

Remain quiet at the time of anger.

16. To Serve *(Seva)* – In fact, this life is just only to serve. ... no person should accept it that he has no power or capability to serve. Each person willing to serve should keep himself entirely away from selfishness. The service should be treated as an ultimate selfishness. A selfish man can never do real service. The people who serve with a desire of reward or wanted its compensation, their service is also not the real service. That is but a method to fulfill a desire. As far as possible, do not disclose about service. Do not make efforts for disclosure. If it is revealed, then feel embarrassed and give its credit to the grace of the God with a true heart. Do not feel pride by serving.

(Bhavrog ki Ramban Dava**)

17. Satisfaction *(Santosh)* – A supreme method to achieve the best happiness in the world is the Satisfaction. A dissatisfied person shall always be just an unhappy. However great or whatever thing or condition may be achieved by him, he always feels shortage of it. But satisfaction is a great hindrance for divine love and in repetition of divine name. Therefore, never satisfied with repetition of chanting name. Just opposite to it, a man attracted to sensual enjoyment is always remain unsatisfied with luxurious world. He always feels shortage of it, whatever and how much he receives but desires even in more quantity. Possessing such dissatisfied nature, he remains increasing his field of area, thereby he is trapped badly from all around himself automatically and is always surrounded by the dejection, fear and worry. He does not perceive peace even in any condition.

(A Stream of Divine Pleasure)

18. Moral conduct *(Sadachar)* – To follow by which a man can be righteous with a virtuous heart is known as moral conduct. In our culture, moral conduct and religion are inseparable. Western religion and ethics are different, but then we considered moral conduct as root of religion and religion is the root of moral conduct. The basic fundamental of this religion and moral conduct is the God. Personal life and social life cannot be two. Moral conduct is such an object which retains them as purest by uniting two into one. According to sage *Manu* with moral conduct a man achieves permanent wealth, people according to one's desire and also the age. Not only this, but untimely death, etc. are also ruined by the moral conduct. A person without every character like knowledge etc. if he is with moral conduct, faithful and without jealousy then he lives for hundred years. (An immediately effective medicine for snares of the world)

19. Not to steal *(Asteya)* – A lack of will for theft is known as non-existence of the theft. To deprive the personal identity of others is known as robbery. Robbery is of many types – to take away other's items, concealment from speech, to arrange theft openly, to gaze other's object through mind, etc. are all just the various type of thefts. Due to support of civilised state, how many thefts have occurred by escaping from the law, if these can be counted then one can find that probably progress of society is increasing with high intensity towards the theft. As much as new laws are framed, just as much as, that new methods for thefts are invented. During earlier times, there was a different community of thieves which was looked upon with a sight of hatred, but at present the whole society has been over powered by such defects like an epidemic disease. The thefts with cleverness have begun even in small villages. These are bad symptoms. The society do not curse such thieves, rather one who can embezzle the right of others very easily, is considered just as much more clever and intelligent.

(A Human Religion*)

20. The Meal *(Aahar)* – The mind is formed just according to the food. Food is genuine or with malevolence, food is earned by whom, who is the cook and how was his/her mental state during cooking, how is the place, who have accompanied during meal and who is the server of food and his intention at the time of meal. All these factors, etc. are questionable? Such question cannot be passed off with a joke. Nowadays anyone can eat any substance, brought by waiter for his master, considering it suitable to eat or drink. No restriction exists for remnants of food nor for any other thing. In fact, it is big negligence. In the way, as will be it's the quality of money earned for food, in the way who will cook the food, in the way how will be the food material and place, of just that sort, will be an effect on the mind. Though, there is just an effect of existent power (*Vastu-shakti*) rather it also happens to this extent that the person who took meal is also affected by the will power and mentality of the host person.

(A Reform of the World Paradise* – Part-3)

21. An assembly of virtuous people *(Satsang)* – It is an extremely rare to meet a person who is supporter of one's own religion, virtuous man with noble nature, possesses a divine wealth, but with due efforts somewhat learned persons like righteous person, person following Vedas which relates to ceremonial acts and sacrificial rites, can also be found. But to encounter such a true and affectionate saint is an extremely difficult whose blessings can grant a divine love which is most deserved by ascetics, scholars and all and is also supremely rare. Therefore, an encounter with such saints is considered very rare. If such saints may be found somewhere then it is very difficult to recognise them. But fortunately, if such saintly person meets somewhere then his meeting, even unknowingly, may never go in vain. By the unknowing company of the God- loving scholar also provides light from the sun consisting of knowledge and an affectionate supreme treasure, due to distraction of sin and darkness without knowledge, but until it is not known, till then a person will not get real pleasure due to his unawareness of such benefit.

(Vision of Love*)

22. **The Hindu culture** – Spiritually oriented religion, well- cultured way and behavioural pattern, being maintained from the immemorial tradition and diffused in every field of life is known as just a Hindu culture. Such clear stream of Hindu culture is flowing uninterruptedly since the extreme ancient times. The main and only object of a human life, in this culture is to achieve an emancipation, wisdom or the achievement of the God. For this very reason, every action and efforts of this life are attempted with a concentration for such an aim. Therefore, in our fourth stage of life towards the final goal of a man, the highest place is designated to the salvation. Religion, wealth, desire and then an emancipation.

(Hindu Sanskriti ka Swarup**)

23. **A visit to pilgrims *(Tirth-sevan)*** – Pilgrims have a definite glory. They destroy the sin of everyone just by their natural power and grant them result as desired by the heart and even bestowed an emancipation. Who have been, when and how and in which way were benefitted in pilgrims and how and which pilgrims appeared, about this, an excessively clear description in very a beautiful manner is available in Hindu scriptures. As much as this glory of pilgrims prevailed, due to the reason because the great high souled, realised scholars and saints have lived there or the Lord have made them highly auspicious, making them His field of acts (Leela kshetra) by appearing their sometimes in some forms. Pilgrims are of three types – (i) Moving or living; (ii) Mental; and (iii) Immovable. (A special number of '*Kalyan*' – '*Tirthank*'**)

24. **The Human Religion *(Manav Dharma)*** – Normal religion, which can be followed by a human only, its other name is human religion.

A mong compilers of scriptures have shown eight characters, someone ten, someone twelve, others 15-16 or even more than that of characters for normal religion. According to sage Manu – A holding, forgiveness, self-control, away from the theft, a hygiene, control over mind senses, an ability to bear, the understanding, truth and non-anger are such ten characters. These are such religions in which no caste or community can object. Development of humanity in men can be possible only by the practice of religions. When there was leading status of these religions among human-race then there had existed a kingdom of happiness and peace in the world, somehow or the other the human race has averted their faces in fostering these religions, in the same way, grief and restlessness have begun to increase in that and at present human beings of the world, due to the destruction of these religions in higher amount to fulfill their petty interests and becoming blood thirsty like violent animals and giving support to mutual hostility, are being trained to devour one-another and for this very reason in the human colonies, who considered themselves as an intelligent, no comforts can be seen generally in anywhere.

(Human Religion*)

25. **Current education** ***(Vartman Shiksha)*** – The aim of an education according to an ancient culture is over and all development (physical, mental, economic and moral) in this world and supremely and utterly meritorious – an achievement of the emancipation in paradise. According to sages, that is the knowledge which can liberate us from ignorance. Such a hallucination has occurred that it has become an indication of our mental progress today to fall in a deep pit of destruction. The knot of hairs and the sacred threads which could not be cut even by the sword of Muslims, but the same are being cut today for the sake of progress, just by the educated arrogant Hindus themselves. Not even a slightest blaze could touch a virtue of Indian women by lying in the red flames of fire pit, rather it got more brilliance, but that very virtuous religion has become a burdensome to our sisters and daughters due to result of present education and efforts are being made to walk away with a step in a well-collective manner all around to dismount it. Children should be imparted with that sort of knowledge which can develop with them religious devotion, religion, moral conduct, sacrifice and self-control, etc.

[*Vartman Shiksha* (Current system of Education*)]

P.S. – Name of the books given in bracket at the end of each head (1-25) and has been marked with single asterisk are the books available in Hindi language while those marked with two asterisks are the original names of the books in Hindi.

❒

132
Philosophical Thoughts of Bhaijee

The supremely deserved ultimate Brahma is totally inexpressible. He is all-containing, entirely detached, entirely skilled, entirely beyond the virtue (a title for unqualified Supreme Being), eternal, inconceivable, accomplished simultaneously, mutually different, identity of talent for spiritual dependence. He is an unqualified formless (ultimate being) – qualified formless, qualified visible and also beyond from all this. Since very ancient times our sages, great saints, scholars and intellectuals have interpreted this very supreme spirit from their different point of view. Their point of view is only called thought or opinion. The chief among them are – (1) Monism of Shri Shankaracharya; (2) Special dualism of Ramanujacharya; (3) Dualism by Madhvacharya; (4) Dual-dualism by Shri Nimbarkacharya; (5) Pure dualism by Ballabhacharya; (6) Inconceivable distinct dessensalism of Shri Chaitanya Mahaprabhu.

Among the tradition of such great scholars, an accomplished saint moved with passionate religious devotion like Bhaijee, is also near the front-line. Chaitanya Mahaprabhu had not promoted for any system of opinion in his life. Such was also occurred in the life time of Shri Poddarji. Though Shri Poddarji then has not promoted any thought, however a clear hint is definitely and nearly spread through, in his texts regarding principles.

There were many texts written and edited by Shri Poddarji and his philosophical views can be seen in these texts, but their description and criticism have been made specially in his three main texts – *Shri Radha-Madhav Chintan*, *Gita Chintan* and in *Pad-Ratnakar*. The ultimate highest state of the divine love is considered as proper state of an emotional dualism *(Rasadwaitya)* by him. He has written –

"Just after perceiving yourself and the God in real sense, the true love occurs but is not possible to acquaint it truly, without love. There is mutually feasible act of achieving-relationship in this love and knowledge. Firstly, a love achieved on being little aware of knowledge, real knowledge comes after attainment of love and supreme love which is proximity to real knowledge, that very is the highest love. That very love is called as an emotional dualism

(Rasadwaitya) by the devotees. Here the love and abode of love have become united. Both of them are mutually merged with one another."

(Gita Chintan)

(To ponder on *Gita*, Page – 562)

Thereafter, the situation which remains in the form of dualism between love and adobe of love, that is only for the enjoyment of an act. The scholars in religious devotion (*bhakti*) Shri Ramanuja, etc., all the great writers have not considered the indifference of the soul form of the God, not only just in restrained condition, rather in free condition. Such is also an opinion of Shri Poddarji as well. He writes –

"A saint released from future birth, can be equal to *Brahma* for knowledge of real nature of things by spiritual point of view, can be indictment with bliss by crossing toils of world but can never be the Supreme Being. The power of creation and destruction of the world is in only with perpetually sacred (*Nitysiddha*) almighty. *For this very reason, this much can be said that a soul can be Brahma but can never be an almighty or the God.*

(*To Ponder on Gita*, Page – 437)

He has written on another place:

I have immersed in the ocean of love and become a form of love,

This can be called an emotional dualism when there remain no different forms.

Love is the God and the God is love, you are both as the lover and a beloved of lover.

Where exists the love, there cannot be a fear of the God of death.

(*Pad-Ratnakar/Premshatak/* Couplet – 664)

Both are also not mutually opposite facts. It is just not an essential unity (*Tatvik ekta*) of lover (Soul) and beloved (The almighty) but it is then an inexpressible integral unity for an enjoyment of acts which is entirely an object of experience. According to Shri Poddarji, there is no difference between love and the almighty. Like the way, it is impossible to describe an all-pervading spirit of universe. In the same way, the love cannot be described through speech. A densely grown pleasure, which is experienced in the heart, that can never be described through speech. Description, which is available for the love that is only symbolic. A lover engrossed in love finds only his charming beloved everywhere. The eyes continuously see to the whole world as consisting of Krishna. People, who are not the traveller of such divine way of emotions, it can be an access of emotion to them but those great scholars, who have been progressive on this way and who have achieved such an attainment state, it is a constant, practical and ultimate truth for them and not an access of emotion.

A will, which was written during the last days of his life by Shri Poddarji, it is written in it – I have been maximally benefitted from the great scholars Shri Shankaracharya and the Lord Chaitanya Dev. It seems that just non-duality (*Adwetya*) of Shri Shankaracharya, becoming cohesive in charm of Shri Chaitanya Dev has ascended to manifest in the form of emotional dualism (*Rasadwetya*) of Shri Poddarji. Those who have impressed him the most, Bhaijee has only confirmed his emotional dualism by the views from both of them. To present his ideas, Shri Poddarji has just never utilised the methods of refutation and elaboration. Many scholars which existed for religious devotion, each of them has criticsed the non-duality of Shri Shankaracharya, so as to establish their opinion. But the delivering practice of Shri Poddarji, is totally different from these scholars. At the time of propagating his views, Shri Poddarji has never criticised the views of any other scholar up to this extent, that he did not criticised even the non-duality of Shri Shankaracharya, on the contrary, it is an extraordinary fact that he had adorned his emotional dualism by accepting his principle of non-duality. Such a method of the adornment in his opinion, is extraordinary specially in the great personality of Shri Poddarji. It can be said in other words that Shri Poddarji, has made a coordination in emotional dualism with scholar devotees for the path of non-dualism (*Adwetyapath*) and the path of religious devotion (*Bhaktipath*). Such way of coordination was a specialty of Shri Poddarji, which is generally not seen in the method of nurturing views of others.

A coordination which is shown amidst various opinions by Shri Poddarji has one motive behind that coordinated method. Such an intention is to think about the welfare of creatures at different levels. Whatever has been said by earlier scholars, it was told from their own experiences for the welfare of creatures entrapped by the illusion. For the benefit of creatures of different nature, an instructure advice is also useful, proposed by various scholars. This very is the reason that there have been innumerable commentary and sub-commentaries for the Shrimad Bhagwat Gita and are also being carried away even today. Just the difference of such interest, is the reason of moving to and fro promotion of different means and methods. Due to result of instincts of infinite births, an attraction for the worldly pleasure of the soul has become very hard. Due to this very reason, it must suffer pain from birth to another birth. Shri Poddarji has experienced that it is not such an easy to get rid of sensual pleasure by the soul, looking to the grief and pain involved in it than to engross with any beautiful object by him. If he could progress towards attractive and lively method of divine love and he could get some interest in it, then it will be very easy for him to get rid of sensual pleasure. According to the principle of emotional dualism (*Rasadwaitya*) of Shri Poddarji, a devotee is remaining continued to move forward on the road of achievement by experiencing its charm, right from the beginning. Taking an existing form of bliss (*Swarupbhut anand*) from all pervading spirit of the universe will be continued as very harsh if its blissful power (*Ehladini shakti*) causing joy is not involved in delighting him. Such savorous dualism (*Rasadwaitya*) is entirely approved by revelation of *Veda* and ancient texts.

Describing mystical savorous – all-pervading spirit of the universe (*Rasbrahma*) a revelation of Veda declares –

Who is known as auspicious? Such a higher all-pervading spirit of universe, the supreme spirit is really blissful, He is only a real bliss.

(Tettireeya upnishad- 2/7/2)

The one who himself is doer, is an element of self-form *(Swayamrup tatva)*, that very is savour (*Rasa*) – is a complete identity for savour *(Purna rassawarup)*. By achieving that form of an essence, the soul becomes blissful.

Such savorous all-pervading spirit of the universe *(Rasbrahma)* is only the supreme being (*Rasrup*). Most charming Lord Shri Krishna Himself declared in the Gita –

'I am installed in the all-pervading spirit of the universe.' Lord Shri Krishna has said in *Brahmapurana* –

"I am always the soul of Radha and (Shri Krishna) my soul definitely and only is Radha, Shri Radha is the Goddess of Vrindavan. Therefore, I worship Radha."

In his text *'Shri Radha-Madhav-Chintan'*, Shri Poddarji has explained extensively that in fact there is no difference between Shri Krishna, Shri Radha, community of herd girls of Braj and their sweetest acts. These have just themselves become taste and tastier. Their several acts are the waves in an ocean of pleasure. The devotee enters in this kingdom of act by the practice with spiritual body *(Bhava-deha)* and has become engrossed in an ultimate bliss (*Parmanand*) by immersing in that public censured sea of act (*Leela sindhu*). In such act of revelation, a unitary state, which occurred on becoming fully absorbed and concerted, is not equal to impenetrable state of the impersonal ultimate being of soul *(Jiva-Brahma)*. Here the perpetual (*Nitya*), though being one, remained also two perpetually. To feel one, though being two and also become two, being one, such an experience does not occur only to an accomplished devotee but rather also with the life of Shri Radha-lighting power (*Ehladni shakti*) of Shri Krishna Himself is sighted with such excellent picture of emotion. Their two of intentions with strong feeling need a careful study. She tells Her beloved Shri Krishna –

"I am a criminal, am a sinner and just definitely disgraced by all means."

(*Pad-Ratnakar*, verse-643)

She again conveys to Her Life Lord –

"Lover, love, an ultimate abode of life, I have no any information but become inspired.

Am I loving Radha or are you only a dear *Nand Kishore*."

(*Pad-Ratnakar*, verse-614)

The state of feeling with passionate religious devotion in duality (*Rasabhavadwetya*) is just not accessible to the revered knowledge.

Such experience can only be possible by the grace of revered supreme twins after realisation of real nature of things (*Tatva darshan*).

The method of such worship is given extensively in *'Shri Radha-Madhav-Chintan'*. It is not possible to describe it due to shortage of space. A symbolic description is given, in a verse of devotional poetry which is being given below –

To first object of devotion is to sacrifice sensual pleasures mentally,

A firm attachment with the virtuous actions (*Satkarm*), which may increase an affection with the God.

To a complete and an utter destruction of different passions of love,

By destroying pride-arrogance, vanity-greed-passion, anger and the honour.

To get rid of discussing others, remove entire desire of sensual pleasures.

To always remember sweet divine name and form, by retaining firm faith with your mind on the God.

To think over for the act and hear for the attributes of God, by developing disinterested passion in essence of acts (*Leela*).

To develop a beloved feeling with *Mohan* continuously by sacrificing the gratification and emancipation.

To feel a complete pleasure just with the happiness of the God, by increasing the devotion unto the feet of the God.

To join the pure company of those intimate saints who are devotee to *Vishnu*.

Who are away of interest in gratification and emancipation. By merging your interest just with their interests.

To think over again on the acts, being a devotee of sacred path of
love.

They can then visualise the acts (*Leela*), by the grace of Shri Krishna and Radha.

Thereafter, they become pure, accomplished and realised by following the feeling of herd girls of Braj by acquiring techniques through passionate religious devotion (*Ras-sadhan*).

Then becomes love form as herd girls, only by perpetual journey through act (*Leela*) of Krishna.

This very is the pure form of love and an ultimate realisation towards the path of love.

(Pad-Ratnakar, verse-730)

Shri Poddarji has progressively considered four extraordinary kingdoms in the accomplishment world (Sadhan-jagat) –

1. Kingdom of action *(KARM-RAJYA)*
2. Kingdom of feeling *(BHAV-RAJYA)*
3. Kingdom of knowledge *(GYAN-RAJYA)*
4. Great and ultimate kingdom of emotion *(MAHAN PARAM BHAV RAJYA)*

The people sensible from the kingdom of action have been accomplishing the act by legal obligations permitted for the householder. They achieved a state without a pledge or any option through total desirelessness. Next to it is the kingdom of feelings, where occurs a preeminence of religious devotion. Through sentimental object of devotion (*Bhav-sadhna*) they achieved here their divine worlds and their deities according to their emotions. They are also totally free from an illusion.

Then comes the kingdom of knowledge. Here the thought-based persons have been standardised as pure form of soul, by feeling the great speech, by four means of practice which includes four-fold ways of self-control. Their souls are not reversible. They become a form of an all-pervading spirit of the universe or obtained beatific state of communion of the soul with the divine being. To become just perceptible even in the life time, there occurs an extreme lacuna of the world and due to a total absence of the practice of ignorance because of proper perception, the soul becomes free from life even retaining the body in the sight of others by setting free of characters for living beings. This very is called knowledge. This very is paramount state in the opinion of non-duality (*Adwaitya*) by Shri Shankaracharya.

Then comes a great sentimental form – Kingdom of divine feeling. The people free from passion of enjoyment-freedom-action-knowledge, etc. are entitled for such supreme kingdom of sentiments. According to Shri Poddarji, that a sage of spiritual wisdom then becomes free from life by meeting with the true knowledge of all pervading spirit of the universe but just with that only, he cannot realise precisely the real nature of that form of the God. Through that supreme devotion, he comes to know me in reality, what and who I am! (The Gita-18/55). That identity assumed by the ultimate being is not perceived exactly from the real nature of human soul. Even in the people free from spiritual wisdom, there sprouts a bud of divine love in few of them only, by which and through the above kingdom of action, feelings and knowledge, they enjoy the acts with the beloved God by entering the former kingdom of divine feelings through their divine body or become helper in his act, remained perpetually engaged in service by relinquishing their different forms just for his happiness. This is such kingdom when even an emancipation must be renounced. According to Shri Poddarji, the eminent persons, dedicating everything, can only enter here, who are free from smell of desire for passion – emancipation to such an extraordinary and great sentimental rare kingdom, they may reach directly flowing in the pure sacrificial stream of love after achieving the knowledge in above kingdom of knowledge by some great means. In this kingdom, continuously and regularly, wandering of an eternal act by the ultimate being with a divine savour of love form *(Premras-swarup)* by Shri Radha Krishna remains continued.

In the field of worship of Shri Radha Krishna, several views have been established till day. On the name of melodious worship *(Madhur Bhava)* or due to other reasons or by time effect in methods of melodious worship, several types of indecencies have entered. Such indecencies caused a great harm, that harm may occur in personal life or in community life. According to the recommendations from the point of alchemist and philosophy, the principle of duality of sentiments by Shri Poddarji has not only removed the confusion but rather shown the brightest love of Shri Radha Krishna, which was duly needed in present age. As such, an eminent scholar of Braj literature Dr. Prabhu Dayal Mittal has written that such narration touching the inner heart, which is made on this subject, in the articles of Shri Poddarji, will now also give a new dimension to the eminent scholars of Braj.

❒

133

Planning of an Accomplishment – Endured Life for the Refuge

As soon as Bhaijee inclined towards religious devotion, since then he had one desire in his mind that all his accompanying persons may spend life endowed with means (*Sadhan-yukta*). Up to this extent that being living in Mumbai for trade purpose, he formed even there an accomplishment committee with his business friends, already committed with the accomplishment (*Sadhan*) seriously. There are about 50 members in this committee. To control these people, engaged in the accomplishment, Bhaijee himself was looking after. A little later, after departure from Mumbai and due to an actual appearance of the God, almost a flood of faith had spread in Gorakhpur. That time people living close to him and main volunteers of Gita press have persuaded to form a committee for devotees under the guidance of Bhaijee and have begun the accomplishment (*Sadhan*) with full sincerity. Few devotees among them like Shri Shukdevji, Shri Ganga Prasadji, Shri Gambhirchandji, etc. have also experienced special perceptions. The zeal of devotees was just fast sometimes or slow sometimes. Accordingly, there have been remain a rise and fall in the committee of devotees as well. Even then, it remained continued in some or other way, then it transformed as an association of devotees and still continued under auspices of the *Gita press*. But Bhaijee was not satisfied by all these. He had been trying again and again that people close to him and coming in special contact should spend sacrificial and befitting way of life for devotees. Not only this, whenever he goes to *Gita Bhawan, Swargashram* for an association of virtuous people (*Satsang*), then even there as well had inspired formal object of devotion to every collective group of people and provided them by publishing the framed ruled to those who wanted to follow them. Then he remains more energetic for some of his closely associated people. But shame to our dirty inner heart, as the rain drops do not stay on slippery earthen pot, in the same manner the sweet drops by that luscious cloud did not even transform us lively and could not provide satisfaction to that generous person. Although according to few devotees, such was the strength of drops in those luscious clouds that they cannot trickle without leaving an effect on it, irrespective of the slipperiness of the earthen pot and I have no idea that how many people will be following his rules today quietly in their homes. I bow unto the feet of all them by my heart, but no such group is seen according to my logical opinion, who are following these rules in toto, infact, few rules are still followed by several devotees. On *Akhsay Tritiya* in 1959, he again inspired his close associates by framing rules for the life of refuge.

During subsequent part of his life when the modes of life of Bhaijee had not retained much at worldly level, he had a throbbing pain of such thing in his heart that his own people are not following an accomplishment endured way of life. Although, such a pious-hearted person like him took all such responsibility on himself. He wrote a letter to his close associate Shri Mohanlal Goyandka in Bankura on 8th June, 1967, which is reproduced here and which indicates the feeling of his heart. Thereafter, also he could not find satisfactory progress. On 9th April, 1967, i.e., prior to 4 years of his heavenly departure, such thing has again appeared in his mind. He has decided that if I follow rules myself, then my close associates will definitely come after. He has begun to follow. It was but natural that his close associates had to become aware about it, while a letter was sent to his distant relatives on 14th April, 1967 through his personal attendant, which is being reproduced as follows –

Gita press, Gorakhpur,
8th June, 1964

Dear brother Mohan,

Let us remember the almighty affectionately. Received your letter. I have not replied timely, so please don't mind it. The world is in very strange condition. Anyone may understand anything but as much as I can understand myself that I have many types of weaknesses, it is entirely true in my opinion and over here I have a great pain in my mind since years and this pain is gradually increasing. It was an old story, I had a great desire to see this country as independently. The childhood had a very pious and sacrificial temperament. With those intentions, I have joined the political field and lived at Shimlapal. Thereafter, also retained very good feelings in Mumbai. A desire to achieve the God remained growing in true sense and I came to Mumbai with an intention to spend my life as a devotee leaving my own business. I had also a clear talk with *Savitri*'s mother to spend an ideal life, living with pure poverty, somewhere alone at the bank of the Ganga. Thereafter, temptations have also been received for a high governmental position and for the earning of crore of rupees. On the other hand, a highly noble soul wanted me to join him with great affection, but the God saved me from all sides. But now, the life over here is becoming just very wretched. More emphasis is given on an achievement in '*Kalyan*'. I wrote in the book. I also preach to people in the association of virtuous people. An association of devotees was also established here, which has many members from outside. The outside people are in impression that we are all realized saints and only saints lived here. Due to such misleading faith, even during pilgrimage train, people did circumambulation of this train, but the fact is that there is no accomplishment in my life and even the life of my accompanying persons may probably also not be connected towards the accomplishment as far as in my opinion. I wanted to a life of refuge. People living over here could be devotee by mind, body and speech. They might have attached to the God, but no other work is being done here according to my opinion except the gratification of passion. It was my desire prior to death that at least in my life and according to my very old wish, to spend my few days at least as self-denying, simple and saintly life which may be as an unattached saint to worldly objects, but that is also not being materialised.

On this end, our life has become a presenter of bad ideals for self and others as well, spoiler of habits, an enhancer for unnecessary needs and poverty and an excessively expensive. Where crore of people like us cannot get a full meal, where two sarees are not available to lacs of sisters, is it not a sin to live such an expensive life style? Sometimes, I am very much worried about it. Looking such things of mine, pictures of those poverty-stricken people have appeared in front of my eyes then tears trickle from the eyes. Everything causes a great pain. Even then, I did not renounce which is a big weakness. Possibly, it is result of money earned un-righteously. Although I don't have much need of mine. By writing two articles each month, earning forty-fifty by it, can manage my everything very easily from a true earning with virtuous feeling, but then an opportunity should also prevail for it.

Why should I blame others, it is all my weakness? People don't have a mutual affection, nor they have a sacrifice, neither have a feeling to serve. The same condition is with press and workers of the press. It seems if I am pretending public at least through my life. I am committing a sin. When I am not proper and spent achievementless expensive life with pleasure then how can I expect such hope from my companions that they should be in an order. I wanted to write all such things to you since many days which I have written here in very brief. If you and … can help me somehow then should try for this work.

I had planned five-seven years ago a thing for a refuge, had framed some rules. There should be an arrangement here for the simple living people and for refuge living. I wrote some very simple rules for refuge living, but even these cannot be applied here. I am enclosing herewith a copy of such rules to you, please go through it.

Respected Shri Sethji is not feeling well. I am also not well. If Shri Sethji feels proper, he could have decided something, it would be then better that who would be responsible of which thing after his demise, what would be arrangements for Calcutta, Gorakhpur and Rishikesh. Otherwise, people will fight mutually due to pride and everyone just knows what the result will be. Though the God is very mindful to me. From time to time, I feel (even suffering with such pain) that it is also just an auspicious rule of the God, why should I worry? But I have just to worry due to pride-passion.

My health is little better than earlier but then weakness still exists.

Savitri's mother is not well at present. Rest is the grace of God.

Yours only, Hanuman

I bow unto the holy feet of respected Sethji. All children will be cheerful. According to the letter from Jaydayal, his health is not well, and the weakness seems to be increased. It is matter of worry.

Rules for refuge:

To get up prior to the sunrise.

Do not sleep beyond six hours.

Don't sleep during the day time.

Do your work by yourself –

Washing long sari and other clothes.

Cleaning utensils.

Cleaning room and other types of hygiene etc.

The Meal – Do not prepare more than four items. Do not eat luxurious items. Do not eat more than six items. Do not eat more than two times a day. Milk, tea, water (lemon), etc. may be taken. Meal should be taken on the leaves as far as possible.

Do not wear luxurious clothes, do not wear more than two clothes, wear clean clothes only. On special need like winter four simple clothes can be used. Do not wear costly clothes. Do not wear clothes made by the mill. Women should not wear costly sari, nylon or transparent clothes. A voluminous skirt must be worn inside the sari.

At least fifty thousand divine names should be repeated daily in morning since awakening till sleep, divine name repetition should be made as much as possible without counting.

Be in a habit to do daily routine as per your habit, i.e., religious rites to be performed in morning, noon and evening, reading religious scriptures, divine name repetition, etc.

To remain silent for two hours, do not indulge in gossiping as far as possible. Do not blame anyone or hear it.

Men should never meet women (except his own wife) alone. Men and women should strongly follow celibacy inside the refuge.

At least on eleventh day of lunar fortnight, fast should be followed and costly fruits, nuts, *halwa*, etc. be avoided.

Must be present daily during assembly of virtuous people (*Satsang*) and group singing of hymns (*Keertan*).

Do not sleep on the cot.

Never use the utensils made of silver, iron, glass or china clay.

Do not use the soap.

Do not use the leather goods.

Utilise your time for the work of responsibility, like repetition of divine name, reading scriptures, in service or management.

Do not retain long hairs.

Do not utilise scented oil from market.

Do not wear ornaments.

You should behave mutually with love and humility while false, theft, theatre, etc. should then just be avoided. Why should there be rules for them?

In refuge, the people coming from outside temporarily can be accommodated till final arrangement is made in refuge. But they will have to follow strictly the codes and ethics of refuge, as long as they would stay in refuge. A person who is even staying for a night should also follow the rules of refuge. There will be no servant except to arrange water and to clean utensils.

Till an arrangement is not made for refuge, those who wish can follow these rules at personal level. Once a refuge is established, the local or an outsider, could follow the refuge rules, if they wish, even living outside of refuge. There is no objection by refuge to follow the refuge rules at home, but it shall be compulsory to follow the refuge rules in refuge.

These rules can be followed willingly, irrespective of your presence at any place.

Gita press, Gorakhpur
Dated – 17th April, 1967

Dear Sir,

I bow to you. Respected Bhaijee has a plan to leave this place on next 21st April and will reach Swargashram at 23rd on Sunday. He had a plan since a long in his mind to spend refuge-life, though a structure of refuge is not established, however, he had framed rules for the residents of refuge. He began to follow them and is following all the rules strictly except two-three rules. Though he does not like to compel, but will be happy if some other men or women will follow these rules completely as much as possible. With his consent a document containing rules is being issued alongwith this letter.

You could apprise me about an information or respected Shri Sethji about those who follow these rules.

Despite this Bhaijee was not satisfied. Prior one year to his long- lasting departure he again planned for the residents of Gita Vatika and recently arrived visitors about which a complete description will be available in his following words –

It is an old story when I have left Mumbai then that time I had a desire, that I should live in somewhere alone at the bank of the Ganga, but the desire is not fulfilled. I have come here to explain the working of '*Kalyan*' but will have to stay here. It seems as if it was just not a strong desire, otherwise had it been firm, then the God might have also helped. Thenceforth, in which pattern it was planned here through my mind, that such condition should prevail, it was just not possible. There was no fault of anyone for this, maybe fault of the firmness of my mind and my devoted striving (*Sadhna*). Then, there was a flow. Such thing appeared in between and many times in mind that there should be a separate refuge. The followers of the rules of refuge should live here. Those people who wish to live for the sake of devoted striving should follow the rules of refuge, domestic people should live separately. Even the people coming from outside – they may live even for five days – but they should follow the rules of refuge if they stay here. Even that could also not be possible. Several rules had been framed for refuge and are stored as such.

The body remains sick and have no idea what will happen next. Type of environment which was expected here and as is expected by outsiders, in fact, it is not like that. As much as, expansion of the spiritualism which was expected here, is just not here in that much of quantity, but in very little quantity and that too in the mind of very few people. Several people have come from outside and they live here leaving everything at distant places. Their intentions were noble but due to faults of ours, these people could not progress that much which they could have done, and which was necessary for further progress due to faulty company.

About 20-25 days ago once, a thought appeared during night like this that 'something should be done here'. The question arises – What to do? I thought that some contact may be made to the people over here with the God and such contact should go on increasing then it is better. There are many such refuges and temples at many places where the repetition of the text of the *Ramayan* is made, repetition of the *Bhagwat* is made, celebration of devotional songs (*Sankeertan*) and divine names is also made. Like this, it may also be held here. Here, the best thing is one – celebration of devotional songs, which is being in process. In addition to this, we should also do it a little bit of it daily. The God is one, not many but people have interest in various forms, have interest in several types of prayers. Various types of cherished forms are there with desires and also without desire as well. Under the category without desire comes various feelings like an achievement of knowledge, an achievement of love and totally without motive – these are many types of emotions. Therefore, as is the feeling of a person, interested in any form of the God, interested in any sacred verse, if people residing here are not sick, then they should do its repetition daily at least for five minutes by coming to this place. I wanted that something should go well throughout entire twenty-four hours of the day. Such people should be groomed, and local people will also agree to cooperate in such task. The people coming from outside have been remain sitting as an idle.

They remained gossiping and did nothing. They can begin reading through the *Ramayan*. Stay for nine days and can finish one complete reading of *Ramayan* in nine days. Can do monthly reading through the Bhagwat. Can do repetition of the *Valmiki Ramayan*. Can do whatever they prefer. Can do 100 repetitions of the *Hanuman Chalisa*, where is the problem?

Likewise, I have put eight pictures of the God with due consideration. Though the statue installation has not been done for them, but everyone should consider them as the God through mind. A person coming in morning should be responsible to burn incense daily and place flowers to each picture. There are two verses each for divine idol, 16-17 verses are in total. Should do the repetition of those verses. If he cannot come some days due to some reason, then may request others to share this responsibility. Few verses have been written, verses are also written for praise. This is requested to everyone – people residing here – requested to ladies and gentlemen that they should definitely do the repetition and reading of the verses in which they are interested by coming in to pavillion, without any gap, daily and regularly as much as they can afford. Minimum for five minutes while there is no limit of too much. If someone may not come due to sickness or under some compulsions, then it does not matter but never neglect it, considering it as secondary or due to laziness or mistake.

Excluding these sacred verses if someone wishes as to recite some other sacred verse then he can do it. These texts are available for reading – the *Shrimad Bhagwat, the Shrimad Bhagwat Gita, the Vishnu Sahastranam, the Durga Saptashati, the Ramrakshastrota, the Ganeshstrota, Shri Radhakripakatakshastavaraj, the Ras Panchadhayayi, Shri Yugalsahastranam, the Ram Charit Manas, the* Hanuman Chalisa, etc. One can study any text in which they are interested. Like this, one may devote as much time in recitation-reading as he can afford, that will be better otherwise spent at least five minutes for it. Devote this time considering it as an unpaid labour, treat it just like that. And if not, then please do it as a favour to me, give it is a begging, people residing here, coming here should all give it as begging. If one can do it without desire for the God, then it can be gradually a very big thing – can help to achieve the God. Recitation of Bhagwat separately, recitation of the Ramayana separately, recitation of the Vishnu Sahastranam separately, recitation of Ram Rakshastotra separately – if there is an enthusiasm inside then every recitation can be managed. This is a plan and today only is its establishment. I still finish to recite fifteenth chapter of the *Gita,* whosoever desires can begin recitation from today, otherwise if not willing, then may start from tomorrow.

What else can be a more better benediction persuasion than this!

Accordingly, he has got it signed on following written announcement by everyone –

It is requested to all ladies and gentlemen residing and coming to this place that they should daily and regularly and without hindrance and as far as possible, coming in to pavillion should do the reading, recitation in low tone of that sacred verses and texts in which each one is interested, at least for five minutes or as much as they can. If they may not come due to sickness or compulsion, then it does not matter, but never ignore it due to laziness – negligence treating it as secondary.

Thursday, Phalgun Shukla 12 Yours, in the year 1969.

Yours
Hanuman Prasad Poddar

❐

134

An Insistence on Abiding

For a long time, Bhaijee had a desire that his close associates should also spend a simple and disciplined life like the people residing in refuge. He tried many times, but a form of refuge cannot be created. At last, Bhaijee decided that he will himself follow the rules firmly. With such intention, he framed rules and begun to follow with firmness since the beginning of 1967. Two times meal in a day with only few items, morning tea, a little bit of fruits in afternoon, this was the only meal at that time for Bhaijee. In addition, there had been more rules as well for which he has begun to follow with firmness. Bhaijee has also dictated letters to his close friends residing outside and sent the details of the rules by which many people started to follow these rules even residing in their homes.

Bhaijee may follow different rules, there was no objection in such case, but he does not also eat well for the protection of rules- for which it was but natural to feel a pain in the mind of his wife. She has requested several times to Bhaijee but Bhaijee was firm in protection of rules. Once a woman had arrived. Bhaijee had special affection for her and she also had a special attention for Bhaijee. Wife of Bhaijee told her – please give him juice to drink as long as you stay here. To follow her advice, she went in afternoon to Bhaijee with orange juice. Bhaijee thought that she has brought water, therefore said – I have just had water. The woman said – You can drink any amount in summer. He tried to ignore several times then finally, Bhaijee said – O.K. give me a half glass of water. The woman has given a drinking glass to Bhaijee. As soon as Bhaijee marked that it is juice, the colour of his face has changed and he said – I will not drink it. Woman persuaded him badly and asked – what is the harm for not drinking it? Bhaijee replied firmly – Why it is not important, it is also necessary, after all, to follow rules. Once a rule is not followed, it will never be followed. In spite of this, when she insisted then said strictly – I will drink just today but I will do fasting in lieu of this for two days, you will then not complain why I am fasting. The woman had no reply and took back the glass.

Such was the firmness for protection of rules by Bhaijee, although he had already been elated several years prior to following these rules. He rose even more than eminence from where even the ancient Indian sacred scriptures become silent but was following so that his close associates may also follow the rules firmly. ❐

135
An Open Invitation of Divine Love

A little change has begun to appear within the external life of Bhaijee, after his return from pilgrimage. He became ill after returning from pilgrimage. Bhaijee went to Ratangarh from Gorakhpur to recover his health. He has become more engrossed in charming and divine sports (*Leela*) of *'Shri Radha-Madhav'*. He found it (to join the act of his deity) more convenient to stay alone in the room due to his sickness. Such scenes (of these acts) have been put in writing as literary composition of verse, most of the verses in devotional poetry coupled with Braj emotions have been created thereafter. Bhaijee has written in an introduction towards his literary composition of verses –

"An auspicious God is an ocean of infinite grace. He has kindly sent such an auspicious disease. I must lie on bed for months. Physicians and ayurvedic consultants have directed me – should live with full comforts in total solitude, people should not be allowed to meet, no work is permitted. Meeting with people is generally almost checked. Found an opportunity to live simply alone. I lived in the closed room just alone for the rest of time except for the time of treatment – medicines and wholesome diet. I spent my time in other work than to think about disease in alone. That work was a self-examination or self-observation. Several types of images of the life have appeared-people have considered me a great saint, devotee or a holy man. Oh! What a big fraud this is! There are number of weaknesses in life, how many stigmas and how many faults and impurities are present here. Looking at all this – the heart is moved by compassion and a natural humility has arisen. Tears trickle from eyes, the soul has surrounded unto the holy feet of naturally kind-hearted, purifying the sinful, store of grace and ocean of compassion, reminded my faults repeatedly with compassionate feelings and has attracted the compassionate attention of the friend of poor (Krishna) towards my wretched condition. Sometimes I have begun just to console myself.

Meanwhile, the sweet smile, the mind captivator for people of the world, an infinite ocean of bliss, Shri *Shyam Sundar* arrives, asked with a smile and putting his supportive hand on my head – Stupid, why are you weeping? Why you have been unhappy becoming a wretched and distressed? Come with me in the Braj; see my divine acts and become engrossed in an ultimate sea of bliss. Hearing just the sweetest words with compact of bliss from the king of Braj, Shri Shyam Sundar, the weakness of the mind runs away. Like an enchanted mind instantly followed him. He leaves behind him in that supremely charming area and becomes engaged in his recreation of acts.

The mind moved freely – sometimes in the courtyard of *Nandbaba,* sometimes in an enclave of *Yashoda*, sometimes in cow pen, sometimes among the comic sentiments of the community of his companions, sc·netimes in courtyard *(Avani)* of the house on returning from forest, sometimes at the bank of *Kalindi,* sometimes among an enactment of round dance, sometimes among the community of loving herd girls of Braj, sometimes in a house of lonely herd girls of Braj, sometimes in the mind of female attendant, sometimes in the sweet loving discussion of female attendants, sometimes below the Banyan tree, sometimes on singing-rope during fifth lunar month of Hindu calendar (July-August), sometimes at swinging-rope during winter season, sometimes during Holi colours, sometimes fragrant of *Vrinda* forest by newly blossomed flowers, sometimes near the better-half, sometimes near Shyam Sundar, sometimes at lonely arbors, sometime at the place for recreation of acts by *Kishore* and *Kishori*, sometimes among sweetest divine utterance held between them, sometimes between the meeting of *Udhav*-herd girls of Braj, sometimes at the meeting of Shri Krishna and Udhav held a Mathura, sometimes for the condition of the love – the anguish of separation between Radha and herd girls of Braj after Shri Krishna departure to Mathura – like such meekness and the flow of act continued daily, day and night for several months. Through mind, seen and understood, various countless and strange acts and splendid abundance of the beauty of Shri Radha-Krishna and have got an opportunity to join in some or other acts. Sometimes have lost myself by entering in an ocean of nectar. What I have seen there that was beyond from mind- speech, entirely rare and divine. Its complete description is not possible. There are no words for it. But whatever could be described through words, just a very small part of it and an appearance of condition of the pitiable state of the mind, has been tried to describe just with very little of thoughts."

As such, it can be said just to explain that prior to this, it was the leading status of a scholar saint in the external life of Bhaijee and, thereafter, as a saint engrossed in sweet flavour with a feeling of Braj. Even, in the discourses during assembly of virtuous people (*satsang*) of Bhaijee, more analysis of feelings for divine love has been made, thereafter. The great festival of *Radhashtami* has also opted more divine and grand shape than earlier. It appeared, if a chapter to distribute divine love openly has been begun prior to his heavenly departure by which sowing a seed of love may be made in those devotees, who have even a little bit of desire in their mind to achieve a divine love. Bhaijee had guided the path of the devotee through the medium of letters in which he also defined more towards feelings of love. All of this, has also begun to show its effect and it was felt in few devotees if a little bit seed of divine love is sowed. Regarding its hint, was received by the letters of few devotees, some part of which is being reproduced as follows – "The sweet flow of nectar, which has been flowing in you by Shyam Sundar, that will remain just continued to flow without an interruption. It has no stoppage nor will be by flowing itself, that is making you eligible to mix inside it, just by itself. It shall just succeed. When that flow moves towards you then you will be already absorbed with that. "Through your letter, I was very much pleased to read the description pointing out a way through the charming condition of an impressive mind and a very sweet of sweetest emotion arising in your mind towards the God. Such of your sacred waves of nectar have agitated my mind and I have submerged in the sea of those waves. Obtained much pleasure as well. It is also just a proof of the ultimate love and an extraordinary kindness of the God for you.

"You have really much more grace of the God that you have got an opportunity of visualisation – thinking of His purest and divinely sweetest acts. You should always be thankful for such great kindness of the God and should become blessed by dedicating yourself unto his holy feet.

"You have been wandering in such world of emotions, which had only happiness, charm, smile and madness and if it can be transformed in an identity of life then that will be just an abode of act for an enchanting Shyam Sundar."

"..... of an amazingly complete change are all the real miracles of divine help. Such emotional flow of you all, will be flowing more and more with higher intensity towards perpetual and an uninterrupted infinity then will provide very unique and excellent thing. But this all, should be limited just with you people. Never compare these most precious charming gems of sentimental abode of nectar within the market of boorish people. Then only their beauty will be more and more refined by making progress for an ultimate purity.

"An identity of divine love is a natural alienation from the sensual pleasure of the world, destruction of a feeling of happiness in them. An experience of divine pleasure always and everywhere, sweet remembrance of the God, daily visualisation of the God through human eyes. An increase of divine wealth. Thus, it is being apparent naturally with you people, which shows you people have excellent grace of the God and His very sacred love is entering in your life.

"........ of boatman-act and .... an act of a horseman, both were just very impressive. Putting her hand on the shoulder of boatman by Shri Radha and enjoying the sweet beauty of beloved through her eyes was certainly and excellently beautiful but to enjoy an essence of binding just in one stroke by Shyam Sundar was more beautiful than that. 'That has become a refreshment of that day'. It is alright. He remains then in search of such refreshment. His thirst remains ever increasing towards such an enjoyment of essence. Long live such divine enjoyment of an essence. But, on the other side, the same condition also prevails in the offering of an essence. Such desires for the enjoyment of an essence (*Ras-pan*) and the offering an essence (*Ras-dan*) are never fulfilled nor will be.

"My mind is also being drawn towards you people. I had a very sweet memory. By recollecting of one which helps to achieve the God, by accompanying to one, which helps to achieve the God, he is just definitely most respected well-wisher. I have reminded a very sweet memory of the God by recollecting you people, therefore, remembering you, is also an ultimately valuable to me. ... I always wrote through my heart to you and precisely just to other loving persons and remained talking by meeting them. The topic of conversation remains one only – sweet acts by the beloved Shri Radha Madhav. I could not write as it requires the facility of time, etc. but everything can be possible at any time mentally and that very only prevails. If you people could come to *Rishikesh,* then it will be very pleasant, but I will be dealing there with public panchayat. How and when I will meet you people, I have no information. But, in fact, I will be meeting just daily, which is the fact." From such an expression with strong feelings of few personal letters, some hint is available for such sowing of seeds through personal conversation, in addition to letters. A conversation held in January, 1969 with such devotees is being given here –

Question: What should we do from our end so that our life may be entirely conformable to you?

Answer: You people are then, just, conformable. What do you do against me? I then treat you just conformable.

Question: I have requested explaining the real state of affairs – in the way we enjoy this world, that is just not conformable with you.

Answer: Yes, such an attachment is not proper. It is due to the result of instinct already then acquired from the infinite births. It should not be tolerated and should have faith in mind that his grace will make it alright. One should not spare shortage of efforts from his side and never give up dependence of his kindness. What is happening, treat it as his kindness. Never pride in anything. The God does not like the pride. A work which comes in front, should never be attempted if it has a forbidden action. Three things should be remembered during working for other activities. O! *Arjun*, do you perform your duty sincerely without any attachment for the sake of sacrifice, alone (*Gita*-3/19). Whatever work is attempted, should be attempted with your best, without any attachment and only for the pleasure of the almighty. There should not be any happiness or sorrow in success or failure. The feeling should be that he is just demanding to serve through such duty. Then his service will begin to commence automatically, and it will also be felt that in which way, he desires to be served.

Question: Our movement is just very slow. Such speed is not sufficient for the life?

Answer: The life will be over, such things should not be presumed. Looking to your speed, it may appear, but you are not required to worry about it. When He begins to worry then it won't take much time. His pledge (*sankalp*) and grant of pledge both are completed simultaneously. When He has accepted you then He will arrange everything Himself by His grace. Yes, we should accept slow progress and should always consider our speed as slow. Actually, it is also a fact that our progress is not as much as it should have been, it is still slow. Such slow speed, which comes into sight, it is an indication of an alertness and such attention should always be maintained.

Question: People may fall, who already gained height, by making all such prudent enquiry I feel disappointed in mind.

Answer: The people who had not been really advanced in devoted striving (*Sadhna*) and were just pretending with pride, it is useless to talk about them but who were really advanced, there are three reasons for their descending. Firstly, there appears somewhat pride for devoted striving and secondly that there appears some ostentation. The God does never accept the pride of His devotees. Such thing should be known very clearly that if the devotee is dedicated truly, then his fall is also a basis of his second ascending. He will definitely rise again. There is no doubt in it. The third reason to fall can be that there comes a decline in his faith.

Question: When one feels pride for himself, then what should be done?

Answer: Always look towards a highly realised person and request the almighty for the protection.

Question: A success that is obtained on the path of the achievement after a few days of practice is discontinued, if it is disclosed. How then has this occurred?

Answer: It occurred due to an increase and decrease of purity, passion and malevolent qualities. At the time of discussion with others, if you possess superiority complex then in that case hindrance is likely to appear. On the contrary if it is discussed mutually in the form of a virtuous conversation then an obstruction may not occur due to it.

Question: During similar discussion, such temperament may appear in mind that I am proceeding well while others are not?

Answer: If such things occur in mind then assume like this that if the accomplishment and singing of hymns (*sadhan-bhajan*) are being properly maintained in my life just by his grace, then it will also be maintained for others as well. If a habit of pride is awakened inside yourself, then the way is blocked.

Question: It appears nice to hear about dedication but how one can do a total dedication?

Answer: To talk about dedication, it is just best but it is also simple and is difficult as well. It is simple because nothing is to be done in it and difficult because you must leave every faith. The real dedication is just to surrender the faith.

O Lord, it is a humble request,

I should have every hope and faith in you and let me free from an inertness.

Then He is ready to bear a complete burden by Himself. ***I bear the acquisition and keeping of those, whoever united constantly and continuously in thought with me. (Gita-9/22)*** But whose burden He is ready to bear? Who is remain perpetually accused, who has been eternally, continuously attached to Him. As the child grasped the hands of his mother, then he may move as she wishes. If it is not so, then in that case, even advanced people may also fall due to an effect of shelter by the God. It is said in spiritual praise (*Ved-stuti*) that advanced people have been also found to fall without the divine support.

O Lord Vishnu, even after obtaining of divinely rare position by you, we have found ourselves falling from that place. (Ram Charit Manas/ Uttarkand/12)

The actual dedication is not made, it then occurs automatically. Be fully ready from your end and you will automatically be accepted by Him. In fact, one should have a desire for a true dedication. As much as desire with you, is observed by Him, He is ready to accept with the same intensity but never compels for it. However, as much as preparation is observed, just as that much is accepted.

Question: Is dedication also occurred in the form of 1/4 or 1/3? **Answer:** Prior to total dedication 1/4 or 1/3 dedication is also possible. Like you have believed on His power means that very will happen, whatever He will prefer, however, it also appears in mind that if such happens then it will be alright. This is an incomplete dedication.

There should not be a separate desire, then, in dedication.

(During this conversation, Bhaijee had remain smiling gently and mildly. To remember that sweet face, the mind has begun to wander just at some divine level.)

Question: One thing often comes to my mind that why should we worry about ourselves in your presence?

Answer: Look, one thing should be remembered that all such feelings should be towards the God only.

Question: We have indeed not seen the God then how we can trust on Him? We have certainly seen you and whatever is achieved, it is due to you. Therefore, we certainly recognised you only.

Answer: I am repeating you today, one thing as conveyed by Baba. The thing which Baba had told many people in alone, according to his opinion, who cannot visualise *Neelsundar* in this structure, they don't possess 'sight'.

A divine feeling can be made through this structure and there is no objection, nor any objection can be raised, but it is not proper to consider this structure as 'Shri Krishna'. Such hypothesis is totally harmful. By accepting this, you people will consider yourself without shelter, once this structure is destroyed. If the divine feeling will be true and at proper level, then the God will take care by coming in this form after the destruction of this structure. Baba has been telling that Hanuman Prasad, has long been dead. Lord Shri Krishna is active in this structure and this structure is retained due to an oath (*sankalp*) by Shri Krishna. The moment he checked such bequeath, then structure will fall at the same moment. Such thing can be understanding by an example. The chariot of *Arjun* had long back burnt by the arrows of paternal grandfather – *Bhishma*. Due to the pledge of Lord Shri Krishna that chariot could be detained for several days even after an injury of paternal grandfather – Bhishma. On the conclusion of war and on his arrival back to the camp, he asked Arjun to descend first and when Lord Krishna alighted that chariot turned to ashes, just after of his descending.

Everything is possible due to power of an oath by the God. An active body due to power of an oath by the God and an energetic body by the method of entry to other's body, both have a great difference. In a glance, it will appear that both types of bodies have been sitting, standing, moving, etc. like us, but, in fact, both are not one. Shri Adi Shankaracharya was required to enter in the dead body of a king. He wanted to know something about the domestic life, to win a doctrinal debate, which was not possible in the life of an ascetic. Therefore, he entered in the dead body of the king. It was an entry into the body of others and it is a method of Yoga. An energetic body through the medium of Yoga methodology, by entering the body of others cannot be compared of that body, which is active due to power of bequeath of the God. A method of entry to other's body is constrained due to the limit of some special country-time-person, is totally restricted but no such restriction is applicable for the power of bequeath by the God. Everything is possible to the God. To pass to and fro anywhere, anytime and in any form is entirely possible with a power of his bequeath.

Shri Laxminarayan Garde was residing at Varanasi. He had some feeling of sin in his mind and he proceeded from his home. On his descending from stairs, I have revealed in a clear form to him not emotionally and took him back. Thereafter, I have not appeared for him. I have even no information of this event and his return to upstairs. He wrote a letter to me, then only I could know. Like this, there is an event of a person from Mumbai. I have also meet him like this in night, but I had even no information. He had written to me then I could know. I assume this only that the God had acted to appear in front of him according to his faith. There is also an event of *Nandgaon*. When we went upstairs, *Baba* had seen this structure (of Bhaijee) in place of divine idol present in conferment room and when he came out of temple then Baba has visualised divine idol in place of this structure. I could know such details only through, just by the description of Baba. Baba had then many such experiences on this subject, out of which few contexts have been given to Shiv Kumar Kedia in writing. Some of them had been retained by Baba in writing. These all were burnt by me. A context of Shri Vijay Krishna Goswami is specially needed to be mentioned here. He had appeared in that very form in front of his pupil Shri Satish Mukharjee on his remembrance, even after his death and had explained many things about an act of accomplishment to his disciple. If the level of faith, is at right level then such structure will continue appearing in that very form according to faith even after the destruction of this structure and no dejection will appear inside you.

An ocean of parental affection from Bhaijee was gushing out today while talking. A programme of weekly meeting had remained continued in Calcutta in which a discussion for an assembly of virtuous people had took place. Taking consideration of that discussion for the assembly of virtuous people, a person said – You had assured last time that you would be sending your feelings from here, in writing to us for the discussion in assembly of virtuous people.

Respected Bhaijee said – I just did not find time for writing letter to you people, then what I can say about this? I am highly compelled, but I remained still sending through mind. What I have been doing for you people from my end, it just cannot be described. What I must do from my side that I continue to perform. What you are supposed to do from your end, that is to be continued.

Question: I don't know anything. My responsibility is just on you.

Answer: When we enter in the lift, then is it necessary to climb the stairs?

All these talks were held on 20th January, 1961 in his room of Bhaijee. We all have sat on a place coming back from respected Bhaijee and have written all these things by learning through heart. On 21st January, respected Bhaijee remain engrossed in profound meditation (*Bhava-Samadhi*) throughout the day, therefore, could not talk. We had to return on 22nd January, therefore, had full hope that the time will definitely be available today.

About 8 o'clock, after a long waiting, he has begun to talk with four of us. He was sitting in a very pleasant mood and was smiling slightly. When one of us spoke, then he would remain smiling sweetly by closing his eyes. But when it comes to his chance, then he had opened his eyes.

Question: The conversations of day before yesterday appeared very sweet. We have written these things in brief after our return from your place and have been also discussing lively and mutually during night for a long time.

Answer: Yes, these talks were then just interesting as well.

Question: Now, current of savour (*ras*) should flow in life?

Answer: Let the current of savour may flow in life. Never stop in between. Decide through your mind that current of savour shall just flow in life. A decision through mind is less strong than the decision through soul. By attempting a little bit, if it is presumed that we have tried, then it will not make any difference. It means this that our desire and ourselves have been under the power of mind. It occurs due to forgetfulness of self-identity.

Question: What should we do from our end?

Answer: There is deficiency both in efforts being made from your end and also in considering yourself totally dependent of the God. Do not make any deficiency in your efforts from your end and never feel any pride. Pride causes a devotee to fall. The beads of string, etc. are just helpful. In fact, it happens due to his grace. In reality, an achievement of truth is normal. When that thing is precisely a truth then what is the problem in obtaining it? There is a deficiency of intensity for both – dependency of the God and self-efforts.

Question: How to achieve savour (*ras*) in life?

Answer: There should be desire for it. Sincere longing is just the main reason. Then savour will be achieved automatically. Sincere desire means this, that there should be restlessness in mind without its achievement. Such faith should be maintained that such an intense desire will also be arranged by Him as well. He will certainly bring about the wish of that sort if you may retain faith in mind.

Question: Regarding faith in the God and a desire for savour are such things that to accomplish this, appears to be difficult, being living with snares of the world. In domestic life one better than another type of hindrances has remain continued to appear in front.

Answer: A hindrance do come but one who removes the hindrances will automatically destroy them. Do not worry for the hindrances. Worry to remain continue with your practice and a devotee should increase his practice more and more. The God has said in the Gita –

I myself arrange wellbeing for those who have constantly and continuously ponder on me with single mind. (Gita – 9/22)

I am equally present in all beings; there is none hateful or dear to Me.

They, however, who devoutly worship me, abide in Me, and I too stand revealed in them. (Gita – 9/29)

Overall, all living beings are equal to Him. No one is dear or despised by Him but who worship Him affectionately, special words are said for him. Therefore, retain a little desire in your mind, then He will fulfill it automatically. Therefore, make a wish, do an intense desire more and more.

Question: You had narrated that day about "more hope and faith, etc". Such thing then seems very difficult to give up hope and faith from all and others.

Answer: It is indeed very simple. It is also very easy. What is difficult in it. Everything is then just complete with the God, you may ask then just anything. If there is any type of difficulty with the God, then only one should expect hope and faith from others, but when everything can be available then why should one have an incomplete, doubtful trust of others. There is only now a need of trust. The work shall be done once you have firm faith.

Question: How a firmness can be developed for this, in mind?

Answer: A firmness of mind will also be accomplished by Him only.

Question: When there is an increase of perplexion in occupation then there appears a lot of problems.

Answer: One should retain such feeling that I am working for Him only. The work should be performed retaining a feeling of dedication in mind. It should be assumed through mind that the real owner is just Him, a higher than to present owner. Then, what is the problem in front of you to do His work. When there is a fault in child then mother tried to remove that fault than to make him angry. A current of her love flows of just that way only. The flow of current of mother does not stop or reduced due to fault of children. You should never make any deficiency in your efforts. When in this world, your mother does not expect more than your capacity, then that mother who is the real source of affection for infinite mothers will never expect more than your capability.

Question: It was mentioned in a letter several days ago that nothing is needed to please him, it is only sufficient to treat yourself that you belong to him.

Answer: Yes, it is quite true. To be owned by him means there will be no right of others on me. Nobody should have any right on you like of sex, of anger, of family. At present, many have this right on us. In fact, nothing is to be done. Concentrate your total attention in him only and he only and exclusively should remain belong to you. Do not make any fault from your end. Always remember that there should not be only negligence in service. We should do as much as possible. There should not be any deficiency in it and that too, should be done due to his strength, not yours. Our responsibility is then this much, is to maintain as much as of agility as we can afford. He is just Himself readily standing to help for the remaining. How much an ant can move?

Question: From the point of view of an accomplishment, how much acquaintance should be made mutually?

Answer: There is no harm to maintain spiritual relation. A part of worldly concerns can spoil the relations. Devotee should maintain little worldly relation amongst them. Spiritual relations should be maintained. There is no harm to serve if an occasion comes, but do not expect to be served.

It seems that Bhaijee had planted a seed of feelings in the life of few devotees or had made such efforts. Such activities have remained continued for several years.

❒

136

A Unique Plan to Encourage Repetition of Divine Name

A clear instruction was given to Bhaijee by the God to spread the divine name if you wish something good to this world. Its complete description has already been given in previous pages. Several types of planning, therefore, have been made to spread the divine name by Bhaijee. Some description about it has already been given earlier. Bhaijee had a strong feeling that name of the God is not only his inseparable identity, but it is more powerful and affluent than even the God due to power it contains. There have been many such saints who have accepted an importance of divine name through their hearts and have openly endorsed in their texts. But I have no information that anyone of them have ever and anywhere made this much of efforts to spread the divine name. There is only one saint who often comes to mind for this type of work – Shri *Chaitanya Mahaprabhu*. In the life of Bhaijee, dedication towards divine name was just like Mahaprabhu and like him respected Bhaijee has not only taken the shelter through strong inspiration by the repetition of divine name, etc. in his discourses or solitary discussion, during trips to spread divine name, solitary group singing of hymns, community group singing of hymns and during group singing of hymns in the city, but there are even some other things which highly assert about the excellence of Bhaijee. According to religion of era, Bhaijee has very much extended the area of publicity techniques, utilising recent facilities. One of such methods was the request made by Bhaijee to the people of every house through '*Kalyan*' magazine for the repetition of divine name. Since the year 1929, Bhaijee had been making a request of repetition for divine name in each house by publishing an information for repetition of divine name every year in *'Kalyan'*. Such rite for chanting of divine name is used to continue for two-and-a-half months every year. Everyone did the repetition of the great sacred verse *'Hare Rama'* and then sent information to the office of '*Kalyan*, after a definite period. By addition to that, the name of every place and total number of repetition of divine name was published in '*Kalyan*' every year. According to published information, 455 crores repetition of divine name has been made in 1929. During 1969-70, number of repetitions of divine name has gradually reached to 729 crores. If we take an average of the number in 1929, then more than 16,360 crores repetition of divine name has been done through this medium, in the life of Bhaijee. Thirty-seven years have been passed since the departure of Bhaijee and such tradition is still continued even today. In addition to this, it is difficult to count that how much repetition of divine name has been made by how many people through daily discourses, personal letters or conversations. Several devotees repeat one lakh divine names daily due to his inspiration till today. Not only this, I have myself seen that Bhaijee had arranged beads of string from *Tulsi* in hundreds of numbers from Vrindavan, retained with him and inspired for daily repetition of divine name by giving a string of beads to anyone who shows even a little interest. A spread has been made for repetition of divine name beyond imagination by all such methods. How many people are repeating the divine name till today, it is also difficult to imagine.

❐

137
An Ultimate Limit of Detachment

It was just not possible to manage external dealings satisfactorily by Bhaijee, due to his great sentimental condition (*Mahabhavmayi*) in which he had prevailed. The fact is this that a new and an ideal example was to present by Shri Krishna in front of this world, through his medium. Result of this very reason was that presentation of new ideas, though servicing in various fields, was made possible through the life of Bhaijee even remaining in that inexpressible condition. After near – about 1952-53, the mode of life has been repeatedly abandoning this world. Under such condition, hindrances have begun to appear in managing the activities of outer world. Some portions from the letter of Bhaijee are being given as follows, which can help to understand something about his state –

He wrote in a letter of 12th June, 1960 – Dear………,

Let us remember divine name with great affection. My health is then generally alright. But the mental attachment for passion, dearness to a secluded place and an absent-mindedness are increasing. Sometimes I forget this world. Forget while talking. Should speak something else, should think something else but did and think just something else. Such is this condition.

This was happening in the life of Bhaijee because now Shyam Sundar was permitting him to enjoy His sweet acts continuously.

Hints of the present sentimental condition of Bhaijee are available in many letters. He wrote in the letter of 16th November, 1964 –

Dear Brother,

Let us remember divine name with great affection. Received your several letters. Over here, I have not written to anyone. External senses used to respond well, only for five-six hours in a day. I did the press work that time as much as possible. Could not write letters, etc., it is very agonising. The room is remaining closed for most of the time. Even for assembly of virtuous people, I can go for sometimes after two-four days. Respected Jay Dayal and mother of Vishnu have come but I could not meet them. Such is the state.

It is also surprising if I do not forget nowadays. I put on writing quite otherwise in letters. Even made mistakes while writing names on the envelopes.

Bhaijee wrote a letter on 24th April, 1962 to the same relative – Dear Brother,

Let us remember the Supreme Being with a great affection. Received your letters. I could not write letters, therefore please excuse me, looking at my condition. I am very much fond of writing to such kind-hearted people like you and it is also proper. Therefore, I have not stopped totally to write letter – the circumstances have compelled. It is difficult to imagine my circumstances completely. The flow of mental state causing complete forgetfulness of the world at every moment, to check forcibly the normal speed of this state and to flow, thereby the conditions responsible to trap the world, revolution through the mind and conflict, my consent for important work to respective minds of everyone due to failure to imagine my condition, request for cooperation and help, various kinds of manifested conditions, etc. due to variability of world, dislike and desire for the work due to forgetfulness of the method and need of work from time to time, suitably managing the work by forcible involvement in work with full sincerity. It is a symbolic state of my condition. Now tell me how I can think and what can I write. Today at this time, I have decided to write four-five letters. This is the first letter to you. Will write or not, I don't know. Such of my state cannot be explained to anyone nor someone will understand it, this is my frank opinion......... .

* * * *

It was not that Bhaijee had expressed through letters only, In fact, his state has become like this. He had remained continuously present in the supremely divine kingdom of sentiments (*Bhavrajya*). A letter was written by him under such precise condition, in which in place of Hanuman, it was written – Radha Madhav. This letter dated 22nd July, 1961 is being given here –

Dear.......... Absolutely all, all mistresses, Radha Madhav is present in everyone, sweet charming act of Radha Madhav exhibits in everyone.

Radha Madhav, Madhav Radha have completely covered the time and region from all around,

An exhilarated Radha is dancing while mind captivator is imploring through his flute.

You should always look and hear in everyone as both of pilgrimages are full everywhere, with bliss,

The sweet charming face always showers sweet and beautiful nectar in the form of a sound by the flute.

Everyone is remaining just sportive in an act while sportive is everywhere with an act,

Such an act is remaining prevailed just with supreme being who performed several strange acts.

In daily rituals to talk gently, see and touch gently with endless new feelings,
In daily rituals to meet fresh again, a desire to meet daily with a fresh longing for tasting a fresh flavour of the Supreme Being.

Radha-Madhav
(*Pad-Ratnakar/p.n.197)*

The mode of life in Bhaijee generally had given up worldly and bodily surface but now has remain detached even something more from the physical surface of five elements of this world. The affectionate people, who had been receiving three-four letters every week or even daily, they were receiving letters after months. Trips have been adjourning even for important assignments. Involvement has been gradually winding up from all important duties except *'Kalyan'*. He had not even talked to the people coming to meet him for cooperation and for important consultation from distant places.

❐

138

The Divine Perceptions

It can be said undisputedly that a clear and an excessive description which respected Bhaijee did in his self-created literary composition of verses, about his divine spiritual feelings and achievements, he had not written that much in prose. If we observe by descending a little deeper, then the verses of *'Pad-Ratnakar'* are the real picture of his divine state. Some of these pictures are so extraordinary that an appraisal and description he has made for the feelings of Shri Radhaji in his text – *'Shri Radha Madhav-Chintan'*, such divine feelings were not only just present in his own experience, but rather he had been taking a walk himself with them.

A beginning of serious devoted striving (*sadhna*) by Bhaijee had begun in 1916 during time of surveillance at *Shimlapal*. He had become ensconced of many steps in devoted striving by residing there for about one and three quarters of the year, but he had almost pressed down for few years due to professionally dominant life after his arrival in Mumbai. Since 1920, the feelings for devoted striving have been restored again due to contact of Shri Sethji and from January, 1922, Bhaijee became again engaged and closely attached to an accomplishment with special attention. Poetry creation also began at this very time. By persuading his mind, he writes –

O lovely mind, why you are wandering here and there, confused and without any aim,

O stupid, why you are unnecessarily wasting a precious opportunity of the life.

* * * * *

Renouncing the fear, confusion and discrimination, you should continuously drink the joyous nectar,

And become peaceful – immortal by regular singing a collective praise for the holy feet of divine pair by dedicating yourself.

(*Pad-Ratnakar/1048*)

On becoming engaged with the act of accomplishing, he has progressed with so much sincerity and speed that he started singing just within short duration –

I have one desire in my mind.

To gaze Natnagar constantly below banyan tree and at the bank of Kalindi.

To forget consciousness of the body fully by hearing the sweet melody of the flute.

To sacrifice enraptured body and mind by assuring a glimpse of His (Krishna's) body and its part at every moment.

(*Pad-Ratnakar/1052*)

It seems as if an instinct of devoted striving from his earlier births has become vigilant and whatever was left for name sake, the God has been pulling him intensely towards Him to fulfill it. When the God Himself wishes to pull then, there cannot be any delay? His mind has become full of intense asceticism and he has become restless to leave the snares of the world. Although, due to an auspicious beginning of '*Kalyan*' a new responsibility had arrived on the name of spiritualism but even then, decision was taken to accept the asceticism, leaving every confinement after serious consideration and a wooden pot was also purchased for it. Permission was also obtained just in 1927 from Shri Sethji, to live in some solitary places at the bank of the Ganga. Now he was waiting for that very day when such an auspicious moment may come in front. This very restlessness of the heart has manifested itself-

When will be that auspicious day, auspicious time that this deceptive mind will become meek,

Will be sacred by get rid of an attachment and will be immersed at the sacred feet of the God.

* * * * *

When will it reside solitarily at that sacred land honoured by the saints,

When all the sins will be destroyed by the sacred stream of the Ganga.

* * * * *

When all malice will be washed by the piercing brilliance of an accomplishment,

When the mind will achieve a pure religious devotion (Bhakti) of the God becoming indifferent from sensual enjoyment.

(*Pad-Ratnaskar – 141*)

(*Time of creation – Year 1927*)

Left Mumbai under such condition and came to *Gorakhpur* to look after the assignment. The mind has become restless for visualization of the God soon after on arrival to Gorakhpur. I had now no liking for anything nor there was any desire. Mind remains always uneasy, which we can never imagine. A true longing of the heart has uttered through poetic language –

Now I do not like anything, there is only one whom I like,

My soul remains pouring out from one place to another to meet you.

I am tossed like fish without water, why you are now teasing me, Why you are delaying to appear, why you are now torturing more? I bet even if your mind accepts for this very thing,
Then there is also no grudge, let the mind may be sad as much as possible.
I am pleased in your happiness but my soul wails for you, O my beloved, do not sow thorns in your happiness for me.
You can treat it as bet or my decision for meeting you, my soul,
I have become restless at every moment, I am very much ambitious for your appearance.
It needs to run by breaking the binds and do not listen to anyone, It has been wandering like a bird throughout twenty-four hours and even blinking of the eyes is considered as a harm.
It is my stake! My mind is ever ready in your satisfaction,
O my beloved, you are just the treasure of my life in both the worlds.
It is then your wish if I don't achieve, but I dedicate my stake, mind and life to you,
You are just my world-Veda and you are also my supreme gem. Why should I fly like a pied cuckoo, why should not I turn my face?
You may trouble, beat or agitate me, even then I will not break such an affection.
You may tease repeatedly, even then I will not leave you.
I will not even look towards the little finger and will attach my soul only with you.

(Pad-Ratnakar/418)
(Time of creation – Ashwin Krishna 1, Year 1927)
(Five days prior to the actual appearance)

As the fish is intent on tossing itself without water, of just that way, the mind is agitating to meet the God, the soul is becoming restless, the real picture of such condition is in verse of devotional poetry, but such an experience is with those fortunate only who have ever achieved such state. In addition to this one, important thing which must be mentioned here, is the comfort concerned, contented feeling (*Tatsukh Sukhiya Bhava*) even during such restlessness. A very high feeling of love, which *Naradji* has shown, i.e., He remains happy only with his (beloved) happiness – is clearly seen here. The God, is yet to appear and still longing for it but even then – "I am happy in your happiness and O my beloved, for my sake do not sow thorn in your happiness," my soul is agitating every moment due to strong desire for visualisation but my dear! even then I am happy in your happiness. You may take my life by tantalising me, even then I will not look to another side. An intention of such feelings of love had occurred in 1927 prior to the actual visualisation.

The God cannot be far away from such feelings. He indeed waits for such emotion by which a true pleasure can be achieved from the visualisation. A few days later to this, an actual visualisation of Lord Vishnu was occurred at Jasidih on 16th September, 1927. That delight of visualisation has come in the form of verses for a poem –

Had retained a hope of visualisation since many births,

Who had a desire to immerse in a beautiful ocean of nectar with the God.

The one, who had filled the restlessness in mind of his meeting, Which had flared an air of separation in his whole body.

* * * * *

This was without an act accomplishment (Sadhan) due to an indefinite reason,

It was definitely an oceanic kindness of pervading spirit of the universe (Brahmrup) – the spiritual guide.

Due to his cord of love, the God Himself must be tied instantly, And has to put His grand hand on his bowed head, to become fearless.

Must make devotee as perpetual carefree by touching through his tender hand,

Have become trouble free by touching His feet and by fearless assurance by His sweet blessings.

Speech is helpless to describe that incalculable and a complete supreme beauty,

You can never measure an unsurpassed sky through hands. Those eyes are fortunate, who have seen such excellent and brilliant beauty,

Become satisfied but cannot describe as I am unable to narrate. Speech may try a little with the help of eyes,

By immersing in the sweet memory to the unfathomable beauty of Manmohan.

Mind has become instantly engrossed in the beauty, by turning in to that memory,

Once the mind halts, the work through speech can no more be carried away.

The pen has stopped writing while the hand does not move forward, An affectionate reader and a simple female reader with good disposition will pardon me.

Everyone with full affection should jointly request Him to appear, By which the supreme God may again appear simply in front of all.

(*Pad-Ratnakar/859*)

What else can be such a clear confession and description of the visualisation (*darshan*)? Visualisation, contact and conversation, etc. have been continued for some time with the Lord Vishnu and then Shri Shyam Sundar had begun to appear in the form of Manmohan. Now, the descriptions of experiences have also been appearing in that very form. The vision of lovely face of Shri Krishna has also begun to appear at any time, everywhere even in an extreme activity of outside –

An intimate curtain of the attachment moved away, all types of confusion and delusion of mind have also abolished,
That imaginary unsurpassed disturbances of mind are now no more interrupting.
Even during an extreme activity – a pleasant peace causing happiness is retained,
Because I can see the facial luster of Shyam Sundar.
(*Pad-Ratnakar/1228*)

Thereafter, Shri Krishna has met him in the beloved form. A craving of life has been fulfilled on an achievement to his beloved. Bhaijee has accepted it clearly –

I got the charming, becoming mine, my beloved God,
A craving of life has been fulfilled, satisfied each desire.
By drinking a sweet luster of divine beauty, the flame of every bit of poison is extinguished,
A pious ray from the body is scattered due to divinely beautiful and supremely great radiance.
An extremely cool shinning is spread everywhere which has eliminated all darkness and ignorance,
Now the mind captivator Shyam Sundar has come into sight, everywhere.
(*Pad-Ratnakar/1218*)

He has clearly written without any high-flown language that all my desires have been fulfilled and Shri Shyam Sundar has come into sight of me, everywhere. A little later, the love and the beloved have both appeared in place of Shyam Sundar. Following couplet also contains its clear description –

O Lord! You have blessed me; an obstruction is removed, and snares of the world are cut off.
Nandlal is seen unveiling, by playing the sweet and frenzied flute. Shyam is present in everyone, ever and everywhere and is performing various acts delightfully.
Has been playing in Himself uninterruptedly coupled with lips full of beautiful smile.
By performing with various disguises and equipments, accompanied with an immediate contemporary community.
His singing instantly causes a noise of thunder and often creating and erasing the mystery.
He is a perpetual from of an essence, a cream full of feelings, He is only a supreme spirit and nothing else.
O Blackish – fair-complexioned, paired mind captivator, You are pouring out a stream of bliss at every place.

On the whole, there is just one emperor in the whole universe though has become two.

O king of elegance (Krishna), by attending the great act, I have become successful and all tasks have been abolished.

(*Pad-Ratnakar/1126*)

It is clearly mentioned that not only this life has become successful by the visualisation of dear one and the beloved, but rather even no any other duty is left. Nothing remains as dues nor any duty. It is not so that such condition prevails only in solitude in a closed room. Look to the next verse –

It may be in journey, may reside even anywhere, at home or in the forest;
I do not live alone; the Lord always lives near to me.

(*Pad-Ratnakar/1227*)

It was not just the matter that visualisation of dear one and beloved only had been occurring or they remain live with. Their acts had always been remaining on the field of vision. Therefore, mind cannot come out –

A very sweet and excellent play is being played in the soul,
How can that silent and without characteristics, can be seen outside.
Who can tell? To whom? Various kinds of experiences from there, Cannot come even for a moment, by leaving that ever new feeling. That act has placed a prohibition at the time of coming outside, That lovely act with good disposition is just roaming inside.
It is very difficult and impossible to get rid of that act, Therefore, nothing is possible to mention outside.
The new, beautiful and an unlimited act is continued daily,
Why only just in the pool with flowers but also in an unaccounted top arbour forest.
Sweet charming act immersed with nectar was performed daily, Mode of life was awakened due to it only while it sleeps in outer world.
The mind, senses, every organ and intelligence are all engrossed just due to it,
All such works of external intelligence have been in tune due to this very reason.

(*Pad-Ratnakar/1128*)

Regarding it, Bhaijee had clearly written in prose as well in 1958, mentioning the background of his devotional poetry that "Hundreds of hundreds, various strange acts and peerless beauty with charm of Shri Radha Krishna had seen, understood by me and have also got an opportunity to join in some or the other acts" (P.S. – Request of Bhaijee made in '*Pad-Ratnakar*'). Such state has then remained continued even in future. The mind was not ready to come out even for a moment. There are not only one but several such verses –

Mohan remained accompanying me always and does not spare even for a moment,
No discrimination between a country or time while an immeasurable elation has risen every moment.
At home or in front, outside-inside during busy schedule or without work,
During sleep or awake, during eating-drinking Shyam remains accompanied me always.
Passion, sensual pleasure is all erased, even the confusion for emancipation is erased,
Only He, Nagar Natwar remains perpetually and constantly existed without separation.
There remains no meaning of anyone, anywhere or the world or the paradise,
Everywhere and every time, He is dancing Himself purely for a higher truth.
Senses, mind and intelligence all have been greatly blessed, becoming a form of the Shyam,
There remains no living creatures or matter, only an incomparable Shyam is left behind.

(*Pad-Ratnakar/1121*)

There was also no any consideration of day or night, morning or evening just at many times. Because it may be an awakening condition or dreaming, only Shyam Sundar is evident. Then how can one, even remember his own name. Example can be seen as follows –

There is no any clue of day or night, no clue of morning or an evening;
During dreaming or an awakening my heart stealing Shyam is always evident.
I have forgotten my name, place also forgotten the identity,
By playing through eyes, stealing my soul, He is laughing, while standing by retaining silence.
How sweet was His face, how much was His strange form, pleasing to mind?
Eyes remained flowing and constantly trickling by remembering that peerless beauty.
Religion is erased by piercing an inner heart and smashed the entire pride,
An honour of people, family prestige is all abolished, there remains no any recollection of self or others.
Alas! How was such charming body full of the nectar who is wandering at the bank of Kalindi river?
Broken all bands and whole of possessions, abolished every custom of shore.

My full body has remain constantly associated mentally with the body of my beloved,
The constant company of Shyam never separates and is retained by every means.
The passionate religious devotion (Rasik) prevailing in ocean of savour with the Krishna (Rasarnav) has become savorous (Rasmay) everywhere by achieving an eternal bless,
A savorous content from an abrosial river has wandered immersing everything, leaving no end.
There is even no any enquiry anywhere, anything at all, whether I exist or Shyam existed,
Shyam becomes me, I have become Shyam, becoming homogenous, remained as an eminent.

(Pad-Ratnakar/505)

Beloved Shyam do not leave me, even for a moment,
Such jewel (Krishna) always resides with me during sleep-awake and also during eating-drinking.
Has remain exhibiting constantly his excessively sacred act- like a paradise,
Has been uninterruptedly bestowing happiness outside-inside in the body and in the mind, as well.

(Pad-Ratnakar/1125)

May live anywhere, in any condition, my Lord eternally lives with me,
I always see that very sweet and great image of Him, wherever I go.
Lives always inside me while also resides outsides of me,
Every type of affection-attachment of world have abolished, achieved full faith in the God.
Sin-fever, fear-grief have also destroyed along with attachment, from the roots,
Dangerous activities due to attachment are erased along with the pangs of every births.
Attractive or terrible, whatever may be a change of the world, today,
But I perceive them all as an act-equipment just by the sweet actful God.
By the visualization, touching and meeting with the God, all daily hostilities of the world have abolished
The constant, complete and astonishing bliss has spread with an ultimate peace.

(Pad-Ratnakar/1189)

The Lord has remain residing with me continuously, never put me at a distance even for a moment,

During awakening, sleeping and in every situation, He always arranged to experience about Himself.
May live anywhere, in any condition, perpetually He remain resides with me,
Remain always surrounds me from outside-inside from all around. How He has become of mine, how can I explain it,
Though experienced but cannot describe like a dumb.

(*Pad-Ratnakar/1172*)

Some of the above verses of devotional poetry have been mentioned, just to remind. There are even more verses of poetry in '*Pad-Ratnakar*'. Under the heading 'Anubhuti', more than one hundred and twenty-five verses are there. Bhaijee had to fight for maintaining his mode of life at worldly level during last ten-twelve years of life. But even after such fight, modes of life have moved forcibly in that very kingdom of act. It was an excellent compulsion. It was such a strange thing which is just not possible to describe through words. An ocean of beauty-flavour (*roop-ras*) had been remain rippling inside him –

There is crore of crores suns are present while it is extremely dark night outside,
The doors of that savorous place, within are open while strong doors are applied from outside,
There is solitary peace from outside while it is an exhibition of beauty from inside.

A thing that is also beyond mind and intelligence is not said as an expressible but also as unimaginable, that cannot be take up through speech, nor there are words just to explain it. As much as which can be explained through words, Bhaijee has spared nothing in it.

Mine auspicious, blissful God just resides always with me, Granted perpetually ever new sweet pleasure by performing various divine revelations.
Remained immersed Himself and also caused me to sink on both ends,
Normally performed clear, very pure recreation of supremely divine pleasure.
Not allowed other to observe nor He perceives,
Has remain always carried through sweetest, divine and pleasant conversation with me.
Never assigned even a little feeling of difference or distinction between me and Him,
A total unification is achieved, and all false detachment and concealment are abolished.

(*Pad-Ratnakar/1220*)

During the last 10-12 years, he had very much reduced to reply letters to sentimental persons. However, he had replied many letters through medium as verses of poetry. The creation of such verses of poetry has been made in larger quantity, which have been used only through letters. Those verses of poetry had been noted by Bhaijee in his diary. Due to publication of '*Pad-Ratnakar*', such of these verses of poetry, have become available to everyone, otherwise it is written in many letters that such poetry should not be read by other person or it was instructed that this verse of poetry can only be read by certain people. The main reason was possibly this, that these verses of poetry had contained a clear description of experiences and state of self. Such verses of poetry though had been published in '*Kalyan*' from time to time, but due to absence of the name of writer, no one could guess it that these are the creation or experiences of Bhaijee himself. Not only this, a collection of literary composition in verses written by Bhaijee was published in his life but his name was also not given in anywhere. Therefore, publication of '*Pad-Ratnakar*' has surprised eminent scholars in Hindi that respected Bhaijee has also written a literary composition at such a large scale. One such letter is being given as an example –

"The reverend almighty"

Gorakhpur, 21-11-1959

Dear.......

Let us remember the Supreme Being affectionately. Over here, I could not write a letter to you through post. Written indeed, many letters mentally. Written even very long letters but what was written I don't remember. Also written to.... But there was lot of work, free time was just not available. Therefore, have not written by pen and paper.... Heard that you are also proceeding for an assembly of virtuous people (*satsang*). It is a very good thing. You will achieve an ultimate benefit from the assembly of virtuous people. I indeed don't have spare time, just due to prevailing work and hence deprived with an assembly of virtuous people. Secondly, there is one more thing – When and how can I conduct an assembly of virtuous people, as well. When one thing is withdrawn, then only I can talk for the other.

I can see something else only when He moves away from infront, When He is always settled in mind then how can I think for others? I don't even find time just with a conversation to Him as well, Then how my tongue can move in discussion for others?
He always tells me the sweetest and savorous thing,
Then how can I listen and for whom, leaving that sweet and excellent pleasure?
I cannot find time even for a moment due to His duty, To whom I can even serve by neglecting Him?
I am now no more of any use to anyone,

Whatever I had, is already dedicated everything to Him.

(*Pad-Ratnakar/482*)

By moving I observe, the day is passed as an awakening while night is passed as dreaming and sleeping,

But that dark and beautiful image do not move away here or there from my heart even for a moment.

But here then it is not only a talk about a heart. When it prevails both in heart and outside then what can be done. I remained lying by closing the door. Brother, you are lucky that you can attend an assembly of virtuous people. Here then –

A home is looted, nothing remains, commotion remained stirred up constantly and everywhere. He is continuously playing naughtiness day and night while all those checks have been put to defeat.

No one is found to be saved from such an ocean of Shyam after drowning. Nobody has become wise once he is crushed by such an intoxication. If someone has become shrewd, it means he did not even taste the alcohol of love.

The memory of you people is no more retained in the form of recollection. That has become a nature and no more remains a mode of life. What can be done, it is also excellent?

Yours,

Hanuman

It is also very clear from the above letter that the creation of such verses of poetry has been done by Bhaijee just to describe his state. The classification of such verses of poetry has been done under – "Sweet waves in the ocean of the love" in '*Pad-Ratnakar*'. This particular thing is applicable towards most of his verses of poetry, as well. Like this, a description for the acts of Shri Radha Madhav and an expression of strong feeling of love by Radha Rani are pictures of dialogues heard and seen by Bhaijee himself, about which an indication is evident, through the request made by him in '*Pad-Ratnakar*'. Not only this, it was clearly mentioned for few verses of poetry that one by one words of such verses of poetry are the same by Shri Krishna or Shri Radha Rani. Therefore, such verses of poetry are not only support to the devotees of Braj feelings but are their real souls based on which, they can run blind-folded.

An enthusiastic perception for the highest feelings of divine love with great and full of emotions for Shri Radha was perceived by Bhaijee himself. His such single emotion was called a true understanding of love (*Premvachitya*). The scholars of Vaishnava sect have written by defining it –

Due to an elation of love, even living with his beloved, a throbbing of separation occurs with a feeling, as he is not present and, thereby, causing a development of various types of separation disorders then it is known as an intense love (prem vachitya) *that brings about a sudden grief due to fear of separation.*

(Ujjawala Neelmani)

In it, Shri Radha Rani has begun to experience a perception of non-contact in the state of hindrance-free meeting with Shri Krishna in the thicket. Though, under name of strong feeling of Shri Radhaji at that time, there is then, already a clear description in '*Pad-Ratnakar*', Bhaijee also described of this sort at intervals about his perception –

Day and night have passed in suffering and thinking caused due to non-contact of the beloved,
Those feelings do not turn aside due to sweet, attractive image of the beloved.

* * * * *

Such sacred and loving perception of non-contact, during constant meeting,
An ultimately sweet, ideal, excellent and pure perception in the kingdom of love is felt.
I can only feel the grief and pleasure occurred due to this, I feel uneasy even for a moment without you.

* * * * *

An intense flame of disagreeable separation is burning in the heart, sometimes during weeping;
Have been laughing sometimes between meeting and become like a garland at once mutually, round the neck.
We have mutually become love and the abode of love, performing new act, daily,
To hide, to appear sometimes but as a result always retains reconciliation.

(*Pad-Ratnakar/1134*)

Some eminent persons are of the opinion due to this sort of description, that the genuine life of Bhaijee is then '*Pad-Ratnakar*' only.

Just one Sanskrit couplet has appeared two times in the Shrimad Bhagwat –

We can even forego alike a heaven or salvation in lieu of the company just for a moment with the devotees of the God.

(Shrimad Bhagwat- 1-17-13/4-30-34)

If the company of the God realised person can be available even for a moment only, then its comparison cannot be made even with a heaven and as such question does not arise of its comparison with worldly gratification, but rather cannot be made even with non- repeatable emancipation. It cannot be understood with normal intelligence that by whose company, even for a moment, has been praised by the creator of Bhagwat extravagantly than emancipation. The biggest opportunity and manliness of the devotees of Supreme Being is an emancipation only. An intelligence can explain somehow by deep observation of above perception, that the company of the God realised person like Bhaijee can only be said an extravagantly better than an emancipation because his company even for a moment will permit the entry in the kingdom of acts (of Radha Krishna) and such perception is not necessarily realised, even to every devotee of all pervading spirit of the universe (*Brahmnishtha*).

The reputation and popularity of Bhaijee has become established as a true saint and guide, just in his life time. Such was the control of his sweet and rare personality on the memory of public that they wanted to solve their most confidential problems either through personal meetings or through letters from Bhaijee. Bhaijee had also been fully and satisfactorily solving it, as much as possible through letters or on query. But the work of letter writing was generally almost discontinued during previous years. Due to his long stay in instinctive ecstatic consciousness (*bhav-samadhi*), solution of the problems for people, coming to meet him, was solved if Bhaijee remains at worldly level otherwise people must feel disappointed to obtain a solution. His compulsion and its expression can be seen in this verse –

O Lord, how much of compassion and what sort of an unweighable endowment you have granted to me,
The curtain of false illusion is removed while you have yourself granted, the knowledge and visualisation.
Nothing remains now except one i.e., you,
People wandering happily in false world should not retain with false intelligence-judgement.
People arriving here have been telling their strange problems, To solve them, they humbly ask for solution by prostrating.
What can I say or how can I convince them, when there appears no any true content,
That mind which had been solving their problems, is completely paralysed.
(*Pad-Ratnakar/1246*)

In fact, then it is true that the life of Bhaijee had become so much divine and rare that it cannot be perceived by natural words or natural mind-intelligence, nor can be tried to perceive. At last, Bhaijee has begun to write –

It has become of no use and may be spared,
Even if retained, then you will get always disappointment.
All my worldly intelligence has turned to ashes as it was placed on fire,
Now no more feelings, enjoyment or region are left in it.
It can no more decide the least that what to do and what no to do, It remains just always instinctively detached by tolerating everything.

Whatever will be, will be, it will be just due to Him only, It has no interest in to live or to be dead.
It has now also no interest with any conflict, Whatever may happen, it is then now always fearless.
He alone writes and enables to write, He alone does and gets it done;
Do not know what is wrong, do not know what is right.

(*Pad-Ratnakar/1150*)

Written even more clearly –
Through me is speaking only mine God,
Through me is playing sweet tone by His flute.
In my life now, then He has only a place,
Therefore, all minute and great activities only of Him, have been constantly occurring inside me.

(*Pad-Ratnakar/1124*)

Whatever you have asked me to convey, I have conveyed that very exactly,
Whatever you have asked me to do, I have done that very without deception.
Whatever you have asked me to learn, I have learnt entirely that very only,
Whatever you have asked me to see, I have with senses seen that very only.
Whatever I have said, did, learnt, seen, O beloved, That was all your excellent act just by yourself.
How can I be self-willed when I have even no existence of myself, The body has just become your home of happiness, in which only you are always present.

(*Pad-Ratnakar/1146*)

It was known through a realised source that whenever Bhaijee returns to consciousness, from non-existence state of outer consciousness (*bahya chetna shunya stithi*) to instinctive profound meditation (*bhava samadhi*), then many verses of poetry were found written in front of him. He explained that these verses of poetry have never been written by him in senses. Which power had activated his pen in consciousness condition, it is matter of kingdom of emotion (*bhav-rajya*). Most of verses among them, he had thrown by tearing to pieces because they do not deserve to be retained. Some verses of poetry were retained. Such fact was also confirmed with certainty that Bhaijee was just not in habit that he may reveal even to his very close associate of solitude that only the God is now speaking through me, then question to reveal such style of writing does not arise. It was against to his habit. But here, he has written clearly that "He alone writes and enables to write, He alone does and gets it done." On what else, whatever I said, done – or seen are your acts, O beloved which you have just done with yourself. Now my inner mode of life has remained maddened totally and constantly in relishing only one essence.

The sun rises, the night arrives, wheel of time moves unobstructed, The living creatures have been performing all sorts of work – good or bad according to their interests.
But an inner mode of life does not proceed towards time of death, action or creator of the world,
It remains eternally maddened in relishing only just one essence. All the activities remain simply continued during sleep-awake by the natural instinct,
But some other extraordinary remains took to heart throughout twenty-four hours in mind.
Neither it is driven back nor itself gets driven aside even for a moment, not released in any way;
He has remained bestowing unchangingly a pure ultimate grief and an eternally supreme happiness.

(*Pad-Ratnakar/1199*)

This is just a very brief description of his divine perceptions.

❒

139

A State with an Ecstatic Love

The ultimate mystery of love has always been undisclosed. Nobody has merely described it completely. This very in the reason that sage *Narad* defined an identity of divine love as entirely inexpressible. If deeply versed, passionately religious persons ever find a little of opportunity to put the dust particles of the beautiful but complicated law of that perceptible and supremely minute love, then according to them, in proportion as the seriousness develops in love, just then its manifestation became continued from its sincere to most sincere form through its freshly serious form. An evaluation and excessive defining was made for different serious forms of love for the chemistry accomplished by those passionately religious and deeply versed devotees. The birth of passion in the heart towards the holy feet of the eminent and most supreme Lord, is known as love. Such love becomes gradually serious and by becoming serious, it achieves an identity of the great ecstatic love (*mahabhava*) by gradually surpassing the layers of emotion and affection, respect, love, passion and the attachment. Great ecstatic love (*mahabhava*) has been defined in the form of a highest state of love in scriptures dealing with chemistry of savour (*ras-shastra*).

In this highest state of love with a great emotion, such state of Bhaijee has been achieved long back. A devotee and maddened saint of *'Giridhar Gopal' Meerabai* appeared in front of supremely blessed saint in 1940 and said that subtle body of Hanuman Prasad is transformed into an identity of Shri Priyaji. For about twenty years, Bhaijee has remained hiding his divine public censured state. In fact, he had a desire to hide himself just permanently, but he was helpless in front of inconceivable planning of his life lord and beloved Shri Shyam Sundar. Such divine condition in the kingdom of love is just not the object to be expressed and Bhaijee tried his level best to hide it, but the desire by his treasure of life and beloved Shyam Sundar was something else. Bhaijee has just not disclosed that state but even after his reluctance and according to divine wish that divine state has come to light in front of the world.

The state of Bhaijee remained very strange during last ten-twelve years of life. Bhaijee had a desire and attempt was made according to such desire that his modes of life should be engaged in services activities of this world but his modes of life had forcibly reached with that kingdom of acts of Shri Krishna. Contrary to the expectation of Bhaijee, the modes of life of Bhaijee had become disappeared in the deep ocean of the sweet acts of Shri Radha Madhav. How was such a strange compulsion? Once his modes of life disappeared in the ocean of act, every work related with worldly service had been retained as unaltered. Bhaijee had a longing to serve this world and an effort was also made sincerely for this reason, even then, a strange compulsion had prevailed. Such was the compulsion, which does not allow to serve, though he had genuine desire for it, whenever it is attempted, then it was observed that the body of Bhaijee is motionless, steady, there is no activity or trembling except to breath in and out. Such motionless state had been retained for hours. Adjacent close associates have begun to call such motionless steady state as an instinctive profound meditation (*bhav- samadhi*).

Once such instinctive profound meditation had acquired, then in addition to this, it was also remaining helping Bhaijee just to do his activities for public welfare.

The life of Bhaijee is an excellent example as patron against virtue or duty which is an aspect of possession for special qualities. There is a poetry of by Shri Narayan Swami, some lines of it are as follows –

The one who with engrossed in Ghanshyam,
Step moves off to one direction but goes another way, forgotten the memory of a place or residence,
By looking to His sweet image, I found no interest in worldly activities nor I have any recollection, of time, day or night,
O Narayan, I am wandering like a mad and have become useless for anything.

A person who has achieved a real affection with Ghanshyam does not remember about his body, nor he remembers about his residence, nor he finds any interest in the world and not aware of time. Such mad person is just useless to anyone for anything. But in the life of Bhaijee, an identity of fulfillment of both the parties is evident. To manage the social organisations, helping the needy, cooperation to volunteers engaged in social service, looking after the people with family, completing religious rites, managing cow protection movement, encouraging devotees, the exposition and editing of '*Kalyan*' and enlisting the society through publishing religious texts – several public well-being activities of this type had been remain performed by Bhaijee. Remain engrossed in a former ocean of acts from this world on one side, being remain immersed in the kingdom of acts on another side, an attentiveness to pursue a duty for multifarious fields related with this world, a flow of these two opposite streams is an entirely strange fact in the life of Bhaijee. Such wonderful fact has connected the life of Bhaijee with the characteristic public censure. Where else can one find an example of such an ideal saint? In domestic category, Bhaijee is indeed a unique example of a domestic saint.

It is also very important to point out about one fact related with the divine condition of Bhaijee. The modes of life of Bhaijee had remain engrossed in an ocean of acts of Shri Radha Madhav during his state of the instinctive profound meditation (*bhav-samadhi*) so much so that he had also no sense of his body and worldly affairs have also given up. Bhaijee remained immersed in such state of an instructive profound meditation (*Bhava-samadhi*) for hours together, but when such condition had not prevailed, then we have found him busy in editing '*Kalyan*'. By observing that, it had appeared that Bhaijee is in normal state. Looking at different works, burden and various activities being managed by Bhaijee one may presume that his state is normal, but the fact is that mind of Bhaijee had been remain strolling with the kingdom of acts of Shri Radha Madhav. In that normal condition, if several works of public had been accomplished by his body, then with that, his mind had been remained crossing over the waves of ocean with the acts of Shri Radha Madhav. On crossing over the waves, when his mind gets deeply absorbed by moving deeper to unfathomable bottom in the ocean of acts of Shri Radha Madhav then condition cannot also support him to accomplish external trades and his body would become motionless and steady. During such instinctive profound meditation, there was no limit of time. During subsequent years of life, Bhaijee has never been just separated from the kingdom of acts of Shri Radha Madhav, only this happens that his engrossment with the kingdom of acts becomes sometimes grown dense while sometimes it remains almost simple.

Bhaijee had a desire that his modes of life should not descend deep, but it was beyond his control and he was helpless. Sometimes he had to fight between himself and the condition of instinctive profound meditation, though it was tried to avoid in vain but had been generally incarnated. Someone would have probably got a chance to see-hear, or read such an information related to the life of a saint. When they are trying themselves to attach their modes of life with worldliness, even then the instinctive profound meditation (*bhava-samadhi*) is set in. Bhaijee has gone to meet some sick person and while returning his mode of life has left bodily level even inside the car. Bhaijee is giving discourse in front of sincere devotees in Gita Vatika by coming out from solitude of room so that mode of life remained intact with worldly level, but the body senses have abandoned their activities and the group of audiences are looking intently to motionless and steady Poddarji. Bhaijee is washing hands with the soil after returning from toilet, but during washing hands, forgetfulness of body occurred, and modes of life have been taking away to the kingdom of acts of Shri Radha Madhav. Bhaijee is walking on the roof, but suddenly became stood like a statue during walking then close associates must be ready to look after his motionless-steady body. Bhaijee is editing '*Kalyan*', sitting on the seat, his pen is writing on the paper, during writing, the pen fell on the paper due to escaping from fingers and Bhaijee has become engrossed in instinctive profound meditation for a long duration. In fact, such condition of Bhaijee is entirely beyond to human eyes and is at level from beyond mind, intelligence and soul. It is a complete fact that through natural words, by natural mind and intelligence, identity of that unnatural condition can just never be understood.

Shri Vishwanath Das had been the Governor of Uttar Pradesh and was a famous politician from *Odisha*. He had established'Indian four adobes building trust for Vedas' for spreading scriptural knowledge with competent cooperation of Bhaijee. His persuasion was that Poddarji should manage the work of trust by accepting joint-secretary ship. Bhaijee had written a letter on 5th May 1967 expressing his helplessness. Bhaijee has just pointed himself of his inexpressible condition in that letter. A part of the letter is being given below –

"For many years over here, my inner heart is being free from final beatitude. Therefore, I generally remained inside a closed room daily in solitude for most of the time. Mode of life does not encourage to meet people. In addition, over here, one more and divinely inspired strange condition has developed since a few years. I do not want to describe it; therefore, I have given it a name 'malfunctioning of the brain'. The fact is that suddenly such thing happens that the entire activities of mind and senses are stopped. The world disappears entirely, only the breath sustains. In such a condition, as I was in beginning, I remained lying or sitting just like this. If eyes are open, even then nothing is seen because no one is there to observe. It can be said as profound meditation (*samadhi*) or something else. Sometimes previously, I was longing for such a state – I was making efforts for it, now even without making any efforts, sometimes such thing happens suddenly, even when efforts are made to embrace the modes of life with the world forcibly. And such state is also continued from minutes to 15-20 hours. That time the body, mind and intelligence have remained entirely inactive. Previously such condition had occurred after many days but now it has been occurring very often. Therefore, I must be very alert. In such condition and, therefore, just an entire sacrifice of activities from active life is expected and is helpful. But, as I am engaged in the activities for active life. Therefore, have to try many times to retain the modes of life, forcibly within the world."

How extraordinary is such an identity of the life of Bhaijee? A saint deeply versed in sacred scriptures said once that such an example is never available for reading on the pages of scriptures. Once Bhaijee was engrossed in instinctive profound meditation (*bhava-samadhi*) in Dalmia building, Swargashram, some of his close associates were sitting near to him and observing Bhaijee as engrossed in profound meditation. At that very time, his profound meditation has become relaxed. One devotee expressed his desire to know about the state of instinctive profound meditation. Looking at the persuasion of query by the devotee, Bhaijee has told with great shyness –

I am helpless to describe it in detail about such state. What and how such things happened due to divine grace is only known to the God. I found myself in a state of an inexpressible bliss, but sometimes forcibly the work of all senses stopped suddenly and where and which condition I was, I remained under that very condition. During that condition, cannot see even with open eyes, cannot hear through ears, cannot experience of touch through skin. Like this, when the activities from senses stopped, then the mind becomes inactive and the intelligence also becomes inactive due to inactive mind. Sometimes during change in turning off the work by all senses, the performance of every senses has also brought to an end. There is no any order in discontinuation. Mode of life is diverted from senses and becomes concentrated in *'there'*. Meaning of *'there'* or its identity cannot be explained. When an external knowledge is fulfilled, then the memory of 'there' is no more and when an incomplete external knowledge is achieved, though it is some recollection of *'there'*, but cannot be explained through speech, it is also not simple to describe it. To bring back the mode of life, sometimes a little mode of life prevails, sometimes just entire mode of life returns altogether.

When mode of life returns then it does also not appear in mind that where I am. Who is in front, but this is also not a real picture of that time because discontinuation in the working of the senses, to renounce the world entirely from the modes of life by mind and intelligence and a complete attachment through mode of life with 'there', is also just not a Vaisnavee state (*Bhagwati* sthiti). If there is a relinquishing of instinctive (*Vrittijanya*) sacrifice and acceptance of instinctive 'there' till then a state only prevails in kingdom of nature (*Prakriti rajya*). During Vaisnavee state, no state exists for mind- intelligence-pride; divine power prevails over that place about which a knowledge only realised during divine power and not to anyone else. Nowadays mode of life attracts less to the world and inclined more to 'there' and becomes Vaishnavee state.

When the state of Bhaijee prevails on normal level then the people had been coming to him to obtain solution of their problems. Those who are attached through affection, it was just natural to them to come with some hope. But, now the mind of Bhaijee was no more at such surface that he can tell the solution of those worldly problems.

During performing daily routine, Bhaijee had become engrossed in instinctive profound meditation (*Bhava-samadhi*), but many times he was also found engrossed in instinctive profound meditation even in between bitter circumstances. Cow protection movement was in progress at all-India level in 1967. Bhaijee was one of the chiefs among seven thread holders. When the movement was at its peak, then preoccupation of Bhaijee had more advanced. Even editorial work of '*Kalyan*' also became secondary. Not only this, even the meal and rest were reduced. Letter, writing, giving statement, encouragement, etc., all these activities had remained continued sincerely throughout the day. Checked and typed papers had to be sent to different places of country after putting proper signatures on them. Once such preoccupation remains continued from morning till 10 o'clock at night. As soon as the last envelope was dispatched by Bhaijee, it was found that Bhaijee was engrossed in meditation. The close associates were very much surprised. It appears if spirit of dissension in Bhaijee is totally finished to differentiate between conflicting condition and peaceful condition and according to him, sensuousness within act of his treasure of life, Shri Shyam Sundar was active in both these conditions. It was an improbable event. Really, Bhaijee had remained always and entirely been engrossed with the sweet acts of his beloved. Last ten-twelve years of his life have been passed just with this very type of act-engrossment.

❐

140

An Accomplishment of Special Task

Bhaijee never gave any hint up till 1969 about that special work for which Bhaijee was sent through the medium of his body made up of five elements. Even thereafter, what was that special duty? Bhaijee remained completely silent in this context. Under such condition, to write anything with one's imagination about 'that' special duty, will be just an unauthorised effort. To describe anything about an inner world of Bhaijee, will be beyond an imagination. Something can be written about the work only, which has been accomplished in his external life.

One important work was to show an evidence of brightest identity of sweet love by Shri Radha Krishna and to expose the feasibility of its achievement. One of a passionate religious scholar from Braj has said up to this extent that 'our Radha shape has become such that to present it, in front of public and educated class has often caused a harassment. But such an identity of Radha was presented by Bhaijee that one feels pride to present that shape without longing of self-pleasure in front of anyone in our country and in abroad as well'.

Just with this, a description is found in 'Patalkhand' of '*Padma Puran*' pointing for the achievement of the love of herd girls of *Braj*, as extremely difficult and that *'Brahmvidya'* made an ascetic fervor for a longer duration. When an ultimate friend of the God, Arjun had expressed a desire in front of Him for its visualisation, then the God has given this very reply that it is not in His hands and he will have to worship with the feelings of herd girls of Braj for it and when Arjun did such worship becoming *Arjuni*, then he could only just visualise it. Due to many such examples, a normal person like us can just not dare for such worship. But with such simplicity Bhaijee has assessed, such worship through his discourses and texts, that the mind of an average person also feels a longing by hearing or reading it. For the sake of respectful greetings towards Radha Baba, he has consecrated of that feeling, not only just description, due to his eligibility by touching his feet which Radha Baba himself had considered an object of illusory world up to that time. Being even a staunch follower of '*Vedanta*', he is adhered, after some time, to worship for charming emotion of Shri Radha Krishna by making a permanent change in his methods of worship. It was such 'an important duty' that was not accomplished in this manner by any other saint.

The second important work which was accomplished by Bhaijee was the protection of our religious scriptures and arranging their feasibility to an average person. Our entire religious texts are in Sanskrit and those were not perceptible (*Bodhgamaya*) for an average man and for this very reason, people had no more interest to protect them. In addition to this, these were even not easily available to the people well versed in Sanskrit. The condition had reached up to this extent that even name of those scriptures had no more retained in the memory of normal public. At such time, Bhaijee had find a track of authentic copies of these scriptures through his far-sighted vision and an authentic Hindi translation of these was done by the reputed scholars. For the publication of these scriptures, Bhaijee has given special attention for three things. Text should be correct and authentic, meaning should be conformable both of grammar and the ancient religious scriptures and full attention had been given to the dignity, during interpretation. Full attention was also given to dignity during translation of events related with an adornment, etc. For the sake of authenticity, he has not made any change in traditionally acknowledged original text. By publishing most of the texts, as special issues of 'Kalyan', these were delivered to millions of houses. Some of these important texts have also been exhibited as books, so that those who are not the customers of '*Kalyan*' can also obtain them according to their interest.

Some of the important text had also been translated in English by a scholar like Chimmanlal Goswami and published so that the foreigners can also obtain them easily. He has arranged to deliver texts like '*Ram Charit Manas*' in every house, by making it easily available only for fifty paise. Looking to such propagation exclusively, a realised saint from Bengal Shri Sita Ram Das Onkar Nath Maharaj has written – The work Bhaijee, did everywhere towards the publicity of religion and religious scriptures during such painful age of Kali, I have not seen such thing in any historical scripture and also not heard if any religious proclaim had ever done for such type of worldwide publicity of religion. Today, the condition is such that the whole country may be destroyed by someone completely by atom bomb, but our religious scriptures will be safe until catastrophe. Looking to such novel and extensive work, it seems, that it can also be an important duty, performed by Bhaijee.

The third important work accomplished by Bhaijee was the publicity of divine name and religious devotion (*bhakti*) to every house. On the whole, such work was also performed absolutely by all saints in some or the other way, but in such an extensive way, and the way, it was performed by Bhaijee, is not seen elsewhere. The God Himself has met him personally for the publicity of divine name and said – "**If you wish to do anything good for this world, then spread the divine name without any discrimination. Declare among the people that everything will be done just by the divine name, in this age**." Therefore, several plans, which have been made by Bhaijee for the publicity of divine name and also implemented them, that was an excellent job about, which you have already read some of its description in earlier pages. Specially, after personal meeting and conversation with sage Narad, the publicity for religious devotion and divine name have been performed in a strange manner. What type of conversation held between reverend Naradji and respected Bhaijee, its authentic description is not available anywhere. But, the work which was performed, thereafter, one can guess that whatever Naradji has said here to Godess of religious devotion (*bhakti devi*) may be as follows –

> *O lovely lady of religious devotion! There is no age like Kali age, I would establish you in the heart of every person and from house to house during this age.*
>
> *Look, if I have not spreaded in this world suppressing all other religions and putting ahead the great festivals,*
>
> *Concerned with religious devotion then I am not a disciple of the Lord Vishnu.*
>
> (*Shrimad Bhagwat Mahapuran/Mahatmya/2-13-14*)

Such conversation may be held with Bhaijee and he (Narad) might have inspired Bhaijee for it. It may be the result of such inspiration or may be some other direction from the inner world, the work, which has been performed by Bhaijee in this direction, that was a unique work by itself.

Whether all these were important duties or was any one or two among them, it is difficult to categorize. This much has been accepted by Bhaijee in his will – "Most of His work has been accomplished due to His grace and power. Although not perceived as was expected and was desired by me... although whatever has been done for the betterment of the world, it is done up to very far and its effect will be extensive and long-lasting."

It is not justified to write further than this due to failure of receipt of any hint by Bhaijee in this context.

❐

141
The Preparation of the Great Journey

The famous saints of the world have suffered with terrible diseases and pain prior to heavenly departure. Bhaijee had also joined such saintly tradition. The God also desired that the mortal body of Bhaijee should also suffer with such disease prior to his departure so that everyone may witness that he was entirely uninfluenced by it. Everybody realised that he was only a spectator of the disease.

Bhaijee checked out his life, pretending for such terrible disease, which was first observed in Rishikesh on 22nd April, 1969. Later, its bouts continued occurring constantly. The fearsome ravages, which were seen on 4th November 1970, thereafter Bhaijee was not found in normal physical condition. Physicians were suspecting stomach cancer. When the eyes of physician have become moist during last week of January 1971, then Bhaijee said – You have all came here affectionately for my treatment then I also let you to show affectionately…it is my firm belief that whatever is to be happen, that just will be…terrible pain is there, but I have great pleasure from inside. I am feeling a contact with the God in such form of pain.

Bhaijee had remained suggesting means (*sadhan*) to physicians, convenient to them at that time as well. You people have been receiving patients, to serve them is to serve the God. In fact, the God needs your services in the form of a patient. Such of your service will help you achieve the God.

Looking at the worried physicians in the first week of February, Bhaijee said – When you people come to see me, I remember the disease that time, otherwise when I am alone in a closed room during the day then generally I don't remember the disease. I remain busy '*in my work*'– remembering the divine name.

It was apparent that physical body of Bhaijee had to be concluded soon as desires by the God. The body was proceeding to that end. No treatment was successful. Family members, friends, relatives, attendants, physicians were all worried, but if someone was carefree even during such terrible state, it was Bhaijee only. There was no effect on him due to such disease. Up to here that when there is a discussion to call a physician from outside, then Bhaijee suggested – the money which will be spent to call a physician from outside should be spent to the service of the poor.

The sickness was gradually increasing, and nourishing elements were also not making their way into the body in any form. Due to this, Bhaijee was also feeling pain in speaking. Suddenly, he decided in mind on 8th March that his current perception should be known to this world in writing. Under condition with an extreme weakness, he took a pen with trembling hands and has written two verses of poetry while lying down, which are the living pictures of his mental state. These are two of his last spiritual instructions for the world. Unfortunately, because of illegible writing due to trembling hands and in Bengali language, these cannot be understood fully. Whatever part of it can be made legible is being given here –

This time o beloved! You have come adorned with pain...disease, You have remained imitating, which has amused me.
Looking to your such form, family members have shaken,
By abandoning this body, I will permanently achieve you and then sink happily and silently,
...I would happily accompany to depart from this life.
But how can I explain to children, friends and family members? How can I console and disclose the mystery to them?

* * * * * *

Please console them by hearing my pity request,
.... Explain some of your ultimate mystery to all. They will be blessed to know your hidden mystery,
It will immediately eliminate their every confusion-grief, attachment and sorrow.
O beloved! They may achieve knowledge-love, happiness and a proper abode with you,
And an unreal abode of suffering may also be abolished forever from every end.
O beloved! You can never harm to anyone,
But remain constantly granting a good fortune....
You have become everything here; an enjoyer, to be enjoyed and an enjoyment,
You have become toys.... You even just play. Sometimes...becoming everything remain dancing, singing by Yourself,
Sometimes as disease...remain lying with a sob adorned with grief, sorrow and with an attachment.
O actful! You have remain always performing a willful act, Why You are making such a creation, what an enjoyment you receive,
If someone exists.... then may understand it, somehow.

❐

142
The Heavenly Departure *(Nityalilaleen)*

All the close associates, devotees had been informed that the mortal body of Bhaijee is on the way to calmness. People had been coming from distant places to see him. It appears if Poddarji is extending an opportunity of his last visualisation (*antim darshan*) to all, even suffering from terrible disease-pain. On the night of 13th March, Poddarji had addressed to the members of his own family present there – "All those persons to whom I have given assurance for an abode of the God, they will definitely achieve it, they should trust it." It appeared to everyone if he is bidding farewell. Everyone was weeping. During night of 14th March at 12.30 hrs when Dr. Chakravarty was making an unsuccessful attempt to feel his pulse, Poddarji told in slow voice – "Thinking power is alright, power of memory remains alright sometimes, sometimes failed. I am unable to speak." Saying this, he enquired with the physician through his trembling right hand – "Have you taken your meal?" Where everyone was counting hours and minutes, Poddarji was worried for the meal of the physician. Such was the glimpse of a state with him.

Reverence for divine name has remain continued to the last breath by Poddarji. It occurred on the night of 20th March. The lips of Bhaijee were stirring, it looked as if trembling. Dr. Chakravarty thought that lips were shaking due to absence of teeth. He said to Poddarji – "Your lips are stirring, can I put on denture? Stirring will cause weaknesses." Poddarji explained the fact – "I am repeating the divine name." It occurred at that time every cell of his body was longing for each and single drop of water. Water was being poured drop by drop in his mouth, through dropper. On the afternoon of 21st March, the pulse near the wrist had disappeared and blood pressure had very much reduced. Gradually, the pulse had left the place of elbow, but the power of thinking by Poddarji remained as such. At 11.00 hrs at night (means nine hours prior to his heavenly departure), when Dr. Chakravarty and Dr. Sharma were examining him, he enquired with a sign from right hand – "Have you people took meal or not?" Such an affectionate care by Poddarji had churned the heart of doctors. They started weeping.

Morning began with 22nd March. Speed of breath had increased. Everybody realised that the time of departure of his body is not far away. At about seven-and-a-half, respected Baba also arrived. At last, Poddarji had raised his trembling hands, joined them – said farewell to all. At about 7.55 hrs., the eyes which had been showering affection uninterruptedly, had closed forever, had been engrossed in an eternal act of his beloved.

People, thousands in number, were present in Gita Vatika. Everybody was weeping. At about 14.00 hrs. After performing the rites like bathing, etc., the mortal body of Poddarji was placed on pier. The pier was brought downstairs in verandah where everybody had offered regards, bowed and walked around in reverence. The pier was brought from there to pavillion, thereafter funeral rites were performed in the precincts of Govardhan hills in Gita Vatika while a touching group singing for divine names was already in progress. Due to ordinance of fate, the nuclei and atoms of the body of Poddarji had been dedicated just to his main place of achievement, in Gita Vatika only. A grand memorial is built in the form of an entombment at that very place where millions of devotees are receiving inspiration in accordance to their individual sentiments.

❐

143

Extraordinary Perceptions After Joining in the Divine Act with His Deity

Due to divine inspiration of noble soul, which was sent to perform some special duties apart of his destiny, has become immersed within the eternal acts of his deity (*nityalilaleen*) after the completion of its duty within 78 years, six months and five days. Thereafter, where someone was crying on one side of the Gita Vatika, someone sobbing with compassion, the stream of tears of someone were also not halting, someone sat as motionless like a stone, someone or two persons to whom Bhaijee had given some responsibility at the time of departure, they were so much engrossed in it if nothing has happened. On the other hand, some remote saints had experienced extraordinary perceptions. The chief of Radha Madhav Committee for celebration of devotional songs (*sankeertan*), a resident of Ghaziabad, Shri Murlidharji Malhotra is my very close friend. He performed celebrational circumambulation (*parikrama*) of the king of the mountain with devotional songs alongwith his companions, every month of the *Govardhan*. Prior to start, he had been bowing to the oldest and most accepted saint Shri Gaya Prasadji. He had told me that once, prior to beginning with circumambulation, he was sitting with respected saint Gaya Prasadji. At that very discussion, he began to discuss about Bhaijee. During conversation, Panditji narrated while describing the identity of Bhaijee – You should not treat Bhaijee as a normal saint. He was a herd girl of Braj. He did every work just with a feeling of herd girls of Braj. The day on which he had left his mortal body, on that day I have myself seen him going through sky route in morning towards *Barsana* as in the form of herd girl of Braj. At the time of conversation, the age of Panditji was just more than ninety years. Such an ultimate saint, whom we have treated as living form of Shri Govardhan Mountain, he can never utter false words from his mouth. Such was his firm belief. The second extraordinary experience occurred to a saint of Vrindavan Shri Balkrishna Dasji Maharaj. He narrated it to his close friend Thakur Shri Ghanshyam Dasji that he experienced in the morning at

5 o'clock on 22nd March that *Shri Priyaji (Shri Radha)* is going to *Yamunaji* along with four of her female friends. One more female friend behind Shri Priyaji is being escorted by four other female friends. He feels restlessness in his mind about the identity of that female friend? At that moment when such eagerness appeared, Bhaijee had looked towards him, moving with that divine identity as in that female friend and had shown a glimpse of her divine identity just by such sight. Contentedness of such divine perception was made when a message was received from a place for singing and praising of the deities *(Bhajnashram)* that Bhaijee had renounced his body of five elements today morning at 8 o'clock.

A third experience occurred to a high category devotee. He was devoting most of his time in devoted striving (*Sadhna*). About six months in a year at *Radhakund* or some other solitary place of Braj, he was residing and had performed devoted striving. He told me, "In the morning of 22nd March 1971, I was seated chanting in my room. Suddenly, I have seen a sight. A procession was arriving. In it, there were all without a single man. Every woman had various types of items in their hands like a bell, a gong, a conch, a trumpet, etc. Gradually, the procession had continued to come nearer. Absolutely all women had been dancing and leading pleasantly. I had seen a man among them, sitting in a litter, who was accepting greetings by everyone, with folded hands. A woman was proceeding behind his back and moving in a series of circles putting her face in front of that man. I was extremely surprised to note that this man was the respected Bhaijee and the woman was Radha Rani herself, who was moving in a series of circles. I could not yet have forgotten the appearance of that lively form. I was surprised with my fortune."

❐

144

An Opinion of Foreign People Towards Respected Bhaijee

Whoever and in the way, by which anyone met Bhaijee, was not left unimpressed. Aloofness can be clearly seen in language of speech and language of his life. The words exploded by his speech had affected like a magic on the people. Like this, who had never been in his contact personally, even those have been so much impressed by reading his articles that way of life for most of them has even changed. Such miraculous change has occurred due to comprehensibility, significant and shining thoughts of Bhaijee. Such change has not only occurred with the native and religious *Sanatandharmi people* but also with the foreigners and the followers of other path. Some of the events with foreigners are being cited as follows –

Dr. Herman Hill (Between 1933 and 1938)

A German scholar, Dr. Herman Hill lived in Chicago city. At that time, he was there as a President of medical association. In the manner of which he was a scholar, of just that sort, he was also a generous and rich person. He was not visiting Church on Sunday because of the ill- behaviour of his father with him. Due to this very reason, he had an opinion that he can never address the God as "our father in heaven". His conscious says if the God is like his father, then it is better not to call him.

Meanwhile, Dr. Hill met an Indian scholar related with Chicago University, Dr. Mahanamvratji Brahmachari. Dr. Brahmachari, realising his feelings, suggested that you can address the God as mother or brother, instead of father or you can presume him as your most loving child. Such type of relation can be maintained with God. Realising this, he became enchanted. When he tried to look some text for more information about this subject. Brahmachariji gave him *'Kalyan-Kalptaru'* to study.

He read articles in '*Kalyan-Kalptaru*' attentively and shed tears like an uninterrupted stream. By reading articles from Bhaijee Hanuman Prasad Poddar, he said that he had never read such articles in his life. He derived such pleasure from the articles of Bhaijee that he has developed an unbreakable relation with it and he has realised that he got his mentor which was his object. Gradually, he became a *Vaishnava*. A string of beads for divine name has been embellished around his neck and hands. The direction and condition of his life has been changed.

Now, the experiences of the following dignitaries from their own pen, regarding Shri Bhaijee –

Mr. Carl G. Zeiss, Larsch (Germany)

I had found an opportunity to see that great soul prior to fifteen years in 1956. Fifteen years of duration is long-lasting, in the life of a person. During this period, I have met several people and eminent persons. I can vouch this now in the later part of my life that meeting with Bhaijee was very important for me. During the initial days of my trip to India, an Indian had told me in Mumbai – 'Shri Hanuman Prasad is an extraordinary person' and I found him just so, with my contact. I had just seen an extraordinary person in his personality and I obtained a saint in his form. The people who met him, even once, can never forget that generous soul. His such words for me are not simple words – You are a member of this family. I never felt myself as foreigner-stranger in India, due to his intimate hospitality. In addition to this, I have seen a real picture of such country due to his hospitality, which was built in the form of an extraordinary temple of human spiritualism by the saints, sages and philosophers since centuries. An importance of services made by Bhaijee towards wretched and poor people could only be realised, just by those persons who have actually received his services and help. I was looking for such sources of inspiration, by which Bhaijee had been receiving, inspiring strength for such great activities. I have tried to study his teachings seriously and found the reply of my search in a small booklet – "Anand ki Lahrein" written by him.

"Do not neglect or hate or trouble anyone by your rough behaviour, if you found a leper, handicapped, wretched or distressed, thinking like that he is repenting his bad deeds, as he did so he will get. He may be the greatest sinner of early birth, it is not your business to look at his sin. Your duty is just to serve him and to be good to him with your best ability."

Who can locate such spring with such excellent thoughts? Shri Bhaijee has proved such statement of Gita – "The God Himself resides in every living being" through his life.

Who would fulfill the space created due to his heavenly departure? Those people have been greatly harmed by his death from this destructive world, who had personal contact with him. I honour Shri Bhaijee in the form of a symbol with best peculiarities of lively Hindu religion. But he belongs to entire humanity and not only to India. The need is for this thing that every person having good will for his spiritual instructions, should listen and obey. He has offered his best contribution for the human salvation.

I wanted to publish books of Bhaijee by translating them in German language, but I cannot translate well. Therefore, such desire has not been fulfilled. The books of Bhaijee will also be very beneficial to German people. German language should have also been learned by saints like Bhaijee. I treat him as the highest messenger among all for Indian culture.

I would well protect the books by Bhaijee and several of his hand- written letters in the form of a personal pledge to that great soul.

Mr. Rudolf Swash, Lucerne (Switzerland)

Shri Poddarji will always remain in my memory and an opportunity, which I had found to live with him, I could never forget. I have not only obtained his affection, his love and his thoughts, but an introduction of his lifestyle within a little time only which I had spent with him.

I had met an Indian gentleman named Cameron in Jerusalem, while travelling to India. He had given me the address of Gita press. I had reached Gorakhpur on 17.03.1963 via my journey from Ayodhya. I have found an opportunity to see the complete Gita press. I found it like a museum. I still remember the memory of those stones of marble, on which complete *Gita* has been engraved. At evening, when I have expressed my desire to spend my night in Gorakhpur itself I was told that an arrangement has been made in the guest house of Shri Bhaijee situated in front of Gita Vatika.

When the darkness was near to approach in that pleasant garden (Gita Vatika), I have seen there, first time Shri Poddarji, sitting with some other eminent people in verandah. I was very much impressed by him. When I bowed him and was ready to move, after my night halt, I was surprised to note that a lot of fresh fruits and too much edibles had been placed, inside my car.

I returned to Gorakhpur on 8th November, 1963 (probably it was *Durga navmi*) after the completion my Nepal trip. I was given such a welcome there in Gita Vatika, as if some family member had returned from abroad. I had also met there to Baba Chakradharji Maharaj. I also joined with Shri Poddarji in Durga Navmi celebration. On that day as well, I stayed in guest house and on next day, bid farewell from there by evening train after spending there three full days.

Even today, I also often remember Bhaijee and his family and I have generally been remain praising him and his associates. I have faith that his thoughts and activities will be spread in the world as well as in future by his reputed friends and fellow workers.

❒

145

Shri Bhaijee in the Opinion of Eminent Persons

Regarding Bhaijee, so much has been written by prestigious persons from different categories which are difficult to find for someone else. It seems that he had charmed of all contemporary and important eminent scholars. Some part of such expressions with strong feelings are being given below –

(1)

There will be just any rare person in the religious world who is not aware about respected and virtuous Shri Hanuman Prasadji Poddar. He revived of spiritual thinking and religious faith throughout India and outside as well, through the medium of *'Kalyan'*. Through his articles, millions of people have become prudent and religious. Whatever he says, of just like this, was also done by him. There was no difference in his saying and doing. His conduct was an example for others and is today as well.

—Hon'ble Shri Shankaracharya Swami
Shri Vidyatirthji Maharaj
Shardapeeth, Shringeri

(2)

In the history of modern India, the name of Shri Hanuman Prasadji Poddar is definitely deserved to be mentioned. His name will remain long memorable in religious literary field. He was a real uplifter of the existing form of old Indian culture.

—Hon'ble teacher of world, Shri Shankaracharya Swami Shri
Abhinav Sachchidananda Teerthji Maharaj
Shardapeeth, Dwarkapuri

(3)

Whatever may be written, heard or said in praise of Shri Hanuman Prasad Poddar, even that, being most of all, is also very little. He was an entirely devoted worshipper of the God, religion, nation, civilisation, culture, conduct and tradition, etc. of Indian dominions. His faith, feeling for religious devotion and dedication were exceptional. The service to the nation which he did in his lifetime, through the medium of English – '*Kalyan-Kalptaru*' and the best monthly magazine *'Kalyan'* for the Hindu culture, Hindu civilisation and Hindu religion can never be performed by any other person.

Even during first meeting of his mild personality, deceitless, honest and nature without trickery and hypocrisy, Shri Poddarji was revealed in front of everyone.

—Hon'ble teacher of the world Shri Shankaracharyaji
Swami Niranjandev Tirthji Maharaj
Govardhan Peeth, Jagannathpuri

(4)

Non-attached, disinterested performer for his own duty, Shri Hanuman Prasad Poddar was a priceless treasure of Indian tradition of thinking. He was a living example of divine love *(madhura bhakti)* and a simple Vaishnav mode of life.

—The world teacher, Shri Shankaracharya Swami
Shri Shantanandji Maharaj
Jyotishpeeth, Badrikashram (Uttarakhand)

(5)

Due to untimely death of Shri Hanuman Prasad Poddar, a brilliant editor of '*Kalyan*', a pillar of the immemorial religion has been demolished. He was an industrious servant of the country, as well as scholar of eminence. There was a great need of such an able and fearless person today, like him but the cruel death has snatched him from us. His body may not be here as the destruction of the body is bound to occur, but his teachings will be providing inspiration and enthusiasm to the people for a long duration.

—Swami Karpatriji Maharaj

(6)

A devoted, generous, most affectionate dear Bhaijee has gone from among us. What was he? From where has he come? This is known to him only, but he was everything to the affectionate people. An inspiration for the unmoved faith of divine love remained inspiring to the devotees, through his life.

—Swami Sharnanandji

(7)

Such is his entry, in the region of my inner heart and gained a place there – his mental image has been established in such a way that I did not even believe it, as per your statement that he has gone to some heavenly world.

—Swami Akhandanandji Saraswati

(8)

He was a spiritual person. I have found his spirituality in real form even during actual and not visible conflicts. He was a coordinator. He had a feeling of respect in his mind for every religion of India. He did invaluable services to scriptural religion and literature, even then his mode of life was full of generosity with an extensive point of view.

—Jain saint, ProfessorTulsi

(9)

The contribution which Shri Poddarji has made towards spreading and publicity for culture and religion, that is extremely very important.

—Jain saint, Shri Sushil Kumarji Maharaj

(10)

Shri Bhaijee was a true and real representative of truth and religion. It is very difficult to find a person like him in the present era of non- theistic real existence (*Anishwarwadi Bhoutikta*). His body had definitely a divine light within.

—Swami Krishnanand
Divine Life Society, Rishikesh

(11)

Shri Poddarji was a living source of savorous worship (*rasopasna*). He was an ideal for an existence of devotees. The public had been able to reach in the sentimental world (*bhav jagat*) just by observing his simple and lively way of life. Those who have attended a historical great festival of *Radhashtami*, they will realise that how much eminent person of a high category he was. I have also attended the great festival of Radhashtami in Gita Vatika, at *Gorakhpur*. On that day, every person had witnessed there with the feeling of Shri Radha, by entering the kingdom of bliss (*anand rajya*). The distribution about the feelings of Shri Radha – a lively religious devotion (*saras bhakti*) of the religious world, which he had made with such generosity, that it is now rare to find it's another example.

—Swami Sitaram Sharanji Maharaj
Laxman Fort, Ayodhya

(12)

Respected Bhaijee Shri Hanuman Prasadji Poddar had come from divine world and returned to that very place. I have not met Bhaijee in person, but have read his literature. Whatever he had done for Hindu religion and Hindu caste, he will always be remembered for it.

—Respected Shri Ramchandra Keshav Dongreji Maharaj

(13)

This servant considers him to be a holy incarnation only, who had descended on this earth for divine activity towards public welfare.

—Veena Maharaj Shri Ramduttji Parvatikar

(14)

If someone can be capable to write and remain just continue to write, regarding respected Shri Bhaijee, even then he will say that – even then, there is no any extent of his virtues.

—Shri Madhavrao Sadashivrao Golvalkar

(15)

Shri Hanuman Prasad Poddar has done memorable services to the cause of Hinduism and it is but right that his services should be suitably recognised.

—C. Rajagopalachari
First Governor General of Independent India

(16)

Nowadays, it has become a fashion to ignore the religious texts, on the name of secularism. To develop a totally religious equality, it is important that we should make a thoughtful and accurate study of literature of other religions in addition to our own religion. Gita press has done an important duty by publishing and publication of religious scriptures, at a large scale and its main credit, is due to personality and devoted life of Shri Hanuman Prasadji Poddar.

—Jay Prakash Narayan

(17)

As a founder editor of famous monthly magazine 'Kalyan', the services rendered by Shri Poddarji towards the revival of our culture shall be remembered for a lengthy period. For a nominal price, he had managed the availability of religious scriptures alongwith commentary to millions of people in Hindi and did an unequalled service to popularise our religious texts.

—Varah Venkat Giri, The President of India

(18)

Shri Poddarji was an ideal person. He did always beneficence from every direction and inclined towards the welfare of others, during his lifetime. He had been spreading, fragrance among others by rubbing himself like a sandalwood. Our culture, which is still living and yet flourishing, its credit without doubt goes to an eminent person like Shri Poddarji.

—Gopal Swaroop Pathak
Ex-Vice President of India

(19)

Shri Poddarji did an important work in the field of social service and religious awakening. The service, which he rendered for Indian citizens, he will be long memorable for it.

—Mohanlal Sukhadia
Chief Minister, Rajasthan

(20)

Shri Hanuman Prasad Poddar was a priceless treasure of our country. His services shall always be remembered for the motherland. We are proud that he was a part of Bikaner.

—King of Bikaner Shri Karni Singhji & the Queen

(21)

I can vouch that the life of Shri Poddarji was totally dedicated towards a progressive – great object – a staunch Hindu, who can aspire to be something. He was a good example of it.

—An emperor, the King of *Nepal*

(22)

A great performer for religious observances renouncing Hindu culture and of Hindu religion has been departed, due to death of Shri Poddarji. Shri Poddarji has tried throughout his life, to publicise and spread of Hindu religion in the world which will always be protected in our Indian history. Shri Poddarji was a living example of simple living and high thinking.

—Atal Bihari Vajpayee
President, Indian Jansangh

(23)

I am happy to learn that in the auspicious memory of the founder of '*Kalyan*' – Shri Hanuman Prasad Poddar, – it has been planned to publish an issue as a reverential offering. Shri Poddarji was a person with religious thinking who did great work to serve nation and society with simple and peaceful attitude, throughout his life. He did notable services to the Indian culture, country and society, through '*Kalyan*' and other publications of Gita press. I wish a success of this issue for a reverential offering.

—Bansilal
Chief Minister, Haryana

(24)

The way Shri Bhaijee spent his life in service to caste, religion, society, country and the literature deserves to be followed.

—Raj Bahadur
Minister, Government of India

(25)

His contribution to the revival of Indian glory is so great that he could truly be called another personality like Hanumanji of the Ramayan fame.

—K. Hanumanthaiya

(26)

I am quite familiar with his work. He was greatly responsible for popularising religious literature among the younger men while the Gita press and the *'Kalyan'* magazine are the legacy left to us by him – the eloquent monuments of his vision and devotion to our ancient religion.

—B. Gopal Reddy
Governor, U.P.

(27)

The mortal body of respected Hanuman Prasad Poddar has merged with five elements. His fame is changeless and immortal. He was a great light-house of the Indian culture. His contribution in popularising and spreading of spiritual thoughts and instincts shall be long memorable.

—Shri Mannarayan,
Governor of Gujarat

(28)

During his well-prolonged lifetime, Bhaijee served only mankind in various ways and provided the highest gift to Indian saint tradition for general public. His personality as public collector shall remain always inspiring to all of us.

—Satya Narayan Singh
Governor, Madhya Pradesh

(29)

Shri Hanuman Prasad Poddar was one of the truly great men of *Bharat*. He believed in doing his duties without the least desire for a material reward or fame. He was a true *karmyogi*.

—Shanti S. Dhavan
Governor, West Bengal

(30)

The name of Hanuman Prasad Poddar will be placed among those eminent people who have been proclaimer and cultivator of Indian culture and civilisation.

—Devkant Barua
Governor, Bihar

(31)

The installation and publication of '*Kalyan*' and management of Gitapress has made Poddarji immortal. The progress of national language has been done by him and for which the whole nation would be indebted to him for a period of centuries. The priceless gems which have been provided by him for the literary storehouse in Hindi through '*Kalyan*', they have become beneficial and long-lasting auspicious for its present and future life to the whole country and the world.

—Kamlapati Tripathi
Chief Minister, Uttar Pradesh

(32)

Shri Hanuman Prasad Poddar is one of the greatest sons of India in recent times. Shri Poddar practiced what he preached. I found in him a highly religious and pious personality.

—M. Ananthasayanam Ayyangar
Ex-Governor

(33)

There are only very rare humbles agitated in other's distress and simple-hearted person like him. He had a deep study of Hindu religion. Whatever is written by him contains influence of his belief towards the almighty.

—Haribhau Upadhyay
Gandhi-Ashram, Hatundi, Ajmer

(34)

He was an indifferent social worker. He had always been helping by distributing free blankets, meal and habitation to the poor people for flood-affected areas in Gorakhpur, Deoria and Basti. He has also established and managed centre of leprosy and many social organisations. Even by doing this much, he had also no pride or longing for reputation.

—Chaudhary Charan Singh
Lucknow

(35)

An extraordinary devotee, a real embodiment of disinterested performer of his proper deed, an ocean of kindness, a dominion of humanity, symbol of selfless love, lord of knowledge and an ideal for service has departed.

—Nanaji Deshmukh, Secretary
Bhartiya Jansangh

(36)

Shri Hanuman Prasad was my old friend. He did unequalled services in the field of publicity for religious literature.

—Ghanshyam Das Birla

(37)

I have come to his contact about 30 years ago. Since then his profound love and affection has been bestowed on me. In fact, our whole Birla family has remained very intimate with him.

Shri Hanuman Prasadji was always very careful of one thing that in which way the person in front would be happy. He thinks this only that there should not be any feeling of pain or distress in the mind of a visitor. Considering all religions as an identity of the God, he had shown equal respect towards them, treating them as various ways to achieve only one ultimate reality.

—Basant Kumar Birla

(38)

He was shining like a touchstone among us. Everybody was charmed due to his supremely soft behaviour and an attraction towards his personality, moved with the compassion.

—Padma Bhushan Seth Shri Mugturamji Jaipuria

(39)

Shri Bhaijee was a real example of the humanity. A *triveni* of religious, cultural and socially useful literature, which was initiated by him, that has given internal peace and inspiration to millions of people.

—Padmapati Singhania

(40)

Whatever is said about Shri Bhaijee would never suffice. He was a great person and had spent his life in divine worship and about its deliberations. Such people are very rare, who believe in the God and remain live with love, simplicity and good conduct.

—Narsinghdas Bangur

(41)

A calm person of the Shrimad Bhagwat Gita and the God's valued devotee like him, presumingly and bodily, was illuminating all the directions. His good deeds in the form of '*Kalyan*' would be guiding eternally to every religious Hindu, else just to human beings.

—Giridharilal Mehta

(42)

Respected Bhaijee had contact with many people and he had loved them all but whenever we had to go to meet him, it appeared as if he was loving us the most than others. Such was his greatness. Though, during meeting and hearing, his discourses in relation to the act of achievement, the peace definitely appeared once in the mind of worldly people like us.

He was so generous and kind that whosever had gone to meet him with any desire, his desire was fulfilled.

In my opinion, such rare and eminent persons have come to this world for some time only for the welfare of human beings and then returned to divine world after completion of the work, as desired by the God.

—Hanuman Prasad Dhanuka

(43)

My personal contact with respected Bhaijee has been about 35-40 years old. The service of our ancient Indian culture which he rendered through a monthly magazine '*Kalyan*', that would always be inscribed with golden words in history. It is a great achievement to obtain about one and three quarter millions of customers for a pure and excellently religious magazine like '*Kalyan*', which is a good achievement of his continuous efforts.

—Shri Gajadhar Somani

(44)

The life of Bhaijee was simple, clear and distinct. There were not even any minutest pretention, forgery or any displaying, while cunningness or false conduct have not even touched him. Amidst feeling, devotion and faith, the children, ladies and gents, younger and the old, had been visiting him and with such peace and satisfaction, most of them have been returning from him, was seen myself as well, and by this, it was not difficult to understand that how deep input has been created on the people by the personality and thinking of Bhaijee.

—Kamal Nayan Bajaj

(45)

In the chain of indifferent saints and eminent scholars, released from the future births, who prevailed in existing form of Indian culture, I can also place the life of respected Hanuman Prasad Poddar. He was a household, lived in this world but his full life, his thoughts, duty and ideals have been like such as a saint, who is released from future births, who has engrossed and merged his everything, himself in the divine illusory form (*srishtirupi*) of the God and who had not left now any personal duty or personality. He has become immortal by sacrificing his life towards a complete service of human beings only.

—Seth Govind Dasji

(46)

Most of the credit to bring *'Kalyan'* and 'Gita press' up to this status is due to respected Bhaijee only. He had offered his life for this purpose. To sleep by 11-12 o'clock at night while still working and begin to work at 3-4 o'clock in the morning, by picking papers already placed below the head was his daily practice. Even during rest for a while after meal, he remained working for '*Kalyan*' by holding papers in hand. Editing for new articles, writing independent articles, selection of pictures, guidance in preparation of pictures to artist at every step, inspection of galley proof and page proofs, etc., all such activities he was doing himself.

—Shri Jaydayalji Dalmia

❐

146

Dissertation on Respected Bhaijee

The growth which has been made by respected Bhaijee in Hindi literature could not yet be evaluated from the literary point of view, till the present moment. Recently, the attention of research scholars of Hindi has been attracted over here. Till now, nine dissertations have been produced for Bhaijee. Their short description is given here:

(1)

1. **Subject of Research:** Shri Hanuman Prasad Poddar: Editor of 'Kalyan'
2. Number of pages in dissertation: 454
3. **Name of research scholar:** Shri Sadanand Gupta
4. **Guide:** Dr. Bhagwati Prasad Singh, Professor & HOD, Gorakhpur University, Gorakhpur
5. **Year of award:** 1979
6. **Institution:** Gorakhpur University, Gorakhpur.

This dissertation consists of seven chapters: (1) Hindi Journalism: Origin and its development; (2) Shri Hanuman Prasad Poddar: A brief introduction; (3) A religious spiritual journalism, initiation of 'Kalyan' and the establishment of Gita Press; (4) Principles for editing by Hanuman Prasad Poddar; (5) A historical development of 'Kalyan', edited by Shri Hanuman Prasad Poddar; (6) Some special columns of 'Kalyan'; and (7) Mystery for popularity of 'Kalyan'.

By such dissertation, a conclusion was made about the contribution of Poddarji in Hindi literature, culture and journalism, through the medium of 'Kalyan' that a new dimension is added in the field of religious journalism by the publication of 'Kalyan'. That has caused a new turn to the current life of the people. Bhaijee has published forty- five special issues in his lifetime which were related to various subjects. He did a remarkable service to Hindi literature and culture through those special and normal issues. He was successful in publicising of Indian spiritual literature not only in India, but also in the world. He awakened the cultural recollection and has expressed the valuable facts, from the spiritual point of view through modern terminology. A new path has been shown to the editors by righteous, spiritual, fearless, firmly dutiful, devoted to work, courteous, humble and reverent personality of Bhaijee. The priceless gems, which have been provided by him, to the store house of Hindi literature, all those have become permanently auspicious form for the present and future life of entire country and world. The sufficient and beneficial literature which is available for the protection of Indian people, to save them from the curse of western culture based on licentiousness, its full credit goes to Shri Bhaijee.

(2)

1. **Subject of Research:** A religious literature of Shri Hanuman Prasad Poddar: A critical evaluation
2. Number of pages in dissertation: 461
3. **Name of research scholar:** Ms. Pushpa Bhartiya
4. **Guide:** Dr. Bhagwati Prasad Singh, Ex. Professor & HOD, Gorakhpur University, Gorakhpur
5. **Year of award:** 1984
6. **Institution:** Gorakhpur University, Gorakhpur.

There are seven chapters in total, in this dissertation:

(1) Introduction; (2) Biography; (3) Literature characterised by religious devotion of Poddarji; (4) Developmental studies of devotionalism; Scriptural practice of literature, characterised by religious devotion from Bhaijee; (6) An evaluation of literature characterised by religious devotion of Poddarji; (7) The conclusion consists of contribution by Poddarji for literature and the society.

Ms. Pushpa Bhartiya has concluded that Poddarji was a great dominion. His personality was unlimited. His body in action enjoined by religion was so much multifaced that it is surprising to note its field and expansion. He was an ideal worker, scholar and a *Yogi*, in addition to an affectionate devotee of high caliber. He was a linguist for many. He was protector of the cows, was ultimate prudent, was a scholar, was also an editor. He has an extraordinary coordination of ancient times and recent era. He was bodiless (remained always engrossed with divine bliss), though he was a householder. His life was an interpretation of religion. Bestowed for respect to everyone, he himself was without pride. His life was coordinated with every ideal.

Poddarji has guided countless persons who have been strayed away from their path by his matured thinking, his brilliant speech and powerful writing. Satisfied the thirst of knowledge for the enquirers. Explained the depth of religious devotion of devotees, stated the mystery of knowledge to learned persons. He has established a highest record in the journalism and also arranged a high quality but cheap literature of public welfare, to general public for an extremely cheap price. Poddarji has revived the cultural values and existing form of an old religion. He had reestablished the ethical values in declining society. This is a great contribution without any doubt for this Indian society.

Poddarji has said while defining the religion that it is the religion which has remained engaged for the welfare of all beings. He had considered the religion as an essential base and life of human culture. He had acknowledged the existing form of old religion as an extremely useful and very necessary for the complete progress of society and men.

Specialty of literature for religious devotion (*Bhakti*) of Poddarji is an extraordinary coordination between the scripturalness and perceptions. His work can be classified as a special meritorious contribution to the Hindi literature, as an evidence to the inexpressible love. He has established the scope of love in its original scriptural limits. The finest, brightest and idealistic form of religiously devoted love has been defined by his literary world. Purity and its extreme remarkability along with an introduction to the most secret condition of the travellers on this path, is the most important quality of his literature. He has defined that supremely radiant savour of act (*Leela Ras*) which is rare to observe in Indian literature. An important attempt, which he did through the literature, to show an extraordinary fundamental scriptural similarity among various Gods and Goddesses and by clarifying to fundamental unity among all communities and by doing this, Poddarji has produced an unfailing sacred verse for coordination and the unity to Indian society.

(3)

1. **Subject of Research:** Shri Hanuman Prasad Poddar: Personality and his contribution. Number of pages in dissertation: 497
2. **Name of research scholar:** Shri Sadguru Sharan Vidyarthi
3. **Guide:** Dr. B.B. Lal, Ex-Vice Chancellor, Bundelkhand University, Jhansi
4. **Year of award:** 1987
5. **Institution:** Bundelkhand University, Jhansi.

This dissertation consists of two parts for personality and contribution and eleven chapters: (1) Personality : A devout *Vaishnav* and saintly personality; (2) Personality of Poddarji on the basis of external and internal evidences; (3) Personality of Hanuman Prasadji; (4) Human personality; (5) An ascetic personality; (6) His personality as a devotee and saint; (7) Significant form of expansion; (8) His contribution else related with a published personality; (9) Revelation of literary work;

Continuous study of the work; (11) Statistical study.

Shri Vidyarthi has mentioned in his dissertation that Poddarji was entirely one with his saying and doing and it is the most important characteristic of his personality. The rules, which he had framed, those were the natural parts of his conduct. No such weaknesses of human personality can be referred to which may give suffering or pain of penitence and can be a stigma on his preceding personality. He had carefully avoided the occasions, towards his praise and commemoration in his life. Bhaijee has not initiated any sect or opinion from his end. To obey the order and inspiration from the supreme Lord, with a feeling of non-attachment, was he longed for, in which he had carefully guarded for not acquiring any impression of his personality or himself and even never allowed any such feeling to prevail in his mind.

Shri Poddarji was an authoritative messenger and most of all, a preliminary person of the supreme Lord and had been evoking an auspicious desire, to achieve the God and a curiosity to realise His divine form in the heart of living beings. He had achieved such a high state where there remains no difference between the God and a saint, both have become in one thread and one tone. The God becomes active in the form of a saint and did salvation of human being.

One very important characteristic in the literature of Poddarji has remained like this that he is found as clearly peeping through it. Savorous duality (*Rasadwetya*) is a new direction and original thinking towards Radha Krishna is his great contribution to this era.

Shri Vidyarthi has concluded from the statistical data that there are 19,670 total lines in his principal literary composition of verses, i.e., *'Pad-Ratnakar'*, which are 19,205 more than the total lines of 12,582, 3,229 and 3,402 gradually from principal literary gems like *Ramcharitmanas, Vinay Patrika* and *Gitawali,* respectively by *Goswami Tulsidasji*. In addition, Poddarji has also an extensive room for prosaic literature.

National language has definitely achieved more honour, due to rich literature of Shri Poddarji and remarkable enrichment has been made on top of religious literature, which is an ideal for succeeding literary world.

(4)

1. **Subject of Research:** A critical study of the poetic work by Shri Bhaijee, with special reference to *'Pad-Ratnakar'*
2. Number of pages in dissertation: 356
3. **Name of research scholar:** Miss V. Kamalamma
4. **Guide:** Dr. N.S. Dakshinmurti, Reader, Department of Hindi, Manas Gangotri, Mysore University, Mysore
5. **Year of award:** 1989
6. **Institution:** Mysore University, Mysore.

This dissertation contains seven chapters: (1) Special characteristics of Bhaijee; (2) Literary work of Bhaijee; (3) Poetic form of '*Pad-Ratnakar*' and the subject appraisal; (4) Characters of '*Pad- Ratnakar*'; (5) Sentiments and figure of speech in '*Pad-Ratnakar*'; (6) Linguistic style of '*Pad-Ratnakar*'; (7) Influence and position of '*Pad-Ratnakar*'.

There are a total 1,557 verses of poetry in '*Pad-Ratnakar*'. It does not consist the description of a complete biography of only one hero. A comparative study has been made of *'Pad-Ratnakar'* with *Shrimad Bhagwat* and *Soorsagar*. In *'Pad-Ratnakar'*, characters are in lyrical poetry because Poddarji has not created this great literature with an intention for creation, he had described for the description of the act to *Radha Madhav*, being delightfully inspired with self-bliss (*Atmanand*) and his object was the human welfare.

Linguistic style of '*Pad-Ratnakar*' consists a mixture of informal language, Braj and of *Rajasthan*. By its matured identity, one can get an introduction of the command on language by the poet. Like *Surdas*, to bring change in language according to character is an artistic skill acquired by Bhaijee. Though *Shri Radha Krishna* are the favoured deities of the poet, Shri Bhaijee of '*Pad-Ratnakar*', even then he has described about other Gods and Goddesses with a high respect. As in *Bhagwat*, the opinion of coordination is expounded, in such a way, that a coordination is also evident in his poetry. With a view of coordination, Shri Bhaijee has even achieved a better high status than opting for a divine form (*Bhagvatakar*), because by declaring *Arhat, Buddha,* Jesus, *Ahurmazd, Allah* all as different identities for only one truth, he has not only coordinated the Hindu religion, but rather every religion.

Though the texts of *Shrimad Bhagwat, Soorsagar* (*Sursagar*), *'Pad-Ratnakar'* appear different from outside, but the main essence is just one and that is an affirmation of religious devotion. Description of parental affection by *Soordas* and Bhaijee is a priceless gem of Hindi literature.

'*Pad-Ratnakar*' is not only a text for stimulation of religious devotion (*Bhakti*), but is rather a greatly contribution which is also abundant from both points of view of artistic favour and sentimental favour in the literary composition of verses. Composed and based on great epics like *Vedopanishad, Nanapuran, Narad Bhakti Sutra*, etc., this text is not a translation or initiation of anyone. The poet has composed the poems from cooking of his literary knowledge and worldly experiences. Though devotional nectar (*Bhakti ras*) is also an acknowledged flavour of this text, there is also a presence of beautiful cooking of other flavours as well. It is decorated with several figures of speech.

'*Pad-Ratnakar*', contributed by a prominent devotee and saint Shri Poddarji is a priceless treasure of modern Hindi literature.

(5)

1. **Subject of Research:** Savourous feeling of duality (*Ras- Bhavadwaetya*) and the contribution of Hanuman Prasad Poddar in it.
2. Number of pages in dissertation: 319
3. **Name of research scholar:** Miss Ranjana Gupta
4. **Guide:** Dr. (Smt.) Sarla Shukla, Ex-Professor & HOD, Department of Hindi and modern Indian language, Lucknow University, Lucknow.
5. **Year of award:** 1992

6. **Institution:** Lucknow University, Lucknow.

There are seven chapters in the present dissertation: (1) The time and contribution of Hanuman Prasad Poddar; (2) Savour of religious devotion (*Bhakti-ras*) and savorous feeling of duality (*Ras bhavadwetya*); (3) A savorous all-pervading spirit of universe (*Rasbrahma*) and great emotion of Radha; (4) Savorous feeling of duality (*Ras-bhavadwetya*) and the supreme spirit *(Yugal tatva);* (5) An influence of regular order of ritual and philosophy, etc. on savorous feeling of duality; (6) The savorous feeling of duality (*Ras-bhavadwetya*) by Poddarji (7) Conclusion.

It was concluded in the dissertation that a tradition by which religious devotion with a savour has been composed boldly and led during sixteenth century by *Goswamiji, Poddarji* was also a new emancipator of that very great tradition. Through the savour of *Radha Madhav,* savorous of duality feeling has begun to appear continuously in the inspired heart of him. Poddarji has liberalised the image of Radha Krishna throughout his life by willful intelligence. Most of the part of Hindi literature is related with the religious devotion of Radha Krishna and such soft embellishing feeling of Poddarji is a prominent contribution in this context to Hindi literature.

Shri Poddarji is another great saint of modern era who is remain engrossed in an ocean of frenzy after *Mahaprabhu Chaitanya*. Being eternally immersed with great divine *Vaishnav* state characterised by emotions, saint Shri Poddarji – successful in evocation of a savour (Ras-siddha) and whose heart itself had been transformed in the shape of dance committee and where daily new and beautiful wandering acts – had always been continued by the queen of dance-crown of savour (*Ras shekhar*) Shri Radha-Madhav. Like this, heart of Poddarji had become a stage for actual staging of divine flavour with sentimental duality (*Bhava dwetya*). He was a witness of this great and extraordinary act of savour, at every moment. Savorous duality (*Rasa dwetya*) was evident in the life of Poddarji.

In fact, monism *(Adetwyavad)* of *Shankaracharya* was a favourite principle of Poddarji, but he did not propagate this knowledge as a path of arrival to such state than religious devotion and love. According to him, due to rising of Sun for love, the mind reaches up to a great sentimental form after being melted by its heat and has acquired to an excellence. Poddarji was of opinion that the God manifests Himself in two forms the man – woman for the sake of an act only. His harmony is the only reason of savourous feeling of duality. Due to such extraordinary establishment, he is also completely with Vedic tradition and also separated from it. Savourous feeling of duality (*Ras bhava dwetya*) is such a divine creation by Poddarji, from where, the love of entire universe appears as a spot only.

Due to his illustrious principles, through philosophy of savorous duality (*Rasadwetya*), Poddarji has presented a new and entirely uncommon interpretation of religious devotion so that the existence of divine lover is perpetually retained as feeling of duality (*Dwetya Bhava*)) in the form of devotee and abode of love instead of its termination in an ocean like a spot.

Delighting is just not possible, being solitary during wandering in an act (*Leela Bhava*) by deity, there is a perpetual necessity of the presence of two; the supplier and legislator of bliss. A lover to the abode of love and abode of love to the lover, both keep on providing pleasure to each other, during wandering of the act by deity. Being inspired and reflected by complete and continuous instant pleasure, there remains also no trace of an imagination to acquire a compassion in such exchange of pleasure.

Through the medium of savorous feeling of duality *(Rasa Bhava Dwetya)*, Shri Poddarji has given a message of a universal love to the universal humanity. In a series of devotees for Vedic religious saviour and public saviour, the name of Poddarji is leading. He has saved a complete race which was ready to enter in the face of complete destruction by the establishments of his religious devotion and socially useful personality.

(6)

1. **Subject of Research:** A critical study of the prosaic work by Shri Bhaijee with special reference to the collection of essays.
2. Number of pages in dissertation: 418
3. **Name of research scholar:** Smt. Vijay Kumari
4. **Guide:** Dr. N.S. Dakshinmurti, Acting Head, Department of Hindi, Manas Gangotri, Mysore University, Mysore.
5. **Year of award:** 1994
6. **Institution:** Mysore University, *Mysore.*

This dissertation consists six of chapters: (1) Short biography and personality of Shri *Bhaijee Hanuman Prasad Poddarji;* (2) Literature of Shri Bhaijee; (3) Literary essays by Shri Bhaijee; (4) Literary form of the work of Shri Bhaijee; (5) Nature and comprehensiveness of dispersed essays by Shri Bhaijee; (6) Contribution of Shri Bhaijee to Hindi literature.

It is mentioned in the dissertation that only language is such a prominent way to the authors, by which they have expressed their thoughts and feelings to the readers. Individuality of the language is its identity. The presence of continuity and attraction of language have the power to confine itself with readers and also influenced and govern their activities and thoughts. We have found many of such distinctly attractive properties in the language of Bhaijee. The language of Bhaijee is simple, clear and correct.

Most of the essays of Bhaijee are thought-based. He had been expressing his thoughts, logic and principles in an order and in clear form. Compelling his readers to move along, he influences as well by his thoughts. A serious care has been taken of the grammar in his writing and an attention has also been given in the use of figures of speech and power of words. No violation has been made of literary rules, at any place. He had adopted various rules of literature in a very simple manner and revised it at the highest level by following the literary limitations. With deep thinking and reflection, the creation of serious spiritual literature, which was produced by Bhaijee, there is no comparison of it. Others have obtained an inspiration for correction of the articles, deep thinking, reflection and sincere work from the literature of Bhaijee.

Everyone has lavishly praised of his vast literary contribution and has accepted him as a saviour of an incarnation for Indian tradition.

The language of Bhaijee is simple, sweet and can be easily understood. There is no place for difficult or pretension, at any place. According to depth of subject, the change is evident in its nature. While defining spiritual subject, its depth was expressed by utilising and assembling words from Sanskrit root and its seriousness was revealed while describing social subjects, its modern identity was explained by using words from English, Arabic, etc. The readers have definitely realised one thing that it is an ineffective effort to change one word by another word in sentences of Bhaijee. It gives an introduction of his command on language.

(7)

1. **Subject of Research:** Shri *Hanuman Prasad Poddar* and his literary composition in verses on Krishna
2. Number of pages in dissertation: 363
3. **Name of research scholar:** Shri Shailesh Kumar Upadhyay
4. **Guide:** Dr. Tribhuvan Ojha, HOD & Reader, Department of Hindi, Karim City College
5. **Year of award:** 1997
6. **Institution:** Ranchi University.

There are five chapters in total in this dissertation: (1) The life and philosophy of life of Shri Hanuman Prasad Poddar; (2) Development of literary personality of Hanuman Prasad Poddar; (3) Reflection of literary composition in verses of Krishna by Hanuman Prasad Poddar;

Internal and external examination of literary composition in verse of Krishna by Hanuman Prasad Poddar; (5) Creation of literary composition in verses of Krishna in Hindi and religious literary composition in verses devoted for Krishna by Poddarji.

It is concluded in this dissertation that Shri Poddarji has considered the religious devotion for Krishna as an ultimate goal of the human life. The entire literary composition in verses, religiously devoted for Krishna and combined with the character of lyrical poetry, is mainly in manner of verses not connected by subject matter of others. The selection of words in verses has been done with extreme expertise which has given life to the verses of devotional poetry. In his literary composition of verses, soft and sweet language to express soft feeling while serious and effective language to express serious feelings have been used. In his literary composition of verses, there is a real and suitable inclusion of literary images. A profound appropriation for disposition of language has placed his literary composition of verses to a particular position. Even this all happened, when his aim was not to formulate the literature, but rather only to express his breathing of heart towards his deity Shri Krishna and Shri Radha. In his literary composition of verses, figures of speech, depending for its effect on sounds rather than on meanings, are present everywhere.

Despite the similarity of occasion, Poddarji has made a notable effort to describe special event regarding mental confusion in love for Shri Radha, which separates him from other contemporary poets.

In the modern era, he has abundantly endowed a praiseworthy work by establishing literary composition of verses amidst religious devotion (*Bhakti Kavya*) with his full dignity and influence. His lyrical poem 'Pad-Ratnakar' is a priceless treasure in Hindi after *Soor-Sagar* of the period characterised by religious devotion due to which the coming generation will absorb and put this source of religious and spiritual occasion at the same category as *Soor* and *Tulsi*.

Poddarji is a devoted poet of twentieth century but his high feeling for religious devotion and originality in his literary composition of verses has placed him on the same category, somewhere among the best devoted poets like *Soordas, Tulsi, Hitharivansh, Raskhan* and *Meera*.

(8)

1. **Subject of Research:** A cultural awareness coupled with religious thought in literary composition of verses by Shri Hanuman Prasad Poddar
2. Number of pages in dissertation: 264
3. **Name of research scholar:** Smt. Kamlesh Gaggad, Lecturer in Hindi, Govt. Bangur P.G. College, Deendwana (Rajasthan)
4. **Guide:** Dr. Umakant Gupta, Govt. Doongar P.G. College, Bikaner (Rajasthan)
5. **Year of award:** 2000
6. **Institution:** M.D.S. University, Ajmer

This dissertation consists of six chapters in total: (1) Hanuman Prasad Poddar: Personality and the contribution; (2) Various dimensions for inspiration of creation of literature by Poddarji; (3) An evaluation of the elements of religious devotion (*Bhakti tatva vivechan*) in the literature of Poddarji; (4) The nature for philosophy of life in the literature of Poddarji; (5) Cultural awareness in the literature of Poddarji; (6) Conclusion, achievements and possibilities from this study. It is shown in this dissertation that India has been an established center for divine accomplishment of spiritualism, philosophy and the art for sages, saints, great scholars and top thinkers. Our saints, high- souled persons and poets have made a priceless contribution in the construction for a honourable shape of Indian culture, by taking care for the immortal values of life. For it, they have presented a rare gift, mainly by self-purification, self-discipline, self-research and self-realisation, inspired by a thought process for upgradation of the people. Under the tradition of such saints, spiritual aspirants, the name of a modern saint of highest calibre with varied talents, Shri Hanuman Prasad Poddar is on top. A famous person among general public, by his pet name 'Bhaijee', Shri Hanuman Prasad Poddar was a son of desert in Rajasthan, though his centre of the spiritual practice and place of working have remained in Gita Vatika and Gita press, Gorakhpur. A credit to hurl a flag of immemorial religion, not only in India, but throughout the world, goes to Shri Poddarji. Like Aurbindo Ashram, Puddicherry of south India, which is the main centre of Yogic treasure and spiritual science, in the same way Gita press, Gorakhpur can be called a meeting place for three rivers of duty, knowledge and religious devotion. In the south, a great Yogi and the saint of high calibre, Shri Aurbindo has spread the divine light of spiritualism, developed from perceptual consciousness, in the same way, Bhaijee has flowed down a sacred river of religious feeling for Radha Madhav.

The personality of Shri Hanuman Prasad Poddar is so extraordinary and multi-faceted that he can altogether be called an incomparable great personality of Indian culture and art, promoter of national language, commentator, editor, original thinker, freedom fighter, competent litterateur, saint and religious devotee. Poddarji has continuously enriched the store house for Goddess of learning through the medium of immortal creations.

It has been clear by the study of poetic composition of Bhaijee that philosophy is naturally evident in it. He has supported non-dualistic philosophy only in the world of living being, Brahma, in his poetic composition. In addition, he has been specially persuading pure dualism. His Shri Krishna (a Brahma) is in pure conscious form, full of bliss and full of pure love and in the same way to herd girls of Braj (the souls) are also pure conscious, full of bliss and full of sacred love.

Likewise, he has not only shown meaningful thoughts on basic elements of the Indian culture, but also expressed strong persuasion towards reputation of those cultural high ideals. Bhaijee has presented ancient customs of Hindu religion, four designated duties of human beings, an importance to woman and humanistic attitude in relation to a feeling of public welfare and universal brotherhood. He has awakened the Indians towards eternal moral values like truth, non-violence, love, compassion, affection, sympathy, good deeds, service to guests and the cow protection. Sanctity of moral conduct, religion and spiritual thinking had been the main basis of his poetic composition.

Publication of '*Kalyan*' is an extraordinary event among the tradition of Indian literature. Bhaijee had not only germinated '*Kalyan*' and '*Kalyan Kalptaru*' but had also provided sufficient water through body, mind and wealth alongwith his self-accomplishment (*Atmsadhna*) which is now flourishing like a huge Banyan tree. Under the shadow of his thoughts, not only the body but soul as well, have felt fully satisfied. Bhaijee has given the life to Hinduism enriched with Indian immemorial religion and customs, through the editing of '*Kalyan*'.

To establish a new humanism, Bhaijee has made an excellent contribution through magazine like '*Kalyan*'. Such is the strong assumption of the scholar.

Dr. Haribansh Rai Bachchan has called him a shining star in the sky of the Indian literature. In this present era of atheist, a nectar through voice which has been pronounced by Poddarji to general public in their own and simple language, the people and the admirers of literature shall be indebted to him till eternity.

The golden era (an era of religious devotion) of Hindi literature and in the sincere dealing with the poetic composition of religious devotion, a summation of stream of creation is definitely delightful and praiseworthy. In fact, and with the same context, a continuous search and research are needed towards Poddarji's literature in the direction of public welfare coupled with motivational speeches and for creative justification.

(9)

The ninth dissertation about Bhaijee is not directly related to him, rather than for '*Kalyan*'. Because Bhaijee and '*Kalyan*' are synonyms to each other, therefore, this dissertation is being also included here.

1. **Subject of Research:** Contribution by a religious magazine '*Kalyan*' towards the field of journalism.
2. Number of pages in dissertation: 453
3. **Name of research scholar:** Rajneesh Kumar Chaturvedi
4. **Guide:** Prof. Ram Mohan Pathak, Director, Madan Mohan Malviya Institute of Hindi Journalism Mahatma Gandhi Kashi Vidyapeeth, Varanasi
5. **Year of award:** 2006
6. **Institution:** Madan Mohan Malviya Institute of Hindi Journalism, Mahatma Gandhi Kashi Vidyapeeth, Varanasi.

There are eight chapters in this dissertation excluding the introduction: (1) Hindi journalism of India; (2) Religious spiritualistic journalism of Hindi in India; (3) Contribution of the founder editor-Shri Hanuman Prasad Poddar; (4) Editorial policy and criteria of '*Kalyan*'; (5) Special issues of '*Kalyan*'; (6) Contents of '*Kalyan*'; (7) The role and contribution of '*Kalyan*' in the field of journalism; Conclusion.

It is concluded by this dissertation after a study of issues for eighty years of '*Kalyan*' that it has got a success to achieve the basic aim of journalism. In fact, the journalism is a mission by which discipline, mutual harmony and the moral values are established, in addition to spread a feeling of nationality in the society. '*Kalyan*' is constantly working for such of its mission. Among this era of commercial journalism, only no-commercial journalism can fulfil its mission for the journalism. '*Kalyan*' is such an example.

It has become very clear by the study of '*Kalyan*' that this is an important magazine for mysticism. This is a magazine of philosophy, history and culture as well as of literature which has fulfilled its responsibility for a healthy society. '*Kalyan*' has been a magazine to put forward an aim to establish a value-based society, to spread the feeling of nationality and, finally, to vouch a message of universal fostering. This is evident with literary, cultural, spiritual, philosophical and linguistic related essays published in it.

'*Kalyan*' has put forward the real form of Hindu philosophy and its living methodology in front of the world, by bringing the basic elements of Indian culture into limelight due to which many misunderstandings spread in it, have been eradicated and its reputation has enhanced in the opinion of non-Hindus.

Such an effect by '*Kalyan*' through journalism has given a new direction for journalism to spread spiritual feeling in the heart of general public. In this way, an anarchy is increasing nowadays in the field of journalism and a code of conduct is discussed to control it. It is clear by putting a sight for the principles and policies of '*Kalyan*' that it has itself implemented most of the things for code of conduct, framed for the journalism. Now, if it is pronounced that there is a code of conduct for principle and policy in the field of journalism by '*Kalyan*', then it will not be unjustified.

In fact, '*Kalyan*' is such a religious magazine which has a patronage for Indian cultural way of life. Spiritual knowledge of ancient Hindu literature (Vedas, Puranas) is being received to seekers, through the medium of '*Kalyan*'. '*Kalyan*' has placed the religious view of Indian subjects and facts in simple language. It is an achievement beyond imagination by itself to obtain such a high object through the medium of journalism.

❐

147

Honourable Mother – Ramdei Poddar

Like there is never any difference in fire and power of burning, Sun and its rays, moon and its moonlight, water and its coolness, milk and its brilliance, which are always one, in the very same way, there was no any difference between Bhaijee and mother. Characteristically being even two, they were one-power and powerful.

Where Bhaijee has brought and erected the flag of a huge Hindu religion like a Himalayan height at the world horizon, due to his continuous and sincere activities, mother has also installed there a prominent record for the characteristics of Indian Hindu woman by her dedicated life. Where Bhaijee has arranged to deliver Indian scriptures composed by saints and sages, the high ideals and defined code for good conduct, approved by the scriptures up to the world community, through the '*Kalyan*' and Gita press and praised the path over there, respected mother has also expressed and sufficiently defined her behaviour about the coordinated nature of an ideal Indian woman as described by the scriptures – like the supreme soul Ramkrishna and mother Sharda, both had perfectly best ways of thinning. In the same manner, absolutely all aspects of both Bhaijee and mother were warp and woof with eminences.

Bhaijee had to spend a life of prison and under surveillance, after two-and-a-half months of marriage due to his involvement in revolutionary activities. During that awesome period, respected mother was completely tolerant, she had no fear, no grief or worry, for herself and was perfectly dedicated towards Bhaijee.

After a duration of fifteen months of surveillance, the English government has granted permission to mother, to live with him in Shimlapal due to good conduct shown by Bhaijee. She lived in a small hut with Bhaijee. In addition to the help, she rendered to Bhaijee, she also took share in servicing patients with Bhaijee. The English government has expelled Bhaijee from Bengal after one and three quarters of year. Absolutely, every villagers had tears in eyes at the time of farewell from Shimlapal, they had pain, they are losing a treasure like Bhaijee and mother. Bhaijee reached Ratangarh (Rajasthan) along with his grandmother, two sisters and wife. He had then no business there or funds. Surveillance allowance was also discontinued by the government. During that time of scarcity, the sad period does not appear as causing grief to Bhaijee, due to cooperation of mother. There was even not any wrinkle or restlessness of scarcity on the face of the mother. She was happy in every situation with Bhaijee.

Bhaijee had begun to wear *Khadi* even about one and half year prior to Gandhiji. Khadi was very scanty at that time and whatever was available that was very rough, like sacking. That time mother had gone to her maternal place. Bhaijee also sent a parcel to mother containing two sarees of *Khadi*. Parents of mother have become very sad to look to those sarees – how our daughter will bear such rough clothes. But mother had no ill-will looking at those sarees, she has placed them on her head. She has humbly convinced her parents that there is no harm in wearing them.

Mother was not behind from Bhaijee at the time of boycotting the foreign goods, due to an inspiration of Gandhiji. Mother had happily dedicated every foreign item of the home into fire. Bhaijee has taken the eye on a left-over foreign item – a saree worn by mother. Mother has understood his hint. She instantly exchanged it from another saree while that foreign saree was also hurled into fire, very happily. Liking of Bhaijee was her way of living.

Life of Bhaijee was wealthy during his time of departure from Mumbai. Absolutely all types of useful items, like a beautiful home, servants were available. Mother had also seen such days of happiness. But, due to longing of an ascetic solitary life Bhaijee had been residing in the garden of Mr. Kantibabu, in a narrow and muddy lane near Asuran Pokhra in Gorakhpur. Mother was even also happy there, in the service to Bhaijee. Mother had done absolutely every type of duty by herself like service to guests, services to Bhaijee, etc. There was no any trace of pain for her due to such activities. During his solitary living, Bhaijee had sent his wife many times to serve her mother in Ratangarh – his wife had served his mother-in-law with devotion.

Editing of *'Kalyan'* was then done by Bhaijee. Cooperation of mother had caused an extraordinary progress for such work. Mother had been protective for comfort of every senior member of editorial department like Shri Shantanu Bihariji Dwivedi (Swami Akhandanandji), Shri Madhavji, Shri Devdharji, Shri Munnilalji (Swami Sanatan Devji), Shri Giridhari Baba, etc. Not only this, senior managers of Gita press like Shri Shukdevji, Shri Ganga Babu were deeply satisfied by the behaviour of mother. Thus, such happiness prevailed amidst them, had caused to do a task, more than several times by all of them. Those people had remained absorbed to serve '*Kalyan*' and Gita press with their mind and body.

A grand arrangement is held every year for the great ceremony of Shri Radhashatmi in Gita Vatika. It was a rare sight due to arrival of hundreds of guests, during those days from different states of India. Mother had been extending full support for maintenance of everyone, alongwith Bhaijee. An arrangement of meal was made by the insinuation of mother. She herself prepares meal several times for the service of guests and then had put them to sleep after entertaining with a meal.

The married life of mother and Bhaijee had been dispersing sweet fragrance. It had retained an excellence, at every aspect of domestic life. Away from cunningness, the life of mother was full of an ascetic fervour. She had been donating generously – had no wish to save anything with her.

Respected Swami Ramsukhdasji had pronounced sometimes that Look! A radiance of loyalty to husband is evident on the forehead of mother. He had encouraged the people residing with him to serve mother. He had treated them as fortunate who serve her sincerely.

Respected Swami Akhandanandji Maharaj had been remembering the sweet and generous behaviour of mother several times in his discourses. Respected Swami Sharnanandji came to meet the mother after the heavenly departure of Bhaijee. He declared that respected mother was wife of respected Bhaijee, for as many as this day but Bhaijee has now entered in mother after his departure. She is now a complete body. She is now an identity of respected Bhaijee.

In Hindu culture and an existing form of old religion, a power- woman has always maintained a particular status. A woman has always been honoured. Lord Shri Ram has given more importance for the service of mother of world Goddess Sita than to His service. When Hanuman returned from Lanka after finding track of Sita, then Lord Shri Ram told him –

Listen my dear (Monkey God), there is no one who is helpful, as you, among the Gods, men, sages or any living creatures.

What can I give in return to you?

As even my mind (a seat of perception) cannot face you.

Bhaijee has written about mother in his will. Perhaps my body may depart and mother of Savitri lives then I would like that who have faith, love, good wishes, consolation or kindness for me, all those family members and outsiders should also try in such way by which mother of Savitri may live happily. Mother of Savitri is a virtuous wife with simple heart, without cunningness and of just, with very virtuous nature. With such desireless feeling and with so much devotion, mother of Savitri has served me that has no comparison anywhere. She has many such ideal qualities which are even not present in me. Therefore, to serve her would give me more pleasure than of my service. In fact, those who could do so, they would be just very fortunate.

Baba had considered mother as an identity of the mother of world – Shri Lalitamba. Mother has herself been arranged, going about for begging daily, to Baba. When mother was remaining unwell then sometimes Bai (Smt. Savitri Bai Fogla), sometimes Bhaijee had to go, to arrange his going about, for begging. Baba gave words to Bhaijee, to look after the welfare of mother. Being remained near the place of funeral of Bhaijee in Gita Vatika, Baba had also been just coming, to look after the mother, at least once in a day. If Baba was unable to come, due to sickness, then the mother had been herself visiting to Baba. A unique and wonderful example to fulfill his promise which Baba had made to Bhaijee, is evident. Mother has concluded her life on 26th September, 1992 and Baba has vanished forever on 13th October, 1992, after 17 days of her demise. Respected Baba has written, praising mother in the beginning of his great literary composition in verses '*Jai- Jai Priyatam*' –

I pay a homage to my own form, most praiseworthy, beautiful Goddess of three worlds, like Goddess Lalitamba, a virtuous woman and my lawful mother known as Ramdatta (Ramdei).

❐

148

A Short Biography of Shri Sethji Jaidayal Goyandka

An eminent saint Shri Sethji Jaidayal Goyandka was such a Marwari saint to whom the people also do not recognize deliberately. Everyone has his own opinion. Few treated him as an expert merchant and there will be big profit in trade by his advice. Someone thinks that he is very clever, honest and impartial, if we could make him jury for our conflicts then he would solve it. Someone thought that he is an upright man with good moral, there would be a benefit of his company. There was one such category who wanted to achieve spiritual benefit, considering him as a realised saint. His way of living, dress, Hindi language mixed with Marwari was so simple that most of the people had not identified, even from a very close distance that he is an exceptional divinity of spiritual world.

A saint has narrated an event that once he was coming to *Churu* and the train had halted at *Bhiwani* station. Both were travelling in third class compartment, as there was no rush during those days. A person entered in that compartment and raised some spiritual questions from the saint sitting nearby. Shri Sethji sitting near window was talking to public, standing outside at the station. The saint did not reply instead pointed towards him, to enquire. The person asked – Who is he? He replied that he is Shri Jaidayalji Goyandka. Listening to this only, the person immersed with surprise. He got down and looked towards his face and again mounted and again got down and has begun to observe him seriously. Again, he boarded the train and enquired the saint if he is really Shri Jaidayalji? The saint has begun to laugh and said – Why don't you ask him? That person has led to discretion, meanwhile the train is set in motion. That person asked him with shyness – What is your good name please? To his reply, he heard the words full of humility – People called me Jaidayal Goyandka. Now, there was no limit of surprise to that person.

He had read many of his heart-touching articles in '*Kalyan*' and had made a very high opinion about the author. He was unable to understand that an author of such secret spiritual articles, can be a so simple person. His pleasure knows no limit of joy with his conversation to him. So, be it!

❐

149

The Birth and an Introduction to His Family

Shri Jaiydayal Goyandka was born at 9 o'clock in the night of *Vikramaditya* year 1885 on *Jyeshta* 6th of Wednesday in a small city named Churu in Rajasthan. Shri Khoobchand Goyandka has a rare honour to become his father. The forefather of Jaydayalji, Shri Salagram Goyandka was a devotee of high category. He reads handwritten *Panchratna Gita* and also repeating 108 times string of beads for the sacred verse, '*Hare Ram*' in low tone, daily. Such worth-seeing text was very carefully preserved by Shri Sethji and was exhibited to those who were keen to see. He used to take out water by himself with his hands from the well and if somebody else was present there, then also helps to let him bath. He used to go daily to temple at night to help to perform sleeping ceremony held in worshipping of the God. While returning from there, he used to go cremation ground and checked if there was sufficient water available for cattle and birds or not and if it was not there, then he arranged for it, instantly. He was a very fearless person. Once his brother Shri Harakchand had got down with fever due to fear, on enquiring he told that he had seen a ghost. When asked – Where you have seen? he replied – in front of the castle. Shri Salagramji instantly went in the castle on the opposite side and found that an ankle-length skirt was hanging and a black earthenware cooking pot was placed on its head. When he took away and showed it, his fever was gone. When Shri Salagramji was once repeating the sacred name in low tone, his father asked him for water, but he could not hear it. Due to such petty thing, his father has stopped talking to him. When he went to him to press his feet in night he did not agree and said – There is no need to press my feet, you should do repetition of divine name. He apologised that he had not heard, otherwise he would have arranged for water. But he did not just speak to him for the rest of his life. Shri Salagramji died in *samvat* 1932, at the age of about sixty years.

❐

150

An Introduction of His Father

Shir Salagram had only one son – Shri Laxmichandji. He died at young age in *samvat* 1934 when he was about 30-32 years old. He had two sons – Shri Khoobchandji and Shri Lalchandji and a daughter – Laxmibai. Shri Khoobchandji was about twelve years old at the time of the death of his father. His mother also died after one year. Then his old grandmother looked after the house and children. Shri Khoobchand began to look after the business at the age of sixteen years. His ready cash was ruined at that period and only a small amount was left for him. He worked as broker. Alittle later, he had sent his brother Lalchand to Calcutta to do some job. He started sending handloom woven clothes from Calcutta and he sold in Churu. Though he had no knowledge of Sanskrit but could do reading and writing in Hindi. He had been carrying out ceremony in honour and for the benefit of deceased relatives. He had a very good dedication to speak the truth. He was firm in the fulfilment of promise. He was also very careful about conduct in purification act. Once he had gone to a marriage party and water was touched by a leather tap. He then did not take the meal there. Many people had pretended to outcaste him, but he remained firm at his decision. He was expert in following the ethics. He was very well aware of the rules. It was not possible for anyone to become non-religious under his control. He had very much hate for other's property. If there occurred some conflicts with someone, then he did not cooperate but never forgot to help at the time of his difficulty. He did not believe in receiving. He had also been renouncing the materials for gratification. He had also good patience. He was never worried of death of anyone or an occurrence of loss. He had made a trip in the month of *Vaisakha* in the year 1911 to *Badrikashram* and died in the same year in *Phalgun* month.

❐

151

Childhood

Shri Sethji had been narrating sometimes about his childhood that how he had been moving outside to play, mentioning several excuses to his father. His maternal grandfather was a *Bajoria* of Ratangarh. At about six years of age, he had gone to maternal place in Ratangarh. His maternal grandmother has collected some money and placed it to somewhere. He took some from it. When maternal grandmother was searching, he was laughing sitting nearby. He said, if you don't beat, then I can tell you the truth. When she promised, he told that I had took away. When she enquired – What have you done? he said – Distributed among children. Such nature of donation was retained till his last day. His friends had been telling that he had a keen interest for truth right from his childhood. He did not like injustice even in sports and recognised a support for the truth. Once his father was unwell and had asked him to fan. He has begun to fan, and his father has managed to sleep, deeply. He had remained fanning him throughout the night. On awakening at morning, his father found that he was fanning him with the same devotion. The mystery was revealed on questioning. Since then, his father pronounced that if he fell asleep next time, then you are free to leave.

His education was conducted in a very simple manner. Practice of Sanskrit had been made by him later, by his own efforts. Marwari community during those days had a custom of child marriage. In accordance, his marriage was also performed at the age of twelve years. He used to read *Mahabharat* during day time just after marriage. Even after many years of marriage, his father had a faith that he was not involved in sexual relation with his wife. He asked his friend Hanuman Das Goyandka to arrange an *attar* for him. Hanuman gave him a packet of *attar*. Shri Sethji told at the age of sixty years that the packet is still lying as such in *Churu*. ❐

152

An Achievement by Devotion and Realisation

In fact, his spiritual practice had begun precisely since childhood, but was evident in practice at the age of 14-15 years of age, due to instinct of his earlier birth. In the beginning, he had done worship of Hanumanji. Once he had visualised Shri Hanumanji in the form of a monkey in dream. His mind was filled with fear and doubt. *Hanumanji* asked – You have decided to distribute *Prasad*, why you have not done it? He replied – I will do it now. By hearing it, Hanumanji disappeared. Thereafter, he worshipped *Lord Shiva*. Then he read a story of Sun-worship in the Mahabharat and then from 1899 to 1909, he did Sun-worship. Such was a hard rule of him for ten years that he took meal only after visualisation of the Sun. He has to remain hungry for several times during this period. He prayed to Sun that O Lord! If I make any relation with another's wife, then my body may be burnt to ashes. When he looked at the Sun, by closing his eyes, a mass of bliss, full of radiance, was seen. This helped him for the meditation of a brilliant formless impersonal ultimate being (*Prakashmay Nirakaar Brahma*). He did an innate study of the Mahabharat with great respect and love. He had been a regular visitor to temple of Lord Shiva. He had not considered any difference between *Shiva-Vishnu*. Lord Shiva had also appeared in his dream.

When he began to study the Ramayan, he observed this thing that Lord Shiva and Hanumanji are disciples of Lord Rama. Then he developed particular faith towards Ramji. Considering this that Ramji is the actual supreme Lord, he kept on repeating of the name of Rama and continued his meditation for Him only. The state of meditation had become very good at the age of 17-18 years. Modes of life had become so much concentrated at that time that if he wished to discontinue meditation, even then it was not distracted. Once he was meditating Lord Rama, sitting on the roof at home. He had such a firm faith that Lord Ram is standing in front. It was clear through his mental eyes. It was evening. His mother called him for meal. In the beginning, he did not reply, but when mother called him repeatedly, he began to move down just as sitting, so that mode of meditation may not be interrupted. Thereafter, when he began to dine, the intensity of meditation had reduced gradually. Thereafter, he had begun to meditate the form of the God alongwith the repetition of divine name, even during his movement on the road. People had been displaying him with a fear to become mad, but he had never given any attention to those things. He also visualised Lord Ram in dream and had conversation for a very long duration.

Thereafter, he had begun to study *'Yogvashishtha'*. When he found more glory of formless impersonal ultimate being (*Nirakaar Brahma*) in it, then his mind had begun to move for the worship of formless. More studies have been made of the texts related to monistic philosophy and theology based on the *Upanishad*. Even at that time, he had not differentiated between without form (non-visible as the ultimate being) and having form (visible). Due to some special reason, he had started meditation on the form of Lord Vishnu.

Now time has come in life for a change. A saint of a high status from Nath-sect Shri Mangalnathji Maharaj was in Churu during that period. He was a living example of renouncing, asceticism and knowledge. Company of a true saint even for a moment is unfailing. Shri Jaidayalji had long discussion with him, did *satsang*. He was deeply impressed by the asceticism and renunciation by Mangalnathji Maharaj and instantly decided to be also like him. Such event occurred in the year 1899. Thereafter, an attentiveness had increased in his act of achievement (*sadhna*). A little later, his state for the practice of without form has become highly advanced. Once he realised such that he had achieved impersonal ultimate being (Brahma). On appearing such thoughts instantly, he had such sudden outward and forward moves in mind that such realisation can never occur to him, who has achieved the impersonal ultimate being that "I have achieved the impersonal ultimate being". Therefore, it is just my illusion. In 1907, he was inside the upper porch of the home at Churu at that time and in an entirely vigilant condition, he achieved a supreme opportunity of actual visualisation of Lord Vishnu. His face was covered by a bedsheet at that time. Such was an enchanted condition due to the ecstasy which is not possible to describe. It appeared in his mind how the God had arrived without an invitation. A beat with strong rhythm appeared in mind that it was for the propagation of desireless religious devotion (*Nishkam bhakti*).

❑

153

A Close Friend

When he was twelve years old, at that very time, he became friend with Shri Hanuman Das Goyandka, who was fourteen years old. He was born in Churu on *Chaitra, Shukla* 1, in *Samvat* 1940. The friendship of childhood gradually changed to close friendship and had become more intimate along with the progress of spiritual practice. Just after two-four years, spiritual conversation had become a principal subject. Even, if they remain aloof, they often met in between and did intimate spiritual discussion. In 1906, the spiritual practice of Hanuman Dasji also achieved attentiveness and this world started appearing as a mere dream to him. He had written everything in a letter to Shri Jaidayalji. In reply Jaidayalji had written that he wanted to meet him once. Either he may come, or I may arrive. The love which I have with you at this moment, no one at home or outside, deserves that much love. Shri Hanuman Dasji was at Calcutta at that period. He was very much impressed by receiving such letter and came to Churu to meet him. On meeting, he asked – Why you have called me? He replied – Look! The work for which you have come in this world, should be completed at first. That work is to visualise the God. Both friends had been discussing a lot of things for the love – influence of the God during those days. Both the friends mostly stayed in solitude throughout day and night. Ultimate thing of the inner heart for spirituality were discussed. Deep and mysterious conversations were also held regarding the visualisation of the God, but Shri Jaidayalji had strongly instructed to keep all things as secret. Even *Vedanta* was also discussed. What are the qualities of a sage during 1st, 2nd, 3rd and 4th roles of knowledge – such things had also been explained by Jaidayalji to him. Due to these things and by hearing things about the visualisation of the God, a strong desire has awakened in the mind of Shri Hanuman Dasji, to live in solitude. He had been persuading Jaidayalji continuously for renunciation of the world to become an ascetic. Looking at his strong persuasion, Shri Jaidayalji told that you should make your state as firm, by continuous singing of hymns and meditation by living here for six months. This will very much help you to accept asceticism. Religious talks along with intense practice had remained continued for four months. On completion of four months, he again began to persuade for asceticism. Shri Jaidayalji was remaining absorbed in thought for some time and then said – A sudden blaze is appearing in my mind about the things of your future. It is not good for you to opt for the asceticism. You would not succeed in it because your asceticism is not permanent, but he remains continuing his persuasion. In response to his persuasion, Shri Jaidayalji told – Look! I have promised to accompany you and I will come along if you insist but it is compulsory for you to enjoy the gratification. If you accept asceticism, then you have to return again in domestic life and if I opt for asceticism, then I shall not return. If at all I become, then I will opt to be a deaf, dumb and lame ascetic. I have a sudden blaze of things of earlier life about me and you. About two thousand years ago, you were the King and I was your minister. We both had accepted the asceticism during that period, leaving behind the kingly state. Several people had been coming to us for the assembly of virtuous people (*satsang*) during asceticism. An assembly of virtuous people was held below the tree. I died after some time. You were then left alone. People had done extreme honour for you. When I was alive, I was also given much respect, but I was not accepting it through mind. You have begun to accept honour after my death, that means you have begun to enjoy good type of foods, mattress and pillows even in that abode of renouncing, due to earlier instinct, which has caused a great harm to you. You have declined. You died on time. Since then, after the death till now, you have not been obtained a human birth. You have remained wandering in renunciation as cattle, birds, etc., but I just lived in a higher world during those days. Now after this much time and with an intervention of fate, your auspicious deeds have revealed, and you are blessed by a human birth and I have also arrived. Now, if you still insist, then I will accept asceticism due to my promise but accept it as a bare fact that you will have to return while I shall not. Our company would be disassociated. Discussion had remained continued for a long duration due to such things. At last, the decision for asceticism had been abandoned. It was decided that Jaidayalji will stay in Bankura and Hanuman Dasji at Calcutta. They may remain meeting from time to time. Such routine remains continued for several years. Whenever they met then the whole night at many times, elapses for divine discussion, even then the things remained incomplete. Even both had been visiting to Churu, generally together.

Shri Hanuman Dasji was sick due to venereal disease in 1907. He had an extreme pain and then told to Jaidayalji – I have faith that if you say from your mouth that my disease should go, then my disease can be cured. There should not be any harm with your saying in singing of hymns and worship, he replied – alright your disease can definitely be cured but to cure it, prior to completion of suffering from sins, you have to suffer its residual part in next birth and I cannot make such an effort that you should again take another birth. Yes, there is another solution, you can transfer this disease to me. Hanuman

Dasji then replied – how can I give my such terrible disease to you, I cannot accept it. Jaidayalji then said – alright, you are refusing it, but what I say right now, please do not refuse it, you must agree to it. You must share half of your disease to me and I will accept it. A half of the pain will be reduced due to this. With just completion of such talk, instantly a half of the disease is, in fact, really transferred on the body of Jaidayalji. His penis has instantly received half of his wound, while half of the wound of Hanuman Dasji was healed and the pain was also reduced to half. Jaidayalji told – throw away the bottles of medicines. It was obeyed. Hanuman Dasji was listening to his talks being immersed with surprise. He was very much surprised to note that the wound was completely healed within five to seven days.

In 1908, when Hanuman Dasji was in Churu, he got suddenly sick due to cholera. He had an immense pain. There was no help of his life by 12 o'clock at night. The ayurvedic doctors have also given up every hope due to their failure. During that time, Jaidayalji was in Chakradharpur. His father Shri Khoobchandji was with Hanuman Dasji. He asked him – tell me if you have any last wish. On persuasion, Hanuman Dasji replied – I don't have any wish except that I could meet Jaidayalji, at least once. Khoobchandji said – He cannot come as he is at present in Chakradharpur. He had uttered this much only that Hanuman Dasji observed – Jaidayalji is standing in front of him with his body and said why I cannot arrive? Then both friends began to talk to themselves, intimately. Jaidayalji said – you should not worry; your disease will be cured. Surprisingly, it was so that everyone can hear the words spoken by Hanuman Dasji, but the words told by Shri Sethji can be heard by Hanuman Dasji only and nobody else. Due to this, everyone presumed that he is affected with a disease of bodily humours. Hanuman Dasji fell fast asleep after such conversation. On awakening, he declared that he has no pain. In fact, he became alright. When Jaidayalji was asked about this event then he replied – I have no information about this thing.

Though Hanuman Dasji had faith in Jaidayalji, his family members had no faith. Once he told his wife that Jaidayalji can tell the feelings of other's mind, but his wife has no confidence on such thing and said that if he can tell the things of my mind, then I would treat it as the truth. For a trial, she thought about some special thing and Jaidayalji described that thing in its true form. Since then, his wife had also developed faith in him.

During an event of assembly of virtuous people (satsang), Jaidayalji has told once to his wife to do meditation for the God. She told – meditation is possible for that which has been seen previously. How can I meditate for the God when I have never seen him earlier? Jaidayalji has tried to explain that with such feelings it is very difficult to visualise the God. But remain supporting her statement, she said that it may not be in person but if I could visualise even in dream, then can meditate accordingly. At last Jaidayalji told – alright, if you visualise the God in dream, then will you meditate? She replied instantly – I will do it then definitely. It would not be inappropriate to mention that on the same day, Lord Vishnu appeared during dream in her sleep.

When Jaidayalji was 20-22 years old, since then his mode of life was used to be so much engrossed in meditation that he sits on the road many times or moves by holding the shoulder of someone. Once he was moving on the street by grasping the shoulder of Hanuman Dasji and already reminded him to be alert, as his modes of life were being concentrating with meditation. Like this, while moving on the road, father of Lalji Goyandka was returning after bath. His head has knocked together with his head. He abused – can't you see? He said – I did it by mistake, please excuse me. Then reminded Hanuman Dasji – I have already told that my modes of life are being concentrated in meditation, you should be alert, but even then, you did not care.

❐

154
The Business

In 1903, Shri Jaidayalji had gone to his maternal uncle in Bankura (Bengal) from Churu to do some work. There he learned the work for some days and then began his own business, separately. From 1910- 1920, he had lived for 10 years in Chakradharpur for the business. He developed difference of opinion with his father in business, due to his point of view of truthfulness. When he observed to bargain his father with the customers as he tells some more price than for which he would like to sell while if a customer enquires for a fixed price, then he tells a fixed price. He did not reduce to even a single paise after declaring a fixed price. If more profit is received by haggler, then the extra money is returned with a smile. But Jaidayalji was in a habit to tell only a fixed price to his customers. Retaining suitable profit after disclosing the fixed price, not even a little change is made in it. Both father and son have remained firm in their dealings. Due to this, his reputation increased in the business. His devotee called him by his nickname 'Sethji'. His business though remained just in Bankura, but after a few years, he had been spending his most of the time to spread the divine message, leaving behind his business to his family members.

❐

155

The Assembly of Virtuous People (*Satsang*) and the Exposition (*Pravachan*)

When Shri Sethji was twenty-two years old, since then he began to speak among the assembly of virtuous people and in expositions. Gradually and just as the people increased their interest in listening, he spent most of his time in exposition. Wherever he lives, an assembly of virtuous people had been accomplished at that very place and an attendance has also begun to increase. In 1910, when he began to live in Chakradharpur then he goes from there to *Kharagpur* in evening while persons interested in the assembly of virtuous people also arrived at Kharagpur from Calcutta. The discussion was held there about the assembly of virtuous people. Thereafter, everyone would go back to their destinations. In the beginning, his exposition was held at 174, Harrison Road in Calcutta. Shri Sethji was sleeping in the office of Shri Atmaramji Khemka and an assembly of virtuous people was held at that very place. The shop of Suraj Mal, father of Hiralalji Goyandka was inside Manohardas Katra and the assembly of virtuous people was held there as well. In the beginning, there was a presence of about twenty-thirty people. Four-five close associates were sleeping in the office of Shri Atmaramji. He had been talking two hours, each of them solitarily with everyone, keeping awake during night. Like this, whenever he went to Calcutta, he discussed about assembly of virtuous people, keeping awake for several nights. During the day, he was also telling about the assembly of virtuous people by visiting different families. Gradually, people interested in the assembly of virtuous people have begun to increase and another arrangement was required for this purpose. Then a place was hired on the name of '*Govind Bhawan*' in Banstalla Lane. This place became a main centre for assembly of virtuous people for Shri Sethji in Calcutta. Hanuman Dasji was serving at that time with Shri Atmaramji. Whenever, Shri Sethji goes to Calcutta, then Hanuman Dasji accompanied him throughout the day. He had already informed to Atmaramji that whenever Shri Sethji will come in Calcutta, then I will not work during that period and would accompany him.

During those days, Shri Sethji had been replying to devotees in writing by his hands. An exchange of ideas was made towards the feelings in those letters, when devotees were assembled. As the meaning of verses of the *Gita* is perceived, in the same manner, the meaning of his written words was developed. Most of the correspondence was made with Shri Hanuman Dasji Goyandka, Shri Atmaramji Khemka and Shri Jwala Prasadji Kanodia, etc. His letters had been dispatched by registered post amongst devotees for reading, then called them back. People had a high respect at that time.

❐

156

An Implicit Confidence by the Venerable People

Father of Shri Sethji was an earlier member of Arya Samaj. He had been reading '*Satyarth Prakash*'.Later, when he heard the talks on the assembly of virtuous people by Shri Sethji and saw his impact, then he was very much impressed by it and has developed faith in him. Shri Sethji had been narrating that there are very few persons who had faith like him. His father has told his wife that do not treat him, as son, he is an incarnation in our home. Since 1914, he began repetition of sacred verse *'Hare Ram'* in low tone, being impressed by Shri Sethji. His faith has more increased, due to his propagation made for *satsang,* etc. When he was sick once, then he asked Shri Sethji whether he would be alive or not? Shri Sethji replied – I don't know. His father said – you then disclosed to Hanuman as he is your friend, but I am also somehow related to you. Instantly, Shri Sethji felt in his mind that he will not die by this disease.

Prior to one month of his death, when he enquired again if he will live or not? Shri Sethji replied – there is no benefit to disclose it. If I say that he will die, then devotion in his service by us would be decreased because he is nearly to die. If I will say that he won't die, then also devotion in service would be decreased as he will yet to live. Therefore, there is no benefit to point out. When he has not disclosed him, then he asked his mother to enquire as he would not disclose to me. His mother asked him two-three times separately that your father has asked, again and again. Thereafter, when his father enquired, he told, it seems, that you would now not retain your body. He did not sleep, prior to one day to his death with an apprehension to lose his life in sleep. Shri Sethji insisted him to sleep. He said – if you can assure me, then only I can sleep. He has then fallen asleep on his assurance. When he got up next day, Shri Sethji told him – your body may leave today, please do not sleep today, I cannot assure today. He was put to bed on ground. He had such a bliss and an enchantment which cannot be disclosed. Prior to his death, he told his wife that do not treat him like a son, treat him as an incarnation. He also told his maternal uncle Shri Narmalji Bajoria – Please do not treat him as a nephew.

He was incarnated in our home. All of us would obtain salvation. There exists just a happiness beyond description, right from the first day.

When Shri Ghanshyam dasji Jalan would not obey to his father, then father of Shri Sethji would remind him – you accompany him, but neither you follow his instruction, nor you imitate, then what would be benefit of his company?

Shri Heeralalji Goyandka was one of the close friend? from Satsang – he had a lot of faith. His father, Shri Suraj Malji had even more faith than him. He had been summoning people, by appreciating the influence and properties of Shri Sethji and had initiated them for the assembly of virtuous people. Shri Sethji told him – please don't praise me. He replied – I will accept your all instructions except this one. Prior four-five hours to his death, Shri Sethji was sitting with him. He was narrating the things about the supreme Lord. He had shown a picture of Lord Vishnu and said that now see the god. He said – it is only a picture then Shri Sethji has taken off his own glasses and put on to him, then said – Look now. On wearing glasses, he told – I am now visualising.

In 1916, Shri Jhabarmalji Singhania was in Purulia. He was attacked by plague and the doctors have shown their helplessness to cure him. Shri Sethji was in Churu at that time and his father was not well. Shri Jhabarmalji has sent a telegram to call Shri Sethji that I want to meet you, my condition is very serious. Shri Sethji has shown this telegram to his father. Father said with a sidelong glance at him – you should just go, he is your friend. Shri Sethji corrected him – I have not shown my inclination to go. His father then asked – Where was then a need to read this telegram in front of me? Thereafter, Shri Sethji has not gone. Later, Shri Jhabarmalji narrated that after sending the telegram, he saw that messengers of Yama had arrived. Then, he observed that Shri Sethji is arriving, along with the god. Looking at them, the messengers have run away. He became alright.

Once Shri Badridasji Goyandka, who had faith in Shri Sethji has washed his sandal and drank that water. This thing has been noted by the younger brother of Shri Sethji – Shri Harikrishna Dasji. He had complained it to Shri Sethji. Shri Sethji called him and said, you should not do such thing. A thing, which I treated as bad, should not be adopted by you people. If wealth can be obtained by theft, even then one should not steal. Later on, he could understand the facts.

❐

157
A Confidential Letter to a Close Friend

In about 1915, Shri Sethji from Churu wrote a very confidential letter to his intimate friend, Shri Hanuman Dasji Goyandka to Calcutta. Such a clear confession is difficult to found by the pen of Shri Sethji. An important part of this letter is being taken up –

To

Dear Hanuman at Calcutta Harbour,

Very affectionate greetings from Jaidayal in *Churu*, Please always remember the supreme Lord….

And it is not your fault. You should not mind anything if there is something between our relations. Everything has been done according to my instruction and you are not accountable for any mistake later.

I have told you in train that you had also not developed that much of love like me. There would be no delay once, you have given up the whole deviation. If you could realise its full impact, then there is left nothing. In worldly opinion, you have great love, more than others.

If you have full faith in the God, then that God is existed everywhere. Once you visualise Him, then there remains no worry. Once you could believe in my words and have love and faith in me, then there is nothing left, to be done in this world. You can understand in this way. If you have some query, then you should be ready with letter. You can also discuss it with an expert.

❐

158

A Set-up of the Gitapress

Shri Sethji was very much fond of the *Gita* since his childhood, being it as a speech through the God Himself. He had been reading it very seriously. When he thinks over the verses number 68-69 in 18th chapter, during his study where the God had declared – the person who would spread the mysterious scriptures of Gita amongst my devotees, there will be no one to do any other favour to me amongst the men nor there will be anyone than him, then a thought appears in his mind, to be also like such type. He decided that it was only possible, when I could change my life according to the Gita. He has himself first readily made his life of just that way. Within a short time, he became a living example for the principles of the Gita. Thereafter, he has begun to spread the principles of the Gita by visiting various places. For that, there was a need of or correct text of the Gita, which was not available at that period. Shri Sethji has arranged to publish an edition of its commentary written by him according to his impulse of emotions for five thousand copies from Vanik Press, Calcutta. Even with great care, he has become disturbed, looking at the mistakes in the book by the printer. In the second edition as well, entire mistakes could not be eliminated even with due efforts. Then he decided that if there is no possibility of personal press, till then, such work is not possible. Though his business was in Bankura, he had remained unable to stay for a long time at any place due to his wandering to promote the assembly of virtuous people to many places. Therefore, the problem was where to establish such press. Shri Ghanshyam Dasji Jalan has suggested that if the press is installed at Gorakhpur, then I could look after the work related its arrangement, along with my business, Shri Sethji has approved his suggestion and it was decided to start press at Gorakhpur.

In 1922, Shri Sethji registered a trust on the name of 'Govind Bhawan office' for the spread of assembly of virtuous people, under the Society Registration Act. The Gita press was established in 1923 at Gorakhpur, within this trust. In the beginning, a house was taken on rent at the rate of rupees ten per month in Urdu Bazar and in it, the hand-press printing machine was purchased at first and then the work has begun in September, 1923. Due to dissatisfaction in printing, a treadle machine was purchased on top priority for two thousand rupees and was installed in the same area. Even then there was no satisfactory progress in the work. A pan-flat-bed cylinder machine in the size of 20-30 inches was purchased on 10th January, 1924 for rupees seven thousand. It has made an improvement in printing of Gita and several editions in small and large sizes of the Gita have begun to publish. Then, there was need to purchase a personal building, as a very small space was available in the rented house and the present eastern part of Gita press was purchased for rupees ten thousand on 12th July, 1926. At that time then that home was accounted more than the current need, but due to expansion of work, even that part was found after some time insignificant. Therefore, and as per the need, more land was gradually purchased near to the present building and an expansion continued. In addition to the Gita, books written by Shri Sethji and Bhaijee, several editions of Ramayan, '*Kalyan*' and books of other saints have begun to publish. During the lifetime of Shri Sethji, almost five hundred books in various sizes have been published, which had continued to publicise the divine wealth. Twenty automatic machines in various shapes were installed gradually due to expansion. In addition, there were several machines for folding, stitching and cutting. For the proper functioning of such a great work, it was supremely necessary to arrange a sufficient fund. The common sense and foresight of Shri Sethji should be exceptionally appreciated. Due to joining of an intimate companion like Shri Bhaijee, the progress of work has been heightened.

Shri Sethji already realised in the beginning that the life of an organisation, dependable on contribution or donation, is not long-standing. Neither there remains a permanent source of income nor its principles can always be firm when it is dependent on donation. Donor influences the ethics of organisation due to power of wealth. Therefore, from the beginning only, this pair of dominion has adopted such ethics that the foundation stone of Gita press should remain firm from financial point of view. In addition, books were to be made available at the price even below an investment so that these may be publicised more and more due to their cheap price. To materialise such dream, an agency was obtained for paper from Titagarh paper mill. In addition, for the practical publicity of non-violence, a shop was opened in Govind Bhawan at Calcutta for shoes sans leather, bangles without lac and the ayurvedic medicines. Such was the success of this economic practice that any help was never asked for the progress of Gita press. When the work was expanded by accepting the principles of 'no profit-no loss', then to fulfill its loss, a trade begun for handloom clothes in consultation with Bhaijee, once it is duly approved by Shri Sethji. Due to influence of his extraordinary personality, several desireless and industrious people have joined Gita press with a feeling to serve. Shri Ghanshyam Dasji Jalan had been ever looking after the work seriously, throughout his life. In addition, chief persons were Shri Sukhdevji Agrawal, Shri Ganga Prasadji Agrawal and Shri Shambhunathji Chaturvedi.

❒

159

His Physical Strength

During his youth, Shri Sethji also had an extraordinary strength. By grasping the rope of cot through his mouth, he had revolved it all around. He lifted two boys on his two palms and then displayed them up. He had also been casually displaying the movement of pulse of his forehead and neck. He had also been demonstrating sweat production from the feet. People have observed it by touching his body, which sometimes become almost hot while sometimes almost cold. Sometimes he shows his lower part of his body as cold and an upper half of his body as hot. Sometimes he had displayed an unbroken stream of tears through eyes. When he was asked to disclose the mystery behind these actions, Shri Sethji told – There is no importance of action in it, I can do it as I wish only due to power of resolve.

❒

160

A Help in the Meditation

Once Shri Hanuman Dasji Goyandka has gone to meet Shri Sethji at Chakradharpur. He asked one day – People practise meditation, please also help me for meditation in the same way. Shri Sethji replied – meditation can be done in two ways. The first is, with the help of restraining the breath from the method of Yoga while other can be achieved due to disappearance of external senses being immersed in the bliss, on meditating the virtuous identity (*sagun swarup*) of the God. I can help you meditate by other method, in your efforts for meditation, but I am not aware to bring back, from the meditation. If you have become fixed in meditation and could not be brought down then the people may burn your body, treating you as dead. Therefore, just forget the meditation. Hanuman Dasji enquired – if the people immersed under such type of meditation are burnt, then what would be their ending? Shri Sethji told – overall, the person will achieve the God because his modes of life have remained immersed within the form of the God. It is just the benefit for that person because his life became successful. On hearing this, his curiosity has further increased. He has begun to persuade to put him in meditation. Looking to an excessive persuasion, Shri Sethji agreed. In the house he was living, there was another home near to it. People believed it is a haunted house. Shri Sethji asked him to accompany in that very house, as there was no possibility of anyone to come. Both people went there, cleaned some space and have sat on the unrolled bedsheet. Shri Sethji has begun to talk impressively about the things in connection with meditation regarding the virtuous God. A little time passed but his meditation was not successful. By observing this, Shri Sethji has got up from his place and asked him to sit at the place where he was himself sitting previously and he sat himself on his place. Therefore, as soon as he began to talk about meditation, Hanuman Dasji was thrilled with an ecstasy and tears of love rolled down from his eyes and meditation has begun, later on profound meditation (Samadhi) like state began to approach. Shri Sethji told – you should now stop the efforts for profound meditation in my opinion because people would never believe that you are under profound meditation. They will arrange for your burning, treating you as the dead. Your family members would be very sad. People will stop coming to me, due to fear and they would be deprived of the little spiritual help which they received. I don't want that you should be responsible for such work. There is not at all any doubt in your salvation. What happens if it occurs today? And how it matters if happened a little later? Therefore, you should agree to my advice. As I have already promised. Therefore, it would be better to stop it, with your consent only. He could not ignore that affectionate advice. Shri Sethji has put a stop to the efforts towards his involvement for profound meditation. A little later, Shri Sethji said – in fact, a man had become ghost by dying in this house. Till now, he was here. By listening to the divine conversation which we had just now, he has achieved good fortune (*sadgati*), leaving the birth of a ghost. Therefore, our efforts have become successful.

❐

161

An Observance for the Health

Shri Sethji had taken seriously ill after the publication of first issue of '*Kalyan*'. The treatment was as it should be, but there was no benefit by it. People involved in the assembly of virtuous people were also worried along with his family members. Other close persons also started worrying. Pandit Ganesh Duttji Vyas from Bikaner was his mentor for investiture of youth with sacred thread and he had high affection on Shri Sethji. Looking at his sickness, he has also become worried. Vyasji was himself a scholar in astrology alongwith magical and mystical scriptures. He reached on a conclusion, looking through a prudent enquiry of his horoscope that Shri Sethji will not be cured, without an observance to appease the inauspicious planetary influences. Therefore, he inspired family members of Shri Sethji for this. Although family members had strong faith in Shri Vyasji even then, no one encouraged to conduct the rite. There was no problem of money. Any amount of money can be spent, but the things were obstructive taking consideration of mainly due to an ideal. Shri Sethji was abundantly characteristic of, with principle of leisurelessness. He had then considered, principles of worship only for worship of the God. He never believed to do worship of the God for the mortal body nor had ever encouraged. Therefore, question did not arise to show partiality towards a desirous worship of planets. No one can dare from his family, to encourage Vyasji directly or indirectly. Vyasji became somewhat disappointed, due to non-receipt of approval because such rite was financially dependent. He himself does not possess that much of funds and no family members have accepted to help. In addition, he wanted to see Shri Sethji to become healthy again and also had a desire to give him the best treatment of his knowledge. Suddenly, Bhaijee came to his mind. He has written complete description and sent it to Bhaijee that he can perform the rite, if Bhaijee can bear its expenses. On the receipts of letter, Bhaijee has quietly arranged a complete financial requirement, as demanded by Vyasji without informing anyone. The rite was completed. Precisely in very truth, Shri Sethji has become completely healthy soon after the completion of the rite.

❐

162

An Advice to the Agrawal General Assembly

Marwari Agrawal General Assembly had been divided into two groups – one group was in favour of the marriage of widows, etc. while the other group was opposing treating it, as dangerous to Aryan culture. The annual convention was to be held on *Chaitra Shukla* in the *Vikramaditya* year 1984 at Calcutta. Shri Sethji received a letter from other group that please do not cooperate in general assembly nor you should even attend it. Shri Sethji sent a telegram to Bhaijee in Mumbai that if there is not much harm of the work and if mother is well and she can permit, then you should reach to general assembly in time. On the same day, he has proceeded to Bankura in afternoon. A discussion was held by Shri Sethji with Bhaijee, brother Shri Harikrishna Das and Hanuman Dasji Goyandka, etc. At last, it was decided to proceed to Calcutta. A very strong demonstration was being held against the people joining the general assembly. Therefore, these people have alighted at Rajaramtalla station, prior to arrival of Howrah station due to peaceful defense. People involved in the assembly of virtuous people had already been informed, therefore, about 10-15 people have reached at Rajaramtalla station. From there, they reached to Govind Building by car. Bhaijee was sent to convince both the groups. He tried his best to maintain peace and the convention was concluded peacefully. Shri Sethji had a full plan to attend this convention, but it was changed, observing a support for marriage of widows by a lecture of president. ❐

163

A Fire in Harijan Colony

Shri Sethji had been visiting Churu generally, every year. Once he was in Churu. At that very time, colony of *Harijans* caught fire. All the huts of Harijans burnt to ashes. Even to provide shelter to their children has become a strong problem for them. Shri Sethji was informed about such misfortunate condition. His heart like a fresh butter melted. He immediately arranged to build new huts for Harijans. Harijans have begun again to spend their livelihood peacefully, after the construction of new huts.

It is said that bad days start, then their chain does not end soon. What can be said about the misfortune of Harijans. The new huts which have been built by Shri Sethji again caught fire. These Harijans have become again without shelter. As soon as Shri Sethji could have learnt that Harijans were rendered shelterless due to fire, Shri Sethji has again made their huts, with absolute generosity. The hearts of Harijans became full of extreme gratification.

But to lament, for the chain of misfortune. Their huts again caught fire and Harijans have again became shelterless. Now, how they can dare to convey their plight to Shri Sethji? Harijans may not dare to say, but information of such plight has reached to Shri Sethji. Shri Sethji said just normally with absolute generosity that new huts should again be built for these Harijans. Listening to this, a close companion said that the God is also not of such opinion that Harijans should live in some shelter house. Therefore, the fire flares up repeatedly in the huts built for them. Therefore, no new huts should be made for them.

For this, the perfect devotee Shri Sethji has replied – it is not our duty to observe what is destined or what is being done by the God. Our duty is to fix our sight on our goal and to help enthusiastically, as much as possible, to those who are in trouble. This is an opportunity, being extended by the God, to serve and as such should be presumed.

His close companion was then speechless. As per his decision, Shri Sethji again arranged to make their huts. This time their huts could not catch fire and they have been spending their livelihood pleasantly, without forgetting the obligation by Shri Sethji.

❐

164

The Publicity for Non-Violence

When Shri Sethji could know that cows and calves are killed to prepare leather shoes, he took a vow for not to wear the leather shoes. The shoes worn by him have been left at that very place. Shoes without leather were not easily available those days. Therefore, Shri Sethji remained wandering without shoes for several days. Thereafter, with great effort, an arrangement was made to make such shoes, for which there is no utility of leather.

Like this, *lac* bangles had been prepared for which animals are killed for its production. Non-violent heart of Shri Sethji could not tolerate this thing. To wear lac bangles was symbol of happy state for a married woman, during those days in Marwari community. Shri Sethji has eliminated such attitude, by his discourses and in lieu of this, an attempt was made to obtain bangles from the places where glass bangles were prepared. A little later, an arrangement was made to sale shoes and *chappals* sans leather and glass bangles in the shop of Govind Bhawan at Calcutta.

❒

165

Religious Deliberations about Gita at Prayag-Kumbh

During Kumbh, lacs of people are accumulated from distant places at the king of pilgrimage, *Prayag*. Considering it to be a very good opportunity to spread the divine name of the God, religious discussion for *Gita* was arranged there in consultation with Shri Sethji. He himself arrived in *Magh*, in Vikramaditya year 1986, while Bhaijee had already arrived. During day time, Shri Sethji gives his exposition. Gita exhibition was also arranged. Mother of Pandit Jawaharlal Nehru, Smt. Swaroop Rani had been attending it regularly.

It had become a successful arrangement Bhaijee had a longing to live at the bank of *Ganga*, solitarily. He had been continuously requesting Shri Sethji through letters for his kind permission. In reply, Shri Sethji has written on *Paush Shukla* 4, in *Vikramaditya year* 1986 – "You have written that it is almost difficult to pursue your duty, any further…how can I advise you about your plan to leave Gorakhpur. I am experiencing more benefit to this world, from the 'Press' and '*Kalyan*'. In my opinion, you should look after the work and can live solitarily in Gorakhpur as well. … if both of us can come to *Prayag* at the same time, then everything can be discussed there in solitude."

When both met in Prayag and Shri Sethji was ready to depart for Bankura after regularising all arrangements on *Magh Krishna* 30, in *Vikramaditya* year 1986, then Bhaijee put his heartiest longing in front of him in solitude. Shri Sethji has said with great affection – I don't approve your departure to anywhere, by leaving such a great work of Gorakhpur. Looking at your strong persuasion, I don't treat it proper to suppress you longing and, as such, a leave can be granted for few days. But, it is your responsibility to edit the *'Ramayanank'* which you can do from any place. Bhaijee had high regards to his advice and as such, his persuasion for a solitude is postponed.

❐

166

The Family

Shri Sethji had three brothers and three sisters. Younger brother of Shri Sethji, Shri Harikrishna Dasji was a very religious person and also a scholar. He had a good study of religious texts. Had a good knowledge of Sanskrit. He had translated several texts of Sanskrit to Hindi which was published by Gitap ress. Keeping himself sometime busy in business, he had spent most of his time reading religious texts. Shri Shivdayalji was younger to him. He died in 1943 in Churu. Youngest brother Shri Mohan Lal was born on 6th July, 1908 in Churu. Simplicity and an instinct for truth-loving have been inherited from their father to all brothers. As Shri Sethji had no issue, when Mohan Lal was eight years old at that very time, Shri Sethji adopted him. He studied in *Rishikul Brahmacharyashram at Ratangarh*. After graduation, he returned to Churu in 1926. He was married in 1927. His wife died after three-four months. Due to special persuasion from family members and an indication received from Gandhiji, he married again in the middle of 1927 to Shantibai – daughter of Shri Mohan Lalji Jhunjhunwala. In the beginning, he did a trade of *Khadi*. He had left the home without informing anyone, due to influence of Gandhiji. Gandhiji then advised him to go back to his home. He returned after several months. At the age of 19 years, he began to look after a shop for grains of his maternal uncle, by coming over to Bankura. After about three years of business of grains, he has started a business of yarn by the name of 'Jaidayal Harikrishna' in consultation and approval of his brothers. During that period, the condition of his family was just normal. Thereafter, he begun to work for yarn dyeing. A little later, a factory was installed for production of the vests. Near about 1937-1938, Shri Sethji took complete retirement from the business. In 1938, Shanta, daughter of Shri Harikrishna Dasji, who was only 22 years old, became widow – a wave of grief has galloped in the family. In the same year, Ishwar – second son of Mohan Lal, had died. His patience was to be seen, to believe. He showed steadfastness to everyone. In 1940, 'Goyandka Trust' was established and most of his trade was managed, through such trust only. To serve the public from the income has become his motto. To use untruth in trade was disliked by him as well. In the end of the year 1949, wife of Shri Harikrishna Dasji died. To maintain goodwill and mutual love in the family and retaining this point in his mind, Mohan Lal has proposed an economic partition of the family, in front of his elder brother. Even though being a principal earner of the wealth, he did not claim any share for himself. Everything was decided peacefully in such a way that the people could not know about it, even after many years. Shri Mohan Lalji had also full interest in the activities for public welfare. He constructed, spending a lot of money, for a high- class College 'Goyandka Vidyalaya' in Bankura. In Bankura district, colleges of high category were also established at three other places. There is a large river named Dwarkeshwar in the south of Bankura, the people had to face a lot of problems during summer and rainy season, due to absence of a bridge on it. A high-quality bridge was also constructed at the place named Kumarghat from him, by spending a very huge amount of wealth. An organisation of eye donation camp and a sufficient help at the time of famine, etc. remained continued by him.

❐

167

Satsang Session (Assembly of Virtuous People) at the Swargashram

The Uttarakhand has been remaining a place for devotional practice in our country since centuries. Shri Sethji overall had been already arranging the assembly of virtuous people during his visit to several places, but in the sacred land of Rishikesh at Uttarakhand, Shri Sethji has inaugurated there a session for *satsang*. Such programme which had begun from 1921-22 was continued uninterruptedly till now. Each year, Shri Sethji generally stayed here from *Chaitra* to *Asadha* and a group of virtuous people accumulated here, just with sacred devotion and enjoyed divine savour at the bank, adorned with continuous indistinct noise by the stream of the sacred Ganga. After few days, the same organisation started to occur on the other bank of Ganga which is known as Swargashram. It was there a dense forest at that time, only few huts existed to live. At the bank of the Ganga and beneath the shadow of a huge Banyan tree, the flow of divine nectar would flow ceaselessly. Gradually, the number of people coming to attend the the *satsang* (An assembly of virtuous people) has increased. For their convenience and with the efforts and inspiration of Shri Sethji, construction of a huge building – Gita Bhawan was made on this very place at the bank of the Ganga, for the residence of people coming for Satsang. A huge hall was also constructed for the *satsang* and special embankments were also built for the convenience of bathing. During *satsang* an arrangement has also been made for restaurant.

The programme for *satsang* and discourses which begins at 4-4.30 hrs in morning, remain continued up to 10-10.30 hrs. at night. In between, there was a little break available for meal and personal practice for the accomplishment, hymns singing. Shri Sethji also gave discourses five to six times while Bhaijee, Swami Ramsukh Dasji Maharaj, Swami Sharananandji Maharaj, etc. and other saints also arrived and gave discourses due to persuasion of Shri Sethji. In addition to discourses, Shri Sethji also solved the problems of devotees, came for *satsang* by extending an extra time to them, solitarily.

❐

168

An Evaluation of Philosophical Knowledge of Gita

Swami Ramsukh Dasji had altogether met first time to Shri Sethji in 1934 at Churu, due to an inspiration of Shri Gambhirchandji Dujari. But his special inclination had begun during period of *chaturmas* (four months) of spiritual observance in 1936 towards Shri Sethji. In 1936, Swami Chakradharji Maharaj remained visiting Swami Ramsukh Dasji Maharaj in Govind Bhawan at Calcutta. Govind Bhawan, during those days, was situated in the lane of Banstalla area. Once Shri Ramsukh Dasji Maharaj was narrating few letters of Shri Sethji to a devotee. Baba was also listening, as sitting at that very place. It appeared in the mind of Baba, through listening one of such letter that such letter cannot be written without the realisation of his own form (*Swarupanubhuti*). He asked Swamiji – who has written this letter and where does he live? Swamiji said – this letter belongs to Shri Sethji and he lives in Bankura. Baba asked – I want to meet him. Swamiji was pleased that a young ascetic, full of talent, is awakened with respect towards Shri Sethji. He has made all the arrangements and Baba has reached to Bankura. Baba did a lot of discussion with Shri Sethji in solitude and he has got the confirmation of his inference. He has developed more faith for Shri Sethji. Baba had remained continued, exchange of ideas on divine spirit with Shri Sethji for many days. Shri Sethji had to go to *Ranchi* for *satsang* after three-four days. Baba had also accompanied him due to persuasion of Shri Sethji. Mutual exchange of ideas had remained continued there as well. Baba was enchanted by his thinking-evaluation and towards realisation of his own identity by Shri Sethji. Baba realised that the emotions, thinking and the experience which Shri Sethji had for *the Gita*, if these were not put in writing, then world would be deprived of a divine treasure. He has suggested to Shri Sethji – you may put your thoughts related to the Gita, in writing. Shri Sethji asked – who can do and how it will be? I cannot even properly speak or write a correct Hindi. Baba said – if you approve my writing, then I can do such work. One of the expositions on the Gita by Shri Sethji has been put in writing by Baba and shown it to Shri Sethji. Looking at the skillfulness of expression, command on language and proficiency in subject by Baba, Shri Sethji was pleased. And so, for just that reason, it was decided that commentary on the Gita should be written and it was also decided that such work shall begin at Gorakhpur. Shri Sethji had to go somewhere. Therefore, the date of arrival to Gorakhpur was finalised. Baba was given a rail ticket to Gorakhpur. Shri Sethji also asked him, to meet Bhaijee. Baba reached earlier. Therefore, he went to Gita Vatika, residence of Bhaijee, met him and stayed there.

On arrival of Shri Sethji in Gorakhpur, the work for commentary writing on Gita has begun. Firstly, discussion was held for the meaning of a verse of the Gita in a meeting of scholars. Such seminar was set daily. Such meeting consists of Shri Sethji, Swami Ramsukh Dasji Maharaj, respected Baba, younger and scholar brother of Shri Sethji, Shri Harikrishna Dasji, etc. Bhaijee had also been attending it casually. Pandit Shantanu Bihariji Dwivedi had also attended it for some time. The work allotted to Baba was to explain an interpretation by various scholars in the assembly of the verses on Gita. Thereafter, an exchange of ideas was held mutually for the mystery involved in verses. The opinion of Shri Sethji was always given final approval in such sitting of an enigmatic discussion. Baba had put in writing of these thoughts by Shri Sethji. Necessary correction was made by Bhaijee in the written matter. Shri Sethji had just to go generally here and there for *satsang*. Therefore, even during such visits, as well, the people participating in seminar also accompanied him as far as possible. Like this and after with continuous readiness and involvement, this work was concluded in about two-and-a-half years. Conclusion of written work was made in 1939 at Bankura and at that time, Bhaijee was also at that very place. Such spiritual treasure in the life of Shri Sethji was first published in the year 1940 titled – '*Gita-tatvank*' as a special issue of 14th year of '*Kalyan*'. Later on, and with necessary corrections by Shri Sethji, it was published in the form of a text with a name of '*Gita-tatva-vivechani*' by Gita press.

❐

169

The Mediation

Shri Sethji had acquired an external faith from the society, even when he was not an educated person. To solve various disputes of the family, Shri Sethji was assigned their jury, instead to knock the court of law. Shri Sethji had saved lakhs of rupees from wasting them in court and sent both parties by satisfying them. His sufficient time was used for such activities. Not only this, but he had to intervene many times for reputed persons. Once Pandit Madan Mohan Malviya was making special publicity to give spiritual advice for people of outcaste through meetings, books, lectures and articles, etc. Shri Karpatriji Maharaj did its opposition, due to its incongruity with scriptures. A day was decided by both to do doctrinal debate. Such declaration was held at Rishikesh. Two mediators were selected among them – Shri Jaidayal Goyandka and Shri Gauri Shankar Goyandka. This doctrinal debate continued for many days and both persons have remained present. Both eminent people had been trying to prove their opinions with strong arguments and proofs, being scholars of a high category. At last, Gauri Shankar has given his decision in favour of Shri Karpatriji Maharaj. But Shri Sethji has given somewhat such type of decision – "According to the country and society, Malviyaji has accomplished his views due to matured arguments. The opinion of Shri Karpatriji Maharaj is correct from the scriptural point of view." Shri Karpatriji Maharaj became a little angry due to non-declaration of a clear decision. Karpatriji has stopped writing in '*Kalyan*'. But, later, Shri Sethji has made Karpatriji happy again due to his behavioural skillfulness. Karpatriji had himself once said that Shri Sethji and Bhaijee of Gita press have so much cooperated in cow protection movement that I have become very happy and given up opposing in spite of differences. Even being a staunch follower of existing form of old religion (*Sanatandharmi*), in addition to the humanitarian kindness, national interest and social circumstances, he had never been careless for the hospitality to national leaders and saints.

❑

170

Means to Get Rid of the Suffering

When commentary on *Gita-tatva-vivechani* was being written in Bankura, at that time scholars like Bhaijee, Ramsukh Dasji Maharaj, Baba Chakradharji Maharaj, Pandit Shantanu Bihariji Dwivedi and others were present at that very place. During those days, younger son of Mohan Lalji died. Though Mohan Lalji was a younger brother of Shri Sethji, Shri Sethji adopted him as he had no child of his own. Everyone went to funeral ground along with dead body of the child. On return, Shri Sethji was found very restless. Everybody began to console him. They told him – If you become so much sad like this, then what would people think about you? You are such a devotee of the God, people may ask when his grief is not allayed, then how our sorrow would be eliminated by following a divine path. Shri Sethji replied – if anyone from family or outside will come as sad person, then I will be again sad. Therefore, you should all make a promise that no one will be sad, then I will not be restless. Precisely, the same was done and everybody was satisfied. Shri Sethji had also become entirely normal. On the second day, someone asked him in solitude – Had you become really so much sad yesterday? Shri Sethji replied – I had done an acting of a sad person intentionally. Had I not become restless then all members of the family will weep, and wail and I would have tired in convincing them. When I became sad, then everybody would become intelligent and consoled me. Pain of everybody was eliminated due to my grieving only.

There is even an art to eliminate the grief of others which is known only to some eminent people.

❐

171
The Pilgrimage

A pilgrimage train was arranged by Gita press in about year 1938. Every pilgrimage was covered within about three months. Shri Sethji also accompanied in this. His devotion and purity towards quality of food were popular. He was very much careful about the purity of material in food, cleanness of people and utensils. Due to such of his habit, he never accepted food and water even from anywhere, though it may be a divine offering of the God. Such events had occurred many times when he had to fulfill of mutual behaviour and the decorum for remnant of food, offered to an idol. There he, by his behavioural skillfulness of maintaining decorum for remnant of the food offered to an idol, had retained his customary devotion, without causing any pain in the heart of anyone. Once he went to a temple for worship. When he was coming out after having sight of an idol, the priest appeared almost running to give him the foot-nectar. Shri Sethji took it in hand, being it was as a foot-nectar and poured it on the head, instead of drinking. Looking at his such devotion the people accompaniying him became enchanted. Accompanying persons had been encountering many examples of such type to observe fulfillment of devotion.

Due to persuasion of accompanying persons in pilgrimage, Shri Sethji had visited the royal place of Bhavnagar. Though the king was not present there at that time, a complete arrangement was made. The attendants had very much persuaded Shri Sethji for food and drink. Shri Sethji remained telling – then I have just taken meal and not yet hungry. Finally, those people have determined to request him to drink water. Shri Sethji constantly replying, just one thing – I am not hungry. On his return from there, a gentleman asked – those people had been persuading to drink water while you have remained answering 'not hungry'. What is mystery behind it? Shri Sethji explained – I was thirsty at that time, but I did not like to drink water of that place because I had no knowledge of its purity – then how can I say that I am not thirsty. By his skill of speech, he had escaped without hurting the sentiments of those people.

In *Totadri*, the travellers had kept tin boxes, filled with oil in the train by learning the importance of consecrated oil of that place. No price for oil was charged there. On hearing such activity, Shri Sethji has abused everybody and said – it is against thc decorum of food offered to the deity, is an injustice and is dishonesty. Everyone was asked to pay the price and hundreds of rupees had been deposited in the temple. His devotion for justice was an ideal. Though he had asked to give prize to rail employees but had denied bribing. Shri Sethji was not particularly interested in pilgrimage. But his main object was to spread the *satsang*. Shri Sethji had given an exposition at every station and city. Few people had reached in advance for its management. Shri Sethji went to see the great sage Shri Raman and made discussion regarding the meditation. During journey at many places, Shri Sethji had been inviting the scholars of that very place and treated them with due hospitality and paid for other religious services.

❐

172

A Conversation with Shantanu Bihari Dwivedi (Swami Akhandanand)

Shri Shantanu Bihariji Dwivedi, who became famous after renunciation of the world by the name of Swami Akhandanandji, has come live in Gorakhpur with Bhaijee in 1936, being impressed by his articles published in '*Kalyan*'. He has started to work in editorial department of '*Kalyan*'. In addition, he has also begun to take interest in the act of accomplishing – singing hymns (*sadhan-bhajan*). He had already a particular faith in Bhaijee and had very good faith in Shri Sethji as well. He had been discussing with Shri Sethji many times alone, with his due permission.

Once he asked Shri Sethji – who is your mentor? Shri Sethji replied – I treat Swami Mangal Nathji as my mentor. Earlier, I had full faith, but when he got involved in a law suit of cowshed, my faith has reduced a little. My and his principles are the same on the subject related with the unqualified ultimate being (*nirgun*). To realise the all-pervading spirit of universe, the principle of monistic philosophy is necessary. He also showed utmost faith on Shri Shankaracharyaji. When enquired about the reason, Shri Sethji said – the necessary requirement which was emphasised by Shankaracharyaji for the worldly renouncement by relinquishing the work, to achieve the knowledge for the real nature of things (*tatvagyan*), is not acceptable to me. Such was the nature of Shri Sethji that he had never criticised anything from the early Indian scriptures or Sanskrit literature dealing with the aspect of an ancient Indian history nor he had ever refuted them. His style of speech was – such thing has not become clear to me, I am not interested in this thing. He had an extraordinary skill to dissociate himself from any controversy. Whenever he gave an exposition or did an assembly of virtuous people to any place, he had definitely saved time to pray at sunrise, noon and sunset. He had narrated once that since he had accepted investiture of youth with the sacred thread till now (for about fifty years), there has never been any difference for my praying at sunrise, noon and sunset. I had never gone beyond time as far as possible and then question does not arise about transgression of the duty. During his journey in train, he had performed mental prayer at sunrise, noon and sunset and, thereafter, did it in an actual form. Due to non-availability of water, he had to do an offering with the sand. Such an extraordinary fulfilling of his religion shows only his firm devotion.

When Shri Sethji was dictating Gita, Shri Dwivedi also stayed with him at his residence in Bankura for few months. During his time of return, Shri Sethji and his scholar brother Shri Harikrishnadasji asked him – Panditji! There is going to be a marriage function of a girl in your family. Please visit inside our shop for utensils and select and put aside the number of utensils, you may need, we will send with you. The soul of Dwivediji moved with compassion to note their generosity. Though he had not taken much utensils, but his unrestrained heart was overwhelmed due to their generosity.

Shri Dwivediji heard few things about the earlier births of Shri Sethji, which he has not believed fully. He asked one day to Shri Sethji in alone – many things are said on your name, about your earlier birth. Have you ever told about your earlier birth to anyone? Shri Sethji replied – henceforth, I had said such things about twenty-thirty years ago. He asked – do you still remember your earlier birth? Shri Sethji replied affirmatively – Yes. He said – if you wish, then you can also know about your earlier birth. He then asked – how can it be? Shri Sethji replied – **During continuous renouncing of false understanding, hatred and love, absence of pride and the attachment, an account of birth is manifested, please control yourself according to such an aphorism of Yoga. The truth is manifested in a non-passionate wisdom**. I had hold of such thing in mind sometime. Then I had sudden blaze of the earlier birth. But Shri Sethji had never encouraged to discuss about birth – another birth. But, had always been encouraging to worship the Supreme Being having qualities (*sagun*) – without qualities (*nirgun*). Shri Sethji was opposite to worship of a person. He believed no saint-sage should be worshipped by anyone. To take photographs, to distribute tasted remnants of food, to meet the woman in solitude or to be appreciated themselves had never been appreciated by him (Shri Sethji) for any saint. He was so firm in this direction that he had said without shyness in solitude and also during public meeting to various eminent saints that they should not behave like this. Conflicting events also became evident sometimes due to such type of arguments, but he remained firm in his principles. Once Shri Karpatriji Maharaj had difference of opinion with Shri Sethji during discussion on the early Indian scriptures (*Vedanta*). That difference of opinion was in relation to the behaviour by one who knows the real nature of things (*Tatvagyan*). Shri Sethji was of the opinion – one should be considered as a saint of philosophical knowledge (*Tatvagyan*) whose behaviour can be followed and is an ideal for others. He had a firm faith that a true scholar can never act against scriptures.

Once there was a Kumbh fair at Haridwar. Gita press also installed its book stall, in it. Due to fire in the fair, the stall of Gita press was also burnt to ashes. As the stall was insured, therefore, full amount was refunded. When it was known to Shri Sethji, he has checked full account and instructed to return the money to the insurance company for the books which had been sold out. His instructions were followed. He declared that if the business is carried on with a feeling to serve the God and with honesty, then even a salvation can be achieved by that. He told once being under delight – Swamiji! Many people have some or other type of hobbies. My subject of interest is the assembly of virtuous people (*satsang*). Otherwise why should I have involved in such type of activities? I have been investing also something or the other for this and also spent time.

❑

173
Publication of *Bhagwatank*

Such thinking was gaining strength after the publication of special issue on the *Gita* and the *Ram Charit Manas* by *'Kalyan'* that a special number should also be published for the *Shrimad Bhagwat Mahapuran*. Shri Sethji was very much aware about the importance of the *Shrimad Bhagwat*, but he was a staunch and customary saint. He had an apprehension that crude elements of the society may create senseless environment in the society by misinterpretation of *'Raspanchadhyayi'*. To become trustworthy only, on the criteria of public compilation, he had a plan to publish any section of the text. Due to an inspiration of feeling for public compilation, he had a desire to publish a special number on *Bhagwat,* but it should not contain five chapters dealing with *Shri Maharaas* from the tenth part of this text.

On this topic, Bhaijee had difference of opinion with Shri Sethji. Bhaijee had strong faith and firm opinion that five chapters of Shri *Raspanchadhyayi* are the five breaths of the *Bhagwat*. What authority we have to make any suspicion on the speech of Lord *Vyas*? *In conclusion of Raspanchadhyayi, it is clearly revealed as a consequence that it destroys a heart disease. Shrimad Bhagwat* may not be published, but if it is, then it must contain five chapters. He had remained neutral after expressing his belief. His mode of alienation was strong during those days. Therefore, in September 1939, he went to Dadri with the permission of Shri Sethji for a seclusion. He proceeded further to Ratangarh after staying three months at Dadri. Shri Sethji had observed that editing and publication of '*Kalyan*' are not possible without Bhaijee. Therefore, he visited Gita Vatika one day and instructed to all senior workers of editorial department – you all should go from here to Ratangarh and bring Hanuman back to this place. If it is not possible to do it, then you can all stay there so that the editorial work of '*Kalyan*' may be managed from there itself. The entire editorial department has gone to Ratangarh after such statement by Shri Sethji and everyone had stayed there for five years. In 1940, special number of '*Kalyan*' – *'Sadhanank'* was published. The society was eagerly waiting for *'Bhagwatank'* and Shri Sethji was well aware of such thing. An annual function was held of Rishikul at Churu in 1940 for which Shri Sethji had already been attending it as far as possible. Then Shri Sethji went thereafter to Ratangarh. On meeting Bhaijee, he told in Marwari language in front of all senior members of department – Hanuman! In some way, I am lost, and you have won over! Now publish this *Bhagwatank*. Shri Sethji also said that you should also definitely give an extensive remark from your end, about the act of great round dance of Krishna with herd girls of Braj and also towards act of stealing and taking away the clothes. Shri Sethji had gone after permitting him. Only three-four months were left. To translate the great work, containing eighteen thousand verses, collection of necessary articles, preparation of pictures and then to publish special number with eleven hundred pages on time within this short interval is a strong proof of strength by Bhaijee. Such a voluminous special number had never been published earlier or thereafter. According to the instructions of Shri Sethji, Bhaijee himself also wrote in addition to editing the extensive articles in the form of a commentary on the act of butter stealing and an act of great round dance of Krishna with the herd girls of Braj and also about an act of stealing and taking away the clothes which would be providing a great illumination to the devotees for ages.

❐

174

An Industriousness

Though being a saint devoted to all-pervading spirit of the universe, the industriousness of Shri Sethji was an extraordinary. Such an industriousness is not generally found in a saint, devoted to all-pervading spirit of the universe. Not only in his youth but he was found to work for sixteen hours even after age of seventy years. He got up at 4 o'clock in the morning and spent only two hours in his physical activities and preparation of meal, etc., while rest of the time he was carefully attending to work irrespective his presence during journey or his movements in Bankura. In addition to his daily routine of worship, he was involved to arrange an assembly of virtuous people, to talk with devotees in solitude, to arrange articles and to reply the pending letters. Almost 25-30 letters were received daily. To solve the disputes by arranging a village council, to advice close associates etc., he never slept prior to 10 o'clock at night, due to his involvement in an unlimited number of activities. If devotees arrived during night for discussion, then he would remain continued to discuss with them, irrespective of any care to sleep. He was also found to discuss even up to 1-2 o'clock at night. There was not an ignorance in day, no laziness, no weakness and no indifference. It appeared that he was long-lasting alert, constantly careful. If it can be expressed in one word, then he was a living idol of Gita, was precisely a bodily incarnation of Gita. According to the Gita, such an example of life is definitely rare in the history of Indian culture and practice.

❐

175

An Account of Special Influence

Such an occasion occurred near about in 1943. Respected Shri Sethji had arrived at Gorakhpur prior to few days of *Shri Gita Jayanti*. He had stayed at the residence of Shri Ghanshyam Dasji Jalan. Near about 4th-5th of *Shuklapaksh* of *Margashirsha*, the chief workers of Gita press were talking to Shri Sethji, just at the residence of Shri Ghanshyam Dasji. Shri Sethji told in front of all the affectionate persons that an exhibition of the Gita should be decorated this time in a very good manner on the occasion of Gita Jayanti.

On this, Shri Shukdevji said that Ganga Babu is now proceeding to *Chitrakoot,* then who will decorate the exhibition in such a beautiful manner? Thereafter, Pandit Ladhuramji expressed his dissatisfaction about the allotment of work given to his son Narayan Prasad in the examination committee of *Gita-Ramayan*. Then Badri Prasadji Acharya also expressed his displeasure. Shri Sethji had been listening to all such things silently for some time.

A little later, sitting carefully in a heroic posture, Shri Sethji said that you people have worked with me since many years, have also served *Gita press*, what you people have been thinking about me until now?

1. I am an all-powerful to those who consider me all-powerful.
2. I know the inner thoughts of those who consider me a Supreme Being.
3. I am omniscient to those who consider me as omniscient. I had to take some service for this world from you people. Therefore, I do not permit to develop such faith, otherwise there cannot be any delay even for a moment to accomplish such an implicit confidence.

❐

176

Words for Special Achievement

Once the assembly of virtuous people was held underneath a Banyan tree at the bank of the Ganga in Swargashram. Shri Sethji said – I will tell you all such things in which you have to do nothing, and you would achieve salvation. People have begun to hear with much curiosity that what can be such a thing in which nothing is expected to do, and the salvation is achieved. Shri Sethji said that the thing is this that you should always be happy. Then he asked himself that you people may ask that with which thing one can remain happy? Then that thing is this that you people have so much grace of the God which you cannot even imagine. You should believe it, on this thing, due to my statement and remain always happy by remembering such things.

On other occasion while arranging an assembly of virtuous people below that very Banyan tree, he said – You people, showing grace to me, should decide for one thing that now no more birth of you should occur. Whosoever will opt for such a pledge, he shall never be born again. But if someone will be suspicious that he may or may not get another birth, then it is doubtful in his case.

❐

177

Eye Surgery

Since many days, there was planning about an eye operation for Shri Sethji due to sufficient problem of vision. Finally, in consultation with Shri Sethji, it was decided to operate by an eye specialist at Bhiwani – Bhaijee also accompanied with Shri Sethji from Gorakhpur to Bhiwani on *Phalgun*, *Shukla* 11, in *Vikramaditya* year 2005. Shri Sethji had made an exposition in way through Delhi against Hindu-code-bill. In the presence of Bhaijee, Shri Sethji was operated for eyes at Bhiwani.

❐

178

A Marriage of the Grandson

Marriage of Shri Madhav, the only son of Shri Mohan Lal – and an adopted son of Shri Sethji, was decided to be held on *Shukla* 15, *Chaitra* of *Vikramaditya year* in 2008 with Gayatri daughter of Shri Shriniwasji Bubna. Due to occurrence of marriage ceremony of his grandson after a long time, several people have arrived from distant places to Bankura. Bhaijee and other saints have also arrived. A large group for an assembly of virtuous people has arrived from Calcutta. The sight of marriage group was very pleasing to mind. During departure of marriage party, Shri Dungarmalji Lohia had been managing group singing of hymns (*Sankeertan*) alongwith dancing in front of Shri Sethji and Bhaijee. The marriage party has reached at the site of marriage, just with group singing of hymns. Most of the people have remained there during night due to an occurrence of the auspicious moment after midnight.

❑

179

A Service to Famine-Affected People at Gorakhpur

A relief work was conducted generally from *Gita press* in Gorakhpur area during the time of flood and famine. In 1952, there occurred an aweful famine in Gorakhpur region. Shri Sethji was also there during that period. Therefore, he himself served the famine-affected by his hands with grains and clothes along with Bhaijee, moving through different places in a jeep. The volunteers used to get highly elated due to the presence of Shri Sethji. Like this as well, Shri Sethji had been always helping the petitioners at various occasions.

❐

180

The Traditional Devotion and a Sharp Pain in Stomach

When Shri Sethji was in Gorakhpur in 1952, he became sick once with severe pain in the stomach. Customary faith of Shri Sethji was very harsh. He never utilised medicines from another method of treatment except the ayurvedic medicines, throughout his life. He used only those medicines among ayurvedic medicines which do not contain any impure objects. He had considered decoction group of medicines as impure. Several treatments were given under the guidance of local ayurvedic doctors, but sharp pain was not cured, that had remained aggravating. His physical state has become serious. All his close friends began to worry. Although Shri Sethji had never took allopathic medicines, but some of his intimate friends had called local civil surgeon Captain Rajendra Prasad to cure his illness. Captain Rajendra Prasadji was considered as a very famous doctor. He had thoroughly examined him and had become worried due to increasing pain of stomach. He told his relatives – Shri Sethji should be given allopathic medicines and injections, otherwise his life can be in danger. The relatives expressed their complete helplessness to pressurise him for allopathic medicines, explaining a customary faith of Shri Sethji. Civil surgeon was fully aware of seriousness of his condition. He never preferred to put the life of a saint in danger in the name of customary faith. He went to Shri Sethji and told him in serious tone – Maharaj, you are very intelligent. I can promise that you will not be given any impure object by me. Please accept my medicines. The pain is strong and is being further increasing. Anything can occur due to non-acceptance of proper medicines. Shri Sethji listened to his good advice and replied in a normal manner – Doctor Sahib, nothing will happen more than death by refusing for allopathic medicines. I have already decided up to that extent. Tell me if something can occur more than this. Doctor was surprised to note his such firmness. But Bhaijee had silently arranged a rite by sincere people towards his recovery of health, due to which Shri Sethji had received a prompt benefit in his health.

❐

181

The Construction of New Building for 'Govind Bhawan'

Since 'Govind Bhawan' was established in Calcutta, till then its work was managed in a rented house at Banstalla Lane. Its front portion was used as a shop for shoes sans leather and glass bangles, medicines and books. In due course of time, this place had become insufficient by all means. The work field had been increased and the hall was also not sufficient for an assembly of virtuous people. An exchange of ideas had remained getting on, for a new building for years. Thereafter, a land was purchased for the construction of a new building at Mahatma Gandhi Road by the permission of Shri Sethji. The work of foundation was conducted in *Magh* of *Vikramaditya* year in 2016 (in the year 1959) by the hands of Bhaijee in scriptural manner. A three- storyed building was constructed there after some time.

❐

182

Death of His Wife

The wife of Shri Sethji was also religious, simple and a follower of marital fidelity. In the beginning, when condition of home was normal, then he had prepared meal by herself to the people coming for an assembly of virtuous people. She had always cooperated in publicity of *satsang* by her body and mind to Shri Sethji and never created any problem. She had remained engaged in several activities to serve Shri Sethji by her own hands. In 1960, at about 6 o'clock in the morning after bath, etc. in Bankura during counting beads of string to perform devotion, her blood pressure had raised one day suddenly. Thereafter, she was conscious for about an hour and had lost external senses later. A vomiting of blood occurred between 11 and 2 o'clock in afternoon. Thereafter, the body had become calm by lack of breath. Group- singing of hymns of Lord Narayan was constantly ongoing, outside. Shri Sethji was himself present there. All the formalities related to last rite had been performed by Shri Mohan Lalji.

❐

183

Shri Ghanshyam Dasji Jalan

Shri Ghanshyam Dasji Jalan was an unique devotee, secretary, friend, companion and an unusual follower of Shri Sethji. He was just a counterpart of self-dedication, such an exquisite beauty of dedication cannot be found. He was born in 1891. His father's name was Shri Prithvirajji while mother's name was Smt. Hardei Bai. His ancestors were basically the residents near Ratangarh city of Rajasthan. He had been bestowed an instinct of religious devotion, as paternal inheritance. He had not obtained any type of institutional education. His knowledge was achieved with the deep experiences of life and from the assembly of virtuous people (*satsang*). His business was in Gorakhpur. He was considered to be incomparable in business field for his skill of accounts. Such an expertise is proved later as treasure for Gita press. He was married in 1906 with Smt. Vasanti Devi. At the age of about 20 years, he met Shri Sethji in Churu. The beginning of such an introduction began due to company of saints from Nath-sect. Such a contact has become gradually changed to an intimacy. Due to him, only the Gita press was established in Gorakhpur. He had managed the work related with Gita press with full devotion. How much paper, thread and how much labour would be involved in a particular book – he had maintained a proper account of this. Things about stock of paper, stock of special issues of '*Kalyan*' and the book, etc. were always known to him by heart. His contribution in attainment of books for cheap price was excellent. Due to such type of his expertise, he had remained a printer, publisher of Gita press in addition to be a trustee throughout his life. Being a well-wisher of the workers of Press, he had also been managing the service activities with an interest. It had appeared that an energy of work from Shri Sethji has flashed into him suddenly with brilliance.

During an all-India pilgrimage, he had concluded such rite of Shri Sethji with devotion, by his sick and frail body with age and suffering with 104° fever and cough, etc. His name will be found written in golden letters not only in the history of Gita press but also in visualisation of all the promises and tendencies by Shri Sethji. He spent most of his time generally with Shri Sethji, during late years. He used to cooperate in the activities of Shri Sethji as far as possible, even though being an unhealthy person. On 6th day of *Shukla* of *Jyeshtha* in *Vikramaditya* year in 2015 in Swargashram, Rishikesh, he had renounced his body of five elements, during celebration of devotional songs among the sacred presence of Bhaijee and Shri Sethji, at the bank of *Ganga* in *Gita Bhawan*.

❒

184

Guidance to the Devotees

Shri Sethji used to guide a path to spiritual devotees-investigators for about sixty years. Guidance through letters, the assembly of virtuous people and discourses had begun right at a very young age. He had been replying to each and every letter by devotees. Shri Sethji would also resolve normally to every curiosity. Later on, one-and-a- half to two hours were spent daily, for dictation of the letters. During the exposition, he also resolved the question from devotees collectively. If a devotee wanted solution in seclusion, then he satisfied him by meeting in solitude. Such practice had remained continued uninterruptedly, irrespective of his presence at any place. Thousands of devotees have tried to proceed further towards their goal by obtaining a solution from him. Shri Sethji never showed any irritation irrespective of the quality of question by anyone, but rather satisfied them with pleasant reply.

❑

185

An Ultimate Departure

Shri Sethji was the best public collector and householder of the undivided tradition for practice and Indian culture. Every breath of life, each corpuscle of the body was illuminated and scented by the melody of *Lord Vasudev,* i.e., *the Gita*. Whatever is in the extensive field of practice and whichever is truth, auspicious and beautiful, it is exhibited through his life by assimilating it. Scriptural thinking did not became thinking only but that became an impeccable part of his life. If his body would permit even a little, he used to remain engaged to inseminate the essence of the Gita to the people, to divert their life towards the God. Whenever any devotee or enquirer reached to him, he begins to inseminate him with immortal mandate irrespective of care towards his health.

Gradually, his body has given up. Since 1954, he had begun to be sick. Even after proper treatment, instead of an improvement, his health just continued to deteriorate. Assembly of virtuous people and discourses have also become gradually decreased. The journey also ended. Once he went to *Bankura* from Varanasi and then returned. During such condition of body, his younger brother and adopted son Mohan Lalji was sent to *Midnapore* prison on 23rd September, 1964 without any fault, utilising only punitive measures by the Government. Retaining there for about one month, the government transferred him in Presidency prison of Calcutta. He was very sad due to deprivation of services to Shri Sethji in sick condition, but Shri Sethji had retained of that very happiness on his face.

Since March 1965, it appeared that mortal body of Shri Sethji would not last long. Therefore, he was brought according to his wish from Bankura to Gita-Bhawan situated at the bank of the Ganga in Swargashram. Even under such condition, he had narrated about an act of achievement for the assembly of virtuous people, while proceeding to Swargashram to the people who have come to meet him from Lucknow. He has advised them to do repetition of divine name in low tone, daily and continuously with a desireless feeling along with faith and also to meditate on the idol of the God. Narrated such methods that if followed daily and faithfully with desireless feeling can bestow the God within twelve months.

Shri Sethji reached Gita Bhawan, Swargashram on 31st March, 1965. On the receipt of an information, Bhaijee also reached on 6th April. Close relatives and people related with the assembly of virtuous people also began to reach in abundant quantity and a lot of people have come up at the last. The condition of his body was worsening day by day. With great efforts, Mohan Lalji was released from prison on 7th April, 1965 and reached directly to Swargashram via Delhi. Shri Sethji had listened to letters and remained dictating their reply up to five days prior to his death. Power of speech had decreased and there was an aweful pain in the head, back and stomach, nevertheless, he remained talking slowly and had raised a matter of spiritual instruction. There was a proper facility to the people coming to have a sight of him. Although his eyesight had become weak, even then he had announced to inform the name of people who had come to visit him. He prayed daily at sunrise, noon and sunset and also offered water in front of the Sun. Repetition of divine name in slow tone used to continue till his last breath. Protection of rules for good conduct, etc. continued uninterruptedly till the last hour.

Shri Sethji asked Bhaijee to guide him to meditate during night of 16th April. In the beginning, he could not understand but after receiving the hint, he has pronounced '*Anand-Tatva*' a favourite of Shri Sethji, alongwith the adjectives. He listened, it again and again and became highly pleased. Immediately thereafter again received same hint, then Bhaijee again narrated words for '*Anand-tatva*' several times, then also narrated some revelations, indicated in monistic all-pervading spirit of the universe. *(Adwetya Brahmbodhak)* and explained him his own eternally true nature of all-pervading spirit of the universe *(Brahmswaroop)*. At the time when Bhaijee was narrating him, that time waves of ecstasy can be seen on the face of Shri Sethji. He was extremely happy. Though he was lying, he wanted to embrace Bhaije by pulling and putting his hands around his neck. He told slowly in delighted tone, articulated from emotions, after listening to everything – 'it is alright, it is alright. Everything is just the all-pervading spirit of the universe (*Brahma*). Is is just, the all-pervading spirit of the universe (*Brahma*). Nothing else is there. It is a bliss, just the bliss'.

He was laid in verandah outside the room during day on 17th April so that everyone sitting can have a sight of him uninterruptedly. People related to the assembly of virtuous people remained celebrating devotional songs (*sankeertan*) sitting all around in large numbers. On the bank of the sacred Ganga in Gita Bhawan at 4 o'clock on 17th April, 1965, Shri Sethji has immersed with the all-pervading spirit of the universe (*Brahmaleen*), by renouncing his physical body. His mortal body was met with funeral ceremonies on the bank of the Ganga, in front of his favourite Banyan tree. According to his principle, no mark or symbol was left at that place.

* * * * * *

In the words of Swami Shri Shivanand – 'Whatever has been performed for the revival of Hindu religion, by Shri Sethji, if its comparison is made with the great *Vedvyas,* then there is no exaggeration in it'.

(*Yog-Vedant*, May 1965)

185a :An Expression of Strong Feeling by Bhaijee

Basic founder, manager and life-giver of Gita press, Shri Jaidayalji Goyandka was an emancipated person, was a great saint. Therefore, there was no harm for him due to destruction of physical body. He was just situated in his own form and is just present even now, but an ultimate benefit, which was receiving uninterruptedly to countless people by his behaviour, movement, by his personal instructions and by his religious observance for a long period, that will now be no more available. Though there is not at all any need to express grief or sorrow for him, for us who are deprived of his spiritual instructions, it is a very big loss to us and there is also an aweful pain due to this reason.

He did not accept only allopathic medicines but also rejected those ayurvedic medicines which may contain even some impure objects, even during his most terrible pain. His customs of eating remain unaltered. He was an ideal of good conduct. During his long age of eighty years, a service beyond description, which he did to the God by publishing of views for the cow protection and service to welfare of living beings, etc., service to poor, knowledge, to work without expectation as directed by Gita, religious devotion, spiritual element, existing form of old religion as composed by sages and Indian culture throughout his life, that is entirely an ideal and is never to be forgotten. An importance of religious devotion in practice, desireless and disinterested performance of one's proper deed in principle and monistic devotion in all-pervading spirit of the universe (*Adwetya brahmnishtha*) as the element of own form (*Swaroop tatva*) was established in his life. He did not only publish it, but also experienced and accomplished himself as well. He was a great man and free from future birth.

Now, we should all obtain benefit from his established behaviour of his life by imprinting it, in our life and also from invaluable spiritual and religious literature which he gave to us. This would be an ultimate service to him, would be his real memorial, would be a property suitable with some request, in lieu of his infinite kindness.

❐

186

View of Scholars and Blessings by the Saints from the Abridged Edition of the Book

(1)

Received a book on short biography of respected Bhaijee Hanuman Prasad Poddarji. This biography of Bhaijee is a form of support to any traveller for an auspicious path. With how much devotion Bhaijee moved further on the path of achievement, how he could transform his life in divine form, some of its imagination can be made by this biography. Bhaijee has made the whole India as his debtor, through the medium of '*Kalyan*'. An authentic publication of religious texts which he published for a little price that cannot be compared. I applause for such a beneficial work.

—Dr. Vishnukant Shastri
Governor, Himachal Pradesh

(2)

I pray to such Hanuman Prasad whose heart is filled by dalliance and dance of Radha Krishna along with the herd-girls of Braj.

I have read many texts related with biography, about the heavenly departed soul (*Nitya leelaleen*) Bhaijee Hanuman Prasad Poddar, but the pleasure which I have received by this text 'An introduction to Bhaijee' due to its undoubtful authenticity and with a point of view for the inauguration of significant element (*sar tatva*), of just that type, cannot be found anywhere else.

—Dr. Vishwambhar Sharan Pathak
Vice Chancellor (Retired), Gorakhpur University

(3)

Respected Bhaijee Shri Hanuman Prasad Poddar was a great, divine spiritual divinity. Shri Shyam Sundarji Dujari is also one of those people who had got an opportunity, to be in his vicinity. He has observed Bhaijee with an extreme proximity and took an inspiration from his divine life. His book – *Bhaijee – An Introduction,* based on the facts of the life of Bhaijee, collected by his father, delivered the work and personality of Bhaijee in an extremely effective manner. A lucid account can easily be found on every aspect for the life of Bhaijee by reading this book. Few topics are so much impressive that even the irritated and worried mind has also satisfied with delight instantly. Such an authentic biography is not available elsewhere. To obtain a book '*Sadhan-Path*' written by Bhaijee in dream from a saint by Shri Deshpande and to find that book at his bed on awakening, an instant cure of tuberculosis in vertebral column of a boy on his joining to an unrestrained celebration of devotional songs, etc. during Radhashtami, there are many such events, which are capable to initiate faith in faithless people as we'l. Like this, an expression of strong feelings about Bhaijee by respected Radha Baba is extremely impressive. I believe that this book is extremely initiator and guide, not only to those interested in spiritualism, but also to general public. I hope that people would definitely be benefitted by it.

—**Shri Shiv Kumar Goyal,** Senior Journalist
Editor – '*Agrohadham*', '*Godhan*'
Awarded Shri Hanuman Prasad Poddar
National Service Certificate

(4)

On looking at the complete text titled '*A Brief Biography of Bhaijee Hanuman Prasad Poddar*', I have reached to this conclusion that it is a unique work in relation to attainment and philosophy of life, act of achievement and biography of saint Bhaijee who was successful in evocation to savour (*Ras-sidha*). This much can be said about this subject that it did not occur in the past nor it would occur in future as well.

To throw light on such a work about philosophy of life for a unique scholar of India like Shri Bhaijee, the whole country will always be remaining indebted towards the composer.

With such a unique skill and profound skill, it was displayed by the composer on the attainment and philosophy of life, his lifestyle and his practice on every aspect of life of Bhaijee, that should be praised. It is a unique and worth collecting text for devotees and the scholars. The composer has obtained gems of feeling by entering in the mine for precious stones with sacred perceptions of bliss, by diving in the moments of sacred memory of Shri Bhaijee, only with that very intention that other people should also accomplish a purpose in their life by achieving them.

In composing of this work, the composer showed an introduction of the power of self-perception, going on in his own mind by his powerful pen and such scripture is not only the creation for the sake of scholars only, being away from the narrow line of farsightedness, but also a divine light attained by spiritual links from the dive made in depth of the inner achievement. To work with a lamp of such divine world, a vigilant effort which the composer has done to throw light on philosophy of life and complete biography of Shri

Bhaijee, due to that very only, the mystery of travel for mysterious inner path by Shri Bhaijee has been disclosed, otherwise it was not possible.

For such an excellent work produced by the glorious pen of composer, the forehead is bowed involuntarily, unto the holy feet.

—Dr. Shyamakant Dwivedi,
'Anand' M.A. (Hindi, Sanskrit, Philosophy)
Ph.D., D.Litt., Scholar in literature

(5)

I read the biography of Bhaijee Shri Hanuman Prasad Poddar, written by Shri Shyam Sundar Dujari, from beginning to the end. He showed skill like 'an ocean in a pot', in few pages only. I was very fortunate that I have also came in close contact of Bhaijee. He was synonyms of Gita press.

In this book, Shri Dujariji has provided light in a very beautiful and impressive manner, on every important aspect of his glorious personality and divine work. In addition, writing is so much impressive that it is not possible to stay in between, once you have begun to read this book. I also congratulate Dujariji for writing this book and also insist readers to read this book at least once. They would definitely get divine inspiration by this.

—Yashpal Jain
Secretary, Society for Low Cost Literature, New Delhi

(6)

Shri Dujariji has compiled the biography of Bhaijee based on various events. Such biography consisting of his life and acts is inspiring as well as interesting, coupled with authentic information. By reading such biography, a religious feeling and a normal mode of life for beneficence would be evoked in the mind of a reader. It is a very interesting book. I congratulate the author for such an auspicious work.

—Dr. Vijyendra Snatak, Delhi
Head, Department of Hindi,
Delhi University, Delhi

(7)

I received the book which provides a brief introduction for the biography of a person, Shri Bhaijee, who should be worth remembering daily in the morning. I have considered it to be your sympathy and divine grace on me. I have read the matter given in it, twice, which has impressed and motivated me abundantly. It appeared that his divine personality has casted a shadow on my mind and brain. To hear or read about such divine dominion is like to dive in an ocean of bliss through the mind. In my opinion, Bhaijee became a second important incarnate person after Goswami Tulsidas, who did such a rare work for religion and culture which appears totally impossible by any single person. He had an undivided feeling with Shri Radha Krishna, and Shri Radha Baba also confirmed this fact by his perceptions and philosophy. He made a unique contribution in the field of literature, socicty and spiritualism. He is a source of inspiration of past, present and future and is a light house as well.

This book has presented a good exhibition of his great life. I found this book as entirely useful. I wish that it should be read more by religious public.

—Lallan Prasad Vyas
Editor – '*World Hindu Philosophy*'
Convener, International Ramayan Society

(8)

By compilation-assembly of a socially useful, beneficial for life and an extremely inspiring book like '*An Introduction to Bhaijee*', you have definitely done a praiseworthy work for well-being of public. Such a spiritual pleasure achieved through reading this book at every moment, such an inspirational perception remains continued if the mind is delightingly-wandering in some inexpressible world of bliss away from the physical surface and a transmission is being accomplished with a new uplifter of power. I have become so much overwhelmed in such condition of mental process that due to excess of emotions, stream of tears flowed ceaselessly at several passages. The mind has become pure, peaceful and calm. Your respected father Shri Gambhichandji Dujari has done a great beneficence to devotee, being a witness for practice (*sadhna*) by Bhaijee that he remained continuously put in writing the description based on gradual perception of the steps for practice by Bhaijee. He should be greeted respectfully, he is a lucky person.

A biography of his mentor with long-standing devotion of Bhaijee who was also a great ascetic, Shri Jaidayalji Goyandka caused the mind to be liberal. The description about his spiritual achievement is just, very miraculous. You have also mentioned about other devotees and writers related with Gita press. Description about him, various aspects in the life of Bhaijee, his talent in literary composition of verse, renouncement of worldly pleasure and sacrifice, etc. like many such unlimited things are there which are source of inspiration for us.

In how many words should I express thanks and show my gratitude?

O brother! You have made me aware about
the sacred philosophy of ***Bhaijee****.*
Bhaijee has given a gift of an essence of
spiritualism to this world,
By which, a publicity of Hindu religion
and culture is manifested.

—Dr. Virendra Sharma
Ph.D., Scholar of Literature,
Ex-Ambassador in Turkmenistan, New Delhi

(9)

There was an extreme need of such a book. The biographies of venerable persons are themselves very enlightening. It contains many such useful elements which can be of extreme benefit to the new generation. The character of Bhaijee himself was stimulator and brilliant like a lamp. He never made any publicity of himself. Many friends are also being benefitted by this book.

—Dr. Ramcharan Mahendra
Retd. Principal, Govt. College, Kota

(10)

I believe that literature of Gita press, which is an inexplicable contribution by Bhaijee for the spiritual path and is providing a true inspiration to living beings, the same would also be provided by his pure character. His character is such a light house to those living beings who have devastated from the real path and which would have remained and continuously guiding them.

—Awadh Bihari Lal Kapoor
Vrindavan

(10)

You have collected many important things of his life as corrected form in this book. You have done a great work of beneficence. I am thinking over each word by reading it with great interest in a secluded place.

—Shri Krishna Gopal Mathur
Litterateur, Journalist, Ujjain

(11)

The life of Poddarji was an ideal life of a person dedicated to the society, religion and literature. The present book provides light and insight in simple Hindi language towards his services for literature, religion, society and the country, which would remain providing divine inspiration to readers.

—Dr. Amba Prasad 'Suman'
D.Litt., *Sahityavachaspati*
U.G.C. Professor (Retd.), Saharanpur

(12)

Such text, manifesting various aspects of changeless and immortal Bhaijee, a resident of heaven and who has already given up honour and prizes, has also just affected this phrase 'an ocean in a pot'– in addition, also gives stimulus to follow the ideal properties of that divinely rare personality. Heartiest greetings and an applause for publishing such rare text.

—Dr. Ved Prakash Shastri
Ph.D., D. Litt., Hyderabad

(13)

I have read complete book with great attachment. I have not seen any such book till today, with which words I can thank you, there are no words.

Such is the event of Ms. Chinmaya Devi, which I had never read nor there is any hope to read in future.

—Dr. Hansraj
Gita Bhawan, *Swargashram (Rishikesh)*

(14)

I have completely read the biography of respected Bhaijee. It was very pleasing to me. Such book would promote the feelings of service to those who are engaged in service and feelings of religious devotion, to those who are follower of the path for religious devotion. Swami Shri Sanatan Devji has also read the complete book. He also liked it very much. Your effort is praiseworthy.

—Swami Shankaranand Saraswati
Parmarth-Niketan, Swargashram

(15)

In a book for brief biography of Bhaijee, a tasteful evaluation has been made of some parts of biography of Bhaijee, which is genuine, instructive and furthering the heart. Dujariji has made a praiseworthy attempt to fill 'an ocean in a pot'. The divine devotees who have occurred in recent past and whom, most of us have seen, if their actual character can be found in the book, then it does a lot of welfare to the people because faith-devotion are just in shortfall in the positivism age of today. People don't believe without actual proof and the faith also does not occur without trust. Therefore, when there is no actual observer at present of great devotees, people will not believe on his biography but if actual observers are alive of some great devotees, then question does not arise for disbelief, on their biographies. Distrustful person can verify the biography of great devotees from the actual observers. The devotees and audiences for the character portrayal of proposed book, Bhaijee Shri Hanuman prasad Poddar which is connected with them by great ascetic love, and are thousands in number, are still living. These are just its proof. Publicity of such book is very useful from the point of view for public welfare. Shri Dujariji is the proper person for gratitude and applause.

—Shri Tarinish Jha
Society for Hindi Literature, Allahabad

(16)

Publication of brief biography of Bhaijee is very important because it has made the entire life and work of that literature, religion and religious devotion of the great scholar easily available in totality for a very little price. As respected Bhaijee made the famous text of Hindu religion easily available to public, just like that you have given a shape to that personality which had already discarded his fame and pride, through this book. Your book has a great utility. I hope people would be benefitted by it.

—Tapeshwar Nath, Ph.D., D. Litt.
HOD, Department of Hindi,
Bhagalpur University

(17)

Received the book on brief biography of Shri Bhaijee. I have read it from beginning to end. I can definitely pronounce that whosever will read it, from beginning to end, he may be an atheistic, he could not escape himself undoubtedly once, without presenting respectful greetings unto the holy feet of great Vaishnav Shri Bhaijee. The topics related to divine company and divine visualisation of Shri Bhaijee presented in the book have stirred the ideals, experiences, true facts of life in such a way and provided sweetness, by reviving the light of hope during moments of disappointment. Taking them altogether and from every point, the book is useful and worth collecting. Shri Dujariji is definitely a proper person to be congratulated for providing such a worthy literature for a very little price.

—Prof. Umakant 'Kapidhwaj'
M.A., Ph.D., Kavyaratna

(18)

I have got an opportunity to read '*An Introduction to Bhaijee*' composed by respected Shri Shyam Sunder Dujari – an entirely devoted and inner resident of Gita Vatika. In fact, such is the personality of the eternally immersed within the act of deity (*Nityalilaleen*), an eminent devotee 'Bhaijee' Shri Hanuman Prasad Poddar, to which every Hindu considered it necessary to know about him and any Indian can vouch himself only as a true Indian if he is aware of his contribution and services. Even then, with such a devotion Shri Dujariji has installed the memory of Bhaijee, in the mental status of religious people that it appeared that Shri Dujariji has done the work of an extremely auspicious nature. The reason is clear. In the heart of people who are installed with rare qualities, can only obtain self-knowledge and divine achievement, being away from quarrelling and flaws. A graceful character of a saint from an ascetic era like Bhaijee would always provide a good stimulus to the thinking of people, in every time and country. It is our duty to publish such noble literature, which can preserve the value of Indian livelihood and provide an encouragement to the forthcoming generation.

The guidance and experiences of the honourable Bhaijee should be published for which he was noble-minded.

Shri Dujariji has got an extraordinary success in achieving the introduction of noble-minded, through his praiseworthy writing. I request to the Supreme Lord that the pledge of Bhaijee should be the main reason of social harmony, by becoming an alternative of the society and the writing of indifferent saints like Shri Dujariji may conduct the artistic work to create a religious environment in the society.

—Dr. Surendra Sharma 'Sushil'
Editor – *Shri Tulsipeeth Saurabh*
Ghaziabad

❒

187

Blessing of the Saints Received by the Master of Original Work

(1)

The glory and usefulness of Gita press and *'Kalyan'* magazine is well known to the whole world. Gita press has done a great spiritual awakening in India through its valuable publication of spiritual books. The soul or the moving spirit of such a unique institution is Shri Hanuman Prasad Poddarji, a *bhakta, gyani* and a dynamic *karmayogi*. Hanuman Prasadji is a silent, unstatutory, humble soul who is endowed with many divine qualities. He has done much in the name of *bhakti*, *karmayoga*, *kirtan* and also in the name of God. He is, good writer and a fluent speaker in Hindi. His language is humid and understandable, and style is charming and arresting.

The life of such a glorious personality must be brought out as soon as possible. May he live long peacefully. May Lord bless him.

May the genuine effort of Shri Gambhir Chandji Dujari in publishing it be issued with success.

—Shiva Nand
(Founder of Divine Life Society)

(2)

You are writing a biography of Hanuman Prasad. This is the thing of great pleasure. Hari Baba has indeed been praising him very much. My thousands of blessings are with you that you achieve success for such endeavour.

—Purnanand Teerth (Odia Baba)
Shri Krishna Ashram, Vrindavan
Bhadra Krishna 5, Vikramaditya year 2003

(3)

The birth of saints takes place for the welfare of others. In my opinion, Shri Hanuman Prasadji Poddar is really a true saint, with whom not only the whole religious world is familiar with, but who also did a true welfare of the public by initiating publication of a magazine in the form of *'Kalyan'*.

The efforts which are being made to publish his biography are praiseworthy. The person should also be praised for this. A true reform can be made by the biographies of such saints. We request the supreme Lord that He may help him for such work.

—Shukdevanand
Parmarth Niketan, Swargashram,
Jyeshtha Shukla, Vikramaditya year 2003

(4)

Many eminent people are known and unknown on this world in the present age. If it is said among them that Shri Hanuman Prasad Poddar is only one in this spiritual world, then it will not be an exaggeration, according to my little knowledge. The efforts that you have made to write the biography of such an eminent person – this is really a very special thing. I request to Supreme Lord that biography of Poddarji may be written from beginning to end joyfully and may come out, after publication, in front of the world so that spiritual seekers should easily find a path for salvation.

—Bhajananand
Parmarth Niketan
Jyeshtha Shukla, Vikramaditya year 2003

(5)

I have remained in contact with respected Bhaijee for about seventeen years. He is a personified idol of divine treasure and courtesy. His behaviuor is a true guide for ordinary people. You are compiling the matter for his biography. It is a matter of great pleasure. May the God be helpful in your such good endeavour. A great beneficence can occur to the world by such of your contribution. Shri Bhaijee is truly an eminent person and the life of a great eminent person only is a true guide to the auspicious devotees.

—Sanatan Dev
(Translator for texts written by *Rishis* in Gita press)

❐

188

An Introduction to the Master of Original Work

An entirely devoted follower of Bhaijee, respected Shri Gambhirchand Dujari was born in a religious Maheshwari family in 1901 (On *Bhadrapada Shukla* 8, Friday, *Vikramaditya year* 1958) at the Bikaner city of Rajasthan. He had a longing for *satsang* due to his family instincts right from his childhood. His childhood passed in pain due to death of his mother and father at the age of four years and seven years, respectively. Due to this reason, he could not even obtain proper education. He had begun to study the Gita even at a very young age and has also begun to attend *satsang* with Shri Ichhalal Joshi, Swami Uttamnathji of *Nath sect* and Shri Lali Maiji. Everyone was compassionate towards him. He had to do business at the young age of twelve years due to family reasons. He met Shri Jaidayalji Goyandka in 1922 at Rishikesh. He was very much impressed by his personality. Therefore, when Shri Sethji arrived next year to *Bikaner*, he utilised complete benefit by his *satsang*. His intimacy with Shri Sethji has developed more and more. He met Bhaijee during his trip to Bikaner in 1923. He was so much impressed by Bhaijee that he had dedicated himself, after some time, unto the feet of Bhaijee by renouncing his business forever. Thereafter, whenever Bhaijee comes to Bikaner, he stayed mostly at his residence. He had become a chief associate to Bhaijee after commencement of publication of *'Kalyan'* from Mumbai. He did a lot of hard work for publicity of *'Kalyan'*, made hundreds of customers for *'Kalyan'* by going around to every door. In the earlier issues of *'Kalyan'*, the address of his residence situated at Bikaner was also given, where new customers were enrolled. He had made an important contribution in the progress of Gita press. He had been selling the books published from Gita press by going around from house to house.

He was called from Bikaner by a telegram on visualisation of Lord Vishnu to Bhaijee at Jasideeh on *Ashwin Krishna Paksh* in *Vikramaditya year* of 1984. When he heard from Bhaijee, instantly he took a vow to spend his life in the service of Bhaijee and at that very time, he decided the goal of his life, i.e., to collect the facts related with the life of Bhaijee. He had performed his work with true readiness even in the absence of proper cooperation. When and where Bhaijee goes, when and who comes to meet him, description about the things, which he had said during *satsang,* etc. and had collected copy of letters of Bhaijee regularly. He always tried to accompany Bhaijee and had remained writing each and every small thing and events related to his life. Such of his activity was not interesting to Bhaijee because Bhaijee had not inclined to retain anything of his characteristic symptoms. Therefore, he had to tolerate scolding and rage. He happily accepted the insult and anger being made by a respected person, treating it as a remnant of food (*prasad*) offered to an idol. He had an incomparable faith for Bhaijee. He remained singing mostly according to his faith –

People may understand or may not understand,
But I have this much of understanding.
Bhimkumar *is my God and daughter of*
Siyaram *is my Goddess.*

His main interest was to bring, the wandering and anguished people and sad widows of the world in contact of Bhaijee and Shri Sethji. He did not care even of his insult, in diverting people to this end and remained visiting the residence of people irrespective of proper time which may be 12 o'clock at night or 4 o'clock in the morning. Sethji had remained telling many times. "The maximum number of people, which were persuaded to *satsang* by Dujariji, no one probably did that much of persuasion for such work. He only had introduced Swami Ramsukh Dasji Maharaj to Shri Sethji. Bhaijee has written in his will – 'Dujariji was very much fond of *satsang.* Dujariji is the person who has brought a reputed scholar with good conduct like Shri Chimman Lal Goswami from Bikaner to *'Kalyan'* by persuading him to resign from higher state services. Dujariji also motivated saint Chyawanramji, Shri Ishwar Dasji Daga, Shri Badri Prasadji Acharya and others to this end. Dujariji had been continuing to collect my letters even against my wish. His main interest was only one – to persuade people for *satsang* under any circumstances. Tolerates insult and abuses but never deviated from his normal duty, he was a very devoted person".

Once I have asked my father (Shri Gambhirchand Dujari) – Why you spent day and night for such writing, instead of utilising your time in an act of achievement and singing hymns (*sadhan-bhajan*)? He replied – The aim of my life is to collect the facts related with the life of Bhaijee, instead of a divine achievement. An object which you people would obtain by devotional songs and meditation that will be bestowed on me, by this very work. I said – it is not in conformable to Bhaijee, then why are you engaged in such work? He replied – I don't believe it that to collect and write the facts are not in conformable to

Bhaijee because even aware of my such activity and of my interest, he was kind enough to share many times his most intimate things at numerous occasions. But, of course, it is not in conformable to his mind about the things which I tell or to induce to others. But, this very is my intention that benefit which people can obtain during life time of Bhaijee, by coming in his contact, they may not again obtain such an opportunity. Therefore, I don't detach myself from such work even though being abused by his scolding. Therefore, my father had considered it necessary to accompany Bhaijee as much as possible. Up to this degree that the marriage of my both younger brothers was held on the same day in 1960. I was about 27-28 years old. I had no experience of the work related to marriage. I have written to my father very insistently that he should come to Calcutta so that marriage arrangements may be made properly. But, he has not agreed even with special insistence. Respected Bhaijee was just likely to arrive to join this marriage. Father also arrived with him and then also returned with him. Not only this, but this was his advice to all of three of us that why we are wasting our life. When we will again get such an opportunity to live with Bhaijee?

Due to our misfortune, we have not cooperated him for this work during his life time of our father. An economic condition was not such that he may take help for this work by hiring someone else on salary. He had also no cooperation from anyone or other people for such work. He died in 1962 due to these circumstances. But, it was his firm determination that such work is being accomplished after his heavenly departure.

Father had come to Calcutta to be with us from Gorakhpur, a little earlier to his death. His body was in a helpless condition due to a damage in the bone of his foot. During this very time, he had a heart attack and he became unconscious. Bhaijee was informed by phone. What type of pledge has been made by respected Bhaijee, this is known to him only. Father has got consciousness just on the next day and begun to perform his every activity like prior to the attack. After ten months for the journey to Puri and Mayapur *(Nabadwip)*, respected Bhaijee arrived at Calcutta along with his attendants. He had also come to our residence to meet the father. An adequate discussion was held with Bhaijee. Father told me, after departure of Bhaijee from our home, you all three brothers should go along with your wives to Puri along with Bhaijee. You people will not get such an opportunity again. Your mother is already with me. Although there was also not any apprehension that he will die within two days. On my insistence, he had retained my younger brother Sitaram and his wife with him and we four have gone to Puri with Bhaijee. On the next day, father has read an exposition of Bhaijee published in '*Sanmarg*' newspaper and preserved its cutting with him. Father has awakened next day morning as usual but after some time, had a heart attack, like two months earlier and died instantly. It appeared that Bhaijee has virtually taken a pledge to meet him personally and that was fulfilled.

During evening, when we were going to sea for bathing along with Bhaijee, at that very place Bhaijee informed about the death of my father and sent us immediately to Calcutta. On his return to Calcutta, Bhaijee again came to our home. Some talks were held in front of others. Thereafter he told me alone that when your father had first heart attack and you have informed me by phone, at that very time, I went to Baba, who told me that Dujariji would meet Shri Krishna prior to his sixteenth breath – there is no doubt in it. Listening to such thing through Bhaijee himself, I was very much pleased.

He had an intimate craving in his heart that all the facts, pointing the greatness and divinity of Bhaijee should be published as a special issue of *'Kalyan'* in future, after the death of Bhaijee. Thus millions of its readers may obtain an introduction of such eminent person who has connected their life with the supreme Lord by providing spiritual illumination in their life. Such dream of him could not yet be materialised.

❐

189

An Introduction of Strong Feeling by Respected Bai – Mrs. Savitri Devi Fogla

Today is the birth centenary day of a devoted follower of my father (Bhaijee) – Shri Gambhichand Dujari. When he came to my father (Shri Bhaijee), I was not even born at that time. I had called him as an uncle. He had an extraordinary devotion to my Babujee (Bhaijee). He had treated Babujee just like his deity.

He had made an extensive collection regarding Babujee and he was found, heard and seen always ready for utilising every possible methods for the sake of collection. Babujee had a normal habit to hide his highest spiritual identity completely and, as such, he does not also retain any letter in this connection for expression of compliments, but rather had destroyed by tearing it to pieces. I have noticed that uncle had picked up those pieces thrown after tearing, with thorough selection and had composed that matter suitable for reading by investing hours, in scraping them together. Respected Radha Baba had also drawn his incomparable conduct regarding Babujee in thirteen chapters with great concentration. Due to some reasons, respected Baba had discontinued to write further but how uncle could obtain such rare documents regarding Babujee written by Radha Baba, regarding this respected Baba has written in his literary composition of verse –

'Even then the unrestrained wind had vanished, along with the scattered notes.'

Baba has addressed the uncle as an unrestrained wind. Uncle should get material in connection with Babujee even if he must do anything for this. His treasured wish was only to collect the material about Babujee in any way, even through quarrel, through snatching away, through force, through rebuking, through request, through flattering, through stealing or through hearing secretly, although his collection is praiseworthy and remarkably rare.

Uncle had very sweet barbed remarks with Babujee. When Babujee feels irritated, he utters with anger (although his anger was only for the sake of an acting) –

'Dujariji! Why don't you understand? Why are you possessed with wrong thinking? You should agree with me – do not show your stubbornness'. But Dujariji said – 'I would do it again and again – will you beat me? O.K. then, come on and beat me, beat me'.

Listening to such conversation, my mother said – 'Dujariji! Why do you snap?' By expressing her concern at unwelcome remarks, she asked him – 'Why don't you obey him?' In reply, uncle said – 'You would not understand him. I know how he is?'

Not only his complete family but he had also connected an umpteen number of people in shelter and vicinity of Babujee.

Several years ago, and during lifetime of Babujee, uncle had come once to me in seclusion along with a steel trunk and said – '*Beta*! This is collected asset of my whole life – a priceless treasure. Please arrange to prepare its press copy. Due to some compulsion which I cannot disclose, I could not care for his request, though I have still inclined for it and his priceless collection was retained with me for about six months, which I have returned as such to him. That very collection is now being published at various places by dear brothers *Shyam* and *Hari*.

At the occasion of his birth centenary, I bow to him, to his feelings and efforts because I cannot describe it as such in words. I can say only this much that no one is found as dedicated as him towards Babujee till today.

It is very easy to fulfill the affection during favourable condition, but the real fulfillment of affection occurs (to fulfill an affection) during an adverseness only, thus was stated by respected Baba. Due to what reason, uncle has been deprived of an actual vicinity of his adored at the last juncture of his life is not known.

Prior to one day of the death of uncle, Babujee had gone to Puri from Calcutta for two days and returned two days after the act of cremation. Why and how such was ordained, I don't know, but he was probably also not worried about it and he had retained mind on a proverb towards adored of his adored –

'O beloved! You may keep a distance or may reject,
Or may let out from the home,
May tease very much but please do not
distract me from your mind'.
My father had remained commenting –
Someone else may understand, may not understand,
But this much of understanding is sufficient for me;
*My Lord is **Nand Kishor** while daughter*
*of **Vrishbhan*** is my Goddess.

And one was him (Uncle) who had remained calling and singing – *'My Lord is **Bhimkumar** while my Goddess is the daughter of **Siyaram**'.*

(Bhimkumar means son of Shri Bhimraj, i.e., my Babujee – Bhaijee Shri Hanuman Prasad Poddar and daughter of Siyaram is my mother Smt. Ramdei). Heartful thanks to such faith, recognition and firm confidence.

Bhadra Shukla 8,	*Dear daughter of her Babujee*
Radhashtami,	*(Savitri)*
Vikramaditya year 2057	*Savitri Devi Fogla*

❑

Glossary

WORDS/PHRASESAND THEIR MEANINGS/ SYNONYMS/ RELATED REFERENCES

A:

1. **Angira:** Third 'Manasputra' (born out of divine intellect) of Lord Brahma and formulated fourth Veda called Atharvaveda with sage Atharvan.
2. **Adi Shankaracharya:** He is famous for his non-dualism and as a mendicant and philosopher of great eminence, has united the nation in a religious and cultural framework about 1,300 years ago. He revived the Veda and Sanatan Dharma once again to defeat Buddhist and other adversaries.
3. **Alipore:** It is a place in Kolkata where political prisoners were kept under British rule and still in operation. It is HQ of South 24 Parganas district of south Kolkata.
4. **Asansol:** It is a city in Bardhaman District in the Indian state of West Bengal.
5. **Amritsar:** It is home to the Sikh's holiest shrine, the Golden Temple in the Indian state of Punjab.
6. **Allahabad:** An important place of pilgrimage in the Indian state of Uttar Pradesh.
7. **Ahmedabad:** It is the sixth largest city of the Indian state of Gujarat. Sabarmati Ashram is in this city.
8. **Ajmer:** It is a historical city of central Rajasthan, India. It contains the most important Muslim pilgrimage centre.
9. **Assam:** This state is famous for tea, silk and located in north-eastern part in India.
10. **Aryan:** A noble person.
11. **Ajoyapi:** Gita, chapter-4, verse-6
12. **Aryasamaji:** A member from Arya Samaj.
13. **Aghan or Margashish:** The ninth month of Hindu lunar year (mid-November-mid-December).
14. **Ashvin or Kuar:** The ninth month of Hindu lunar calendar (September-October).

15. **Arjun:** One of the five Pandavas and son of Pandu of the Mahabharata origin.
16. **Arjuni:** Arjun had to disguise as Arjuni to be able to achieve the Gopi Bhava.
17. **Asarh:** The fourth month (Lunar) of the Hindu year (mid-June to mid-July).
18. **Arhat:** A perfect person who has achieved spiritual enlightenment.
19. **Ahurmazd:** The highest God of Zoroastrians.
20. **Ashtang Yoga:** Yoga performed with eight parts of body touching the ground.
21. **Aryan culture:** An ancient culture.
22. **Akshaya tritiya:** An auspicious day of the year when any holy function can be conducted.
23. **Anubhuti:** Perception.
24. **Acharya:** Professor/A man of distinguished learning.
25. **Asuran pond (Pokhra):** A famous area of Gorakhpur.
26. **Arist category:** Decoction group of medicines.
27. **Anand-tatva:** This is a philosophical thought (A prayer for Nirgun Nirakar, which is formulated from ancient Hindu scriptures by Shri Seth Jaydayal Goyandka) most liked by Shri Sethji. It indicates that everything of this creation is blissful.
28. **Ayodhya:** Also known as Saket, is an ancient city and one of the seven most important pilgrimages for Hindus. It is on the right bank of Saryu River and 8 km from Faizabad in the Indian state of Uttar Pradesh.
29. **Aligarh:** It is the city in north Indian state of Uttar Pradesh. It is approx. 90 miles away from the Indian capital, New Delhi.
30. **Ayodhyakand:** It consists of events of the exile of Shri Ram to forest and meeting with his brother, Shri Bharat in Chitrakoot.
31. **Ashwin Shukla:** A light half period during seventh lunar month of the Indian calendar.
32. **Ashwin Krishna:** A dark half period during seventh lunar month of the Indian calendar.
33. **Ashwin (Kuar) sudi:** See point 31 (November-December)
34. **Ashad Sudi:** Alight half period during fourth lunar month of Hindu calendar (June-July).
35. **Ashad Krishna:** A dark half period during fourth lunar month of Hindu calendar (June-July).
36. **Agnipuranank:** It is a Sanskrit text and one of the eighteen major Puranas of Hinduism. It is a medieval era encyclopedia and covers a diverse range of topics.
37. **Almora:** It is a district of Kumaun of Uttarakhand state, India. It is famous for its beauty and views of Himalayas.

38. **Avari Mata:** It is in Bhadesar tehsil of Chittorgarh district of Rajasthan, India. It has a famous temple of Goddess Avari Mata.
39. **Anand Mayee Maa:** She was regarded as self/God- realised master (1896-1982).
40. **Autobiography of a Yogi:** It is an autobiography of Paramhans Yoganand, first published in 1946. It is included in the book '50 Spiritual Classics' by T. Butler Bowdon.
41. **Aana:** It was a currency unit formerly used in India and Pakistan, equal to 1/16 rupee.
42. **Ajanta:** These are the caves in Aurangabad district in Maharashtra of India. There are about 30 rock-cut Buddhist cave monuments.

B:

1. **Bhaijee:** Apet name given to Shri Hanuman Prasad Poddar in Mumbai.
2. **Bhaijee-Pawan Smaran:** A book written on Bhaijee, which was published in his memory, after his death.
3. **Bhava-Samadhi:** Ecstatic consciousness-unconsciousness from other world.
4. **Bengal:** It is the most diversely populated state of India.
5. **Baba:** A respectful form of address to an elder person.
6. **Burdwan:** It is a district of the state of West Bengal in India.
7. **Bhiwani:** It is a district of the State of Haryana in India.
8. **Bohra Community:** Gujarati-speaking caste, originated from Kachchh area of India.
9. **Beawar:** It is a town in the district of Ajmer in Rajasthan state of India.
10. **Bal Gangadhar Tilak:** Father of Indian movement and a popular leader.
11. **Bhramar Gita:** It contains the verses of devotional songs by Soordas in which Udhav was sent to Braj from Mathura with a message by Krishna.
12. **Bhagwat:** Most important classic in India, describing life and times of Lord Krishna (16th-19th centuries).
13. **Ballabh sect:** A path for grace of the Hinduism and is unique in its facets of devotion of Krishna and was established by Ballabh Acharya.
14. **Baba Vishwanath temple:** Famous Hindu temple in Varanasi in the Indian state of Uttar Pradesh.
15. **Brahmin:** It is a caste of people in Hinduism.
16. **Braj:** It is a region around Mathura-Vrindavan in Uttar Pradesh state of India. An area where incarnation of Lord Krishna took place and he spent his childhood.
17. **Beni Madhav:** It is also a name of Lord Krishna.

18. **Badrinath Dham/Badrikashram:** It is the most sacred place for Hindus and situated in Chamoli district of Indian state of Uttarakhand.
19. **Bhakti Yoga:** Means for religious devotion.
20. **Barsana:** It is 21 km to North of Govardhan in Vrindavan near Mathura in Uttar Pradesh state of India. It is said to be the birthplace of Radha.
21. **Bhaktank:** It is a special annual issue of '*Kalyan*', devoted to devotees.
22. **Badi:** Dark half of a lunar month (full to new moon).
23. **Bankura:** District place of Bardhwan division in Indian state of West Bengal.
24. **Bhadrapad or Bhadon:** Sixth month of Hindu lunar year (mid-August to mid-September).
25. **Bhang:** or Cannabis, traditionally and specially used in food and drink during festival in the Indian sub-continent
26. **Bharat:** He was a legendry emperor and founder of Bharat dynasty in Hindu mythology. Hence, India has been called '*Bharatvarsha*'. It is the official name of the Republic of India.
27. **Basti:** It is an important city near Gorakhpur in Uttar Pradesh state, India.
28. **Buddha:** He was a sage and spiritual leader of India.
29. **Bikaner:** It is a desert city of Rajasthan state of India.
30. **Bhagwatank:** A special issue of '*Kalyan*' on '*Bhagwat*'.
31. **Beti:** A respectful form of address with a literal meaning to a young girl.
32. **Bhadra Krishna:** Dark half of lunar month in third and fourth lunar asterisms.
33. **Bajoria:** A known businessman.
34. **Bettiah:** It is a city of West Champaran district near Indo- Nepal border in Bihar state of India.
35. **Barhaj:** A town at the bank of Saryu in Deoria district in Indian state of Uttar Pradesh. (Also known as Gaura Barhaj).
36. **Bandra-Mumbai:** It is a suburb of west Mumbai in the state of Maharashtra, India. It is a posh location.
37. **Bhagwatnamank:** Special issue of '*Kalyan*' devoted to the divine name.
38. **Bhagalpur:** It is situated on southern banks of river Ganga in Indian state of Bihar. It is the third largest city of Bihar.
39. **Borabar (Jodhpur):** It is the nearby railway station to Ladoli in tehsil Makrana of district Nagaur in Rajasthan state of India.
40. **Brahma:** He is the creator God in trimurti of Hinduism. He has four faces, also known as swayambhu (self-born), Vagisa (Lord of speech) and creator of four Vedas, one from each mouth.

41. **Balkand:** It is the first part of Valmiki Ramayan – one of the two great epics of India. It is also the first chapter of the Ramayana by Tulsidasji.
42. **Bihar:** It is a state in East India. A centre of peace, learning and culture in ancient and classical India.
43. **Brahmvaivarta:** It is a voluminous Sanskrit text and a major Mahapurana of Hinduism. It centres around Krishna and Radha in this text.
44. **Bapu:** It is a Hindi word for father and is generally referred to Mahatma Gandhi.
45. **Babar:** Laid the basis of Mughal dynasty in India and became the first Emperor.
46. **Bhubaneswar:** Ancient city and capital of Indian state of Odisha, formerly Orissa.
47. **Buddha temple, Bodh Gaya:** Buddha is said to have attained enlightenment. It is a UNESCO world heritage site and is located about 96 km from Patna.
48. **Bhairawa (Nepal):** It is a place near Indo-Nepal crossing border. It is also famous due to ground water irrigation project.
49. **Bhimraj:** It is the name of the father of Bhaijee.
50. **Beta:** An affectionate way of addressing young boy. Literal meaning is 'son'.
51. **Babujee:** It is an affectionate way of addressing to Bhaijee by her daughter.
52. **Bhim Kumar (Bhimraj):** Name of the father of Bhaijee Shri H.P. Poddar.
53. **Bhadrapada Shukla:** A light half period of the sixth month of Hindu lunar calendar (mid-August-mid September).
54. **Bhadrapada Krishna:** A dark half period of the sixth month of Hindu lunar calendar (mid-August-mid September).
55. **Bhakta:** One who practices Bhakti.
56. **Bhagwatank:** A special issue of 'Kalyan' on Shrimad Bhagwat.
57. **Bhartiya Jansangh:** It was the nationalist political party which existed from 1951 to 1977 and was a political arm of R.S.S. In 1977, it was merged with Janata Party. After its split in 1980, it was reformed as Bharatiya Janata Party (BJP).
58. **Bhabhiji:** An affectionate way of addressing a married lady. (Literal meaning – sister-in-law).
59. **Bulandshahar (Bulandshahar):** It is a city 28 miles away from Noida in Uttar Pradesh state of India.
60. **Brahmapurana:** It is first of the eighteen Puranas except Padma Purana which (in *Patal Khand*) arrogates precedence to itself.

61. **Bhagwannamank:** A special issue of '*Kalyan*' towards the importance of divine name.
62. **Bengla:** One of the Indian languages of people of Bengal.
63. **Bangladesh:** It regained independence in 1971 and became a free country.
64. **Brahman:** It means the concept of transcendent and imminent ultimate reality – a supreme cosmic soul in *advaitya* philosophy.
65. **Bhadra asana:** Also known as gracious pose and is suitable for prolonged period of sitting.
66. **Bahmacharya:** It is known as celibacy.
67. **Brahmanical tradition:** The tradition followed by the Brahmins.
68. **Brahmavidya:** It is also a name given by the Mundaka Upnishad to its own teachings. In its opening verse of Mundaka, Brahma taught this Brahmavidya to his eldest son Atharva, who passed it on to succession to qualified disciple.
69. **Bhado Badi:** Adark half period of the six months of Hindu lunar calendar (mid-August-mid-September).
70. **Bhavnagar:** It is district place of Saurashtra region of Gujarat state of India and is situated 198 kms from capital Gandhinagar.
71. **Bhind:** It is one of the districts of Madhya Pradesh state of India.
72. **Bengaluru:** It is the capital city of Karnataka state of India. Its location is at south Karnataka and is an excellent starting point for tours to south India. It is an important centre for business, science and technology.
73. **Belur:** It is located on the west bank of Hooghly River in the West Bengal state of India.

C:

1. **Chharandi:** Also observed as Saraswati Puja, it highlights the coming of spring and attended to in Magh month.
2. **Chandpur:** It is now a district of south-eastern part of Bangladesh of Chittagong division.
3. **Calcutta (Kolkata – present name):** Capital of Indian state of West Bengal.
4. **Chaitra:** First month of the Hindu lunar year (Mid-March to Mid-April).
5. **Churu:** A city in desert region of Rajasthan state of India, it is the birthplace of Sethji Shri Jaidayal Goyandka.
6. **Chaitanya Mahaprabhu or Chaitanya:** He is none other than Lord Shri Krishna, who appeared in Kali-yuga to inaugurate the *yug dharma* for this age. He appeared at Sridham Mayapur in the city of Navdeep in West Bengal state of India.

7. **Chowpatti (Chaupati):** Best-known public beach, adjoining Marine Drive in Girgaun area of Mumbai, India.
8. **Chitrakoot:** A town of Satna district in the state of Madhya Pradesh in India. A place of religion, culture, historical and archaeological importance.
9. **Chakradharpur:** It is a town in West Singhbhoomi district in the state of Jharkhand, India. It was a quasi-hill station in mid-1900.
10. **Chappar:** It is in Churu district of north-eastern Rajasthan in the Shekhawati region of India.
11. **Chanakya:** He was traditionally identified as Kautilya, Vishnugupta who had written Indian political treatise – the Arthashastra. He was teacher, philosopher, economist and royal advisor. He died in 203 B.C.
12. **Chaitra Shukla:** New moon in the month of Chaitra (first month of Hindu lunar calendar).
13. **Chimmanlal Goswami:** A staunch follower who joined Bhaijee in 1933, leaving his high-class practice forever, he was a scholar in Hindi, Sanskrit and English and helped Bhaijee editorial work of '*Kalyan*' and various religious books.
14. **Chirgaon:** A town and municipal area in Jhansi district in Indian state of Uttar Pradesh.
15. **Chakradhar Maharaj/Baba:** Affectionally called Radha Baba, an ardent devotee of Bhaijee, he was a great scholar in Sanskrit, Bangla and English as well as for spiritual knowledge. Joined Bhaijee on 11th May 1939 and never disassociated even for a day till his death.
16. **Chittorgarh:** It is a city and municipality in Rajasthan state of Western India. It was a former capital of the Sisodia dynasty.

D:

1. **Dhyana:** Meditation – Deeper awareness of oneness.
2. **Dwapar:** It is the third out of four *yugas*, described in Hindu scriptures. It comes between Treta and Kaliyug. Compassion and truthfulness were two pillars during this era.
3. **Devi:** Respectful form of address to a woman.
4. **Dhruva:** Devotee of Supreme Lord Vishnu and son of King Uttanpada. He was given a place in sky to shine for taking care of his parents.
5. **Dehli/Delhi:** National capital territory of India.
6. **Draupadi:** A tritagonist according to Hindu epic Mahabharata. She is fire-born daughter of Drupada, king of Panchal. She is one of the most important female characters in the Hindu epic, Mahabharata.
7. **Duryodhana:** A kingpin of Kauravas in the Mahabharata and the eldest son of blind king Dhritrashtra and queen Gandhari.

8. **Dhani:** A distant secluded place from the residential area.
9. **Durga Saptashati:** It contains 700 verses describing the victory of Goddess Durga over demon Mahishasura.
10. **Dadri:** It is a town in district Bhiwani in Haryana state of India.
11. **Dhoti:** Traditional men's garment, chiefly worn by Indian Hindu people. A long cloth typically wrapped around the waist, passed between legs and tucked in waistline.
12. **Deonagri script:** It is abugida alphabet of India, written from left to right, and has a symmetrical rounded shape within squared outlines.
13. **Dasavatar stotram:** Prayer made in praise of all the incarnations.
14. **Dohavali:** A famous text by Goswami Tulsidas.
15. **Dalmia:** One of the leading cement producers in India.
16. **Dhanvantari**: An incarnation of Vishnu in Hinduism. He appears as the physician of the Gods.
17. **Durga navmi:** It is the final day for worship of Goddess Durga.
18. **Deoria:** It is a district of Uttar Pradesh, India. This place is also famous due to renowned saint Deoraha Baba.
19. **Durga Puja:** It is an annual Hindu festival that celebrates worship of Hindu Goddess Durga from sixth to tenth day of bright lunar fortnight in Ashwin.
20. **Dujariji:** It generally refers to the master (collector) of the original Hindi version – the late Shri Gambhirchandji Dujari.
21. **Dhruva Narayan:** Dhruva Narayan is a devotee of supreme Lord Vishnu and a son of Uttanpad. His tale is recorded in Vishnu Purana and Bhagwat Purana. Narayan is the Vedic Supreme God.
22. **Dibrugarh:** It is a city and HQ of Dibrugarh district in the state of Assam in India.
23. **Didwana:** It is town in Nagaur district of Rajasthan in India in the Thar Desert. It is thought to be 500 years old.
24. **Dwarkadhish temple:** It is one of the oldest and largest temples of Mathura city in Uttar Pradesh state of India.
25. **Damodar tank:** It is a sacred lake, located at foot-hills of Girnar hills, near Junagarh in Gujarat state of India.
26. **Dwarka/Dwarkapuri:** It is one of the foremost *char- dhams* (four sacred pilgrimage sites) and seventh most ancient religious cities in India.
27. **Daulatpur (Rai Bareli):** It is a small village in Sareni tehsil in Rai Bareli District of Uttar Pradesh state of India.
28. **Dhundhiraj Ganesh:** It is a lesser known but an ancient Ganesh Temple and lies just a few minutes away from acclaimed Kashi Vishwanath temple.

G:

1. **Gaya:** It is a city of ancient historical and mythological importance and a major pilgrimage city of Bihar for Hindus and Buddhists. It is a ritual place and famous for funeral offerings for benefits of soul of the deceased.
2. **Ganpati:** A synonym for Lord Ganesh.
3. **Giridhar Gopal:** A synonym for Lord Shri Krishna.
4. **Gita press:** Famous publisher of religious books related to Hinduism, situated in Gorakhpur of Uttar Pradesh state of India.
5. **Gorakhnath temple:** It is situated in Gorakhpur.
6. **Gorakhpur:** It is a city along the bank of Rapti River in eastern part of Indian state of Uttar Pradesh.
7. **Giriraj:** It is also called Govardhan hill – a sacred Hindu site. It is famous for 21 km-long circumambulations. It is a form of worship to walk around Govardhan hill. It extends four-five miles and is in Mathura district of Uttar Pradesh state of India.
8. **Gyan Yagya:** Means yagya for true knowledge.
9. **Ganesh Stotra:** A prayer in praise of Lord Ganesh.
10. **Gushainji:** Nickname of Tulsidasji.
11. **Govardhan Peeth, Jagannath Puri:** It is a monastery located at Puri in Odisha state of India. It is associated with Jagannath temple and one of the four cardinal mathas founded by Adi Shankaracharya in 8th century C.E. Its territory is whole eastern part of Indian subcontinent.
12. **Gandhi Ashram, Hatundi:** It is situated at Hatundi in Ajmer in Rajasthan state of India for people to live group life with religious spirit in widest sense.
13. **Gyanottar Bhava Rajya:** A final state once you have achieved the real wisdom.
14. **Goswami Tulsidas:** Believed to be an incarnation of sage Valmiki, Tulsidas wrote 'The Ram Charit Manas', 'Dohawali', 'Gitawali' and 'Vinay Patrika', etc.
15. **Gandhi:** His real name was Mohandas Karamchand Gandhi and is also known as Mahatma Gandhi. A prominent leader of Indian independence movement in British-ruled India.
16. **Ganga:** A great and sacred river, personified as Goddess known as the Ganga. Flows from Gangotri to Brahmaputra River.
17. **Gita:** It is a message delivered through 700 verses of a rare Hindu scripture in Sanskrit and is a part of Hindu epic, the Mahabharata.
18. **Gita Jayanti:** Birthday of the Bhagwat-Gita, it is celebrated on the 11th day of waxing moon of Margashirsha month. (December-January).

19. **Gitawali:** It is a second important text next to Ramayana from the point of its framework by Tulsidas. It is also described as the complete Ramayana in devotional poetry in a graceful manner.
20. **Gayatri mantra:** It is a very popular devotional chant, meaningful and is said to be very powerful. It is a verse from a sukta of Rigveda.
21. **Gauhati or Gauhaty:** The largest city, it is a major riverine port city of Assam, India.
22. **Gita Vatika:** It is situated about 4 kms from city's railway station on Gorakhpur-Pipraich Road near the Asuran Chowk in Gorakhpur. It was established by the founder editor of '*Kalyan*', Bhaijee Hanuman Prasad Poddar, who lived here for 45 years. A magnificent temple of Radha Krishna in Nagra style of North India has been set up by HPP Memorial Committee. One can also see a small hall in which divotees sing *Sankeertan* continously for 24 hours since 1968. This place is also important and famous for two more reasons. Firstly, due to Radhastami festival which is being celebrated every year with great pomp and show since 1941. Secondly, it has a unique place where the great sage Angira and saint Narada had met Bhaijee first time personally in 1936 and disclosed him many secret things which are not available in ancient Hindu scriptures. It is also managing various charitable orgnisations successfully like: RAM DEI ANNA KSHETRA, SADHNA MANDIR, HELP TO THE POOR CANCER PATIENTS, HELP TO THE COWS AND PAD RATNAKAR SHODH SANSTHAN. Anyone can join and extend a helping hand to such reputed organisations.
23. **Giridhar Gopal:** Synonym for Lord Krishna.
24. **Gopinath Kaviraj:** He was a Sanskrit-tantra scholar, Indologist and a philosopher. Starting as a librarian, he later remained a Principal of Government Sanskrit College, Varanasi from 1923 to 1937.
25. **Ganeshank:** A special annual issue of '*Kalyan*' devoted to Lord Ganesha.
26. **Golaghat (Ayodhya):** This place lies with Faizabad district in Uttar Pradesh state of India.
27. **Golaghat (Assam):** It is a full-fledged district of Assam (1987) state of India. It has the earliest post mail services and telecommunication system in Assam since 1876.
28. **Gita tatwank:** A special issue of '*Kalyan*' on the Gita.
29. **Govardhan Peeth:** It is a monastery located in the city of Puri in Odisha state (India). One of the four cardinal *Mathas* founded by Adi Shankaracharya in 8th century C.E.
30. **Gajendra mokshastotram:** It is one of the most sacred books in Hinduism and one of the famous exploits of Lord Vishnu.

31. **Gujarat:** It is one of the westernmost states, has varied terrain and many sacred sites.
32. **Golden temple, Amritsar:** Shri Harminder Sahib is the holiest Gurudwara of Sikhism, located in the city of Amritsar in Punjab state of India.
33. **Gujarati:** Language spoken by the people of Gujarat.
34. **Giriraj:** It means king of mountain and is located near Vrindavan in Mathura district of Uttar Pradesh state of India.
35. **Gour sect:** It belongs to Gaudia Vaishnava tradition that practices philosophy and principles as enunciated by Shri Chaitanya.
36. **Garh Kola, Magrayar (Unnao):** It is a village in Bighapur tehsil in Unnao district of Uttar Pradesh state in India.
37. **Gita Chintan:** This is an excellent book by Shri H.P. Poddar with brilliant articles on Gita.
38. **Ghaziabad:** It is a city in Indian state of Uttar Pradesh. It is close to New Delhi and, hence, it is sometimes also referred to as capital of Uttar Pradesh.
39. **Ghanshyam:** Synonym of Lord Krishna.
40. **Greece:** It is a country of south-eastern Europe. Athens – its capital retains landmarks including 5th century B.C. Acropolis citadel with Parthenon temple.
41. **Gambhir Chand Dujari:** Master and original compiler of the Hindi version.
42. **Ganeshstotra:** It is a prayer to Lord Ganesha to get rid of all evils.
43. **Gurumukhi:** It is an alphabetical abugida, can be translated as 'mouth of Guru'. It is a script used by Sikhs.
44. **Gitank:** A special issue of '*Kalyan*', devoted to the Gita.
45. **Gusainji:** His real name was Vitthalnath. He was born in Varanasi. He was mentioned in 'Agnipurana'.
46. **Govind Bhawan:** It is an office-cum-*satsang* centre established by Jaydayal Goyandka firstly in 1940 in a rented house at Banstalla Lane in Kolkata to sell Gita press books, glass bangles and shoes sans leather. Later on, a land was purchased, and foundation ceremony was done by Bhaijee in 1959 for a new building. It is now situated in M.G. Road, Burrabazar, Kolkata.
47. **Gayatri Yajna:** It is one of the most auspicious *yajnas*. It helps and assists one on one's spiritual path to burn and clear *Karma*.
48. **Goddess Durga:** She is the warrior manifestation of Goddess Adi Shakti. It means the invisible one.
49. **Guru Yukteshwar:** It is the monastic name of Priyanath Sarkar (1855-1936) who was the Guru of Paramhans Yoganand. He was a *Kriya Yogi*, Vedic astrologer, a scholar of Gita and the Bible.

50. **Gita Bhawan:** It is situated on the bank of holy river Ganges amidst Himalayan Mountains of Swargashram, Risikesh. It consists of a very large complex comprising discourse halls and 1,000 rooms available free of charge for the stay of devotees. It is in Uttarakhand state of India.

H:

1. **Hoshiarpur:** It is the district of Punjab state in northern India and one of the oldest districts of Punjab.
2. **Hanuman Prasad Poddar:** Real name of Bhaijee.
3. **Hanuman Stotra:** Verses in praise of Lord Hanuman.
4. **Hyderabad:** Capital of Telangana in southern state of India.
5. **Hindu:** Anyone who regards himself/herself as culturally, ethnically and religiously, adhering to aspect of Hinduism.
6. **Holi:** A special festival of India, also known as festival of colours.
7. **Hanuman kavach:** It has ability to provide abundance, wealth, son, joy and victory everywhere.
8. **Hare Ram Hare Ram Rama Rama ----------Hare Hare (Mahamantra)** – It is known as a chief sacred verse. It is a sixteen-word Vaishnawa mantra which first appears in Kali- Sanatana Upnishad in 16th century during Bhakti movement.
9. **Hari Sharnam:** It is a devotional verse devoted to Lord Rama, Krishna or Vishnu. It asks that we be bought to Hari's shelter, a place of refuge, who removes all anxieties.
10. **Hanumanji:** Also known as Mahavira or Bajrangbali is a Hindu God and an ardent devotee of Lord Rama.
11. **Hanuman Chalisa:** Literary forty quatrains written as two rhyming lines of verses, each contains sixteen metrical instants.
12. **Halwa:** Indian sweet dessert, prepared in different forms. The recipe uses flour, melted butter, ghee, sugar and dry nuts.
13. **Hit Harivansh (Mahaprabhu):** Founder of the Radhaballabh sect. Born in Badgram on 11th day of Vaishakh in Samvat 150, he was the incarnation of The Lord Krishna's flute. A follower of Prem-Bhakti and devotee of Radha Rani.
14. **Himalaya:** The highest mountain in the world which also contains Mount Everest.
15. **Harijan:** A term popularised by Indian revolutionary leader Mahatma Gandhi for referring Dalits, traditionally considered to be untouchable.
16. **Hindi:** It is also called modern standard. Hindi is a standardised and official language in India.
17. **Himachal Pradesh:** It is a state of north-western India and offers much for those looking to experience the Himalayas.

18. **Haryana:** It is a north-Indian state surrounding New Delhi on three sides. The city of Chandigarh is its capital.
19. **Hyderabad:** It is the capital of southern India's Telangana state. A major centre for technology industries. Its historic sites include Golkunda fort and Charminar – a 16th-century mosque.
20. **Hanuman Temple:** A temple built for Lord HH Hanuman Hanumanji.
21. **Hari Krishna Dujari:** Commonly known as 'Hari Baba' is the younger brother of late Shri Shyam Sunder Dujari who had compiled and merged different parts of the Hindi script left behind by his father Shri Gambhir Chand Dujari and published it as a text – EK ALOKIK VIBHUTI. Hari baba is living in Gitavatika since 1968 and extending his services wholeheartedly for the welfare of the sacred, lively working environment established by Bhaijee. In addition, He is planning and continously busy to publish the important remaing parts of the script by Bhaijee, lying with him as a treasure beyond price.
22. **Howrah:** It is an industrial city in the Howrah district of West Bengal, India. It is a twin city to Kolkata and is connected by four bridges on river Ganga.
23. **Hrishikesh:** Synonym for Lord Krishna.
24. **Hanuman/Hanuman Prasad/Hanuman Prasad Poddar:** Synonyms for Bhaijee.
25. **Harinam:** Name of divine Lord/the Almighty/the God.
26. **Hanuman Garhi:** It is a temple of Lord Hanuman in Ayodhya, located in Uttar Pradesh state of India.
27. **Hinduism:** It is the oldest religion of the world and some scholars and practitioners refer to it as Sanatan Dharma.
28. **Haridwar:** It is an ancient city of Uttarakhand state of India. It is one of the seven holiest places (*Saptpuri*) of Hindus.
29. **Hira Singh Markam:** Party president of Gondwana Gantantra Party, which pleads for the rights of Gond people. He lives at Tivarta in Korba district of Chhattisgarh state of India.

I:

1. **Indore:** It is one of the major cities in the state of Madhya Pradesh in India.
2. **Ishwarank:** A special issue of 'Kalyan', it is devoted to sacred text of various religions.
3. **Indira Gandhi:** She was the third Prime Minister of India.

J:

1. **Jabalpur:** An ancient city in central India situated on the shores of holy river Narmada.
2. **(Jalandhar):** A city in north-central Punjab state in north-western part of India.

3. **Janmashtami:** It commemorates earthy appearance of Lord Krishna.
4. **Janki:** It means Goddess Sita in India.
5. **Jasidih:** A city in Deoghar district of Jharkhand where the God had virtually appeared before Bhaijee twice.
6. **Jeth/Jyeshtha:** Third month of Hindu lunar year (mid- May mid-June).
7. **Jhunsi:** It is a town of Allahabad district in the Indian state of Uttar Pradesh.
8. **Jyotish Peeth Badrikashram, Uttarakhand:** A place for astrological decisions.
9. **Juhu:** It is suburb of Mumbai and famous for sprawling beaches.
10. **Jagannath Puri/Jagannathji:** It is situated in Indian state of Odisha.
11. **Jawaharlal Nehru/Nehru:** First Prime Minister of India.
12. **Jaydayalji/Jaidayal Goyandka:** He was such a Marwari and householder saint whom the people have not recognised deliberately. He was the founder of Gita press. He was popularly known as Sethji.
13. **Jyestha Badi:**A dark half period of the third month of Hindu lunar calendar (May-June).
14. **Jyestha Sudi/Shukla:** Alight half period of the third month of Hindu lunar calendar (May-June).
15. **Jyotish Peeth:** It is a very old institute situated at Joshimath in Uttarakhand state of India.
16. **Jhansi:** It is a historic city of Uttar Pradesh state of India. Famous Rani Lakshmi Bai ruled it (1857-1858).
17. **Jain temples, Abu:** These are located about 2½ km from Mount Abu in Rajasthan state of India.
18. **Jagannath temple:** It is an ancient temple of Lord Jagannath in Puri, Odisha, India.

K:

1. **Kshatriya:** A Hindu of upper caste traditionally assigned to governing the military occupation.
2. **Kalighat temple:** A Hindu temple in West Bengal, India, dedicated to Hindu Goddess Kali.
3. **Kanya Pathshala:** A school for the girls.
4. **Khadi:** A term for hand-spun and hand-woven cloth from India.
5. **Kheer:** A south-Asian rice pudding, made by boiling rice with milk, sugar and dry nuts.
6. **Kaliyuga/Kali age:** It is preceded by *Sat*, *Treta* and *Dwapar*. It is associated with apocalyptic demon *Kali*.
7. **Krishna:** He was the eighth incarnation of Lord Vishnu and was born in Dwapar Yuga.

8. **Kumbha:** It is a holy time for many Hindus. It is the oldest and longest gathering of people. It is held once in twelve years at five places in India.
9. **Kalindi:** It is a tidal estuarine river in and around the Sundarbans in North 24 Parganas district in Indian state of West Bengal.
10. **Kartik:** Eight month of the Hindu lunar year (mid-October mid-November).
11. **Kalpbheda:** Various ages and forms.
12. **Kaurav:** A legendary King Kuru, who was the ancestor of many characters of the Mahabharata, like Duryodhana, etc.
13. **Karma Yoga:** Disinterested performance of one's proper duty. It concerns day-to-day activities in normal life, which are to be dealt with balanced behaviour.
14. **Kishore and Kishori:** Lord Krishna and Radhaji.
15. **Krishna Paksha:** Dark half of the lunar month.
16. **Krishna Chandrika:** Name of a text.
17. **Karmyogi:** Day-to-day activities of a person which are dealt with balanced behaviour.
18. **Kanpur:** It is the biggest city of Indian state of Uttar Pradesh and situated on the bank of Ganga River.
19. **Kharagpur:** Important industrial town in Paschim Medinipur district of West Bengal state of India.
20. **Kalyan:** Famous spiritual magazine of Gorakhpur since 1926, published by Gita press.
21. **Kshetra sannyas:** Exclusive renunciation (to an area).
22. **Krishnank:** A special issue of '*Kalyan*' devoted to Lord Krishna
23. **Kusum sarovar:** It is a huge water tank (450 metres), which is said to belong to the period of Lord Krishna.
24. **Karimabad:** It is a historical place in Govardhan in Mathura district of Uttar Pradesh of India.
25. **Kashi:** Synonym for Varanasi/Banaras.
26. **Kalyan Kalptaru:** The publication of this English magazine, which is at par to '*Kalyan*', began in January, 1933. It is being published regularly with a special number followed by eleven monthly issues.
27. **Kankroli:** It is located in district Rajsamand in Rajasthan state of India. A beautiful temple of Dwarkadheesh is there along Rajsamand Lake.
28. **Kali temple, Dakshineshwar:** It is a Hindu temple near Kolkata. It was built in 1855 by Rani Rashmoni and famous due to its association with Ram Krishna, a mystic of 19th century.
29. **Kriya Yogi:** A Yogi who follows an ancient Yoga system revived in modern times by Mahavatar Babaji through his disciple Lahiri Mahasaya.

30. **Korba:** It is a city in Indian state of Chhattisgarh.
31. **Kailash Mansarovar:** Kailash Mountain is in Himalayan mountain ranges of remote south-western corner of Tibet. It is not only the highest part of the world but is also one of the most significant spiritual spots in the planet. Just 20 kms away from Kailash, the sacred blue and emerald green Mansarovar lake that lies at a height of 15,015 ft. is known to be an epitome of purity.
32. **Karvi:** It is the district headquarter of Chitrakoot district in Uttar Pradesh state of India. A very famous place for Hindu pilgrimage.
33. **Kaldi (Kerala):** It is a census town located east of Periyar River in Ernakulam district of Kerala state of India.
34. **Krishnacharitamrit:** A text related to primary biographies detailing life and teachings of Shri Chaitanya Mahaprabhu (1486-1533).
35. **Kishore:** Synonym for Lord Krishna.
36. **Kishori:** Synonym for Goddess Radha/Radha Rani.
37. **Kartik Badi:** A dark half period during eighth month of the Hindu calendar year (October-November).
38. **Kartik Sudi:** A light half period during eighth month of the Hindu calendar year (October-November).
39. **Kartik Krishna:** Synonym for Kartik Badi in Deonagari script.
40. **Kabul:** It is the capital of Afghanistan. It is over 3,500 years old.
41. **Kota:** It is a city located in south-east of northern Indian state of Rajasthan. It is a major coaching hub of India.
42. **Kanchidham:** It is a beautiful secluded mountain refuge, located in Kumaun hills in Uttarakhand state of India. It is a place where the late Neem Karoli Baba lived till 1973.

L:

1. **Leela:** A play (creative play by divine absolute).
2. **Leela Sindhu:** An ocean of play.
3. **Loharganj (Narpara):** Also known as Lauharganj, it is in Munshiganj district of Dhaka, now in Bangladesh.
4. **Lala Lajpat Rai:** A leader in Indian independence movement.
5. **Laxmangarh:** It is a town in Sikar district of Indian state of Rajasthan.
6. **Laddoo:** These are ball-shaped sweets popular in Indian subcontinent. *Laddoos* are made of flour, minced dough, sugar and dry fruits.
7. **Lakshman:** He is brother of Rama in Indian epic, the Ramayana.
8. **Lalitaji:** A confidante of Shri Radhaji.
9. **Lokmanya Tilak:** An Indian freedom fighter born in Ratnagiri in Maharashtra state of India.
10. **Lord Shankar:** The God who dwells at Kailash Mountain.
11. **Lord Brahma:** The creator God, having four faces. He is self-born, Lord of speech and a creator of four Vedas.

12. **Lahore:** The second largest city of Pakistan and capital of Punjab province. It has vacant temple dedicated to Lava, son of Hindu God Rama.
13. **Laxman fort, Ayodhya:** It is near Sarayu River in Faizabad district of Indian state of Uttar Pradesh.
14. **Leningrad:** Also known as St. Petersburg, there are many man-made rivers or canals.
15. **Lanka (Sri Lanka):** It is in southern Asia. Isolated country in Indian Ocean, South of India.
16. **Lucknow:** A capital of Uttar Pradesh, it thrives along the bank of Gomti.
17. **Lord Vishnu:** Protector of the world and restorer of moral order and is supreme Lord.
18. **Liluah:** It is a town in Howrah district, West Bengal, India.
19. **Laxminarayan:** He is manifestation of Lord Vishnu.
20. **Lohaganj/Lohagunj:** It is a place in Chamoli district in the interiors of Uttarakhand state of India. It is situated in the base of Garhwal Himalayas.
21. **Losal:** It is a city in Sikar district in Indian state of Rajasthan.
22. **Lingraj temple:** It is a Hindu temple dedicated to Lord Shiva and Vishnu in Bhubaneswar, the capital of East Indian state of Odisha.
23. **Lord Vasudev:** Synonym of Lord Krishna.
24. **Lahiri Mahasaya:** His real name was Shyama Charan Lihiri (1828-1895) and was an Indian Yogi and a disciple of Mahavatar Babaji. Popularly known as Kashi Baba, he revived the Yogic science of Kriya Yoga which he learned from Mahavatar Babaji. He was a mentor of Guru Yukteshwar Giri.

M:

1. **Mathura:** A district in Indian state of Uttar Pradesh. It is the birthplace of Shri Krishna at the centre of Braj-bhoomi.
2. **Mahatma:** A great soul.
3. **Manu Yajnavalkya:** Manu is the name given to a progenitor of humanity; hence, the first human to appear in the world after universal destruction. Fourteen Manus appear in each Kalp. Yajnavalkya was a sage and philosopher and pupil of sage Vaisampayana.
4. **Mumbai:** A densely populated city on India's west coast.
5. **Mahatma Gandhi:** Also known as Father of Nation, his adherence to non-violence defeated the British and secured Indian independence.
6. **Medinipur:** It is under Paschim Medinipur district of Indian state of West Bengal.
7. **Mogul/Moghul/Mughal:** It is a corruption of Persian word used for Mongol. The central Asian tribe and descendants of warriors

like Chengiz Khan and Timur. Other examples: Babar, Humayun, Jahangir, Shahjahan, etc.

8. **Muslims:** These follow Islam religion based on the Quran, recited by the God to Prophet Muhammad.
9. **Mahabharata:** One of the two major Sanskrit epics of ancient India. The other being the Ramayana. It is an epic narration of the war in Kurukshetra and fates of Kauravas and Pandavas.
10. **Mhow:** It is a cantonment in Indore district of Indian state of Madhya Pradesh.
11. **Maharajji:** Respectful form of address to a noble and religious person.
12. **Margashirsha or Aghan:** Ninth month of Hindu lunar year (mid-November to mid-December).
13. **Marwari:** Indian ethnic group that originates from Rajasthan region of India. Their traditional occupation has been as traders.
14. **Manas:** Denotes the general thinking ability/a common name assigned to famous Hindi epic Ram Charit Manas.
15. **Mahamrityunjay:** It is a prayer to Lord Shiva for healing and overcoming death.
16. **Madhusudan:** A synonym for Lord Krishna.
17. **Meera:** A Hindu mystic poet and devotee of Krishna in 16th century. She was born in royal family of Kudki, district of Pali in Rajasthan, India.
18. **Maagh:** Eleventh month of Hindu lunar year (mid-January to mid-February).
19. **Maharaas:** It is a chief dance associated with the play of Krishna, Radha and herd-girls of Braj at Vrindavan.
20. **Mahapurana:** It is deemed to be upper corpus of Puranas. Traditionally, there are 18 Mahapuranas.
21. **Mundwa:** Also known as Mundya Marwar, it is a Tehsil of Nagaur district in the Indian state of Rajasthan.
22. **Mahaprabhu Chaitanya:** He was a spiritual teacher who founded Gaudia Vaishnavism. He was believed by his devotees to be Krishna Himself.
23. **Mantra:** A sound, word or prayer that is repeated by someone who is praying or meditating.
24. **Mahadevi Bai:** It is the name of first wife of Bhaijee who died just after five years of marriage.
25. **Madan Mohan Malaviya/Malaviyaji/Mahamanaji:** He was an Indian educationist, politician, notable for his role in the Indian independence movement and two-time President of Indian National Congress.

26. **Makrera:** It is village/town in Nagaur district of Rajasthan state of India.
27. **Maa Annapurna:** She is a Hindu Goddess of nourishment. She is an incarnation of Parvati, the wife of Lord Shiva.
28. **Mahaprabhu Vallabhacharya:** He was also known as Vallabh, a devotional philosopher and founded Krishna- centred Pushti sect of Vaishnavism in Braj region of India.
29. **Maheshwari:** One who follows Maheshwarism – a religion originated in Rajasthan region of India – mainly in Khandela Marwar.
30. **Lord Mahesh:** Synonym of Lord Shankar.
31. **Manas temple, Varanasi:** It is one of the most famous temples in holy city of Varanasi. Hindi epic Ramcharitmans was originally written at this place by Goswami Tulsidas.
32. **Meerut:** It is a city in Indian state of Uttar Pradesh. It is an ancient city with settlement dating back to the Indus Valley civilisation, having been found in and around the area.
33. **Marathi:** It is an Indus-Aryan language spoken mainly by Marathi people of Maharashtra state of India.
34. **Maithilisharan Gupt:** He was one of the most important modern Hindi poets. He is a pioneer of *khari boli* (plain dialect). Mahatma Gandhi addressed him as national poet in 1936.
35. **Manu:** It is a term found with various meanings in different mythologies of Hinduism. It refers to the first man (progenitor of humanity).
36. **Mohan/Madhav/Manmohan/Madhusudan:** A synonyms of Lord Krishna.
37. **Madhya Pradesh:** It is a centrally situated state of India.
38. **Mysore (Mysure):** A famous capital of Wodeyar dynasty. It has been home to one of the longest established empires in Indian history. It is the third most populous city of Karnataka state of India.
39. **Magh Krishna:** A dark half period during eleventh month of the Hindu calendar year.
40. **Margashirsha Shukla:** A light half period during eleventh month of the Hindu calendar year.
41. **Madhvacharya:** He was a great religious reformer and philosopher of 13th century A.D. He was a proponent for Dwaitavad school of Bhakti philosophy.
42. **Meenakshi temple, Madurai:** It is the most important temple situated in Madurai, Tamil Nadu, India.
43. **Mahadev Temple, Khajuraho:** It is the largest, holiest and finest temple of Khajuraho in Madhya Pradesh state of India.

44. **Mahakal Temple, Ujjain:** It is one of the most famous Hindu temples dedicated to Lord Shiva, located in ancient city of Ujjain in state of Madhya Pradesh, India.
45. **Muktinath (Uttarakhand):** It is a sacred place both for Hindus and Buddhists, located in Muktinath valley in Mustang, Nepal.
46. **Muzzafarnagar:** It is the largest city in the Indian state of Uttar Pradesh.
47. **Malihabad:** It is a town in Lucknow district of Uttar Pradesh state of India.
48. **Maulasar:** It is a village in Didwana tehsil of Nagaur district of Rajasthan.

N:

1. **Narad:** He is a saint who can travel everywhere unrestrained. He is a liberated space man, a son of Brahma and devotee of Lord Vishnu.
2. **Nimbark sect:** It is the most ancient Vaishnava sect and based on *dvaita-advaita* philosophy.
3. **Nath Yogi:** Yogi primarily associated with Yogic tradition, promoted by Nath saints.
4. **Nasik:** It is situated on the bank of holy Godawari River. It is in North-West Maharashtra state of India.
5. **Nagpur:** It is the second capital and third largest city of Indian state of Maharashtra.
6. **Navdweep (Nabadwip):** It is in Nadia district, West Bengal state of India. It is the birthplace of Chaitanya Mahaprabhu.
7. **Navratri:** A Hindu festival of nine nights, dedicated to the glorification of Shakti, the feminine form of the divine Goddess.
8. **Nar-Narayan:** A Hindu deity pair, it is the twin brother incarnation of Lord Vishnu on earth. In this concept, the human soul Nara is the eternal companion of the divine Narayan.
9. **Narayan:** A Sanskrit name of Lord Vishnu.
10. **Narsingh Jayanti:** It celebrates the victory of good over evil and divine appearance day of Lord Narsimha Deo. It is held in May every year.
11. **Nat-Nagar:** A synonym of Lord Shri Krishna.
12. **Nand Kishore:** A synonym of Lord Shri Krishna.
13. **Narad-Bhakti-Sutras:** These are the heart and soul of the path for spiritual devotion, within the tradition of Hinduism.
14. **Neti-neti:** "Neither this, nor that" – is the method of Vedic analysis of negation.
15. **Nand-Baba:** Head of cow-herds of Braj. He is popularly known as foster father of Shri Krishna.
16. **Neel Sundar:** A synonym of Lord Shri Krishna.

17. **Narad Purana:** It is one of the eighteen Mahapuranas. It deals with places of pilgrimage. It is presented in a style of dialogue between Narad and Sanat Kumar.
18. **Nalbar:** It is a small place in Indian state of Assam (also known as Nalbari or Navdeep).
19. **Navgaon:** It is a city in Indian state of Assam.
20. **Naogaon:** Naogaon is also a town in Bangladesh.
21. **Naini prison:** It is one of the most important prisons and a correctional institution in Uttar Pradesh state of India.
22. **Nandgaon:** It is a town in Nagar panchayat in Mathura district in the Indian state of Uttar Pradesh.
23. **Naamchintamani Krishna:** The holy name of Krishna is transdentally blissful.
24. **Nathdwara:** It is famous for Krishna temple and located in Aravali hills in western state of Rajasthan, India.
25. **Novakhali:** It is a district in south-eastern Bangladesh.
26. **Nritya Gopal:** A synonym of Lord Krishna.
27. **Narsi Mehta:** A poet saint and Adi Kavi of Gujarat state of India and an exponent of Vaishnava poetry.
28. **Nainital:** A Himalayan resort town in Kumaun region of India's Uttarakhand state.
29. **Nath sect:** It is founded by Matsyendranath and developed by Gorakhnath.
30. **NatwarNagar/Nandlal/Neelsundar:** A synonym of Lord Krishna.
31. **Nityanand:** He was an Indian guru. His teachings are published in "*Chidakash Gita*".
32. **Nanapurana:** This word means different Puranas.
33. **Nimbarkacharya:** He is known for propagating Vaishnav theory of Dwaitadwaita or dualistic nondualism.

O:

1. **Om Namo Bhagwate Vasudevay:** Sacred verse for Lord Vishnu and Shri Krishna both. It means Om, I bow to Lord Vasudeva and Lord Shri Krishna.
2. **Oriya Gita:** Preachings of the Shrimad Bhagwat Gita with Oriya poetic theme.
3. **Om Shri Parmatmane Namah:** 'My respect for Vasudeva, the divine Lord'.
4. **Outram Ghat:** It is located to the south of Balughat of Kolkata's premier riverside entertainment spot.
5. **Odisha:** It is an eastern Indian state on the Bay of Bengal. It has many ancient Hindu temples.
6. **Om Klim Shri Krishnabhyam Namah:** It means salutation to Lord Krishna.

P:

1. **Prem-Yoga:** A theory of love.
2. **Phalgun:** Twelfth month of Hindu lunar year (February- March).
3. **Prahlad:** Famous devotee of Vishnu, son of Hiranyakashyapu.
4. **Purulia:** It lies in the west of state of West Bengal and is surrounded by Bankura and Paschim Medinipur districts to east.
5. **Panditji:** A title of respect to a learned Brahmin.
6. **Pondicherry:** It is now known as Puducherry. It is a city and capital of Pondicherry, union territory of south India. A choicest holiday destination.
7. **Pagyapatti:** It is a wholesale hub area in Burrabazar in Kolkata.
8. **Puranas:** A class of voluminous work in Sanskrit, dealing with aspect of ancient Indian history, legends, mythology or theology.
9. **Prem Darshan:** A very famous book published by Gita press on commentary of Narad Bhakti Sutras by Bhaijee.
10. **Prasad:** It denotes everything first offered to deity/saint and distributed in his/her name to their followers or others as a good sign.
11. **Peda:** It is a sweet from India and prepared in thick, semi- soft pieces. The main ingredients are khoya, sugar, cardamom nuts, etc.
12. **Puri:** An abode city of Odisha state in India, famous for pilgrimage; also known as Jagannathpuri.
13. **Prem Bhakti Prakash:** Afamous book written by Jaidayal Goyandka and published by Gitapress.
14. **Prayag:** A city in Indian state of Uttar Pradesh; also called Allahabad and with a meeting point of three sacred rivers: the Ganga, the Yamuna, the Saraswati.
15. **Puri/Puree:** It is a small round cake of unleavened wheat flour and deep-fried in oil.
16. **Paus/Pus/Pausya:** Tenth month of the Hindu lunar year in order of sequence (mid-December-January).
17. **Padma Purana:** Also known as Gita Mahatmya (Majesty of Gita), it is one of the major eighteen Puranas.
18. **Punjabi:** A native inhabitant of Punjab state in India.
19. **Parmatma:** It is absolute *atman* or supreme soul or spirit in Vedant and Yoga philosophy of India.
20. **Paisa:** A monetary unit in India equal to one-hundredth part of a rupee at present.
21. **Pad-Ratnakar:** An excellent and epic text about Radha Rani and herd-girls of Braj. Original devotional poetry for Radha-Krishna created by saint Shri Bhaijee and published by Gita press.
22. **Pravachan:** Speaking an exposition on religious texts or topics/ discourse/sermon.

23. **Purushottam Das Tandon:** He was a freedom fighter from Uttar Pradesh state of India. He is remembered for his efforts in achieving the official language of India status for Hindi. He was awarded 'Bharat Ratna' and given title of Rajarshi.
24. **Pandit Motilal Nehru:** He was the father of our first Prime Minister of India, the late Jawaharlal Nehru.
25. **Parsees/Paris:** They are the followers of Iranian prophet Zoroaster. They migrated to India to avoid religious persecution by Muslims.
26. **Pandurna:** It is a city in Chhindwara district of Madhya Pradesh state of India.
27. **Pushkar:** It is a town bordering Thar desert of Ajmer district in Rajasthan state of India. It also has a 14th century Jagatpita Brahma temple dedicated to Lord Brahma.
28. **Punjab:** It is a state in North India. It is a site of the holiest Gurudwara, the Golden temple in Amritsar.
29. **Pushottam Tatva:** Elements of Supreme Godliness.
30. **Prabhudatt Brahmachari:** He was Indian Guru and freedom fighter. He stood against Nehru on cow protection and against Hindu Code Bill.
31. **Parmarth Niketan:** It is an *ashram* located in Rishikesh, Uttarakhand, India. It was founded in 1942 in the lap of lush Himalayas.
32. **Poddarji/Poddar Baba:** Pet name affectionately given to Shri H.P. Poddar.
33. **Pandit Govind Vallabh Pant:** He was an Indian freedom fighter and one of the architects of modern India.
34. **Premchand:** He was an Indian writer famous for his modern Indian Hindi, Urdu literature. He was one of the most celebrated writers on the Indian subcontinent.
35. **Prarthana Piyush:** Afamous book which contains various prayers for different deities.
36. **Pus/Paushya Badi:** A dark half period of the tenth lunar month of the Hindu calendar year (December-January).
37. **Paushya Shukla:** A light half period of the tenth lunar month of the Hindu calendar year (December-January).
38. **Phalgun:** The twelfth lunar month of Indian calendar (February-March).
39. **Phalgun Shukla:** A light half period of the twelfth lunar month of the Hindu calendar.
40. **Phalgun Badi:** A dark half period of the twelfth lunar month of the Hindu calendar.
41. **Phalgun sudi:** See point 39.
42. **Phalgun Krishna:** See point 40.

43. **Panchratna Gita:** There are five jewels that surround Shri Bhagwat Gita, Vishnu Sahastranam, Bhishma Stavaraja, Anu Smriti and Gajendra Moksha. These ornaments create a *Sadhna* which is a stepping stone to the Chandi Samput.
44. **Prachya Vidya:** Ancient knowledge.
45. **P.K. Hazra:** A disciple of Paramhans Yoganand and a direct disciple of Gyanvatar Shri Shri Yukteshwarji. His name appeared five times in the book '*Autobiography of a Yogi*'. This is an example showing that a man with full- fledged family can achieve the highest state of *samadhi* (profound meditation) in modern times.

R:

1. **Ram Kaur Devi:** Grandmother of Bhaijee. In fact, she was the wife of uncle Shri Kaniramji of Bhaijee, i.e., his grandmother, but Bhaijee treated her like mother throughout his life due to an early death of his mother Rikhi Bai.
2. **Rishikesh:** It is a tehsil of Dehradun district of Indian state of Uttarakhand, located at the foothills of Himalayas.
3. **Rikhi Bai:** Mother of Bhaijee.
4. **Ramdei:** She was the wife of Bhaijee on his third marriage after the death of his second wife.
5. **Rajput:** Member of the patrilineal clans of the western, central and Northern India.
6. **Ramgarh:** It is a city in Sikar district in the Indian state of Rajasthan. It came up in 1872 and was built by Poddar chhatri.
7. **Rishikul:** Rishikul Vidyapeeth is one of the ancient and best institutes of Laxmangarh. Rishikul Brahmcharya Ashram is part and parcel of it. It is in Sikar district of Rajasthan state of India.
8. **Ram/Lord Ram:** Also known as Raghav, He is the seventh incarnation of Hindu God Vishnu and a king of Ayodhya.
9. **Ramnavmi:** Birthday of Lord Rama falls on the 9th day of bright fortnight of Chaitra (mid-March-April).
10. **Radha:** Also known as Radha Rani is a Hindu Goddess and is almost always depicted along with Shri Krishna.
11. **Ramcharitmanas or Manas:** It is an epic poem in Awadhi dialect of Hindi composed by the 16th century Bhakta poet, Goswami Tulsidas.
12. **Ramgarh (Rajasthan):** It is a city and a municipality in Sikar district in Indian state of Rajasthan.
13. **Rakhi or Rakshabandhan:** It is used to celebrate brother- sister relationship between men and women who are relatives or biologically unrelated. On this day, sisters tie a sacred thread on their brothers' wrists.

14. **Radha-Madhav-Chintan:** The transcedental love between Radha and Krishna has been depicted in this book and published by Gita press.
15. **Ramrakshastotra:** It is a hymn of praise, used as a prayer to Lord Rama.
16. **Ras Panchadhyayi:** It is based on the speeches by Bhaijee in original text. It is worth reading for devotees who wish to worship Lord Krishna, Gopi Bhava and Ras Sadhna. It is an essence of Shrimad Bhagwat.
17. **Radha Kripa:** Prayer for merciful side long glance of Shri Radha.
18. **Radha Kunda:** A town in Mathura district in the Indian state of Uttar Pradesh.
19. **Ratangarh:** A town in Churu district in Rajasthan. It is famous for grand mansions. A field of activity and place of accomplishment by Bhaijee.
20. **Radha Kunj:** It is in Haridwar in the Indian state of Uttarakhand.
21. **Ranchi:** The capital of Jharkhand state of India. It is also capital city of waterfalls and lakes.
22. **Radhashtami:** Celebrated as appearance anniversary of Shri Radha Rani, the lover-consort of Lord Shri Krishna.
23. **Rajarshi:** A person having qualities of a royal saint and *rishi*.
24. **Raskhan:** He was a poet who was both a Muslim and a follower of Lord Shri Krishna.
25. **Ramayan:** It is a Sanskrit epic poem ascribed to Hindu sage and Sanskrit poet Valmiki.
26. **Rajasthan:** The largest state of India, located on the western side of the country, which comprises most of the wide Thar Desert.
27. **Ravi Verma (Raja Ravi Verma Koil Thampuran):** A celebrity and established artist and a painter in Indian history of art.
28. **Radha Baba/Radhe Baba:** Pet name given to Shri Chakradhar Maharaj.
29. **Radhe Krishan/Radha Madhav:** A synonym of supreme couple.
30. **Rajgarh:** It is a town and tehsil in district Churu in northern Rajasthan, India. Its railway station is named as Sadulpur.
31. **Dr. Rajendra Prasad:** He was the first President of independent India.
32. **Ramanuj sect:** There exists plurity and distinction between soul (*atman*) and ultimate reality (*Brahman*). There is unity of souls and individual soul has the potential to realise identity with the Brahman.
33. **Rewari:** It is a city in Indian state of Haryana.
34. **Rohtak:** It is a city in Indian state of Haryana. It was founded by Jat people.

35. **Ramayananak:** A special issue of '*Kalyan*' devoted to Lord Rama.
36. **Rajpur:** It is a village in Kanpur dehat district in state of Uttar Pradesh in India. The nearest railway station is Pukhrayan.
37. **Roopmanzari Devi:** A confidante of Shri Radha.
38. **Radhasudhanidhi:** It is a text written by Shri Prabhodanand Saraswatipade. He taught us how to follow the footsteps of Shri Radha Rani and always remember her. This book teaches us how to become qualified for eternal Vrijseva in our perfected spiritual forms.
39. **Ramsukh Das:** A close friend of Shri Gambhirchand Dujari who introduced him to Shri Goyandkaji in 1934 and then to Bhaijee. He was a *sannyasi* and had written many books on the Gita.
40. **Ramnaam:** The sacred name of Lord Rama.
41. **Rickshaw:** A light two-three-wheeled hooded vehicle drawn by one person.
42. **Rameswaram:** It is in south India and has most well- known and revered Rameswaram temple, which is the only Shiva temple.
43. **Ramcharitamritank:** A special issue about the various events of the life of Lord Rama.
44. **Ramanujacharya**- He was an Indian theologian philosopher and one of the most important exponents of Shri Vaishnavism tradition with Hinduism.
45. **Radha Kripa Katakshastavaraj:** It is the most famous strota of Vrindavan and all *sadhus* and devoted women know it by heart. It was spoken by Lord Shiva to Parvati in the *tantra* named *Urdhvamnaya-tantra.*
46. **Rajarshi Tandon:** *See* Purushottam Das Tandon.
47. **Ramkrishna and Sharda:** He was an Indian mystic and Yogi (1836-1886) during the 19th century. He was given to spiritual ecstasies from a young age and was influenced towards Kali, Tantra and Vaishnava Bhakti. His chief disciple was Swami Vivekananda. Though he was married to Sharda Devi whom he regarded as divine mother in person and addressed her as a holy mother.
48. **Rai Sahib:** It was a title of honour issued during the era of British rule in India to a person who performed great service to visionary leadership of the nation.
49. **Rai Bahadur:** It is a title of honour bestowed during British rule in India to persons for their services to the Empire.
50. **Rawatpura:** The name has emerged from ancient temple of Hanumanji which is situated in Rawatpura village of Chambal region in Madhya Pradesh state of India. It is about 100 kms from two major cities – Gwalior and Jhansi. It has a popular place known as

'Rawatpura Sarkar Dham'. It is situated in Lahar tehsil of district Bhind in Gwalior division of Madhya Pradesh state.

51. **Raipur:** It is capital city of state of Chhattisgarh in India.
52. **R.H. Nixon:** He was later known as Krishna Prem, was a British spiritual aspirant who went to India in early 20th century together with his spiritual teacher Yashoda Ma. He founded an *ashram* in Mir Tola, near Almora, India.
53. **Rudra Prayag:** It is a district in Indian state of Uttarakhand and a point of confluence for the sacred rivers Alaknanda and Mandakini.

S:

1. **Sat Yuga:** It is the age or era of truth when the humanity is governed by the God.
2. **Samadhi:** A state of intense concentration (profound meditation) through meditation.
3. **Shillong:** Capital and hill station of Meghalaya state and birthplace of Bhaijee.
4. **Shri Sign:** A mark of Shree or Sri or Shri is a word of Sanskrit origin, used in India as polite form of address equivalent to 'Mr.' or 'Ms' in written or spoken language or as title of veneration of deities (translated as holy).
5. **Sandalwood Tilak:** It is applied with sandalwood tilak (bindi) on forehead which is a common practice in India.
6. **Surya/Suryanarayana:** Sun, also known as Aditya, Bhanu or Ravi, is the chief solar deity in Hinduism.
7. **Shiva/Lord Shankar:** Also known as Mahadev.
8. **Suvati Bai:** Name of wife of Bhaijee on second marriage after death of his first wife.
9. **Savitri:** Name for the daughter of Bhaijee.
10. **Surdas/Soordas:** Surdas was late 15th century blind saint, poet and musician known for devotional songs, dedicated to Lord Shri Krishna. He is said to have written and composed songs in his magnum opus 'Sur-Sagar'.
11. **Sadhna:** A devoted striving.
12. **Soham-Soham:** It means I am he/that, when used in meditation, it acts as a natural mantra. It controls one's breathing pattern to gain concentration.
13. **Sarhi (Sari)/Saree:** It is a south Asian female garment that consists of drapes varying five-nine yards in length, and two-four feet in breadth. It is wrapped around the waist with one end draped over shoulder.
14. **Sikh:** One who believes in Guru Govind Singh Sahib.
15. **Sita:** Also known as Vaidehi, Janki, Maithili, she is the central female character of Hindu epic, the Ramayana and daughter of Janak.

16. **Shri Ram/Ram:** Seventh incarnation of Hindu God Vishnu.
17. **Shesha:** Also known as Sheshnaga or Adi Shesha is the king of all nagas (*serpents*) and one of the primal beings of creation. He is said to have descended to Earth as Lakshman and Balram.
18. **Shankh Chakram:** Salutation to Lord Vishnu who holds conch and discus.
19. **Shri Krishna Govind Hare Murari Hey Nath Narayan Vasudeva:** O attractive, O pleasure of my senses, who takes away all sufferings, O renounce of all obstacles, O Master, the resting place of all creations, creator of Universe. It is a complete sacred verse.
20. **Socrates:** He was a classical Greek (Athencian) philosopher and one of the founders of western philosophy.
21. **Swargashram:** It is a small township located 3 km from Rishikesh on the left bank of the Ganges.
22. **Shri Hari:** Honorific prefix to Lord Vishnu.
23. **Sewa Kunj:** It is a forest and has a temple of Radha Krishna. It is believed that Radha-Krishna visit here every night. It is in Vrindavan near Mathura, Uttar Pradesh, India.
24. **Sadhan Path:** A text written by Bhaijee.
25. **Sankadi Sages:** Four *Manas putras* (mind-born sons) or spiritual sons of Lord Brahma according to Bhagwat Purana. Knowledge comes to these Rishis by itself (without being dependent on study). They are preceptors of scriptures on duty.
26. **Skanda Purana:** One of the eighteen Hindu Puranas, is devoted to the *lilas* (divine act) of Kartikeya, son of Lord Shiva and Parvati.
27. **Shukla Paksha:** Light half of the lunar month.
28. **Sajjan goth:** It is a Hindu wedding ritual where the groom side is seated in arrangement and the bride side makes sure that they eat well.
29. **Sita Ram:** This is an Indian name, meaning Princess Sita of Mithila, Nepal and Prince Ram of Ayodhya.
30. **Shri Ganesh:** Also known as Vinayaka or Ganpati, He is revered as remover of obstacles and God of intellect and wisdom.
31. **Shantakaram Bhujagendra Shayanam Padmanbham – Sarvaloki Kanatham:** A prayer of Lord Vishnu.
32. **Saryu:** It flows through Indian states of Uttarakhand and Uttar Pradesh. It has ancient significance. Ayodhya is situated on the bank of this river.
33. **Shrimad Bhagwat Mahapurana:** It is one of the eighteen great texts of Hinduism. It is composed in Sanskrit and promotes *bhakti* (emotional loving devotion) to Lord Vishnu in the incarnation of Shri Krishna. It is the very essence of all Vedanta literature.

34. **Shrimad Bhagwat Gita:** It is referred to as simply the Gita.
35. **Shravan:** Fifth month of lunar year.
36. **Samvat (Vikram Samvat):** It is an Indian calendar started in 57 BC. It is said to have been framed by King Vikramaditya. It uses lunar months and solar side real year.
37. **Stotravali:** A book of hymns and prayers.
38. **Shivank:** Special issue of '*Kalyan*' devoted to Lord Shiva.
39. **Swami Chakradharji:** Commonly known as Radha Baba.
40. **Shardapeeth Shringeri:** It is a southern Monastery established by Adi Shankaracharya in 8th century A.D. The *math* is on the bank of Tunga River in Chikkmaglur district, Karnataka state of India.
41. **Shankaracharya:** He is the head of monastery called math. The title derives from Adi Shankaracharya. He is honoured as '*Jagat Guru*'.
42. **Shardapeeth Dwarkapuri:** It is also called Shardapeeth. It is an ancient monastery situated in the coastal city of Dwarka in Gujarat state of India. It is one of the four cardinal seats of learning and represents Sama Veda.
43. **Sur Sagar/Soorsagar:** Surdas (1483-1563), a follower of Vallabh school of Vedant, is known for his collection of poems (*Sur Sagar*) based on the stories of Shri Krishna's childhood, found in the Bhagwat Purana.
44. **Shimlapal:** A city of West Bengal in India where Bhaijee was placed under surveillance.
45. **Sethji:** People having faith in Shri Jaidayal Goyandka called him by a nickname 'Sethji'.
46. **Satsang:** *Satsang* (An association of virtuous people) in Indian religion is being in the company of the truth or the good, by sitting together with the *guru* or group of religious people.
47. **Sahitya Vachaspati:** Atop literary honour of Prayag Hindi Sahitya Sammelan, Allahabad.
48. **Sage Angira:** He is a *rishi* who along with sage Atharvan is credited to have formulated (heard) most of the fourth Veda called Atharva Veda.
49. **Saint Narada:** He is depicted carrying *khartal* and *veena* which he uses to accompany his singing of hymns, prayers and mantras as an act of devotion to Lord Vishnu. He is the most travelled sage to the world and realms.
50. **Sraddh:** Libation and offering of pindas are made to the spirits of the deceased and of the food and gifts to Brahmin officiates and to relatives.
51. **Sanatan Dharma:** It is used to denote the absolute set of duties or religiously ordained practices incumbent upon all Hindus.

52. **Shri Yugal Sahastranaam:** A sacred verse in 1,000 words in praise of Shri Radha and Shri Krishna.
53. **Sanatan Dharmi:** It is used to denote the people who believe in eternal duties or religious ordained practices incumbent upon all Hindus irrespective of class, caste or creed.
54. **Sudi:** Light half of the lunar month.
55. **Sanawad:** A city in Khargone district in Madhya Pradesh state of India. It is a place where the original collector of this book Shri Gambhir Chand Dujari worked prior, of his arrival to Mumbai, forever to extend full cooperation throughout his life to Bhaijee.
56. **Shri Radha Kripa-Kataksha-Stav-Raja:** A prayer for the merciful sidelong glance of Shri Radha.
57. **Seth Sanwaliaji temple:** It is a renowned temple of dark Krishna situated on Chittorgarh-Udaipur highway in the town of Mandaphia.
58. **Sargana:** It is a tehsil in Alwar district of Rajasthan.
59. **Sadhan Path:** This book is written by Shri Bhaijee and published by Gita press, Gorakhpur.
60. **Satkathank:** A special Issue of '*Kalyan*' devoted to the true stories.
61. **Sanat Kumara:** According to post 1,900 publications of theosophy, Lord Sanat Kumara is an advanced being at the ninth level initiation who is regarded as Lord and is thought to be the head of the spiritual hierarchy of Earth.
62. **Sandwa:** It is a town in Churu district in Shekhawati region of Indian state of Rajasthan.
63. **Sunder Kand:** It means beautiful episode/book. It is the story of Lord Hanuman finding Sitaji.
64. **Sevakunj Bihari/Shyam Sunder:** A synonym for Lord Krishna.
65. **Swami Chakradharji:** He was affectionately called Radha Baba and was an ardent devotee of Bhaijee.
66. **Siropova:** Such reward that is bestowed to a respectable person by the royal office for his dedication to the society, it contains a complete attire from head to toe, that is a coat, a turban, a pajama and a shawl.
67. **Santi:** An honorific way of expression in Sanskrit for plural of 'is' (are).
68. **Sanskrit:** It is the primary and sacred language of Hinduism and Mahayana Buddhism, a philosophical language of Hinduism, Janism, Buddhism and Sikhism.
69. **Shri Priyaji/Priyaji:** Respectful address to Shri Radha Rani.
70. **Sabarmati refuge:** It is also known as Gandhi Ashram, located in Sabarmati suburb of Ahmedabad in Gujarat state of India. This had been one of the residences of Mahatma Gandhi for about 12 years.

71. **Sardar Patel:** He was an Indian barrister, leader of Indian National Congress and formerly father of the Republic of India. Played a role in India's struggle for independence.
72. **Sun Temple of Konark:** It is a 13th century temple at Konark in Odisha state of India. It is dedicated to the Sun God.
73. **Stoopa of Sanchi:** The Buddhist *vihara* of Sanchi, famous for great Stoopa, is in Sanchi town in Raisen district of Indian state of Madhya Pradesh.
74. **Shiv temple, Kedarnath:** It is a Hindu temple dedicated to Lord Shiva. It is on the Garhwal Himalayan range near Mandakini River in Kedarnath, Uttarakhand in India.
75. **Sheshadri:** It is the name of a hill in Andhra Pradesh state. It has a well-known temple of Lord Vishnu.
76. **Sandal paste:** It is made from sandalwood powder.
77. **Shri Radhaji:** Divine consort of Shri Krishna.
78. **Shri Krishnank:** A special issue of '*Kalyan*' devoted to Lord Krishna.
79. **Shivank:** A special issue of '*Kalyan*' devoted to Lord Shiva.
80. **Shakti ank:** Aspecial issue of '*Kalyan*' devoted to Goddess Durga.
81. **Sakshi Gopal:** It is a medieval temple dedicated to Lord Gopal/ Krishna located in town of Sakshi Gopal on Puri- Bhubanewar highway in Odisha state of India.
82. **Shri rangam:** It an island and part of city of Tiruchirappalli in south India.
83. **Shyam/Shyam Sunder:** A synonym of Lord Krishna.
84. **Shravan Sudi:** Light half period in the fifth month of lunar year.
85. **Sujangarh:** It is a city in Churu district in Shekhawati region of Rajasthan state of India.
86. **Shri Prahlad:** He was a son of *daitya* king Hiranyakashyapu. He was known for his piety and *bhakti* to Lord Vishnu.
87. **Sharda Bill:** It was passed on 20th September, 1929 by British India Legislature, which fixed the marriage age of girl to 14 years.
88. **Sahebganj:** This is the locality of Gorakhpur city in which Gita press is situated.
89. **Shringeri:** It is a hill town in Chikkamangaluru district of Indian state of Karnataka. It is the site of first *math* (Sharda Peeth) established by Adi Shankaracharya.
90. **Sitaram:** The God incarnation of divine couple as Ram and Sita.
91. **Swami Ramsukhdas:** He was born in Madepura in Nagaur district of Rajasthan in 1940 A.D. He went from village to village and city to city and kept pouring the nectar of *Satsang*.
92. **Satyarth Prakash:** A book that has been written by Swami Dayanand Saraswati (founder of Arya Samaj) containing information about

Vedas which he has perceived from hypotheses through sages and saints.

93. **Sadhnank:** A special issue of '*Kalyan*' devoted to spiritual practices.
94. **Shyam/Shyam Sundar Dujari:** Compiler and combining for the original Hindi text-EK ALAUKIK VIBHOOTI collected by his father Shri Gambhir Chandji Dujari.
95. **Saharanpur:** It is a city in state of Uttar Pradesh in northern India. It is famous for wood-carving.
96. **Sankeertan:** It is a 'call and response' style song set to music for which multiple singers recite in a legend.
97. **Sagar:** It is a city in state of Madhya Pradesh in central India.
98. **Siyaram:** It refers here to the wife of Bhaijee who was the daughter of Shri Sitaramji Sanganeria (Siyaram).
99. **Shravan Krishna Paksha:** Dark half part in the fifth month of lunar year.

T:

1. **Tulsidas:** Also known as Goswami Tulsidas, he was a Hindu poet, saint, reformer, and philosopher from Ramanand sect devoted to Lord Ram. He is best known as the creator of epic the Ramcharit Manas.
2. **Treta Yuga:** It began from *Baishakh Shukla Tritya*. In the 78th pedigree from Manu Shri Ram ruled in Ayodhya and we have the first great epic, the Ramayana.
3. **Tutia Maharaj:** A holy saint living with Nath Yogis at Ratangarh.
4. **Triveni Sangam:** It is a confluence of three rivers. One such place is in Prayag (Allahabad), which has two physical rivers Ganga, Yamuna and the invisible/mythical Saraswati river. An important site of Kumbh fair, held every 12th year.
5. **Twameo Mata – Mam Deva Deva:** This sacred verse was spoken by queen Gandhari to Shri Krishna.
6. **Tulsi-Dal:** A famous text by Hanuman Prasad Poddar.
7. **Tulsi:** A shurb plant or holy basil (Ocimum temiflorum), it is a sacred shrub in Hindu belief. It is a consort of God Vishnu. The offering of its leaves is mandatory in ritualistic worship of Vishnu, Krishna and Vithoba.
8. **Tatwa-Vivachani:** A commentary on the Gita by Shri Sethji.
9. **Tazia:** A Muslim passion play celebrated by Shia in Muharram as a replica of tomb of Hussain, the martyred son of Muhammad, which is carried as a procession during Muharram.
10. **Totadri Math:** A famous Vaishnava temple situated at Nanguneri-Taluka HQ in district of Tirunelveli in the Indian state of Tamil Nadu.
11. **Thelasar:** It is a village located in Churu district of Indian state of Rajasthan.

12. **Triveni:** A confluence of three sacred rivers.
13. **Tatwa Chintamani:** It is a tantric treatise composed in Sanskrit verses by 16th-century sad Baka of Bengal Paramhans Purnanand. It contains 26 chapters including the most important known as Satchakranirupana.
14. **Tinsukia:** It is a city in Assam state of India. It is called by this name as one of the ministers dug a triangular pond known as Tinsukia Pukhuri.
15. **Tamil:** It is a Dravidian language mainly spoken by Tamil people of India and Shri Lanka.
16. **Tirthank:** A special issue of '*Kalyan*' devoted to details about various pilgrims of India.
17. **Tanjore:** Now known as Thanjavur, it is a city in south Indian state of Tamil Nadu and is famous for south Indian religion, art and culture.
18. **Titagarh:** It is a city in North Kolkata. The Titagarh Paper Mill was set up in Titagarh and Kakinada in 1882.

U:

1. **Upanishads:** Collection of texts containing central philosophical concepts of Hinduism. These are also referred to as Vedantas. The concept of *Brahman* (ultimate reality) and *atman* (soul) are the central ideas in all the Upanishads. More than 200 are known, of which 12 or so are the oldest and most important.
2. **Uma:** The Goddess and consort of Lord Shiva.
3. **Uttarkashi:** It is a town in Uttarkhand, India. It is a district headquarter and situated on the bank of river Bhagirathi.
4. **Ujjain:** It is an ancient city on the eastern bank of Kshipra River in Malwa region of Indian state of Madhya Pradesh. Important place of pilgrimage.
5. **Uddhava/Oodhav:** A friend and counsellor of Shri Krishna. He taught the process of Yoga and *bhakti* directed by Shri Krishna.
6. **Ujjwal Neel Mani:** To elaborate and explain every aspect of *Madhur-ras*, Rasikacharya Rup Goswami wrote this book. It is only a definite guide to *rasa* and *rasmayi-bhakti* to those who dive into the deep ocean of *Bhakti*.
7. **Uttar Pradesh:** It is the most popular state of India, created in 1937 as United Province and renamed as Uttar Pradesh in 1950. In 2000, a new state Uttarakhand was carried out.
8. **Udaipur:** It is a major city in Indian state of Rajasthan. It is known for its history and culture, scenic locations.
9. **Urdu:** It is a standardised register of Hindustani language. It is also one of the 22 official languages recognised in the Constitution of India.

10. **Uttarakhand:** Formerly known as Uttaranchal, it is a state of northern part of India, also referred to as "*Devbhumi*" (Land of the Gods) due to many Hindu temples and pilgrimage centres.

V:

1. **Vaman:** Fifth incarnation of Lord Vishnu and first incarnation of second age, i.e., Treta Yuga. He is the first incarnation to appear as human and appears as dwarf Brahmin.
2. **Vedvyas or Vyas:** He is a central and revered figure in most Hindu traditions. It means the one who classified the Vedas. He is considered to be scribe of both Vedas and Puranas and an author and character of the Mahabharata. He is also considered to be an incarnation of Lord Vishnu and one of the seven immortals, who are still in existence according to Hindu belief.
3. **Vaishya:** They were assigned traditional role of agriculture and cattle rearing, but over time, they came to be landowners and traders, etc.
4. **Vishnu Sahastranaam:** It contains 1,000 names (*sahastranaam*) of Lord Vishnu and one of the most commonly chanted *stotras* in Hinduism.
5. **Varanasi:** Also known as Banaras, it is a north Indian city on the bank of the Ganga in the Indian state of Uttar Pradesh. It is one of the oldest and continuously inhabited cities of the world. The spiritual capital of India.
6. **Vellore:** District headquarters of Indian state of Tamil Nadu.
7. **Vrindavan/Vrindavan Dham:** A town in Mathura district of Indian state of Uttar Pradesh. Lord Krishna spent His childhood at this place.
8. **Vaishakh:** Second month of Hindu lunar year (mid-April to mid-May).
9. **Vaishnava:** He is follower of major branches of Hinduism. He is focused on veneration of Lord Vishnu.
10. **Vedanta:** It is also known as *Uttar Mimansa*. It is one of the six schools of Hindu philosophy. The term 'Ved' means 'knowledge' and '*anta*' means 'end'.
11. **Valmiki Ratnakar:** It is a Sanskrit epic poem ascribed to Hindu sage and Sanskrit poet Valmiki.
12. **Vishnu Yajna:** For the well-being of life, such rite is highly recommended. It is done by reading 1,000 names of Lord Vishnu.
13. **Vedas:** These are the large bodies of text originating in ancient India and composed of Vedic Sanskrit. These are also called *Shruti* (what is heard).**Vaishnavi state:** See point 9.
14. **Ved-Bhawan:** Important schools of Vedic *yagna*, astrology and education of Vedas, are active at Badrinath, Jagannath Puri, Dwarka,

Rameshwaram, Rudra Prayag, Shri rangam, Prayag and Kalri (Kerala).

15. **Vidur:** A central character in Mahabharata. His name means skilled, intelligent. He was uncle of Pandavas and Kauravas and minister of Hastinapur.
16. **Vinay Patrika:** Devotional poem composed by Goswami Tulsidas for different deities, specially for Lord Rama with extreme humility.
17. **Vashishtha:** He is one of the seven great *rishis* and *manas putras* of Lord Brahma.
18. **Vikramaditya Year:** The system of Hindu calendar was started by King Vikramaditya of Ujjain.
19. **Vishnu:** He is the supreme Lord and also known as Narayan or Lord Hari.
20. **Vishakhaji:** A confidante or female attendant of Shri Radhaji.
21. **Vagdaan:** In this Hindu ceremony, the couple exchange gold rings and flower garlands. This ensures both parties that the girl and boy are now engaged.
22. **Vyawar (Beawar):** It was financial capital of Marwar state of Rajputana (Rajasthan state of India).
23. **Vishnu ank:** A special issue of '*Kalyan*' devoted to Lord Vishnu.
24. **Vrindavan Bihari:** A synonym of Lord Krishna.
25. **Vrinda:** It is a Hindi name for girls meaning Basil, Goddess Radha, Tulsi.
26. **Vastugun:** Nature of property for a specific thing.
27. **Vaishakh Krishna:** Adark half period of the second lunar month of Hindu calendar (April-May).
28. **Vaishakh Badi:** A dark half period of the second lunar month of Hindu calendar (April-May).
29. **Vaishakh Shukla:** A light half period of the second lunar month of Hindu calendar (April-May).
30. **Vinoba Bhave (1895-1982):** He was an Indian advocate of non-violence and human rights. He is best known for Bhoodan movement.
31. **Vallabhacharya:** Also known as Vallabha, he was a devotional philosopher who founded the Krishna-centred Pushti sect of Vaishnavism in the Braj region of India and philosophy of dualism.
32. **Vedant ank:** Aspecial issue of '*Kalyan*' devoted to ancient religious Hindu scriptures.
33. **Vrishbhanu:** Radha was the daughter of Vrishbhanu, who was king of Suchendra in his previous life.
34. **Vishalakshi Temple:** It is a Hindu temple dedicated to Goddess Vishalakshi (an aspect of Goddess Parvati) at Mir Ghat on the bank of the Ganges at Varanasi, U.P., India). It is regarded as Shakti peeth.

35. **Vedic scholar:** Scholar of the Vedas, considered to be root of Hinduism.
36. **Vedo-Upanishad:** A large body of texts spawning four Vedas and related scriptures that date to roughly 1700-500 BCE is called Vedic literature developed by ancient *rishi lineages*. Vedas speak about the underlying principles (roots) of creation mechanism, understanding of which influenced our ancient way of life. Upanishad means sitting beside master. Upanishads elaborate on techniques employed to explore and realise their underlying principles.
37. **Vastu God:** A deity related with the science of architecture.
38. **Vishuddhanand Paramhans (1853-1937):** He was popularly known as Gandhi Baba (the perfume saint) and a *yogi*. He was teacher of Gopinath Kaviraj.
39. **Vishuddhanand Kanan Ashram:** This is a very unique and sacred place in Maldahiya area of Varanasi. The entry is strictly prohibited to general public for which a notice with a due warning can be seen at its entrance.

W:

1. **West Bengal:** It is an Indian state located in East India in the Bay of Bengal.

Y:

1. **Yamlarjun:** It is a famous tale Ukhal *Bandhan* and salvation of Yamlarjun from Bhagwat Purana (one of the sons of Kuber-Nal Kuber and Manigreev).
2. **Yashoda:** Foster mother of Lord Shri Krishna and wife of Nand of Gokul.
3. **Yogvashishtha:** A text ascribed to Valmiki. It is narrated as discourse of sage Vashishtha to Prince Rama.
4. **Yogi:** Refers to an ascetic, practitioner of meditation.
5. **Yama:** Also known as Yamraja, He is the God of death. His parents are the Sun God Surya and Sanjana, daughter of Vishwakarma.
6. **Yoga-Vedant:** Name of a magazine.
7. **Yada-Yada:** It means 'whenever'. It is in the Bhagwat Gita chapter 4, verses 7-8. The meaning of these two verses (*shlokas*) is – '*Whenever there is a decay of righteousness, O Bharath.....for the sake of firmly establishing righteousness, I am born from age to age*'.
8. **Yarvada Prison:** It is a noted high-security prison in Yarvada, Pune in Maharashtra state of India and one of the largest prisons of south Asia.
9. **Yugsahastranaam:** It contains 1,000 names of divine couple (Radha-Krishna from the Narad Purana).

10. **Yamunaji:** It is the longest and second largest tributary river of the Ganges in northern India.
11. **Yoganand:** Paramhans Yoganand (1893-1952) was an Indian Yogi and Guru who introduced millions of westners to the teaching of Meditation and Kriya Yoga through his famous book '*Autobiography of a Yogi*'. He became a disciple of Guru, Swami Yukteshwar Giri in 1910 at the age of 17.

❑❑❑

Shri Gambhirchandji Dujari –
A resident of the heaven (1901-1962)

We had not completely understood during your lifetime what is the importance of the work for which you are spending your entire life. Now a little is coming into our minds that the facts of life of two paramount saints of the present era would have not just taken a form in front of the world, if you had not dedicated your life for this work. In a particular form, for which you had a longing to publish this matter, that could not be just possible but as I could manage:

"With heartfelt prostration,
I am offering to you which is entirely yours."